# WAYS OF READING

## An Anthology for Writers

### Second Edition

David Bartholomae

UNIVERSITY OF PITTSBURGH

Anthony Petrosky

UNIVERSITY OF PITTSBURGH

BEDFORD BOOKS OF ST. MARTIN'S PRESS

Boston

**For Bedford Books**

*Publisher:* Charles H. Christensen
*Associate Publisher:* Joan E. Feinberg
*Managing Editor:* Elizabeth M. Schaaf
*Production Editor:* Tara L. Masih
*Copyeditor:* Susan M. S. Brown
*Text Design:* Anna Post-George
*Cover Design:* Volney Croswell, Paul Shilale (Hamilton Shilale)

Library of Congress Catalog Card Number: 88–63081
Copyright © 1990 by Bedford Books *of* St. Martin's Press
Manufactured in the United States of America
4 3 2 1
f e

*For information, write:* St. Martin's Press, Inc.
175 Fifth Avenue, New York, NY 10010

*Editorial Offices:* Bedford Books *of* St. Martin's Press
29 Winchester Street, Boston, MA 02116

ISBN: 0–312–03077–0

## ACKNOWLEDGMENTS

Roland Barthes, "The World of Wrestling" and "Striptease." From *Mythologies* by Roland Barthes. Translation copyright © 1972 by Jonathan Cape Ltd. Reprinted by permission of Farrar, Straus and Giroux, Inc., the Estate of Roland Barthes, translator Annette Lavers, and Jonathan Cape Ltd.
Saul Bellow, "A Silver Dish." From *Him with His Foot in His Mouth* by Saul Bellow. Copyright © 1974, 1978, 1982, 1984 by Saul Bellow Ltd. Reprinted by permission of Harper & Row, Publishers, Inc.
John Berger, "Ways of Seeing." From *Ways of Seeing* by John Berger. Copyright © 1972 by Penguin Books Ltd. Reprinted by permission of Viking Penguin, a division of Penguin Books USA, Inc. Botticelli, *Venus and Mars;* Leonardo da Vinci, *Virgin of the Rocks* and *The Virgin and Child with St. Anne and St. John the Baptist.* Reproduced by courtesy of the Trustees, The National Gallery, London. Leonardo da Vinci, *Virgin of the Rocks.* Reprinted by permission of the Louvre Museum. Pierre Bourdieu and Alain Darbel, from *L'Amour de l'Art.* Reprinted by permission of Éditions de Minuit. Pieter Breughel the Elder, *The Procession to Calvary.* Reprinted by permission of Kunst Historisches Museum, Vienna. Frans Hals, *Regents of the Old Men's Alms House* and *Regentesses of the Old Men's Alms House.* Reprinted by permission of Frans Halsmuseum. Vincent van Gogh, *Wheatfield with Crows.* Vincent van Gogh Foundation/National Museum Vincent van Gogh, Amsterdam. Reprinted by permission of Stedelijk Museum. Jan Vermeer, *Woman Pouring Milk.* Reprinted by permission of Rijksmuseum-Stichting.
Robert Coles, "Entitlement." From *Privileged Ones,* Vol. 5 of *Children of Crisis* by Robert Coles. Copyright © 1977 by Robert Coles. By permission of Little, Brown and Company.
Thomas J. Cottle and Stephen L. Klineberg, "Ted and Ellie Graziano." Reprinted with permission of The Free Press, a division of Macmillan, Inc., from *The Present of Things Future: Explorations of Time*

*Acknowledgments and copyrights are continued at the back of the book on page 768, which constitutes an extension of the copyright page.*

# Preface

*Ways of Reading* is designed for a course where students are given the opportunity to work on what they read, and to work on it by writing. When we began developing such courses, we realized the problems our students had when asked to write or talk about what they read were not "reading problems," at least not as these are strictly defined. Our students knew how to move from one page to the next. They could read sentences. They had, obviously, been able to carry out many of the versions of reading required for their education—skimming textbooks, cramming for tests, strip-mining books for term papers.

Our students, however, felt powerless in the face of serious writing, in the face of long and complicated texts—the kinds of texts we thought they should find interesting and challenging. We thought (as many teachers have thought) that if we just, finally, gave them something good to read—something rich and meaty—they would change forever their ways of thinking about English. It didn't work, of course. The issue is not only *what* students read, but what they can learn to *do* with what they read. We learned that the problems our students had lay not in the reading material (it was too hard) or in the students (they were poorly prepared) but in the classroom—in the ways we and they imagined what it meant to work on an essay.

There is no better place to work on reading than in a writing course, and this book is intended to provide occasions for readers to write. You will find a number of distinctive features in *Ways of Reading*. For one thing, it contains selections you don't usually see in a college reader: long, powerful, mysterious pieces like John Berger's "Ways of Seeing," Stanley Fish's "How to Recognize a Poem When You See One," Adrienne Rich's "When We Dead Awaken: Writing as Re-Vision," Clifford Geertz's "Deep Play:

Notes on the Balinese Cockfight," Thomas Kuhn's "The Historical Structure of Scientific Discovery," John Edgar Wideman's "Our Time," Julia Kristeva's "Stabat Mater," and Saul Bellow's "A Silver Dish." These are the sorts of readings we talk about when we talk with our colleagues. We have learned that we can talk about them with our students as well.

When we chose the essays and stories, we were looking for "readable" texts—that is, texts that leave some work for a reader to do. We wanted selections that invite students to be active, critical readers, that present powerful readings of common experience, that open up the familiar world and make it puzzling, rich, and problematic. We wanted to choose selections that invite students to be active readers and to take responsibility for their acts of interpretation. So we avoided the short set-pieces you find in so many anthologies. In a sense, those short selections misrepresent the act of reading. They can be read in a single sitting; they make arguments that can be easily paraphrased; they solve all the problems they raise; they wrap up Life and put it into a box; and so they turn reading into an act of appreciation, where the most that seems to be required is a nod of the head. And they suggest that a writer's job is to do just that, to write a piece that is similarly tight and neat and self-contained. We wanted to avoid pieces that were so plainly written or tightly bound that there was little for students to do but "get the point."

We learned that if our students had reading problems when faced with long and complex texts, the problems lay in the way they imagined a reader—the role a reader plays, what a reader does, why a reader reads (if not simply to satisfy the requirements of a course). When, for example, our students were puzzled by what they read, they took this as a sign of failure. ("It doesn't make any sense," they would say, as though the sense were supposed to be waiting on the page, ready for them the first time they read through.) And our students were haunted by the thought that they couldn't remember everything they had read (as though one could store all of Geertz's "Deep Play" in memory); or if they did remember bits and pieces, they felt that the fragmented text they possessed was evidence that they could not do what they were supposed to do. Our students were confronting the experience of reading, in other words, but they were taking the problems of reading—problems all readers face—and concluding that there was nothing for them to do but give up.

As expert readers, we have all learned what to do with a complex text. We know that we can go back to a text; we don't have to remember it— in fact, we've learned to mark up a text to ease that re-entry. We know that a reader is a person who puts together fragments. Those coherent readings we construct begin with confusion and puzzlement, and we construct those readings by writing and rewriting—by working on a text.

These are the lessons our students need to learn, and this is why a course in reading is also a course in writing. Our students need to learn that there is something they can do once they have first read through a complicated text; successful reading is not just a matter of "getting" an essay the first time. In a very real sense, you can't begin to feel the power a reader has until you realize the problems, until you realize that no one "gets" Geertz or Rich or Kuhn or Wideman all at once. You work on what you read, and then what you have at the end is something that is yours, something you made. And this is what the teaching apparatus in *Ways of Reading* is designed to do. In a sense, it says to students, "OK, let's get to work on these essays; let's see what you can make of them."

This, then, is the second distinctive feature you will find in *Ways of Reading:* reading and writing assignments designed to give students access to the essays and stories. After each selection, for example, you will find "Questions for a Second Reading." We wanted to acknowledge that re-reading is a natural way of carrying out the work of a reader, just as re-writing is a natural way of completing the work of a writer. It is not something done out of despair or as a punishment for not getting things right the first time. The questions we have written highlight what we see as central textual or interpretive problems. Geertz, for example, divides his essay into seven sections, each written in a different style. By going back through the essay with this in mind and by asking what Geertz is doing in each case (what his method is and what it enables him to accomplish), a student is in a position to see the essay as the enactment of a method and not just as a long argument with its point hidden away at the end. These questions might serve as preparations for class discussion or ways of directing students' work in journals. Whatever the case, they both honor and direct the work of rereading.

Each selection is also followed by two sets of writing assignments, "Assignments for Writing" and "Making Connections." The first set directs students back into the work they have just read. While the assignments vary, there are some basic principles behind them. They ask students to work on the essay by focusing on difficult or problematic moments in the text; they ask students to work on the author's examples, extending and testing his or her methods of analysis; or they ask students to apply the method of the essay (its way of seeing and understanding the world) to settings or experiences of their own. Students are asked, for example, to give a "Geertzian" reading to scenes from their own immediate culture (the behavior of teenagers at a shopping mall, characteristic styles in decorating a dorm room) and they are asked to imagine that they are working alongside Geertz and making his project their own. Or they are asked to consider the key examples in Rich's "When We Dead Awaken" (poems from various points in her career) to see how as writers they might use the key terms of her argument ("structures of oppression," "re-naming") in representing their own experience. The last assignments—"Making Connections"—invite students to read one essay in the context of another, to see, for example, if Kuhn's account of the "historical structure" of a discovery might be used to chart the stages in the development of Rich's poems or in Geertz's work on the Balinese cockfight. In a sense, then, the essays are offered as models, but not as "prose models" in the strictest sense. What they model is a way of seeing or reading the world, of both imagining problems and imagining methods to make those problems available to a writer.

At the end of the book, we have included several longer assignment sequences and a goodly number of shorter sequences. In some cases these incorporate single assignments from earlier in the book; in most cases they involve students in projects that extend anywhere from two to three weeks for the shorter sequences to an entire semester's worth of work for the longer ones. Almost all the sequences include several of the stories or essays in the anthology and require a series of separate drafts and revisions. In academic life, readers seldom read single essays in isolation, as though one were "finished" with Geertz after a week or two. Rather, they read with a purpose—with a project in mind or a problem to solve. The assignment sequences are designed to give students a feel for the rhythm and texture of an extended academic project. They offer, that is, one more way of reading and writing. Because these sequences lead students through intellectual projects proceeding from one week to the next, they enable them to develop authority as specialists, to feel the difference between being an expert and being a "common" reader on a single subject. And, with the luxury of time available for self-reflection, students can look back on what they have done, not only to revise what they know and the methods that enable what they know but also to take stock and comment on the value and direction of their work.

Because of their diversity, it is difficult to summarize the assignment sequences. Perhaps the best way to see what we have done is to turn to the back of the book and look at them. We have made them short enough to leave room for an individual instructor's desire to add assignments, to spend additional time on single essays, or to mix one sequence with another. They are meant to frame a project for students but to leave open possibilities for new directions.

You will also notice that there are few "glosses" appended to the essays. We have not added many editors' notes to define difficult words or to identify names or allusions to other authors or artists. We've omitted them because their presence suggests something we feel is false about reading. They suggest that good readers know all the words or pick up all the allusions or recognize every name that is mentioned. This is not true. Good readers do what they can and try their best to fill in the blanks; they ignore seemingly unimportant references and look up the important ones. There is no reason for students to feel they lack the knowledge necessary to complete a reading of these texts. We have translated foreign phrases and glossed some technical terms, but we have kept the selections as clean and open as possible.

Several of our reviewers asked us why we had included short stories in the collection. Perhaps the best answer is because we love to teach them. We think of them as having a status similar to that of the nonfiction case studies in the book: Thomas Cottle and Stephen Klineberg's on Ted and Ellie Graziano, John Edgar Wideman's on his brother Robby, Gloria Steinem's on her mother, or Robert Cole's on the children of privileged families. They offer thick, readable slices of life—material rich enough for a reader's time and effort. We realize that we are ignoring traditional distinctions between fiction and nonfiction, but we are not sure that these are key distinctions in a course that presents reading as an action to be completed by writing. Students can work on Bellow's story about Woody Selbst just as they can work on Cottle and Klineberg's representation of the Grazianos.

We have also been asked on several occasions whether the readings aren't finally just too hard for students. The answer is no. Students will have to work on the selections, but that is the point of the course and the reason, as we said before, why a reading course is also a course in writing. College students want to believe that they can strike out on their own, make their mark, do something they have never done before. They want to *be* experts, not just hear from them. This is the great pleasure, as well as the great challenge, of undergraduate instruction. It is not hard to convince students they ought to be able to speak alongside of (or even speak back to) Clifford Geertz, Adrienne Rich, or Roland Barthes. And, if a teacher is patient and forgiving—willing, that is, to let a student work out a reading of Barthes, willing to keep from saying, "No, that's not it" and filling the silence with the "right" reading—then students can, with care and assistance, learn to speak for themselves. It takes a certain kind of classroom, to be sure. A teacher who teaches this book will have to be comfortable turning the essays over to the students, even with the knowledge that they will not do immediately on their own what a professional could do—at least not completely, or with the same grace and authority.

In our own teaching, we have learned that we do not have to be experts on every figure or every area of inquiry represented in this book. And, frankly, that has come as a great relief. We can have intelligent, responsible conversations about Geertz's "Deep Play" without being experts on Geertz or on anthropology or ethnography. We needed to prepare ourselves to engage and direct students as readers, but we did not have to prepare ourselves to lecture on Kristeva or Geertz or Rich or Kuhn and what they have to say. The classes we have been teaching, and they have been some of the most exciting we have ever taught, have been classes where students—together and with their instructors—work on what these essays might mean.

So here we are, imagining students working shoulder to shoulder with Geertz and Rich and Kristeva, even talking back to them as the occasion arises. There is a wonderful Emersonian bravado in all this. But such is the case with strong and active readers. If we allow students to work on powerful texts, they will want to share the power. This is the heady fun of academic life, the real pleasure of thinking, reading, and writing. There is no reason to keep it secret from our students.

**Note to the Second Edition.** The second edition of *Ways of Reading* contains eleven new selections, including essays by Roland Barthes, Jean Franco, Simon Frith, Harriet Jacobs, Julia Kristeva, Mark Crispin Miller, Jane Tompkins, and Virginia Woolf and a new short story by Carlos Fuentes. Our principle of selection remained the same—we were looking for "readable" texts, pieces that instructors and students would find compelling for their subjects and methodologies, pieces, that is, that struck us as deserving of extended work. There are two new semester-long assignment sequences: one on gender and writing and one on cultural criticism. We have also added a number of shorter, "mini" sequences that vary in length by the number of selections they use and the number of assignments they ask for. The shortest of these might engage a class for two to three weeks, the longest for a month or two. We wrote these mini sequences at the request of instructors who had used the first edition and wanted more flexibility with the sequences and a wider range of projects to present to their students.

We've also updated and expanded *Resources for Teaching Ways of Reading*, adding four new essays by graduate students (including three on their work with the new assignment sequences). These essays offer advice to other graduate assistants on how to work with the book. They stand best, however, as examples of graduate students speaking frankly about their teaching with *Ways of Reading* and as examples of the kinds of papers graduate students can write when they use this book in teaching seminars.

With our colleagues, we have taught every selection in this book, including the new ones. Several of us worked together to prepare the new assignment sequences; they, too, have been tested in class. As we have traveled around giving talks, we've met many people who have used *Ways of Reading*. We have been delighted to hear them talk about how it has served their teaching, and we have learned much from their example. It is an unusual and exciting experience to see one's course turned into text, to be read, critiqued, deconstructed, and explained. We have many people to thank, but the list that follows can't begin to name all those to whom we owe a debt, and it can't begin to express our gratitude.

**Acknowledgments.** We owe much to the friendship and wisdom of the people with whom we have worked at Pitt, particularly Jean Ferguson Carr, Steve Carr, John Champagne, Nick Coles, Joe Harris, Michael Helfand, Paul Kameen, Mariolina Salvatori, Bill Smith, and Phil Smith; Rita Capezzi, Steve Harless, Richard Miller, Donna Dunbar-Odom, Carolyn Ball, Christine Conklin, Alpana Sharma, and Kathleen Welsch.

We also owe much to colleagues at other schools who have followed our work with interest and offered their support and criticism, particularly Nancy Sommers, Patricia Bizzell, Kurt Spellmeyer, Donald McQuade, Ben McClelland, Dolores Schriner, Louise Smith, Kathryn Flannery, Mike Rose, Charles Schuster, James Slevin, James Parlett, and Louise Wetherbee Phelps. Donald McQuade gave a close and careful reading to early drafts of the first edition of the book. Kathryn Flannery was the spirit presiding over the waters of the second edition. She is a remarkable reader and a wise and savvy teacher. Three of our graduate students worked on the new assignment sequences: John Champagne, Richard Miller, and Kathleen Welsch. They helped choose material and write assignments; we learned much from them.

We were fortunate to have a number of outstanding reviewers on the project. We would first like to thank those who did in-depth reviews of the first edition: Patricia Bizzell, Ben McClelland, Thomas Recchio, Sylvia G. Robins, Carolyn Smith, and Louise Smith. We're also grateful for the help of Linda Spargo, Deborah Pope, and the other graduate students at the University of Mississippi. We would also like to thank those who responded to our questionnaire: Kathy Abuschinow, Rutgers University; Jay Balderson, Western Illinois University; Sara M. Bates, Geneva College; Sonia Benson, University of Michigan; Kathryn N. Benzel, Kearney State College; Susan Bernstein, Tufts University; Elizabeth A. Bohls, Stanford University; Dolores M. Burton, Boston University; Rita A. Capezzi, University of Pittsburgh; Toni-Lee Capossela, Boston University; William W. Combs, Western Michigan University; Tom Crochunis, Rutgers University; Robert Crooks, Bentley College; Jim Crosswhite, University of California at San Diego; Rose Doyle Didero, Purdue University; Donna Dunbar-Odom, University of Pittsburgh; Suzanne Edwards, The Citadel; Judith Goleman, University of Massachusetts at Boston; Philip Greene, Adelphi University; Kay Halasek, University of Texas at Austin; Pamela Hardman, Cleveland State University; Steven R. Harless, University of Pittsburgh; Joseph Harris, University of Pittsburgh; Valerie Jablow, Rutgers University; Sharon Kane, Syracuse University; Ellen Kreitler, Rutgers University; Andrew Lakritz, Miami University; Scott Larkin, University of Mississippi; Leslie Lewis,

Indiana University; Dusky Loebel, Tulane University; Ken Luebbering, Lincoln University; Deborah McCollister, University of Mississippi; Robert McDonell, University of San Diego; David Martin, University of Wisconsin at Milwaukee; James Mauch, Foothill College; Verner D. Mitchell, U.S. Air Force Academy; Lolly Ockerstrom, Northeastern University; Patrick Pacheco, Santa Rosa Junior College; George Peranteau, College of DuPage; Robert C. Petersen, Middle Tennessee State University; Deborah Pope, University of Mississippi; Dave Powell, University of Mississippi; Donna Qualley, University of New Hampshire; Vincent Quinn, Brooklyn College; Sarah Rabkin, Crown College/University of California at Santa Cruz; Phoebe Reeves, University of Massachusetts at Boston; Rosalind Reilly, University of Richmond; Sandra M. Ross, University of Southern California; Jacqueline Sadashige, Indiana University; Maureen E. St. Laurent, Vanderbilt University; Norbert Schedler, University of Central Arkansas; Julie Slim, Muhlenberg College; Cornelia P. Spoor, Rutgers University; Joseph Stancliff, University of Mississippi; Gary R. Stephens, New York Institute of Technology; William L. Svitavsky, Syracuse University; Wendolyn E. Tetlow, William Paterson College; John M. Thomson, U.S. Air Force Academy; Myron Tuman, University of Alabama; Sandra Van Pelt, University of Mississippi; Kathleen Vollmer, Fairfield University; Julia Wagner, University of Pittsburgh; Nancy Ware, California State Poly University; Robert Whitney, Millsaps College; Melinda Wolf-Taylor, Grand Valley State University; Merla Wolk, University of Michigan; Portia Wright, University of Wisconsin at Milwaukee; David Zauhar, Gustavus Adolphus College.

Chuck Christensen of Bedford Books remains the best in the business. We owe our greatest debt to Joan Feinberg, a fine and thoughtful friend as well as a fine and thoughtful editor. As always, she was quick to understand what we wanted to do in our book and quick to understand when we didn't know what we wanted to do, and she managed all of the negotiations from start to finish with her characteristic grace and good humor. Riikka Melartin kept the project on track and kept a careful eye on the manuscript. Tara Masih skillfully guided the book through production. Susan M. S. Brown was a remarkable copy editor, quick to understand the quirks of our prose and with an amazing memory for pattern and detail. We are also grateful to Chris Rutigliano for her careful handling of the permissions.

And, finally, we are grateful to Joyce Dunlop Bartholomae and Jesse, Daniel, and Catherine Bartholomae; to Ellen Bishop and Matthew and Benjamin Petrosky, for their love and support and for seeing to it that life went on even when we were sitting in front of our computers.

# Contents

## *Assignment Sequences*   673

CONTENTS

# Introduction:
# Ways of Reading

## *Making a Mark*

*R*EADING involves a fair measure of push and shove. You make your mark on a book and it makes its mark on you. Reading is not simply a matter of hanging back and waiting for a piece, or its author, to tell you what the writing has to say. In fact, one of the difficult things about reading is that the pages before you will begin to speak only when the authors are silent and you begin to speak in their place, sometimes for them—doing their work, continuing their projects—and sometimes for yourself, following your own agenda.

This is an unusual way to talk about reading, we know. We have not mentioned finding information or locating an author's purpose or identifying main ideas, useful though these skills are, because the purpose of our book is to offer you occasions to imagine other ways of reading. We think of reading as a social interaction—sometimes peaceful and polite, sometimes not so peaceful and polite.

We'd like you to imagine that when you read the essays and stories

1

we've collected here, somebody is saying something to you, and we'd like you to imagine that you are in a position to speak back, to say something of your own in turn. In other words, we are not presenting our book as a miniature library (a place to find information) and we do not think of you, the reader, as a term-paper writer (a person looking for information to write down on three-by-five cards).

When you read, you hear an author's voice as you move along; you believe a person with something to say is talking to you. You pay attention, even when you don't completely understand what is being said, trusting that it will all make sense in the end, relating what the author says to what you already know or expect to hear or learn. Even if you don't quite grasp everything you are reading at every moment (and you won't), and even if you don't remember everything you've read (no reader does—at least not in long, complex pieces), you begin to see the outlines of the author's project, the patterns and rhythms of that particular way of seeing and interpreting the world.

When you stop to talk or write about what you've read, the author is silent; you take over—it is your turn to write, to begin to respond to what the author said. At that point this author and his or her text become something you construct out of what you remember or what you notice as you go back through the text a second time, working from passages or examples but filtering them through your own predisposition to see or read in particular ways.

In "The Achievement of Desire," one of the essays in this book, Richard Rodriguez tells the story of his education, of how he was drawn to imitate his teachers because of his desire to think and speak like them. His is not a simple story of hard work and success, however. In a sense, Rodriguez's education gave him what he wanted—status, knowledge, a way of understanding himself and his position in the world. At the same time, his education made it difficult to talk to his parents, to share their point of view; and to a degree, he felt himself becoming consumed by the powerful ways of seeing and understanding represented by his reading and his education. The essay can be seen as Rodriguez's attempt to weigh what he had gained against what he had lost.

If ten of us read his essay, each would begin with the same words on the page, but when we discuss the chapter (or write about it), each will retell and interpret Rodriguez's story differently; we emphasize different sections—some, for instance, would want to discuss the strange way Rodriguez learned to read, others would be taken by his difficult and changing relations to his teachers, and still others would want to think about Rodriguez's remarks about his mother and father.

Each of us will come to his or her own sense of what is significant, of what the point is, and the odds are good that what each of us makes of the essay will vary from one to another. Each of us will understand Rodriguez's story in his or her own way, even though we read the same piece. At the same time, if we are working with Rodriguez's essay (and not putting it aside or ignoring its peculiar way of thinking about education), we will be working within a framework he has established, one that makes education stand, metaphorically, for a complicated interplay between permanence and change, imitation and freedom, loss and achievement.

In "The Achievement of Desire," Rodriguez tells of reading a book by Richard Hoggart, *The Uses of Literacy*. He was captivated by a section of this book in which Hoggart defines a particular kind of student, the "scholarship boy." Here is what Rodriguez says:

> Then one day, leafing through Richard Hoggart's *The Uses of Literacy*, I found, in his description of the scholarship boy, myself. For the first time I realized that there were other students like me, and so I was able to frame the meaning of my academic success, its consequent price—the loss.

For Rodriguez, this phrase, "scholarship boy," became the focus of Hoggart's book. Other people, to be sure, would read that book and take different phrases or sections as the key to what Hoggart has to say. Some might argue that Rodriguez misread the book; that it is really about something else, about British culture, for example, or about the class system in England. The power and value of Rodriguez's reading, however, are represented by what he was able to *do* with what he read, and what he was able to do was not record information or summarize main ideas but, as he says, "frame the meaning of my academic success." Hoggart provided a frame, a way for Rodriguez to think and talk about his own history as a student. As he goes on in his essay, Rodriguez not only uses this frame to talk about his experience, but he resists it, argues with it. He casts his experience in Hoggart's terms but then makes those terms work for him by seeing both what they can and cannot do. This combination of reading, thinking, and writing is what we mean by *strong reading*, a way of reading we like to encourage in our students.

When we have taught "The Achievement of Desire" to our students, it has been almost impossible for them not to see themselves in Rodriguez's description of the scholarship boy (and this was true of students who were not minority students and not literally on scholarships). They, too, have found a way of framing (even inventing) their own lives as students—students whose histories involve both success and loss. When we have asked our students to write about this essay, however, some students have argued, and quite convincingly, that Rodriguez had either to abandon his family and culture or to remain ignorant. Other students have argued equally convincingly that Rodriguez's anguish was destructive and self-serving, that he was trapped into seeing his situation in terms that he might have replaced with others. He did not necessarily have to turn his back on his family. Some have contended that Rodriguez's problems with his family had nothing to do with what he says about education, that he himself shows how imitation need not blindly lead a person away from his culture, and these student essays, too, have been convincing.

Reading, in other words, can be the occasion for you to put things together, to notice this idea or theme rather than that one, to follow a writer's announced or secret ends while simultaneously following your own. When this happens, when you forge a reading of a story or an essay, you make your mark on it, casting it in your terms. But the story makes its mark on you as well, teaching you not only about a subject (Rodriguez's struggles with his teachers and his parents, for example) but about a way of seeing and understanding a subject. The text provides the opportunity for you to see through someone else's powerful language, to imagine your own familiar settings through the images, metaphors, and ideas of others. Rodriguez's essay, in other words, can make its mark on readers, but they, too, if they are strong, active readers, can make theirs on it.

Readers learn to put things together by writing. It is not something you can do, at least not to any degree, while you are reading. It requires that you work on what you have read, and that work best takes shape when you sit down to write. We will have more to say about this kind of thinking in a later section of the introduction, but for now let us say that writing gives you a way of going to work on the text you have read. To write about a story or essay, you go back to what you have read to find phrases or passages that define what for you are the key moments, that help you interpret sections that seem difficult or troublesome or mysterious. If you are writing an essay of your own, the work that you are doing gives a purpose and a structure to that rereading.

Writing also, however, gives you a way of going back to work on the text of your own reading. It allows you to be self-critical. You can revise not just to make your essay neat or tight or tidy but to see what kind of reader you have been, to examine the pattern and consequences in the choices you have made. Revision, in other words, gives you the chance to work on your essay, but it also gives you an opportunity to work on your reading—to qualify or extend or question your interpretation of, say, "The Achievement of Desire."

We can describe this process of "re-vision," or re-seeing, fairly simply. You should not expect to read "The Achievement of Desire" once and completely understand the essay or know what you want to say. You will work out what you have to say while you write. And once you have constructed a reading—once you have completed a draft of your essay, in other words—you can step back, see what you have done, and go back to work on it. Through this activity—writing and rewriting—we have seen our students become strong, active, and critical readers.

Not everything a reader reads is worth that kind of effort. The essays and stories we have chosen for this book all provide, we feel, powerful ways of seeing (or framing) our common experience. The selections cannot be quickly summarized. They are striking, surprising, sometimes troubling in how they challenge common ways of seeing the world. Some of them (we're thinking of pieces by Adrienne Rich, Stanley Fish, Clifford Geertz, and Virginia Woolf) have captured and altered the way our culture sees and understands daily experience. The essays have changed the ways people think and write. In fact, every selection in the book is one that has given us, our students, and colleagues that dramatic experience, almost like a discovery, when we suddenly saw things as we had never seen them before and, as a consequence, we had to work hard to understand what had happened and how our thinking had changed.

If we recall, for example, the first time we read Virginia Woolf's "A Room of One's Own," or John Berger's "Ways of Seeing," we know that they have radically shaped our thinking. We carry these essays with us in our minds, mulling over them, working through them, hearing Woolf and Berger in sentences we write or sentences we read; we introduce the essays in classes we teach whenever we can; we are surprised, reading them for the third or fourth time, to find things we didn't see before. It's not that we failed to "get" these essays the first time around. In fact, we're not sure we have captured them yet, at least not in any final sense, and we disagree in basic ways about what Woolf and Berger are saying or about how these essays might best be used. Essays like these are not the sort that you can "get" like a loaf of bread at the store. We're each convinced that the essays are ours in that we know best what's going on in them, and yet we have also become theirs, creatures of these essays, because of the ways they have come to dominate our seeing, talking, reading, and writing. This captivity is something we welcome, yet it is also something we resist.

Our experience with these texts is a remarkable one and certainly hard to provide for others, but the challenges and surprises are reasons we read—we hope to be taken and changed in just these ways. Or, to be more accurate, it is why we read outside the daily requirements to keep up with the news or conduct our business. And it is why we bring reading into our writing courses.

## *Ways of Reading*

Before explaining how we organized this book, we would like to say more about the purpose and place of the kind of strong, aggressive, labor-intensive reading we've been referring to.

Readers face many kinds of experiences, and certain texts are written with specific situations in mind and invite specific ways of reading. Some texts, for instance, serve very practical purposes—they give directions or information. Others, like the short descriptive essays often used in English textbooks and anthologies, celebrate common ways of seeing and thinking and ask primarily to be admired. These texts seem self-contained; they announce their own meanings with little effort and ask little from the reader, making it clear how they want to be read and what they have to say. They ask only for a nod of the head or for the reader to take notes and give a sigh of admiration ("yes, that was very well said"). They are clear and direct. It is as though the authors could anticipate all the questions their own essays might raise and solve all the problems a reader might imagine. There is not much work for a reader to do, in other words, except, perhaps, to take notes and, in the case of textbooks, to work step-by-step, trying to remember as much as possible.

This is how assigned readings are often presented in university classrooms. Introductory textbooks (in biology or business, for instance) are good examples of books that ask little of readers outside of note-taking and memorization. In these texts the writers are experts and your job, as novice, is to digest what they have to say. And, appropriately, the task set before you is to summarize—so you can speak again what the author said, so you can better remember what you read. Essay tests are an example of the writing tasks that often follow this kind of reading. You might, for instance, study the human nervous system through textbook readings and lectures and then be asked to write a summary of what you know from both sources. Or a teacher might ask you during a class discussion to paraphrase a paragraph from a textbook describing chemical cell communication to see if you understand what you've read.

Another typical classroom form of reading is reading for main ideas. With this kind of reading you are expected to figure out what most people (or most people within a certain specialized group of readers) would take as the main idea of a selection. There are good reasons to read for main ideas. For one, it is a way to learn how to imagine and anticipate the values and habits of a particular group—test-makers or, if you're studying business, Keynesian economists, perhaps. If you are studying business, to continue this example, you must learn to notice what Keynesian economists notice—for instance, when they analyze the problems of growing government debt—to share key terms, to know the theoretical positions they take, and to adopt for yourself their common examples and interpretations, their jargon, and their established findings.

There is certainly nothing wrong with reading for information or reading to learn what experts have to say about their fields of inquiry. These are not, however, the only ways to read, although they are the ones most often taught. Perhaps because we think of ourselves as writing teachers, we are concerned with presenting other ways of reading in the college and university curriculum.

A danger arises in assuming that reading is only a search for information or main ideas. There are ways of thinking through problems and working with written texts which are essential to academic life, but which are not represented by summary and paraphrase or by note-taking and essay exams.

Student readers, for example, can take responsibility for determining the meaning of the text. They can work as though they were doing something other than finding ideas already there on the page and they can be guided by their own impressions or questions as they read. We are not, now, talking about finding hidden meanings. If such things as hidden meanings can be said to exist, they are hidden by readers' habits and prejudices (by readers' assumptions that what they read should tell them what they already know), or by readers' timidity and passivity (by their unwillingness to take the responsibility to speak their minds and say what they notice).

Reading to locate meaning in the text places a premium on memory, yet a strong reader is not necessarily a person with a good memory. This point may seem minor, but we have seen too many students haunted because they could not remember everything they read or retain a complete essay in their minds. A reader could set herself the task of remembering as much as she could from Percy's "The Loss of the Creature," an essay filled with stories about tourists at the Grand Canyon and students in a biology class, but a reader could also do other things with that essay; a reader might figure out, for example, how both students and tourists might be said to have a common problem seeing what they want to see. Students who read Percy's essay as a memory test end up worrying about bits and pieces (bits and pieces they could go back and find if they had to) and turn their attention away from the more pressing problem of how to make sense of a difficult and often ambiguous essay.

A reader who needs to have access to something in the essay can use simple memory aids. A reader can go back and scan, for one thing, to find passages or examples that might be worth reconsidering. Or a reader can construct a personal index, making marks in the margin or underlining passages that seem interesting or mysterious or difficult. A mark is a way of saying, "This is something I might want to work on later." If you mark the selections in this book as you read them, you will give yourself a working record of what, at the first moment of reading, you felt might be worth a second reading.

If Percy's essay presents problems for a reader, they are problems of a different order from summary and recall altogether. The essay is not the sort that tells you what it says. You would have difficulty finding one sentence that sums up or announces, in a loud and clear voice, what he is talking about. At the point you think Percy is about to summarize, he turns to one more example that complicates the picture, as though what he is discussing defies his attempts to sum things up. Percy is talking about tourists and students, about such things as individual "sovereignty" and our media culture's "symbolic packages," but if he has a point to make, it cannot be stated in a sentence or two.

In fact, Percy's essay is challenging reading in part because it does not have a single, easily identifiable main idea. A reader could infer that it has several points to make, none of which can be said easily and some of which, perhaps, are contradictory. To search for information, or to ignore the rough edges in search of a single, paraphrasable idea, is to divert attention from the task at hand, which is not to remember what Percy says but to speak about the essay and what it means to you, the reader. In this sense, the Percy essay is not the sum of its individual parts; it is, more accurately, what its readers make of it.

A reader could go to an expert on Percy to solve the problem of what to make of the essay—perhaps to a teacher, perhaps to a book in the library. And if the reader pays attention, he could remember what the expert said or she could put down notes on paper. But in doing either, the reader only rehearses what he or she has been told, abandoning the responsibility to make the essay meaningful. There are ways of reading, in other words, in which Percy's essay, "The Loss of the Creature," is not what it means to the experts but what it means to you as a reader willing to take the chance to construct a reading. You can be the authority on Percy; you don't have to turn to others. The meaning of the essay, then, is something you develop as you go along, something for which you must take final responsibility. The meaning is forged from reading the essay, to be sure, but it is determined by what you do with the essay, by the connections you can make and your explanation of why those connections are important, and by your account of what Percy might mean when he talks about "symbolic packages" or a "loss of sovereignty" (phrases Percy uses as key terms in the essay). This version of Percy's essay will finally be yours; it will not be exactly what Percy said. (Only his words in the order he wrote them would say exactly what he said.) You will choose the path to take through his essay and support it as you can with arguments, explanations, examples, and commentary.

If an essay or story is not the sum of its parts but something you as a reader create by putting together those parts that seem to matter personally, then the way to begin, once you have read a selection in this collection, is by reviewing what you recall, by going back to those places that stick in your memory—or, perhaps, to those sections you marked with checks or notes in the margins. You begin by seeing what you can make of these memories and notes. You should realize that with essays as long and complex as those we've included in this book, you will never feel, after a single reading, as though you have command of everything you read. This is not a problem. After four or five readings (should you give any single essay that much attention), you may still feel that there are parts you missed or don't understand. This sense of incompleteness is part of the experience of reading, at least the experience of reading serious work. And it is part of the experience of a strong reader. No reader could retain one of these essays in her mind, no matter how proficient her memory or how experienced she might be. No reader, at least no reader we would trust, would admit that he understood everything that Adrienne Rich or Clifford Geertz or John Edgar Wideman had to say. What strong readers know is that they have to begin, and they have to begin regardless of their doubts or hesitations. What you have after your first reading of an essay is a starting place, and you begin with your marked passages or examples or notes, with questions to answer, or with problems to solve. Strong readings, in other words, put a premium on individual acts of attention and composition.

## Strong Readers, Strong Texts

We chose essays and stories for this book that invite strong readings. Our selections require more attention (or a different form of attention) than a written summary, a reduction to gist, or a recitation of main ideas. They are not "easy" reading. The challenges they present, however, do not make them inaccessible to college students. The essays are not specialized studies; they have interested, pleased, or piqued general and specialist audiences alike. To say that they are challenging is to say, then, that they leave some work for a reader to do. They are designed to teach a reader new ways to read (or to step outside habitual ways of reading), and they anticipate readers willing to take the time to learn. These readers need not be experts on the subject matter. Perhaps the most difficult problem for students is to believe that this is true.

You do not need experts to explain these stories and essays, although you could probably go to the library and find an expert guide to most of the selections we've included. Let's take, for example, Adrienne Rich's, "When We Dead Awaken: Writing as Re-Vision." This essay looks at the history of women's writing (and at Rich's development as a poet). It argues that women have been trapped within a patriarchal culture—speaking in men's voices and telling stories prepared by men—and, as a consequence, according to Rich, "We need to know the writing of the past, and know it differently than we have ever known it; not to pass on a tradition but to break its hold over us."

You could go to the library to find out how Rich is regarded by experts, by literary critics or feminist scholars, for example; you could learn how her work fits into an established body of work on women's writing and the representation of women in modern culture. You could see what others have said about the writers she cites: Virginia Woolf, Jane Austen, and Elizabeth Bishop. You could see how others have read and made use of Rich's essay. You could see how others have interpreted the poems she includes as part of her argument. You could look for standard definitions of key terms, like "patriarchy" or "formalism."

Though it is often important to seek out other texts and to know what other people are saying or have said, it is often necessary and even desirable to begin on your own. Rich can also be read outside any official system of interpretation. She is talking, after all, about our daily experience. And when she addresses the reader, she addresses a person—not a term-paper writer. When she says, "We need to know the writing of the past, and know it differently than we have ever known it," she means us and what we know and how we know what we know. (Actually the "we" of her essay refers most accurately to women readers, leading men to feel the kind of exclusion women must feel when the reader is always "he." But it is us, the men who are in the act of reading this essay, who feel and respond to this pressure.)

The question, then, is not what Rich's words might mean to a literary critic, or generally to those who study contemporary American culture. The question is what you, the reader, can make of those words and Rich's use of them in the essay, given your own experience, your goals, and the work you do with what she has written. In this sense, "When We Dead Awaken: Writing as Re-Vision" is not what it means to others (those who have already decided what it means) but what it means to you, and this meaning is something you compose when you write about the essay; it is your account of what Rich says and how what she says might be said to make sense.

A teacher, poet, and critic we admire, I. A. Richards, once said, "Read as though it made sense and perhaps it will." To take command of complex material like the essays and stories in this book, you need not subordinate yourself to experts; you can assume the authority to provide such a reading on your own. This means you must allow yourself a certain tentativeness and recognize your limits. You should not assume that it is your job to solve the problems between men and women. You can speak with authority while still acknowledging that complex issues *are* complex.

There is a paradox here. On the one hand, the essays are rich, magnificent, too big for anyone to completely grasp all at once, and before them, as before inspiring spectacles, it seems appropriate to stand humbly, admiringly. And yet, on the other hand, a reader must speak with authority.

In "The American Scholar" (an essay included in this book), Ralph Waldo Emerson says, "Meek young men grow up in libraries, believing in their duty to accept the views, which Cicero, which Locke, which Bacon, have given, forgetful that Cicero, Locke, and Bacon were only young men in libraries when they wrote these books." What Emerson offers here is not a fact but an attitude. There is creative reading, he says, as well as creative writing. It is up to you to treat authors as your equals, as people who will allow you to speak too. At the same time, you must respect the difficulty and complexity of their texts and of the issues and questions they examine. Little is to be gained, in other words, by turning Rich's essay into a message that would fit on a poster in a dorm room: "Be Yourself" or "Stand on Your Own Two Feet."

## Reading with and against the Grain

From this pushing and shoving with and against texts, we come then to a difficult mix of authority and humility. A reader takes charge of a text; a reader gives generous attention to someone else's (a writer's) key terms and methods, commits his time to her examples, tries to think in her language, imagines that this strange work is important, compelling, at least for the moment.

Most of the questions in *Ways of Reading* will have you moving back and forth in these two modes, reading with and against the grain of a text, reproducing an author's methods, questioning his or her direction and authority. With the essay "When We Dead Awaken," for example, we have asked students to give a more complete and detailed reading of Rich's poems (the poems included in the essay) than she does, to put her terms to work, to extend her essay by extending the discussion of her examples. We have asked students to give themselves over to her essay—recognizing that this is not necessarily an easy thing to do. Or, again in Rich's name, we have asked students to tell a story of their own experience, a story similar to the one she tells, one that can be used as an example of the ways a person is positioned by a dominant culture. Here we are saying, in effect, read your world in Rich's terms. Notice what she would notice. Ask the questions she would ask. Try out her conclusions.

And we have asked students to turn back against Rich's project, to ask questions that they believe might come as a surprise, to engage her, through a discussion of her examples, in a dialogue. How might her poems be read to counter what she wants to say about them? If her essay argues for a new language for women, how is this language represented in the final poem or the final paragraphs, when the poem seems unreadable and

**11**

the final paragraph sounds familiarly like the usual political rhetoric? If Rich is arguing for a collective movement, a "we" represented by the "we" of her essay, who is included and who is excluded by the terms and strategies of her writing? To what degree might you say that this is a conscious or necessary strategy?

Many of the essays in this book provide examples of writers working against the grain of the common readings or everyday language. This is true of Roland Barthes and John Berger, for example, who define the material of our culture (striptease for Barthes and art museums for Berger) against what they take to be the usual misreadings of them. It is true of John Edgar Wideman, who reads against his own text while he writes it— asking questions that disturb the story as it emerges on the page. It is true of Harriet Jacobs, Julia Kristeva, and Virginia Woolf, whose writing shows the signs of their efforts to work against the grain of the standard essay, habitual ways of representing what it means to know something, to be somebody, to speak before others.

This, we've found, is the most difficult work for students to do, this work against the grain. For good reasons and bad, students typically define their skill by reproducing rather than questioning or revising the work of their teachers (or the work of those their teachers ask them to read). It is important to read generously and carefully and to learn to submit to projects that others have begun. But it is also important to know what you are doing—to understand where this work comes from, whose interests it serves, how and where it is kept together by will rather than desire, and what it might have to do with you. To fail to ask the fundamental questions—where am I in this? how can I make my mark? whose interests are represented? what can I learn by reading with or against the grain?—to fail to ask these questions is to mistake skill for understanding, and it is to misunderstand the goals of a liberal education. All of the essays in this book, we would argue, ask to be read, not simply reproduced; they ask to be read and to be read with a difference. Our goal is to make that difference possible.

## Reading and Writing:
## The Questions and Assignments

Strong readers, we've said, remake what they have read to serve their own ends, putting things together, figuring out how ideas and examples relate, explaining as best they can material that is difficult or problematic, translating phrases like Richard Rodriguez's "scholarship boy" into their own terms. At these moments, it is hard to distinguish the act of reading from the act of writing. In fact, the connection between reading and writing can be seen as almost a literal one, since the best way you can show your reading of a rich and dense essay like "The Achievement of Desire" is by writing down your thoughts, placing one idea against another, commenting on what you've done, taking examples into account, looking back at where you began, perhaps changing your mind, and moving on.

Readers, however, seldom read a single essay in isolation, as though their own job were to arrive at some sense of what an essay has to say. Although we couldn't begin to provide examples of all the various uses of reading in academic life, it is often the case that readings provide information and direction for investigative projects, whether they are philosophical or scientific in nature. The reading and writing assignments that follow each selection in this book are designed to point you in certain directions, to give you ideas and projects to work with, and to challenge you to see one writer's ideas through another's.

Strong readers often read critically, weighing, for example, an author's claims and interpretations against evidence—evidence provided by the author in the text, evidence drawn from other sources, or the evidence that is assumed to be part of a reader's own knowledge and experience. Critical reading can produce results as far-reaching as a biochemist publicly challenging the findings and interpretations in an article on cancer research in the *New England Journal of Medicine* or as quiet as a student offering a personal interpretation of a story in class discussion.

You will find that the questions we have included in our reading and writing assignments often direct you to test what you think an author is saying by measuring it against your own experience. Paulo Freire, for example, in "The 'Banking' Concept of Education," talks about the experience of the student, and one way for you to develop or test your reading of his essay is to place what he says in the context of your own experience, searching for examples that are similar to his and examples that differ from his. If the writers in this book are urging you to give strong readings of your common experience, you have access to what they say because they are talking not only to you but about you. Freire has a method that he employs when he talks about the classroom—one that compares "banking" education with "problem-posing" education. You can try out his method and his terms on examples of your own, continuing his argument as though you were working with him on a common project. Or you can test his argument as though you want to see not only where and how it will work but where and how it will not.

You will also find questions that ask you to extend the argument of the essay by looking in detail at some of the essay's own examples. John Berger, for example, gives a detailed analysis of two paintings by Frans Hals in "Ways of Seeing." Other paintings in the essay he refers to only briefly. One way of working on his essay is to look at the other examples, trying to do with them what he has done for you earlier.

Readers seldom, however, read an essay in isolation, as though, having once worked out a reading of Virginia Woolf's "A Room of One's Own," they could go on to something else, something unrelated. It is unusual for anyone, at least in an academic setting, to read in so random a fashion. Readers read most often because they have a project in hand—a question they are working on or a problem they are trying to solve. For example, if as a result of reading Woolf's essay you become interested in the difference between women's writing and men's writing, and you begin to notice things you would not have noticed before, then you can read other essays in the book through this frame. If you have a project in mind, that project will help determine how you read these other essays. Sections of an essay that might otherwise seem unimportant suddenly become important— Emerson's unusual prose style, Rich's references to Woolf, the moments when Harriet Jacobs addresses the "women of the North." Woolf may enable you to read Jacobs's narrative differently. Jacobs may spur you to rethink Woolf.

In a sense, then, you do have the chance to become an expert reader, a reader with a project in hand, one who has already done some reading, who has watched others at work, and who has begun to develop a method of analysis and a set of key terms. You might read Carlos Fuentes's story, "The Son of Andrés Aparicio," for example, in the context of Jean Franco's discussion of the Latin American "imaginary," or use Thomas Kuhn's system for charting the internal structure of a discovery to examine the process of Clifford Geertz's discoveries concerning cockfights in Bali, or use Robert Coles's concept of entitlement to understand Richard Rodriguez and his concern about what he did and did not deserve to get from his education. Imagining yourself operating alongside some of the major figures in contemporary thought can be great fun and heady work—particularly when you have the occasion to speak back to them.

In every case, then, the material we provide to direct your work on the essay or story will have you constructing a reading, but then doing something with what you have read—using the selection as a frame through which you can understand (through which you can "read") your own experience, the examples of others, or the ideas and methods of other writers.

You may find that you have to alter your sense of who a writer is and what a writer does as you work on your own writing. Writers are often told that they need to begin with a clear sense of what they want to do and what they want to say. The writing assignments we've written, we believe, give you a sense of what you want (or need) to do. We define a problem for you to work on, and the problem will frame the task for you. You will have to decide where you will go in the texts you have read to find materials to work with, the primary materials that will give you a place to begin as you work on your essay. It would be best, however, if you did not feel that you need to have a clear sense of what you want to say before you begin. You may begin to develop a sense of what you want to say while you are writing—as you begin, for example, to examine how and why Emerson's essay could be said to be difficult to read, and what that difficulty might enable you to say about what Emerson expects of a reader. It may also be the case, however, that the subjects you will be writing about are too big for you to assume that you need to have all the answers or that it is up to you to have the final word or to solve the problems once and for all. When you work on your essays, you should cast yourself in the role of one who is exploring a question, examining what might be said, and speculating on possible rather than certain conclusions. If you consider your responses to be provisional, examples of what might be said by a bright and serious student at this point in time, you will be in a position to learn more, as will those who read what you write. Think of yourself, then, as a writer intent on opening a subject up rather than closing one down.

Let us turn briefly now to the various categories of reading and writing assignments you will find in the book.

## Questions for a Second Reading

Immediately following each selection are questions designed to guide your second reading. You may, as we've said, prefer to follow your own instincts as you search for the materials to build your understanding of the essay or story. These questions are meant to assist that process or develop those instincts. Most of the essays and stories in the book are longer and more difficult than those you may be accustomed to reading. They are difficult enough that any reader would have to reread them and work to understand them; the second reading questions are meant to suggest ways of beginning that work.

The second reading questions characteristically ask you to consider the relations between ideas and examples in what you have read or to test specific statements in the essays against your own experience (so that you can get a sense of the author's habit of mind, his or her way of thinking about subjects that are available to you, too). Some turn your attention to what we take to be key terms or concepts, asking you to define these terms by observing how the writer uses them throughout the essay.

These are the questions that seemed "natural" to us; they reflect our habitual way of reading and, we believe, the general habits of mind of the academic community. These questions have no simple answers; you will not find a correct answer hidden somewhere in the selection. In short, they are not the sorts of questions asked on SAT or ACT exams. They are real questions, questions that ask about the basic methods of an essay or about the issues the essay raises. They pose problems for interpretation or indicate sections where, to our minds, there is some interesting work for a reader to do. They are meant to reveal possible ways of reading the text, not to indicate that there is only one correct way, and that we have it.

You may find it useful to take notes as you read through each selection a second time, perhaps in a journal you can keep as a sourcebook for more formal written work.

## Assignments for Writing

This book actually offers three different kinds of writing assignments: assignments that ask you to write about a single essay or story; assignments that ask you to read one selection through the frame of another; and longer sequences of assignments that define a project within which three or four of the selections serve as primary sources. All of these assignments serve a dual purpose. Like the second reading questions, they suggest a way for you to reconsider the stories or essays; they give you access from a different perspective. The assignments also encourage you to be strong readers and actively interpret what you have read. In one way or another, they all invite you to use a story or an essay as a way of framing experience, as a source of terms and methods to enable you to interpret something else—some other text, events and objects around you, or your own memories and experience. The assignment sequences can be found at the end of the book. The others (titled Assignments for Writing and Making Connections) come immediately after each selection.

Assignments for Writing ask you to write about a single selection. Although some of these assignments call for you to paraphrase or reconstruct difficult passages, most ask you to interpret what you have read with a specific purpose in mind. The work you are to do is generally of two sorts. For most of the essays, one question asks you to interpret a moment from your own experience through the frame of the essay. This, you will remember, is the use that Rodriguez made of Richard Hoggart's *The Uses of Literacy.*

An essay by Thomas Kuhn, "The Historical Structure of Scientific Discovery," provides a method for analyzing the internal structure of scientific discoveries. Although we cannot assume that you have made a scientific discovery, we can assume that at some point you have discovered something—about yourself, your friends, your school, or the world around you. Thus, one assignment asks you to describe a discovery that gave you a new view of something familiar and to then give that discovery a Kuhnian analysis, to examine it as though you were continuing Kuhn's work in a project of your own. The point of this exercise is to develop your command

16

of Kuhn's method and key terms by applying them to a separate case, by seeing how this essay on great moments in science might connect with moments in your own life. We believe that by doing such an assignment you will learn about Kuhn and the work he does, but we also believe that through Kuhn you can come to a new understanding of your own experience.

Other assignments, however, ask you to turn an essay back on itself or to extend the conclusions of the essay by reconsidering the examples the writer has used to make his or her case. Adrienne Rich's essay, "When We Dead Awaken: Writing as Re-Vision," is built around a series of poems she wrote at various stages in her career. She says that the development represented by these poems reflects her growing understanding of the problems women in a patriarchal society have in finding a language for their own experience. She presents the poems as examples but offers little detailed discussion of them. One of the assignments, then, asks you to describe the key differences in these poems. It next asks you to comment on the development of her work and to compare your account of that development with hers.

In her essay, Rich also says that writing is "re-naming." This is an interesting and, one senses, a potentially powerful term. For it to be useful, however, a reader must put it to work, to see what results when you accept the challenge of the essay and think about writing as re-naming. Another assignment, then, asks you to apply this term to one of her poems and to discuss the poem as an act of re-naming. The purpose of this assignment is not primarily to develop your skill as a reader of poems but to develop your sense of the method and key terms of Rich's argument.

## Making Connections

The connections questions will have you work with two or more readings at a time. These are not so much questions that ask you to compare or contrast the essays or stories as they are directions on how you might use one text as the context for interpreting another. Franco, for example, talks in "Killing Priests, Nuns, Women, Children" about a "Latin American imaginary," an imaginary topography that serves as a set of references for thinking about, organizing, and valuing space. And Carlos Fuentes's story, "The Son of Andrés Aparicio," might be called a "Latin American imaginary," a story that offers an imaginary Latin American topography. Accordingly, there is an assignment that asks you to use Fuentes's story to test or extend Franco's presentation of the Latin American imaginary and to examine the degree to which Fuentes's story reflects (or revises, or resists) the changes Franco says came with the political violence of the 1960s. Other assignments follow this pattern. You are asked to use Clifford

Geertz's methods to interpret the examples that John Berger provides of the ways in which our culture reproduces and uses images from the past. Geertz can provide insight into a way of looking at Berger that you would not have been able to invent on your own. In another assignment you are asked to examine the case study of Ted and Ellie Graziano in the context of Gloria Steinem's argument about the "formidable forces" arrayed against her mother, which are responsible for her transformation from an "energetic, fun-loving, book-loving woman . . . into someone who was afraid to be alone . . . and who could rarely concentrate enough to read a book."

The purpose of all of these assignments is to demonstrate how the work of one author can be used as a frame for reading and interpreting the work of another. This can be exciting work, and it demonstrates a basic principle of liberal arts education: students should be given the opportunity to adopt different points of view, including those of scholars and writers who have helped to shape modern thought. These kinds of assignments give you the chance, even as a novice, to try your hand at the work of professionals.

## The Assignment Sequences

The assignment sequences are more broad-ranging versions of the making connections assignments; in the sequences several reading and writing assignments are linked and directed toward a single goal. They allow you to work on projects that require more time and incorporate more readings than would be possible in a single assignment. And they encourage you to develop your own point of view in concert with those of the professionals who wrote the essays and stories you are reading.

The assignments in a sequence build on one another, each relying on the ones before. In one sequence, for example, you begin with Walker Percy's essay, "The Loss of the Creature," an essay that considers the problems tourists and students have in seeing and understanding that which lies before them. You are given the chance to work on the essay, to determine what, so far as you are concerned, it is saying about both the nature of this problem and how it might be overcome. The second assignment asks you to comment on experiences you have had as a student or a tourist using Percy's terms, writing about yourself as though you were carrying out a project Percy had begun.

The opening assignments are followed by others that have you working on essays by other writers who consider why people do or don't see things. You have a chance to look at a student (Richard Rodriguez) and a tourist (Clifford Geertz) in order to test Percy's views and those of the other writers. And, finally, you are asked to carve out a position of your own, to see what, after studying all these essays, you might add to an ongoing con-

18

versation about tourists and students and the problems people have seeing and understanding the world around them.

The sequences allow you to participate in an extended academic project, one in which you take a position, revise it, look at a new example, hear what someone else has to say, revise it again, and see what conclusions you can draw about your subject. These projects always take time—they go through stages and revisions as a writer develops a command over his or her material, pushing against habitual ways of thinking, learning to examine an issue from different angles, rejecting quick conclusions, seeing the power of understanding that comes from repeated effort, and feeling the pleasure writers take when they find their own place in the context of others whose work they admire. This is the closest approximation we can give you of the rhythm and texture of academic life, and we offer our book as an introduction to its characteristic ways of reading, thinking, and writing.

# The Readings

# ROLAND
# BARTHES

$R$OLAND BARTHES (b. 1915) was born in Cherbourg, France, and studied French literature and classics at the University of Paris. He taught French in Romania and Egypt before joining the Centre National de la Recherche Scientifique to work in sociology and linguistics. After the success of his early work in the 1960s, Barthes taught at the Sorbonne, the University of Paris, the Collège de France, and Johns Hopkins University in Baltimore.

Barthes was a distinguished scholar ("the founder of French and modern semiotics"), but he was also a public figure, a brilliant, extravagant, and popular essayist whose work was read widely outside the academy. There was plenty to read. In his lifetime he published over 150 articles and seventeen books, including Writing Degree Zero, Elements of Semiology, The Pleasure of the Text, The Fashion System, Image-Music-Text, and Mythologies, from which the following excerpts were taken. He was also a contributor to Tel Quel, the influential French journal with which Julia Kristeva was associated. Barthes died in 1980.

Barthes wrote about language, linguistics, and literature, about music, film, and painting, but he was also instrumental in extending the study of culture to the everyday, particularly in Mythologies, where he demonstrated possibilities for reading the common material of culture: the Eiffel Tower, the face of Greta Garbo, an advertisement for margarine. In the introduction to Mythologies, Barthes says, "The starting point of these reflections was usually a feeling of impatience at the sight of the 'naturalness' with which newspapers, art and common sense constantly dress up a reality which, even though it is the one we live in, is undoubtedly determined by history. . . . I resented seeing Nature and History confused at every turn, and I wanted to track down, in the decorative display of what-goes-without-saying, the ideological abuse, which, in my view, is hidden there."

Barthes's work asks us to think of predictable, routine, organized events like a wrestling match as though they were texts, texts created not by a single author but by some other, larger agency (called "history" in the passage just quoted). These "texts" reproduce a tradition, assume an audience, and must be read, Barthes argues. He asks us to "read" a wrestling match, for example, in the same way we'd read a literary text. When we fail to "read" these nonlinguistic texts, we mistake "History" for "Nature." We forget that nonlinguistic texts are written—even if we cannot find their author, they embody design and intention; they are constructed to create effects, to produce certain ends, shaping both what and how we think. Barthes's Mythologies insists on the importance of learning to read the social text, lest we confuse the world that we and others have constructed for one that seems "naturally" and inevitably and peacefully there.

# The World of Wrestling

The grandiloquent truth of gestures
on life's great occasions.
— BAUDELAIRE

The virtue of all-in wrestling is that it is the spectacle of excess. Here we find a grandiloquence which must have been that of ancient theaters. And in fact wrestling is an open-air spectacle, for what makes the circus or the arena what they are is not the sky (a romantic value suited rather to fashionable occasions), it is the drenching and vertical quality of the flood of light. Even hidden in the most squalid Parisian halls, wrestling partakes of the nature of the great solar spectacles, Greek drama and bullfights: in both, a light without shadow generates an emotion without reserve.

There are people who think that wrestling is an ignoble sport. Wrestling is not a sport, it is a spectacle, and it is no more ignoble to attend a wrestled performance of Suffering than a performance of the sorrows of Arnolphe or Andromaque. [1] Of course, there exists a false wrestling, in which the participants unnecessarily go to great lengths to make a show of a fair fight; this is of no interest. True wrestling, wrongly called amateur wrestling, is performed in second-rate halls, where the public spontaneously attunes itself to the spectacular nature of the contest, like the audience at a suburban cinema. Then these same people wax indignant because wrestling is a stage-managed sport (which ought, by the way, to mitigate its ignominy). The public is completely uninterested in knowing whether the contest is rigged or not, and rightly so; it abandons itself to the primary virtue of the spectacle, which is to abolish all motives and all consequences: what matters is not what it thinks but what it sees.

This public knows very well the distinction between wrestling and boxing; it knows that boxing is a Jansenist° sport, based on a demonstration of excellence. One can bet on the outcome of a boxing match: with wrestling, it would make no sense. A boxing match is a story which is constructed before the eyes of the spectator; in wrestling, on the contrary, it is each moment which is intelligible, not the passage of time. The spectator is not interested in the rise and fall of fortunes; he expects the transient image of certain passions. Wrestling therefore demands an immediate reading of the juxtaposed meanings, so that there is no need to connect them. The logical conclusion of the contest does not interest the wrestling fan, while on the contrary a boxing match always implies a science of the future. In other words, wrestling is a sum of spectacles, of which no single one is a function: each moment imposes the total knowledge of a passion which rises erect and alone, without ever extending to the crowning moment of a result.

Thus the function of the wrestler is not to win; it is to go exactly through the motions which are expected of him. It is said that judo contains a hidden symbolic aspect; even in the midst of efficiency, its gestures are measured, precise but restricted, drawn accurately but by a stroke without volume. Wrestling, on the contrary, offers excessive gestures, exploited to the limit of their meaning. In judo, a man who is down is hardly down at all, he rolls over, he draws back, he eludes defeat, or, if the latter is obvious, he immediately disappears; in wrestling, a man who is down is exaggeratedly so, and completely fills the eyes of the spectators with the intolerable spectacle of his powerlessness.

This function of grandiloquence is indeed the same as that of ancient theater, whose principle, language, and props (masks and buskins) concurred in the exaggeratedly visible explanation of a Necessity. The gesture

---

**Jansenist** From a seventeenth-century religious movement that stressed austerity and predestination.

of the vanquished wrestler signifying to the world a defeat which, far from disguising, he emphasizes and holds like a pause in music, corresponds to the mask of antiquity meant to signify the tragic mode of the spectacle. In suffering, one knows how to cry, one has a liking for tears.

Each sign in wrestling is therefore endowed with an absolute clarity, since one must always understand everything on the spot. As soon as the adversaries are in the ring, the public is overwhelmed with the obviousness of the roles. As in the theater, each physical type expresses to excess the part which has been assigned to the contestant. Thauvin, a fifty-year-old with an obese and sagging body, whose type of asexual hideousness always inspires feminine nicknames, displays in his flesh the characters of baseness, for his part is to represent what, in the classical concept of the *salaud*, the "bastard" (the key concept of any wrestling match), appears as organically repugnant. The nausea voluntarily provoked by Thauvin shows therefore a very extended use of signs: not only is ugliness used here in order to signify baseness, but in addition ugliness is wholly gathered into a particularly repulsive quality of matter: the pallid collapse of dead flesh (the public calls Thauvin *la barbaque*, "stinking meat"), so that the passionate condemnation of the crowd no longer stems from its judgment, but instead from the very depth of its humors. It will thereafter let itself be frenetically embroiled in an idea of Thauvin which will conform entirely with this physical origin; his actions will perfectly correspond to the essential viscosity of his personage.

It is therefore in the body of the wrestler that we find the first key to the contest. I know from the start that all of Thauvin's actions, his treacheries, cruelties, and acts of cowardice, will not fail to measure up to the first image of ignobility he gave me; I can trust him to carry out intelligently and to the last detail all the gestures of a kind of amorphous baseness, and thus fill to the brim the image of the most repugnant bastard there is: the bastard octopus. Wrestlers therefore have a physique as peremptory as those of the characters of the *Commedia dell'Arte,* who display in advance, in their costumes and attitudes, the future contents of their parts: just as Pantaloon can never be anything but a ridiculous cuckold, Harlequin an astute servant and the Doctor a stupid pedant, in the same way Thauvin will never be anything but an ignoble traitor, Reinières (a tall blond fellow with a limp body and unkempt hair) the moving image of passivity, Mazaud (short and arrogant like a cock) that of grotesque conceit, and Orsano (an effeminate teddy-boy first seen in a blue-and-pink dressing-gown) that, doubly humorous, of a vindictive *salope,* or bitch (for I do not think that the public of the Elysée-Montmartre, like Littré, believes the word *salope* to be a masculine).

The physique of the wrestlers therefore constitutes a basic sign, which like a seed contains the whole fight. But this seed proliferates, for it is at every turn during the fight, in each new situation, that the body of the wrestler casts to the public the magical entertainment of a temperament which finds its natural expression in a gesture. The different strata of meaning throw light on each other, and form the most intelligible of spectacles. Wrestling is like a diacritic writing: above the fundamental meaning of his body, the wrestler arranges comments which are episodic but always opportune, and constantly help the reading of the fight by means of gestures, attitudes, and mimicry which make the intention utterly obvious. Sometimes the wrestler triumphs with a repulsive sneer while kneeling on the good sportsman; sometimes he gives the crowd a conceited smile which forebodes an early revenge; sometimes, pinned to the ground, he hits the floor ostentatiously to make evident to all the intolerable nature of his situation; and sometimes he erects a complicated set of signs meant to make the public understand that he legitimately personifies the ever-entertaining image of the grumbler, endlessly confabulating about his displeasure.

We are therefore dealing with a real Human Comedy, where the most socially inspired nuances of passion (conceit, rightfulness, refined cruelty, a sense of "paying one's debts") always felicitously find the clearest sign which can receive them, express them, and triumphantly carry them to the confines of the hall. It is obvious that at such a pitch, it no longer matters whether the passion is genuine or not. What the public wants is the image of passion, not passion itself. There is no more a problem of truth in wrestling than in the theater. In both, what is expected is the intelligible representation of moral situations which are usually private. This emptying out of interiority to the benefit of its exterior signs, this exhaustion of the content by the form, is the very principle of triumphant classical art. Wrestling is an immediate pantomime, infinitely more efficient than the dramatic pantomime, for the wrestler's gesture needs no anecdote, no decor, in short no transference in order to appear true.

Each moment in wrestling is therefore like an algebra which instantaneously unveils the relationship between a cause and its represented effect. Wrestling fans certainly experience a kind of intellectual pleasure in *seeing* the moral mechanism function so perfectly. Some wrestlers, who are great comedians, entertain as much as a Molière character, because they succeed in imposing an immediate reading of their inner nature: Armand Mazaud, a wrestler of an arrogant and ridiculous character (as one says that Harpagon [2] is a character), always delights the audience by the mathematical rigor of his transcriptions, carrying the form of his gestures to the furthest reaches of their meaning, and giving to his manner of fighting the kind of vehemence and precision found in a great scholastic disputation, in which what is at stake is at once the triumph of pride and the formal concern with truth.

What is thus displayed for the public is the great spectacle of Suffering,

Defeat, and Justice. Wrestling presents man's suffering with all the amplification of tragic masks. The wrestler who suffers in a hold which is
reputedly cruel (an arm lock, a twisted leg) offers an excessive portrayal of
Suffering; like a primitive Pietà, he exhibits for all to see his face, exaggeratedly contorted by an intolerable affliction. It is obvious, of course, that
in wrestling reserve would be out of place, since it is opposed to the voluntary ostentation of the spectacle, to this Exhibition of Suffering which is
the very aim of the fight. This is why all the actions which produce suffering are particularly spectacular, like the gesture of a conjurer who holds
out his cards clearly to the public. Suffering which appeared without intelligible cause would not be understood; a concealed action that was actually cruel would transgress the unwritten rules of wrestling and would
have no more sociological efficacy than a mad or parasitic gesture. On the
contrary suffering appears as inflicted with emphasis and conviction, for
everyone must not only see that the man suffers, but also and above all
understand why he suffers. What wrestlers call a hold, that is, any figure
which allows one to immobilize the adversary indefinitely and to have him
at one's mercy, has precisely the function of preparing in a conventional,
therefore intelligible, fashion the spectacle of suffering, of methodically establishing the conditions of suffering. The inertia of the vanquished allows
the (temporary) victor to settle in his cruelty and to convey to the public
this terrifying slowness of the torturer who is certain about the outcome
of his actions; to grind the face of one's powerless adversary or to scrape
his spine with one's fist with a deep and regular movement, or at least to
produce the superficial appearance of such gestures: wrestling is the only
sport which gives such an externalized image of torture. But here again,
only the image is involved in the game, and the spectator does not wish
for the actual suffering of the contestant; he only enjoys the perfection of
an iconography. It is not true that wrestling is a sadistic spectacle: it is only
an intelligible spectacle.

There is another figure, more spectacular still than a hold; it is the forearm smash, this loud slap of the forearm, this embryonic punch with which
one clouts the chest of one's adversary, and which is accompanied by a
dull noise and the exaggerated sagging of a vanquished body. In the forearm smash, catastrophe is brought to the point of maximum obviousness,
so much so that ultimately the gesture appears as no more than a symbol;
this is going too far, this is transgressing the moral rules of wrestling,
where all signs must be excessively clear, but must not let the intention of
clarity be seen. The public then shouts "He's laying it on!" not because it
regrets the absence of real suffering, but because it condemns artifice: as
in the theater, one fails to put the part across as much by an excess of
sincerity as by an excess of formalism.

We have already seen to what extent wrestlers exploit the resources of a given physical style, developed and put to use in order to unfold before the eyes of the public a total image of Defeat. The flaccidity of tall white bodies which collapse with one blow or crash into the ropes with arms flailing, the inertia of massive wrestlers rebounding pitiably off all the elastic surfaces of the ring, nothing can signify more clearly and more passionately the exemplary abasement of the vanquished. Deprived of all resilience, the wrestler's flesh is no longer anything but an unspeakable heap spread out on the floor, where it solicits relentless reviling and jubilation. There is here a paroxysm of meaning in the style of antiquity, which can only recall the heavily underlined intentions in Roman triumphs. At other times, there is another ancient posture which appears in the coupling of the wrestlers, that of the suppliant who, at the mercy of his opponent, on bended knees, his arms raised above his head, is slowly brought down by the vertical pressure of the victor. In wrestling, unlike judo, Defeat is not a conventional sign, abandoned as soon as it is understood; it is not an outcome, but quite the contrary, it is a duration, a display, it takes up the ancient myths of public Suffering and Humiliation: the cross and the pillory. It is as if the wrestler is crucified in broad daylight and in the sight of all. I have heard it said of a wrestler stretched on the ground: "He is dead, little Jesus, there, on the cross," and these ironic words revealed the hidden roots of a spectacle which enacts the exact gestures of the most ancient purifications.

But what wrestling is above all meant to portray is a purely moral concept: that of justice. The idea of "paying" is essential to wrestling, and the crowd's "Give it to him" means above all else "Make him pay." This is therefore, needless to say, an immanent justice. The baser the action of the "bastard," the more delighted the public is by the blow which he justly receives in return. If the villain—who is of course a coward—takes refuge behind the ropes, claiming unfairly to have a right to do so by a brazen mimicry, he is inexorably pursued there and caught, and the crowd is jubilant at seeing the rules broken for the sake of a deserved punishment. Wrestlers know very well how to play up to the capacity for indignation of the public by presenting the very limit of the concept of Justice, this outermost zone of confrontation where it is enough to infringe the rules a little more to open the gates of a world without restraints. For a wrestling fan, nothing is finer than the revengeful fury of a betrayed fighter who throws himself vehemently not on a successful opponent but on the smarting image of foul play. Naturally, it is the pattern of Justice which matters here, much more than its content: wrestling is above all a quantitative sequence of compensations (an eye for an eye, a tooth for a tooth). This explains why sudden changes of circumstances have in the eyes of wrestling habitués a sort of moral beauty: they enjoy them as they would enjoy an inspired episode in a novel, and the greater the contrast between the success of a move and the reversal of fortune, the nearer the good luck of a contestant to his downfall, the more satisfying the dramatic mime is felt to be. Justice is therefore the embodiment of a possible transgression; it is from the fact that there is a Law that the spectacle of the passions which infringe it derives its value.

It is therefore easy to understand why out of five wrestling matches, only about one is fair. One must realize, let it be repeated, that "fairness" here is a role or a genre, as in the theater: the rules do not at all constitute a real constraint; they are the conventional appearance of fairness. So that in actual fact a fair fight is nothing but an exaggeratedly polite one: the contestants confront each other with zeal, not rage; they can remain in control of their passions, they do not punish their beaten opponent relentlessly, they stop fighting as soon as they are ordered to do so, and congratulate each other at the end of a particularly arduous episode, during which, however, they have not ceased to be fair. One must of course understand here that all these polite actions are brought to the notice of the public by the most conventional gestures of fairness: shaking hands, raising the arms, ostensibly avoiding a fruitless hold which would detract from the perfection of the contest.

Conversely, foul play exists only in its excessive signs: administering a big kick to one's beaten opponent, taking refuge behind the ropes while ostensibly invoking a purely formal right, refusing to shake hands with one's opponent before or after the fight, taking advantage of the end of the round to rush treacherously at the adversary from behind, fouling him while the referee is not looking (a move which obviously only has any value or function because in fact half the audience can see it and get indignant about it). Since Evil is the natural climate of wrestling, a fair fight has chiefly the value of being an exception. It surprises the aficionado, who greets it when he sees it as an anachronism and a rather sentimental throwback to the sporting tradition ("Aren't they playing fair, those two"); he feels suddenly moved at the sight of the general kindness of the world, but would probably die of boredom and indifference if wrestlers did not quickly return to the orgy of evil which alone makes good wrestling.

Extrapolated, fair wrestling could lead only to boxing or judo, whereas true wrestling derives its originality from all the excesses which make it a spectacle and not a sport. The ending of a boxing match or a judo contest is abrupt, like the full stop which closes a demonstration. The rhythm of wrestling is quite different, for its natural meaning is that of rhetorical amplification: the emotional magniloquence, the repeated paroxysms, the exasperation of the retorts can only find their natural outcome in the most baroque confusion. Some fights, among the most successful kind, are crowned by a final charivari, a sort of unrestrained fantasia where the rules, the laws of the genre, the referee's censuring, and the limits of the ring are abolished, swept away by a triumphant disorder which overflows into the hall and carries off pell-mell wrestlers, seconds, referee, and spectators.

It has already been noted that in America wrestling represents a sort of mythological fight between Good and Evil (of a quasi-political nature, the "bad" wrestler always being supposed to be a Red). The process of creating heroes in French wrestling is very different, being based on ethics and not on politics. What the public is looking for here is the gradual construction of a highly moral image: that of the perfect "bastard." One comes to wrestling in order to attend the continuing adventures of a single major leading character, permanent and multiform like Punch or Scapino, inventive in unexpected figures and yet always faithful to his role. The "bastard" is here revealed as a Molière character or a "portrait" by La Bruyère, that is to say as a classical entity, an essence, whose acts are only significant epiphenomena arranged in time. This stylized character does not belong to any particular nation or party, and whether the wrestler is called Kuzchenko (nicknamed Mustache after Stalin), Yerpazian, Gaspardi, Jo Vignola, or Nollières, the aficionado does not attribute to him any country except "fairness"—observing the rules.

What then is a "bastard" for this audience composed in part, we are told, of people who are themselves outside the rules of society? Essentially someone unstable, who accepts the rules only when they are useful to him and transgresses the formal continuity of attitudes. He is unpredictable, therefore asocial. He takes refuge behind the law when he considers that it is in his favor, and breaks it when he finds it useful to do so. Sometimes he rejects the formal boundaries of the ring and goes on hitting an adversary legally protected by the ropes, sometimes he reestablishes these boundaries and claims the protection of what he did not respect a few minutes earlier. This inconsistency, far more than treachery or cruelty, sends the audience beside itself with rage: offended not in its morality but in its logic, it considers the contradiction of arguments as the basest of crimes. The forbidden move becomes dirty only when it destroys a quantitative equilibrium and disturbs the rigorous reckoning of compensations; what is condemned by the audience is not at all the transgression of insipid official rules, it is the lack of revenge, the absence of a punishment. So that there is nothing more exciting for a crowd than the grandiloquent kick given to a vanquished "bastard"; the joy of punishing is at its climax when it is supported by a mathematical justification; contempt is then unrestrained. One is no longer dealing with a *salaud* but with a *salope*—the verbal gesture of the ultimate degradation.

Such a precise finality demands that wrestling should be exactly what the public expects of it. Wrestlers, who are very experienced, know perfectly how to direct the spontaneous episodes of the fight so as to make them conform to the image which the public has of the great legendary themes of its mythology. A wrestler can irritate or disgust, he never disappoints, for he always accomplishes completely, by a progressive solidification of signs, what the public expects of him. In wrestling, nothing exists except in the absolute, there is no symbol, no allusion, everything is presented exhaustively. Leaving nothing in the shade, each action discards all parasitic meanings and ceremonially offers to the public a pure and full signification, rounded like Nature. This grandiloquence is nothing but the popular and age-old image of the perfect intelligibility of reality. What is portrayed by wrestling is therefore an ideal understanding of things; it is the euphoria of men raised for a while above the constitutive ambiguity of everyday situations and placed before the panoramic view of a univocal Nature, in which signs at last correspond to causes, without obstacle, without evasion, without contradiction.

When the hero or the villain of the drama, the man who was seen a few minutes earlier possessed by moral rage, magnified into a sort of metaphysical sign, leaves the wrestling hall, impassive, anonymous, carrying a small suitcase and arm-in-arm with his wife, no one can doubt that wrestling holds that power of transmutation which is common to the Spectacle and to Religious Worship. In the ring, and even in the depths of their voluntary ignominy, wrestlers remain gods because they are, for a few moments, the key which opens Nature, the pure gesture which separates Good from Evil, and unveils the form of a Justice which is at last intelligible.

NOTES

[1] In Molière's *L'École des Femmes* and Racine's *Andromaque*.
[2] In Molière's *L'Avare*.

# *Striptease*

Striptease—at least Parisian striptease—is based on a contradiction: Woman is desexualized at the very moment when she is stripped naked. We may therefore say that we are dealing in a sense with a spectacle based on fear, or rather on the pretense of fear, as if eroticism here went no further than a sort of delicious terror, whose ritual signs have only to be announced to evoke at once the idea of sex and its conjuration.

It is only the time taken in shedding clothes which makes voyeurs of the public; but here, as in any mystifying spectacle, the decor, the props and the stereotypes intervene to contradict the initially provocative intention and eventually bury it in insignificance: evil is *advertised* the better to impede and exorcize it. French striptease seems to stem from . . . a mystifying device which consists in inoculating the public with a touch of evil, the better to plunge it afterwards into a permanently immune Moral Good: a few particles of eroticism, highlighted by the very situation on which the show is based, are in fact absorbed in a reassuring ritual which negates the flesh as surely as the vaccine or the taboo circumscribe and control the illness or the crime.

There will therefore be in striptease a whole series of coverings placed upon the body of the woman in proportion as she pretends to strip it bare. Exoticism is the first of these barriers, for it is always of a petrified kind which transports the body into the world of legend or romance: a Chinese woman equipped with an opium pipe (the indispensable symbol of "Sininess"), an undulating vamp with a gigantic cigarette holder, a Venetian decor complete with gondola, a dress with panniers, and a singer of serenades: all aim at establishing the woman *right from the start* as an object in disguise. The end of the striptease is then no longer to drag into the light a hidden depth, but to signify, through the shedding of an incongruous and artificial clothing, nakedness as a *natural* vesture of woman, which amounts in the end to regaining a perfectly chaste state of the flesh.

The classic props of the music hall, which are invariably rounded up here, constantly make the unveiled body more remote, and force it back into the all-pervading ease of a well-known rite: the furs, the fans, the gloves, the feathers, the fishnet stockings, in short the whole spectrum of adornment, constantly makes the living body return to the category of luxurious objects which surround man with a magical decor. Covered with feathers or gloved, the woman identifies herself here as a stereotyped element of music hall, and to shed objects as ritualistic as these is no longer a part of a further, genuine undressing. Feathers, furs, and gloves go on pervading the woman with their magical virtue even once removed, and give her something like the enveloping memory of a luxurious shell, for it is a self-evident law that the whole of striptease is given in the very nature of the initial garment: if the latter is improbable, as in the case of the Chinese woman or the woman in furs, the nakedness which follows remains itself unreal, smooth, and enclosed like a beautiful slippery object, withdrawn by its very extravagance from human use: this is the underlying significance of the G-String covered with diamonds or sequins which is the very end of striptease. This ultimate triangle, by its pure and geometrical shape, by its hard and shiny material, bars the way to the sexual parts like a sword of purity, and definitively drives the woman back into a mineral world, the (precious) stone being here the irrefutable symbol of the absolute object, that which serves no purpose.

Contrary to the common prejudice, the dance which accompanies the striptease from beginning to end is in no way an erotic element. It is probably quite the reverse: the faintly rhythmical undulation in this case exorcises the fear of immobility. Not only does it give to the show the alibi of Art (the dances in strip shows are always "artistic"), but above all it constitutes the last barrier, and the most efficient of all: the dance, consisting of ritual gestures which have been seen a thousand times, acts on movements as a cosmetic, it hides nudity, and smothers the spectacle under a glaze of superfluous yet essential gestures, for the act of becoming bare is here relegated to the rank of parasitical operations carried out in an improbable background. Thus we see the professionals of striptease wrap themselves in the miraculous ease which constantly clothes them, makes them remote, gives them the icy indifference of skillful practitioners, haughtily taking refuge in the sureness of their technique: their science clothes them like a garment.

All this, this meticulous exorcism of sex, can be verified *a contrario* in the "popular contests" [*sic*] of amateur striptease: there, "beginners" undress in front of a few hundred spectators without resorting or resorting very clumsily to magic, which unquestionably restores to the spectacle its erotic power. Here we find at the beginning far fewer Chinese or Spanish women, no feathers or furs (sensible suits, ordinary coats), few disguises as a starting point—gauche steps, unsatisfactory dancing, girls constantly threatened by immobility, and above all by a "technical" awkwardness (the resistance of briefs, dress, or bra) which gives to the gestures of unveiling an unexpected importance, denying the woman the alibi of art and the refuge of being an object, imprisoning her in a condition of weakness and timorousness.

And yet, at the *Moulin Rouge,* we see hints of another kind of exorcism, probably typically French, and one which in actual fact tends less to nullify eroticism than to tame it: the compère tries to give striptease a reassuring petit-bourgeois status. To start with, striptease is a *sport*: there is a Striptease Club, which organizes healthy contests whose winners come out crowned and rewarded with edifying prizes (a subscription to physical training lessons), a novel (which can only be Robbe-Grillet's *Voyeur*), or useful prizes (a pair of nylons, five thousand francs). Then striptease is identified with a *career* (beginners, semiprofessionals, professionals), that is, to the honorable practice of a specialization (strippers are skilled workers). One can even give them the magical alibi of work: *vocation*; one girl is, say *"doing well"* or *"well on the way to fulfilling her promise,"* or on the contrary *"taking her first steps"* on the arduous path of striptease. Finally and above all, the competitors are socially situated: one is a salesgirl, another a secretary (there are many secretaries in the Striptease Club). Striptease here is made to rejoin the world of the public, is made familiar and bourgeois, as if the French, unlike the American public (at least according to what one hears), following an irresistible tendency of their social status, could not conceive eroticism except as a household property, sanctioned by the alibi of weekly sport much more than by that of a magical spectacle: and this is how, in France, striptease is nationalized.

. . . . . . . . . . .

### QUESTIONS FOR A SECOND READING

1. While the subject of "The World of Wrestling" could be said to be relatively common, the essay is at places difficult to read and to understand. The language is difficult. There are many allusions to French literature. It's hard to place this "Roland Barthes" and what he is doing; he seems excessive in his interpretations, and it is hard to find where and how he is getting to the point.

   As you go back to this text, mark the sections that seem to provide the greatest difficulties for you as a reader and use them as an index to what is new or unusually demanding in Barthes's project and Barthes's methods. Go back to them with both a generous and a critical eye. Go back first, that is, assuming that there is something to be gained in understanding what Barthes is doing. He is doing something new and unconventional; therefore, it requires an extra effort to follow. And then go back in a less generous mode, assuming that the problem is not yours but his, that he is failing his reader and his task in some fundamental way. What do you make of it now? What do you take to have been his responsibilities and yours?

2. These essays "The World of Wrestling," and "Striptease," rest on certain devices, figures Barthes creates in order to conduct his analysis. He refers regularly, for instance, to the "public" as though this were a single, homogenous group whose thoughts and wishes he completely understands: "This public knows very well the distinction between wrestling and boxing; it knows that boxing is a Jansenist sport, based on a demonstration of excellence"; "What the public wants is the image of passion, not passion itself." Likewise he refers to what the "spectator" thinks or what "we" know. And, as he accounts for wrestling as a conventional narrative, a drama, he needs to refer to its "author": "But what wrestling is above all meant to portray is a purely moral concept: that of justice."

   As you reread the essays, look for similar devices and mark them so that you can go back and examine them as a group. What is Barthes doing here? Let's assume that what enables him to do his work is a method, not genius or inspiration. If he is constructing something in these essays (that is, if what he is doing is not "natural," a natural way of experiencing culture), what has he made? How has he made it? and to what ends? What is his agenda, both hidden and open?

## ASSIGNMENTS FOR WRITING

1. In *Mythologies*, Barthes "reads" some characteristic examples of French popular culture. He reads against what he takes to be a common but false understanding (what some people think), and he reads in the name of the "public" or the "spectator," whose experience he comes to understand in a way he believes they cannot.

   As a way of testing your sense of Barthes's method, and of testing the usefulness of his examples, write an essay (or perhaps a series of "mythologies") that provides a similar reading of an example (or related examples) of American culture—MTV, skateboarding, the Superbowl, Pee Wee Herman, etc. You might ask, "What would Barthes notice in my examples? What would he say about these significant features?"

   You can imagine that you are either extending and reproducing or commenting on and challenging Barthes's project in *Mythologies*. You like what he is doing and you are going to take it one step further. Or you think there is someting wrong with what he is doing and you are going to show him a better way. In either case you should make some reference to Barthes and what he would do. Your example, that is, should serve as commentary on Barthes.

2. In these two excerpts from *Mythologies*, Barthes "reads" the spectacle of wrestling and striptease. These excerpts, however, could themselves be read as examples of mythic spectacle—that is, they could be read as the characteristic spectacle of a man watching and taking possession of what he sees.

   In the essays on wrestling and striptease Barthes argues that his reading reveals something essential in these events, but he writes about wrestling and striptease without calling into question the degree to which he, too, is implicated in a familiar story, the way he becomes a familiar figure, a man watching events designed to please the male spectator. These events, one could argue, ritualize the ways in which men watch men or men watch women. Barthes does not stand outside of that ritual. He is part of the myth and, in that sense, not its critic. He remains a familiar figure—the man watching.

   Barthes obviously takes some pleasure in telling the inside story, uncovering the hidden agenda as he sees it in the myths of wrestling and striptease. In a similar spirit, write a "mythology" of your own, this one on the common figure of the male spectator, with Barthes as your central figure. You might think of similar figures, such as intellectuals, teachers, artists or writers. There are others, however, who serve the same role: doctors or detectives, figures in paintings or advertisements, characters from stories or movies, any of several representatives of what you might call the "male gaze."

## MAKING CONNECTIONS

1. Barthes in his analysis of wrestling and striptease, Stanley Fish in his analysis of the classroom (p. 179) and Mark Crispin Miller in his analysis of the soap ad and the *Cosby* show (p. 400) could all be said to be engaged in similar activities of cultural criticism. It is interesting, however, to work out the differences in what these three authors do and to ask what those differences represent, particularly as they could be said to represent a different agenda, different concerns, a different sense of the function of culture and cultural critique—something other, that is, than different quirks or personalities in the authors.

   Write an essay in which you very precisely represent what each author is doing—for example, Barthes with wrestling, Fish with the classroom, and Miller with the *Cosby* show. You may want to work with all three authors, or you may want to work with only Barthes and one of the others. After presenting the work of each, go on then to parse out the key differences in the work of each and to speculate on what these differences might be said to represent.

2. In "'Indians': Textualism, Morality, and the Problem of History," (p. 561), Jane Tompkins writes a very different kind of essay than Barthes, although she too is concerned with the difficulty and necessity of reading myths that seem to be not myths at all but facts, truths self-evident to members of the culture. Write an essay in which you work out, in careful detail, the different ways of working represented in Barthes's and Tompkins's essays. The point, of course, is not to demonstrate that people are different or that different people work differently, but that each represents projects with different goals and methods. How would you describe their goals and methods? How would you describe what those goals and methods allow the writers to "see" and what they keep them from "seeing"?

# SAUL
# BELLOW

$S$AUL BELLOW *is one of our most celebrated contemporary American writers. He won the Nobel Prize for literature in 1976, the Pulitzer Prize for fiction (for* Humboldt's Gift), *and several National Book Awards (for* The Adventures of Augie March, Herzog, *and* Mr. Sammler's Planet). *Bellow was born in Lachine, Quebec, in 1915, but grew up in Chicago, which is the setting for much of his fiction.*

*Bellow earned a B.S. in sociology and anthropology from Northwestern University in 1937. He abandoned his studies after a short stay in graduate school— because, he said, "every time I worked on my thesis, it turned out to be a story." While he made a career telling stories, his writing has always exemplified the social scientist's concern for closely observed, carefully recorded scenes of daily life. Bellow's fiction is not showy or self-consciously experimental. He seems to invite a reader into familiar territory; these familiar landscapes, however, become rich, mysterious, and unsettling. Bellow once commented that "perhaps the deepest readers are those who are least sure of themselves." Bellow's great talent is telling stories of ordinary people and places that allow readers those deep, if disquieting, moments of uncertainty.*

*After working in the WPA Writer's Project during the Great Depression and serving with the Merchant Marine in World War II, Bellow taught at the University of Minnesota, New York University, and Princeton University, among others, and has been a member of the University of Chicago's English department since 1963. Bellow's most recent work includes the novel* More Die of Heartbreak, *the* Foreword *to* The Closing of the American Mind, *a critique of higher education written by Bellow's colleague Allan Bloom, and* A Theft, *a novella.* A Theft *is Bellow's fourteenth book. The following story, "A Silver Dish," appeared in Bellow's* Him with His Foot in His Mouth and Other Stories.

# A Silver Dish

What do you do about death—in this case, the death of an old father? If you're a modern person, sixty years of age, and a man who's been around, like Woody Selbst, what do you do? Take this matter of mourning, and take it against a contemporary background. How, against a contemporary background, do you mourn an octogenarian father, nearly blind, his heart enlarged, his lungs filling with fluid, who creeps, stumbles, gives off the odors, the moldiness or gassiness, of old men. I *mean!* As Woody put it, be realistic. Think what times these are. The papers daily give it to you—the Lufthansa pilot in Aden is described by the hostages on his knees, begging the Palestinian terrorists not to execute him, but they shoot him through the head. Later they themselves are killed. And still others shoot others, or shoot themselves. That's what you read in the press, see on the tube, mention at dinner. We know now what goes daily through the whole of the human community, like a global death-peristalsis.

Woody, a businessman in South Chicago, was not an ignorant person. He knew more such phrases than you would expect a tile contractor (offices, lobbies, lavatories) to know. The kind of knowledge he had was not the kind for which you get academic degrees. Although Woody had studied for two years in a seminary, preparing to be a minister. Two years of college during the Depression was more than most high-school graduates could afford. After that, in his own vital, picturesque, original way (Morris, his old man, was also, in his days of nature, vital and picturesque), Woody had read up on many subjects, subscribed to *Science* and other magazines that gave real information, and had taken night courses at De Paul and Northwestern in ecology, criminology, existentialism. Also he had traveled extensively in Japan, Mexico, and Africa, and there was an African experience that was especially relevant to mourning. It was this: on a launch

39

near the Murchison Falls in Uganda, he had seen a buffalo calf seized by a crocodile from the bank of the White Nile. There were giraffes along the tropical river, and hippopotamuses, and baboons, and flamingos and other brilliant birds crossing the bright air in the heat of the morning, when the calf, stepping into the river to drink, was grabbed by the hoof and dragged down. The parent buffaloes couldn't figure it out. Under the water the calf still threshed, fought, churned the mud. Woody, the robust traveler, took this in as he sailed by, and to him it looked as if the parent cattle were asking each other dumbly what had happened. He chose to assume that there was pain in this, he read brute grief into it. On the White Nile, Woody had the impression that he had gone back to the pre-Adamite past, and he brought reflections on this impression home to South Chicago. He brought also a bundle of hashish from Kampala. In this he took a chance with the customs inspectors, banking perhaps on his broad build, frank face, high color. He didn't look like a wrongdoer, a bad guy; he looked like a good guy. But he liked taking chances. Risk was a wonderful stimulus. He threw down his trenchcoat on the customs counter. If the inspectors searched the pockets, he was prepared to say that the coat wasn't his. But he got away with it, and the Thanksgiving turkey was stuffed with hashish. This was much enjoyed. That was practically the last feast at which Pop, who also relished risk or defiance, was present. The hashish Woody had tried to raise in his backyard from the Africa seeds didn't take. But behind his warehouse, where the Lincoln Continental was parked, he kept a patch of marijuana. There was no harm at all in Woody, but he didn't like being entirely within the law. It was simply a question of self-respect.

After that Thanksgiving, Pop gradually sank as if he had a slow leak. This went on for some years. In and out of the hospital, he dwindled, his mind wandered, he couldn't even concentrate enough to complain, except in exceptional moments on the Sundays Woody regularly devoted to him. Morris, an amateur who once was taken seriously by Willie Hoppe, the great pro himself, couldn't execute the simplest billiard shots anymore. He could only conceive shots; he began to theorize about impossible three-cushion combinations. Halina, the Polish woman with whom Morris had lived for over forty years as man and wife, was too old herself now to run to the hospital. So Woody had to do it. There was Woody's mother, too—a Christian convert—needing care; she was over eighty and frequently hospitalized. Everybody had diabetes and pleurisy and arthritis and cataracts and cardiac pacemakers. And everybody had lived by the body, but the body was giving out.

There were Woody's two sisters as well, unmarried, in their fifties, very Christian, very straight, still living with Mama in an entirely Christian bungalow. Woody, who took full responsibility for them all, occasionally had to put one of the girls (they had become sick girls) in a mental institution. Nothing severe. The sisters were wonderful women, both of them gorgeous once, but neither of the poor things was playing with a full deck. And all the factions had to be kept separate—Mama, the Christian convert; the fundamentalist sisters; Pop, who read the Yiddish paper as long as he could still see print; Halina, a good Catholic. Woody, the seminary forty years behind him, described himself as an agnostic. Pop had no more religion than you could find in the Yiddish paper, but he made Woody promise to bury him among Jews, and that was where he lay now, in the Hawaiian shirt Woody had bought for him at the tilers' convention in Honolulu. Woody would allow no undertaker's assistant to dress him, but came to the parlor and buttoned the stiff into the shirt himself, and the old man went down looking like Ben-Gurion in a simple wooden coffin, sure to rot fast. That was how Woody wanted it all. At the graveside, he had taken off and folded his jacket, rolled up his sleeves on thick freckled biceps, waved back the little tractor standing by, and shoveled the dirt himself. His big face, broad at the bottom, narrowed upward like a Dutch house. And, his small good lower teeth taking hold of the upper lip in his exertion, he performed the final duty of a son. He was very fit, so it must have been emotion, not the shoveling, that made him redden so. After the funeral, he went home with Halina and her son, a decent Polack like his mother, and talented, too—Mitosh played the organ at hockey and basketball games in the Stadium, which took a smart man because it was a rabble-rousing kind of occupation—and they had some drinks and comforted the old girl. Halina was true blue, always one hundred percent for Morris.

Then for the rest of the week Woody was busy, had jobs to run, office responsibilities, family responsibilities. He lived alone; as did his wife; as did his mistress: everybody in a separate establishment. Since his wife, after fifteen years of separation, had not learned to take care of herself, Woody did her shopping on Fridays, filled her freezer. He had to take her this week to buy shoes. Also, Friday night he always spent with Helen—Helen was his wife de facto. Saturday he did his big weekly shopping. Saturday night he devoted to Mom and his sisters. So he was too busy to attend to his own feelings except, intermittently, to note to himself, "First Thursday in the grave." "First Friday, and fine weather." "First Saturday; he's got to be getting used to it." Under his breath he occasionally said, "Oh, Pop."

But it was Sunday that hit him, when the bells rang all over South Chicago—the Ukrainian, Roman Catholic, Greek, Russian, African Methodist churches, sounding off one after another. Woody had his offices in his warehouse, and there had built an apartment for himself, very spacious and convenient, in the top story. Because he left every Sunday morning at

seven to spend the day with Pop, he had forgotten by how many churches
Selbst Tile Company was surrounded. He was still in bed when he heard
the bells, and all at once he knew how heartbroken he was. This sudden
big heartache in a man of sixty, a practical, physical, healthy-minded, and
experienced man, was deeply unpleasant. When he had an unpleasant condition, he believed in taking something for it. So he thought: What shall I
take? There were plenty of remedies available. His cellar was stocked with
cases of Scotch whisky, Polish vodka, Armagnac, Moselle, Burgundy.
There were also freezers with steaks and with game and with Alaskan king
crab. He bought with a broad hand—by the crate and by the dozen. But
in the end, when he got out of bed, he took nothing but a cup of coffee.
While the kettle was heating, he put on his Japanese judo-style suit and
sat down to reflect.

Woody was moved when things were *honest*. Bearing beams were honest, undisguised concrete pillars inside high-rise apartments were honest.
It was bad to cover up anything. He hated faking. Stone was honest. Metal
was honest. These Sunday bells were very straight. They broke loose, they
wagged and rocked, and the vibrations and the banging did something for
him—cleansed his insides, purified his blood. A bell was a one-way throat,
had only one thing to tell you and simply told it. He listened.

He had had some connections with bells and churches. He was after
all something of a Christian. Born a Jew, he was a Jew facially, with a hint
of Iroquois or Cherokee, but his mother had been converted more than
fifty years ago by her brother-in-law, the Reverend Doctor Kovner. Kovner,
a rabbinical student who had left the Hebrew Union College in Cincinnati
to become a minister and establish a mission, had given Woody a partly
Christian upbringing. Now, Pop was on the outs with these fundamentalists. He said that the Jews came to the mission to get coffee, bacon,
canned pineapple, day-old bread, and dairy products. And if they had to
listen to sermons, that was okay—this was the Depression and you
couldn't be too particular—but he knew they sold the bacon.

The Gospels said it plainly: "Salvation is from the Jews."

Backing the Reverend Doctor were wealthy fundamentalists, mainly
Swedes, eager to speed up the Second Coming by converting all Jews. The
foremost of Kovner's backers was Mrs. Skoglund, who had inherited a
large dairy business from her late husband. Woody was under her special
protection.

Woody was fourteen years of age when Pop took off with Halina, who
worked in his shop, leaving his difficult Christian wife and his converted
son and his small daughters. He came to Woody in the backyard one spring
day and said, "From now on you're the man of the house." Woody was
practicing with a golf club, knocking off the heads of dandelions. Pop came

into the yard in his good suit, which was too hot for the weather, and when he took off his fedora the skin of his head was marked with a deep ring and the sweat was sprinkled over his scalp—more drops than hairs. He said, "I'm going to move out." Pop was anxious, but he was set to go— determined. "It's no use. I can't live a life like this." Envisioning the life Pop simply *had* to live, his free life, Woody was able to picture him in the billiard parlor, under the El tracks in a crap game, or playing poker at Brown and Koppel's upstairs. "You're going to be the man of the house," said Pop. "It's okay. I put you all on welfare. I just got back from Wabansia Avenue, from the relief station." Hence the suit and the hat. "They're send- ing out a caseworker." Then he said, "You got to lend me money to buy gasoline—the caddie money you saved."

Understanding that Pop couldn't get away without his help, Woody turned over to him all he had earned at the Sunset Ridge Country Club in Winnetka. Pop felt that the valuable life lesson he was transmitting was worth far more than these dollars, and whenever he was conning his boy a sort of high-priest expression came down over his bent nose, his ruddy face. The children, who got their finest ideas at the movies, called him Richard Dix. Later, when the comic strip came out, they said he was Dick Tracy.

As Woody now saw it, under the tumbling bells, he had bankrolled his own desertion. Ha ha! He found this delightful; and especially Pop's atti- tude of "That'll teach you to trust your father." For this was a demonstra- tion on behalf of real life and free instincts, against religion and hypocrisy. But mainly it was aimed against being a fool, the disgrace of foolishness. Pop had it in for the Reverend Doctor Kovner, not because he was an apos- tate (Pop couldn't have cared less), not because the mission was a racket (he admitted that the Reverend Doctor was personally honest), but because Doctor Kovner behaved foolishly, spoke like a fool, and acted like a fiddler. He tossed his hair like a Paganini (this was Woody's addition; Pop had never heard of Paganini). Proof that he was not a spiritual leader was that he converted Jewish women by stealing their hearts. "He works up all those broads," said Pop. "He doesn't even know it himself, I swear he doesn't know how he gets them."

From the other side, Kovner often warned Woody, "Your father is a dangerous person. Of course, you love him; you should love him and for- give him, Voodrow, but you are old enough to understand he is leading a life of wice."

It was all petty stuff: Pop's sinning was on a boy's level and therefore made a big impression on a boy. And on Mother. Are wives children, or what? Mother often said, "I hope you put that brute in your prayers. Look what he has done to us. But only pray for him, don't see him." But he saw him all the time. Woodrow was leading a double life, sacred and profane. He accepted Jesus Christ as his personal redeemer. Aunt Rebecca took advantage of this. She made him work. He had to work under Aunt Rebecca. He filled in for the janitor at the mission and settlement house. In winter, he had to feed the coal furnace, and on some nights he slept near the furnace room, on the pool table. He also picked the lock of the storeroom. He took canned pineapple and cut bacon from the flitch with his pocket-knife. He crammed himself with uncooked bacon. He had a big frame to fill out.

Only now, sipping Melitta coffee, he asked himself: Had he been so hungry? No, he loved being reckless. He was fighting Aunt Rebecca Kovner when he took out his knife and got on a box to reach the bacon. She didn't know, she couldn't prove that Woody, such a frank, strong, positive boy, who looked you in the eye, so direct, was a thief also. But he was also a thief. Whenever she looked at him, he knew that she was seeing his father. In the curve of his nose, the movements of his eyes, the thickness of his body, in his healthy face, she saw that wicked savage Morris.

Morris, you see, had been a street boy in Liverpool—Woody's mother and her sister were British by birth. Morris's Polish family, on their way to America, abandoned him in Liverpool because he had an eye infection and they would all have been sent back from Ellis Island. They stopped awhile in England, but his eyes kept running and they ditched him. They slipped away, and he had to make out alone in Liverpool at the age of twelve. Mother came of better people. Pop, who slept in the cellar of her house, fell in love with her. At sixteen, scabbing during a seamen's strike, he shoveled his way across the Atlantic and jumped ship in Brooklyn. He became an American, and America never knew it. He voted without papers, he drove without a license, he paid no taxes, he cut every corner. Horses, cards, billiards, and women were his lifelong interests, in ascending order. Did he love anyone (he was so busy)? Yes, he loved Halina. He loved his son. To this day, Mother believed that he had loved her most and always wanted to come back. This gave her a chance to act the queen, with her plump wrists and faded Queen Victoria face. "The girls are instructed never to admit him," she said. The Empress of India speaking.

Bell-battered Woodrow's soul was whirling this Sunday morning, indoors and out, to the past, back to his upper corner of the warehouse, laid out with such originality—the bells coming and going, metal on naked metal, until the bell circle expanded over the whole of steel-making, oil-refining, power-producing mid-autumn South Chicago, and all its Croatians, Ukrainians, Greeks, Poles, and respectable blacks heading for their churches to hear Mass or to sing hymns.

Woody himself had been a good hymn singer. He still knew the hymns.

He had testified, too. He was often sent by Aunt Rebecca to get up and tell a churchful of Scandihoovians that he, a Jewish lad, accepted Jesus Christ. For this she paid him fifty cents. She made the disbursement. She was the bookkeeper, fiscal chief, general manager of the mission. The Reverend Doctor didn't know a thing about the operation. What the Doctor supplied was the fervor. He was genuine, a wonderful preacher. And what about Woody himself? He also had fervor. He was drawn to the Reverend Doctor. The Reverend Doctor taught him to lift up his eyes, gave him his higher life. Apart from this higher life, the rest was Chicago—the ways of Chicago, which came so natural that nobody thought to question them. So, for instance, in 1933 (what ancient, ancient times!), at the Century of Progress World's Fair, when Woody was a coolie and pulled a rickshaw, wearing a peaked straw hat and trotting with powerful, thick legs, while the brawny red farmers—his boozing passengers—were laughing their heads off and pestered him for whores, he, although a freshman at the seminary, saw nothing wrong, when girls asked him to steer a little business their way, in making dates and accepting tips from both sides. He necked in Grant Park with a powerful girl who had to go home quickly to nurse her baby. Smelling of milk, she rode beside him on the streetcar to the West Side, squeezing his rickshaw puller's thigh and wetting her blouse. This was the Roosevelt Road car. Then, in the apartment where she lived with her mother, he couldn't remember that there were any husbands around. What he did remember was the strong milk odor. Without inconsistency, next morning he did New Testament Greek: The light shineth in darkness—*to fos en te skotia fainei*—and the darkness comprehended it not.

And all the while he trotted between the shafts on the fairgrounds he had one idea, nothing to do with these horny giants having a big time in the city: that the goal, the project, the purpose was (and he couldn't explain why he thought so; all evidence was against it)—God's idea was that this world should be a love world, that it should eventually recover and be entirely a world of love. He wouldn't have said this to a soul, for he could see himself how stupid it was—personal and stupid. Nevertheless, there it was at the center of his feelings. And at the same time, Aunt Rebecca was right when she said to him, strictly private, close to his ear even, "You're a little crook, like your father."

There was some evidence for this, or what stood for evidence to an impatient person like Rebecca. Woody matured quickly—he had to—but how could you expect a boy of seventeen, he wondered, to interpret the viewpoint, the feelings, of a middle-aged woman, and one whose breast had been removed? Morris told him that this happened only to neglected women, and was a sign. Morris said that if titties were not fondled and kissed, they got cancer in protest. It was a cry of the flesh. And this had seemed true to Woody. When his imagination tried the theory on the Reverend Doctor, it worked out—he couldn't see the Reverend Doctor behaving in that way to Aunt Rebecca's breasts! Morris's theory kept Woody looking from bosoms to husbands and from husbands to bosoms. He still did that. It's an exceptionally smart man who isn't marked forever by the sexual theories he hears from his father, and Woody wasn't all that smart. He knew this himself. Personally he had gone far out of his way to do right by women in this regard. What nature demanded. He and Pop were common, thick men, but there's nobody too gross to have ideas of delicacy.

The Reverend Doctor preached, Rebecca preached, rich Mrs. Skoglund preached from Evanston, Mother preached. Pop also was on a soapbox. Everyone was doing it. Up and down Division Street, under every lamp, almost, speakers were giving out: anarchists, Socialists, Stalinists, single-taxers, Zionists, Tolstoyans, vegetarians, and fundamentalist Christian preachers—you name it. A beef, a hope, a way of life or salvation, a protest. How was it that the accumulated gripes of all the ages took off so when transplanted to America?

And that fine Swedish immigrant Aase (Osie, they pronounced it), who had been the Skoglunds' cook and married the eldest son, to become his rich, religious widow—she supported the Reverend Doctor. In her time she must have been built like a chorus girl. And women seem to have lost the secret of putting up their hair in the high basketry fence of braid she wore. Aase took Woody under her special protection and paid his tuition at the seminary. And Pop said . . . But on this Sunday, at peace as soon as the bells stopped banging, this velvet autumn day when the grass was finest and thickest, silky green: before the first frost, and the blood in your lungs is redder than summer air can make it and smarts with oxygen, as if the iron in your system was hungry for it, and the chill was sticking it to you in every breath . . . Pop, six feet under, would never feel this blissful sting again. The last of the bells still had the bright air streaming with vibrations.

On weekends, the institutional vacancy of decades came back to the warehouse and crept under the door of Woody's apartment. It felt as empty on Sunday as churches were during the week. Before each business day, before the trucks and the crews got started, Woody jogged five miles in his Adidas suit. Not on this day still reserved for Pop, however. Although it was tempting to go out and run off the grief. Being alone hit Woody hard this morning. He thought: Me and the world; the world and me. Meaning that there always was some activity to interpose, an errand or a visit, a picture to paint (he was a creative amateur), a massage, a meal—a shield between himself and that troublesome solitude which used the world as its reservoir. But Pop! Last Tuesday, Woody had gotten into the hospital bed with Pop because he kept pulling out the intravenous needles.

Nurses stuck them back, and then Woody astonished them all by climbing into bed to hold the struggling old guy in his arms. "Easy, Morris, Morris, go easy." But Pop still groped feebly for the pipes.

When the tolling stopped, Woody didn't notice that a great lake of quiet had come over his kingdom, the Selbst Tile warehouse. What he heard and saw was an old red Chicago streetcar, one of those trams the color of a stockyard steer. Cars of this type went out before Pearl Harbor—clumsy, big-bellied, with tough rattan seats and brass grips for the standing passengers. Those cars used to make four stops to the mile, and ran with a wallowing motion. They stank of carbolic or ozone and throbbed when the air compressors were being charged. The conductor had his knotted signal cord to pull, and the motorman beat the foot gong with his mad heel.

Woody recognized himself on the Western Avenue line and riding through a blizzard with his father, both in sheepskins and with hands and faces raw, the snow blowing in from the rear platform when the doors opened and getting into the longitudinal cleats on the floor. There wasn't warmth enough inside to melt it. And Western Avenue was the longest car line in the world, the boosters said, as if it was a thing to brag about. Twenty-three miles long, made by a draftsman with a T square, lined with factories, storage buildings, machine shops, used-car lots, trolley barns, gas stations, funeral parlors, six-flats, utility buildings, and junkyards, on and on from the prairies on the south to Evanston on the north. Woodrow and his father were going north to Evanston, to Howard Street, and then some, to see Mrs. Skoglund. At the end of the line they would still have about five blocks to hike. The purpose of the trip? To raise money for Pop. Pop had talked him into this. When they found out, Mother and Aunt Rebecca would be furious, and Woody was afraid, but he couldn't help it.

Morris had come and said, "Son, I'm in trouble. It's bad."

"What's bad, Pop?"

"Halina took money from her husband for me and has to put it back before old Bujak misses it. He could kill her."

"What did she do it for?"

"Son, you know how the bookies collect? They send a goon. They'll break my head open."

"Pop! You know I can't take you to Mrs. Skoglund."

"Why not? You're my kid, aren't you? The old broad wants to adopt you, doesn't she? Shouldn't I get something out of it for my trouble? What am I—outside? And what about Halina? She puts her life on the line, but my own kid says no."

"Oh, Bujak wouldn't hurt her."

"Woody, he'd beat her to death."

Bujak? Uniform in color with his dark-gray work clothes, short in the legs, his whole strength in his tool-and-die-maker's forearms and black fingers; and beat-looking—there was Bujak for you. But, according to Pop, there was big, big violence in Bujak, a regular boiling Bessemer inside his narrow chest. Woody could never see the violence in him. Bujak wanted no trouble. If anything, maybe he was afraid that Morris and Halina would gang up on him and kill him, screaming. But Pop was no desperado murderer. And Halina was a calm, serious woman. Bujak kept his savings in the cellar (banks were going out of business). The worst they did was to take some of his money, intending to put it back. As Woody saw him, Bujak was trying to be sensible. He accepted his sorrow. He set minimum requirements for Halina: cook the meals, clean the house, show respect. But at stealing Bujak might have drawn the line, for money was different, money was vital substance. If they stole his savings he might have had to take action, out of respect for the substance, for himself—self-respect. But you couldn't be sure that Pop hadn't invented the bookie, the goon, the theft—the whole thing. He was capable of it, and you'd be a fool not to suspect him. Morris knew that Mother and Aunt Rebecca had told Mrs. Skoglund how wicked he was. They had painted him for her in poster colors—purple for vice, black for his soul, red for Hell flames: a gambler, smoker, drinker, deserter, screwer of women, and atheist. So Pop was determined to reach her. It was risky for everybody. The Reverend Doctor's operating costs were met by Skoglund Dairies. The widow paid Woody's seminary tuition; she bought dresses for the little sisters.

Woody, now sixty, fleshy and big, like a figure for the victory of American materialism, sunk in his lounge chair, the leather of its armrests softer to his fingertips than a woman's skin, was puzzled and, in his depths, combining pain and amusement in his breast (how did *that* get there?). Intense thought puckered the skin between his eyes with a strain bordering on headache. Why had he let Pop have his way? Why did he agree to meet him that day, in the dim rear of the poolroom?

"But what will you tell Mrs. Skoglund?"

"That old broad? Don't worry, there's plenty to tell her, and it's all true. Ain't I trying to save my little laundry-and-cleaning shop? Isn't the bailiff coming for the fixtures next week?" And Pop rehearsed his pitch on the Western Avenue car. He counted on Woody's health and his freshness. Such a straightforward-looking body was perfect for a con.

Did they still have such winter storms in Chicago as they used to have? Now they somehow seemed less fierce. Blizzards used to come straight down from Ontario, from the Arctic, and drop five feet of snow in an afternoon. Then the rusty green platform cars, with revolving brushes at both ends, came out of the barns to sweep the tracks. Ten or twelve streetcars followed in slow processions, or waited, block after block.

There was a long delay at the gates of Riverview Park, all the amusements covered for the winter, boarded up—the dragon's-back high-rides, the Bobs, the Chute, the Tilt-a-Whirl, all the fun machinery put together by mechanics and electricians, men like Bujak the tool-and-die-maker, good with engines. The blizzard was having it all its own way, behind the gates, and you couldn't see far inside; only a few bulbs burned behind the palings. When Woody wiped the vapor from the glass, the wire mesh of the window guards was stuffed solid at eye level with snow. Looking higher, you saw mostly the streaked wind horizontally driving from the north. In the seat ahead, two black coal heavers, both in leather Lindbergh flying helmets, sat with shovels between their legs, returning from a job. They smelled of sweat, burlap sacking, and coal. Mostly dull with black dust, they also sparkled here and there.

There weren't many riders. People weren't leaving the house. This was a day to sit legs stuck out beside the stove, mummified by both the outdoor and the indoor forces. Only a fellow with an angle, like Pop, would go and buck such weather. A storm like this was out of the compass, and you kept the human scale by having a scheme to raise fifty bucks. Fifty soldiers! Real money in 1933.

"That woman is crazy for you," said Pop.

"She's just a good woman, sweet to all of us."

"Who knows what she's got in mind. You're a husky kid. Not such a kid, either."

"She's a religious woman. She really has religion."

"Well, your mother isn't your only parent. She and Rebecca and Kovner aren't going to fill you up with their ideas. I know your mother wants to wipe me out of your life. Unless I take a hand, you won't even understand what life is. Because they don't know—those silly Christers."

"Yes, Pop."

"The girls I can't help. They're too young. I'm sorry about them, but I can't do anything. With you it's different."

He wanted me like himself, an American.

They were stalled in the storm, while the cattle-colored car waited to have the trolley reset in the crazy wind, which boomed, tingled, blasted. At Howard Street they would have to walk straight into it, due north.

"You'll do the talking at first," said Pop.

Woody had the makings of a salesman, a pitchman. He was aware of this when he got to his feet in church to testify before fifty or sixty people. Even though Aunt Rebecca made it worth his while, he moved his own heart when he spoke up about his faith. But occasionally, without notice, his heart went away as he spoke religion and he couldn't find it anywhere. In its absence, sincere behavior got him through. He had to rely for delivery on his face, his voice—on behavior. Then his eyes came closer and closer together. And in this approach of eye to eye he felt the strain of hypocrisy. The twisting of his face threatened to betray him. It took everything he had to keep looking honest. So, since he couldn't bear the cynicism of it, he fell back on mischievousness. Mischief was where Pop came in. Pop passed straight through all those divided fields, gap after gap, and arrived at his side, bent-nosed and broad-faced. In regard to Pop, you thought of neither sincerity nor insincerity. Pop was like the man in the song: he wanted what he wanted when he wanted it. Pop was physical; Pop was digestive, circulatory, sexual. If Pop got serious, he talked to you about washing under the arms or in the crotch or of drying between your toes or of cooking supper, of baked beans and fried onions, of draw poker or of a certain horse in the fifth race at Arlington. Pop was elemental. That was why he gave such relief from religion and paradoxes, and things like that. Now, Mother *thought* she was spiritual, but Woody knew that she was kidding herself. Oh, yes, in the British accent she never gave up she was always talking to God or about Him—please God, God willing, praise God. But she was a big substantial bread-and-butter down-to-earth woman, with down-to-earth duties like feeding the girls, protecting, refining, keeping pure the girls. And those two protected doves grew up so overweight, heavy in the hips and thighs, that their poor heads looked long and slim. And mad. Sweet but cuckoo—Paula cheerfully cuckoo, Joanna depressed and having episodes.

"I'll do my best by you, but you have to promise, Pop, not to get me in Dutch with Mrs. Skoglund."

"You worried because I speak bad English? Embarrassed? I have a mockie accent?"

"It's not that. Kovner has a heavy accent, and she doesn't mind."

"Who the hell are those freaks to look down on me? You're practically a man and your dad has a right to expect help from you. He's in a fix. And you bring him to her house because she's bighearted, and you haven't got anybody else to go to."

"I got you, Pop."

The two coal trimmers stood up at Devon Avenue. One of them wore a woman's coat. Men wore women's clothing in those years, and women men's, when there was no choice. The fur collar was spiky with the wet, and sprinkled with soot. Heavy, they dragged their shovels and got off at the front. The slow car ground on, very slow. It was after four when they reached the end of the line, and somewhere between gray and black, with snow spouting and whirling under the street lamps. In Howard Street, autos were stalled at all angles and abandoned. The sidewalks were blocked. Woody led the way into Evanston, and Pop followed him up the middle of the street in the furrows made earlier by trucks. For four blocks they bucked the wind and then Woody broke through the drifts to the snowbound mansion, where they both had to push the wrought-iron gate because of the drift behind it. Twenty rooms or more in this dignified house and nobody in them but Mrs. Skoglund and her servant Hjordis, also religious.

As Woody and Pop waited, brushing the slush from their sheepskin collars and Pop wiping his big eyebrows with the ends of his scarf, sweating and freezing, the chains began to rattle and Hjordis uncovered the air holes of the glass storm door by turning a wooden bar. Woody called her "monk-faced." You no longer see women like that, who put no female touch on the face. She came plain, as God made her. She said, "Who is it and what do you want?"

"It's Woodrow Selbst. Hjordis? It's Woody.

"You're not expected."

"No, but we're here."

"What do you want?"

"We came to see Mrs. Skoglund."

"What for do you want to see her?"

"Just tell her we're here."

"I have to tell her what you came for, without calling up first."

"Why don't you say it's Woody with his father, and we wouldn't come in a snowstorm like this if it wasn't important."

The understandable caution of women who live alone. Respectable old-time women, too. There was no such respectability now in those Evanston houses, with their big verandas and deep years and with a servant like Hjordis, who carried at her belt keys to the pantry and to every closet and every dresser drawer and every padlocked bin in the cellar. And in High Episcopal Christian Science Women's Temperance Evanston, no tradespeople rang at the front door. Only invited guests. And here, after a ten-mile grind through the blizzard, came two tramps from the West Side. To this mansion where a Swedish immigrant lady, herself once a cook and now a philanthropic widow, dreamed, snowbound, while frozen lilac twigs clapped at her storm windows, of a new Jerusalem and a Second Coming and a Resurrection and a Last Judgment. To hasten the Second Coming, and all the rest, you had to reach the hearts of these scheming bums arriving in a snowstorm.

Sure, they let us in.

Then in the heat that swam suddenly up to their muffled chins Pop and Woody felt the blizzard for what it was; their cheeks were frozen slabs. They stood beat, itching, trickling in the front hall that *was* a hall, with a carved newel post staircase and a big stained-glass window at the top. Picturing Jesus with the Samaritan woman. There was a kind of Gentile closeness to the air. Perhaps when he was with Pop, Woody made more Jewish observations that he would otherwise. Although Pop's most Jewish characteristic was that Yiddish was the only language he could read a paper in. Pop was with Polish Halina, and Mother was with Jesus Christ, and

Woody ate uncooked bacon from the flitch. Still, now and then he had a Jewish impression.

Mrs. Skoglund was the cleanest of women—her fingernails, her white neck, her ears—and Pop's sexual hints to Woody all went wrong because she was so intensely clean, and made Woody think of a waterfall, large as she was, and grandly built. Her bust was big. Woody's imagination had investigated this. He thought she kept things tied down tight, very tight. But she lifted both arms once to raise a window and there it was, her bust, beside him, the whole unbindable thing. Her hair was like the raffia you had to soak before you could weave with it in a basket class—pale, pale. Pop, as he took his sheepskin off, was in sweaters, no jacket. His darting looks made him seem crooked. Hardest of all for these Selbsts with their bent noses and big, apparently straightforward faces was to look honest. All the signs of dishonesty played over them. Woody had often puzzled about it. Did it go back to the muscles, was it fundamentally a jaw problem—the projecting angles of the jaws? Or was it the angling that went on in the heart? The girls called Pop Dick Tracy, but Dick Tracy was a good guy. Whom could Pop convince? Here Woody caught a possibility as it flitted by. Precisely because of the way Pop looked, a sensitive person might feel remorse for condemning unfairly or judging unkindly. Just because of a face? Some must have bent over backward. Then he had them. Not Hjordis. She would have put Pop into the street then and there, storm or no storm. Hjordis was religious, but she was wised up, too. She hadn't come over in steerage and worked forty years in Chicago for nothing.

Mrs. Skoglund, Aase (Osie), led the visitors into the front room. This, the biggest room in the house, needed supplementary heating. Because of fifteen-foot ceilings and high windows, Hjordis had kept the parlor stove burning. It was one of those elegant parlor stoves that wore a nickel crown, or miter, and this miter, when you moved it aside, automatically raised the hinge of an iron stove lid. That stove lid underneath the crown was all soot and rust, the same as any other stove lid. Into this hold you tipped the scuttle and the anthracite chestnut rattled down. It made a cake or dome of fire visible through the small isinglass frames. It was a pretty room, three-quarters paneled in wood. The stove was plugged into the flue of the marble fireplace, and there were parquet floors and Axminster carpets and cranberry-colored tufted Victorian upholstery, and a kind of Chinese étagère, inside a cabinet, lined with mirrors and containing silver pitchers and goblets. There were Bibles and pictures of Jesus and the Holy Land and that faint Gentile odor, as if things had been rinsed in a weak vinegar solution.

"Mrs. Skoglund, I brought my dad to you. I don't think you ever met him," said Woody.

"Yes, Missus, that's me, Selbst."

Pop stood short but masterful in the sweaters, and his belly sticking out, not soft but hard. He was a man of the hard-bellied type. Nobody intimidated Pop. He never presented himself as a beggar. There wasn't a cringe in him anywhere. He let her see at once by the way he said "Missus" that he was independent and that he knew his way around. He communicated that he was able to handle himself with women. Handsome Mrs. Skoglund, carrying a basket woven of her own hair, was in her fifties—eight, maybe ten years his senior.

"I asked my son to bring me because I know you do the kid a lot of good. It's natural you should know both of his parents."

"Mrs. Skoglund, my dad is in a tight corner and I don't know anybody else to ask for help."

This was all the preliminary Pop wanted. He took over and told the widow his story about the laundry-and-cleaning business and payments overdue, and explained about the fixtures and the attachment notice, and the bailiff's office and what they were going to do to him; and he said, "I'm a small man trying to make a living."

"You don't support your children," said Mrs. Skoglund.

"That's right," said Hjordis.

"I haven't got it. If I had it, wouldn't I give it? There's bread lines and soup lines all over town. Is it just me? What I have I divvy with. I give the kids. A bad father? You think my son would bring me if I was a bad father into your house? He loves his dad, he trusts his dad, he knows his dad is a good dad. Every time I start a little business going I get wiped out. This one is a good little business, if I could hold on to that little business. Three people work for me, I meet a payroll, and three people will be on the street, too, if I close down. Missus, I can sign a note and pay you in two months. I'm a common man, but I'm a hard worker and a fellow you can trust."

Woody was startled when Pop used the word "trust." It was as if from all four corners a Sousa band blew a blast to warn the entire world: "Crook! This is a crook!" But Mrs. Skoglund, on account of her religious preoccupations, was remote. She heard nothing. Although everybody in this part of the world, unless he was crazy, led a practical life, and you'd have nothing to say to anyone, your neighbors would have nothing to say to you, if communications were not of a practical sort, Mrs. Skoglund, with all her money, was unworldly—two-thirds out of this world.

"Give me a chance to show what's in me," said Pop, "and you'll see what I do for my kids."

So Mrs. Skoglund hesitated, and then she said she'd have to go upstairs, she'd have to go to her room and pray on it and ask for guidance—would they sit down and wait. There were two rocking chairs by the stove. Hjordis gave Pop a grim look (a dangerous person) and Woody a blaming one (he brought a dangerous stranger and disrupter to injure two kind Christian ladies). Then she went out with Mrs. Skoglund.

As soon as they left, Pop jumped up from the rocker and said in anger, "What's this with the praying? She has to ask God to lend me fifty bucks?"

Woody said, "It's not you, Pop, it's the way these religious people do."

"No," said Pop. "She'll come back and say that God wouldn't let her."

Woody didn't like that; he thought Pop was being gross and he said, "No, she's sincere. Pop, try to understand: she's emotional, nervous, and sincere, and tries to do right by everybody."

And Pop said, "That servant will talk her out of it. She's a toughie. It's all over her face that we're a couple of chiselers."

"What's the use of us arguing," said Woody. He drew the rocker closer to the stove. His shoes were wet through and would never dry. The blue flames fluttered like a school of fishes in the coal fire. But Pop went over to the Chinese-style cabinet or étagère and tried the handle, and then opened the blade of his penknife and in a second had forced the lock of the curved glass door. He took out a silver dish.

"Pop, what is this?" said Woody.

Pop, cool and level, knew exactly what this was. He relocked the étagère, crossed the carpet, listened. He stuffed the dish under his belt and pushed it down into his trousers. He put the side of his short thick finger to his mouth.

So Woody kept his voice down, but he was all shook up. He went to Pop and took him by the edge of his hand. As he looked into Pop's face, he felt his eyes growing smaller and smaller, as if something were contracting all the skin on his head. They call it hyperventilation when everything feels tight and light and close and dizzy. Hardly breathing, he said, "Put it back, Pop."

Pop said. "It's solid silver; it's worth dough."

"Pop, you said you wouldn't get me in Dutch."

"It's only insurance in case she comes back from praying and tells me no. If she says yes, I'll put it back."

"How?"

"It'll get back. If I don't put it back, you will."

"You picked the lock. I couldn't. I don't know how."

"There's nothing to it."

"We're going to put it back now. Give it here."

"Woody, it's under my fly, inside my underpants. Don't make such a noise about nothing."

"Pop, I can't believe this."

"For cry-ninety-nine, shut your mouth. If I didn't trust you I wouldn't have let you watch me do it. You don't understand a thing. What's with you?"

"Before they come down, Pop, will you dig that dish out of your long johns."

Pop turned stiff on him. He became absolutely military. He said, "Look, I order you!"

Before he knew it, Woody had jumped his father and begun to wrestle with him. It was dangerous to clutch your own father, to put a heel behind him, to force him to the wall. Pop was taken by surprise and said loudly, "You want Halina killed? Kill her! Go on, you be responsible." He began to resist, angry, and they turned about several times, when Woody, with a trick he had learned in a Western movie and used once on the playground, tripped him and they fell to the ground. Woody, who already outweighed the old man by twenty pounds, was on top. They landed on the floor beside the stove, which stood on a tray of decorated tin to protect the carpet. In this position, pressing Pop's hard belly, Woody recognized that to have wrestled him to the floor counted for nothing. It was impossible to thrust his hand under Pop's belt to recover the dish. And now Pop had turned furious, as a father has every right to be when his son is violent with him, and he freed his hand and hit Woody in the face. He hit him three or four times in midface. Then Woody dug his head into Pop's shoulder and held tight only to keep from being struck and began to say in his ear, "Jesus, Pop, for Christ sake remember where you are. Those women will be back!" But Pop brought up his short knee and fought and butted him with his chin and rattled Woody's teeth. Woody thought the old man was about to bite him. And because he was a seminarian, he thought: Like an unclean spirit. And held tight. Gradually Pop stopped threshing and struggling. His eyes stuck out and his mouth was open, sullen. Like a stout fish. Woody released him and gave him a hand up. He was then overcome with many bad feelings of a sort he knew the old man never suffered. Never, never. Pop never had these groveling emotions. There was his whole superiority. Pop had no such feelings. He was like a horseman from Central Asia, a bandit from China. It was Mother, from Liverpool, who had the refinement, the English manners. It was the preaching Reverend Doctor in his black suit. You have refinements, and all they do is oppress you? The hell with that.

The long door opened and Mrs. Skoglund stepped in, saying, "Did I imagine, or did something shake the house?"

"I was lifting the scuttle to put coal on the fire and it fell out of my hand. I'm sorry I was so clumsy," said Woody.

Pop was too huffy to speak. With his eyes big and sore and the thin hair down over his forehead, you could see by the tightness of his belly how angrily he was fetching his breath, though his mouth was shut.

"I prayed," said Mrs. Skoglund.

"I hope it came out well," said Woody.

"Well, I don't do anything without guidance, but the answer was yes, and I feel right about it now. So if you'll wait, I'll go to my office and write a check. I asked Hjordis to bring you a cup of coffee. Coming in such a storm."

And Pop, consistently a terrible little man, as soon as she shut the door, said, "A check? Hell with a check. Get me the greenbacks."

"They don't keep money in the house. You can cash it in her bank tomorrow. But if they miss that dish, Pop, they'll stop the check, and then where are you?"

As Pop was reaching below the belt, Hjordis brought in the tray. She was very sharp with him. She said, "Is this a place to adjust clothing, Mister? A men's washroom?"

"Well, which way is the toilet, then?" said Pop.

She had served the coffee in the seamiest mugs in the pantry, and she bumped down the tray and led Pop down the corridor, standing guard at the bathroom door so that he shouldn't wander about the house.

Mrs. Skoglund called Woody to her office and after she had given him the folded check said that they should pray together for Morris. So once more he was on his knees, under rows and rows of musty marbled-cardboard files, by the glass lamp by the edge of the desk, the shade with flounced edges, like the candy dish. Mrs. Skoglund, in her Scandinavian accent—an emotional contralto—raising her voice to Jesus-uh Christ-uh, as the wind lashed the trees, kicked the side of the house, and drove the snow seething on the windowpanes, to send light-uh, give guidance-uh, put a new heart-uh in Pop's bosom. Woody asked God only to make Pop put the dish back. He kept Mrs. Skoglund on her knees as long as possible. Then he thanked her, shining with candor (as much as ke knew how), for her Christian generosity and he said, "I know that Hjordis has a cousin who works at the Evanston YMCA. Could she please phone him and try to get us a room tonight so that we don't have to fight the blizzard all the way back? We're almost as close to the Y as to the car line. Maybe the cars have even stopped running."

Suspicious Hjordis, coming when Mrs. Skoglund called to her, was burning now. First they barged in, made themselves at home, asked for money, had to have coffee, probably left gonorrhea on the toilet seat. Hjordis, Woody remembered, was a woman who wiped the doorknobs with rubbing alcohol after guests had left. Nevertheless, she telephoned the Y and got them a room with two cots for six bits.

Pop had plenty of time, therefore, to reopen the étagère, lined with reflecting glass or German silver (something exquisitely delicate and tricky), and as soon as the two Selbsts had said thank you and goodbye and were in midstreet again up to the knees in snow, Woody said, "Well, I covered for you. Is that thing back?"

"Of course it is," said Pop.

They fought their way to the small Y building, shut up in wire grille and resembling a police station—about the same dimensions. It was locked, but they made a racket on the grille, and a small black man let them in and shuffled them upstairs to a cement corridor with low doors. It was like the small-mammal house in Lincoln Park. He said there was nothing to eat, so they took off their wet pants, wrapped themselves tightly in the khaki army blankets, and passed out on their cots.

First thing in the morning, they went to the Evanston National Bank and got the fifty dollars. Not without difficulties. The teller went to call Mrs. Skoglund and was absent a long time from the wicket. "Where the hell has he gone?" said Pop.

But when the fellow came back, he said, "How do you want it?"

Pop said, "Singles." He told Woody, "Bujak stashes it in one-dollar bills."

But by now Woody no longer believed Halina had stolen the old man's money.

Then they went into the street, where the snow-removal crews were at work. The sun shone broad, broad, out of the morning blue, and all Chicago would be releasing itself from the temporary beauty of those vast drifts.

"You shouldn't have jumped me last night, Sonny."

"I know, Pop, but you promised you wouldn't get me in Dutch."

"Well, it's okay. We can forget it, seeing you stood by me."

Only, Pop had taken the silver dish. Of course he had, and in a few days Mrs. Skoglund and Hjordis knew it, and later in the week they were all waiting for Woody in Kovner's office at the settlement house. The group included the Reverend Doctor Crabbie, head of the seminary, and Woody, who had been flying along, level and smooth, was shot down in flames. He told them he was innocent. Even as he was falling, he warned that they were wronging him. He denied that he or Pop had touched Mrs. Skoglund's property. The missing object—he didn't even know what it was—had probably been misplaced, and they would be very sorry on the day it turned up. After the others were done with him, Dr. Crabbie said that until he was able to tell the truth he would be suspended from the seminary, where his work had been unsatisfactory anyway. Aunt Rebecca took him aside and said to him, "You are a little crook, like your father. The door is closed to you here."

To this Pop's comment was "So what, kid?"

"Pop, you shouldn't have done it."

"No? Well, I don't give a care, if you want to know. You can have the dish if you want to go back and square yourself with all those hypocrites."

"I didn't like doing Mrs. Skoglund in the eye, she was so kind to us."

"Kind?"

"Kind."

"Kind has a price tag."

Well, there was no winning such arguments with Pop. But they debated it in various moods and from various elevations and perspectives for forty years and more, as their intimacy changed, developed, matured.

"Why did you do it, Pop? For the money? What did you do with the fifty bucks?" Woody, decades later, asked him that.

"I settled with the bookie, and the rest I put in the business."

"You tried a few more horses."

"I maybe did, but it was a double, Woody. I didn't hurt myself, and at the same time did you a favor."

"It was for me?"

"It was too strange of a life. That life wasn't *you*, Woody. All those women . . . Kovner was no man, he was an in-between. Suppose they made you a minister? Some Christian minister! First of all, you wouldn't have been able to stand it, and second, they would throw you out sooner or later."

"Maybe so."

"And you wouldn't have converted the Jews, which was the main thing they wanted."

"And what a time to bother the Jews," Woody said. "At least *I* didn't bug them."

Pop had carried him back to his side of the line, blood of his blood, the same thick body walls, the same coarse grain. Not cut out for a spiritual life. Simply not up to it.

Pop was no worse than Woody, and Woody was no better than Pop. Pop wanted no relation to theory, and yet he was always pointing Woody toward a position—a jolly, hearty, natural, likable, unprincipled position. If Woody had a weakness, it was to be unselfish. This worked to Pop's advantage, but he criticized Woody for it, nevertheless. "You take too much on yourself," Pop was always saying. And it's true that Woody gave Pop his heart because Pop was so selfish. It's usually the selfish people who are loved the most. They do what you deny yourself, and you love them for it. You give them your heart.

Remembering the pawn ticket for the silver dish, Woody startled himself with a laugh so sudden that it made him cough. Pop said to him after his expulsion from the seminary and banishment from the settlement house, "You want in again? Here's the ticket. I hocked that thing. It wasn't so valuable as I thought."

"What did they give?"

"Twelve-fifty was all I could get. But if you want it you'll have to raise the dough yourself, because I haven't got anymore."

"You must have been sweating in the bank when the teller went to call Mrs. Skoglund about the check."

"I was a little nervous," said Pop. "But I didn't think they could miss the thing so soon."

That theft was part of Pop's war with Mother. With Mother, and Aunt Rebecca, and the Reverend Doctor. Pop took his stand on realism. Mother represented the forces of religion and hypochondria. In four decades, the fighting never stopped. In the course of time, Mother and the girls turned into welfare personalities and lost their individual outlines. Ah, the poor things, they became dependents and cranks. In the meantime, Woody, the sinful man, was their dutiful and loving son and brother. He maintained the bungalow—this took in roofing, pointing, wiring, insulation, air-conditioning—and he paid for heat and light and food, and dressed them all out of Sears, Roebuck and Wieboldt's, and bought them a TV, which they watched as devoutly as they prayed. Paula took courses to learn skills like macramé-making and needlepoint, and sometimes got a little job as recreational worker in a nursing home. But she wasn't steady enough to keep it. Wicked Pop spent most of his life removing stains from people's clothing. He and Halina in the last years ran a Cleanomat in West Rogers Park— a so-so business resembling a laundromat—which gave him leisure for billiards, the horses, rummy and pinochle. Every morning he went behind the partition to check out the filters of the cleaning equipment. He found amusing things that had been thrown into the vats with the clothing— sometimes, when he got lucky, a locket chain or a brooch. And when he had fortified the cleaning fluid, pouring all that blue and pink stuff in from plastic jugs, he read the *Forward* over a second cup of coffee, and went out, leaving Halina in charge. When they needed help with the rent, Woody gave it.

After the new Disney World was opened in Florida, Woody treated all his dependents to a holiday. He sent them down in separate batches, of course. Halina enjoyed this more than anybody else. She couldn't stop talking about the address given by an Abraham Lincoln automaton. "Wonderful, how he stood up and moved his hands, and his mouth. So real! And how beautiful he talked." Of them all, Halina was the soundest, the most human, the most honest. Now that Pop was gone, Woody and Halina's son, Mitosh, the organist at the Stadium, took care of her needs over and above Social Security, splitting expenses. In Pop's opinion, insurance was a racket. He left Halina nothing but some out-of-date equipment.

Woody treated himself, too. Once a year, and sometimes oftener, he left his business to run itself, arranged with the trust department at the bank to take care of his gang, and went off. He did that in style, imaginatively, expensively. In Japan, he wasted little time on Tokyo. He spent three weeks in Kyoto and stayed at the Tawaraya Inn, dating from the seventeenth century or so. There he slept on the floor, the Japanese way, and bathed in scalding water. He saw the dirtiest strip show on earth, as well as the holy places and the temple gardens. He visited also Istanbul, Jerusalem, Delphi, and went to Burma and Uganda and Kenya on safari, on democratic terms with drivers, Bedouins, bazaar merchants. Open, lavish, familiar, fleshier and fleshier but (he jogged, he lifted weights) still muscular—in his naked person beginning to resemble a Renaissance courtier in full costume—becoming ruddier every year, an outdoor type with freckles on his back and spots across the flaming forehead and the honest nose. In Addis Ababa he took an Ethiopian beauty to his room from the street and washed her, getting into the shower with her to soap her with his broad, kindly hands. In Kenya he taught certain American obscenities to a black woman so that she could shout them out during the act. On the Nile, below Murchison Falls, those fever trees rose huge from the mud, and hippos on the sandbars belched at the passing launch, hostile. One of them danced on his spit of sand, springing from the ground and coming down heavy, on all fours. There, Woody saw the buffalo calf disappear, snatched by the crocodile.

Mother, soon to follow Pop, was being lighthearted these days. In company, she spoke of Woody as her boy—"What do you think of my Sonny?"—as though he was ten years old. She was silly with him, her behavior was frivolous, almost flirtatious. She just didn't seem to know the facts. And behind her all the others, like kids at the playground, were waiting their turn to go down the slide: one on each step, and moving toward the top.

Over Woody's residence and place of business there had gathered a pool of silence of the same perimeter as the church bells while they were ringing, and he mourned under it, this melancholy morning of sun and autumn. Doing a life survey, taking a deliberate look at the gross side of his case—of the other side as well, what there was of it. But if this heartache continued, he'd go out and run it off. A three-mile jog—five, if necessary. And you'd think that this jogging was an entirely physical activity, wouldn't you? But there was something else in it. Because, when he was a seminarian, between the shafts of his World's Fair rickshaw, he used to receive, pulling along (capable and stable), his religious experiences while he trotted. Maybe it was all a single experience repeated. He felt truth coming to him from the sun. He received a communication that was also light and warmth. It made him very remote from his horny Wisconsin passengers, those farmers whose whoops and whore cries he could hardly hear when he was in one of his states. And again out of the flaming of the sun would come to him a secret certainty that the goal set for this earth was that it should be filled with good, saturated with it. After everything preposterous, after dog had eaten dog, after the crocodile death had pulled everyone into his mud. It wouldn't conclude as Mrs. Skoglund, bribing him to round up the Jews and hasten the Second Coming, imagined it, but in another way. This was his clumsy intuition. It went no further. Subsequently, he proceeded though life as life seemed to want him to do it.

There remained one thing more this morning, which was explicitly physical, occurring first as a sensation in his arms and against his breast and, from the pressure, passing into him and going into his breast.

It was like this: When he came into the hospital room and saw Pop with the sides of his bed raised, like a crib, and Pop, so very feeble, and writhing, and toothless, like a baby, and the dirt already cast into his face, into the wrinkles—Pop wanted to pluck out the intravenous needles and he was piping his weak death noise. The gauze patches taped over the needles were soiled with dark blood. Then Woody took off his shoes, lowered the side of the bed, and climbed in and held him in his arms to soothe and still him. As if he were Pop's father, he said to him, "Now, Pop, Pop." Then it was like the wrestle in Mrs. Skoglund's parlor, when Pop turned angry like an unclean spirit and Woody tried to appease him, and warn him, saying, "Those women will be back!" Beside the coal stove, when Pop hit Woody in the teeth with his head and then became sullen, like a stout fish. But this struggle in the hospital was weak—so weak! In his great pity, Woody held Pop, who was fluttering and shivering. From those people, Pop had told him, you'll never find out what life is, because they don't know what it is. Yes, Pop—well, what is it, Pop? Hard to comprehend that Pop, who was dug in for eighty-three years and had done all he could to stay, should now want nothing but to free himself. How could Woody allow the old man to pull the intravenous needles out? Willful Pop, he wanted what he wanted when he wanted it. But what he wanted at the very last Woody failed to follow, it was such a switch.

After a time, Pop's resistance ended. He subsided and subsided. He rested against his son, his small body curled there. Nurses came and looked. They disapproved, but Woody, who couldn't spare a hand to wave them out, motioned with his head toward the door. Pop, whom Woody thought he had stilled, only had found a better way to get around him. Loss of heat was the way he did it. His heat was leaving him. As can happen with small animals while you hold them in your hand. Woody presently felt him cooling. Then, as Woody did his best to restrain him, and thought he was succeeding, Pop divided himself. And when he was separated from his warmth, he slipped into death. And there was his

**61**

elderly, large muscular son, still holding and pressing him when there was nothing anymore to press. You could never pin down that self-willed man. When he was ready to make his move, he made it—always on his own terms. And always, always, something up his sleeve. That was how he was.

· · · · · · · · · · ·

## QUESTIONS FOR A SECOND READING

1. The story begins with a question: "What do you do about death—in this case, the death of an old father? If you're a modern person, sixty years of age, and a man who's been around, like Woody Selbst, what do you do?" What *does* Woody do about the death of his father? What does the story offer as his characteristic ways of thinking and acting in this situation? And what can you conclude from this about Woody Selbst?

2. What attitude do you suppose Bellow intends you to take toward Woody? (How, for example, are you supposed to read the reference to Woody as a "modern person," "a man who's been around"? Are these references ironic?) As you read back through the story, mark those passages that best represent the narrator's attitude (or attitudes) toward Woody. What attitude do you think the narrator expects the reader to take in each case? What attitudes *do* you take, and how do they change or develop as you read from the first page to the last?

## ASSIGNMENTS FOR WRITING

1. Aunt Rebecca said that Woody was a "little crook," just like his father. Woody said that Pop "wanted me like himself, an American." Is Woody like his father? What part of his father does Woody carry with him? What lessons? Write an essay in which you discuss what Woody inherits from his father and explain what he does (or does not do) with his inheritance.

2. At one point (on page 58) the narrator says:

> Pop was no worse than Woody, and Woody was no better than Pop. Pop wanted no relation to theory, and yet he was always pointing Woody toward a position—a jolly, hearty, natural, likable, unprincipled position. If Woody had a weakness, it was to be unselfish. This worked to Pop's advantage, but he criticized Woody for it, nevertheless. "You take too much on yourself," Pop was always saying. And it's true that Woody gave Pop his heart because Pop was so selfish. It's usually the selfish people who are loved the most.

They do what you deny yourself, and you love them for it. You give
them your heart.

This paragraph sounds like one of the statements an author makes to sum
up a chapter—in this case, to give the final word on Woody Selbst and his
relationship to his father. Write an essay in which you discuss whether you
think this summation is an adequate description of the relationship. What
parts of Woody's behavior does it seem to explain? What won't it account
for? (Who is speaking in that passage? to what end?)

## MAKING CONNECTIONS

1. John Berger, in "Ways of Seeing" (p. 66), says, "The past is never there
waiting to be discovered, to be recognized for exactly what it is. History
always constitutes the relation between a present and its past." If the past
is not just *there*, waiting to be recognized for exactly what it is, then the
past has to be created, or re-created, by a person with a particular point
of view, a particular way of reading the memories, stories, documents, or
artifacts that provide a connection to a time that would otherwise be gone.

   John Edgar Wideman, in "Our Time" (p. 596), says that he is writing
to "recover" his brother Robby from the past. Woody Selbst, it might be
said, is doing the same thing. As the story "A Silver Dish" takes us inside
his thinking and his memories, we watch him trying to put together his
past and, in doing so, understand his father.

   Take John Edgar Wideman and Woody Selbst as examples of people
working on the past. (To do this, you will have to assume that "A Silver
Dish" represents Woody's train of thought.) Pay particular attention to the
characteristic ways that each one selects, arranges, and interprets (or comments on) the material he gathers to represent the past. Write an essay,
then, in which you use these two texts, "Our Time" and "A Silver Dish,"
to address the problems of recovering the past and constructing a history.

2. Clifford Geertz, in his essay "Deep Play: Notes on the Balinese Cockfight"
(p. 272), approaches cockfights in Bali as a reader might approach a text—
he begins by assuming that they "say something of something," that they
represent more than just the fact of cockfights. After mapping out his evidence, he concludes that they are dramatizations of status concerns, that,
in other words, they enact the culture's appointments of power and rank,
and, as such, that they use emotion for cognitive ends. A cockfight's function, as Geertz says, "is interpretive: it is a Balinese reading of Balinese
experience: a story they tell themselves about themselves."

   The narrator in Bellow's story is invisible; we don't see him as a character in the story, but it is nevertheless his story, and although he announces that it is a story of a man dealing with his father's death, it could
be, if we take a Geertzian perspective, a story about something else, a story
that might say something about the narrator and his culture.

   Take the invisible narrator of this story and make him visible by "reading" him as a cultural artifact, as a particular person telling a particular story that could be said to dramatize or enact something significant about him and his culture. Like Geertz, you'll have to approach the story not only as a story but also as a metaphorical representation of the author in his culture. And, like Geertz, you might begin by asking what the narrator offers you for evidence to read his story as a metaphoric representation. What, for example, are his significant metaphors? How do they represent him? the culture he is embedded in? What are the significant events and relationships he offers? How can you read them as saying something about a narrator in a culture?

Write an essay in which you use the narrator's story and his creations—the metaphors, events, and relationships he uses—to do a Geertzian reading of him in his culture. In what ways might the narrator be said to be a representative of his culture? And what is it that he represents?

# JOHN

# BERGER

*J*OHN BERGER (b. 1926), like few other art critics, elicits strong and contradictory reactions to his writing. He has been called (and sometimes in the same
review) "preposterous" as well as "stimulating," "pompous" yet "exciting." He
has been accused of falling prey to "ideological excesses" and of being a victim of
his own "lack of objectivity," but he has been praised for his "scrupulous" and
"cogent" observations on art and culture. He is one of Europe's most influential
Marxist critics, yet his work has been heralded and damned by leftists and conser-
vatives alike. Although Berger's work speaks powerfully, its tone is quiet, thoughtful, measured. According to the poet and critic Peter Schjeldahl, "The most mysterious element in Mr. Berger's criticism has always been the personality of the
critic himself, a man of strenuous conviction so loath to bully that even his most
provocative arguments sit feather-light on the mind."

The following selection is the first chapter from Ways of Seeing, a book which
began as a series on BBC television. In fact, the show was a forerunner of those
encyclopedic television series later popular on public television stations in the
United States: Civilization, The Ascent of Man, Cosmos. Berger's show was
less glittery and ambitious, but in its way it was more serious in its claims to be
educational. As you watched the screen, you saw a series of images (like those in

*the following text). These were sometimes presented with commentary, but some-
times in silence, so that you constantly saw one image in the context of another—
for example, classic presentations of women in oil paintings interspersed with images of women from contemporary art, advertising, movies, and "men's magazines." The goal of the exercise, according to Berger, was to "start a process of
questioning," to focus his viewer's attention not on a single painting in isolation
but on "ways of seeing" in general, on the ways we have learned to look at and
understand the images that surround us, and on the culture that teaches us to see
things as we do. The method of* Ways of Seeing, *a book of art history, was used
by Berger in another book,* A Seventh Man, *to document the situation of the
migrant worker in Europe.*

*Berger has written poems, novels, essays, and film scripts, including* G, A
Fortunate Man, The Success and Failure of Picasso, *and* About Looking. *He
lived and worked in England for years, but he currently lives in Quincy, a small
peasant village in Haute-Savoie, France, where he has, for the past few years, been
writing a trilogy of books on peasant life. Berger has tentatively entitled the trilogy*
Into Their Labours. *The first book in the series,* Pig Earth, *is a collection of
essays, poems, and stories set in Haute-Savoie. The second,* Once in Europa,
*consists of five peasant tales that take love as their subject. The third and final book
in the trilogy, tentatively entitled* An Old Wives' Tale of a City, *will be a novel
about the migration of the peasants to the city.*

# Ways of Seeing

Seeing comes before words. The child looks and recognizes before it
can speak.

But there is also another sense in which seeing comes before words. It
is seeing which establishes our place in the surrounding world; we explain
that world with words, but words can never undo the fact that we are
surrounded by it. The relation between what we see and what we know
is never settled. Each evening we *see* the sun set. We *know* that the earth
is turning away from it. Yet the knowledge, the explanation, never quite
fits the sight. The Surrealist painter Magritte commented on this always-
present gap between words and seeing in a painting called *The Key of
Dreams.*

The way we see things is affected by what we know or what we believe.
In the Middle Ages when men believed in the physical existence of Hell
the sight of fire must have meant something different from what it means
today. Nevertheless their idea of Hell owed a lot to the sight of fire con-

*The Key of Dreams* by Magritte 1898–1967

suming and the ashes remaining—as well as to their experience of the pain of burns.

When in love, the sight of the beloved has a completeness which no words and no embrace can match: a completeness which only the act of making love can temporarily accommodate.

Yet this seeing which comes before words, and can never be quite covered by them, is not a question of mechanically reacting to stimuli. (It can only be thought of in this way if one isolates the small part of the process which concerns the eye's retina.) We only see what we look at. To look is an act of choice. As a result of this act, what we see is brought within our reach—though not necessarily within arm's reach. To touch something is to situate oneself in relation to it. (Close your eyes, move round the room and notice how the faculty of touch is like a static, limited form of sight.) We never look at just one thing; we are always looking at the relation between things and ourselves. Our vision is continually active, continually moving, continually holding things in a circle around itself, constituting what is present to us as we are.

Soon after we can see, we are aware that we can also be seen. The eye of the other combines with our own eye to make it fully credible that we are part of the visible world.

If we accept that we can see that hill over there, we propose that from that hill we can be seen. The reciprocal nature of vision is more funda-

mental than that of spoken dialogue. And often dialogue is an attempt to verbalize this—an attempt to explain how, either metaphorically or literally, "you see things," and an attempt to discover how "he sees things."

In the sense in which we use the word in this book, all images are manmade [see above]. An image is a sight which has been recreated or reproduced. It is an appearance, or a set of appearances, which has been detached from the place and time in which it first made its appearance and preserved—for a few moments or a few centuries. Every image embodies a way of seeing. Even a photograph. For photographs are not, as is often assumed, a mechanical record. Every time we look at a photograph, we are aware, however slightly, of the photographer selecting that sight from an infinity of other possible sights. This is true even in the most casual family snapshot. The photographer's way of seeing is reflected in his choice of subject. The painter's way of seeing is reconstituted by the marks he makes on the canvas or paper. Yet, although every image embodies a way of seeing, our perception or appreciation of an image depends also upon our own way of seeing. (It may be, for example, that Sheila is one figure among twenty; but for our own reasons she is the one we have eyes for.)

Images were first made to conjure up the appearances of something that was absent. Gradually it became evident that an image could outlast what it represented; it then showed how something or somebody had once looked—and thus by implication how the subject had once been seen by other people. Later still the specific vision of the image-maker was also recognized as part of the record. An image became a record of how X had seen Y. This was the result of an increasing consciousness of individuality, accompanying an increasing awareness of history. It would be rash to try to date this last development precisely. But certainly in Europe such consciousness has existed since the beginning of the Renaissance.

No other kind of relic or text from the past can offer such a direct testimony about the world which surrounded other people at other times. In this respect images are more precise and richer than literature. To say this is not to deny the expressive or imaginative quality of art, treating it as mere documentary evidence; the more imaginative the work, the more profoundly it allows us to share the artist's experience of the visible.

Yet when an image is presented as a work of art, the way people look at it is affected by a whole series of learnt assumptions about art. Assumptions concerning:

> Beauty
> Truth
> Genius
> Civilization
> Form
> Status
> Taste, etc.

Many of these assumptions no longer accord with the world as it is. (The world-as-it-is is more than pure objective fact, it includes consciousness.) Out of true with the present, these assumptions obscure the past. They mystify rather than clarify. The past is never there waiting to be discovered, to be recognized for exactly what it is. History always constitutes the relation between a present and its past. Consequently fear of the present leads to mystification of the past. The past is not for living in; it is a well of conclusions from which we draw in order to act. Cultural mystification of the past entails a double loss. Works of art are made unnecessarily remote. And the past offers us fewer conclusions to complete in action.

When we "see" a landscape, we situate ourselves in it. If we "saw" the art of the past, we would situate ourselves in history. When we are prevented from seeing it, we are being deprived of the history which belongs to us. Who benefits from this deprivation? In the end, the art of the past is being mystified because a privileged minority is striving to invent a history which can retrospectively justify the role of the ruling classes, and such a justification can no longer make sense in modern terms. And so, inevitably, it mystifies.

Let us consider a typical example of such mystification. A two-volume

*Regents of the Old Men's Alms House* by Hals 1580–1666

*Regentesses of the Old Men's Alms House* by Hals 1580–1666

study was recently published on Frans Hals. [1] It is the authoritative **work** to date on this painter. As a book of specialized art history it is no **better** and no worse than the average.

The last two great paintings by Frans Hals [above] portray the Governors and the Governesses of an Alms House for old paupers in the Dutch seventeenth-century city of Haarlem. They were officially commissioned portraits. Hals, an old man of over eighty, was destitute. Most of his life he had been in debt. During the winter of 1664, the year he began painting

70

these pictures, he obtained three loads of peat on public charity, otherwise he would have frozen to death. Those who now sat for him were administrators of such public charity.

The author records these facts and then explicitly says that it would be incorrect to read into the paintings any criticism of the sitters. There is no evidence, he says, that Hals painted them in a spirit of bitterness. The author considers them, however, remarkable works of art and explains why. Here he writes of the Regentesses:

> Each woman speaks to us of the human condition with equal importance. Each woman stands out with equal clarity against the *enormous* dark surface, yet they are linked by a firm rhythmical arrangement and the subdued diagonal pattern formed by their heads and hands. Subtle modulations of the *deep,* glowing blacks contribute to the *harmonious fusion* of the whole and form an *unforgettable contrast* with the *powerful* whites and vivid flesh tones where the detached strokes reach *a peak of breadth and strength.* [Berger's italics]

The compositional unity of a painting contributes fundamentally to the power of its image. It is reasonable to consider a painting's composition. But here the composition is written about as though it were in itself the emotional charge of the painting. Terms like *harmonious fusion, unforgettable contrast,* reaching *a peak of breadth and strength* transfer the emotion provoked by the image from the plane of lived experience, to that of disinterested "art appreciation." All conflict disappears. One is left with the unchanging "human condition," and the painting considered as a marvellously made object.

Very little is known about Hals or the Regents who commissioned him. It is not possible to produce circumstantial evidence to establish what their relations were. But there is the evidence of the paintings themselves: the evidence of a group of men and a group of women as seen by another man, the painter. Study this evidence and judge for yourself [p. 70].

The art historian fears such direct judgement:

> As in so many other pictures by Hals, the penetrating characterizations almost seduce us into believing that we know the personality traits and even the habits of the men and women portrayed.

What is this "seduction" he writes of? It is nothing less than the paintings working upon us. They work upon us because we accept the way Hals saw his sitters. We do not accept this innocently. We accept it in so far as it corresponds to our own observation of people, gestures, faces, institutions. This is possible because we still live in a society of comparable social

relations and moral values. And it is precisely this which gives the paintings their psychological and social urgency. It is this—not the painter's skill as a "seducer"—which convinces us that we *can* know the people portrayed.

The author continues:

> In the case of some critics the seduction has been a total success. It has, for example, been asserted that the Regent in the tipped slouch hat, which hardly covers any of his long, lank hair, and whose curiously set eyes do not focus, was shown in a drunken state. [p. 73]

This, he suggests, is a libel. He argues that it was a fashion at that time to wear hats on the side of the head. He cites medical opinion to prove that the Regent's expression could well be the result of a facial paralysis. He insists that the painting would have been unacceptable to the Regents if one of them had been portrayed drunk. One might go on discussing each of these points for pages. (Men in seventeenth-century Holland wore their hats on the side of their heads in order to be thought of as adventurous and pleasure-loving. Heavy drinking was an approved practice. Etcetera.) But such a discussion would take us even farther away from the only confrontation which matters and which the author is determined to evade.

In this confrontation the Regents and Regentesses stare at Hals, a destitute old painter who has lost his reputation and lives off public charity; he examines them through the eyes of a pauper who must nevertheless try to be objective; i.e., must try to surmount the way he sees as a pauper.

This is the drama of these paintings. A drama of an "unforgettable contrast."

Mystification has little to do with the vocabulary used. Mystification is the process of explaining away what might otherwise be evident. Hals was the first portraitist to paint the new characters and expressions created by capitalism. He did in pictorial terms what Balzac did two centuries later in literature. Yet the author of the authoritative work on these paintings sums up the artist's achievement by referring to

> Hals's unwavering commitment to his personal vision, which
> enriches our consciousness of our fellow men and heightens
> our awe for the ever-increasing power of the mighty impulses
> that enabled him to give us a close view of life's vital forces.

That is mystification.

In order to avoid mystifying the past (which can equally well suffer pseudo-Marxist mystification) let us now examine the particular relation which now exists, so far as pictorial images are concerned, between the present and the past. If we can see the present clearly enough, we shall ask the right questions of the past.

Today we see the art of the past as nobody saw it before. We actually perceive it in a different way.

This difference can be illustrated in terms of what was thought of as perspective. The convention of perspective, which is unique to European art and which was first established in the early Renaissance, centres everything on the eye of the beholder. It is like a beam from a lighthouse—only instead of light travelling outwards, appearances travel in. The conventions called those appearances *reality*. Perspective makes the single eye the centre of the visible world. Everything converges on to the eye as to the vanishing point of infinity. The visible world is arranged for the spectator as the universe was once thought to be arranged for God.

According to the convention of perspective there is no visual reciprocity. There is no need for God to situate himself in relation to others: he is himself the situation. The inherent contradiction in perspective was that it structured all images of reality to address a single spectator who, unlike God, could only be in one place at a time.

After the invention of the camera this contradiction gradually became apparent.

I'm an eye. A mechanical eye. I, the machine, show you a world the way only I can see it. I free myself for today and

Still from *Man with a Movie Camera* by Vertov

forever from human immobility. I'm in constant movement.
I approach and pull away from objects. I creep under them.
I move alongside a running horse's mouth. I fall and rise with
the falling and rising bodies. This is I, the machine, ma-
noeuvring in the chaotic movements, recording one movement after another in the most complex combinations.

Freed from the boundaries of time and space, I coordinate
any and all points of the universe, wherever I want them to
be. My way leads towards the creation of a fresh perception
of the world. Thus I explain in a new way the world unknown to you.[2]

The camera isolated momentary appearances and in so doing destroyed the
idea that images were timeless. Or, to put it another way, the camera
showed that the notion of time passing was inseparable from the experience of the visual (except in paintings). What you saw depended upon
where you were when. What you saw was relative to your position in time
and space. It was no longer possible to imagine everything converging on
the human eye as on the vanishing point of infinity.

This is not to say that before the invention of the camera men believed
that everyone could see everything. But perspective organized the visual
field as though that were indeed the ideal. Every drawing or painting that
used perspective proposed to the spectator that he was the unique centre
of the world. The camera—and more particularly the movie camera—demonstrated that there was no centre.

The invention of the camera changed the way men saw. The visible
came to mean something different to them. This was immediately reflected
in painting.

For the Impressionists the visible no longer presented itself to man in
order to be seen. On the contrary, the visible, in continual flux, became
fugitive. For the Cubists the visible was no longer what confronted the
single eye, but the totality of possible views taken from points all round
the object (or person) being depicted [p. 76, top].

The invention of the camera also changed the way in which men saw
paintings painted long before the camera was invented. Originally paintings were an integral part of the building for which they were designed.
Sometimes in an early Renaissance church or chapel one has the feeling
that the images on the wall are records of the building's interior life, that
together they make up the building's memory—so much are they part of
the particularity of the building [p. 76, bottom].

The uniqueness of every painting was once part of the uniqueness of
the place where it resided. Sometimes the painting was transportable. But
it could never be seen in two places at the same time. When the camera
reproduces a painting, it destroys the uniqueness of its image. As a result

*Still Life with Wicker Chair* by Picasso 1881–1973

Church of St. Francis at Assisi

its meaning changes. Or, more exactly, its meaning multiplies and fragments into many meanings.

This is vividly illustrated by what happens when a painting is shown on a television screen. The painting enters each viewer's house. There it is surrounded by his wallpaper, his furniture, his mementoes. It enters the atmosphere of his family. It becomes their talking point. It lends its meaning to their meaning. At the same time it enters a million other houses and, in each of them, is seen in a different context. Because of the camera, the painting now travels to the spectator rather than the spectator to the painting. In its travels, its meaning is diversified.

One might argue that all reproductions more or less distort, and that therefore the original painting is still in a sense unique. Here [p. 78] is a reproduction of the *Virgin of the Rocks* by Leonardo da Vinci.

Having seen this reproduction, one can go to the National Gallery to look at the original and there discover what the reproduction lacks. Alternatively one can forget about the quality of the reproduction and simply be reminded, when one sees the original, that it is a famous painting of which somewhere one has already seen a reproduction. But in either case the uniqueness of the original now lies in it being *the original of a reproduction*. It is no longer what its image shows that strikes one as unique; its first meaning is no longer to be found in what it says, but in what it is.

This new status of the original work is the perfectly rational consequence of the new means of reproduction. But it is at this point that a process of mystification again enters. The meaning of the original work no longer lies in what it uniquely says but in what it uniquely is. How is its unique existence evaluated and defined in our present culture? It is defined as an object whose value depends upon its rarity. This market is affirmed and gauged by the price it fetches on the market. But because it is nevertheless "a work of art"—and art is thought to be greater than commerce—its market price is said to be a reflection of its spiritual value. Yet the spiritual value of an object, as distinct from a message or an example, can only

*Virgin of the Rocks* by Leonardo da Vinci 1452–1519. Reproduced by
courtesy of the Trustees, The National Gallery, London

be explained in terms of magic or religion. And since in modern society
neither of these is a living force, the art object, the "work of art," is enveloped in an atmosphere of entirely bogus religiosity. Works of art are
discussed and presented as though they were holy relics: relics which are
first and foremost evidence of their own survival. The past in which they
originated is studied in order to prove their survival genuine. They are
declared art when their line of descent can be certified.

Before the *Virgin of the Rocks* the visitor to the National Gallery would
be encouraged by nearly everything he might have heard and read about
the painting to feel something like this: "I am in front of it. I can see it.
This painting by Leonardo is unlike any other in the world. The National
Gallery has the real one. If I look at this painting hard enough, I should
somehow be able to feel its authenticity. The *Virgin of the Rocks* by Leonardo
da Vinci: it is authentic and therefore it is beautiful."

To dismiss such feelings as naïve would be quite wrong. They accord
perfectly with the sophisticated culture of art experts for whom the National Gallery catalogue is written. The entry on the *Virgin of the Rocks* is
one of the longest entries. It consists of fourteen closely printed pages.
They do not deal with the meaning of the image. They deal with who
commissioned the painting, legal squabbles, who owned it, its likely date,
the families of its owners. Behind this information lie years of research.

National Gallery

*Virgin of the Rocks* by Leonardo da Vinci 1452–1519.
Louvre Museum

The aim of the research is to prove beyond any shadow of doubt that the painting is a genuine Leonardo. The secondary aim is to prove that an almost identical painting in the Louvre is a replica of the National Gallery version.

French art historians try to prove the opposite [see above].

The National Gallery sells more reproductions of Leonardo's cartoon of *The Virgin and Child with St. Anne and St. John the Baptist* [p. 80] than any other picture in their collection. A few years ago it was known only to scholars. It became famous because an American wanted to buy it for two and a half million pounds.

Now it hangs in a room by itself. The room is like a chapel. The drawing is behind bullet-proof perspex. It has acquired a new kind of impressiveness. Not because of what it shows—not because of the meaning of its image. It has become impressive, mysterious, because of its market value.

The bogus religiosity which now surrounds original works of art, and which is ultimately dependent upon their market value, has become the

*The Virgin and Child with St. Anne and St. John the Baptist* by Leonardo da Vinci 1452–1519. Reproduced by courtesy of the Trustees, The National Gallery, London.

substitute for what paintings lost when the camera made them reproducible. Its function is nostalgic. It is the final empty claim for the continuing values of an oligarchic, undemocratic culture. If the image is no longer unique and exclusive, the art object, the thing, must be made mysteriously so.

The majority of the population do not visit art museums. The following table [p. 81, top] shows how closely an interest in art is related to privileged education.

The majority take it as axiomatic that the museums are full of holy relics which refer to a mystery which excludes them: the mystery of unaccountable wealth. Or, to put this another way, they believe that original masterpieces belong to the preserve (both materially and spiritually) of the rich. Another table [p. 81, bottom] indicates what the idea of an art gallery suggests to each social class.

In the age of pictorial reproduction the meaning of paintings is no longer attached to them; their meaning becomes transmittable: that is to say it becomes information of a sort, and, like all information, it is either put to use or ignored; information carries no special authority within itself. When a painting is put to use, its meaning is either modified or totally changed. One should be quite clear about what this involves. It is not a

National proportion of art museum visitors according to level of education:
Percentage of each educational category who visit art museums

| | Greece | Poland | France | Holland | | Greece | Poland | France | Holland |
|---|---|---|---|---|---|---|---|---|---|
| With no educational qualification | 0.02 | 0.12 | 0.15 | — | Only secondary education | 10.5 | 10.4 | 10 | 20 |
| Only primary education | 0.30 | 1.50 | 0.45 | 0.50 | Further and higher education | 11.5 | 11.7 | 12.5 | 17.3 |

*Source:* Pierre Bourdieu and Alain Darbel, *L'Amour de l'Art*, Editions de Minuit, Paris 1969, Appendix 5, table 4

question of reproduction failing to reproduce certain aspects of an image faithfully; it is a question of reproduction making it possible, even inevitable, that an image will be used for many different purposes and that the reproduced image, unlike an original work, can lend itself to them all. Let us examine some of the ways in which the reproduced image lends itself to such usage.

Reproduction isolates a detail of a painting from the whole. The detail is transformed. An allegorical figure becomes a portrait of a girl [p. 82].

When a painting is reproduced by a film camera it inevitably becomes material for the film-maker's argument.

A film which reproduces images of a painting leads the spectator,

Of the places listed below which does a museum remind you of most?

| | Manual workers | Skilled and white collar workers | Professional and upper managerial |
|---|---|---|---|
| | % | % | % |
| Church | 66 | 45 | 30.5 |
| Library | 9 | 34 | 28 |
| Lecture hall | — | 4 | 4.5 |
| Department store or entrance hall in public building | — | 7 | 2 |
| Church and library | 9 | 2 | 4.5 |
| Church and lecture hall | 4 | 2 | — |
| Library and lecture hall | — | — | 2 |
| None of these | 4 | 2 | 19.5 |
| No reply | 8 | 4 | 9 |
| | 100 (n = 53) | 100 (n = 98) | 100 (n = 99) |

*Source:* as above, Appendix 4, table 8

through the painting, to the film-maker's own conclusions. The painting lends authority to the film-maker. This is because a film unfolds in time and a painting does not. In a film the way one image follows another, their succession, constructs an argument which becomes irreversible. In a painting all its elements are there to be seen simultaneously. The spectator may need time to examine each element of the painting but whenever he reaches a conclusion, the simultaneity of the whole painting is there to reverse or qualify his conclusion. The painting maintains its own authority

*Venus and Mars* by Botticelli 1445–1510. Reproduced by courtesy of the Trustees, The National Gallery, London

[below]. Paintings are often reproduced with words around them [p. 84, top].

This is a landscape of a cornfield with birds flying out of it. Look at it for a moment [p. 84, bottom]. Then turn the page [p. 85 top].

It is hard to define exactly how the words have changed the image but undoubtedly they have. The image now illustrates the sentence.

In this essay each image reproduced has become part of an argument which has little or nothing to do with the painting's original independent meaning. The words have quoted the paintings to confirm their own verbal authority. . . .

Reproduced paintings, like all information, have to hold their own against all the other information being continually transmitted [p. 85, bottom].

Consequently a reproduction, as well as making its own references to

*Procession to Calvary* by Breughel 1525–1569

the image of its original, becomes itself the reference point for other images. The meaning of an image is changed according to what one sees immediately beside it or what comes immediately after it. Such authority as it retains, is distributed over the whole context in which it appears [see p. 86].

Because works of art are reproducible, they can, theoretically, be used by anybody. Yet mostly—in art books, magazines, films, or within gilt frames in living-rooms—reproductions are still used to bolster the illusion that nothing has changed, that art, with its unique undiminished authority, justifies most other forms of authority, that art makes inequality seem noble

*Wheatfield with Crows* by Van Gogh 1853–1890

*This is the last picture that Van Gogh painted before he killed himself.*

and hierarchies seem thrilling. For example, the whole concept of the National Cultural Heritage exploits the authority of art to glorify the present social system and its priorities.

The means of reproduction are used politically and commercially to disguise or deny what their existence makes possible. But sometimes individuals use them differently [p. 87].

Adults and children sometimes have boards in their bedrooms or living-rooms on which they pin pieces of paper: letters, snapshots, reproductions of paintings, newspaper cuttings, original drawings, postcards. On each board all the images belong to the same language and all are more or less equal within it, because they have been chosen in a highly personal way to match and express the experience of the room's inhabitant. Logically, these boards should replace museums.

What are we saying by that? Let us first be sure about what we are not saying.

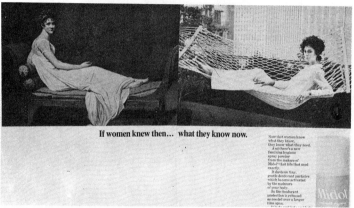

We are not saying that there is nothing left to experience before original works of art except a sense of awe because they have survived. The way original works of art are usually approached—through museum catalogues, guides, hired cassettes, etc.—is not the only way they might be approached. When the art of the past ceases to be viewed nostalgically, the works will cease to be holy relics—although they will never re-become what they were before the age of reproduction. We are not saying original works of art are now useless.

Original paintings are silent and still in a sense that information never is. Even a reproduction hung on a wall is not comparable in this respect for in the original the silence and stillness permeate the actual material, the paint, in which one follows the traces of the painter's immediate gestures. This has the effect of closing the distance in time between the painting of the picture and one's own act of looking at it. In this special sense all paintings are contemporary. Hence the immediacy of their testimony. Their historical moment is literally there before our eyes. Cézanne made a similar observation from the painter's point of view. "A minute in the world's life

passes! To paint it in its reality, and forget everything for that! To become that minute, to be the sensitive plate . . . give the image of what we see, forgetting everything that has appeared before our time . . ." What we make of that painted moment when it is before our eyes depends upon what we expect of art, and that in turn depends today upon how we have already experienced the meaning of paintings through reproductions.

Nor are we saying that all art can be understood spontaneously. We are not claiming that to cut out a magazine reproduction of an archaic Greek head, because it is reminiscent of some personal experience, and to pin it to a board beside other disparate images, is to come to terms with the full meaning of that head.

The idea of innocence faces two ways. By refusing to enter a conspiracy, one remains innocent of that conspiracy. But to remain innocent may also be to remain ignorant. The issue is not between innocence and knowledge (or between the natural and the cultural) but between a total approach to art which attempts to relate it to every aspect of experience and the esoteric approach of few specialized experts who are the clerks of the nostalgia of a ruling class in decline. (In decline, not before the proletariat, but before the new power of the corporation and the state.) The real question is: to whom does the meaning of the art of the past properly belong? To those who can apply it to their own lives, or to a cultural hierarchy of relic specialists?

The visual arts have always existed within a certain preserve; originally this preserve was magical or sacred. But it was also physical: it was the place, the cave, the building, in which, or for which, the work was made.

87

*Woman Pouring Milk* by Vermeer 1632–1675

The experience of art, which at first was the experience of ritual, was set apart from the rest of life—precisely in order to be able to exercise power over it. Later the preserve of art become a social one. It entered the culture of the ruling class, whilst physically it was set apart and isolated in their palaces and houses. During all this history the authority of art was inseparable from the particular authority of the preserve.

What the modern means of reproduction have done is to destroy the authority of art and to remove it—or, rather, to remove its images which they reproduce—from any preserve. For the first time ever, images of art have become ephemeral, ubiquitous, insubstantial, available, valueless, free. They surround us in the same way as a language surrounds us. They have entered the mainstream of life over which they no longer, in themselves, have power.

Yet very few people are aware of what has happened because the means of reproduction are used nearly all the time to promote the illusion that nothing has changed except that the masses, thanks to reproductions, can now begin to appreciate art as the cultured minority once did. Understandably, the masses remain uninterested and sceptical.

If the new language of images were used differently, it would, through its use, confer a new kind of power. Within it we could begin to define our experiences more precisely in areas where words are inadequate. (Seeing comes from words.) Not only personal experience, but also the essential historical experience of our relation to the past: that is to say the experience of seeking to give meaning to our lives, of trying to understand the history of which we can become the active agents.

The art of the past no longer exists as it once did. Its authority is lost. In its place there is a language of images. What matters now is who uses that language for what purpose. This touches upon questions of copyright for reproduction, the ownership of art presses and publishers, the total policy of public art galleries and museums. As usually presented, these are narrow professional matters. One of the aims of this essay has been to show that what is really at stake is much larger. A people or a class which is cut off from its own past is far less free to choose and to act as a people or class than one that has been able to situate itself in history. This is why— and this is the only reason why—the entire art of the past has now become a political issue.

*Many of the ideas in the preceding essay have been taken from another, written over forty years ago by the German critic and philosopher Walter Benjamin.*

*His essay was entitled* The Work of Art in the Age of Mechanical Reproduction. *This essay is available in English in a collection called* Illuminations *(Cape, London, 1970).*

NOTES

[1] Seymour Slive, *Frans Hals* (Phaidon, London)

[2] This quotation is from an article written in 1923 by Dziga Vertov, the revolutionary Soviet film director.

. . . . . . . . . . .

## QUESTIONS FOR A SECOND READING

1. Berger says, "The past is never there waiting to be discovered, to be recognized for exactly what it is. History always constitutes the relation between a present and its past (p. 69)." And he says, "If we 'saw' the art of the past, we would situate ourselves in history. When we are prevented from seeing it, we are being deprived of the history which belongs to us (p. 69)." As you reread this essay, pay particular attention to Berger's uses of the word "history." What does it stand for? What does it have to do with looking at pictures? How might you define the term if your definition were based on its use in this essay?

   You might take Berger's discussion of the Hals painting as a case in point. What is the relation Berger establishes between the past and the present? If he has not "discovered" the past or recognized it for exactly what it is, what has Berger done in writing about these paintings? What might it mean to say that he has "situated" us in history or has returned a history that belongs to us? And in what way might this be said to be a political act?

2. Berger argues forcefully that the account of the Hals painting offered by the unnamed art historian is a case of "mystification." How would you characterize Berger's account of that same painting? Would you say that he sees what is "really" there? If so, why wasn't it self-evident? Why does it take an expert to see "clearly"? As you read back over the essay, look for passages you could use to characterize the way Berger looks at images or paintings. If, as he says, "The way we see things is affected by what we know or what we believe," what does he know and what does he believe?

## ASSIGNMENTS FOR WRITING

1. Berger says that the real question is this: "To whom does the meaning of the art of the past properly belong?" Let's say, in Berger's spirit, that it belongs to you. Look again at the painting by Vermeer, *Woman Pouring Milk*, that is included in the essay (p. 88). Berger includes the painting but without much discussion, as though he were, in fact, leaving it for you. Write an essay that shows others how they might best understand that painting. You should offer this lesson in the spirit of John Berger. Imagine that you are doing this work for him, perhaps as his apprentice.

2.    Original paintings are silent and still in a sense that information never is. Even a reproduction hung on a wall is not comparable in this respect for in the original the silence and stillness permeate the

actual material, the paint, in which one follows the traces of the painter's immediate gestures. This has the effect of closing the distance in time between the painting of the picture and one's own act of looking at it. . . . What we make of that painted moment when it is before our eyes depends on what we expect of art, and that in turn depends today on how we have already experienced the meaning of paintings through reproductions (pp. 86–87).

While Berger describes original paintings as silent in this passage, it is clear that these paintings begin to speak if one approaches them properly, if one learns to ask "the right questions of the past." Berger demonstrates one route of approach, for example, in his reading of the Hals paintings, where he asks questions about the people and objects and their relationship to the painter and the viewer. What the paintings might be made to say, however, depends upon the viewer's expectations, his or her sense of the questions that seem appropriate or possible. Berger argues that, because of the way art is currently displayed, discussed, and reproduced, the viewer expects only to be mystified.

For this paper, imagine that you are working against the silence and mystification Berger describes. Go to a museum—or, if that is not possible, to a large-format book of reproductions in the library (or, if that is not possible, to the reproductions in this essay)—and select a painting that seems silent and still, yet invites conversation. Your job is to figure out what sorts of questions to ask, to interrogate the painting, to get it to speak, to engage with the past in some form of dialogue. Write an essay in which you record this process and what you have learned from it. Somewhere in your paper, perhaps at the end, turn back to Berger's essay and speak to it about how this process has or hasn't confirmed what you take to be Berger's expectations.

Note: If possible, include with your essay a reproduction of the painting you select. (Check the postcards at the museum gift shop.) In any event, you want to make sure that you describe the painting in sufficient detail for your readers to follow what you say.

## MAKING CONNECTIONS

1. Walker Percy, in "The Loss of the Creature" (p. 462), like Berger in "Ways of Seeing," talks about the problems people have seeing things. "How can the sightseer recover the Grand Canyon?" Percy asks. "He can recover it in any number of ways, all sharing the common strategem of avoiding the approved confrontation of the tour and the Park Service." There is a way in which Berger also tells a story about tourists—tourists going to a museum to see paintings, to buy postcards, gallery guides, reprints, and T-shirts featuring the image of the Mona Lisa. "The way original works of art are usually approached—through museum catalogues, guides, hired

cassettes, etc.—is not the only way they might be approached. When the art of the past ceases to be viewed nostalgically, the works will cease to be holy relics—although they will never re-become what they were before the age of reproduction."

Write an essay in which you describe possible "approaches" to a painting in a museum, approaches that could provide for a better understanding or a more complete "recovery" of that painting than would be possible to a casual viewer, to someone who just wandered in, for example, with no strategy in mind. You should think of your essay as providing real advice to a real person. (You might, if you can, work with a particular painting in a particular museum.) What should that person do? How should that person prepare? What would the consequences be?

At least one of your approaches should reflect Percy's best advice to a viewer who wanted to develop a successful strategy, and at least one should represent the best you feel Berger would have to offer. When you've finished explaining these approaches, go on in your essay to examine the differences between those you associate with Percy and those you associate with Berger. What are the key differences? And what do they say about the different ways these two thinkers approach the problem of why we do or do not see that which lies before us?

2. Clifford Geertz, in "Deep Play: Notes on the Balinese Cockfight" (p. 272), argues that the cockfights are a "Balinese reading of Balinese experience; a story they tell themselves about themselves." They are not, then, just cockfights. Or, as Geertz says, the cockfights can be seen as texts "saying something of something." Berger's essay, "Ways of Seeing," offers a view of our culture and, in particular, of the way our culture reproduces and uses images from the past. They are placed in museums, on bulletin boards, on T-shirts, and in advertisements. They are described by experts in certain predictable tones or phrases. It is interesting to look at our use of those images as a story we tell ourselves about ourselves, as a practice that says something about something else.

Geertz's analysis of the cockfight demonstrates this way of seeing and interpreting a feature of a culture. Write an essay in which you use Geertz's methods to interpret the examples that Berger provides of the ways our culture reproduces and uses images from the past. If these practices say something about something else, what do they say, and about what do they say it? What story might we be telling ourselves about ourselves?

Note: For this assignment, you should avoid rushing to the conclusion Berger draws—that the story told here is a story about the ruling class and its conspiracy against the proletariat. You should see, that is, what other interpretation you can provide. You may, if you choose, return to Berger's conclusions in your paper, but only after you have worked on some of your own.

# ROBERT
# COLES

*R*OBERT COLES *spent seven years following migrant workers north from Florida to gather material for the second volume—*Migrants, Sharecroppers,
Mountaineers*—of his remarkable series of books,* Children of Crisis. *He learned
about the workers' lives, he says, by visiting "certain homes week after week until
it [had] come to pass that I [had] known certain families for many years." The
sacrifice, patience, compassion, and discipline required for his massive project—a
study of American children—transform the usual business of research into something saintly, magnificent.*

*Coles's project began when he was stationed at Keesler Air Force Base in Biloxi,
Mississippi. He was, he says, a "rather smug and all too self-satisfied child psychiatrist, just out of medical training." He was in the South at the beginning of
the civil rights movement, and the scenes that he witnessed led him to abandon his
plans to return to New England and to remain instead in the South to find out
how children responded to social and political crisis. He began with standard psychiatric questions, such as "How did these children respond to stress?" but soon
realized, he said, "that I was meeting families whose assumptions, hopes, fears, and
expectations were quite definitely strange to me. I realized, too, how arbitrarily I*

*was fitting the lives of various individuals into my psychiatric categories—a useful practice under certain circumstances, but now, for me, a distinct hindrance. I was unwittingly setting severe, maybe crippling, limits on what I would allow myself to see, try to comprehend."* He learned, through the children, to abandon his care-fully rehearsed questions and to talk and listen. The stories he learned to tell are remarkable and moving, and his commentary on those stories, represented here by his remarks on the stories he has told of wealthy, privileged children, have an au-thority available to few writers. As Walker Percy once said of Coles, *"like Freud, he is humble before the facts. . . . He treads a narrow path between theorizing and novelizing and emerges as what in fact he is: a physician, and a wise and gentle one. He is doctor to the worst of our ills."*

Born in 1929, Coles graduated from Harvard in 1950 and earned an M.D. degree from Columbia University in 1954. He has published articles in the Atlantic Monthly, The New Yorker, the New Republic, the American Poetry Review, and Harper's, and he has written nearly forty books. A recipient of a MacArthur Fellowship, Coles teaches at Harvard University. His most recent books include Women of Crisis, which he coauthored with his wife, Jane Hallowell Coles, and The Call of Stories: Teaching and the Moral Imagination. His multivolume work Children of Crisis won the Pulitzer Prize in 1972. "Entitlement" is one of the concluding chapters of Volume 5, Privileged Ones.

# *Entitlement*

The poor both are and are not alike. On the one hand they struggle against the same odds—hunger and malnutrition in the worst instances, or a marginal life that poses constant threats. Yet Eskimos do not regard their poverty in the same way that Appalachian yeomen do, or Chicanos in Texas or southern California. In the four volumes that have preceded this one° I have tried to show how the common social and economic vul-nerability of the poor does not make for a uniform pattern of child-rearing. Historical precedents, cultural experiences, religious convictions exert their influence on parents and children, make boys and girls differ in all sorts of respects, depending on where they live and who their parents are. The same holds for the well-to-do or the rich. It won't do to talk of *the* affluent ones in America (never mind the world!). It won't do to say that in our

---

Coles is referring to the first four volumes of the series, *Children of Crisis: A Study of Courage and Fear; Migrants, Sharecroppers, Mountaineers; The South Goes North,* and *Eskimos, Chicanos, Indians.*

upper-middle-class suburbs, or among our wealthy, one observes clearcut, consistent psychological or cultural characteristics. Even in relatively homogeneous suburbs, there are substantial differences in home life, in values taught, hobbies encouraged, beliefs advocated or virtually instilled.

But there are indeed distinct groups among the well-off—equivalent in their way to the various kinds of poor people. It is the obligation of someone who wants to know how children make sense of their lives—agricultural migrancy, Indian reservation life in the Southwest, the upper-income life of large homes amid ample acreage in rich towns or in wealthy urban enclaves—to document as faithfully as possible the way the common heritage of money and power affects the assumptions of individual boys and girls. Each child, however, is also influenced by certain social, racial, cultural, or religious traditions, or thoroughly idiosyncratic ones—a given *family's* tastes, sentiments, ideals, say. The issue is "class"; but the issue is not only "class."

Many of the influences, even some of the more idiosyncratic ones, that distinguish some children from others are themselves subject to side influences—a "rebound effect," one rather prosperous Illinois Mormon called it. He was anxious for me to know (just as he could not forget) that there was only so much his faith could resist. He took pains, constantly, to tell his children that he was not like his father; that he was not like his brother either, who lives in Salt Lake City and works for a bank. To live near Chicago and be a doctor, to be a Mormon living in a highly secular upper-middle-class world, was to be an exile. He felt stronger in his faith, but also weaker; he felt like his neighbors in many ways, but unlike them in critically important preferences and articles of faith.

What binds together a Mormon banker in Utah with his brother, or other coreligionists in Illinois or Massachusetts? What distinguishes such people, one from the other? Old New Orleans upper-class families are not in certain respects like families who live in, say, Wellesley Hills, Massachusetts, or Haverford, Pennsylvania, or up the hills outside San Antonio. There *are* resemblances, based on class, occupation, religion, common experiences, expectations, ideas conveyed to children. And yet, again, there are distinctions, shades of feeling and thinking, emphases of one sort or another—even within those families and well-to-do neighborhoods.

I use the word "entitlement" to describe what, perhaps, all quite well-off American families transmit to their children—an important psychological common denominator, I believe: an emotional expression, really, of those familiar, class-bound prerogatives, money and power. The word was given to me, amid much soul-searching, by the rather rich parents of a child I began to talk with almost two decades ago, in 1959. I have watched those parents become grandparents, seen what they described as "the responsibilities of entitlement" get handed down to a new generation. When the father, a lawyer and stockbroker from a prominent and quietly influential family, referred to the "entitlement" his children were growing up with, he had in mind a social rather than a psychological phenomenon: the various juries or committees that select the Mardi Gras participants in New Orleans's annual parade and celebration. He knew that his daughter was "entitled" to be invited here, to attend a dance there, to feel part of a carefully limited and sometimes self-important social scene.

He wanted, however, to go beyond that social fact; he wanted his children to feel obligated by how fortunate they were, and would no doubt always be, all things being equal—or unequal! He talked about what he had received from his parents and what he would give to his children, "automatically, without any thought," and what they too would pass on. The father was careful to distinguish between the social entitlement and "something else," a "something else" he couldn't quite define but knew he had to try to evoke if he were to be psychologically candid: "Our children have a good life ahead of them; and I think they know it now. I think they did when they were three or four, too. It's *entitlement*, that's what I call it. My wife didn't know what I was talking about when I first used the word. She thought it had something to do with our ancestry! Maybe it does! I don't mean to be snide. I just think our children grow up taking a lot for granted, and it can be good that they do, and it can be bad. It's like anything else, it all depends. I mean, you can have spoiled brats for children, or you can have kids who want to share what they have. I don't mean give away all their money! I mean be responsible, and try to live up to their ideals, and not just sit around wondering which island in the Caribbean to visit this year, and where to go next summer to get away from the heat and humidity here in New Orleans."

At the time he said no more. It was 1960, and I was interested mainly in what his son and his daughter thought about black children—and about the violence then being inflicted on a few black children brave enough and stubborn enough to walk past mobs into two elementary schools. But as months became years, I came back to that word "entitlement," especially because it was one I had heard years earlier, in Boston, when I was receiving my training in child psychiatry. "Narcissistic entitlement" was the phrase I had been taught to be familiar with, to use occasionally when speaking of a particular kind of "disturbed" child. The term could be used in place of more conventional, blunter ones that everyone else uses from time to time: a smug, self-satisfied child; or a child who thinks he (or she) owns the world, or will one day; or a self-centered child who expects a lot from just about everyone.

I recall a boy of eight I was treating in Boston, before I went South; my supervisor, a child psychoanalyst who had worked with a similar child for three years, and anticipated, alas, another year or two, at least, of thrice weekly office visits, told me that I was being naïvely hopeful, and a touch simpleminded, when I remarked upon the curiosity of the boy, his evident willingness to ask me questions about all sorts of persons, places, things—and so his capacity for engagement with the world around him. Yes, she pointed out, there was indeed a measure of that, but it was best that *we* ask questions about the nature of *his* questions. As we did, they all came back to him—to quite specific experiences he had gone through and wanted to talk about. And he had told me that, actually; he never asked a question out of intellectual interest—rather, in his words, "because I like to know what might happen next to me."

It is hard to describe the special fearfulness and sadness such a child struggles with. He was not the "ordinary" child; he was quite troubled. And I suppose the parents of such children (even if those mothers and fathers have other, relatively solid children, psychologically speaking) must be disqualified as "normal" or "average." They may be like anyone else on the street; may be rather knowing, psychiatrically—able to sense something "wrong" with a child's "behavior" and go do something about it by seeking out a doctor. But the analyst-supervisor I was myself "seeing" once a week was convinced that there was a "special narcissism," she called it, that a certain kind of parent offers a child: "Narcissism is something we all struggle with; but some people have more of it than others, and some children come from homes that have so much that all the money and possessions, all the rugs and furniture and toys and vacations and savings accounts and insurance policies come crashing on the child's head. There is a shift from narcissism to narcissistic entitlement."

I wasn't sure exactly what she meant, or how the "shift" she had mentioned did indeed take place. I know, because she is someone I still discuss psychoanalytic theory with, that she was not sure herself what the exact dimensions were of that childhood journey. But she knew even then, before there were "fields" like "social psychiatry" or "community psychiatry," that at some point a family's psychology and psychopathology engage with its social and economic life; and that when a migrant child or a ghetto child has to contend with narcissism, it will take on a certain flavor (narcissistic despair, for instance); whereas for a child who lives in a big house and whose parents have a lot and want to give a lot to their offspring, "narcissistic entitlement" may well be a possibility. The child withdraws not only into himself or herself but, by extension, into a certain world of objects, habits and rituals—the comfortable world of room, a home, a way of life. The child has much, but wants and expects more—only to feel no great gratitude, but a desire for yet more: an inheritance the world is expected to provide. One's parents will oblige, as intermediaries. And if underneath there lie apprehension and gloom and, not least, a strain of gnawing worthlessness, that is of no matter to many children whose "narcissistic entitlement" becomes what psychoanalytic theorists refer to as a "character trait," rather than a "symptom" that prompts a visit to a doctor. That is, the child is regarded by everyone, psychiatrists included, as "normal," as "all right," or different, but not all *that* different. One doesn't send every cocksure, greedy, self-centered child to a child psychiatrist.

In many other well-to-do homes I've visited, parents have known in their bones what child psychiatrists think and wonder as they talk with their children. Will a certain child get too much—so much that he or she runs the danger of turning away from life, forsaking people for a life of passionate involvement with objects? Less ominously, might a mild tendency in that direction become especially evident when things get tough, psychologically, for one reason or another? Will the child be willing to reach for people, and get along with them, but always with certain limits on the involvement? Often when children are four, five, and six, parents who have felt able to offer them virtually anything begin to pull back, in concern if not outright horror. A son not only has become increasingly demanding or petulant; even when he is quiet he seems to be sitting on a throne of sorts—expecting things to happen, wondering with annoyance why they don't, reassuring himself that they will, or, if they haven't, shrugging his shoulders and waiting for the next event.

It was just such an impasse—not dramatic, but quite definite and worrisome—that prompted that New Orleans father to use the word "entitlement." He had himself been born to wealth, as will future generations of his family be, unless the American economic system changes drastically. But he was worried about what a lot of money can do to a person's "personality"; he uses that word as a layman, but he knows exactly what he has in mind. It isn't so much a matter of spoiling or indulging children; he is willing to let that happen, "within limits." But he knew precisely what those limits were: when the child begins to let his or her situation, the life that he or she lives, "go to the head." It is then that children begin "to act as if they have royal blood in them." And conservative though he is, for him each generation has to prove itself—not necessarily by finding new worlds to conquer or by becoming extraordinarily successful. He has wanted his children to show an interest in the world, to reach out and touch others, to develop their own initiatives, however circumscribed, undramatic, and conventional. It is those kinds of initiative he naturally finds appealing. He is rather satisfied with the life he was born to. He finds each day to be pleasant, interesting, and by his lights, quite useful. He has, however, worried at times that his children were taking *too* much for granted. When his young daughter, during a Mardi Gras season, kept *assuming* she would one day receive this honor and that honor—indeed, become a Mardi Gras queen—he realized that his notion of "entitlement" was not quite hers. *Noblesse oblige* requires a gesture toward others. Had a parent sensed the danger of what my supervisor referred to as a "shift" from "entitlement" to "narcissistic entitlement"?

He would not be the only parent to express such a concern to me in the course of my work. In homes where mothers and fathers profess no explicit reformist persuasions (to say the least!) they nevertheless worry about what happens to children who grow up surrounded by just about everything they want, virtually, on demand. And if much of the apprehension is conventional—that the child will become "spoiled"—there is an element of uneasiness that runs deeper. The parents may begin to regard spoiled behavior as but a symptom: "I don't mind if my children become a little spoiled. That's bound to happen. I worry that they will think that everything is coming to them; that they will grow up with the idea that if they're frustrated, or if they want something, then all they have to do is say a few words, and they'll have what they asked for. When they're like that, they've gone from spoiled to spoiled rotten—and beyond, to some state I don't even know how to describe.

When children are two and three they become increasingly conscious of what belongs to whom. They also become, usually, more and more willing and able to leave themselves behind, so to speak—reach out for objects as well as individuals. They develop their first friends, their first interests or regular and cherished activities. They learn too, most of them, a variety of restraints and frustrations. They must gain control of their bodies, manage without diapers, remember to empty their bladders before going to bed, and get up at night and do likewise in the bathroom rather than on the sheet and mattress. They must learn not to touch hot stoves; not to leave refrigerator doors open; not to spill things, break things, step on things; not to intrude on what belongs to others; not to confuse their prerogatives or possessions with the rights and property of parents, brothers and sisters, friends. At three and four, children from homes like those in New Orleans's Garden District have often started nursery school, have also started making visits to other homes or receiving visitors at their own homes. There are toys to share, games to play, a sandbox or a lawn or indeed a swimming pool or a paddock with its animals. All children have to struggle with themselves for the strength to offer as well as take, or to yield with tact and even a touch of gratitude what has been loaned rather than made an outright gift.

But for some children, a relative handful of the world's, such obligations and struggles are muted. Obviously it is possible for parents to have a lot of money yet avoid bringing up their children in such a way that they feel like members of a royal family. Yet even parents determined not to spoil their children often recognize what might be called the existential (as opposed to strictly psychological) aspects of their situation, and that of their children. A father may begin rather early on lecturing his children about the meaning of money; a mother may do her share by saying no, even when yes is so easy to say—but the child may well sense eventually what the parents know quite well: the difference between a voluntary posture and an utterly necessary one.

Such a child, by the age of five or six, has very definite notions of what is possible, even if not always permitted; possible because there is plenty of money that can be spent. That child, in conversation and without embarrassment or the kind of reticence and secretiveness that comes later, may reveal a substantial knowledge of economic affairs. A six-year-old girl in New Orleans knew that she would at twenty-one inherit a half a million dollars. She also knew that her father "only" gave her twenty-five cents a week—whereas some friends of hers received as much as a dollar. She was vexed; she asked her parents why they were so "strict." One friend had even used the word "stingy" for the parents. The father, in a matter-of-fact way, pointed out to the daughter that she did, after all, get "anything she really wants." Why, then, the need for an extravagant allowance? The girl was won over, told her friends thereafter that it was no matter to her whether she even received an allowance; the important point was the future and what it had to offer. The friends then checked back with their parents, who were rather alarmed—that such young children were talking so freely and openly about family financial matters.

As a result the girl learned from her friends that she had disclosed what ought to be kept firmly under wraps. She decided on the basis of such declarations that her friends may well be "comfortable," but they are not as rich as her parents are or as she will one day be. They in turn explained to her that she had gone beyond the bounds of available evidence. The friends may simply have been told to keep quiet about their family's monetary status—a good idea, the girl was reminded by her parents. The girl agreed, but was not really prepared at the time to follow such advice. She had heard her parents talk with *their* parents about money matters and had been told that it is best that she, too, gradually understand what her financial situation is and will be. That being the case, she wondered out loud why it wasn't appropriate for her to share what she had learned about her future prospects with those she considered good friends. Her parents could only repeat their conviction that certain matters are quite definitely and properly kept within the confines of the family.

Such conversations between young children and their parents help consolidate in boys and girls a conviction of present and future affluence. It obviously never occurs to these children that they won't have food at some point in the near or distant future. Nor do they ever really lack for anything. There are differences in amount, and lectures and sermons may accompany parental acts of generosity. But admonitions don't modify the quite shrewd appraisal children make of what they are heir to, and don't at all diminish the sense of entitlement.

In an Appalachian mine-owner's home, for instance, a boy of seven made the following comment in 1963, after his father's mine had suffered an explosion, killing two men and injuring seriously nine others: "I heard my mother saying she felt sorry for the families of the miners. I feel sorry for them, too. I hope the men who got hurt get better. I'm sure they will. My father has called in doctors from Lexington. He wants the best doctors in all Kentucky for those miners. Daddy says it was the miners' fault; they get careless, and the next thing you know, there's an explosion. It's too bad. I guess there are a lot of kids who are praying hard for their fathers. I wish God was nice to everyone. He's been very good to us. My Daddy says it's been hard work, running the mine and another one he has. It's just as hard to run a mine as it is to go down and dig the coal! I'm glad my father is the owner, though. I wouldn't want him to get killed or hurt bad down there, way underground. Daddy has given us a good life. We have a lot of fun coming up, he says, in the next few years. We're going on some trips. Daddy deserves his vacations. He says he's happy because he can keep us happy, and he does. If we want something really bad, we go tell him or Mum, and they oblige us almost all the time. That's what Daddy always says—that he's glad to oblige my sister and me!"

The father is not *always* "glad to oblige"; he can be quite stern at times, but the children have learned that his lectures have only a limited applicability to their life. Yes, there are restraints; not every request for money or a present is granted forthwith. On the other hand, their life is sufficiently comfortable to belie the parents' insistence on caution, lest there be nothing left. In fact, the lectures only seem to reinforce in the children a certain materialistic preoccupation. Having been told to make do with what they already have in such abundance, the boy and girl (and their counterparts in the homes I have visited in other parts of the United States) retreat to their respective rooms, get out their possessions, and begin to use them as well as simply gaze at them. The boy can be quite pointed and expressive about what he has—and is doing with what he has—at such moments: "I have my soldiers, and my trucks, and the tanks and the helicopters. I get them lined up. I build a fort. I have the blocks and the logs, and I make the fort strong. I have my helicopter pad. I make sure the pad is protected by tanks and some men with machine guns. Some terrorists might come and try to attack, and destroy the pad and the helicopter. It's best to keep a few planes in the air, to scout. You have to keep your eyes open, or there will be a surprise attack. I surround the fort with men, and I have these bushes and trees, and I put men behind them. And I have some men on horses."

He stops and looks at what he has done. He is rather proud of himself. He has thought at times of working toward a military career, but he knows that he "most likely" will follow in his father's footsteps. There is a profitable coal company to run and his father has told him that, in the boy's words, "coal has a big future now because there's an energy problem." That observation prompts him to worry about his fort. Does *it* have enough energy or might there one day be a shortage? No, he is sure that his fort will be able to manage successfully. There is a large stack of wood set aside in the stockade. As for the tanks, helicopters, airplanes, they will not lack fuel; there is an oil well nearby. And in the event that should give out, the boy is certain that oil can be flown in or, if necessary, a "secret pipeline" could be built, just in case some disaster should come upon the airfield-landing pad.

His sister has on some occasions become provocative, even truculent. She has asked him, after watching him "declare war" on an unseen enemy, why he always wins. He has replied that the answer is quite simple; he has the best army. She will occasionally express her misgivings: there might be, just *might* be, an army that could overcome his army, with its nine-teenth-century fort and twentieth-century military hardware. The boy replies with scorn that his sister is being far too literal-minded. Anyway, America has never lost a war, he knows for sure, and he is an American and does not intend to lose one either. Nor has his father, when brought into the argument later, been anything but encouraging. True, Vietnam was "a mess"; but the country was never "really determined" to win—and maybe never should have involved itself in such a struggle, waged in "distant jungles." The sister has by then lost all interest in her younger (by one year) brother's "game."

The boy is not obsessed with the war game, either. He has many other opportunities to play—other games or, more personally, friends to have over, to go visit. When he plays the war game with them, however, there is invariably a battle of wits, a stalemate. The boy and his friend are tireless in the resourcefulness they summon to their encounters. If necessary, they find themselves in possession of atomic bombs, supersonic planes, surprise tunnels, magical weapons of all kinds, secret supply bases, hidden contingents of men. Eventually, they each declare the other "a winner." The boy realizes: "I know there has to be a losing side. My sister is right. You can't win all the time. But she doesn't like to lose, either. She's always saying her guinea pig is the prettiest, and she says she can ride her bike faster than anyone. I hope I'll get a five-speed bike soon; as soon as I'm a little taller, I'll get one. Then you can really go zoom, zoom down the roads. They say that when I'm grown up, we'll be landing on the moon all the time and we'll be landing on the planets—Mars, for sure. This country will do it! Maybe I could be an astronaut for a while, and then come back and help Daddy in his business. He says he may buy a couple more mines, and by the time I'm out of college, there will be a lot to do. He says I should plan to be a lawyer, because it really helps you, if you have a business, to know how to go to court and protect yourself. The unions want to interfere a lot, and Daddy has to fight them. He has to give some ground, but he's the boss, and they can't push too hard or he'll close up his mines. Then they'd all be out of work! And Daddy could hire some other miners. There are a lot of people who would be glad to get a job!"

So it goes: an abundance of energy for his fort and air force base and an abundance of workers for his father's mines. Abundance is his destiny, he has every reason to believe. He may even land on the stars. Certainly he has traveled widely in this country. He associates the seasons with travel, among other events. In winter, for instance, there is a trip South, to one or another Caribbean island. Winters can be long and hard in Appalachia, and a respite is invigorating—and "healthy." The boy watches his father exercise, hears his mother talk about certain foods, and remarks upon something else that has to do with his future: he may well live to be over a century old. Why not?

His parents are not health faddists, or unusually self-preoccupied: given exercise, a careful diet, and medical progress, one will do (in the father's words) "right well." As an additional boost to the family's collective health, a sauna has been installed, and the children are entranced with it. They also are preoccupied with their two dogs, and their other animals—the guinea pigs, hamsters, rabbits, chickens. There is always someone in the house, a maid, a handyman. Still, it is sad to say good-bye. Now, if the family owned a plane, the animals could come along on those trips!

The boy doesn't really believe that his father ever will own a Lear jet; yet, at moments he can imagine himself wrong. And he can construct a fantasy: suddenly an announcement, most likely at breakfast, of a "surprise." It is a familiar sequence. The boy has come to associate breakfast with good news. What is ahead for the day? When does a certain vacation start? During one breakfast the father announced that he had a surprise. The children were all ears. So was their mother; she knew of no forthcoming surprise. The father paused, waited for a bit of suspense to build up, then made his announcement: a new car—a red MG, a fast car that takes curves well and seats only two, in which he would take his wife and children for rides, one at a time.

Yet the boy had apparently been hoping for another kind of surprise: "I woke up and it was very funny, I remembered that I'd just had this dream. In it I was walking through the woods with Daddy, and all of a sudden there was an open field, and I looked, and I saw a hawk, and it was circling and circling. I like going hunting with Daddy, and I thought we were hunting. But when I looked at him, he didn't have his gun. Then he pointed at the hawk, and it was coming down. It landed ahead of us, and it was real strange—because the hawk turned into an airplane! I couldn't believe it. We went toward the plane, and Daddy said we could get a ride any time we wanted, because it was ours; he'd just bought it. That's when I woke up, I think. I even forgot about the dream until I looked at my fort and the airplanes, and then I remembered the dream, and once I remembered it, I didn't forget it again."

Dreams evoke a social as well as psychological reality. Dreams show what a child can hope for, unashamedly expect. It so happens that among rich children one day's apparently fatuous, excessive fantasy or dream can turn into the next day's actuality. Four years after that boy had dreamed that his father owned a plane, the father got one. The boom of the 1970s in the coal fields made his father even richer. The boy was of course eager to go on flying trips; eager also to learn to fly. The family owned a horse farm by then, near Lexington, Kentucky, and when the boy and girl were not flying, they were riding. The girl learned to jump well, the boy to ride quite fast. At thirteen he dreamed (by day) of becoming an astronaut or of becoming the manager of his father's horse farm or of going to the Air Force Academy and afterward becoming a "supersonic pilot."

He would never become a commercial pilot, however; and his reasons were interesting: "I've gone on a lot of commercial flights, and there are a lot of people on board, and the pilot has to be nice to everyone, and he makes all these announcements about the seat belts, and stuff like that. My dad's pilot was in the air force, and then he flew commercial. He was glad to get out, though. He says you have to be like a waiter; you have to answer complaints from the customers and apologize to them, just because the ride gets bumpy. It's best to work for yourself, or work for another person, if you trust him and like him. If you go commercial, like our pilot says, you're a servant. You can't really speak your mind. I'd like to fly, but I'm worried about going into the air force. Our pilot says it can be fun, or it can be murder, depending on your superior officer. If I got a bad one, I guess I'd just quit. They can't keep you in forever against your will."

He has only confidence about the future, no real sense of danger. At times he talks (at thirteen) as if he could simultaneously hold down several jobs. He would run the family horse farm. He would take part in any number of races and hunts. He would also fly his own plane. He would learn how to parachute; he might even become a professional parachutist. He met one at a fair, and found the man not only brave, but "real nice to talk to." In more restrained (realistic?) moments, he forgets the horse farm, forgets the airplanes or just plain air; he talks about law school—the place his father would like him to race to, land upon. When only an eighth-grade student he imagined himself, one day, owning an airplane, flying it back and forth from law school (at the University of Kentucky) to his father's horse farm, some fifty miles away.

He has never had any patience for lines, for traffic jams, for crowded stores. Many of the children I have worked with are similarly disposed; they do not like large groups of people in public places—in fact, have been taught the distinct value not only of privacy but the quiet that goes with being relatively alone. Some of the children are afraid of those crowds, can't imagine how it would be possible to survive them. Of course, what is strange, unknown, or portrayed as unattractive, uncomfortable, or just to be avoided as a nuisance can for a given child become a source of curiosity, even an event to be experienced at all costs. An eight-year-old girl who lived well outside Boston, even beyond its suburbs, on a farm, wanted desperately to go to the city and see Santa Claus—not because she believed in him, but because she wanted to see "those crowds" she had in fact seen on television. She got her wish, was excited at first, then quite disappointed, and ultimately made rather uncomfortable. She didn't like being jostled, shoved, pushed, and ignored when she protested. She was only too glad when her mother suggested that they had gone through quite enough. Yes, they had, the daughter agreed. Soon they were in a cab, then on a commuter train. The latter was going to be the limit for the girl thereafter; if she would venture into the world, the train would be its microcosm. She would travel by train to Boston, then turn right around and travel back—unless, of course, she were going to a restaurant or an art gallery or to her parents' club. In those places one is not overcome by people who shout, and step on the feet of others, and ignore any protests made.

A week after the girl had gone through her Boston "adventure" (as she had called the trip *before* she embarked upon it), each student in her third-grade class was asked to draw a picture in some way connected to the Christmas season, and the girl obliged eagerly. She drew Santa Claus standing beside a pile of packages, presents for the many children who stood near him. They blended into one another—a mob scene. Watching them but removed from them was one child, bigger and on a higher level—suspended in space, it seemed, and partially surrounded by a thin but visible line. The girl wrote on the bottom of the drawing "I saw Santa Claus." She made it quite clear what she had intended to portray: "He was standing there, handing out these gifts. They were all the same, I think, and they were plastic squirt guns for the boys and little dolls for the girls. I felt sorry for the kids. I asked my mother why kids wanted to push each other, just to get that junk. My mother said a lot of people just don't know any better. I was going to force my way up to that Santa Claus and tell him to stop being so dumb! My mother said he was probably a drunk, trying to make a few dollars, so he could spend it in a bar nearby that evening! I don't want to be in a store like that again. We went up to a balcony and watched, and then we got out of the place and came home. I told my mother that I didn't care if I ever went to Boston again. I have two friends, and they've never been in Boston, and they don't want to go there, except to ride through on the way to the airport."

She sounds at that moment more aloof, condescending, and downright snobbish than she ordinarily is. She spends some of her time with two or three girls who live on nearby "estates." Those girls don't see each other regularly, and each of them is quite able to be alone—in fact, rather as anxious to be by themselves, do things by themselves, as to be with one another and find things to work on together. Sometimes a day or two goes by with no formal arrangement to play. They meet in school, and that seems to be enough. Each girl has obligations—a horse to groom, a stall to work on. They are quite "self-sufficient," a word they have heard used repeatedly by their parents. Even within one's own social circle there is no point in surrendering to excessive gregariousness!

The girls meet by accident (or unacknowledged design) on various riding trails. On such daily expeditions one learns to be very much alone with one's thoughts. In the beginning they have to do with riding; but eventually they embrace the weather, the landscape, and, almost always, the child's body: "I think of my leg muscles, my hold on the horse. It's funny how you can forget a lot of your muscles until you mount that horse. Once up there you notice your feet and your knees and your hips, and you watch your arms and hands, and you think of your head and back—how straight are you sitting. It's your whole body that's on your mind, like the teacher says. It's a little like that with skiing, and a lot like that with ballet lessons; but for me, riding is when I'm most in touch with my body! And I'm also in touch with the horse's body. We're sort of one!"

Once up on the horse, riding, she is (by her own description) in her "own world." She has heard her mother use that expression. The mother is not boasting, or dismissing others who live in other worlds. The mother is describing, as does the child, a state of progressive withdrawal from people and, selectively, the familiar routines or objects of the environment, in favor of a mixture of reverie and disciplined activity. And when the girl, for one reason or another, is unable to ride, she misses not only the sport, but the state of mind that goes with riding.

Her mother is more explicit about what happens; she tells her daughter, at times, that she wants to "leave everything" and go riding. She tells her daughter that when she is on the horse, cantering across the field or trotting down a trail, she has a "feeling" that is "better than being on a plane." She finds that she can put everyone and everything into "perspective." Nothing seems impossible, burdensome, difficult. There are no distractions, nuisances, petty or boring details to attend to. One is not only away from it all, but above it all. And one is closer to one's "self." The mother talks about the "self" and the child does too. "It is strange," the girl comments, "because you forget yourself riding or skiing, but you also remember yourself the way you don't when you're just sitting around watching television or reading or playing in your room."

With none of the other American children I have worked with have I heard such a continuous and strong emphasis put on the "self." In fact, other children rarely if ever think about themselves in the way children of well-to-do and rich parents do—with insistence, regularity, and, not least, out of a learned sense of obligation. These privileged ones are children who live in homes with many mirrors. They have mirrors in their rooms, large mirrors in adjoining bathrooms. When they were three or four they were taught to use them; taught to wash their faces, brush their teeth, comb their hair. Personal appearance matters and becomes a central objective for such children. A boy of eight expresses his rebelliousness by clinging to sloppy clothes, but leaves the house every day for school in a neat and well-fitted uniform. A good number of these children wear them—shirts or sweaters with a school's name and/or insignia on them. Even when the child relaxes, comes home, and changes into "old" clothes, there is an air of decisiveness about the act—and certainly, the issue is one of choice: to wear *this*, or *that*; to look a particular way, in keeping with a particular mood, time of day, event.

The issue also is that of the "self"—its display, its possibilities, its cultivation and development, even the repeated use of the word. A ten-year-old boy who lives in the outermost part of Westchester County made this very clear. I had originally met him because his parents, both lawyers, were active in the civil rights movement. His father, a patrician Yankee, very much endorsed the students who went South in the early 1960s and, nearer to home, worked on behalf of integrated school up North. His own children, however, attended private schools—a source of anguish to both the father and the son, who do not lend themselves easily to a description that only emphasizes the hypocritical element in their lives.

The boy knew that he also *would* be (as opposed to wanted to be!) a lawyer. He was quick to perceive and acknowledge his situation, and as he did so he brought himself (his "self") right into the discussion: "I don't want to tell other kids what to do. I told my father I should be going to the public schools myself. Then I could say anything. Then I could ask why we don't have black kids with us in school. But you have to try to do what's best for your *own* life, even if you can't speak up for the black people. When I'm growing up, I'll be like my father; I'll help the black people all I can. It's this way: first you build *yourself* up. You learn all you can. Later, you can *give of yourself*. That's what Dad says: you can't help others until you've learned to help *yourself*. It's not that you're being self-ish. People say you're selfish, if you're going to a private school and your parents have a lot of money. We had a maid here, and she wasn't right in the head. She lost her temper and told Dad that he's a phony, and he's out for *himself* and no one else, and the same goes for my sister and me. Then she quit. Daddy tried to get her to talk with us, but she wouldn't. She said that's all we ever do—talk, talk. I told Daddy she was contradicting herself; because she told me a few weeks ago that I'm always doing something, and I should sit down and talk with her. But I didn't know what to say to her! I think she got angry with me because I was putting on my skis for cross-country skiing, and she said I had too much, that was my problem. I asked her where the regular skis were, and she said she wouldn't tell me, even if she knew! It's too bad, what happened to her.

"I feel sorry for her, though. Like my sister said, it's no fun to be a maid! The poor woman doesn't look very good. She weighs too much. She's only forty, my mother thinks, but she looks as if she's sixty, and is sick. She should take better care of herself. She said my sister and I make big messes in the bathroom. But that's because we *use* the bathroom! And her breath—God, it's terrible. She isn't as clean as she should be. My mother wanted to get her some deodorant, but we were afraid she'd just blow up at us. But she did anyway. So it didn't make any difference! Like my Dad said, it's too bad about her; she didn't know how to take care of herself and now she's thrown away this job, and she told my mother last year that it was the best one she'd ever had, so she's her own worst enemy. I wonder what she'll think when she looks at herself in the mirror and tries to figure out what to do next."

He was no budding egotist. If anything, he was less self-centered, at ten, than many other children of his community or others like it. He was willing to think about, at least, others less fortunate than himself—the maid, and black people in general. True, he would often repeat uncritically his father's words, or a version of them. But he was trying to respond to his father's wishes and beliefs as well as his words. It was impossible for him, no matter how compassionate his nature, to conceive of life as others live it—the maid, and yes, millions of children his age, who don't look in the mirror very often and may not even own one; who don't worry about what is worn, and how one looks, and what is said and how one sounds, and what is done (in the bathroom) and how one smells.

Sometimes minor details of life tell more than larger attitudes spoken and duly recorded by outside observers. A boy's fingernails, for instance; or his sister's skin—in each instance, a reflection of much more. Here is the boy from Westchester County, at eleven, talking about the new pair of scissors he has received from his father: "I like them. I didn't want my mother to clip my fingernails any longer. I'd rather take care of myself! I'll be shaving soon. I look forward to that! I've watched my father a lot. He showed me how to use the scissors and end up with nails that aren't too short and aren't too long. There's a kid in my class, he lets his nails get longer and longer and there's a lot of dirt under them, and you wonder how long they'll get, and then all of a sudden, one day, you notice that they've been cut off. His parents have got a divorce, and they have a maid taking care of him and his kid brother, and she runs the house and there's no one supervising her. You have to tell the help what to do, because if you don't, they forget and they don't live up to your standards, and they're acting as if they were back in their own homes."

So it happens—a boy's developing sense of himself as against a collective, amorphous "them." It is a "sense" that has both sociological and psychological dimensions to it. The former are perhaps more painful to spell out but also more readily apparent. The boy has learned that in the ghetto people live who don't use his parents' kind of judgment, and don't, either, have the same personal habits or concerns. The boy's sister has a similar kind of knowledge. At twelve she could be quite pointed: "We've had a couple of maids, and they don't know why I use my mother's Vaseline lotion on my arms and hands—and in winter on my face, too. They say I've got a wonderful complexion; but I don't think they know how to look real carefully at my skin—or their own either. Maybe they don't have the time. But I see them taking a 'break,' and what do they do? They go put on a prize show in the morning or a 'story' in the afternoon. I don't know how they can stand looking at that stuff! I've got a lot of chores. We're not spoiled here! I have to clean out the stalls and brush the horses carefully before we go riding. I have to pick up my room. My mother told me when I was real little, before I even was old enough to go to school, that she wasn't going to have me sitting and looking at television while the maid was straightening out my room. The same goes for outside the house; we have a gardener, but he's not allowed to come into the barn and help us with the animals.

"We had one maid, and she said we spent more time with the animals than she does with her children. I felt sad when she told me that. She has no understanding of what an animal needs. She was the one who was always telling me I was beautiful, and so I didn't need any lotion on my skin. I wanted to give her the lotion. She needs it. Her skin is in terrible shape. It's so dried and cracked. My mother says you can be poor and still know how to take care of yourself. It's not the money; it's the attitude you have toward yourself. If our maid stopped buying a lot of candy and potato chips, she could afford to get herself some skin lotion. And she wouldn't be so fat!"

A child has learned to distinguish between her own inclinations or preferences and those of another person—a whole category of people. This girl was, at the time, not quite an adolescent; for years, however, she had been prepared for that time, for adulthood as well—prepared by parents who not only wanted her to know how to use skin lotions, or choose "tasteful" lipstick, or shun anything but "natural" fingernail polish, or learn how to care for her hair and wash it, and pay attention to the scalp as well. Those parents wanted her to give an enormous amount of attention to *herself*—to her thoughts, which she has been taught are worthy of being spoken, and to her body, which is going to be, one day, "attractive." So she has been told by several maids—far too emphatically to suit the taste of her parents. They prefer a more understated, indirect approach. They remind the girl that she looks like her grandmother ("a handsome lady") or her aunt ("who was quite beautiful"). They let her know how graceful she is as a young dancing student, how agile and accomplished a rider she has become, how fast and accurate a game of tennis she has developed, even at her age. They smile at pictures of her smiling, applaud her once again when watching home movies. Her picture is on the mantle over the living room fireplace, on her father's desk, on her mother's desk, and is on her own desk, for that matter.

When she was six and seven she asked a lot of questions about herself. They were answered patiently, thoughtfully, and often with enthusiastic pride—a contrast indeed with many poor children, whose parents are tired, embittered, sad, or all too resigned to their fate, and hardly able to boast about the circumstances of life. The girl's questions occur to all children, rich or poor—are the banal inquiries we never quite stop asking ourselves: who am I, why am I here, whence do I come, and where am I going—the continuing preoccupations of philosophers, novelists, and painters. Children prefer the painters' approach. They sometimes don't pay much attention to the answers to their questions. After all too verbal family meals they retire to a desk or table, draw pictures meant to suggest what life is and will be about. When the girl mentioned above wonders who she is or has questions about her future, she picks up crayons and draws herself with care and affection—on a horse, in a garden, high up in a tower, surveying the countryside.

In doing so she draws upon her concrete, day-to-day experiences. She also uses those experiences in order to suggest something larger about her particular life. Especially noteworthy is the care she and others like her take with themselves as they draw. So often poor children treat themselves cursorily; they quickly sketch a rather unflattering self-portrait. Sometimes they are unwilling to complete what they have begun—as if they are unsure of life itself. A migrant child once told me in a matter-of-fact way that he had no expectation of living beyond twenty. He was simply a child who knew the score. The children of doctors and lawyers and business executives have learned the score too. The girl mentioned above spends a half hour drawing herself, moves her eyes toward a mirror every once in a while to check on how she actually does look, and is eventually quite proud of what she has drawn. She also spends long periods of time looking at old photographs—of herself, her parents, her grandparents. Such observations and bits of anecdotal family history have become consolidated in the girl's mind. She regards herself—though she has learned to be affectingly modest—as a rather attractive person. No wonder she once posed herself, in a picture, beside a giant sunflower. She was in no way overshadowed by the flower; if anything, it adorned her own luminous presence.

When that girl became ill with chicken pox the anguish of her mental state was noticeable and instructive. She wanted to scratch the many lesions on her face and arms but was told, of course, by her parents that she must not. She heeded their advice. In the beginning she did scratch one pustule midway on her upper right arm. Her mother became quite upset. Before the mother could say a word, the child spoke up, acknowledged her awareness of the future implications of her deed. She had lost control, and she would suffer. Her description of that talk and of her later, more successful, bout with the disease, has struck me as a classic of sorts: "I don't want to look ugly. If I had scratched my face, like I did my right arm, I'd look a mess for life. I knew that. But I had *such* a bad case! The doctor said it was one of the worst he'd seen in the last few years. He told me he had seen even worse than mine, and I was sort of disappointed. I figured that I'd like to go through the biggest challenge, and come out on top!

"After a day or two, I began to wonder if I'd be able to survive! I got very weepy. I began to wonder whether I'd done anything wrong—to deserve this punishment. I couldn't look myself in the mirror. I didn't want to wash at all. I felt so dirty and horrible looking. I asked my brother and my parents not to look at me! My brother tried to kid me out of my mood. He came in with his Polaroid camera and said he'd take a picture of me, and I could keep it, and when I was over the disease, I could just laugh! Instead I started crying, right in front of him. He apologized.

"The worst part of the chicken pox was the waiting and the trying to keep control. My mother sat with me, and my Dad did too, when he got home. On the worst day, he offered to stay with me and not go to his office. I said no, I'd be all right. But he decided to stay anyway. He just sat there and read to me. We watched some television—the news and a cooking class. We talked a little. Dad kept telling me I was great, and not to worry; he was sure I was going to have a wonderful life, because I've got everything going for me. I told him 'not the chicken pox,' when he said that. But he just laughed and told me that the chicken pox would soon be a bad memory, and I'd forget about it completely in a couple of months. I'm not sure I ever will, though. I have this scar on my arm, and I'll always have it. My mother says no one will notice; but *I* do! She got angry the other day. She said I was worrying too much. But I've seen her worry a lot too. If a dress doesn't fit her, she sends it right back. She's always either on a diet or coming off one, or getting ready to go on one again. We have scales in every bathroom, and one in her bedroom. I told her I don't need to weigh myself and my brother doesn't; but she wants us to get in the habit, so we'll know later when to start being careful about food. She tells the maid to give us cookies only when she's not around; she doesn't want to be tempted. And her hair—well that's 'a whole subject,' as my Daddy says. When he was with me that day, I asked him why Mom worries so much about her hair, and dyes it. Who cares if there's some gray in her hair! But Dad said that gray hair for Mom is like the chicken pox for me. I could see what he meant, but it's not exactly the same."

She did not for long insist upon the difference; she went along with her father's comparison. She did so not reluctantly, but with the detachment that goes with complete recovery—a feeling of remove from what was once painful. Her mother has always been regarded as a rather lovely woman; the girl was prepared to emphasize that fact in her mind, and associate her own present and future appearance with her mother's deserved reputation. The girl was also prepared to acknowledge quite candidly what a relatively severe case of a basically benign disease could do to her thoughts about herself: "I began to worry whether I really was as pretty as everyone had been saying. It was a mood; I'm over it now. I do have a few bad memories. Dad says they'll go. I hope so. I look at myself in the mirror and I'll suddenly be afraid that the chicken pox is coming back. I get scared. It's silly. I know I'm never going to get the chicken pox again!

"I wish I hadn't scratched that one place. It's such a small scar. But it gives me nightmares! I woke up the other night and my parents were in my room. I guess I'd been crying or shouting. In the morning my mother said I'd half-awakened, and I'd told them that a cat had been chasing me, and scratched me, and I was afraid there'd be a scar. I wonder a lot about the man I'll marry. Will he have brown hair or blond hair or black hair? My mother asked me if it makes any difference; I told her I like brown hair and green eyes, and I hope he'll be tall and thin. I wouldn't even want to go out once with a man who was overweight!"

This is no petty, superficial, half-witted, or empty-headed girl. She has gone to very good private schools—each of which has high academic standards and expectations. She can be serious, thoughtful, and idealistic—that is, worried about others less fortunate and hopeful that they somehow get to live better lives. As a child she can hardly be expected to come up with solutions for the world's various problems, but some of those problems do at times weigh upon her. Yet she can, all of a sudden, move from writing a composition about "world hunger" to discussing with her mother the virtues of various cosmetics or the appropriateness of certain dresses for one or another social occasion. She can also, rather disarmingly, stop thinking about "the troubles in America" her teacher has asked the class to write about, because her parakeet needs food or water, her two gerbils require new bedding, her alarm clock has to be set, her desk is cluttered and ought be straightened out, or her phone has rung. She has a room with its own demands and requirements, with a bureau mirror and one on the back of the door, a full-length mirror. Sometimes she gets tired of thinking of arithmetic problems and social problems, and spelling problems, of coming up with ideas meant to straighten out society.

The last word, incidentally, has two meanings for her. She started, at ten, dancing lessons. She was aware then that later on she would be going to parties, would become a debutante. Her mother plays down that word, debutante. Her mother is a New Englander who doesn't like "fuss," abhors elaborate, pretentious parties, the stuff of social climbing; but she also has a keen eye for who is acceptable to whom in her social circle, what name elicits deference, and whose "situation" is what mixture of "position" and "real wealth."

Those words are used discreetly, but they do not go unnoticed by a ten- or eleven-year-old child. The girl asks questions about her family, its origins and "place" in the social and economic system. "Our minister tells us to think of others, but it's hard, because I've never seen the poor. I gave half of some money I saved for Christmas to the starving people of Africa. Daddy said he was real proud of me. He gave me the money I'd contributed. He says that when I grow up I should marry a man who is kind and worries about other people, not just himself; that's the type of man who makes a good husband. I agree. It's best to marry someone who's pretty much like yourself, though. Otherwise you might run into trouble. He'll think one way, and you'll think another. There are a lot of divorces that take place. My parents have a lot of friends whose marriages aren't good. If you marry a person who thinks like you, and he has the same beliefs, then you have a better chance of staying married.

"When I leave this room and stay at a friend's, or when we go up skiing or down to our summer house, I get a funny feeling. I really miss my dolls and my bureau—the shells and dishes my parents have brought me when they have come back from trips. I have all kinds of shells, from all the Caribbean beaches. I have dishes and ashtrays from a lot of countries. I have posters; I love French posters. I hope I learn to speak French fluently. It's a beautiful language. It's strange, leaving your room and sleeping in a place that hasn't got much of anything that belongs to you, that's yours, that's *you*."

That last progression deserves respectful attention as a rather forceful, intelligent, and exact analysis of the complicated psychology of class-connected "narcissistic entitlement." She and others like her grow up surrounded by possessions, animate as well as inanimate. They have learned to live with them, to look after them, and to depend upon them for support. They have also learned to give of themselves to those "objects." When they leave for a winter or summer vacation they try to take some of their most treasured belongings with them, but often still experience a sense of emptiness or a feeling of being alone, isolated, bereft. Child psychiatrists use the expresson "transitional object" to refer to a child's blanket or teddy bear or doll—taken to bed, carried around, held tight at the age of four, five, six.

Few children are unable to find those "transitional objects." I have seen the poorest of American children, living the most uprooted of lives, cling to a dirty old rag, a stick, a rock, the cheapest of plastic toys, often obtained secondhand, maybe from someone's trash barrel. Children of working-class parents or of so-called "middle-income" families seldom experience such sad desperation. On the other hand, many of those children share rooms with brothers and sisters and by no means assume that they are to be recipients of an apparently endless succession of gifts, vacations, pleasant surprises. In the homes of the rich, in contrast, the children almost invariably have their own rooms and the quantitative difference in their material acquisitions prompts a qualitative psychological difference: an enhanced expectation of what life has to offer, and with that, a strong inclination to build a sanctuary out of one's room and one's property. The girl is subtle but sharp and exact when she distinguishes between what belongs to her (a piece of property) and what has become hers—an existential psychological transformation. The next step is of course an ironic act of personal surrender: the object and the person merge somewhat—from "that's yours" to "that's *you*."

All children struggle when very young—starting at a little under a year, in fact—to distinguish between themselves and their parents. They begin to realize, at two and three, that it is *they* who exist—individuals who crawl and walk and make noises and talk. As they separate, to a degree, from their mothers, especially then, at two or three, they first know loneliness. Certainly, thereafter, for most children, there are reattachments to the mother, new attachments to other persons—and to things. But the child turns inward too upon occasion, makes an effort to find comfort and even pleasure in a newfound solitariness. Freud, at one point, referred to "the purified pleasure ego"—by which he meant a child's delight in the various excitements or satisfactions he or she can manage to find. I recall a four-year-old boy in one home I visited, not far from that of the girl quoted just above, who slid up and down a wonderfully solid, circular staircase, shouting me, me, me; he was in love with the dizzying speed, with the feeling of control and power he had—with himself.

Later on, at five and six, such a child becomes quite conscious of rights and wrongs, of what ought to be done to please parents and teachers, not to mention one's own developing conscience. Psychoanalysts describe the "idealized parent image"—the part of the child's mind that holds up examples, insists upon directions. The child absorbs from significant persons his or her notions of what matters and how he or she should in general be trying to live—and tries to go along. The "you" that the girl mentioned above at age ten—a summary, almost, of which belongings had become part of her "self"—was preceded by the earlier "you" comprehended at the age of six: "I'd like to do good in school, and learn to ski, and ride my bike fast, and get to make real tasty cookies with the maid, and then I'll be good, and people will say, she's doing everything she should be doing, and I'll say that to myself. When I'm finished brushing my teeth, they'll be clean, and my mother will soon be upstairs and check me out, and I'll say to myself: you're doing okay. And a few minutes later my mother says the same thing: 'You're doing okay!'"

That child has had ample opportunities—beyond using a toothbrush well—to prove herself, as well as find pleasure in competence. She has been taught tennis and swimming by coaches, cooking by a maid, riding by her mother. The girl has also learned how to draw and paint, play the piano, "do" ballet. She has gone abroad often, has mastered words, used her own passport. She has become acquainted with forms of etiquette, with new protocols. She knows when to defer, when to speak up. She knows how to recognize various songs, symphonies, operatic pieces. She knows how to walk the corridors of museums, recognize the work of certain artists. And too, she has acquired some of the psychological judgment good hostesses have: who is like whom, who belongs near whom at the table, who will be a "disaster" with whom. She used that word sometimes, when eleven and twelve, and in so doing revealed more than a "prepubescent" affinity for a way of talking, or a superficial cleverness about people. In fact, she was indicating something significant about her sense of *herself*.

One such "disaster" was her mother's much younger cousin, and the girl knew why: "She's sloppy. She's always been sloppy. She speaks sloppy. She had a harelip, and that was what ruined her. The parents didn't take her to the right doctor, and the girl became shy, and she didn't want to talk to anyone, and when she was a teenager she became even worse. She just stayed in her room a lot. Then she got religious, in a weird way. She was always praying. My mother says they should have sent her to a doctor. She decided to become a nun, I think. She wanted to convert and be a Catholic, and then be a nun. They talked her out of that. She came to life a little. She began to go out and meet people. Then she met this guy, and he was a music teacher, and he was poor, and they fell in love, and they wanted to get married. He was a disaster, my mother says. He could barely open his mouth, and he didn't know which fork to use, and he wore real funny clothes, and he had a bad complexion, and the worst case of dandruff my mother has ever seen. He just sat there, and it didn't even seem to bother him that he didn't talk. But my mother's cousin was a disaster, too. She was just an oddball, that's what. They got married, and my mother says they've been good for each other.

"They would be poor now, if it wasn't that my mother's aunt left them some money. I think they have enough to get by. We see them sometimes; they come to visit my grandmother. We have to keep a straight face. We can't laugh. That would be bad. You should feel sorry for people who aren't as fortunate as you are. If you don't, then you are rude and you don't have charity. If you're not nice to someone, you've lost. You sink down to the other person's level. That's what Daddy tells us, and he gets angry if we don't pay attention. He says we've got a responsibility to show good manners at all times. I'd never call someone a 'disaster' in front of him; at least while we're having supper. Sometimes he'll be having a drink, and then even he will call someone a fool or *no good*; that's *his* way of calling someone he knows and doesn't like a 'disaster.'"

In "Forms and Transformations of Narcissism" (*Journal of the American Psychoanalytic Association*, April, 1966), Heinz Kohut observes that the "form and content of the psychic representation of the idealized parent thus vary with the maturational stage of the child's cognitive apparatus." Then he adds, significantly, that the form and content "are also influenced by environmental factors that affect the choice of internalizations and their intensity." There may seem, at first glance, a considerable distance in substance if not tone between the child's reflections on her second cousin and a psychoanalyst's theoretical observations, addressed to his scholarly colleagues. But the psychiatrist is trying to formulate what the child is living through and occasionally able to comment upon. Even as a migrant child or ghetto child learns to feel weak and vulnerable, a child of well-off parents learns to feel, in many respects, confident. There are idiosyncratic variations, of course. One can be rich and psychotic, for instance, and instill fear, apprehension, and a sense of worthlessness in one's children. Yet even among the disturbed young children of well-to-do parents there are concerns and expectations that contrast profoundly with the notions of other children, from other backgrounds, possess about themselves. At a certain point in every child's life, as Dr. Kohut suggests, and as Freud repeatedly pointed out, culture and class became matters of a child's fantasy life and affect the tone of his or her self regard. The girl who wants to look a certain way, speak a certain way, who anticipates a certain way of life, and who derives personal strength and competence from the sense of herself she has learned to have, is a person whose "narcissism," whose "idealized parent image," has drawn upon many daily conversations and experiences, rewards and lessons.

At another point in his paper Dr. Kohut points out that our "ambitions and ideals" don't just appear out of nowhere. They have a psychological history, not to mention a social and economic background. He refers to their "preconscious correlates" and locates them (structurally speaking) in the "narcissistic self," whose various "ego ideals" have, of course, been acquired over countless intimate encounters—the family involvements that set the stage for a child's view of what "life" is going to be like. Dr. Kohut points out that ambitions do not always coincide with ideals. A child whose parents are poor or of working-class background may have heard a mother or father (or, rather often, a teacher) say that anyone can be President in this country, or rise to the top of a company, or become a doctor, a lawyer, a "success"—given "hard work." But the child has seen and heard much evidence to the contrary. The child has seen his or her parents curbed, scorned, exhausted, frustrated, embittered. The child has heard that "life" is no picnic, that wages don't keep up with prices, that the factory is laying off more and more people, including his or her father or mother. The child has heard, upon breaking a dish or a toy, upon failing to follow instructions, or falling short at school, that soon enough the difficulties and tensions of grown-up life will fall upon him or her. In contrast, privileged children, far fewer in number, are destined for quite another fate. In his own manner, Dr. Kohut approaches their lives; speaking of their "ambitions and ideals," he observes that "they are at times hard to distinguish, not only because ambitions are often disguised as ideals but also because there are indeed lucky moments in our lives, or lucky periods in the lives of the very fortunate, in which ambitions and ideals coincide."

For those "lucky," a sense of entitlement develops—the merger of what they have learned would be "ideal" and what they have actually experienced, into an ongoing attitude toward the world. Let others feel diminished, impeded, burdened; or let them long for a different kind of life, knowing all too clearly by the age of six or seven the difference between a castle in Spain and a ranch house in Levittown, or a ghetto tenement, or a tenant farmer's shack. For privileged children, there is every reason to feel entitlement. But let us not forget that entitlement is perfectly compatible with doubts, misgivings, despair. A child can feel—being realistic—entitled to a certain kind of life and yet have other reasons to be confused or hurt. Even schizophrenics experience the distinctions that have to do with class and caste, race and place of residence. The girl whose words I called upon above had her own thoughts, one day, about these theoretical issues of mental life—after she had heard, at the age of twelve, that her father was sick and required surgery: "I hope he'll be all right. It's serious, my mother told me. I can tell it is; Daddy hasn't been smiling much. He's been worried. He's been talking lot about his insurance, and he took my brother and me to the bank, and he told us we'll be going there for the rest of our lives, or calling them up and asking them to send us over some money. He says that if we're careful, our children will have the same amount of money we have. It's best to use the interest and not the capital. The bank knows how to keep your money invested in the best stocks.

"Daddy will be all right. He's strong. He has the best doctor in the country; he's the best surgeon. I met him, and he was very nice. He gave my brother and me a book he'd written, about the seashore and the clams and oysters and lobsters you find in the water and the sand. He owns a lot of land by the ocean, and he's a marine biologist, my father says, besides being a surgeon. And he's an artist, too. I wouldn't mind being a doctor myself, but I don't know if I'd want to operate on anyone. The surgeon offered to show my brother and me how he operates; we could watch him—but not when he works on Daddy. My brother says yes, but I said no. I'd rather not be there, if anything goes wrong; then, when Daddy is being operated on, I'd worry even more.

"We'll be all right. My mother says everything will turn out good. Daddy may not be home for a couple of weeks, but we can go and see him all the time. We can eat with him in his room. It'll be like going out to a restaurant. He'll have television and his own phone. We can talk with him any time we want. He says he'll get a lot of reading done. He'll have a nice view from his room, and he'll get all the rest he'll need. Then, when he gets home, we're going away. Daddy says we'll be in Barbados for two weeks. He's promised to take us out of school. We'll get all our homework, and we won't fall back at all. My mother says it may turn out to be a blessing in disguise that Daddy got sick; he'll get a lot of rest, and he'll be much stronger. I hope so."

She was not about to acknowledge, even to herself, how worried she sensed her mother to be. But she (and her mother) had resources that very much ameliorated an anxious period of waiting. The dreaded outcome of the father's illness, a malignancy, did not materialize. All the money in the world could not have converted cancerous cells into normal ones. But during those days that preceded surgery the girl and her brother felt more hope than dread, and had quite valid sources of support for that hope. And during the father's convalescence, instead of hearing their mother and father lamenting bills, expressing worries about the loss of a job, or complaining about the "conditions" in the hospital, their time of trouble became for everyone concerned an opportunity for pleasure, relaxation, new initiatives and accomplishments. The girl and her brother ended up becoming scuba divers in the warm Caribbean water; went on motorcycle rides such as they had never had before; began to realize more exactly than ever how well-off their parents are and they as children are. "It all came out for the best," the girl said, weeks after her father was pronounced able to return to his work as a business executive. In a sense the words are a slogan of sorts, constantly kept in mind by her and others: life works out "for the best," mostly—and one has a right to conclude that if one has had ample confirming evidence.

For some of these children, the privileged life presents a danger of what clinicians have referred to as "secondary narcissism"—the "narcissistic entitlement" I mentioned at the beginning of this section. However, on the evidence of the privileged children I have come to know, I would emphasize the possibility that a feeling of "entitlement" may develop in a child without the potentially treacherous development of an excessively narcissistic tone. When a feeling of "entitlement" becomes "narcissistic," it has departed from what James Agee called "human actuality." Suppose the girl whose father had taken ill began, for her own reasons, to imagine that her father's illness would be associated with some extraordinary development: a call to the theater or television as a young actress; a medal of honor awarded by the school she attended; a party given her as an expression of her popularity. Suppose that girl, alternatively, expected the surgeon to cure her father, no matter *what* was discovered upon operating. Suppose that girl began crying constantly before her father entered the hospital; and did so petulantly, plaintively, as if less interested in her father's troubles than her own. At that point her narcissism would have taken its form from her private experiences, although the same child in other moments might lose her despairing self-centeredness. The point to emphasize is the mind's capacity to appreciate the reality of a certain kind of life. The mind can of course undercut a good thing, make a bad thing even worse, or make the best of it.

It is important that a privileged child's normal sense of "entitlement" be distinguished not only from pathological narcissism, but from the more common phenomenon known as being "spoiled." It is a matter of degree; "spoiled" children are self-centered all right, petulant and demanding—but not saddled with the grandiose illusions (or delusions) clinicians have in mind when using the phrase "narcissistic entitlement." The rich, the "well-to-do" are all too commonly charged with producing spoiled children. Yet one sees spoiled children everywhere, among the very poor as well as the inordinately rich. A child can be spoiled by a mother's attitude. What the child is "given" can be called excessive instinctual leeway or, in everyday words, however politicized in recent years, "permissive indulgence." I remember a migrant mother who knew precisely and uncannily what she was doing "wrong"—knew, indeed, to call it all "wrong." She told me one day that she had given birth to a particular child with more pain than usual and had been in lower spirits than ever before in her life during the first months of that child's life. When the baby began to notice the mother and the world, start crawling and separating himself from her, she felt a fierce desire within herself, expressed with unforgettable intensity, "to let that boy have anything he wants, anything he can lay his hands on." She was careful, for all her lack of education and her troubled spirits, to qualify herself. She moved quickly, immediately, from "anything he wants" to "anything he can lay his hands on." She knew that in the first or second year of life the child would have all he could do to reach and hold on to what he wanted.

But soon enough a child begins to see things that others have; on a rented, only half-working television set the migrant child saw a lot, and looked around the room and realized a lot. His was no blessed life! He continued, however, to want to take what little he could get. And of course children (or adults) can want things that are psychological in lieu of what is "material." They can become demanding, possessive, insistent, if allowed to be. They can compete with others for attention, push hard against others who try to assert themselves. They can make every effort to obtain center stage at all times. The migrant mother developed, deep within her hurt and sad self, a pride about her child and his stubborn, indulged, expropriative, loud-mouthed, and at times impossibly egotistical behavior.

He was the child who would shout and scream and swagger, shake his fists, really, at the wretched world he had been born to. No matter that such behavior, whether allowed or even encouraged, is hardly a guarantee of a future rise to success. On the contrary, a child of migrant parents who acts like that one is headed, quite likely, for future trouble. The mother knew that too. She knew that migrants are virtually peons; that they submit to endless demands and manipulations. Perhaps one of her children would be so "spoiled" that he would be utterly incapable of becoming a migrant or lasting as one for very long. She answered along those lines when her husband asked her why she doesn't spank the "spoiled one" as she does the other children.

He in turn mentioned the grim likelihood that the boy would not indeed last as a migrant. He would instead end up in jail—or soon dead. All right, better a last stand, the mother replied. But she knew that really there was no point to such a hope; it would never even come to that, because the boy would either learn to mind his manners, and submit to the only life he would most likely ever know, or go down not in defiant resistance but through the slow attrition of cheap wine and harmless side-of-the-road braggadoccio—the "maladjusted" migrant who works inefficiently, goes to the bars before and after work, dies in a car accident or drowns drunk in one of the hundreds of irrigation canals that crisscross the agricultural counties of Florida, where this particular family spent its winters.

The parallel with spoiled children of upper-income families is not so farfetched. In one of the first such families I came to know there was a girl who was described by both parents as "spoiled." At the time, I fear, I was ready to pronounce every child in New Orleans's Garden District spoiled.

Nevertheless, I soon began to realize that it wouldn't do to call one set of children spoiled, by virtue of their social and economic background—as against another set of children who were obviously less privileged. Though one meets among the poor any number of spoiled children, one also meets among the rich restrained, disciplined children; sometimes, even, boys and girls who have learned to be self-critical, even ascetic—anything but "spoiled" in the conventional sense of the word. True, one can find a touch and more of arrogance in those apparently Spartan boys and girls, who seem quite anxious to deny themselves all sorts of apparently accessible privileges. But one also finds in these children a consistent willingness to place serious and not always pleasant burdens on themselves. They often struck me, as I came to their homes fresh from visits with much poorer age-mates, as remarkably *less* spoiled: not so much whining or crying; fewer demands for candy or other sweets; even sometimes a relative indifference to toys, a disregard of television—so often demanded by the children I was seeing across the city, on the other side of the tracks.

Those children from prominent families appeared, even at the age of four or five, to put their energies in the service of " constructive" play or "useful" activities. They had begun to learn at two and three how important it was for them to do "right" as against "wrong"; to build rather than destroy; to concentrate their energies, devote them to particular tasks, which were to be finished rather than started and abandoned. They had, in some instances, even learned to take care of their own rooms—keep them neat, pick up after themselves, be conscious of what belongs where. Maids came to help, or lived with the family, but sometimes a particular boy or girl, as young as five or six, was a taskmaster to the maid rather than, certainly, a helpless or indulged child. And sometimes the maid herself became astonished by the example set by such children—and became their strong admirer.

A New Orleans black woman said to me in 1961: "I don't know how to figure out these rich, white kids. They're something! I used to think, before I took a job with this family, that the only difference between a rich kid and a poor kid is that the rich kid knows he has a lot of money and he grows up and he becomes spoiled rotten. That's what my mother told me; she took care of a white girl, and the girl was an only child, and her father owned a department store in McComb, Mississippi, and that girl thought she was God's special creature. My mother used to come home and tell us about the 'little princess'; but she turned out to be no good. She was so pampered she couldn't do a thing for herself. All she knew how to do was order people around. It's different with these two children here in New Orleans. I've never seen such a boy and such a girl. They think they're the best ones who ever lived—like that girl in McComb—but they don't behave like her. They're never asking me to do much of anything. They even ask if *they* can help *me*! They tell me that they want to know how to do everything. The girl says she wants to learn how to run the washing machine and the dishwasher. She says she wants to learn all my secret recipes. She says she'd like to give the best parties in the Garden District when she grows up, and she'd like to be able to give them without anyone's help. She says I could serve the food, but she would like to make it. The boy says he's going to be a lawyer and a banker, so he wants to know how much everything costs. He doesn't want to waste anything. He'll see me throw something away, and he wants to know why. I wish my own kids were like him!

"I wish my kids weren't so lazy; they don't care what's going on; they just want to play and play, and they waste a lot of food, and they break the toys I get them real fast. I even told my children I wish they could learn from these two children here. But these children here are special, and don't they know it! That's what being rich is: you know you're different from most people. These two kids are even more special, because they act as if they're going to be tops in everything, and they're pleased as can be with themselves, because there is nothing they can't do, and there's nothing they can't get, and there's nothing they can't win, and they're always showing off what they can do, and then before you can tell them how good they are, they're telling the same thing to themselves. It's confusing! They're not spoiled one bit, but oh, they have a high opinion of themselves!

"And I'll have to admit, there are times when I have the same high opinion of them! I'll look at them, and I'll say that they could be dropped on an island in the middle of a big ocean, and they'd know what to do, and if they didn't have anyone around to be pleased with them, they'd be all right because they'd be pleased with themselves! And it wouldn't take them long to know where to go and what to do on that island, because they are just so sure of themselves and so full of themselves that they always have their chins up, and they're happy, and they know where they're going, and they know what's ahead—that everything will come out fine in the end. When you have that kind of spirit in you, then you'll always get out of any jam you're in, and you'll always end up on top, because that's where you started, and that's where you believe you're going to end up, and if it's in your mind that it is like that, and it's *going* to be like that, and if you're willing to work hard, like these kids are, and if you're careful about everything, like they are, then you just *can't* lose, and don't these kids know it, I'll tell you!"

Actually the children she speaks of aren't as confident of themselves as she thinks, though she certainly has accurately conveyed their appearance. The kind of children she knows so well are extraordinarily privileged by virtue of background and money, are also intelligent and of attractive appearance; but those children have demons that occasionally urge them on, and their nature is not always easy to divine. Boys and girls may seem without anxiety or self-doubt at, say, eight or nine. Yet, there are moments of hesitation, if not apprehension. An eleven-year-old boy from a prominent and quite brilliant Massachusetts family (three generations of first-rate lawyers) told his teachers in an autobiographical composition about the vicissitudes of "entitlement": "I don't always do everything right. I'd like to be able to say I don't make any mistakes, but I do, and when I do, I feel bad. My father and mother say that if you train yourself, you can be right *almost* 100% of the time. Even they make mistakes, though. I like to be first in sports. I like to beat my brothers at skiing. But I don't always go down the slopes as fast as I could and I sometimes fall down. Last year I broke my leg. That was the first time I'd ever gone to a hospital and stayed there. It was my mother who reminded me that I'd been in the hospital for a week just after I was born! I'd forgotten! I was saying that I'd *never* been in the hospital overnight, and she corrected me.

"My great-greatfather is eighty-four, and he's in the best of health. It worries me that I have bad sinus trouble a lot of times after I get flu. I'd hate to be sick when I'm older. There's too much to do; if you get sick, you can't do much of anything, except stay home and rest. When I get a bad cold, I feel disappointed in myself. I don't think it's right to be easy on yourself. If you are, then you slip back, and you don't get a lot of the rewards in life. If you really work for the rewards, you'll get them."

His teachers have often given him that kind of platitude. In the fourth grade, for instance, his teacher had written on the blackboard (and kept it there for weeks): "Those who want something badly enough get it, provided they are willing to wait and work." The boy has been brought up to believe that it will be like that for him. He knows that others are not so lucky, but he hasn't really met those "others," and they don't cross his mind. What does occur to him sometimes is the need for constant exertion, lest he fail to "measure up." The expression is a family one, used repeatedly. No matter how difficult a task, no matter how frustrating it is for others, one "measures up" when one does it well. One "measures up" when one tries hard, succeeds. One measures up because one *must*. No allowance is made for any possible lack of ability or endowment. The assumption is that one has been "given a lot" (another family expression) and so a "return" is obligatory if justice is to be done. If one slackens or stumbles, one ought take oneself to task. The emphasis is on a quick and efficient moment of scrutiny followed by "a fast pickup," yet another admonitory injunction handed down.

Such counsel is not as callous or psychologically insensitive as it may sound—or even as it may have been *intended* to sound. The child who hears it gets briefly upset, but "a fast pickup" does indeed take place quite often. Again, it is a matter of feeling "entitled." A child who has been told repeatedly that all he or she needs to do is try hard does not feel inclined to allow himself or herself much skeptical self-examination. The point is to feel *entitled*—then act upon that feeling. The boy whose composition was just quoted from wrote again, apparently about his younger (aged five) brother: "I was watching my brother from my bedroom window. He was climbing up the fence we built for our corral. He got to the top, and then he just stood there and waved and shouted. No one was there. He was talking to himself. He was very happy. Then he would fall. He would be upset for a few seconds, but he would climb right back up again. Then he would be even happier! He was entitled to be happy. It is his fence, and he has learned to climb it, and stay up, and balance himself."

The little brother was indeed happy on top of the fence. He would talk to himself with obvious pleasure—tell nameless, invisible people that they are stupid and inadequate because, unlike him, they are unable to climb the fence and stay there and enjoy themselves. Yes, he was obviously talking to himself. He was also speaking to an earlier version of himself, to the boy of four who had wanted to climb that fence, wanted to get on top, and, just as important, stay there and enjoy the experience. Once he had succeeded, he enjoyed his new-found competence. He would practically never be curbed, humiliated, denied interesting or engaging occasions because of the "reality" of the world around him. Quite the contrary; there would be one inviting adventure after another over the months and years. One day, as a matter of fact, he ran across the field after he had shown himself able to climb a particular fence with ease—in search of a taller, slightly more precarious fence on the other side of the corral. And when that climb was "nothing" and the position of balance a giant bore, he predicted quite casually that he would never see a fence that he couldn't rather quickly master. His father did not want the boy to be completely unrealistic, however. To whistle in the dark, to assume that one can always triumph, is to be vulnerable—the weakness of the overconfident. One ought to have a great deal of drive and ambition, a conviction that the world will eventually be made to oblige—but only after a substantial effort.

It is absurd to say that all children whose parents make a certain amount of money or work at certain occupations, or live in a certain neighborhood, possess an attitude of mind (and an attitude toward the world) that might be sensibly tucked into the generalization referred to here as "entitlement." More than once I have insisted that each individual has his or her unique way of pulling together the various elements of mental life. I have wanted, however, to suggest a common manner of response toward life among children of a certain class and background. I realize that the particular word "entitlement" has complicated psychoanalytic implications or, for some, pejorative social or political implications, or indeed, for others, quite defensible and justifiable implications. For the children I have worked with, however, the word is simply a description of a certain actuality. There are both social and psychological dimensions to that actuality, and deep down these children know them rather well.

I have in mind especially the son of a powerful Florida grower. When the child was five he kept using the words "I'm entitled to." His parents were much annoyed. The father did not want his son using such a peremptory, self-important, demanding expression. He began interrupting the boy, telling him that he was not "entitled" to *anything*, that he must ask for what he wanted, and be grateful when he got it. The boy kept asking why, why. The father kept explaining—a litany of oughts and musts. The boy in turn fell back upon his considerable intelligence and powers of observation. He reminded his father of his own words: "If you earn something, you are entitled to keep it." Had not the boy "earned" the right to make his various requests—by trying to be "good" or "quiet"? Had not the father told him on a number of occasions that he was "coming along nicely," that he was "making his parents proud"?

The boy spoke up for himself in fits and starts, but he got his message across, because his father eventually settled for an ironic statement: "A boy who stands up for himself like that boy has—well, he's entitled to say every once in a while, that he's *entitled* to something!" It must be rather obvious—it was to the grower, for all his lack of interest in the plight of the hundreds of impoverished migrants who worked his land so long and hard—that not every father can be grateful for his son's outspokenness, his young son's assumption that he was entitled to political freedom, social equality, economic privilege.

· · · · · · · · · · ·

### QUESTIONS FOR A SECOND READING

1. Coles tells the stories of a number of children: the son of an Appalachian mine owner, an eight-year-old son from a Boston suburb, a boy and a girl from a family living in Westchester County. As you reread the essay, closely review what he has to say about one of these cases. What is there in his account that you can now—after you've read it a second time—identify as predictable, as evidence of Coles's particular method and bias, his way of looking at and interpreting, or reading, the evidence he gathers from his interviews? What, then, do you suppose he fails to see? or per-

haps keeps secret? What didn't he look for that you think he might have? And, finally, what conclusions can you draw then about Coles's *method*— about what it both can and can't do?

2. Would you want to argue that any of these children is "sick" or "disturbed" or that somehow the child is not psychologically healthy? Which one? Where is the evidence? How do you read the evidence to draw this conclusion? What's the borderline between health and sickness in this case? Is Coles any help in making this distinction? Why, or why not?

## ASSIGNMENTS FOR WRITING

1. The key word in this chapter is, obviously, "entitlement," and Coles builds a variety of uses for it as the chapter proceeds. In a sense, Coles works out his analysis of these children by working out the possible uses of the term. At the end of the essay, he says,

> More than once I have insisted that each individual has his or her unique way of pulling together the various elements of mental life. I have wanted, however, to suggest a common manner of response toward life among children of a certain class and background. I realize that the particular word "entitlement" has complicated psychoanalytic implications or, for some, pejorative social or political implications, or indeed, for others, quite defensible and justifiable implications. For the children I have worked with, however, the word is simply a description of a certain actuality. There are both social and psychological dimensions to that actuality, and deep down these children know them rather well (pp. 124–125).

As you read Coles's argument, what are the social and psychological dimensions of "entitlement"? To explore what Coles's term "entitlement" might mean, write an essay that identifies as many varieties of social and psychological entitlement as Coles's chapter will justify. You should look at his uses of the term along with the cases they describe.

2. It's hard to read these cases without thinking of your own life. If you extend Coles's use of "entitlements" to refer to any social, political, or economic "actuality," to any set of expectations (not only those of wealthy children), how would you explain the way entitlements influenced your childhood?

   Write an essay in which you extend Coles's project by telling your story of entitlements. What experiences and what influences can you identify as key in the development of your expectations? How would you use Coles's terms to account for those experiences? Were they social? political? economic? some combination of these? Once you have told your story, go on to discuss the most significant differences between your experiences as a child and the experiences of the children Coles discusses. What factors do you think account for those differences—is it money? class? entitlement? some combination of these?

## MAKING CONNECTIONS

1. We might see "entitlements" as sets of expectations—psychological, social, economic. In Joyce Carol Oates's story, "Theft" (p. 420), Marya and Imogene come from different social classes and apparently have different expectations for themselves and for others. Write an essay in which you explain what these women expect and how their expectations determine who they are and how they act. Your job, in other words, is to study them the way Coles studies the children in "Entitlement." How, as a reader of Coles, might you tell their stories or explain their cases?

2. In "Our Time" (p. 596), John Edgar Wideman tells his brother Robby's story. Robby is in prison, and through John he looks back at the major influences in his life—his mother; his grandfather John French; his best friend, Garth; and his neighborhood. Write an essay in which you extend Coles's project in "Entitlement" by retelling Robby's story as a story of his entitlements.

   How might you, in other words, account for Robby's experiences through Coles's terms? What experiences of Robby's would you identify as key, and how would you "read" them as Coles might, as examples of Robby's "unique way of pulling together the various elements of mental life"?

# THOMAS COTTLE
# AND STEPHEN
# KLINEBERG

*T*HOMAS COTTLE *was born in Chicago in 1937. He received his B.A. from Harvard University in 1959, then returned to his hometown to attend graduate school at the University of Chicago, eventually completing a Ph.D. in sociology in 1968. Once described as a "specialist in children's rights," Cottle is the author of a number of books on children, including* Children in Jail *and* Black Children, White Dreams. *More recently, he has written about adults from a variety of Boston neighborhoods, all in an attempt to tell the stories of people whose lives would otherwise go unnoticed* (Private Lives and Public Accounts *and* The Present of Things Future: Explorations of Time in Human Experience). *Cottle is also a regular fixture on television; he has had a series of syndicated shows, including a children's show, "Hot Hero Sandwich," and shows for adults: "Up Close," "Soapbox," and "The Tom Cottle Show."*

*As a writer, Cottle is at his best when he writes case studies like the study of the Grazianos here. Cottle begins these studies by collecting data—by spending as much time as he can with his subjects, even living with them for extended periods of time. In the end, however, what he does is to tell the story of people's lives and to do so as truthfully and accurately as he can. These case studies serve as the raw material from which social scientists make generalizations about people or society. Some critics have found his work patronizing—Sara Blackburn, for instance, writes, "We don't need more studies by experts, no matter how caring, of how bright, sensitive, and thus worthy of salvation are the victims of our political and social crimes." But Cottle is more often praised for his compassion, his sensitivity, and his concern for both the people he writes about and the ethical implications of his participation in their lives.*

The Present of Things Future, *from which the Grazianos' case study is drawn, was cowritten with Stephen Klineberg (born 1940), a social psychologist who teaches at Rice University. Klineberg completed a Ph.D. in social psychology at Harvard University, and his work has appeared in the* Journal of Personality and Social Psychology *and* The Key Reporter. *Cottle and Klineberg began with a general interest in the way people perceive and experience time. They have collaborated on a second book about this subject,* The Perception of Time. *Of* The Present of Things Future, *one critic wrote, "The authors make an excellent point of showing the social and cultural limitations which frequently profoundly influence anticipations of the future. An aspect of the study which may give rise to some controversy is the suggestion that the male and female may experience time quite differently."*

# *Ted and Ellie Graziano*

I had been late arriving at the Grazianos' house on Poplar Street. Some unexpected traffic, which I had cursed, held me up, and that fact, coupled with the uncongenial design of Boston's streets, was enough to make me almost forty-five minutes behind schedule. Theodore Graziano, his good friends call him Mushy, had Tuesdays off from work and so the moments I could spend with him and his wife Eleanor together were precious. Normally, I would see one of them alone.

For about fifteen years, Ted Graziano has worked for a Boston newspaper. Starting as a stockroom boy (he was almost twenty-five at the time), he had worked his way up to where now, at thirty-nine, he was foreman of the shipping operation. Salaries had risen over the last years. Several threatened strikes and union pressure on management had brought his take-home pay to a level at which he could just about get by. The important thing for him was the security, a factor he had mentioned several times when we spoke in his office.

"This is not the time to be sitting on any gamble," he said as we began eating our sandwiches. "This is the time when the economy of the country demands that you get yourself a job that looks like it's got to hold out. Doctors, lawyers, judges, they got it best. The working man, like always, he's going to be the first to get hit. Unemployment starts at the bottom and works its way up. It's like a disease that they can't find a cure for. You know it's out there and you just got to do the best you can to avoid getting it. Stay warm, eat good food. . . ." He smiled at me, enjoying his humor. His strong hands held the sandwich he had made that morning. His black hair was thick, his forehead low, and only the thin lines around his eyes and mouth revealed his true age. It was hard to believe that Ted was approaching forty.

"Yeah, forty," Ted reflected when I raised the issue with him once. "I guess that means something. I still feel young though, and you know what they say about feeling your age."

"Yeah, I do. But I feel old."

"Maybe you ought to see a doctor," he laughed.

"Or stay away from young-feeling guys like you." I remember that particular remark. It had sounded patronizing, but he had enjoyed it. Still, the more I played out in my mind a conversation that might have ensued, the more patronizing it became. I think often, for example, that maybe the "good life" is working with one's hands, witnessing real accomplishment, and going home with no lingering thoughts about work until the next morning when you get up and repeat it. But that is precisely the point on which Ted Graziano had long ago put an end to my naïve notions.

"You take a job like this," he had said, waving his right arm about as if to take in the enormous shipping area, partitioned offices, and truck docks, "it's one helluvan operation. I got real responsibility here. You ask any man they got working here and they'll tell you about that responsibility. I tell you though, in the beginning, ten years ago or so, it was one helluva challenge. Couple nights there I got so damn excited with the prospect of it all I could barely sleep. Now, it's just another job to me. Plasterer gets up each morning and slops that shit on the walls; butcher goes cutting up his meat; I direct the newspaper business down here. It's a job, not much more. Every day you get a little excitement, but when you go to think about it day in and day out, it's routine. Man, there are times I'm working down here thinking about how nice it would be to be anywhere else. Sitting in the sun or taking care of people. Doing what you're doing, you know, walking around, talking to people. That'd be nice. I'd like that. But most of the time I have to take those thoughts and crush 'em up like little paper balls and throw 'em away." He shook his head from side to side, crumpling an imaginary sheet of paper in one of his hands. Then he looked back at me.

"Tell you what gets me—I know you're interested in this. It's the time thing. Two things about time I can tell you. First, is how slow it goes most of the time. Look there, once you start to use that word it just keeps coming back on you. Lots of ways you can use that word, though. Like wasting time. Boy, I must say that to the guys here twenty times a day." He had heard the word again and grinned. "Well, I ain't about to go commenting on my verbal skills. Wasting time is one thing, but it's not as important to me, really, as the way time passes so slowly most of the time. Clock seems to die on me every day. I'll be working and just check it out, then work long and hard and check it out again, and see only about fifteen minutes have passed when a good hour should have." He smiled. "You can't beat it. You just can't beat it." A feeling of resignation could be heard in his voice. The muscles of his powerful forearms moved slightly as he pulled his watch band higher on his wrist. "Here's the devil," he said. "Right here's our number one nemesis. Nothing I can do, it seems, to make the seconds go by any faster. 'Course, I'm sure that in a few years I'll be wishing I could slow the whole mess down."

"Yeah," I responded, "I guess lots of us know that feeling right now."

"Funny, I don't. Not yet anyway. Probably will pretty soon. Ain't getting younger just sitting here, but, like, you could say I'm still in the stage of life when I want time to speed up. You know, you could probably categorize people just by asking them, 'Do you want time to speed up or slow down?' I'll bet you'd discover some pretty interesting things. Of course, you'd have to take account of the fact that lots of times a person is doing things where he wants time to speed up or slow down. Still, I'll bet you'd find that lots of people feel the same way most of the time. Like me, I want it to speed up. It's true even when I'm home."

On another occasion, as we sat together on the concrete edge of the truck dock, with the last truck having departed and Ted ready to head for home, he offered another thought about his involvement with time. As usual, his tone with me was formal, for he never forgot that I was not one of his close friends.

"Maybe the worst part of the job is not that time passes slowly. The worst part of my life, really, is that I can see the whole thing laying out before me. See, if I were to tell you that the job is boring, monotonous, that wouldn't really capture the feelings I have when I think about it. And man, you *make* me think about it." He slapped my leg. "I always feel talking with you that I'm back in school writing one of those themes for an English teacher, and I'm trying my best to dig out the big words. Funny about that, too, that being back in school, 'cause like right now, trying to answer your questions, I want to give a good impression. . . . "

"Like getting a good grade?" I interrupted.

"Just like it. But there's more, too, because when I wrote those themes, or tried to write them," he smiled, "it was like I was talking to myself in a very deep and special way. This is all, now, different from working for a good grade. When you write, you know, you begin to know yourself in private. It's not like talking." I could see his thoughts beginning to overtake him. Perhaps he was saying that tenderness as well as anger can come out in writing. Hurt can, too, in ways that day-by-day encounters and friendships often do not allow.

"Anyway, let me get to this one thing. The rotten part of my job here is that everything is so predictable. I can see long, long stretches of time. Maybe the next ten, fifteen, twenty years. I can see them. Work and work, the same job. That's the monotonous part. If every day were the same, like it is, it would still be all right if I didn't ever have to wonder about how all the days string together. But it's the line of days, one after the other, each one repeating, and then the ability to be able to look down the road and see exactly what's coming. Jesus, that's, that's . . . Honest to God, man, it just about frightens me to death, because it means I can see the days leading right down to the end.

"You know you can't live every day of your life thinking only about that single day. That's part of the crap they feed you. You can't do it. You can't keep your mind from focusing on tomorrow and next week, next year. That's what I'm thinking about. You don't think that way in this life. You've got to think about the future. That's where the possibilities are. That's where anything that might be resembling hope is. This business of living day by day, even in a job like mine, can't make it. You can't make it that way. So now I got the problem of being born with a vision that looks down the road, way down the road, and being able to see everything that's coming. They got lots of guys, I'm sure, give their right eye to be able to see what's coming up for them. Well, I can see, and just being able to see is more of a curse than it is anything else. An evil curse. You know what I mean? You got this inborn thing that drives you to get yourself set for the future, right?"

I nodded yes. I thought, too, of the connection between one's images of the future and one's present mood. For when things go particularly well I am able to foresee the future—almost as if the sense of possibility cannot be contained by anything as finite as a future allotment of time.

"Yessir. Every man does," Ted went on. "But *you* don't know what's going to be. Today you talk with me and I tell you something. Tomorrow maybe you talk with Ellie or some kid and you don't know what they're up to. And in a week from now we may not even be seeing one another. You'll go get yourself another family or go do a story about something else. But you can be sure as hell I'll be right here. Two weeks vacation in July each year and then I'll be here. That gets to a guy, that knowing that you might be moving up, like I have, in an organization, and still you're not actually changing that much. I think that's why so many of us liked being in the army so much. Didn't anybody want to get killed naturally, but it *was* a change. Everything that led up to the army stopped once I got in, and what would come after no one could see. I thought about my future plenty then. Oh brother, we had a million conversations about the future. But no one could tell us the way it was going to be. The future was all a mystery. I remember, that was my word for it: 'the mysterious future.' It made you kind of scared. But now that I think about it, those little jittery feelings were exactly the feelings I needed to get me going. They give you a kind of push, a motivation. Now, my whole life is like a car running along a highway. Things going pretty smooth, no complaints, but pretty soon the scenery gets monotonous. So what do you think about? You think about the way it used to be, or maybe you start to wonder just how long it's going to be before your car runs out of gas." He stopped talking, although the movement of his face told me of the thoughts that preoccupied him.

My own thoughts, however, were turning to this method of inquiring about another person. Despite the care one takes, it is clear that many questions or concerns simply do not touch the lives of those with whom one speaks. Nonetheless, in response, they work hard at providing answers. And so those whose lives we may or may not gently invade transform disinterest or irrelevance into unpreparedness, and communicate to us that it is their fault and not ours that a gracious or beguiling response is not forthcoming.

For Ted, the subject of time was central and preoccupying. I had not fished for inquiries that might, somehow, conjoin his world with my own. I had, as they say, struck a chord, a reservoir he had not only wondered about, but seriously considered. I would hear his reflections on time again on the afternoon I reached the Grazianos' forty-five minutes late. His orientation to the future, and what he meant by a transparent future, were not capricious notions for him. In particular, a temporal orientation predicated on personal experience was forming even in the midst of the random flow of those conversations that often seemed to me to be heading in no discernable direction.

Our home meetings took place in the kitchen, so I entered through the back door as the family members did. Alone in the house, Ted had been sitting in the kitchen reading the newspaper. Two glasses of milk and a cake covered with tin foil were on the kitchen table along with plates and forks. Early in our friendship, Eleanor Graziano had learned from Ted of my love for apple cakes and apple pies, and so something freshly baked regularly awaited my arrival. Today the smell in the kitchen was especially tantalizing. Ted watched me and grinned with pride. "Quite a lady, huh?"

"You better believe it," I replied.

"She'll be here in a minute. Something came up at her mother's. She left a note." Ted handed me a page from a calendar on which Ellie had written: "I will be back in a minute. Milk and cake are for you. I have not forgotten."

"Come on, let's eat the cake. I've been waiting for you dying with hunger here." Ted took great pleasure in cutting the cake and gently laying a piece on a plate. He reached over and placed a fork on the plate and then pushed one of the glasses of milk toward me. When I was taken care of, he prepared a piece, considerably smaller, for himself.

"So what do we talk about today, or shouldn't we say anything until Ellie gets here?" Ted asked, his mouth full of cake.

"Talk about anything you like, Mr. Graziano," I said. "I'm not listening anyway with this cake here."

"Eat it up. There's lots more where it came from. Your wife cooks, though, doesn't she?"

"Yes, she does."

"Well, then you aren't hurting too much." He sighed deeply, wiping some crumbs from his chin. "Lots of guys have it pretty bad. I told myself a long time ago, though, no wife of mine is going to work. Ever! No matter how bad it is, a man provides in his way, a woman in hers. Ellie doesn't need to go cleaning or secretarying, or work at the phone company like her girlfriends. We'll manage. Eight thousand years, and I'll have this house paid off, and when I die she'll be set up. She don't ever have to work if she don't want to. That's the way it's supposed to be. You agree?"

"Well, I guess I believe people have to work it out the way they want," I answered him. "Men live their way, women theirs."

"Now you're not going to tell me you're one of these liberation people, are you?" He smiled at me.

"Well, I guess in a way I am. Men and women, it seems to me, have to enhance one another, support each other to be what they want."

"Now, *that* I like. *That* I'll buy. That's all right. I like that enhancing business. You know, now that you mention it, that's maybe like my biggest gripe. I never did have anyone enhance my life. I can look back at it now, forty years next July, I can't see a person there anywhere enhanced me, helped me to get anything. Parents never gave a damn. When they died it made no difference in my life at all. No teachers ever cared about what I was doing in school. Priest couldn't have cared less about the whole group of us kids."

"You have Ellie," I said.

His eyes were closed slightly as several thoughts seem to touch him at once. "Yeah, I got Ellie, all right. Probably a good thing for me, too. But it's not really enhancement. That's not what I call the kind of support I'm talking about. A wife is a wife, she doesn't help you out there." He pointed in the direction of the kitchen window above the sink. "That's not what I mean."

"What is it then, Ted? Can you talk about it?"

"Let me get the words first." He paused, looking through his glass at the filmy layer of milk on the bottom. "The living day by day that women do is not what helps a man, or at least a man like me. There's a way a man has to get his whole life together. It's all got to fit somehow, make sense. You know what I mean?" He didn't wait for an answer. "It's got to be set up so that every move you make has some reason in a plan that you have to formulate somewhere along the line. It has to build toward something. Even when you're a little kid, people are asking you what you're going to be when you get older. I did the same thing with my kids. I remember holding Tony on my knee one night, I'll bet he wasn't six months old, and telling him about some of the things he might think about doing when he gets older. Now, here he is, what? Fifteen? He still doesn't know what he's going to do or be. But it doesn't make any difference, see, 'cause he knows he has to become something. That *I* put into his head, starting when he was six months. That's the important thing. He knows he's got to have a plan for when he gets older.

"My problem maybe was I never had one, really, although I did have this thing about making sure that you're living your life to prepare. That's about the only good thing my Dad ever did for me. He made me understand that you got to have something out there waiting for you, and that nothing is going to be out there unless you make the preparations, do the ground work, like they say."

"It makes sense to me."

"Sure. It's got to make sense to you 'cause you're a man. You know about these things. You may be richer than I am. I'll bet you are, too," he looked at me, "and you may have a more interesting job, which I know you do. I even told you once, remember?"

"Yes. In the shop."

"At the office, right," he corrected me.

"Office," I said quietly.

"But the important thing is that a man knows what it means to arrange for his life. That, no woman knows! That I know for sure." A melancholy feeling was taking the place of anger. "There's a kicker in it though, you know?"

"Which is?"

"Which is that a life that asks us to make sure that pasts and presents and futures fit together in some logical way has a price. You know, yourself, as time goes on it gets harder and harder to just live each day and get the most out of it. Can't be done. You don't live each day like that when you're a man. What you live is your work at the moment, your plans, what you call your prospects, *and* your regrets, what you should have done. You think about having bits of time back again to work with. You think how nice it would be to see what the future holds, even in a job like mine where I practically know how everything's going to turn out. Still, you'd like to take a little peek. Maybe just to know whether all those connections you're making are really sticking. You follow me?"

"Yes I do," I answered him.

"So you don't say the hell with what was and what will be. Like that song, what will be, will be. That's the way you think when you go out drinking. At least, that's the way it is for me. I go out and get a little in the bag," he started to smile. I smiled too, as I saw his face take on a look of pride. "That's when my future disappears and my past disappears and I got once and for all my present moment and nothing else, goddamn it, to be concerned about!" He shouted the words as he straightened up in the chair. "But now, I ask you, how long's a man with any self-respect going to run around in the bag? So you come home, and you sleep, and you drink coffee, and you make nice to your wife, and there you are the next day, thinking the same things all over again, how it all fits together, how you wish you could be young again, and how great it would be to know what the future's got waiting for you. And there you are, right back where you started, if you got any strength, that is."

"That's one helluvan analysis," I said, moving about in my chair and wishing, for the moment, to take a second piece of cake.

"Well, I don't know I'd call it an analysis, exactly," he said. "Nothing mysterious about what I've been saying. You keep your eye on the future. That's what men are for. You keep an eye on the future because the name of the game is that since you don't have much to say about dying, you have to fill in as many of the empty spaces out there as you can. You don't leave things to chance. Ellie always talks to me when I get in a huff about God or fate. 'Things will just happen,' she says all the time. 'Things are just going to happen.' Sure. They are. Lots of things are just going to happen. Like the roof might fall in on our heads, right here in the kitchen. But the odds aren't pure chance. The odds are against it because *I* fix the roof, *I* make certain things like that *won't* happen. That's what you do with the day. You fix things so that some things will happen and some things won't.

"The difference between Ellie and me is she waits. She waits for the roof to fall in. Then, when it happens, she does something. Or, she'll say, there's nothing I can do, so I shouldn't worry. What are you going to do? Men worry. They worry because they have to reorganize their lives to make the future better or safer or whatever they're after. Women bake cakes. You like her cake, she's pleased, that's enough for one day. Men worry too, because they have a plan which they have to put into operation." Ted rose from the table and went to the sink to wash his hands. I remembered being in this house one afternoon when the sink faucets were leaking and his temper, like my own on many occasions, had exploded. "No, now they see the operation taking place. Maybe it works, maybe it doesn't. The point is that with one part of their brain they're wondering what they could do *now* to make next week or next year work out better. They're starting new plans, if you know what I mean." He dried his hands on a blue towel that hung on the handle of the refrigerator door.

"Now with the other part of their brain," he resumed, seating himself opposite me, "they wonder what it would be like having the past back again so they might fix a few things, maybe play it all out a little differently. But what a man does that a woman doesn't have the faintest idea about is, that when he has the chance, I mean, *if* he had the chance to live it again, he's still working it around so that the present might be better. I should have gone this way rather than that way, he'll say. Do this instead of that."

"I think I do that myself."

"Sure you do. But you know what a woman does? She gets a chance to be young again, she'll just do it all over the same way. You ask Ellie. She'll tell you exactly what I'm telling you now. All the things from the past that she liked, she'll just do them all over again. And all the bad things too." He anticipated my question. "She'll just say you have to live through the good things and the bad things, or whatever that expression is. Take the good with the bad."

"You know what it's like, Tom? It's like football. There's a good reason why men like football. It's not just the violence. It's a man's game because it's played the way men think. Look what you got in football. First, you got competition. You got a chance to win or lose, and a man is practically born with the idea in his head that you got to win. Then, everybody's got a fair chance. But now here's the subtle part of that game. You have a game plan. Plan. See, there it is again. Now, this plan takes in your purpose, your goal, the way you're going to work it out. And you stick with it unitl you have to find a new one. And that's the point right there. You don't scrap a plan. A new plan simply means you have to find new patterns, new ways for things to stick together. And it's all leading up to something. Something you could practically predict. That's what football is. If you move here, I'll move there. You move here, I'll move there." He pushed his fingers against the table top, his right hand representing my team, his left hand representing his team. "You can make predictions. It's not a game of chance, like gambling. You know how something ought to work out. Here's another thing. What do they do when the game's over?"

"I don't know. They think about what's gone on."

"That's exactly right. They see the movies of the game, the replays like they call them. They use those films to change their plans and, in your words, to try to make the future come to pass in a different way." He paused. "Here, I got some more milk."

"That a great metaphor, Ted. I've never thought of football in those terms. It's absolutely true."

"I guess I've been thinking about ways to carry our last discussion from the office forward a little bit. I can't say these things to Ellie. Of course, the kids don't want to hear about it. I talk with some of my friends, but, as you can imagine, not too many of them are as smart as you. I guess you know better than most of us how little schooling we all had. Our kids, I hope, will be different. Oops, I'm starting to sound like the old lady. Hoping instead of arranging."

"Well," I tried to assure him, "there's got to be a place for hope in the plan."

"Sure," he said with resignation, "of course there's a place for hope. But first you make preparations, then, whatever is left over that you can't control for, that falls over into the hope category. A fellow in my position ought to be able to say without fail, I can predict that my kids will go to college. I will get money somehow for them to go, whether it is good for them or not—and, believe me, I got lots of questions for you on that one—I can arrange the future for them. I don't need God or prayer, or hope. This is exactly what I'm talking about. I can arrange for all of this."

He rested his elbows on the table and held his hands up as though shaking a loaf of bread. "I can get all of this to happen. Fate's got no place in here. But baby, I'll tell you, sometimes it makes me wonder why we're here, and why we're doing what we're doing. You got to get out once in a while. I don't mean, don't misunderstand me, I don't mean just out of the house. . . . "

"I know what you mean."

"I mean out of the path of the ball, you know? Go this way for once, or that way, any way to break the monotony. Go backward or forward if that makes any difference. That's what I mean by getting out. In time!"

For a moment, Ted was silent. Then he resumed. "Prediction. That may be the key. Each man his own computer, able to see what's coming up at any point in his life. There are lots of guys who tell you that you can't go around predicting. They say it's bad luck. They're superstitious. Predict something good about your life and you'll see, something bad is always supposed to happen. That's what they say, anyway. Ellie goes along with this. Only God predicts, is probably what she'd tell you if you ever asked her about it. Now, don't get me wrong. You don't want to go around predicting. But predicting is like I was telling you before. It's like hope. It's part of what's left over. You have plans that you might like to see how they come out, but I'm not so sure you have to go around predicting. Still, like that football things of ours, what'd you call it?"

"Game plan, you mean?"

"No, that other, like the picture I was describing."

"Metaphor?"

"Metaphor. Football metaphor." He seemed relieved. "I remember that from school. Similes and metaphors. Right?"

"Right."

"I never got straight which is which. Anyway, prediction. When you get to be a man they've got this future thing so pushed down your throat, the feeling of making a prediction just isn't so weird as it seems at first. Anything like a . . . technique that had to do with working out the future is something a man quickly gets used to. Not women. Hope's still the last resort though. Just like they say. When all else fails, maybe you better start praying. But when they say that all else fails, they mean that they've been working at something that isn't going to work now. You don't start with prayer. You may see those football players pray at the start of the game, like to get a little boost from the Good Lord. That's all right. Little superstition never killed anyone. God, Ellie better not hear my say that. They may be praying, but you and I know they've been practicing all week long. Not praying! Practicing! They've been getting themselves all set for Sunday. So if they make predictions, it's because they feel they have ways of fixing the outcomes. You get what I mean?"

We had been speaking almost an hour when the back door opened, and Eleanor Graziano entered the kitchen. Her face was flushed and she was out of breath.

"Please, please excuse me. I'm so late. I went over to my mother's for a minute. I didn't even take my coat off and before you know it an hour's gone." I nodded to her and started to say something about my own lateness. Bracing herself in the doorway, she leaned down to remove her boots. "Did you find the cake?"

"Did we!" I replied.

"Was it all right?" she asked modestly.

I grinned at her. "Fair. It was fair, Ellie." She laughed and turned her face downward. Ted laughed too.

"A couple of jokesters I got here. Two little boys with no place to go and nothing to do but eat cake and get fat."

I couldn't resist: "Oh, you love it and you know it, Mrs. G."

"You I love," she laughed. "Mushy I'm not so sure about." Ted and I laughed again and looked at each other.

"You better be careful, wife, or I'll tell you what I've been telling Tom here for the last hour about *you*."

"Yeah, and what's that?" she asked her husband, throwing her boots in the back hallway.

"Oh," he started, "about people enhancing one another's lives. Game plans, you know, the usual." He winked at me.

"Game plans?" she asked. "Football? Is that it?"

"That's it," I said.

"Not quite," Ted said.

"Then what is it?" she wanted to know.

"Sit down, Ellie. You and Tom talk. I'm going to the corner for cigars. When I come back we'll continue with this. It's time for a commercial."

"Commercial? Tom, will you please tell me what he's babbling about?"

"I will."

"Go on then," she said to her husband. "I've got a few things for Tom *you* don't have to know about."

"Yeah, like what?" Ted demanded.

Ellie was silent for a moment. Then she exploded the one word. "Hockey!"

The three of us roared with laughter.

Eleanor Graziano moved about the kitchen, looking into cabinets at canned goods, glasses, and plates.

"Will you stay for dinner?" she asked.

"No, I can't, Ellie, but I promise I will another time."

"Can't seem to find . . . don't tell me I forgot to get . . . if I don't make a list when I go to the store I'm dead. Can you beat this? I'm not forty yet and my mother, who is almost seventy, has a brain in better shape than mine."

"I doubt that."

"No, it's true," she protested without looking back. "So what do we speak about today? Are you still asking the same questions?"

"Same questions, I suppose."

"About working and living and everything, eh?"

"Yeah, that about covers it."

"Well, I don't know what else I can tell you. Mushy's the one with all the answers. There's nothing you could ask him that he wouldn't have an answer for. Everything. Everything he can find something to speak about. Some man, Mr. Graziano."

I watched her lay out supplies and utensils in preparation for making dinner. The counter tops were spotless, the sink empty of dishes and garbage, the faces of the cabinets glistening clean. It was all quite a change from the day when the Grazianos had moved into this house. Four years ago they lived in a four-room apartment less than a mile away. Then, suddenly, Ted had gotten it in his head to buy a house. Ellie argued that they couldn't afford it, but Ted was driven to buy, and with loans and arrangements at work, they managed to purchase this lovely three-bedroom home. Now they "could spread out," as Ellie said, finally admitting her delight. "The children can stay in the same school and we will live better. I'm closer to my mother, too. If we can just manage," she had sighed. "If we can just manage it will be a blessing, *the* blessing of my whole life."

Although Eleanor Chadwick had never known poverty as a child, she also had never imagined that her marriage to Teddy Graziano, "the Mushy man," would ever lead to a home and a kitchen glowing with warmth and pride like this one. Her father had been an elevator operator and starter during the day, a warehouse inspector four nights a week. He had lived his entire life in Boston. His salary allowed his wife and five children to live comfortably enough in a three-story walk-up apartment. A screened-in back porch opened out from the kitchen of that apartment, and on hot summer evenings the family gathered there feeling as cool as one could during a Boston summer. The view from the porch admittedly was rather uninteresting. "Who, after all, likes looking down an alley at a bunch of other apartment houses?" Ellie had said. "But is *was* cool up there. We enjoyed it together very much. That was ever so lovely, just to be together, even when it was so hot you thought you might die. They had a kid, I remember, who lived downstairs, who died of the heat. He just couldn't get enough cool air, the doctor said. So tragic. So tragic. He could have come up to our porch and saved his life. I suppose you could say I long to see my childhood again."

We had had this conversation about her childhood several years ago, on the very day, actually, that the Grazianos moved into their new home. Ellie and I had sat in the kitchen on cardboard boxes filled with supplies and clothes. "I would love to have those days back again," she said on that moving day. "Even before Mushy and all this. So many times I wish that tomorrow would be the beginning of a change, a sort of a change backward. It's not like you might think, that I fear getting older. I don't think I'm different from other people. But no one likes to grow old. When you have children they say it keeps you young. It's not true. Children age you. My, they age you. It's just that they don't give you any time to think about it. They got you running around all the time.

"No, it's just that wonderful feeling or worryless peace, childhood, being a little girl and having those long hours with my father. He was a delight to know. You would have liked him, Tom. I feel that very strongly. You two would have gotten on. 'Course, that's not saying too much, since Dad never had an enemy. He got on with everyone he ever knew. You know, in many ways, he was very much like Mushy; Mushy without the anger. Dad knew, for example, that he would never be rich, that he'd never achieve anything special or wonderful in his life. He knew lots of rich people, too, but I never heard him complain, or compare himself with someone else. The world was the way it was, and he was big enough to accept it. All of that, I'm sure, made for very peaceful living for the rest of us.

"Mushy's the same way, up to a point. I'm sure he feels that he's not going anywhere in his life, at his job, I mean, but he's not about to accept any of that. He wants to achieve something, to be able to show everybody, mostly himself, of course, that he's gotten something out of life. He'll always tell me that if next year's the same as this year, then he's been a failure. There's no other way. That kind of statement I never heard once from my father's mouth. Never once. For me, you see, that's the sign of a good man. If next year's the same as this one, then you thank God. You get down on your knees at night and you thank God that everybody is well, or still alive I should say, and that you have enough to eat, and a comfortable place to sleep. You know that everything is provided for. But Mushy doesn't want it that way. The comfortable things, of course, he wants. That he wants as much as anyone. Like, he wanted this house. . . . "

I remember Ellie looking about at the boxes and cartons and seeing in her face a look of "How are we ever going to get set up again? Why did we ever undertake this move and this severing of attachments?" I saw excitement, too, a controlled excitement as though one were not supposed to ask for such delicious treasures, but could nevertheless enjoy them if they came one's way.

"Well, I'm set here for life. This is it for me. I detest moving. I may be strange or peculiar, maybe I'm some kind of a mental or something, but I become attached to places. I get used to something very quickly and I don't ever want to change. You know something? I can feel in my hands the curtains we used to have in the apartment where I lived as a child. And the tables in the living room and the kitchen, too. That's how strong my memory is, so that must be how strong my attachment to things is. To people, too. It's sort of funny, though. It grieves me, it really does, that the good times are gone and by many, sad to say, forgotten. I think Mush is that way. Something good happens, like maybe a party. He likes it as much as anyone. But then, when it's over, that's sort of the end of it. Yesterday for him, even this morning, might just as well be a thousand years ago. Me, I'm so different from him it's hard to believe we could have gotten along as long as we have. Something important happens, it doesn't matter whether it's good or bad, I hang on to it. I don't ever want to let go. It's just like the house. I wanted to hang on to the old house. It has memories in it. That's what he doesn't understand. I love this, of course, but you give me the largest mansion you can find, a palace, and I'll sit in my bedroom, I mean bedrooms," she laughed, "and I'll be thinking of that little apartment I grew up in, and the porch and the summers, and all the rest of it."

She paused, looking at nothing in particular, screening a series of ideas before selecting one to present.

"You know that my mother will be seventy years old in March? That's even hard for me to believe. It's all so peculiar. I think peculiar's getting to be my favorite word. But it *is* hard for me to believe that she's that old. My mother is always forty. When I think of her she's just forty. She's in that old kitchen—God, that was some horrible place—working at making dinner, or cleaning out the stove, or peeling apples."

"And you're about ten?" I reasoned.

"Yes, I'm ten or eleven, watching my mother and admiring her very, very much. She was a beautiful woman, though no one could see that now. Beautiful, and blessed with endless energy, too. She's still got that, even now. But you know, what's funny is that when I think about her I'm not really remembering those years; I'm actually back there. I'm *really* ten, and she's *really* forty; that's the way it's always going to be. Neither one of us will ever change."

I could see in Ellie's face a sense of peace that bespoke the loveliness of those moments thirty years ago. "You see, I do become attached to places and to certain people and find myself hoping things never have to be any different than they are right now. I remember on many occasions as a child wishing that I didn't ever have to get any older. I even spoke to my mother about it. She always laughed at me. "You're too young to be thinking about that," is about all she could say to me then. Now I'm getting close to her age. Three years and I'll be forty myself, and I have a daughter and . . . well . . . life goes on."

That was part of our conversation of almost four years ago. Now, as we waited together in the same kitchen for Ted to return, I know that we both felt a nostalgia, a longing for something, for the people of four years ago, for the people of our childhoods as well.

"You're pretty deep in thought, young man." Ellie surprised me. "Maybe *I* ought to be asking the questions today. Turn the tables on you." She was smiling.

"Yeah. I guess I was pretty deep into something there. I was remembering my own childhood, and also the discussion we had in here when you first moved. Remember that?"

"Yes." She strained to recover some of those earlier words. "Barely I do. About my childhood and the old place? Isn't that what we talked about once?"

"Yes. And your mother and father," I reminded her.

"Yes. I remember. My days as a little girl I certainly remember. I wonder what Mushy remembers of those days. I'll bet you very little. He sure likes to lock his past away. He thinks only of the future now. That's all. Every night in bed he's got another plan, another dream. Someday we're going to do this; someday we're going to do that. Trips, property, real estate, the kids going to college. This one's going to be a doctor; that one's going to be a nurse. I have to tell him, 'Mushy, its 1970, not 1990. Let time pass already. You're living in an age that isn't even born yet.' Can you hear me saying that to him? 'Give the world a chance to do what it's going to do. What do you want the time to pass by so quickly for, anyway?'

"You know, I begin to think that people who don't have parents want the past to go away, or they avoid thinking about it, somehow, by doing all that planning and preparing. It's like today. I went by to bring my mother some groceries. Days like these it's hard for her to get around. So I brought over a few nothings, a little soup and some coffee. Bread. The usual." She blew out a long breath. "Anyway, when I saw my mother I couldn't help thinking how really old she looks. I see her regularly, almost every day because we live so close, so I can't see the changes taking place that easily. You need to stand back from it. But today, for some reason, maybe because I knew you were coming, I looked especially hard at her. And she's old! It frightens me. It actually begins to scare me. I'm not like my husband, with all his plans. I don't want it to be 1990. I don't want to be thinking about what's it all going to be like then, if we're still here. I don't want to go back, exactly, but I certainly don't want it to be 1990 or 1980 or whatever the king up there is thinking about at night. He wants it to be 1990, that's fine with me, but he can damn well get there without me. I'll just take my own sweet time about it." She ended by pulling extra hard on the tie of her apron strings.

"Ellie, what did you mean, you were thinking about your mother getting older because I was coming this afternoon?"

"I knew you'd ask me that."

"I knew you knew." We smiled at each other.

"Well, you get me thinking, somehow, about time, only I can't always find any complicated ideas in all of it. Time for me, like I told you once, is people. People get older, never younger. You reach a point in your life when you first begin to realize this and then you worry over it. Worry's maybe not the right word. But, you know, you feel bad that your little baby's grown up and is a big girl or boy, and that your mother really starts to look old. There's no denying it. I saw her today; it was almost like I was seeing her for the first time. She's an old lady now. She looks just like these old ladies you see wherever you go. When I was young, my brothers and sisters and me, we used to be playing somewhere and we would laugh at old men and women. I remember that like it was yesterday. When you're young you never think that you'll be one of those old people someday.

You never do. You also don't think that much about your parents getting older. Older maybe, but not *that* old that you'd look at them and laugh. It's funny too, because I remember then, I still do it now, I thought about what it would be like when my parents died. Every child, I'm sure, thinks about things like that. But you don't think about them getting older or looking very old. Shriveled up and all, I mean. At least I didn't. Maybe I'm different. Oh, it's an awful thing to be talking about." She shook her head as if to be rid of these images.

"Well, anyway, just to finish, I make people my calendars, you might say. To see their faces is to see time. You can tell the date by looking at your mother's or your husband's face. You know what I mean? So today when my mother opened the door, I was flabbergasted. Your questions always make me think of the past, of my parents, and going to school, or whatever pops into my mind. I must have been thinking of my mother as a young woman. Forty or so. I think that's all I mean. You know, this is what you and I once talked about. My special way of not remembering, exactly, but of *being* the age of my memories. When they took place, I mean. That's what it was, I think. I'm not crazy, am I? I mean, this sort of thinking doesn't mean that I'm ready for the State Farm already, does it?"

"Well, it's either the State Farm or making apple cakes every day when I come."

"You want some more? Where did he put it, that miser? Funny, he's so busy planning he forgets to think that maybe you'd like some more cake."

"No thanks, I'm full."

"You're not," she said, "but I'm not one to force anybody."

For a while we sat together in silence. Often it feels awkward being in the house of someone with whom one shares intimate things, stories, memories and all. I feel that I should have questions ready at hand, for the other person may take my silence to mean that I'm not doing my job well. They're waiting for me, I tell myself, to keep the time filled and to take the lead. I started to rise from my chair. Through the window above the sink I saw Ted walking through a light rain. Ellie could not see him.

"Here he . . . " I started.

"I know one thing that makes me different from him." She had one last thought, one that Ted would hear later, but that I was meant to hear first. "I worry more than Mushy. I worry about what will happen. I worry there may not be ways to get things done as we want them to. But I don't worry about what I can't see, or about what's not here yet. What's more, and this is very important if you want to really understand us, is that I believe you must live with a belief in God. Some things you can't take care of yourself. Some things only God knows what to do with. Mushy thinks I'm nuts when I say this. So I've stopped saying it in front of him, and, for that matter, in front of the children when he's around. It drives him crazy. He worries, too, but for him it's that there won't be enough time to finish all the things he's planned to do. As for God, he's about as far from God as I am from, from, I don't know what. The President of the United States. It's not easy living with this disagreement either." I saw the top of Ted Graziano's head pass under the window.

"Don't think for one minute I'm telling you little petty businesses in our lives," Ellie continued. "I'm telling you the most important things. This is a very serious difference. We run, you might say, on different clocks. You know, like the East Coast and the West Coast. We're in the same country, speaking the same language most of the time, but we've got clocks inside of us that I'm sure not only run at different speeds, but, if it's possible, in different directions as well. That probably doesn't make any sense to you, but I think it sort of tells what I worry about quite a bit of the time." She hesitated again, although she had more to say. The back door flew open and Ted entered the kitchen.

"A man with cigars," he began, "is a man halfway to heaven." He slammed the door shut, and the latch chain smacked loudly against the glass pane. Shaking off the rain and stomping his feet dry, he was a man doing his best to announce his arrival.

I had turned my body to greet him. Beside me I heard Ellie say quietly: "Two separate clocks, each ticking its own sweet time, each heading off in a direction that would probably confuse the Almighty."

How and when the tension between Ted and Ellie grew to the proportions it would that rainy afternoon I cannot recall. I do know that their ordering of the world, the arrangements they had made with time itself, were now at stake, driving them toward some temporary conclusion, some partial settlement. Just beyond the boundaries of this extended moment lay a special and distinct instant when confrontation would switch off, and the flow of this one eruption would, like water, find a new bed in which to run. No death, no final stopping place, but a life marker, nonetheless; an instant colored with hatred, I suppose, and the anguish that life and people, circumstances and history, combine to create.

In this case, I was at the center of their tension, for I had not only asked the questions on which they had unloaded so many feelings, I had split them apart by speaking intimately with each of them. I knew things about each, they both believed, that they had not confided to each other. Mine was the easy position of being able to listen to someone's everyday world without having to share much of my own. It is that comfortable role of sharing compassion while hiding one's own conflicting or antagonistic attitudes. Ellie was right. People are themselves temporal units, delicate mechanisms in which the experience of duration and the capacity for knowing change, the sense of history and continuity, disruption and evolution are all curiously combined.

To be sure, we possess internal clocks, beating systems of all sorts. But the world that exists beyond us tampers with these systems, leaving us with a peculiar repertoire of rhythms and tempos that dominate our lives, or the style of our lives. And events like marriage and the birth of children cause us to feel a reverberation in these rhythms, as childhood experiences, reveries, and recollections seek to overcome the connections and adjustments that we have finally settled on.

Ellie was seated at the table across from me; Ted was standing in the doorway between the dining space and living room, pacing in and out of our vision, a machine rumbling its engines, dying to lurch forward and, with a deafening rage, be gone.

"You know, Ellie," he was saying, his anger rising, "that's probably where it all goes wrong, every time with every man and every woman."

"Where?" she asked. "Where does *what* go wrong?"

"There! You see, it's right there. That you even have to ask it is what I'm saying."

"I don't see the thread of it either, Ted," I said.

"Look. You and I may come from the same background," he pointed at his wife, "but there are times when we're so different it's almost laughable that we've made it this long."

"Are the kids upstairs?" Ellie questioned.

"Oh, the hell with the kids. Let 'em hear. What the hell's the difference if they hear. What do you want, children who don't know what's going on in their own house?"

"No, I don't." Ellie's voice sounded frightened.

"That's exactly what my parents always did. They tried to keep everything from us, as though we didn't know what was going on. Let 'em hear for once."

"I'm merely. . . ."

"Look, if you'd just let me say this already."

"I'm letting you say anything you want, Ted." Ellie and I watched him walk out of the kitchen, then return.

"You've never been able to understand what my life is made of," he went on. "I tell you my plans, my prospects of what might happen at work, I tell you my dreams. That is, I used to tell you my dreams. Little that you could care."

"I listen to every one of them."

"Listening isn't enough, goddamn it. It's like Tom here. He listens. But it isn't enough. You think my plans are nuts or that I live in the future somehow. Or that I got a lot of pipe dreams."

"I didn't say that."

"You do in your way. You ought to look and listen to yourself so you could see what I see. Here's a stranger comes in this house is more sympathetic to the way I want to work out my future than the woman I married. That's really a laugh. Now that really gets me."

"That's not fair, Ted," I said.

"I don't care about fair," he shot back. "We're way beyond talking about what's fair and what's not fair." Then to me: "I tell you things about my life, you don't come back with all the junk I have to hear from her."

"*Her* is still in this room," Ellie said sharply. "Why don't you speak a little to *her?*"

"I *am* speaking to you. Who the hell you think I'm speaking to? The man in the moon?"

"I thought you might have been speaking to him." She nodded at me.

"When I want to speak with him, I'll speak with him. This is *our* business."

"Hey, maybe I should go," I suggested.

"No sir, you sit right there," Ted insisted. "You want to know about us, you listen to this part too. Every day isn't so rosy. You stay around and see the seamy side, too."

"Ted," Ellie broke in, "you're sounding foolish."

"Oh shut up!" She didn't move. "You stay, Tom. I want you to hear. I work five hard days a week. I ain't got no good prospects for anything like lots of other guys. That newspaper goes under, I'm out a job. I'd like you, Mrs. Know-it-all, to tell me just exactly what I'm supposed to do then. Huh? You got this philosophy you take every day one at a time? Isn't that your usual speech?"

"That's my usual speech," Ellie responded with resignation.

"Yeah. That's it. That's a terrific philosophy. You know where I'd be with that philosophy running my life? Do you know? *Do* you?"

"No, I don't, Ted. Where would you be?"

"You don't care. What's the use?"

"I *do* care. I want to know."

"C'mon, Ted," I said, "we want to hear you."

"O.K. I'd be in the same job I had when I was eleven years old. I'd be delivering for that moron McCrackle or McCarver or whatever the hell his name was."

Ellie began to smile. "Mencken," she corrected him.

"Mencken. McCracken. What the hell's the difference? You don't understand what I'm saying anyway."

"That's not true," his wife answered him. "I do."

"Yeah? Then what am I saying?" He looked at her smugly.

"That if you hadn't had some dream or goal you wouldn't have gone beyond the life you knew as a little boy."

"That's exactly right. So what I'd like to learn from you is, if you understand that, how can you be so, so, I don't know what when it comes to listening to me?"

"I try to listen to you." Ellie's voice was kind.

"Maybe you do then. But our worlds are too different. You can't possibly understand what's in my head."

"I tell you what I believe in the best ways I can."

"That God . . . you mean that God stuff?"

"Yes," she said firmly. "That 'God stuff,' as you call it."

"That's where we part. I mean, that's where it all falls apart."

"Why? Where? What's falling apart, Ted?"

"Us. You, me. The whole thing. It falls apart. You rely on some set of beliefs that bring nothing." His anger, which had subsided, rose again. "God doesn't buy homes. God doesn't pay bills. Men do that. God doesn't provide! Love doesn't provide! You can go to church. . . . "

"I realize that."

"You can go to church every day of the week, my friend, but if I don't work, or you don't work, you don't eat. You ever hear of God throwing down food? Or clothes? Or homes? Does your friend God do *that*?"

"Of course not. That's not why people . . . "

"You see you're wrong there. I'm sorry to correct you, but that's exactly what all those poor slobs go there on Sunday for. They march off to church and give their last pennies to God and beg Him to give them food or shelter, or whatever the hell they ask for."

"I don't think that's what . . . "

"I'll tell you something else. That's exactly why they're poor."

"Who? Who's poor?" Ellie started. "What are you talking about?"

Ted bent over and pointed at her, all the while keeping his distance. "That's why the poor are poor!" he yelled at her. "Am I such a dummy that no one understands me any more? I thought I was being perfectly clear."

"Ted."

"C'mon, Ted," I joined in.

"Ted nothing," he came back. I made another gesture to leave. Ted came at me and grabbed my shoulder, pushing me back in the chair. "You want to think of me as a madman, go ahead. But you'll leave here only when I'm finished."

"C'mon, Ted," I tried again.

"No, *you* listen! Both of you. The reason the poor stay poor is because of what *you* believe," he pointed at Ellie.

"You mean *I'm* the cause of people being poor?" she asked sarcastically.

"That's exactly right. *You're* the cause. All this business of living day by day, of wanting God to solve problems, of not doing things until they actually happen, until they fall into your goddamn lap, *you* believe that, and that's why people like you don't get anywhere. People are making it in this country every day of their lives. You can still have a chance. But this business of laughing at someone 'cause he plans, or praying, that's the end. That's the living end. You hold on to your childhood; you've never let go of it; and we're married almost twenty years. You see your mother as much as you see your husband. I'd love to know what in the hell you two can find to talk about every day. That's something for you to study, Tom. If you *really* want to do an interesting study, that's what you should study: what Ellie and her mother find to talk about every day of every week of every month." Ellie had placed her head in her hands. She made no sound. "But you don't hear me complain about what portion of my salary goes to supporting her, do you?"

"No, I don't hear you complain," Ellie whispered.

"What'd you say?" Ted screamed at her.

She lifted her head and answered him more loudly: "I said, 'No, I don't hear you complain.'"

"No, I don't complain. I just shell out dough left and right for all those little things you bring her every day because that beautiful saint of a father of yours who loved everybody and everybody loved him, never planned, never dreamed. It ain't enough to be nice."

"Don't you dare speak about my father," Ellie said bitterly, staring at him.

"I'll speak about anyone I damn please. Who the hell's paying for this house anyway?"

"You don't have to speak about the dead."

"I'm not speaking about the dead. I'm speaking about poor people; people who think love and niceness and praying in a church are what matter. It's a lot of *shit*! It's all a lot of shit! Your parents were *full* of shit!"

"Ted," she screamed at him. "Stop it!"

"And *my* parents were full of shit too. They all stunk! None of 'em knew what was going on. You know what they did? The led their lives day by day, minded their own business and decided if this is what history brought them, then that's the way it had to be. Destiny is what they call it. They just obeyed their destiny. You go ahead and look around at their children. Who's doing anything worthwhile? Huh? Who's trying to fight? Who's dreaming about the future and not about the past? Huh? You and your mother cause poverty. You sit together like mentals dreaming of the good old days when your father was alive, and none of you seems to give a rat's ass that you were poor."

"Ted, please." Ellie began to weep. My presence made it more difficult for her.

"Ted," I said, "I'm going to go."

"You're not going. I'm not done." We looked at Ellie. "Let her cry. She cries all the time. Maybe we should call her mother over and they could have a good cry together about the old days. Maybe we could make an invention and bring back the dead."

"You're a monster," Ellie sobbed.

"*I'm* the monster? Sure. Of course. *I'm* the monster, because I'm a little different from those idiots who run the church. I speak the truth. I tell you that you *waste* your life. All you have is yesterday and today. That's all all women have. Memories, tears, dreams, MOTHERS! You forget that I remember you as a child. I knew your family. They were doing nothing at all to escape their circumstances. You take a look at rich people someday. You know what they're doing? Right now? I'll tell you, and Tom will back me up, too." He continued to pace up and back across the room. "They're planning so many things for their lives they ain't got time to go to church. They got the lives of their kids planned and their kids' kids. You talk to some rich guy with his insurance policies and his trust funds. You ask them if they live day by day. They're an army, the rich. They march on the future and rip it up, eat it, and spit it out. That's what they do. They beat the future at its own game. Right, Tom? They're there before it. They don't wait to see how their kids are turning out. They put 'em in the best schools, like these finishing schools, so's they can make sure the kids will *have* to turn out right."

"I don't want to hear about the rich," I heard Ellie say.

"Of course you don't. No one wants to hear what really goes on in life. You'd rather believe your daddy's going to come home and give you presents."

"I told you about talking about my father."

"O.K. *My* father then. He came home. . . . When he was alive, he didn't do one goddamn thing to change his life. Not a goddamn thing. Ever! He was supposed to be a perfectly good guy. But he was like you, all caught up with this crap of taking each day one by one and making the best of it you can. You know what you get from that philosophy?"

"Oh, stop already. Please stop."

"Ted . . . " I shouted.

"You get windows over kitchen sinks like this one." I looked at him quizzically. "Windows over kitchen sinks," he repeated, nodding his head up and down. "The rich work to make their lives work out. Everything from their childhood on is bent toward fixing their lives and giving them security. You talk about the ability to make predictions? You should talk to the rich people like I do at work. They've got things figured out you wouldn't even be able to dream of. Believe me, I know. They think in enor-

**151**

mous blocks of time. Not days. Not years, even. They're moving in decades, ten years, all the time left in this century. This ain't no nickel-and-dime stuff. It's all big business. Years at a time they take from the past and add onto the future. That's what their life is based on. Big business. Now, in this shitty little house which is about the best I'm ever going to be able to do, this woman here stands in front of a sink looking out the window all day worrying either about the weather, or whether it's daytime or nighttime. That's all women know. If it's daytime you make breakfast, if it's nighttime you make dinner. Bills, plans, what's going to become of us, they couldn't care less. Nighttime, daytime, all they want to know is what's in the cabinets to eat. Women and children. They're one and the same."

"So what do you want of me, Ted? What do you want of me?" Ellie's voice and tears were frightening to Ted. He moved back, disappearing into the dining area. "O.K., you're a big man, you're doing a great job here in front of us, putting on this big show, probably for Tom. You're doing fine. Now just what is it that you want? Just what do you want me and my mother and *your* children and *my* father to do? Why don't you answer that instead of carrying on here like a mental case? *You* answer, for once. What do *you* want? You want me to work? Is that it? You want the kids to stop going to school and go to work? Here, give me the phone. I'll call up the schools and pull the kids out. That's what you want, isn't it? C'mon, c'mon. Here, big man, give me the phone. Come on!" She held her open hand out in front of her. "HERE!" she screamed. Ted walked toward her.

"Stop it, goddamn it. The both of you." I heard myself yell.

"I'll give you," Ted was saying, "I'll give you the phone, across your fresh mouth is where I'll give you the phone."

"Go ahead," Ellie yelled. "You talk so much. Why don't you do something instead of babbling on like this, like some kind of an escapee from a mental hospital."

Ted's mouth closed; he nodded sarcastically. "Escapee from a mental. . . . This is what I have to take. Every day of my life. I am totally alone, making it possible for four human beings to lead their lives with a little dignity." His voice had quieted somewhat. "Four ungrateful human beings. I don't have a soul to talk to in this house. I see the way people are living. I see the way people are dying, and we're not getting any of it. Either one. I can't even afford to get us ground in the cemetery. Has that, Mrs. Big Mouth, ever crossed that brilliant brain of yours? Where, exactly, would you like them to put my corpse when I die if I don't arrange for a plot? Here? Would you like it in the kitchen maybe? Just where do the poor die? You ever think of that? That, too, is part of the future. Maybe that's what they mean by destiny. Huh? You ever think of that? I got to arrange for that too, pal.

"There's nothing for me to look forward to. I see the future that you and your mother and all those idiots you talk with at church pray to God to take care of you. I *see* the future. I'm already seventy years old and still at the Gazette, still lifting Sunday papers, still dragging my ass around that goddamn hole. You're praying, and I'm working to have enough money to buy a place, and a way to get rid of my body which, if you'd really care to know, was dead a long, long time ago. Let me give you a little lesson." He glared at the two of us before continuing.

"Let me give you both a bit of a lesson. You," he said, pointing to me, "will have to excuse me if I don't sound like some important professor from M.I.T. A man doesn't die when his heart stops. That's not the only death a man has got to look forward to. There are lots of deaths . . . "

"Like when your parents die?" Ellie quietly interrupted.

"NO!" he yelled at her. "Wrong again. Those are the deaths that women fall apart with. Men don't die at the sight of death. You talk to soldiers. They fight with hundreds, thousands of guys falling down all around 'em. No sir, women go to cemeteries and fall apart. Men hold women together because they know more about death than women. They know more about death because they work. They work every damn day of their lives and so they know what it is to reach a point where you can't go any further. Your own little progress is over. Dead. That's the death a man knows. The death of effort. How's that?" he questioned me. "The death of effort. You ever hear of the word incapacitated?" he asked his wife.

"Of course I did," Ellie answered.

"Of course I did," he mocked her in baby talk. "Of course you *didn't*, you mean. You can't know because women can't know the thought every day of your life of something happening and you're not able to work again. That's death, my friend." He glared at Ellie, assured that I, a man, would have to agree. "That's death."

"And women don't have that?" she inquired.

"No, women don't have that. Look at your mother. Someone else has to work so's she can eat. Someone else has to cook. Someone else has to wash up and clean and whatever you do. No sir, women don't have that. You don't know the feelings of these other deaths until you find yourself in a world where you don't have any choice; and you just stay at it, like it or not, knowing you better damn well stay healthy or a whole group of people are going to fall flat on their faces."

"You're talking through your hat," Ellie started. "How hard do you think it would be for all of us to go to work? We could make up the difference. Did *you*, Mr. Bright Ideas, ever think of *that?*"

"Many, many, many times," Ted replied softly. "Many times I've thought about what it would be like having your wife and children working while you sat around the house, sick or something. That, my friend, is another form of death. That may be the worst death of all. When women work it's a fill-in. They're a substitute, and brother, when they put in the substitutes it's because the first team either stinks or can't play. Or maybe," he smiled, "'cause the first team's got a lead they'll never catch. If only it worked that way. If only I could ever get ahead of it, instead of always chasing, chasing, chasing . . . "

"What are you chasing, chasing, chasing?" Ellie asked, at last looking up. "Now that *is* a good question. What is it that you're always after that you can know all these *special* deaths that no one else seems to know anything about? Huh?"

"I'm chasing life!" he yelled back at her. "I'm chasing the rich and the government and my bosses and taxes and bills. That's what I'm chasing. I'm a drowning man. Look at me. I'm a drowning man, chasing after a breath. After air. Is that enough for you? I don't take life day by day and sit back and dream about the beautiful past. Anybody does that has already drowned. You chase, goddamn it. You chase your goals. You chase after the little that might possibly be coming your way. Like a fifty-dollar bonus for Christmas. *I* screw up, lady, and *you* don't get the money that you use to buy Christmas presents. You think bonuses just *come* to you? How do you think it works out there? That somebody just *gives* you things? Things come to you because you work your goddamn ass off, and what's more, and this no woman could ever know, you can work your ass off every day of your life, eight to six every day of your life, and end up with this!" He held his hand up, making a zero sign with his thumb and index finger. "Zero!" he yelled. "Nothing!" You can work and work just like your father did and end up with nothing!"

"He was a happy man on the day he died."

"The hell he was. You don't know anything about your father. You ask your brother Milt about your father. You ask him just how happy he was in his life. He kept it from all of you. Ask your mother. She knows. Maybe now that you're a big girl she'll tell you some of the real facts of life. Go ask her when you see her tomorrow. Go tonight. Go now, for Christ's sake; it's been almost an hour since you've seen the old lady." He glanced up at the kitchen clock. I looked too and he caught me. "One more minute, then you can go too," he ordered me. "When you go there ask your mother about his drinking."

"Shut up, Ted." Ellie was angered and embarrassed. She looked at me. On several occasions we had spoken of her father's alcoholism, but the subject was not to be mentioned, apparently, when the three of us were together.

"I'm not supposed to be saying anything about that, eh? I'm supposed to keep my mouth shut so the world can think that everything around us and our beautiful childhoods was perfect? Well, I can't. You ask your mother about how many times your father died in his life before the Good Lord took him away. Ask her. She'll tell you ten thousand. Ten million. He died every night of his life. Every night he came home to that dump your family lived in, he died. You think it's easy for a man to look around every day at his life, where he worked, where he lives, and be reminded of what a failure he is and always will be? That's the death part, Ellie. And that's the part, reporter, you better write about if you want to understand us. The people like us. It's that double hit; that seeing every day of your life what you got and *knowing*, knowing like your own name, that it ain't ever going to get any better. That's what you live with, and that's what your father had in his mind and in his body every day of his life. That's why a man drinks. Believe me, I know. You keep it from your children just so long. But in this country, there isn't a man who fails and holds his head up. Any man who holds his head up after he loses is just trying to protect himself. No one likes a loser. That's why the rich can't stand us. That's why we moved here. Your home, my house, what we had together all those years were *prisons*. They were advertisements of how much we didn't have. You got any doubts about it, you just turn on the TV and see the way people are living, with their new cars and their boats, and their homes in the country. How many times a day they have to remind you of that, I'd like to know?"

For the first time, Ellie was nodding assent. I had seen her face show relief moments before when, unthinkingly, Ted had used the phrase, "the Good Lord took him away." Now she was her husband's wife, his woman, for at last the direction of his anguish had shifted, and it was America, the rich, social classes, me, that he attacked and held responsible for the perceptions of time that he nurtured. Finally she could feel that connection with a history and with a group of people who struggle precisely because the perceptions, attitudes, and ways of others were more powerful, more successful, perhaps, than they, cause them to struggle. No longer was it men against women; it was the poor against the rich, those who can, with a genuine sense of autonomy and possibility underwriting it, achieve with dignity, and those who must sweat out the work, the waiting, and the decisions of bosses for bonuses and a chance to move ahead slightly.

Ted stood, not exactly next to his wife, but closer to her, leaving me, still seated, the third person. Reflecting on his words, I sought a proper way to excuse myself. For minutes the three of us were silent. Ellie and I staring at the table top, Ted standing near us, motionless. I could hear him breathing, and I could feel my eyebrows rising and falling, as though something in me wanted to signal the two of them. We will all three of us go on from here, is what the silence meant to me. We will all face the forms of death, as Ted had said, that each of us faces, not every day perhaps, but often enough. And we will dream of a past, of homes perhaps where it is warm, and where everyone is content. We will know experiences that make us live moment by moment, for as long as each moment lasts, just as we will think up something for the future, a plan, a prediction, a style of ignoring it, almost as children generate some new idea for a game they have played before.

Ted broke the silence. His voice was even and resolute. "I want you to know, Tom, that you have my permission to write anything you want about this afternoon. All of it. I'm pretty sure Ellie feels the same way."

"I do. Yes, I do," Ellie said.

When I looked up at them they were already looking intently at me. "I appreciate that," I responded. "I don't ever know exactly what I'll be writing, of course."

"I don't know much about writing," Ted began. "I don't want to ever tell a man how to do his work if I don't know how to do that work better than that man. But I think it might just be good for you to take a shot at writing this. Don't worry about us. You go ahead and write what you feel you should. Call us about our meeting next week." That was all he said that afternoon.

Two feelings had come over me, two feelings as distinct as shaking hands with both Grazianos simultaneously, Ted's right hand in my right hand, Ellie's hand in my left hand. I felt, first, that I had been as moved by these two people as I had ever been by anyone or anything, and that because of this resonance deep inside me, our lives were now married. But I felt, too, a desire to make all three of us, through my writing, special and unforgettable; famous, I suppose. I was half-way home, driving through an angry rain that made visibility almost impossible, before the one word that swirled in my head finally came to rest: immortality.

In the end, the overriding dimension of time in human experience is the dimension of freedom. For freedom implies the right to embrace one's past, one's immediate experiences, and one's prospects as one chooses, all according to an equitable reality. Like the word "future," freedom implies possibility. When freedom is denied, therefore, a person's past, present, or future, or all three, may also be denied. And so a past is rejected, prospects are ruled outrageous, and a man and woman remain alone to suffer an anguish they are led to believe each has caused the other. In fact, it is a culture's power and the ways of social systems that sting human possibility and kill the belief in an honorable past, a tolerable present, and the prospect of a generous future.

. . . . . . . . . . . .

## QUESTIONS FOR A SECOND READING

1. Ted locates his life in the future—at least he spends much of his time think-ing about the future and preparing for it. When you go back to the essay, look at those passages (like the one on p. 153) where he talks about the future. What does he say? If you were to take these passages as "keys" to understanding Ted and his view of the world, what would you notice? What would you be able to say?

2. Ted wants to be in control, or feels he has to be. What about Ellie? Review those sections of the essay where she talks about herself, about her beliefs, values, and actions. How does she see herself and her role in their rela-tionship?

3. Reread the sections of the essay where Ted and Ellie offer metaphors for their relationship—the football game for Ted, and the clocks that run on different time for Ellie. What do the metaphors say about the way these two people understand themselves and their differences? What do they allow the Grazianos to see? What do they keep them from seeing? How might you extend these metaphors to serve your own analysis of these two people?

## ASSIGNMENTS FOR WRITING

1. Ted Graziano realizes that he and his wife have managed to keep their marriage together despite what he claims are profound differences. Write an essay in which you define the important differences between the Gra-zianos and explain what these might be said to represent (like the differ-ences, for example, between two personality types, or between men and women of a particular generation, social class, or culture). If you take the Grazianos as a case for study, in other words, what generalizations might you make?

2. Write an essay explaining what you see as the most significant or revealing passage if you are interested in understanding Ted. What do you see in that passage that others might have missed? And what, then, can you say to help others understand Ted as you do?

3. Write an essay explaining what you see as the most significant or revealing passage if you are interested in understanding Ellie. What do you see in that passage that others might have missed? And what, then, can you say to help others understand Ellie as you do?

## MAKING CONNECTIONS

1. Gloria Steinem, in "Ruth's Song (Because She Could Not Sing It)" (p. 542), tells her mother's story in a careful and precise way, and she avoids the temptation to settle for a quick summary and easy conclusions. She identifies moments and stories in her mother's life that seem to her telling or significant in some way, especially in how they might help her understand Ruth's change or transformation and then, later, what she calls the formidable forces arrayed against Ruth.

   Write an essay in which you tell Ellie Graziano's story as Steinem might, especially if she were interested in identifying and explaining what she would call formidable forces arrayed against Ellie. What might they be, and how might Steinem explain them? What moments or incidents from the interview might Steinem choose as telling or significant in her argument about the formidable forces arrayed against Ellie? Would these be the same passages that strike you as important? And what stories of Ellie's might Steinem choose to retell? How would they advance her argument?

2. Roland Barthes, in "The World of Wrestling" and "Striptease" (p. 24), reads fairly common activities—wrestling and striptease—to reveal them as mythologies, and to demonstrate the possibility that events, including the things and people associated with them, are both what they claim to be and not at all what they claim to be. What happens to Ted Graziano if you read him, à la Barthes, as a character in a common and powerful myth?

   Write an essay in which you read this selection as a spectacle or a story, as something made for public consumption. What key passages or moments would you identify as significant for explaining Ted as a character in a myth? How might those passages demonstrate what Barthes calls "juxtaposed meanings," meanings that represent both "common" and "mythic" qualities in the story Cottle and Klineberg have constructed out of interviews with the Grazianos?

# RALPH WALDO EMERSON

$R$ ALPH WALDO EMERSON (1803–1882) is probably one of the most famous, most eloquent, and least read figures in American literature. He was a poet, a preacher, a visionary, and an itinerant lecturer; he left behind a remarkable series of essays, lectures, notebooks, and journals; and yet he is best known for his influence on those who followed him: Melville, Thoreau, Whitman, Dickinson, Frost, Hart Crane, and Wallace Stevens.

Textbooks most often introduce Emerson as the central figure in American transcendentalism. He does not, however, have to be read as a representative philosopher; to do so, in fact, violates his own feisty individualism and his struggle to stay free of schools of thought and the pressure of received opinion. He can be read for the pleasure of his unusual style of speaking and thinking and for the force of his immediate argument. The essay that follows, "The American Scholar," is about education, including university education, and it says some rather surprising things, including the following about the use of books (like the one you are reading right now): "Books are for the scholar's idle times," and "Meek young men grow up in libraries, believing it their duty to accept the views, which Cicero, which Locke, which Bacon, have given, forgetful that Cicero, Locke, and Bacon were only

*young men in libraries when they wrote these books." It is a shame to think that
the only way to read Emerson is as an example of what people once thought (and,
in fact, it is wrong to think that in the nineteenth century most people thought or
said such things). It is possible, alternatively, to read Emerson as a person with
something to say to American scholars at today's colleges and universities.*

*"The American Scholar" was presented as a lecture to the Harvard chapter of
Phi Beta Kappa on August 31, 1837. It has been called "the most influential address
ever made before an American college audience," and America's "intellectual Dec-
laration of Independence." It was also called "misty, dreamy, and unintelligible."
Emerson's prose is not orderly, straightforward, or systematic. It does not easily
or quickly connect one thing to another but puts the responsibility in the hands of
the reader—in your hands—which, according to one of the essay's arguments, is
exactly where it belongs.*

# The American Scholar

An Oration
Delivered Before the Phi Beta Kappa Society,
at Cambridge, August 31, 1837

MR. PRESIDENT, AND GENTLEMEN,

I greet you on the re-commencement of our literary year. Our anniversary is one of hope, and, perhaps, not enough of labor. We do not meet
for games of strength or skill, for the recitation of histories, tragedies and
odes, like the ancient Greeks; for parliaments of love and poesy, like the
Troubadours; nor for the advancement of science, like our contemporaries
in the British and European capitals. Thus far, our holiday has been simply
a friendly sign of the survival of the love of letters amongst a people too
busy to give to letters any more. As such, it is precious as the sign of an
indestructible instinct. Perhaps the time is already come, when it ought to
be, and will be something else; when the sluggard intellect of this continent
will look from under its iron lids and fill the postponed expectation of the
world with something better than the exertions of mechanical skill. Our
day of dependence, our long apprenticeship to the learning of other lands,
draws to a close. The millions that around us are rushing into life, cannot
always be fed on the sere remains of foreign harvests. Events, actions arise,
that must be sung, that will sing themselves. Who can doubt that poetry
will revive and lead in a new age, as the star in the constellation Harp

which now flames in our zenith, astronomers announce, shall one day be the pole-star for a thousand years?

In the light of this hope, I accept the topic which not only usage, but the nature of our association, seem to prescribe to this day—the American Scholar. Year by year, we come up hither to read one more chapter of his biography. Let us inquire what light new days and events have thrown on his character, his duties, and his hopes.

It is one of those fables, which out of an unknown antiquity, convey an unlooked-for wisdom, that the gods, in the beginning, divided Man into men, that he might be more helpful to himself; just as the hand was divided into fingers, the better to answer its end.

The old fable covers a doctrine ever new and sublime; that there is One Man,—present to all particular men only partially, or through one faculty; and that you must take the whole society to find the whole man. Man is not a farmer, or a professor, or an engineer, but he is all. Man is priest, and scholar, and statesman, and producer, and soldier. In the *divided* or social state, these functions are parcelled out to individuals, each of whom aims to do his stint of the joint work, whilst each other performs his. The fable implies that the individual, to possess himself, must sometimes return from his own labor to embrace all the other laborers. But unfortunately, this original unit, this fountain of power, has been so distributed to multitudes, has been so minutely subdivided and peddled out, that it is spilled into drops, and cannot be gathered. The state of society is one in which the members have suffered amputation from the trunk, and strut about so many walking monsters,—a good finger, a neck, a stomach, an elbow, but never a man.

Man is thus metamorphosed into a thing, into many things. The planter, who is Man sent out into the field to gather food, is seldom cheered by any idea of the true dignity of his ministry. He sees his bushel and his cart, and nothing beyond, and sinks into the farmer, instead of Man on the farm. The tradesman scarcely ever gives an ideal worth to his work, but is ridden by the routine of his craft, and the soul is subject to dollars. The priest becomes a form; the attorney, a statute-book; the mechanic, a machine; the sailor, a rope of a ship.

In this distribution of functions, the scholar is the delegated intellect. In the right state, he is, *Man Thinking*. In the degenerate state, when the victim of society, he tends to become a mere thinker, or, still worse, the parrot of other men's thinking.

In this view of him, as Man Thinking, the whole theory of his office is contained. Him nature solicits, with all her placid, all her monitory pictures. Him the past instructs. Him the future invites. Is not, indeed, every man a student, and do not all things exist for the student's behoof? And, finally, is not the true scholar the only true master? But, as the old oracle said, "All things have two handles. Beware of the wrong one." In life, too often, the scholar errs with mankind and forfeits his privilege. Let us see him in his school, and consider him in reference to the main influences he receives.

## I

The first in time and the first in importance of the influences upon the mind is that of nature. Every day, the sun; and, after sunset, night and her stars. Ever the winds blow; ever the grass grows. Every day, men and women, conversing, beholding and beholden. The scholar must needs stand wistful and admiring before this great spectacle. He must settle its value in his mind. What is nature to him? There is never a beginning, there is never an end to the inexplicable continuity of this web of God, but always circular power returning into itself. Therein it resembles his own spirit, whose beginning, whose ending he never can find—so entire, so boundless. Far, too, as her splendors shine, system on system shooting like rays, upward, downward, without centre, without circumference,—in the mass and in the particle nature hastens to render account of herself to the mind. Classification begins. To the young mind, every thing is individual, stands by itself. By and by, it finds how to join two things, and see in them one nature; then three, then three thousand; and so, tyrannized over by its own unifying instinct, it goes on trying things together, diminishing anomalies, discovering roots running under ground, whereby contrary and remote things cohere, and flower out from one stem. It presently learns, that, since the dawn of history, there has been a constant accumulation and classifying of facts. But what is classification but the perceiving that these objects are not chaotic, and are not foreign, but have a law which is also a law of the human mind? The astronomer discovers that geometry, a pure abstraction of the human mind, is the measure of planetary motion. The chemist finds proportions and intelligible method throughout matter: and science is nothing but the finding of analogy, identity in the most remote parts. The ambitious soul sits down before each refractory fact; one after another, reduces all strange constitutions, all new powers, to their class and their law, and goes on forever to animate the last fibre of organization, the outskirts of nature, by insight.

Thus to him, to this school-boy under the bending dome of day, is suggested, that he and it proceed from one root; one is leaf and one is flower; relation, sympathy, stirring in every vein. And what is that Root? Is not that the soul of his soul?—A thought too bold—a dream too wild. Yet when this spiritual light shall have revealed the law of more earthly natures,— when he has learned to worship the soul, and to see that the natural philosophy that now is, is only the first gropings of its gigantic hand, he shall look forward to an ever expanding knowledge as to a becoming creator.

He shall see that nature is the opposite of the soul, answering to it part for part. One is seal, and one is print. Its beauty is the beauty of his own mind. Its laws are the laws of his own mind. Nature then becomes to him the measure of his attainments. So much of nature as he is ignorant of, so much of his own mind does he not yet possess. And, in fine, the ancient precept, "Know thyself," and the modern precept, "Study nature," becomes at last one maxim.

## II

The next great influence into the spirit of the scholar, is, the mind of the Past,—in whatever form, whether of literature, of art, of institutions, that mind is inscribed. Books are the best type of the influence of the past, and perhaps we shall get at the truth—learn the amount of the influence more conveniently—by considering their value alone.

The theory of books is noble. The scholar of the first age received into him the world around; brooded thereon; gave it the new arrangement of his own mind, and uttered it again. It came into him—life; it went out from him—truth. It came to him—short-lived actions; it went out from him—immortal thoughts. It came to him—business; it went from him—poetry. It was—dead fact; now, it is quick thought. It can stand, and it can go. It now endures, it now flies, it now inspires. Precisely in proportion to the depth of mind from which it issued, so high does it soar, so long does it sing.

Or, I might say, it depends on how far the process had gone, of transmuting life into truth. In proportion to the completeness of the distillation, so will the purity and imperishableness of the product be. But none is quite perfect. As no air-pump can by any means make a perfect vacuum, so neither can any artist entirely exclude the conventional, the local, the perishable from his book, or write a book of pure thought that shall be as efficient, in all respects, to a remote posterity, as to contemporaries, or rather to the second age. Each age, it is found, must write its own books; or rather, each generation for the next succeeding. The books of an older period will not fit this.

Yet hence arises a grave mischief. The sacredness which attaches to the act of creation,—the act of thought,—is instantly transferred to the record. The poet chanting, was felt to be a divine man. Henceforth the chant is divine also. The writer was a just and wise spirit. Henceforward it is settled, the book is perfect; as love of the hero corrupts into worship of his statue. Instantly, the book becomes noxious. The guide is a tyrant. We sought a brother, and lo, a governor. The sluggish and perverted mind of the multitude, always slow to open to the incursions of Reason, having once so opened, having once received this book, stands upon it, and makes an outcry, if it is disparaged. Colleges are built on it. Books are written on it by thinkers, not by Man Thinking; by men of talent, that is, who start wrong, who set out from accepted dogmas, not from their own sight of principles. Meek young men grow up in libraries, believing it their duty to accept the views which Cicero, which Locke, which Bacon have given, forgetful that Cicero, Locke and Bacon were only young men in libraries when they wrote these books.

Hence, instead of Man Thinking, we have the bookworm. Hence, the book-learned class, who value books, as such; not as related to nature and the human constitution, but as making a sort of Third Estate with the world and the soul. Hence, the restorers of readings, the emendators, the biblio-maniacs of all degrees.

This is bad; this is worse than it seems. Books are the best of things, well used; abused, among the worst. What is the right use? What is the one end which all means go to effect? They are for nothing but to inspire. I had better never see a book than to be warped by its attraction clean out of my own orbit, and made a satellite instead of a system. The one thing in the world of value, is, the active soul,—the soul, free, sovereign, active. This every man is entitled to; this every man contains within him, although in almost all men, obstructed, and as yet unborn. The soul active sees absolute truth; and utters truth, or creates. In this action, it is genius; not the privilege of here and there a favorite, but the sound estate of every man. In its essence, it is progressive. The book, the college, the school of art, the institution of any kind, stop with some past utterance of genius. This is good, say they,—let us hold by this. They pin me down. They look backward and not forward. But genius always looks forward. The eyes of man are set in his forehead, not in his hindhead. Man hopes. Genius creates. To create,—to create,—is the proof of a divine presence. Whatever talents may be, if the man create not, the pure efflux of the Deity is not his:— cinders and smoke, there may be, but not yet flame. There are creative manners, there are creative actions, and creative words; manners, actions, words, that is, indicative of no custom or authority, but springing spontaneous from the mind's own sense of good and fair.

On the other part, instead of being its own seer, let it receive always from another mind its truth, though it were in torrents of light, without periods of solitude, inquest and self-recovery, and a fatal disservice is done. Genius is always sufficiently the enemy of genius by over-influence. The literature of every nation bear me witness. The English dramatic poets have Shakspearized now for two hundred years.

Undoubtedly there is a right way of reading,—so it be sternly subordinated. Man Thinking must not be subdued by his instruments. Books are for the scholar's idle times. When he can read God directly, the hour is too precious to be wasted in other men's transcripts of their readings. But when the intervals of darkness come, as come they must,—when the soul seeth not, when the sun is hid, and the stars withdraw their shin-ing,—we repair to the lamps which were kindled by their ray to guide our steps to the East again, where the dawn is. We hear that we may speak. The Arabian proverb says, "A fig tree looking on a fig tree, becometh fruit-ful."

It is remarkable, the character of the pleasure we derive from the best books. They impress us ever with the conviction that one nature wrote and the same reads. We read the verses of one of the great English poets, of Chaucer, of Marvell, of Dryden, with the most modern joy,—with a plea-sure, I mean, which is in great part caused by the abstraction of all *time* from their verses. There is some awe mixed with the joy of our surprise, when this poet, who lived in some past world, two or three hundred years ago, says that which lies close to my own soul, that which I also had well-nigh thought and said. But for the evidence thence afforded to the philo-sophical doctrine of the identity of all minds, we should suppose some pre-established harmony, some foresight of souls that were to be, and some preparation of stores for their future wants, like the fact observed in in-sects, who lay up food before death for the young grub they shall never see.

I would not be hurried by any love of system, by any exaggeration of instincts, to underrate the Book. We all know, that as the human body can be nourished on any food, though it were boiled grass and the broth of shoes, so the human mind can be fed by any knowledge. And great and heroic men have existed, who had almost no other information than by the printed page. I only would say, that it needs a strong head to bear that diet. One must be an inventor to read well. As the proverb says, "He that would bring home the wealth of the Indies, must carry out the wealth of the Indies." There is then creative reading, as well as creative writing. When the mind is braced by labor and invention, the page of whatever book we read becomes luminous with manifold allusion. Every sentence is doubly significant, and the sense of our author is as broad as the world. We then see, what is always true, that as the seer's hour of vision is short and rare among heavy days and months, so is its record, perchance, the least part of his volume. The discerning will read in his Plato or Shak-speare, only that least part,—only the authentic utterances of the oracle,—and all the rest he rejects, were it never so many times Plato's and Shak-speare's.

Of course, there is a portion of reading quite indispensable to a wise man. History and exact science he must learn by laborious reading. Col-leges, in like manner, have their indispensable office,—to teach elements. But they can only highly serve us, when they aim not to drill, but to create; when they gather from far every ray of various genius to their hospitable halls, and, by the concentrated fires, set the hearts of their youth on flame.

Thought and knowledge are natures in which apparatus and pretension avail nothing. Gowns, and pecuniary foundations, though of towns of gold, can never countervail the least sentence or syllable of wit. Forget this, and our American colleges will recede in their public importance whilst they grow richer every year.

## III

There goes in the world a notion that the scholar should be a recluse, a valetudinarian,—as unfit for any handiwork or public labor, as a penknife for an axe. The so-called "practical men" sneer at speculative men, as if, because they speculate or *see*, they could do nothing. I have heard it said that the clergy,—who are always more universally than any other class, the scholars of their day,—are addressed as women: that the rough, spontaneous conversation of men they do not hear, but only a mincing and diluted speech. They are often virtually disfranchised; and, indeed, there are advocates for their celibacy. As far as this is true of the studious classes, it is not just and wise. Action is with the scholar subordinate, but it is essential. Without it, he is not yet man. Without it, thought can never ripen into truth. Whilst the world hangs before the eye as a cloud of beauty, we cannot even see its beauty. Inaction is cowardice, but there can be no scholar without the heroic mind. The preamble of thought, the transition through which it passes from the unconscious to the conscious, is action. Only so much do I know, as I have lived. Instantly we know whose words are loaded with life, and whose not.

The world,—this shadow of the soul, or *other me*, lies wide around. Its attractions are the keys which unlock my thoughts and make me acquainted with myself. I run eagerly into the resounding tumult. I grasp the hands of those next to me, and take my place in the ring to suffer and to work, taught by an instinct that so shall the dumb abyss be vocal with speech. I pierce its order; I dissipate its fear; I dispose of it within the circuit of my expanding life. So much only of life as I know by experience, so much of wilderness have I vanquished and planted, or so far have I extended my being, my dominion. I do not see how any man can afford, for the sake of his nerves and his nap, to spare any action in which he can partake. It is pearls and rubies to his discourse. Drudgery, calamity, exasperation, want, are instructers in eloquence and wisdom. The true scholar grudges every opportunity of action past by, as a loss of power.

It is the raw material out of which the intellect moulds her splendid products. A strange process too, this, by which experience is converted into thought, as a mulberry leaf is converted into satin. The manufacture goes forward at all hours.

The actions and events of our childhood and youth are now matters of calmest observation. They lie like fair pictures in the air. Not so with our recent actions,—with the business which we now have in hand. On this we are quite unable to speculate. Our affections as yet circulate through it. We no more feel or know it, than we feel the feet, or the hand, or the brain of our body. The new deed is yet a part of life,—remains for a time immersed in our unconscious life. In some contemplative hour, it detaches itself from the life like a ripe fruit, to become a thought of the mind. Instantly, it is raised, transfigured; the corruptible has put on incorruption. Always now it is an object of beauty, however base its origin and neighborhood. Observe, too, the impossibility of antedating this act. In its grub state, it cannot fly, it cannot shine,—it is a dull grub. But suddenly, without observation, the selfsame thing unfurls beautiful wings, and is an angel of wisdom. So is there no fact, no event, in our private history, which shall not, sooner or later, lose its adhesive inert form, and astonish us by soaring from our body into the empyrean. Cradle and infancy, school and playground, the fear of boys, and dogs, and ferules, the love of little maids and berries, and many another fact that once filled the whole sky, are gone already; friend and relative, profession and party, town and country, nation and world, must also soar and sing.

Of course, he who has put forth his total strength in fit actions, has the richest return of wisdom. I will not shut myself out of this globe of action and transplant an oak into a flower pot, there to hunger and pine; nor trust the revenue of some single faculty, and exhaust one vein of thought, much like those Savoyards, who, getting their livelihood by carving shepherds, shepherdesses, and smoking Dutchmen, for all Europe, went out one day to the mountain to find stock, and discovered that they had whittled up the last of their pine trees. Authors we have in numbers, who have written out their vein, and who, moved by a commendable prudence, sail for Greece or Palestine, follow the trapper into the prairie, or ramble round Algiers to replenish their merchantable stock.

If it were only for a vocabulary the scholar would be covetous of action. Life is our dictionary. Years are well spent in country labors; in town—in the insight into trades and manufactures; in frank intercourse with many men and women; in science; in art; to the one end of mastering in all their facts a language, by which to illustrate and embody our perceptions. I learn immediately from any speaker how much he has already lived, through the poverty or the splendor of his speech. Life lies behind us as the quarry from whence we get tiles and copestones for the masonry of to-day. This is the way to learn grammar. Colleges and books only copy the language which the field and the work-yard made.

But the final value of action, like that of books, and better than books, is, that it is a resource. That great principle of Undulation in nature, that shows itself in the inspiring and expiring of the breath; in desire and satiety; in the ebb and flow of the sea, in day and night, in heat and cold, and as yet more deeply ingrained in every atom and every fluid, is known to us under the name of Polarity,—these "fits of easy transmission and reflection," as Newton called them, are the law of nature because they are the law of spirit.

The mind now thinks; now acts; and each fit reproduces the other. When the artist has exhausted his materials, when the fancy no longer paints, when thoughts are no longer apprehended, and books are a weariness,—he has always the resource *to live*. Character is higher than intellect. Thinking is the function. Living is the functionary. The stream retreats to its source. A great soul will be strong to live, as well as strong to think. Does he lack organ or medium to impart his truths? He can still fall back on this elemental force of living them. This is a total act. Thinking is a partial act. Let the grandeur of justice shine in his affairs. Let the beauty of affection cheer his lowly roof. Those "far from fame" who dwell and act with him, will feel the force of his constitution in the doings and passages of the day better than it can be measured by any public and designed display. Time shall teach him that the scholar loses no hour which the man lives. Herein he unfolds the sacred germ of his instinct, screened from influence. What is lost in seemliness is gained in strength. Not out of those on whom systems of education have exhausted their culture, comes the helpful giant to destroy the old or to build the new, but out of unhand-selled savage nature, out of terrible Druids and Berserkirs, come at last Alfred and Shakspeare.

I hear therefore with joy whatever is beginning to be said of the dignity and necessity of labor to every citizen. There is virtue yet in the hoe and the spade, for learned as well as for unlearned hands. And labor is every where welcome; always we are invited to work; only be this limitation observed, that a man shall not for the sake of wider activity sacrifice any opinion to the popular judgments and modes of action.

I have now spoken of the education of the scholar by nature, by books, and by action. It remains to say somewhat of his duties.

They are such as become Man Thinking. They may all be comprised in self-trust. The office of the scholar is to cheer, to raise, and to guide men by showing them facts amidst appearances. He plies the slow, unhonored, and unpaid task of observation. Flamsteed and Herschel, in their glazed observatories, may catalogue the stars with the praise of all men, and, the results being splendid and useful, honor is sure. But he, in his private observatory, cataloguing obscure and nebulous stars of the human mind, which as yet no man has thought of as such,—watching days and months, sometimes, for a few facts; correcting still his old records;—must relinquish display and immediate fame. In the long period of his preparation, he must betray often an ignorance and shiftlessness in popular arts, incurring the disdain of the able who shoulder him aside. Long he must stammer in his speech; often forego the living for the dead. Worse yet, he must accept—how often! poverty and solitude. For the ease and pleasure of treading the old road, accepting the fashions, the education, the religion of society, he takes the cross of making his own, and, of course, the self-accusation, the faint heart, the frequent uncertainty and loss of time which are the nettles and tangling vines in the way of the self-relying and self-directed; and the state of virtual hostility in which he seems to stand to society, and especially to educated society. For all this loss and scorn, what offset? He is to find consolation in exercising the highest functions of human nature. He is one who raises himself from private considerations, and breathes and lives on public and illustrious thoughts. He is the world's eye. He is the world's heart. He is to resist the vulgar prosperity that retrogrades ever to barbarism, by preserving and communicating heroic sentiments, noble biographies, melodious verse, and the conclusions of history. Whatsoever oracles the human heart in all emergencies, in all solemn hours has uttered as its commentary on the world of actions,—these he shall receive and impart. And whatsoever new verdict Reason from her inviolable seat pronounces on the passing men and events of to-day,—this he shall hear and promulgate.

These being his functions, it becomes him to feel all confidence in himself, and to defer never to the popular cry. He and he only knows the world. The world of any moment is the merest appearance. Some great decorum, some fetish of a government, some ephemeral trade, or war, or man, is cried up by half mankind and cried down by the other half, as if all depended on this particular up or down. The odds are that the whole question is not worth the poorest thought which the scholar has lost in listening to the controversy. Let him not quit his belief that a popgun is a popgun, though the ancient and honorable of the earth affirm it to be the crack of doom. In silence, in steadiness, in severe abstraction, let him hold by himself; add observation to observation, patient of neglect, patient of reproach; and bide his own time,—happy enough if he can satisfy himself alone that this day he has seen something truly. Success treads on every right step. For the instinct is sure that prompts him to tell his brother what he thinks. He then learns that in going down into the secrets of his own mind, he has descended into the secrets of all minds. He learns that he who has mastered any law in his private thoughts, is master to that extent of all men whose language he speaks, and of all into whose language his own can be translated. The poet in utter solitude remembering his spontaneous thoughts and recording them, is found to have recorded that which men in crowded cities find true for them also. The orator distrusts at first the fitness of his frank confessions,—his want of knowledge of the persons he addresses,—until he finds that he is the complement of his hearers;—that they drink his words because he fulfils for them their own nature; the deeper he dives into his privatest secretest presentiment,—to his wonder he finds, this is the most acceptable, most public, and universally true. The people delight in it; the better part of every man feels. This is my music; this is myself.

In self-trust, all the virtues are comprehended. Free should the scholar be,—free and brave. Free even to the definition of freedom, "without any hindrance that does not arise out of his own constitution." Brave; for fear is a thing which a scholar by his very function puts behind him. Fear always springs from ignorace. It is a shame to him if his tranquility, amid dangerous times, arises from the presumption that like children and women, his is a protected class; or if he seek a temporary peace by the diversion of his thoughts from politics or vexed questions, hiding his head like an ostrich in the flowering bushes, peeping into microscopes, and turning rhymes, as a boy whistles to keep his courage up. So is the danger a danger still: so is the fear worse. Manlike let him turn and face it. Let him look into its eye and search its nature, inspect its origin,—see the whelping of this lion,—which lies no great way back; he will then find in himself a perfect comprehension of its nature and extent; he will have made his hands meet on the other side, and can henceforth defy it, and pass on superior. The world is his who can see through its pretension. What deafness, what stone-blind custom, what overgrown error you behold, is there only by sufferance,—by your sufferance. See it to be a lie, and you have already dealt it its mortal blow.

Yes, we are the cowed,—we the trustless. It is a mischievous notion that we are come late into nature; that the world was finished a long time ago. As the world was plastic and fluid in the hands of God, so it is ever to so much of his attributes as we bring to it. To ignorance and sin, it is flint. They adapt themselves to it as they may; but in proportion as a man has anything in him divine, the firmament flows before him, and takes his signet and form. Not he is great who can alter matter, but he who can alter my state of mind. They are the kings of the world who give the color of their present thought to all nature and all art, and persuade men by the cheerful serenity of their carrying the matter, that this thing which they do, is the apple which the ages have desired to pluck, now at last ripe, and inviting nations to the harvest. The great man makes the great thing. Wherever Macdonald sits, there is the head of the table. Linnæus makes botany the most alluring of studies and wins it from the farmer and the herb-woman. Davy, chemistry: and Cuvier, fossils. The day is always his, who works in it with serenity and great aims. The unstable estimates of men crowd to him whose mind is filled with a truth, as the heaped waves of the Atlantic follow the moon.

For this self-trust, the reason is deeper than can be fathomed,—darker than can be enlightened. I might not carry with me the feeling of my audience in stating my own belief. But I have already shown the ground of my hope, in adverting to the doctrine that man is one. I believe man has been wronged: he has wronged himself. He has almost lost the light that can lead him back to his prerogatives. Men are become of no account. Men in history, men in the world of to-day are bugs, are spawn, and are called "the mass" and "the herd." In a century, in a millenium, one or two men; that is to say—one or two approximations to the right state of every man. All the rest behold in the hero or the poet their own green and crude being—ripened; yes, and are content to be less, so *that* may attain to its full stature. What a testimony—full of grandeur, full of pity, is borne to the demands of his own nature, by the poor clansman, the poor partisan, who rejoices in the glory of his chief. The poor and the low find some amends to their immense moral capacity, for their acquiescence in a political and social inferiority. They are content to be brushed like flies from the path of a great person, so that justice shall be done by him to that common nature which it is the dearest desire of all to see enlarged and glorified. They sun themselves in the great man's light, and feel it to be their own element. They cast the dignity of man from their downtrod selves upon the shoulders of a hero, and will perish to add one drop of blood to make that great heart beat, those giant sinews combat and conquer. He lives for us, and we live in him.

Men such as they are, very naturally seek money or power; and power because it is as good as money,—the "spoils," so called, "of office." And why not? for they aspire to the highest, and this, in their sleep-walking, they dream is highest. Wake them, and they shall quit the false good and leap to the true, and leave governments to clerks and desks. This revolution is to be wrought by the gradual domestication of the idea of Culture. The main enterprise of the world for splendor, for extent, is the upbuilding of a man. Here are the materials strown along the ground. The private life of one man shall be a more illustrious monarchy,—more formidable to its enemy, more sweet and serene in its influence to its friend, than any kingdom in history. For a man, rightly viewed, comprehendeth the particular natures of all men. Each philosopher, each bard, each actor, has only done for me, as by a delegate, what one day I can do for myself. The books which once we valued more than the apple of the eye, we have quite exhausted. What is that but saying that we have come up with the point of view which the universal mind took through the eyes of that one scribe; we have been that man, and have passed on. First, one; then, another; we drain all cisterns, and waxing greater by all these supplies, we crave a better and more abundant food. The man has never lived that can feed us ever. The human mind cannot be enshrined in a person who shall set a barrier on any one side to this unbounded, unboundable empire. It is one central fire which flaming now out of the lips of Etna, lightens the capes of Sicily; and now out of the throat of Vesuvius, illuminates the towers and vineyards of Naples. It is one light which beams out of a thousand stars. It is one soul which animates all men.

But I have dwelt perhaps tediously upon this abstraction of the Scholar. I ought not to delay longer to add what I have to say, of nearer reference to the time and to this country.

Historically, there is thought to be a difference in the ideas which predominate over successive epochs, and there are data for marking the genius of the Classic, of the Romantic, and now of the Reflective or Philosophical age. With the views I have intimated of the oneness or the identity of the mind through all individuals, I do not much dwell on these differences. In fact, I believe each individual passes through all three. The boy is a Greek; the youth, romantic; the adult, reflective. I deny not, however, that a revolution in the leading idea may be distinctly enough traced.

Our age is bewailed as the age of Introversion. Must that needs be evil? We, it seems, are critical. We are embarrassed with second thoughts. We cannot enjoy any thing for hankering to know whereof the pleasure consists. We are lined with eyes. We see with our feet. The time is infected with Hamlet's unhappiness,—

"Sicklied o'er with the pale cast of thought."

Is it so bad then? Sight is the last thing to be pitied. Would we be blind? Do we fear lest we should outsee nature and God, and drink truth dry? I look upon the discontent of the literary class as a mere announcement of the fact that they find themselves not in the state of mind of their fathers, and regret the coming state as untried; as a boy dreads the water before he has learned that he can swim. If there is any period one would desire to be born in,—is it not the age of Revolution; when the old and the new stand side by side, and admit of being compared; when the energies of all men are searched by fear and by hope; when the historic glories of the old, can be compensated by the rich possibilities of the new era? This time, like all times, is a very good one, if we but know what to do with it.

I read with joy some of the auspicious signs of the coming days as they glimmer already through poetry and art, through philosophy and science, through church and state.

One of these signs is the fact that the same movement which effected the elevation of what was called the lowest class in the state, assumed in literature a very marked and as benign an aspect. Instead of the sublime and beautiful, the near, the low, the common, was explored and poetized. That which had been negligently trodden under foot by those who were harnessing and provisioning themselves for long journeys into far countries, is suddenly found to be richer than all foreign parts. The literature of the poor, the feelings of the child, the philosophy of the street, the meaning of household life, are the topics of the time. It is a great stride. It is a sign—is it not? of new vigor, when the extremities are made active, when currents of warm life run into the hands and the feet. I ask not for the great, the remote, the romantic; what is doing in Italy or Arabia; what is Greek art, or Provencal Minstrelsy; I embrace the common, I explore and sit at the feet of the familiar, the low. Give me insight into to-day, and you may have the antique and future worlds. What would we really know the meaning of? The meal in the firkin; the milk in the pan; the ballad in the street; the news of the boat; the glance of the eye; the form and the gait of the body;—show me the ultimate reason of these matters;—show me the sublime presence of the highest spiritual cause lurking, as always it does lurk, in these suburbs and extremities of nature; let me see every trifle bristling with the polarity that ranges it instantly on an eternal law; and the shop, the plough, the leger, referred to the like cause by which light undulates and poets sing;—and the world lies no longer a dull miscellany and lumber room, but has form and order; there is no trifle; there is no puzzle; but one design unites and animates the farthest pinnacle and the lowest trench.

This idea has inspired the genius of Goldsmith, Burns, Cowper, and, in a newer time, of Goethe, Wordsworth, and Carlyle. This idea they have differently followed and with various success. In contrast with their writing, the style of Pope, of Johnson, of Gibbon, looks cold and pedantic. This writing is blood-warm. Man is surprised to find that things near are not less beautiful and wondrous than things remote. The near explains the far. The drop is a small ocean. A man is related to all nature. This perception of the worth of the vulgar, is fruitful in discoveries. Goethe, in this very thing the most modern of the moderns, has shown us, as none ever did, the genius of the ancients.

There is one man of genius who has done much for this philosophy of life, whose literary value has never yet been rightly estimated;—I mean Emanuel Swedenborg. The most imaginative of men, yet writing with the precision of a mathematician, he endeavored to engraft a purely philosophical Ethics on the popular Christianity of his time. Such an attempt, of course, must have difficulty which no genius could surmount. But he saw and showed the connexion between nature and the affections of the soul. He pierced the emblematic or spiritual character of the visible, audible, tangible world. Especially did his shade-loving muse hover over and interpret the lower parts of nature; he showed the mysterious bond that allies moral evil to the foul material forms, and has given in epical parables a theory of insanity, of beasts, of unclean and fearful things.

Another sign of our times, also marked by an analogous political movement is, the new importance given to the single person. Every thing that tends to insulate the individual,—to surround him with barriers of natural respect, so that each man shall feel the world is his, and man shall treat with man as a sovereign state with a sovereign state;—tends to true union as well as greatness. "I learned," said the melancholy Pestalozzi, "that no man in God's wide earth is either willing or able to help any other man." Help must come from the bosom alone. The scholar is that man who must take up into himself all the ability of the time, all the contributions of the past, all the hopes of the future. He must be an university of knowledges. If there be one lesson more than another which should pierce his ear, it is, The world is nothing, the man is all; in yourself is the law of all nature, and you know not yet how a globule of sap ascends; in yourself lumbers the whole of Reason; it is for you to know all, it is for you to dare all. Mr. President and Gentlemen, this confidence in the unsearched might of man, belongs by all motives, by all prophecy, by all preparation, to the American Scholar. We have listened too long to the courtly muses of Europe. The spirit of the American freeman is already suspected to be timid, imitative, tame. Public and pirvate avarice make the air we breathe thick and fat. The scholar is decent, indolent, complaisant. See already the tragic consequence. The mind of this country taught to aim at low objects, eats upon itself. There is no work for any but the decorous and the complaisant. Young men of the fairest promise, who begin life upon our shores, inflated by the mountain winds, shined upon by all the stars of God, find the earth below not in unison with these,—but are hindered from action by the disgust which the principles on which business is managed inspire, and turn drudges, or die of disgust,—some of them suicides. What is the remedy? They did not yet see, and thousands of young men as hopeful now crowding to the barriers for the career, do not yet see, that if the single man plant himself indomitably on his instincts, and there abide, the huge world will come round to him. Patience—patience;—with the shades of all the good and great for company; and for solace, the perspective of your own infinite life; and for work, the study and the communication of principles, the making those instincts prevalent, the conversion of the world. Is it not the chief disgrace in the world, not to be an unit;—not to be reckoned one character;—not to yield that peculiar fruit which each man was created to bear, but to be reckoned in the gross, in the hundred, or the thousand, of the party, the section, to which we belong; and our opinion predicted geographically, as the north, or the south. Not so, brothers and friends,— please God, ours shall not be so. We will walk on our own feet; we will work with our own hands; we will speak our own minds. The study of letters shall be no longer a name for pity, for doubt, and for sensual indulgence. The dread of man and the love of man shall be a wall of defence and a wreath of joy around all. A nation of men will for the first time exist, because each believes himself inspired by the Divine Soul which also inspires all men.

· · · · · · · · · · · ·

## QUESTIONS FOR A SECOND READING

1. At the end of his essay, Emerson says "If the single man plant himself indomitably on his instincts, and there abide, the huge world will come round to him." As you reread this essay, what do you come to understand about "instinct," as Emerson refers to it? Could you say, for example, that Emerson is arguing that every student should be free to do what he or she wants? If so, what role would teachers or writers play in a person's education? If not, what should a student do other than take notes, read carefully, and follow the rules?

2. The scholar in this essay is both a person who learns and a person who teaches. (The latter is described most fully in the section on the scholar's duties.) How does Emerson describe the best possible relationship between a scholar and his or her teachers? How does he describe the best possible relationship between the scholar and those he or she would teach? In what ways, if at all, would the scholar change as he or she moved from the role of student into the role of teacher?

3. In section I of the essay, Emerson charts the growth of a young person's mind and at the end concludes that, if all goes well, "Know Thyself" and "Study Nature" become "at last one maxim." What does he mean by this? It sounds lofty and pious, but if you take your own case or the case of a child you know well, how might you use section I to comment on current practices in American education? What would be your most useful and powerful examples?

4. In section II of the essay, Emerson talks about the relationship between the scholar and the "mind of the past" and, in particular, about the proper and improper uses of books. Books, he says, "are the best of things, well used; abused, among the worst." What do you suppose Emerson would say is the best use of this essay? As you read through the essay, what kind of reader does Emerson invite you to be? What would you have to do—specifically and at specific places—to be an "Emersonian" reader of Emerson?

## ASSIGNMENTS FOR WRITING

1. Emerson says that in the three numbered sections of his essay he has "spoken of the education of the scholar by nature, by books and by action." Let's say that you wanted to take Emerson as a guide and imagine an appropriate "Emersonian" curriculum or institution. Write an essay (cast, perhaps, as a position paper or an article for an alumni magazine) that uses "The American Scholar" to comment specifically on the curriculum at your own school. (It might be useful to go to your college catalogue, or whatever documents your school has prepared to explain its curriculum, to see what

they have to say about the role of nature, books, and action in a person's education.)

2. Let's imagine Emerson himself as a teacher who wants to have his students read "The American Scholar" (perhaps along with some other selections from this anthology). What kind of assignment might he give? What, that is, would he ask you to *do* with the readings? What would he do as your teacher? Write an essay that considers both how, in practice, a modern teacher might encourage an Emersonian use of books and why, so far as you are concerned, a modern teacher might want to.

3. There is no question but that Emerson's text is difficult to read, and the difficulty is not simply a matter of big or unusual words. The text just doesn't do what we expect it to do. Some of its elusiveness can be attributed to the time during which it was written—expectations were different then—but this should not keep you from making the most of your own responses as a reader. For one thing, it's not completely true; not everyone in the 1860s wrote like Emerson. For another, it assumes that a nonspecialist cannot or should not read works from the past. One way of imagining your connection to the 1860s is to imagine that your encounter with this text is somehow typical—that you, too, are Emerson's contemporary.

Take a section of the essay that you find characteristically difficult. (Section II is an interesting one to work with.) Reread it, paying close attention to the experience of reading. Where are you surprised? Where are you confused? How might this be part of a strategy, part of Emerson's design? What is Emerson doing? What is he asking you to do? This should be an exercise in close reading. You want to pay attention to how paragraph leads to paragraph, sentence leads to sentence; to notice the ways examples or statements are offered and taken away.

Write an essay in which you describe in close detail the story of what is was like to read this section of "The American Scholar." Tell a story of reading, one where you and Emerson are the main characters—complicated characters, not stick figures (the Innocent Child and the Inscrutable Genius). When you are done, see what connections you can make with Emerson's argument—with what he says is a proper relation between readers and writers. In what ways might his difficulties and yours be said to be unfortunate? In what ways might they be signs of his attempts to get the language (and a reader) to do what he wants them to do?

## MAKING CONNECTIONS

1. Both Emerson in "The American Scholar" and Julia Kristeva in "Stabat Mater" (p. 359) can be said to have written difficult texts. And in both cases the difficulties can be seen as attempts to thwart or resist conventional desires (the desires of readers; the desires of the culture; the desires at the root of language, part of its history, resisting change, insisting on predictability).

Write an essay in which you take a representative section of each selection in order to chart in careful detail the sorts of difficulties each presents (the difficulties that are "in" the text; the difficulties that are "in" the experience of the reader; the difficulties that are "in" the aims and strategies of the writer).

In what ways could Emerson's and Kristeva's writing be said to be similar? In what ways might they be said to be different? How would you explain the differences? How would the authors like them to be explained?

2. Both Emerson, in "The American Scholar," and Paulo Freire, in "The 'Banking' Concept of Education" (p. 207), seem to be arguing for freedom or for a form of education that allows students to be free. If we grant that this is common ground, it may be interesting to consider the significant differences in their arguments. Write an essay in which you compare Emerson's and Freire's accounts of the ideal education. What does "freedom" come to mean for each? And what does this freedom have to do with knowledge or truth, or whatever it is that a student is supposed to gain by an education?

# STANLEY
# FISH

*S TANLEY FISH was born in Providence, Rhode Island, in 1938. He is the*
*author of several books, including* John Skelton's Poetry, Self-Consuming
Artifacts: The Experience of Seventeenth-Century Literature, Surprised by
Sin: The Reader in Paradise Lost, *and* Doing What Comes Naturally:
Change, Rhetoric, and the Practice of Theory in Literary and Legal Studies.
*Formerly William Kenan, Jr., Professor of English at Johns Hopkins University in*
*Baltimore, Fish currently heads the department of English at Duke University in*
*North Carolina.*

*Fish is one of this country's most influential and provocative literary critics.*
*His writing is witty, bold, and straightforward; and he seems to delight in contro-*
*versy. Fish once said, in fact, that his only responsibility as a critic was to be*
*interesting, not to be right. (He later took this statement back—although not the*
*part about being interesting.)*

*The essay included here, "How to Recognize a Poem When You See One," is*
*from a series of lectures he gave at Kenyon College in Ohio in 1979. Fish said that*
*he found the event exhilarating and exhausting and that "apparently, some of the*
*same feelings were shared by the audience, for in an editorial written for the college*

newspaper (titled, 'Fish Baits Audience') *generous praise of my 'intellectual skill' was qualified by the observation that, needless to say, 'it was not always the skill of a gentleman.'"*

*In his recent work, Fish does not write about individual texts and what they mean but about reading itself—about how such texts are read or how they might be read. He begins with the assumption that "good" readers can read the same work and not agree on what it says. When two people read the same story but interpret it differently, Fish would argue, this does not necessarily mean that one reader "got it" and that the other didn't, but that different people read differently—they "make" the story into different stories when they read. The question Fish asks, then, is whether this means that any text can mean anything that anyone says it means— whether meaning is so unstable that a story could be said to have an infinite number of meanings and that no one, not even an English teacher, can tell right from wrong.*

*The following essay is from a book titled* Is There a Text in This Class? *The title comes from a question asked by a student at Johns Hopkins. Her professor responded, "Yes; it's the* Norton Anthology of Literature," *to which the student responded, "No, no. I mean in this class do we believe in poems and things, or is it just us?" "How to Recognize a Poem When You See One" addresses the question of whether there are such things as poems or whether readers make them up as they go along.*

# How to Recognize a Poem When You See One

In the summer of 1971 I was teaching two courses under the joint auspices of the Linguistic Institute of America and the English Department of the State University of New York at Buffalo. I taught these courses in the morning and in the same room. At 9:30 I would meet a group of students who were interested in the relationship between linguistics and literary criticism. Our nominal subject was stylistics but our concerns were finally theoretical and extended to the presuppositions and assumptions which underlie both linguistic and literary practice. At 11:00 these students were replaced by another group whose concerns were exclusively literary and were in fact confined to English religious poetry of the seventeenth century. These students had been learning how to identify Christian symbols and how to recognize typological patterns and how to move from the observation of these symbols and patterns to the specification of a poetic intention that was usually didactic or homiletic. On the day I am thinking about, the only connection between the two classes was an assignment given to the first which was still on the blackboard at the beginning of the second. It read:

Jacobs–Rosenbaum
Levin
Thorne
Hayes
Ohman (?)

I am sure that many of you will have already recognized the names on this list, but for the sake of the record, allow me to identify them. Roderick Jacobs and Peter Rosenbaum are two linguists who have coauthored a number of textbooks and coedited a number of anthologies. Samuel Levin is a linguist who was one of the first to apply the operations of transformational grammar to literary texts. J. P. Thorne is a linguist at Edinburgh who, like Levin, was attempting to extend the rules of transformational grammar to the notorious irregularities of poetic language. Curtis Hayes is a linguist who was then using transformational grammar in order to establish an objective basis for his intuitive impression that the language of Gibbon's *Rise and Fall of the Roman Empire* is more complex than the language of Hemingway's novels. And Richard Ohmann is the literary critic who, more than any other, was responsible for introducing the vocabulary of transformational grammar to the literary community. Ohmann's name was spelled as you see it here because I could not remember whether it contained one or two n's. In other words, the question mark in parenthesis signified nothing more than a faulty memory and a desire on my part to appear scrupulous. The fact that the names appeared in a list that was arranged vertically, and that Levin, Thorne, and Hayes formed a column that was more or less centered in relation to the paired names of Jacobs and Rosenbaum, was similarly accidental and was evidence only of a certain compulsiveness if, indeed, it was evidence of anything at all.

In the time between the two classes I made only one change. I drew a frame around the assignment and wrote on the top of that frame "p. 43." When the members of the second class filed in I told them that what they saw on the blackboard was a religious poem of the kind they had been studying and I asked them to interpret it. Immediately they began to perform in a manner that, for reasons which will become clear, was more or less predictable. The first student to speak pointed out that the poem was probably a hieroglyph, although he was not sure whether it was in the shape of a cross or an altar. This question was set aside as the other students, following his lead, began to concentrate on individual words, interrupting each other with suggestions that came so quickly that they seemed spontaneous. The first line of the poem (the very order of events assumed the already constituted status of the object) received the most attention: Jacobs was explicated as a reference to Jacob's ladder, traditionally allegorized as a figure for the Christian ascent to heaven. In this poem, however, or so my students told me, the means of ascent is not a ladder but a tree, a rose tree or rosenbaum. This was seen to be an obvious reference to the Virgin Mary who was often characterized as a rose without thorns, itself an emblem of the immaculate conception. At this point the poem appeared to the students to be operating in the familiar manner of an iconographic riddle. It at once posed the question, "How is it that a man can climb to heaven by means of a rose tree?" and directed the reader to the inevitable answer: by the fruit of that tree, the fruit of Mary's womb, Jesus. Once this interpretation was established it received support from, and conferred significance on, the word "thorne," which could only be an allusion to the crown of thorns, a symbol of the trial suffered by Jesus and of the price he paid to save us all. It was only a short step (really no step at all) from this insight to the recognition of Levin as a double reference, first to the tribe of Levi, of whose priestly function Christ was the fulfillment, and second to the unleavened bread carried by the children of Israel on their exodus from Egypt, the place of sin, and in response to the call of Moses, perhaps the most familiar of the old testament types of Christ. The final word of the poem was given at least three complementary readings: it could be "omen," especially since so much of the poem is concerned with foreshadowing and prophecy; it could be Oh Man, since it is man's story as it intersects with the divine plan that is the poem's subject; and it could, of course, be simply "amen," the proper conclusion to a poem celebrating the love and mercy shown by a God who gave his only begotten son so that we may live.

In addition to specifying significances for the words of the poem and relating those significances to one another, the students began to discern larger structural patterns. It was noted that of the six names in the poem three—Jacobs, Rosenbaum, and Levin—are Hebrew, two—Thorne and Hayes—are Christian, and one—Ohman—is ambiguous, the ambiguity being marked in the poem itself (as the phrase goes) by the question mark in parenthesis. This division was seen as a reflection of the basic distinction between the old dispensation and the new, the law of sin and the law of love. That distinction, however, is blurred and finally dissolved by the typological perspective which invests the old testament events and heroes with new testament meanings. The structure of the poem, my students concluded, is therefore a double one, establishing and undermining its basic pattern (Hebrew vs. Christian) at the same time. In this context there is finally no pressure to resolve the ambiguity of Ohman since the two possible readings—the name is Hebrew, the name is Christian—are both authorized by the reconciling presence in the poem of Jesus Christ. Finally, I must report that one student took to counting letters and found, to no one's surprise, that the most prominent letters in the poem were S, O, N.

Some of you will have noticed that I have not yet said anything about Hayes. This is because of all the words in the poem it proved the most recalcitrant to interpretation, a fact not without consequence, but one which I will set aside for the moment since I am less interested in the details of the exercise than in the ability of my students to perform it. What is the source of that ability? How is it that they were able to do what they did? What is it that they did? These questions are important because they bear directly on a question often asked in literary theory, What are the distinguishing features of literary language? Or, to put the matter more colloquially, How do you recognize a poem when you see one? The commonsense answer, to which many literary critics and linguists are committed, is that the act of recognition is triggered by the observable presence of distinguishing features. That is, you know a poem when you see one because its language displays the characteristics that you know to be proper to poems. This, however, is a model that quite obviously does not fit the present example. My students did not proceed from the noting of distinguishing features to the recognition that they were confronted by a poem; rather, it was the act of recognition that came first—they knew in advance that they were dealing with a poem—and the distinguishing features then followed.

In other words, acts of recognition, rather than being triggered by formal characteristics, are their source. It is not that the presence of poetic qualities compels a certain kind of attention but that the paying of a certain kind of attention results in the emergence of poetic qualities. As soon as my students were aware that it was poetry they were seeking, they began to look with poetry-seeing eyes, that is, with eyes that saw everything in relation to the properties they knew poems to possess. They knew, for example (because they were told by their teachers), that poems are (or are supposed to be) more densely and intricately organized than ordinary communications; and that knowledge translated itself into a willingness—one might even say a determination—to see connections between one word and another and between every word and the poem's central insight. Moreover, the assumption that there *is* a central insight is itself poetry-specific, and presided over its own realization. Having assumed that the collection of words before them was unified by an informing purpose (because unifying purposes are what poems have), my students proceeded to find one and to formulate it. It was in the light of that purpose (now assumed) that significances for the individual words began to suggest themselves, significances which then fleshed out the assumption that had generated them in the first place. Thus the meanings of the words and the interpretation in which those words were seen to be embedded emerged together, as a consequence of the operations my students began to perform once they were told that this was a poem.

It was almost as if they were following a recipe—if it's a poem do this, if it's a poem, see it that way—and indeed definitions of poetry *are* recipes, for by directing readers as to what to look for in a poem, they instruct them in ways of looking that will produce what they expect to see. If your definition of poetry tells you that the language of poetry is complex, you will scrutinize the language of something identified as a poem in such a way as to bring out the complexity you know to be "there." You will, for example, be on the look-out for latent ambiguities; you will attend to the presence of alliterative and consonantal patterns (there will always be some), and you will try to make something of them (you will always succeed); you will search for meanings that subvert, or exit in a tension with the meanings that first present themselves; and if these operations fail to produce the anticipated complexity, you will even propose a significance for the words that are *not* there, because, as everyone knows, everything about a poem, including its omissions, is significant. Nor, as you do these things, will you have any sense of performing in a willful manner, for you will only be doing what you learned to do in the course of becoming a skilled reader of poetry. Skilled reading is usually thought to be a matter of discerning what is there, but if the example of my students can be generalized, it is a matter of knowing how to *produce* what can thereafter be said to be there. Interpretation is not the art of construing but the art of constructing. Interpreters do not decode poems; they make them.

To many, this will be a distressing conclusion, and there are a number of arguments that could be mounted in order to forestall it. One might point out that the circumstances of my students' performance were special. After all, they had been concerned exclusively with religious poetry for some weeks, and therefore would be uniquely vulnerable to the deception I had practiced on them and uniquely equipped to impose religious themes and patterns on words innocent of either. I must report, however, that I have duplicated this experiment any number of times at nine or ten universities in three countries, and the results are always the same, even when the participants know from the beginning that what they are looking at was originally an assignment. Of course this very fact could itself be turned into an objection: doesn't the reproducibility of the exercise prove that there is something about these words that lead everyone to perform in the same way? Isn't it just a happy accident that names like Thorne and Jacobs have counterparts or near counterparts in biblical names and symbols? And wouldn't my students have been unable to do what they did if the assignment I gave to the first class had been made up of different names? The answer to all of these questions is no. Given a firm belief that they were confronted by a religious poem, my students would have been able to turn any list of names into the kind of poem we have before us now, because they would have read the names within the assumption that they were informed with Christian significances. (This is nothing more than a literary analogue to Augustine's rule of faith.) You can test this assertion by replacing Jacobs-Rosenbaum, Levin, Thorne, Hayes, and Ohman with names drawn from the faculty of Kenyon College—Temple, Jordan, Seymour, Daniels, Star, Church. I will not exhaust my time or your patience by performing a full-dress analysis, which would involve, of course, the relation between those who saw the River Jordan and those who saw *more* by seeing the Star of Bethlehem, thus fulfilling the prophecy by which the temple of Jerusalem was replaced by the inner temple or church built up in the heart of every Christian. Suffice it to say that it could easily be done (you can take the poem home and do it yourself) and that the shape of its doing would be constrained not by the names but by the interpretive assumptions that gave them a significance even before they were seen. This would be true even if there were no names on the list, if the paper or blackboard were blank; the blankness would present no problem to the interpreter, who would immediately see in it the void out of which God created the earth, or the abyss into which unregenerate sinners fall, or, in the best of all possible poems, both.

Even so, one might reply, all you've done is demonstrate how an interpretation, if it is prosecuted with sufficient vigor, can impose itself on material which has its own proper shape. Basically, at the ground level, in the first place, when all is said and done, "Jacobs-Rosenbaum Levin Thorne Hayes Ohman(?)" is an assignment; it is only a trick that allows you to transform it into a poem, and when the effects of the trick have worn off, it will return to its natural form and be seen as an assignment once again. This is a powerful argument because it seems at once to give interpretation its due (as an act of the will) and to maintain the independence of that on which interpretation works. It allows us, in short, to preserve our commonsense intuition that interpretation must be interpretation of *something*. Unfortunately, the argument will not hold because the assignment we all see is no less the product of interpretation than the poem into which it was turned. That is, it requires just as much work, and work of the same kind, to see this as an assignment as it does to see it as a poem. If this seems counterintuitive, it is only because the work required to see it as an assignment is work we have already done, in the course of acquiring the huge amount of background knowledge that enables you and me to function in the academic world. In order to know what an assignment is, that is, in order to know what to do with something identified as an assignment, you must first know what a class is (know that it isn't an economic grouping) and know that classes meet at specified times for so many weeks, and that one's performance in a class is largely a matter of performing between classes.

Think for a moment of how you would explain this last to someone who did not already know it. "Well," you might say, "a class is a group situation in which a number of people are instructed by an informed person in a particular subject." (Of course the notion of "subject" will itself require explication.) "An assignment is something you do when you're not in class." "Oh, I see," your interlocutor might respond, "as assignment is something you do to take your mind off what you've been doing in class." "No, an assignment is a part of a class." "But how can that be if you only do it when the class is not meeting?" Now it would be possible, finally, to answer that question, but only by enlarging the horizons of your explanation to include the very concept of a university, what it is one might be doing there, why one might be doing it instead of doing a thousand other things, and so on. For most of us these matters do not require explanation, and indeed, it is hard for us to imagine someone for whom they do; but that is because our tacit knowledge of what it means to move around in academic life was acquired so gradually and so long ago that it doesn't seem like knowledge at all (and therefore something someone else might *not* know) but a part of the world. You might think that when you're on campus (a phrase that itself requires volumes) that you are simply walking around on the two legs God gave you; but your walking is informed by an internalized awareness of institutional goals and practices, of norms of behavior, of lists of do's and don'ts, of invisible lines and the dangers of crossing them; and, as a result, you see everything as *already* organized in relation to those same goals and practices. It would never occur to you, for example, to wonder if the people pouring out of that building are fleeing from a fire; you *know* that they are exiting from a class (what could be more obvious?) and you know that because your perception of their action occurs within a knowledge of what people in a university could possibly be doing and the reasons they could have for doing it (going to the next class, going back to the dorm, meeting someone in the student union). It is within that same knowledge that an assignment becomes intelligible so that it appears to you immediately as an obligation, as a set of directions, as something with parts, some of which may be more significant than others. That is, it is a proper question to ask of an assignment whether some of its parts might be omitted or slighted, whereas readers of poetry know that no part of a poem can be slighted (the rule is "everything counts") and they do not rest until every part has been given a significance.

In a way this amounts to no more than saying what everyone already knows: poems and assignments are different, but my point is that the differences are a result of the different interpretive operations we perform and not of something inherent in one or the other. An assignment no more compels its own recognition than does a poem; rather, as in the case of a poem, the shape of an assignment emerges when someone looks at something identified as one with assignment-seeing eyes, that is, with eyes which are capable of seeing the words as already embedded within the institutional structure that makes it possible for assignments to have a sense. The ability to see, and therefore to make, an assignment is no less a learned ability than the ability to see, and therefore to make, a poem. Both are constructed artifacts, the products and not the producers of interpretation, and while the differences between them are real, they are interpretive and do not have their source in some bedrock level of objectivity.

Of course one might want to argue that there is a bedrock level at which these names constitute neither an assignment nor a poem but are merely a list. But that argument too fails because a list is no more a natural object—one that wears its meaning on its face and can be recognized by anyone—than an assignment or a poem. In order to see a list, one must already be equipped with the concepts of seriality, hierarchy, subordination, and so on, and while these are by no mean esoteric concepts and seem available to almost everyone, they are nonetheless learned, and if there were someone who had not learned them, he or she would not be able to see a list. The next recourse is to descend still lower (in the direction of atoms) and to claim objectivity for letters, paper, graphite, black marks on white spaces, and so on; but these entities too have palpability and shape only because of the assumption of some or other system of intelligibility, and they are therefore just as available to a deconstructive dissolution as are poems, assignments, and lists.

The conclusion, therefore, is that all objects are made and not found, and that they are made by the interpretive strategies we set in motion. This does not, however, commit me to subjectivity because the means by which they are made are social and conventional. That is, the "you" who does the interpretive work that puts poems and assignments and lists into the world is a communal you and not an isolated individual. No one of us wakes up in the morning and (in French fashion) reinvents poetry or thinks up a new educational system or decides to reject seriality in favor of some other, wholly original, form of organization. We do not do these things because we could not do them, because the mental operations we can perform are limited by the institutions in which we are *already* embedded. These institutions precede us, and it is only by inhabiting them, or being inhabited by them, that we have access to the public and conventional senses they make. Thus while it is true to say that we create poetry (and assignments and lists), we create it through interpretive strategies that are finally not our own but have their source in a publicly available system of intelligibility. Insofar as the system (in this case a literary system) constrains us, it also fashions us, furnishing us with categories of understanding, with which we in turn fashion the entities to which we can then point. In short, to the list of made or constructed objects we must add ourselves, for we no less than the poems and assignments we see are the products of social and cultural patterns of thought.

To put the matter in this way is to see that the opposition between objectivity and subjectivity is a false one because neither exists in the pure form that would give the opposition its point. This is precisely illustrated by my anecdote in which we do *not* have free-standing readers in a relationship of perceptual adequacy or inadequacy to an equally free-standing text. Rather, we have readers whose consciousness are constituted by a set of conventional notions which when put into operation constitute in turn a conventional, and conventionally seen, object. My students could do what they did, and do it in unison, because as members of a literary community they knew what a poem was (their knowledge was public), and that knowledge led them to look in such a way as to populate the landscape with what they knew to be poems.

Of course poems are not the only objects that are constituted in unison by shared ways of seeing. Every object or event that becomes available within an institutional setting can be so characterized. I am thinking, for example, of something that happened in my classroom just the other day. While I was in the course of vigorously making a point, one of my students, William Newlin by name, was just as vigorously waving his hand. When I asked the other members of the class what it was that Mr. Newlin was doing, they all answered that he was seeking permission to speak. I then asked them how they knew that. The immediate reply was that it was obvious; what else could he be thought to be doing? The meaning of his gesture, in other words, was right there on its surface, available for reading by anyone who had the eyes to see. That meaning, however, would not have been available to someone without any knowledge of what was involved in being a student. Such a person might have thought that Mr. Newlin was pointing to the fluorescent lights hanging from the ceiling, or calling our attention to some object that was about to fall ("the sky is falling," "the sky is falling"). And if the someone in question were a child of elementary or middle-school age, Mr. Newlin might well have been seen as seeking permission not to speak but to go to the bathroom, an interpretation or reading that would never occur to a student at Johns Hopkins or any other institution of "higher learning" (and how would we explain to the uninitiated the meaning of *that* phrase).

The point is the one I have made so many times before: it is neither the case that the significance of Mr. Newlin's gesture is imprinted on its surface where it need only be read off, or that the construction put on the gesture by everyone in the room was individual and idiosyncratic. Rather, the source of our interpretive unanimity was a structure of interests and understood goals, a structure whose categories so filled our individual consciousnesses that they were rendered as one, immediately investing phenomena with the significance they *must* have, given the already-in-place assumptions about what someone could possibly be intending (by word or gesture) in a classroom. By seeing Mr. Newlin's raised hand with a single shaping eye, we were demonstrating what Harvey Sacks has characterized as "the fine power of a culture. It does not, so to speak, merely fill brains in roughly the same way, it fills them so that they are alike in fine detail."[1] The occasion of Sacks's observation was the ability of his hearers to understand a sequence of two sentences—"The baby cried. The mommy picked it up."—exactly as he did (assuming, for example that "the 'mommy' who picks up the 'baby' is the mommy of that baby"), despite the fact that alternative ways of understanding were demonstrably possible. That is, the mommy of the second sentence could well have been the mommy of some other baby, and it need not even have been a baby that this "floating" mommy was picking up. One is tempted to say that in the absence of a specific context we are authorized to take the words literally, which is what Sacks's hearers do; but as Sacks observes, it is within the assumption of a context—one so deeply assumed that we are unaware of it—that the words acquire what seems to be their literal meaning. There is nothing *in the words* that tells Sacks and his hearers how to relate the mommy and the baby of this story, just as there is nothing *in the form* of Mr. Newlin's gesture that tells his fellow students how to determine its significance. In both cases the determination (of relation and significance) is the work of categories of organization—the family, being a student—that are from the very first giving shape and value to what is heard and seen.

Indeed, these categories are the very shape of seeing itself, in that we are not to imagine a perceptual ground more basic than the one they afford. That is, we are not to imagine a moment when my students "simply see" a physical configuration of atoms and *then* assign that configuration a significance, according to the situation they happen to be in. To be in the situation (this or any other) is to "see" with the eyes of its interests, its goals, its understood practices, values, and norms, and so to be conferring significance *by* seeing, not after it. The categories of my students' vision are the categories by which they understand themselves to be functioning as students (what Sacks might term "doing studenting"), and objects will appear to them in forms related to that way of functioning rather than in some objective or preinterpretive form. (This is true even when an object is seen as not related, since nonrelation is not a pure but a differential category—the specification of something by enumerating what it is not; in short, nonrelation is merely one form of relation, and its perception is always situation-specific.)

Of course, if someone who was not functioning as a student was to walk into my classroom, he might very well see Mr. Newlin's raised hand (and "raised hand" is already an interpretation-laden description) in some other way, as evidence of a disease, as the salute of a political follower, as a muscle-improving exercise, as an attempt to kill flies; but he would always see it in *some* way, and never as purely physical data waiting for his interpretation. And, moreover, the way of seeing, whatever it was, would never be individual or idiosyncratic, since its source would always be the institutional structure of which the "see-er" was an extending agent. This is what Sacks means when he says that a culture fills brains "so that they are alike in fine detail"; it fills them so that no one's interpretive acts are exclusively his own but fall to him by virtue of his position in some socially organized environment and are therefore always shared and public. It follows, then, that the fear of solipsism, of the imposition by the unconstrained self of its own prejudices, is unfounded because the self does not exist apart from the communal or conventional categories of thought that enable its operations (of thinking, seeing, reading). Once one realizes that the conceptions that fill consciousness, including any conception of its own status, are culturally derived, the very notion of an unconstrained self, of a consciousness wholly and dangerously free, becomes incomprehensible.

But without the notion of the unconstrained self, the arguments of Hirsch, Abrams, and the other proponents of objective interpretation are deprived of their urgency. They are afraid that in the absence of the controls afforded by a normative system of meanings, the self will simply substitute its own meanings for the meanings (usually identified with the intentions of the author) that texts bring with them, the meanings that texts *"have"*; however, if the self is conceived of not as an independent entity but as a social construct whose operations are delimited by the systems of intelligibility that inform it, then the meanings it confers on texts are not its own but have their source in the interpretive community (or communities) of which it is a function. Moreover, these meanings will be neither subjective nor objective, at least in the terms assumed by those who argue within the traditional framework: they will not be objective because they will always have been the product of a point of view rather than having been simply "read off"; and they will not be subjective because that point of view will always be social or institutional. Or by the same reasoning one could say that they are *both* subjective and objective: they are subjective because they inhere in a particular point of view and are therefore not universal; and they are objective because the point of view that delivers them is public and conventional rather than individual or unique.

To put the matter in either way is to see how unhelpful the terms "subjective" and "objective" finally are. Rather than facilitating inquiry, they close it down, by deciding in advance what shape inquiry can possibly take. Specifically, they assume, without being aware that it is an assumption and therefore open to challenge, the very distinction I have been putting into question, the distinction between interpreters and the objects they interpret. That distinction in turn assumes that interpreters and their objects are two different kinds of *a*contextual entities, and within these twin assumptions the issue can only be one of control: will texts be allowed to constrain their own interpretation or will irresponsible interpreters be allowed to obscure and overwhelm texts. In the spectacle that ensues, the spectacle of Anglo-American critical controversy, texts and selves fight it out in the persons or their respective champions, Abrams, Hirsch, Reichert, Graff on the one hand, Holland, Bleich, Slatoff, and (in some characterizations of him) Barthes° on the other. But if selves are constituted by the ways of thinking and seeing that inhere in social organizations, and if these constituted selves in turn constitute texts according to these same ways, then there can be no adversary relationship between text and self because they are the necessarily related products of the same cognitive possibilities. A text cannot be overwhelmed by an irresponsible reader and one need not worry about protecting the purity of a text from a reader's idiosyncracies. It is only the distinction between subject and object that gives rise to these urgencies, and once the distinction is blurred they simply fall away. One can respond with a cheerful yes to the question "Do readers make meanings?" and commit oneself to very little because it would be equally true to say that meanings, in the form of culturally derived interpretive categories, make readers.

Indeed, many things look rather different once the subject-object dichotomy is eliminated as the assumed framework within which critical discussion occurs. Problems disappear, not because they have been solved but because they are shown never to have been problems in the first place. Abrams, for example, wonders how, in the absence of a normative system of stable meanings, two people could ever agree on the interpretation of a work or even a sentence; but the difficulty is only a difficulty if the two (or more) people are thought of as isolated individuals whose agreement must be compelled by something external to them. (There is something of the police state in Abrams's vision, complete with posted rules and boundaries, watchdogs to enforce them, procedures for identifying their violators as criminals.) But if the understandings of the people in question are informed by the same notions of what counts as a fact, of what is central, peripheral, and worthy of being noticed—in short, by the same interpretive principles—then agreement between them will be assured, and its source

---

**Abrams, Hirsch, Reichert, Graff . . . , Holland, Bleich, Slatoff, and . . . Barthes** Central figures in the critical controversy over whether meanings should properly be said to reside in texts or in readers.

will not be a text that enforces its own perception but a way of perceiving that results in the emergence to those who share it (or those whom it shares) of the same text. That text might be a poem, as it was in the case of those who first "saw" "Jacobs-Rosenbaum Levin Thorne Hayes Ohman(?)," or a hand, as it is every day in a thousand classrooms; but whatever it is, the shape and meaning it appears immediately to have will be the "ongoing accomplishment"[2] of those who agree to produce it.

NOTES

[1] "On the Analysability of Stories by Children," in *Ethnomethodology*, ed. Roy Turner (Baltimore: Penguin, 1974), p. 218.

[2] A phrase used by the ethnomethodologists to characterize the interpretive activities that create and maintain the features of everyday life. See, for example, Don H. Zimmerman, "Fact as a Practical Accomplishment," in *Ethnomethodology*, pp. 128–143.

. . . . . . . . . . .

## QUESTIONS FOR A SECOND READING

1. Fish devotes part of this essay to talking about the experience of being a student. He talks, for example, about students "doing studenting" and seeing what they have been taught to see. Does this sound right to you? Does his account of a student's experience seem consistent with your experience, as you understand it? As you reread the essay, think about where and how Fish might be said to have it right or to have it wrong when he talks about the student's experience of the classroom.

2. Surely Fish had several stories to tell when he told this story about what he did in class. In fact, it is safe to say that he had an audience in mind beyond the teachers and students who gathered together to hear him at Kenyon College. He alludes, for example, to people who have a "fear of solipsism" or who are "afraid" of the absence of those controls "afforded by a normative system of meaning." Fish is addressing the special concerns of a special community of literary theorists, but you don't have to know the issues (or share their way of speaking) to read Fish's essay. It is interesting, however, to imagine who these people are and what they argue about. As you read through the essay for a second time, see what conclusions you can draw about this specialized audience. What does Fish expect that they will see in the story he tells? What does he assume will please them, or impress them, or make them nervous? How do you think their questions or concerns are similar to or different from your own? (What points in the essay, for example, make you nervous? or impressed? or pleased?)

## ASSIGNMENTS FOR WRITING

1. Fish seems quite pleased to tell the story that he tells, and he seems quite happy with what his students do with the "poem" on the blackboard. It's not just that he is pleased with his performance as a teacher (although that pleasure is there), but that the story he tells nicely reveals what he takes to be a basic truth about learning or about all classrooms where students are expected to interpret phenomena—books, artifacts, experiments, human behavior—as members of an interpretive community. Fish's unusual example enables us to see something we would otherwise miss in our own routine experience. At least that seems to be the assumption of the essay.

    You have your own expertise in this matter, however, since you've been a student in classrooms for a number of years. Fish assumes that students and teachers are members of the same community. "No one of us," he says, (and that means you, too)

    > wakes up in the morning and (in French fashion) reinvents poetry or thinks up a new educational system or decides to reject seriality in favor of some other, wholly original, form of organization. We do not do these things because we could not do them, because the mental operations we can perform are limited by the institutions in which we are *already* embedded. These institutions precede us, and it is only by inhabiting them, or being inhabited by them, that we have access to the public and conventional senses they make (p. 186).

    And yet, as a student, your relation to poetry or the educational system or forms of organization might be said to be different from that of your teachers. What you would produce would be different as, most likely, would be its reception by the institution. A student's rejection of conventional organization is treated differently than a professor's. It is possible, that is, to reread Fish's examples (and arguments) through students' eyes.

    Write an essay that represents a student's response to Fish's argument. You will want to work with Fish's examples and demonstrate that you understand (and can reproduce) his argument. You can, however, bring in examples of your own. The point is not to push Fish aside (or pretend that his argument is either simply right or simply wrong). The issue is not so much one of right and wrong but of what might be said next if Fish's discussion can be extended by a response from students.

2. Fish tells the story of Mr. Newlin's raised hand as a way of summarizing or recapitulating the story of his class and the "poem." Mr. Newlin's raised hand could be a sign that Mr. Newlin has to go to the bathroom, or that the light is falling from the ceiling, or that he is catching flies. It only "obviously" means that Mr. Newlin has something to say to a teacher to those who see through those eyes (who share a "structure of interests and understood goals . . .").

    Write an essay in which you tell a similar anecdote, one about an everyday sight that has a significance obvious to everyone who sees it, but that could also be interpreted in other ways. In your essay you should examine several possible interpretations, speculate on why the "community" sees

**192**

one but not the others, and discuss the consequences of this single, shaping vision. You should, wherever possible, use Fish's key terms or phrases and try to see through his eyes, at least initially, since this will give you a way of working out some of the more difficult theoretical parts of his argument.

## MAKING CONNECTIONS

1. "Undoubtedly there is a right way of reading," says Emerson in "The American Scholar" (p. 160), "so it be sternly subordinated." Both Emerson and Fish are concerned with how students read, with the limits and possibilities of those acts of reading, and with the role of reading in a general education.

    Let's imagine that two experimental schools have been designed on Emersonian and Fishian principles. We'll call them Emerson University and Fish University.

    What differences would there be in the way students are taught to read (or in the way readings might be assigned) at each school? What would instructors do? How, for example, might they use some of the essays in this book? What would students be asked to do?

    What differences would there be in introductory courses? in courses for seniors? What assumptions would teachers make at each school about the link between introductory and advanced work?

    Write an essay in which you report on the differences between these two programs of study. You could imagine that you are preparing a comparative study for an article on these two experimental schools.

2. Walker Percy, in "The Loss of the Creature" (p. 462), argues that "a student who had the desire to get at a dogfish or a Shakespeare sonnet may have the greatest difficulty in salvaging the creature itself from the educational package in which it is presented." Fish's anecdote seems to provide an almost classic case for Percy. You could say that this teacher took a dogfish, put it on the desk in a Shakespeare class, and his students turned it into a sonnet. Fish says, "Skilled reading is usually thought to be a matter of discerning what is there, but if the example of my students can be generalized, it is a matter of knowing how to *produce* what can thereafter be said to be there. Interpretation is not the art of construing but the art of constructing."

    How would Percy read Fish's account of his poetry class? What would he notice? What would he say? And if Percy's greatest hope is that students can find a way of rescuing their specimens from the "educational package," what might he offer as an alternative for those students whose accomplishments Fish finds so comfortably predictable? Write an essay in which you "read" Fish's anecdote about the poetry class from the point of view of Percy's "The Loss of the Creature." You can imagine that you are carrying on Percy's work and applying his methods and ideas to the case of Fish and his students.

# JEAN
# FRANCO

*J*EAN FRANCO *was born in England in 1924. She received her B.A. from the University of Manchester and her M.A. and Ph.D. from King's College in London. She has taught at the University of London and Stanford University in California and is currently director of the Institute of Iberian and Latin American Studies at Columbia University in New York. In 1984 she served as an investigator in El Salvador and Nicaragua on behalf of the Faculty for Human Rights in El Salvador and Central America.*

*Franco has published widely in Spanish and English and was founder and editor of the journal* Tabloid. *Her books include* César Vallejo, The Modern Culture of Latin America, *and* An Introduction to Spanish-American Literature. *Her most recent book,* Plotting Women, *is a study of representations of Mexican women from the time of the Spanish conquest to the present, looking particularly at what Mexican women have written and the ways they have been written into other people's stories. She has said, "*Plotting Women *is about struggles for interpretive power, struggles waged not on the high plane of theory but very often at the margins of canonical genres—in letters and life stories."*

*"Killing Priests, Nuns, Women, Children" was first published in a collection*

titled On Signs, *edited by Marshall Blonsky. This essay extends Franco's concern for life stories not only as they are written into the culture but as they are acted out in national and political life, particularly in the conflict between the "standard" narrative (of a woman's "proper" life, for example, or those versions of the proper life represented in art or the mass media) and individuals' lived versions of that narrative. For Franco, one powerful example of this conflict is represented in the life of Alaíde Foppa, whose name figures prominently in "Killing Priests, Nuns, Women, Children." Here is what Franco has to say about Foppa in* Plotting Women—*in a chapter titled "Rewriting the Family":*

> State terror against the guerrilla movement went far beyond the armed rebels themselves and deeply affected the civilian population, drawing women into the circle of terror. This was tragically demonstrated by the fate of one of the founders of fem, Alaíde Foppa, a Guatemalan resident in Mexico who was kidnapped and "disappeared" on a visit to Guatemala at the end of 1980, apparently because her children were involved in the guerrilla movement. Alaíde was a poet and literary critic, who in relative isolation had grasped the necessity of forming a women's network that could deal with the specific problems of Latin American women. After initiating a series of radio programs, she helped found fem along with Margarita García Flores. But as women participated more and more actively in political and guerrilla movements, they also found that they could no longer expect immunity from counterinsurgency. Neither her upper-class origins, her age, nor her status as a mother protected Alaíde. She was not unique, however; in Argentina several members of the Mothers' movement would disappear, and in Chile women students received the same rough treatment from the triumphant military as men.

*And, Franco says, "In this environment, the question of where women stand is pertinent." The essay that follows looks closely at "where women stand" in a Latin-American cultural landscape that is both powerfully real and powerfully imaginary.*

# *Killing Priests, Nuns, Women, Children*

The murder of three American nuns in El Salvador in December 1980, the murder of priests in Brazil and Argentina, the torture of pregnant women in Uruguay, the farming out of "terrorists'" children to military families in the southern cone, the admonitory raping of women in front of their families in several Latin American countries, the Mexican army's attack on unarmed male and female students in Tlatelolco in 1968, the recent kidnapping in broad daylight of a well-known writer, university teacher, and feminist, Alaíde Foppa in Guatemala, the dislodging of Indian communities from traditional lands, plus countless other incidents, all appear more and more to be the well-thought-out atrocities of a concerted offensive. It is part of a war that has pitted unequal forces against one another— on the one hand, the overarmed military who have become instruments of the latest stage of capitalist development and, on the other, not only the left but also certain traditional institutions, the Indian community, the family, and the Church (which still provide sanctuary and refuge for resistance). These institutions owe their effectiveness as refuges to historically based moral rights and traditions, rather like the immunities which (before the recent attack on the Spanish embassy in Guatemala) had accrued to diplomatic space. Homes were, of course, never immune from entry and search but until recently, it was generally males who were rounded up and taken away, often leaving women to carry on and even transmit resistance from one generation to another. Families thus inherited opposition as others inherited positions in the government and bureaucracy.

But what is now at stake is the assault on such formerly immune territories. The attack on the Cathedral in El Salvador in 1980 and the assassination of Archbishop Romero, for instance, showed how little the Church could now claim to be a sanctuary. The resettlement of Indians in Guatemala, of working-class families from militant sectors of Buenos Aires, the destruction of the immunity formerly accorded to wives, mothers, children, nuns, and priests have all taken away every immune space. This assault is not as incompatible as it might at first seem with the military government's organization of its discourse around the sanctity of Church and family. Indeed these convenient abstractions, which once referred to well-defined physical spaces, have subtly shifted their range of meaning. Thus, for instance, the "saucepan" demonstrations of Chilean women during the last months of the Allende regime plainly indicated the emergence of the family as consumer in a society which, under Pinochet, was to acquire its symbolic monument—the spiral-shaped tower of the new labyrinthine shopping center. The Church, once clearly identified as the Catholic Church, and the parish as its territory, has now been replaced by a rather more flexible notion of religion. The conversion of massive sectors of the population all over Latin America to one form or another of Protestantism, the endorsement by Rios Montt, when president of Guatemala, of born-again Christianity, and the active encouragement, in other countries, of fundamentalist sects, all indicate a profound transformation which, until recently, had gone almost unnoticed. Radio and television now promote a serialized and privatized religious experience which no longer needs to be anchored in the physical reality of the parish and in the continuity of family life.

This process can be described as "deterritorialization," although I use this term in a sense rather different from that used by Deleuze and Guattari. In their view (see Gilles Deleuze and Félix Guattari, *Anti-Oedipus: Capitalism and Schizophrenia*, New York, 1977), primitive society (the social machine) does not distinguish between the family and the rest of the social and political field, all of which are inscribed on the socius (that is, the social machine that distinguishes people according to status and affiliations). In the primitive tribe, the socius is the mother earth. What Deleuze and Guattari describe is a process of abstraction which takes place with the emergence of the despotic state that now inscribes people according to their residence, and in doing so "divides the earth as an object and subjects men to a new imperial inscription, in other words to the abstract unity of the State." This they call "pseudo-territoriality," and see it as the substitution of abstract signs (e.g., money) for the signs of the earth and a privatization of the earth itself (as state or private property). Advanced capitalism carries this abstraction much further, recoding persons and making repression into self-repression, exercised not only in the workplace and the streets but within the family, the one place under capitalism where desire can be coded and territorialized (as with Oedipus).

What seems unsatisfactory in Deleuze and Guattari's description of the family is that even though, reading these authors, we may recognize the family's restrictive and repressive qualities, we do not recognize the family's power as a space of refuge and shelter. What seduces us about the home (and what seduces some people about the convent) is that it is a refuge, a place for turning one's back on the world. Max Horkheimer saw (albeit in an idealized fashion) that the family could nourish subjectivities that were alien to capitalism. (Thomas Mann's *Buddenbrooks* is a good example of the subversive effects of the mother inculcating into her son all that will make him incapable of reproducing the work ethic.) In Latin America, this sense of refuge and the sacredness that attaches to certain figures like the mother, the virgin, the nun, and the priest acquire even greater significance, both because the Church and the home retained a traditional topography and traditional practices over a very long period, and also because during periods when the state was relatively weak these institutions were the only functioning social organizations. They were states within the state, or even counter-states, since there are certain parishes and certain families which have nourished traditions of resistance to the state and hold on to concepts of "moral right" (E. P. Thompson's term), which account for their opposition to "modernization" (i.e., integration into capitalism). This is not to say that the patriarchal and hierarchical family, whose priority was the reproduction of the social order, has not rooted itself in Latin American soil. But the family has been a powerful rival to the state, somehow more real, often the source of a maternal power which is by no means to be despised, particularly when, as in contemporary Latin America, the disappearance of political spaces has turned the family (and the mother, in particular) into a major institution of resistance.

It is only by recognizing the traditional power of the family and the Church and the association of this power with a particular space (the home, the Church building) that we can begin to understand the significance of recent events in Latin America. Beginning in the fifties and early sixties, "development" brought new sectors of the population, including women, into the labor force. The expansion of transnational companies into Latin America depended on the pool of cheap labor formed from the uprooted peasantry and the ever-growing sector of urban under-classes. The smooth functioning of this new industrial revolution was imperiled by the guerrilla movements and movements of national liberation which, in turn, confronted the counterinsurgency campaigns of the sixties that "modernized" the armies of Latin America, making them pioneers in the newest of torture methods and inventive masters of the art of "disappearance." It is this counterinsurgency movement which has destroyed both the notion of sacred space and the immunity which, in theory if not in practice, belonged to nuns, priests, women, and children.

Though women have never enjoyed complete immunity from state terror—indeed rape has been the casually employed resource of forces of law and order since the Conquest—the rapidity with which the new governments have been able to take immunity away from the traditional institutions of Church and family calls for explanation. Such an explanation would involve understanding not only the particular incidents mentioned at the beginning of this essay, but the profound consequences of destroying what Bachelard, in *The Poetics of Space*, called the "images of felicitous spaces," or topophilia. Bachelard's investigations "seek to determine the human value of the sorts of space that may be grasped, that may be defended against adverse forces, the space we love. For diverse reasons, and with the differences entailed by poetic shadings, this is eulogized space. Attached to its protective value, which can be a positive one, are also imagined values, which soon become dominant" (Introduction, p. xxxiii). In this essay, I want to give these felicitous spaces a more concrete and historical existence than Bachelard's phenomenology allows, for only in this way can we understand the really extraordinary sacrilege that we are now witnessing.

Although it is impossible to separate the literary from the social, literature is a good place to begin to understand this Latin American imaginary with its clearly demarcated spaces. In common with Mediterranean countries, public space in Latin America was strictly separated from the private space of the house (brothel), home, and convent, that is spaces which were clearly marked as "feminine." These spaces gave women a certain territorial but restricted power base and at the same time offered the "felicitous" spaces for the repose of the warrior. Nothing illustrates this better than the description of the return of José Arcadio Buendía's blood to its place of origin in his mother's kitchen in García Márquez's *One Hundred Years of Solitude*. The thread of blood "passed along the street of the Turks, turned a corner to the right and another to the left, made a right angle at the Buendía house, went in under the closed door, crossed through the parlor, hugging the walls so as not to stain the rugs, went on to the other living room, made a wide curve to avoid the dining-room table, went along the porch with the begonias, and passed without being seen under Amaranta's chair as she gave an arithmetic lesson to Aureliano José, and went through the pantry and came out in the kitchen, where Ursula was getting ready to crack thirty-six eggs to make bread."

The blood of one of the most *macho* of the Buendías thus follows the order of "feminine" domesticity, traces its path through the women's peaceful and comforting everyday activities which stand in stark opposition to the male world of physical and intellectual prowess and war (the virile or in its most recent and reduced game-cock version—the *macho*).

To view the home thus as a sanctuary obviously makes it into a male-idealized otherness (the Utopia) whilst locking women into this pacific domesticity. House, home, and convent are undoubtedly constructions produced by a sex-gender system in which feminine categories are organized in relation to the presence/absence of the phallus, understood in this case as the source of symbolic power. The "logic" of this organization can be illustrated by a semiotic quadrangle (see figure).

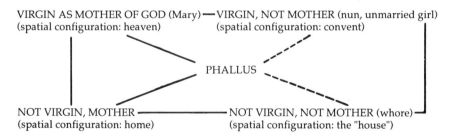

VIRGIN AS MOTHER OF GOD (Mary) — VIRGIN, NOT MOTHER (nun, unmarried girl)
(spatial configuration: heaven)　(spatial configuration: convent)

PHALLUS

NOT VIRGIN, MOTHER ———— NOT VIRGIN, NOT MOTHER (whore)
(spatial configuration: home)　(spatial configuration: the "house")

Because there can only be one mother of God (Mary), all other women fall into one of the three remaining categories of which only one (the mother) can receive the legitimate seed that will allow the system to be reproduced. The extent to which the mother is not only sanctified by this function but is converted into the temple of the species, whose bodily configuration is identical to that of the home, is illustrated in a poem by César Vallejo.

Imagining his return to the family home, his mother's body is reentered as if it were a building:

> Your archways of astonishment expects me,
> The tonsured columns of your cares
> That have eroded life. The patio expects me
> The hallway down below with its indentures and
> its feast-day decorations. My grandfather chair expects me
> that good jowly piece of dynastic leather,
> that stands grumbling at the strapped and strapping
> behind of great great great grandchildren.

The father alone has the right to enter this temple and when he does so, it is on his knees in acknowledgment of an irreversible event.

> Between the colonnade of your bones
> That cannot be brought down even with lamentations
> And into whose side not even Destiny can
> place a single finger!

The reference in the last line is to the doubting finger of Thomas who wished to test the resurrection of Christ by touching the wound. In Vallejo's human mother/temple, no such doubt is possible, for the matrix offers the only unequivocal faith in a chaotic world.

The very structure of the Hispanic house emphasized that it was a private world, shut off from public activity. It was traditionally constructed around two or more patios, the windows onto the street being shuttered or barred. Inside, the patios with their plants and singing birds represented an oasis, a domestic replica of the perfumed garden. Respectable women only emerged from the house when accompanied and when necessary. Their lives were almost as enclosed as those of their counterparts, the brothel whore and the nun. In the fifties, I lived in such a house where windows onto the outside were felt to mark the beginning of danger as indeed, after curfew, they did. A prison yes, but one that could easily be idealized as a sanctuary given the violence of political life.

The convent was also a sanctuary of sorts, one that gathered into itself the old, the homeless, and the dedicated to God. In José Donoso's novel *The Obscene Bird of Night*, the convent has become an extended building housing the archaic, the mythic, and the hallucinating desires which are outlawed from the rest of society. It is this aspect of the Hispanic imaginary which Buñuel's films also capture. Archaic in topography, its huge, empty, decrepit rooms not only sealed it off entirely from the outside world but made it into a taboo territory, the violation of which tempted and terrorized the male imagination.

Finally there was the brothel, the house whose topography mimed that of the convent, with its small cell-like rooms and which, as described by Mario Vargas Llosa in his novel *The Green House*, was another version of the oasis. As the convent gathered to itself the women who were no longer sexual objects, the green house offered them as the common receptacles of a male seed absolved from the strict social rules that governed reproduction.

> Blacks, mulattoes, mixtures of all kinds, drunks, somnolent or frightened half-breeds, skinny Chinese, old men, small groups of young Spaniards and Italians walking through the patios out of curiosity. They walked to and fro passing the open doors of the bedrooms, stopping to look in from time to time. The prostitutes, dressed in cotton dresses, were seated at the back of the rooms on low boxes. Most of them sat with their legs apart showing their sex, the "fox" which was sometimes shaved and sometimes not. (José María Arguedas, *The Fox Above and the Fox Below*)

In describing these spaces, I am not describing categories of women but an imaginary topography in which the "feminine" was rigidly compartmentalized and assigned particular territories. Individual women constantly transgressed these boundaries but the territories themselves were loaded with significance and so inextricably bound to the sacred that they were often taken for spaces of immunity. With the increase in state terrorism in the sixties, mothers used this traditional immunity to protest, abandoning the shelter of homes for the public square, taking charge of the dead and the disappeared and the prisoners whose existence no one else wished to acknowledge. With the seizure of power by the military, the dismantling of political parties and trade unions, this activity acquired a special importance. Homes became hiding places, bomb factories, escape hatches, people's prisons. From the signifier of passivity and peace, mother became a signifier of resistance. Nothing illustrates this in more dramatic fashion than an article by Rodolfo Walsh (an Argentine writer who would himself "disappear" shortly after writing this piece). His daughter, who was the mother of a small child and whose lover had already disappeared, was one of a group of *montoneros*° killed in the army attack on a house, an attack which deployed 150 men, tanks, and helicopters. A soldier who had participated in this battle described the girl's final moments.

> The battle lasted more than an hour and a half. A man and woman were shooting from upstairs. The girl caught our attention because every time she fired and we dodged out of

---

**montoneros**   A resistance movement in opposition to the military dictatorship in Argentina.

the way, she laughed. All at once there was silence. The girl let go of the machine gun, stood up on the parapet, and opened her arms. We stopped firing without being ordered to and we could see her quite well. She was skinny, with short hair and she was wearing a nightdress. She began to talk to us calmly but clearly. I don't remember everything she said, but I remember the last sentence. In fact, I could not sleep for thinking of it. "You are not killing us," she said, "we choose to die." Then she and the man put pistols to their foreheads and killed themselves in front of us.

When the army took over the house, they found a little girl sitting un-harmed on the bed and five dead bodies.

The significance of such an event goes far beyond the rights and wrongs of local politics. Like the murder of the nuns in El Salvador and the kid-napping and killing of Alaíde Foppa in Guatemala, it is a cataclysmic event which makes it impossible to think of the Utopian in terms of space or of the feminine in the traditional sense. Most disconcerting of all, the destruc-tion of these Utopian spaces has been conducted not by the left but by the right-wing military who have nothing left to offer but the unattainable com-modity (unattainable, that is, for all but the army and the technocrats). It is true that the military of some southern-cone countries are now in (tem-porary?) eclipse, but the smell of the cadaver will not be dispelled by the commodity culture, a debt-ridden economy and the forms of restored po-litical democracy.

It is some time since Herbert Marcuse drew attention to the terrors of a desublimated world, one in which such spaces and sanctuaries had been wiped out. His analysis and that of Horkheimer can be seen as overbur-dened with nostalgia for that *gemütlich* interior of European bourgeois fam-ily life in which all the children played instruments in a string quartet. But even if we can no longer accept the now challenged Freudian language of his analysis, he undoubtedly deserves credit for monitoring the first signals from an empty space once occupied by archaic but powerful figures. Fem-inist criticism based on the critique of patriarchy and the traffic in women has rightly shed no tears for this liquidation of mother figures whose power was also servitude. Yet such criticism has perhaps underestimated the op-positional potentialities of these female territories whose importance as the *only* sanctuaries became obvious at the moment of their disappearance.

This is, however, an essay without a conclusion. I wrote it, thinking of an old friend of mine, Alaíde Foppa, who in 1954 provided sanctuary for those of us left behind in Guatemala and trying to get out after the Castillo Armas coup. I have a vivid memory of her reciting a poem about her five children "like the five fingers of her hand." Today there are only three children left. During the 1960s and 1970s, Alaíde became the driving force behind the feminist movement in Mexico. She was used to going back home once a year to Guatemala to visit her mother. In 1980 she did not come back. A Guatemalan newspaper reported that her whereabouts and that of her chauffeur were "unknown." To this day, Alaíde "continues disappeared" in the words of the newspaper, like many other men, women, priests, nuns, and children in Latin America who no longer occupy space but who have a place.

.   .   .   .   .   .   .   .   .   .   .   .

## QUESTIONS FOR A SECOND READING

1. Franco makes a distinction between physical space—actual places—and space as part of an "imaginary"—an imaginary topography, a set of references that belong to a discourse (a habitual way of speaking and thinking) and that organize and value experience. Thus she can talk about house, home, and convent as specific places but also as figures of speech (where a house is different from a home), as "constructions produced by a sex-gender system in which feminine categories are organized in relation to the presence/absence of the phallus, understood in this case as the source of symbolic power." As you reread the essay, pay attention to where and how she makes these references, to how and why a place becomes a figure of speech, and to what the implications of this transformation are for an analysis of political events.

2. The final paragraph of the selection begins "This is, however, an essay without a conclusion." There is, however, a final paragraph. If this is not a conclusion, what is it? And why do you suppose Franco stops the discussion where she does and tries to imagine an ending that is not an ending? One could argue that Franco just ran out of gas or space. But one could also argue that this unusual ending was a careful and complex move on her part. As you reread the essay, think about its organization (and what it says about organization) and see how you might read the gesture represented by this last paragraph.

## ASSIGNMENTS FOR WRITING

1. Bachelard's investigations "seek to determine the human value of the sorts of space that may be grasped, that may be defended against adverse forces, the space we love. For diverse reasons, and with the differences entailed by poetic shadings, this is eulogized space. Attached to its protective value, which can be a positive one, are also imagined values, which soon become dominant." . . . In this essay,

203

I want to give these felicitous spaces a more concrete and historical
existence. . . . (p. 198).

Franco's essay is offered as an attempt to understand a "Latin American
imaginary"—that is, a way of thinking and speaking that is rooted in the
culture and that could be said to *produce* the world experienced as "naturally" there: "House, home, and convent are undoubtedly constructions
produced by a sex-gender system." Her essay could also be read as an
attempt to understand the relationship between the "imaginary," on the
one hand and on the other, history, society, political violence—things that
are materially there in the world.

Write an essay that explores a contemporary North American "imaginary," a topography or "map" produced to organize the landscape into
clearly demarcated spaces. Think of your essay as a response to Franco.
You should imagine your project as an investigation of particular sites or
spaces, bringing forward the system or logic that governs the position and
significance of these sites in the North American imaginary. And, at some
point, you should speculate on the interaction between the imaginary and
the social or political in national life.

2. One can, as in the preceding assignment, use Franco's work to investigate
   a national imaginary. One can also use it to investigate a local site, to see
   what it might represent if a particular arrangement of buildings, rooms, or
   neighborhoods were "read" as part of a discourse, a systematic way of organizing what we see, say, and understand.

   Turn to a set of spaces whose organization you see or sense, even if
   you have never taken the time to work out what that organization might
   mean or what, in terms of that organization, each of the spaces might signify. You might, in fact, make a chart, one inspired by, although not necessarily in imitation of, Franco's. Once you have completed your preliminary research, write an essay in which you present the results of your
   investigations, an essay that presents your topography and examines how
   it might be read.

## MAKING CONNECTIONS

1. Franco says, "Although it is impossible to separate the literary from the
   social, literature is a good place to begin to understand this Latin American
   imaginary with its clearly demarcated spaces." Turn to Carlos Fuentes's
   story, "The Son of Andrés Aparicio" (p. 239). There is no question but that
   this is a man's story—it is about fathers and sons and the ways men organize themselves inside and outside the home.

   Write an essay in which you use Fuentes's story to test or extend Franco's presentation of the Latin American imaginary. In particular, assess the
   degree to which the story reflects (or revises, or resists) the changes Franco
   says came with the political violence of the 1960s.

2. Harriet Jacobs, in "Incidents in the Life of a Slave Girl" (p. 312), represents places and culture of slave society in the South of the United States before the Civil War. Following Franco's lead, how might you chart and read the distribution of spaces in Jacobs's world, particularly those spaces Jacobs fears and desires, spaces imagined as either safe and free or dangerous and limiting? How would you compare Franco's representation of the Latin American imaginary with the imaginary governing this Carolina community?

   Write an essay in which you apply Franco's method of analysis in a close reading of the real and imaginary topography of "Incidents."

# PAULO
# FREIRE

*P*AULO FREIRE *(pronounce it "Fr-air-ah" unless you can make a Portuguese "r") is one of the most influential radical educators of our world. A native of Recife, Brazil, he spent most of his early career working in poverty-stricken areas of his homeland, developing methods for teaching illiterate adults to read and write and (as he would say) to think critically and, thereby, to take power over their own lives. Because he has created a classroom where teachers and students have equal power and equal dignity, his work has stood as a model for educators around the world. It led also to sixteen years of exile after the military coup in Brazil in 1964. During that time he taught in Europe and in the United States and worked for the Allende government in Chile, training the teachers whose job it would be to bring modern agricultural methods to the peasants.*

*Freire was born in 1921. He has worked with the adult education programs of UNESCO, the Chilean Institute of Agrarian Reform, and the World Council of Churches. He is now professor of educational philosophy at the Catholic University of São Paulo. He is the author of* Education for Critical Consciousness, The Politics of Education, *and* The Pedagogy of the Oppressed *(from which the following essay is drawn).*

For Freire, education is not an objective process, if by objective we mean "neutral" or "without bias or prejudice." Because teachers could be said to have something that their students lack, it is impossible to have a "neutral" classroom; and when teachers present a subject to their students, they also present a point of view on that subject. The choice, according to Freire, is fairly simple: teachers either work "for the liberation of the people—their humanization—or for their domestication, their domination." The practice of teaching, however, is anything but simple. According to Freire, a teacher's most crucial skill is his or her ability to assist students' struggle to gain control over the conditions of their lives, and this means helping them not only to know but "to know that they know."

Recently, Freire edited, along with Henry A. Giroux of Miami University in Ohio, a series of books on education and teaching. In Literacy: Reading the Word and the World, a book for the series, Freire describes the interrelationship between reading the written word and understanding the world that surrounds us. "My parents introduced me to reading the word at a certain moment in this rich experience of understanding my immediate world. Deciphering the word flowed naturally from reading my particular world; it was not something superimposed on it. I learned to read and write on the grounds of the backyard of my house, in the shade of the mango trees, with words from my world rather than from the wider world of my parents. The earth was my blackboard, the sticks my chalk." For Freire, reading the written word involves understanding a text in its very particular social and historical context. Thus reading always involves "critical perception, interpretation, and rewriting of what is read."

# The "Banking" Concept of Education

A careful analysis of the teacher-student relationship at any level, inside or outside the school, reveals its fundamentally *narrative* character. This relationship involves a narrating Subject (the teacher) and patient, listening objects (the students). The contents, whether values or empirical dimensions of reality, tend in the process of being narrated to become lifeless and petrified. Education is suffering from narration sickness.

The teacher talks about reality as if it were motionless, static, compartmentalized, and predictable. Or else he expounds on a topic completely alien to the existential experience of the students. His task is to "fill" the students with the contents of his narration—contents which are detached from reality, disconnected from the totality that engendered them and could give them significance. Words are emptied of their concreteness and become a hollow, alienated, and alienating verbosity.

The outstanding characteristic of this narrative education, then, is the sonority of words, not their transforming power. "Four times four is sixteen; the capital of Pará is Belém." The student records, memorizes, and repeats these phrases without perceiving what four times four really means, or realizing the true significance of "capital" in the affirmation "the capital of Pará is Belém," that is, what Belém means for Pará and what Pará means for Brazil.

Narration (with the teacher as narrator) leads the students to memorize mechanically the narrated content. Worse yet, it turns them into "containers," into "receptacles" to be "filled" by the teacher. The more completely he fills the receptacles, the better a teacher he is. The more meekly the receptacles permit themselves to be filled, the better students they are.

Education thus becomes an act of depositing, in which the students are the depositories and the teacher is the depositor. Instead of communicating, the teacher issues communiqués and makes deposits which the students patiently receive, memorize, and repeat. This is the "banking" concept of education, in which the scope of action allowed to the students extends only as far as receiving, filing, and storing the deposits. They do, it is true, have the opportunity to become collectors or cataloguers of the things they store. But in the last analysis, it is men themselves who are filed away through the lack of creativity, transformation, and knowledge in this (at best) misguided system. For apart from inquiry, apart from the praxis, men cannot be truly human. Knowledge emerges only through invention and reinvention, through the restless, impatient, continuing, hopeful inquiry men pursue in the world, with the world, and with each other.

In the banking concept of education, knowledge is a gift bestowed by those who consider themselves knowledgeable upon those whom they consider to know nothing. Projecting an absolute ignorance onto others, a characteristic of the ideology of oppression, negates education and knowledge as processes of inquiry. The teacher presents himself to his students as their necessary opposite; by considering their ignorance absolute, he justifies his own existence. The students, alienated like the slave in the Hegelian dialectic, accept their ignorance as justifying the teacher's existence—but, unlike the slave, they never discover that they educate the teacher.

The *raison d'être* of libertarian education, on the other hand, lies in its drive towards reconciliation. Education must begin with the solution of the teacher-student contradiction, by reconciling the poles of the contradiction so that both are simultaneously teachers *and* students.

This solution is not (nor can it be) found in the banking concept. On the contrary, banking education maintains and even stimulates the contradiction through the following attitudes and practices, which mirror oppressive society as a whole:

a. the teacher teaches and the students are taught;
b. the teacher knows everything and the students know nothing;
c. the teacher thinks and the students are thought about;
d. the teacher talks and the students listen—meekly;
e. the teacher disciplines and the students are disciplined;
f. the teacher chooses and enforces his choice, and the students comply;
g. the teacher acts and the students have the illusion of acting through the action of the teacher;
h. the teacher chooses the program content, and the students (who were not consulted) adapt to it;
i. the teacher confuses the authority of knowledge with his own professional authority, which he sets in opposition to the freedom of the students;
j. the teacher is the Subject of the learning process, while the pupils are mere objects.

It is not surprising that the banking concept of education regards men as adaptable, manageable beings. The more students work at storing the deposits entrusted to them, the less they develop the critical consciousness which would result from their intervention in the world as transformers of that world. The more completely they accept the passive role imposed on them, the more they tend simply to adapt to the world as it is and to the fragmented view of reality deposited in them.

The capability of banking education to minimize or annul the students' creative power and to stimulate their credulity serves the interests of the oppressors, who care neither to have the world revealed nor to see it transformed. The oppressors use their "humanitarianism" to preserve a profitable situation. Thus they react almost instinctively against any experiment in education which stimulates the critical faculties and is not content with a partial view of reality but always seeks out the ties which link one point to another and one problem to another.

Indeed, the interests of the oppressors lie in "changing the consciousness of the oppressed, not the situation which oppresses them";[1] for the more the oppressed can be led to adapt to that situation, the more easily they can be dominated. To achieve this end, the oppressors use the banking concept of education in conjunction with a paternalistic social action apparatus, within which the oppressed receive the euphemistic title of "welfare recipients." They are treated as individual cases, as marginal men who deviate from the general configuration of a "good, organized, and just" society. The oppressed are regarded as the pathology of the healthy society, which must therefore adjust these "incompetent and lazy" folk to its own patterns by changing their mentality. These marginals need to be "integrated," "incorporated" into the healthy society that they have "foresaken."

The truth is, however, that the oppressed are not "marginals," are not men living "outside" society. They have always been "inside"—inside the structure which made them "beings for others." The solution is not to "integrate" them into the structure of oppression, but to transform that structure so that they can become "beings for themselves." Such transformation, of course, would undermine the oppressors' purposes; hence their utilization of the banking concept of education to avoid the threat of student *conscientização.*°

The banking approach to adult education, for example, will never propose to students that they critically consider reality. It will deal instead with such vital questions as whether Roger gave green grass to the goat, and insist upon the importance of learning that, on the contrary, Roger gave green grass to the rabbit. The "humanism" of the banking approach masks the effort to turn men into automatons—the very negation of their ontological vocation to be more fully human.

Those who use the banking approach, knowingly or unknowingly (for there are innumerable well-intentioned bank-clerk teachers who do not realize that they are serving only to dehumanize), fail to perceive that the deposits themselves contain contradictions about reality. But, sooner or later, these contradictions may lead formerly passive students to turn against their domestication and the attempt to domesticate reality. They may discover through existential experience that their present way of life is irreconcilable with their vocation to become fully human. They may perceive through their relations with reality that reality is really a *process*, undergoing constant transformation. If men are searchers and their ontological vocation is humanization, sooner or later they may perceive the contradiction in which banking education seeks to maintain them, and then engage themselves in the struggle for their liberation.

But the humanist, revolutionary educator cannot wait for this possibility to materialize. From the outset, his efforts must coincide with those of the students to engage in critical thinking and the quest for mutual humanization. His efforts must be imbued with a profound trust in men and their

---

**conscientização**  According to Freire's translator, "The term *conscientização* refers to learning to perceive social, political, and economic contradictions, and to take action against the oppressive elements of reality."

creative power. To achieve this, he must be a partner of the students in his relations with them.

The banking concept does not admit to such partnership—and necessarily so. To resolve the teacher-student contradiction, to exchange the role of depositor, prescriber, domesticator, for the role of student among students would be to undermine the power of oppression and serve the cause of liberation.

Implicit in the banking concept is the assumption of a dichotomy between man and the world: man is merely *in* the world, not *with* the world or with others; man is spectator, not re-creator. In this view, man is not a conscious being (*corpo consciente*); he is rather the possessor of *a* consciousness: an empty "mind" passively open to the reception of deposits of reality from the world outside. For example, my desk, my books, my coffee cup, all the objects before me—as bits of the world which surrounds me—would be "inside" me, exactly as I am inside my study right now. This view makes no distinction between being accessible to consciousness and entering consciousness. The distinction, however, is essential: the objects which surround me are simply accessible to my consciousness, not located within it. I am aware of them, but they are not inside me.

It follows logically from the banking notion of consciousness that the educator's role is to regulate the way the world "enters into" the students. His task is to organize a process which already occurs spontaneously, to "fill" the students by making deposits of information which he considers to constitute true knowledge. [2] And since men "receive" the world as passive entities, education should make them more passive still, and adapt them to the world. The educated man is the adapted man, because he is better "fit" for the world. Translated into practice, this concept is well suited to the purposes of the oppressors, whose tranquility rests on how well men fit the world the oppressors have created, and how little they question it.

The more completely the majority adapt to the purposes which the dominant minority prescribe for them (thereby depriving them of the right to their own purposes), the more easily the minority can continue to prescribe. The theory and practice of banking education serve this end quite efficiently. Verbalistic lessons, reading requirements, [3] the methods for evaluating "knowledge," the distance between the teacher and the taught, the criteria for promotion: everything in this ready-to-wear approach serves to obviate thinking.

The bank-clerk educator does not realize that there is no true security in his hypertrophied role, that one must seek to live *with* others in solidarity. One cannot impose oneself, nor even merely co-exist with one's students. Solidarity requires true communication, and the concept by which such an educator is guided fears and proscribes communication.

211

Yet only through communication can human life hold meaning. The teacher's thinking is authenticated only by the authenticity of the students' thinking. The teacher cannot think for his students, nor can he impose his thought on them. Authentic thinking, thinking that is concerned about *reality*, does not take place in ivory tower isolation, but only in communication. If it is true that thought has meaning only when generated by action upon the world, the subordination of students to teachers becomes impossible.

Because banking education begins with a false understanding of men as objects, it cannot promote the development of what Fromm calls "biophily," but instead produces its opposite: "necrophily."

> While life is characterized by growth in a structured, functional manner, the necrophilous person loves all that does not grow, all that is mechanical. The necrophilous person is driven by the desire to transform the organic into the inorganic, to approach life mechanically, as if all living persons were things. . . . Memory, rather than experience; having, rather than being, is what counts. The necrophilous person can relate to an object—a flower or a person—only if he possesses it; hence a threat to his possession is a threat to himself; if he loses possession he loses contact with the world. . . . He loves control, and in the act of controlling he kills life. [4]

Oppression—overwhelming control—is necrophilic; it is nourished by love of death, not life. The banking concept of education, which serves the interests of oppression, is also necrophilic. Based on a mechanistic, static, naturalistic, spatialized view of consciousness, it transforms students into receiving objects. It attempts to control thinking and action, leads men to adjust to the world, and inhibits their creative power.

When their efforts to act responsibly are frustrated, when they find themselves unable to use their faculties, men suffer. "The suffering due to impotence is rooted in the very fact that the human equilibrium has been disturbed." [5] But the inability to act which causes men's anguish also causes them to reject their impotence, by attempting

> . . . to restore [their] capacity to act. But can [they], and how? One way is to submit to and identify with a person or group having power. By this symbolic participation in another person's life, [men have] the illusion of acting, when in reality [they] only submit to and become part of those who act. [6]

Populist manifestations perhaps best exemplify this type of behavior by the oppressed, who, by identifying with charismatic leaders, come to feel that they themselves are active and effective. The rebellion they express as they emerge in the historical process is motivated by that desire to act effectively. The dominant elites consider the remedy to be more domination and repression, carried out in the name of freedom, order, and social peace (that is, the peace of the elites). Thus they can condemn—logically, from their point of view—"the violence of a strike by workers and [can] call upon the state in the same breath to use violence in putting down the strike." [7]

Education as the exercise of domination stimulates the credulity of students, with the ideological intent (often not perceived by educators) of indoctrinating them to adapt to the world of oppression. This accusation is not made in the naïve hope that the dominant elites will thereby simply abandon the practice. Its objective is to call the attention of true humanists to the fact that they cannot use banking educational methods in the pursuit of liberation, for they would only negate that very pursuit. Nor may a revolutionary society inherit these methods from an oppressor society. The revolutionary society which practices banking education is either misguided or mistrusting of men. In either event, it is threatened by the specter of reaction.

Unfortunately, those who espouse the cause of liberation are themselves surrounded and influenced by the climate which generates the banking concept, and often do not perceive its true significance or its dehumanizing power. Paradoxically, then, they utilize this same instrument of alienation in what they consider an effort to liberate. Indeed, some "revolutionaries" brand as "innocents," "dreamers," or even "reactionaries" those who would challenge this educational practice. But one does not liberate men by alienating them. Authentic liberation—the process of humanization—is not another deposit to be made in men. Liberation is a praxis: the action and reflection of men upon their world in order to transform it. Those truly committed to the cause of liberation can accept neither the mechanistic concept of consciousness as an empty vessel to be filled, nor the use of banking methods of domination (propaganda, slogans—deposits) in the name of the liberation.

Those truly committed to liberation must reject the banking concept in its entirety, adopting instead a concept of men as conscious beings, and consciousness as consciousness intent upon the world. They must abandon the educational goal of deposit-making and replace it with the posing of the problems of men in their relations with the world. "Problem-posing" education, responding to the essence of consciousness—*intentionality*—rejects communiqués and embodies communications. It epitomizes the special characteristic of consciousness: being *conscious of,* not only as intent on objects but as turned in upon itself in a Jasperian "split"—consciousness as consciousness *of* consciousness.

Liberating education consists in acts of cognition, not transferrals of information. It is a learning situation in which the cognizable object (far from being the end of the cognitive act) intermediates the cognitive actors—

teacher on the one hand and students on the other. Accordingly, the practice of problem-posing education entails at the outset that the teacher-student contradiction be resolved. Dialogical relations—indispensable to the capacity of cognitive actors to cooperate in perceiving the same cognizable object—are otherwise impossible.

Indeed, problem-posing education, which breaks with the vertical patterns characteristic of banking education, can fulfill its function as the practice of freedom only if it can overcome the above contradiction. Through dialogue, the teacher-of-the-students and the students-of-the-teacher cease to exist and a new term emerges: teacher-students with students-teacher. The teacher is no longer merely the-one-who-teaches, but one who is himself taught in dialogue with the students, who in turn while being taught also teach. They become jointly responsible for a process in which all grow. In this process, arguments based on "authority" are no longer valid; in order to function, authority must be *on the side of* freedom, not *against* it. Here, no one teaches another, nor is anyone self-taught. Men teach each other, mediated by the world, by the cognizable objects which in banking education are "owned" by the teacher.

The banking concept (with its tendency to dichotomize everything) distinguishes two stages in the action of the educator. During the first he cognizes a cognizable object while he prepares his lessons in his study or his laboratory; during the second, he expounds to his students about that object. The students are not called upon to know, but to memorize the contents narrated by the teacher. Nor do the students practice any act of cognition, since the object towards which that act should be directed is the property of the teacher rather than a medium evoking the critical reflection of both teacher and students. Hence in the name of the "preservation of culture and knowledge" we have a system which achieves neither true knowledge nor true culture.

The problem-posing method does not dichotomize the activity of the teacher-student: he is not "cognitive" at one point and "narrative" at another. He is always "cognitive," whether preparing a project or engaging in dialogue with the students. He does not regard cognizable objects as his private property, but as the object of reflection by himself and the students. In this way, the problem-posing educator constantly re-forms his reflections in the reflection of the students. The students—no longer docile listeners—are now critical co-investigators in dialogue with the teacher. The teacher presents the material to the students for their consideration, and re-considers his earlier considerations as the students express their own. The role of the problem-posing educator is to create, together with the students, the conditions under which knowledge at the level of the *doxa* is superseded by true knowledge, at the level of the *logos*.

Whereas banking education anesthetizes and inhibits creative power, problem-posing education involves a constant unveiling of reality. The former attempts to maintain the *submersion* of consciousness; the latter strives for the *emergence* of consciousness and *critical intervention* in reality.

Students, as they are increasingly posed with problems relating to themselves in the world and with the world, will feel increasingly challenged and obliged to respond to that challenge. Because they apprehend the challenge as interrelated to other problems within a total context, not as a theoretical question, the resulting comprehension tends to be increasingly critical and thus constantly less alienated. Their response to the challenge evokes new challenges, followed by new understandings; and gradually the students come to regard themselves as committed.

Education as the practice of freedom—as opposed to education as the practice of domination—denies that man is abstract, isolated, independent, and unattached to the world; it also denies that the world exists as a reality apart from men. Authentic reflection considers neither abstract man nor the world without men, but men in their relations with the world. In these relations consciousness and world are simultaneous: consciousness neither precedes the world nor follows it.

> La conscience et le monde sont donnés d'un même coup: extérieur par essence à la conscience, le monde est, par essence relatif à elle. [8]

In one of our culture circles in Chile, the group was discussing . . . the anthropological concept of culture. In the midst of the discussion, a peasant who by banking standards was completely ignorant said: "Now I see that without man there is no world." When the educator responded: "Let's say, for the sake of argument, that all the men on earth were to die, but that the earth itself remained, together with trees, birds, animals, rivers, seas, the stars . . . wouldn't all this be a world?"

"Oh, no," the peasant replied emphatically. "There would be no one to say: 'This is a world'."

The peasant wished to express the idea that there would be lacking the consciousness of the world which necessarily implies the world of consciousness. *I* cannot exist without a *not-I*. In turn, the *not-I* depends on that existence. The world which brings consciousness into existence becomes the world of that consciousness. Hence, the previously cited affirmation of Sartre: *"La conscience et le monde sont donnés d'un même coup."*

As men, simultaneously reflecting on themselves and on the world, increase the scope of their perception, they begin to direct their observations towards previously inconspicuous phenomena:

> In perception properly so-called, as an explicit awareness [*Gewahren*], I am turned towards the object, to the paper, for in-

215

stance. I apprehend it as being this here and now. The apprehension is a singling out, every object having a background in experience. Around and about the paper lie books, pencils, ink-well, and so forth, and these in a certain sense are also "perceived," perceptually there, in the "field of intuition"; but whilst I was turned towards the paper there was no turning in their direction, nor any apprehending of them, not even in a secondary sense. They appeared and yet were not singled out, were not posited on their own account. Every perception of a thing has such a zone of background intuitions or background awareness, if "intuiting" already includes the state of being turned towards, and this also is a "conscious experience," or more briefly a "consciousness of" all indeed that in point of fact lies in the co-perceived objective background. [9]

That which had existed objectively but had not been perceived in its deeper implications (if indeed it was perceived at all) begins to "stand out," assuming the character of a problem and therefore of challenge. Thus, men begin to single out elements from their "background awarenesses" and to reflect upon them. These elements are now objects of men's consideration, and, as such, objects of their action and cognition.

In problem-posing education, men develop their power to perceive critically *the way they exist* in the world *with which* and *in which* they find themselves; they come to see the world not as a static reality, but as a reality in process, in transformation. Although the dialectical relations of men with the world exist independently of how these relations are perceived (or whether or not they are perceived at all), it is also true that the form of action men adopt is to a large extent a function of how they perceive themselves in the world. Hence, the teacher-students and the students-teacher reflect simultaneously on themselves and the world without dichotomizing this reflection from action, and thus establish an authentic form of thought and action.

Once again, the two educational concepts and practices under analysis come into conflict. Banking education (for obvious reasons) attempts, by mythicizing reality, to conceal certain facts which explain the way men exist in the world; problem-posing education sets itself the task of demythologizing. Banking education resists dialogue; problem-posing education regards dialogue as indispensable to the act of cognition which unveils reality. Banking education treats students as objects of assistance; problem-posing education makes them critical thinkers. Banking education inhibits creativity and domesticates (although it cannot completely destroy) the *intentionality* of consciousness by isolating consciousness from the world, thereby denying men their ontological and historical vocation of becoming more fully human. Problem-posing education bases itself on creativity and stimulates true reflection and action upon reality, thereby responding to the vocation of men as beings who are authentic only when engaged in inquiry and creative transformation. In sum: banking theory and practice, as immobilizing and fixating forces, fail to acknowledge men as historical beings; problem-posing theory and practice take man's historicity as their starting point.

Problem-posing education affirms men as beings in the process of *becoming*—as unfinished, uncompleted beings in and with a likewise unfinished reality. Indeed, in contrast to other animals who are unfinished, but not historical, men know themselves to be unfinished; they are aware of their incompletion. In this incompletion and this awareness lie the very roots of education as an exclusively human manifestation. The unfinished character of men and the transformational character of reality necessitate that education be an ongoing activity.

Education is thus constantly remade in the praxis. In order to *be*, it must *become*. Its "duration" (in the Bergsonian meaning of the word) is found in the interplay of the opposites *permanence* and *change*. The banking method emphasizes permanence and becomes reactionary; problem-posing education—which accepts neither a "well-be-haved" present nor a predetermined future—roots itself in the dynamic present and becomes revolutionary.

Problem-posing education is revolutionary futurity. Hence it is prophetic (and, as such, hopeful). Hence, it corresponds to the historical nature of man. Hence, it affirms men as beings who transcend themselves, who move forward and look ahead, for whom immobility represents a fatal threat, for whom looking at the past must only be a means of understanding more clearly what and who they are so that they can more wisely build a future. Hence, it identifies with the movement which engages men as beings aware of their incompletion—an historical movement which has its point of departure, its Subjects and its objective.

The point of departure of the movement lies in men themselves. But since men do not exist apart from the world, apart from reality, the movement must begin with the men-world relationship. Accordingly, the point of departure must always be with men in the "here and now," which constitutes the situation within which they are submerged, from which they emerge, and in which they intervene. Only by starting from this situation—which determines their perception of it—can they begin to move. To do this authentically they must perceive their state not as fated and unalterable, but merely as limiting—and therefore challenging.

Whereas the banking method directly or indirectly reinforces men's fatalistic perception of their situation, the problem-posing method presents this very situation to them as a problem. As the situation becomes the object of their cognition, the naïve or magical perception which produced their fatalism gives way to perception which is able to perceive itself even as it perceives reality, and can thus be critically objective about that reality.

A deepened consciousness of their situation leads men to apprehend that situation as an historical reality susceptible of transformation. Resignation gives way to the drive for transformation and inquiry, over which men feel themselves to be in control. If men, as historical beings necessarily engaged with other men in a movement of inquiry, did not control that movement, it would be (and is) a violation of men's humanity. Any situation in which some men prevent others from engaging in the process of inquiry is one of violence. The means used are not important; to alienate men from their own decision-making is to change them into objects.

This movement of inquiry must be directed towards humanization—man's historical vocation. The pursuit of full humanity, however, cannot be carried out in isolation or individualism, but only in fellowship and solidarity; therefore it cannot unfold in the antagonistic relations between oppressors and oppressed. No one can be authentically human while he prevents others from being so. Attempting *to be more* human, individualistically, leads to *having more*, egotistically: a form of dehumanization. Not that it is not fundamental *to have* in order *to be* human. Precisely because it *is* necessary, some men's *having* must not be allowed to constitute an obstacle to others' *having*, must not consolidate the power of the former to crush the latter.

Problem-posing education, as a humanist and liberating praxis, posits as fundamental that men subjected to domination must fight for their emancipation. To that end, it enables teachers and students to become Subjects of the educational process by overcoming authoritarianism and an alienating intellectualism; it also enables men to overcome their false perception of reality. The world—no longer something to be described with deceptive words—becomes the object of that transforming action by men which results in their humanization.

Problem-posing education does not and cannot serve the interests of the oppressor. No oppressive order could permit the oppressed to begin to question: Why? While only a revolutionary society can carry out this education in systematic terms, the revolutionary leaders need not take full power before they can employ the method. In the revolutionary process, the leaders cannot utilize the banking method as an interim measure, justified on grounds of expediency, with the intention of *later* behaving in a genuinely revolutionary fashion. They must be revolutionary—that is to say, dialogical—from the outset.

NOTES

¹ Simone de Beauvoir, *La Pensée de Droite, Aujourd'hui* (Paris); ST, *El Pensamiento político de la Derecha* (Buenos Aires, 1963), p. 34.

² This concept corresponds to what Sartre calls the "digestive" or "nutritive" concept of education, in which knowledge is "fed" by the teacher to the students to "fill them out." See Jean-Paul Sartre, "Une idée fondamentale de la phénomenologie de Husserl: L'intentionalité," *Situations I* (Paris, 1947).

³ For example, some professors specify in their reading lists that a book should be read from pages 10 to 15—and do this to "help" their students!

⁴ Eric Fromm, *The Heart of Man* (New York, 1966), p. 41.

⁵ *Ibid.*, p. 31.

⁶ *Ibid.*

⁷ Reinhold Niebuhr, *Moral Man and Immoral Society* (New York, 1960), p. 130.

⁸ Sartre, *op. cit.*, p. 32. [The passage is obscure but could be read as "Consciousness and the world are given at one and the same time: the exterior world as it enters consciousness is relative to our ways of seeing and understanding that world." Editors' note.]

⁹ Edmund Husserl, *Ideas—General Introduction to Pure Phenomenology* (London, 1969), pp. 105–106.


. . . . . . . . . . .


QUESTIONS FOR A SECOND READING

1. While Freire speaks powerfully about the politics of the classroom, he provides few examples of actual classroom situations. As you go back through the essay, try to ground (or to test) what he says with examples of your own. What would take place in a "problem-posing" class in English, history, psychology, or math? What is an "authentic form of thought and action"? How might you describe what Freire refers to as "reflection"? What, really, might teachers be expected to learn from their students? What example can you give of a time when you were "conscious of consciousness" and it made a difference to you with your school work?

   You might also look for moments when Freire does provide examples of his own. On page 211, for example, Freire makes the distinction between a student's role as a "spectator" and as a "re-creator" by referring to his own relationship to the objects on his desk. How might you explain this distinction? Or, how might you use the example of his books and coffee cup to explain the distinction he makes between "being accessible to consciousness" and "entering consciousness"?

2. Freire uses two terms drawn from Marxist literature: *praxis* and *alienation*. From the way these words are used in the essay, how would you define them? And how might they be applied to the study of education?

3. A writer can be thought of as a teacher and a reader as a student. If you think of Freire as your teacher in this essay, does he enact his own principles? Does he speak to you as though he were making deposits in a bank? Or is there a way in which the essay allows for dialogue? Look for sections in the essay you could use to talk about the role Freire casts you in as a reader.

## ASSIGNMENTS FOR WRITING

1. Surely all of us, anyone who has made it through twelve years of formal education, can think of a class, or an occasion outside of class, to serve as a quick example of what Freire calls the "banking" concept of education, where students were turned into "containers" to be "filled" by their teachers. If Freire is to be useful to you, however, he must do more than enable you to call up quick examples. He should allow you to say more than that a teacher once treated you like a container or that a teacher once gave you your freedom.

   Write an essay that focuses on a rich and illustrative incident from your own educational experience and read it (that is, interpret it) as Freire would. You will need to provide careful detail: things that were said and done, perhaps the exact wording of an assignment, a textbook, or a teacher's comments. And you will need to turn to the language of Freire's argument, to take key phrases and passages and see how they might be used to investigate your case.

   To do this you will need to read your account as not simply the story of you and your teacher, since Freire is not writing about individual personalities (an innocent student and a mean teacher, a rude teacher, or a thoughtless teacher) but about the roles we are cast in, whether we choose to be or not, by our culture and its institutions. The key question, then, is not who you were or who your teacher was but what roles you played and how those roles can lead you to better understand the larger narrative or drama of Education (an organized attempt to "regulate the way the world 'enters into' the students (p. 211)."

   Freire would not want you to work passively or mechanically, however, as though you were following orders. He would want you to make your own mark on the work he has begun. Use your example, in other words, as a way of testing and examining what Freire says, *particularly those passages that you find difficult or obscure.*

2. Problem-posing education, according to Freire, "sets itself the task of demythologizing"; it "stimulates true reflection and action"; it allows students to be "engaged in inquiry and creative transformation." These are grand and powerful phrases, and it is interesting to consider what they might mean if applied to the work of a course in reading and writing.

   If the object for study were Freire's essay, "The 'Banking' Concept of Education," what would Freire (or a teacher determined to adapt his practices) ask students to *do* with the essay? What writing assignment might he set for his students? Prepare that assignment, or a set of questions or guidelines or instructions (or whatever) that Freire might prepare for his class.

Once you've prepared the writing assignment, write the essay that you think would best fulfill it. And, once you've completed the essay, go on, finally, to write the teacher's comments on it—to write what you think Freire, or a teacher following his example, might write on a piece of student work.

### MAKING CONNECTIONS

1. Freire says

> Students, as they are increasingly posed with problems relating to themselves in the world and with the world, will feel increasingly challenged and obliged to respond to that challenge. Because they apprehend the challenge as interrelated to other problems within a total context, not as a theoretical question, the resulting comprehension tends to be increasingly critical and thus constantly less alienated.

Students learn to respond, Freire says, through dialogue with their teachers. Freire could be said to serve as your first teacher here. He has raised the issue for you and given you some language you can use to frame questions and to imagine the possibilities of response.

Using one of the essays in this book as a starting point, pose a problem that challenges you and makes you feel obliged to respond, a problem that, in Freire's terms, relates to you "in the world and with the world." This is a chance for you, in other words, to pose a Freirean question and then to write a Freirean essay, all as an exercise in the practice of freedom.

When you are done, you might reread what you have written to see how it resembles or differs from what you are used to writing. What are the indications that you are working with greater freedom? If you find evidence of alienation or "domination," to what would you attribute it and what, then, might you do next to overcome it?

2. Freire writes about the distribution of power and authority in the classroom and argues that education too often alienates individuals from their own historical situation. Richard Rodriguez, in "The Achievement of Desire" (p. 499), writes about his education as a process of difficult but necessary alienation from his home, his childhood, and his family. And he writes about power—about the power that he gained and lost as he became increasingly successful as a student.

But Freire and Rodriguez write about education as a central event in the shaping of an adult life. It is interesting to imagine what they might have to say to each other. Write a dialogue between the two in which they discuss what Rodriguez has written in "The Achievement of Desire." What would they have to say to each other? What questions would they ask? How would they respond to one another in the give-and-take of conversation?

Note: This should be a dialogue, not a debate. Your speakers are trying to learn something about each other and about education. They are not trying to win points or convince a jury.

# SIMON
# FRITH

*S*IMON FRITH, *in the introduction to his book* Sound Effects: Youth, Leisure, *and the* Politics of Rock 'n' Roll, *describes the relationship between his two areas of interest, "academic" sociology and rock music:*

> *When I went to college in 1964 I assumed that I'd reached the end of my teenage bopping days, and I didn't even take my records with me. Rock 'n' roll was heard then, by me too, as youth music—and as working-class music at that; it was time now for me to grow up. Three years later, in 1967, I had an Oxford degree, my entrance ticket to bourgeois culture, and I didn't feel particularly eccentric setting out for California under the inspiration of a pop song, Scott McKenzie's "San Francisco." My use of music hadn't changed after all, and even in England, pop's power was publicly realized. In Berkeley I found a culture in which rock and politics, music and the Movement, pleasure and action were inextricably linked. They have been so for me ever since, and by the time I came back to England again, in 1969, I was sure that rock was the most interesting and most encouraging of the contemporary mass media.*

*In the example of the Oxford graduate, prepared to study the sociology of popular culture, heading off to California under the influence of a pop song, we have a handy illustration of the complex relationship between music, the listener, and culture which Frith has explored through most of his career as a critic and a scholar. Frith's work asks fundamental questions about the origins and effects of rock music: What does rock do to its listeners? What does it say? What is the source of its tremendous appeal? its incredible commercial value? And from where does it come? the individual artist? a particular pocket of the general culture (the working class in England, black culture in the United States)? or an industry (busy shaping rather than being shaped by "youth" culture)?*

*Born in Sussex, England, in 1946, Frith received a B.A. in philosophy, politics, and economics from Oxford University and a Ph.D. in sociology from the University of California at Berkeley. He was senior lecturer in sociology at the University of Warwick. He is currently director of research at the John Logie Baird Centre at Strathclyde University in Glasgow.*

*In addition to his work as a university professor, Frith has maintained a career as a rock journalist. His articles have appeared in* The Village Voice, Creem, *and* In These Times. *His books include* Art into Pop, Music for Pleasure, *and* Facing the Music. *In this last book, which Frith states was inspired by "the suspicion that the rock story is ending," he expresses his belief that "the conventional model of center and periphery on which rock's account of itself as commercially radical depends (the model of heroic independent artists competing with the majors, matching economic muscle with cultural guile) is obsolete. Rock is now the sound of worldwide film and television entertainment: its commercial importance is the most effective way of delivering the right audience to the right advertisers."*

# Rock and Sexuality

## Youth and Sexuality

The girl culture . . . is teenage culture, essentially working-class, but such leisure constraints also apply to student culture, even if the sexual differentiation of economic opportunity is less blatant for middle-class youth. Indeed it was on college campuses in the 1920s that many of the conventions of postwar teenage sexual behavior were first established: it was college girls who first decided which sex acts a respectable girl could enjoy, which were illicit; it was college boys who first organized sex as a collective male activity, turned seductions into "scores"; it was at college that petting (an extraordinary American sexual institution) was first turned into a routine. College youth culture was interpreted at the time as "liberating," particularly for the girls, but they weren't liberated from the double standard.

If girls' leisure is limited by its use as the setting for courtship, courtship itself has to be understood in the context of a particular sort of ideology of marriage, an ideology that does give girls a freedom—the freedom to choose partners. Historians have argued that boys had a youth, a time of transition from childhood to adulthood as they moved from home to work, long before girls. Adolescence as a social status is predicated on a degree of independence, and as long as girls were protected through puberty, confined to one household until they were given away in marriage to another, they had no youth. Girls could only become teenagers when free marital choice became the norm, when marriage was expected to be preceded by love. Only then did a transitional period become necessary for women too, a period when they could play the marriage field for themselves. This ideology only began to be a general norm at the beginning of this century, as ragtime and the dance craze began. Rudi Blesh and Harriet Janis quote the *Sedalia Times* from 1900:

> When the girls walk out evenings with the sole purpose of picking up a young man and continuing the walk, it is time to have a curfew law that will include children over sixteen. The restlessness that comes upon girls upon summer evenings results in lasting trouble unless it is speedily controlled. The right kind of man does not look for a wife on the streets, and the right kind of girl waits till the man comes to her home for her. [1]

Lawrence Stone, in his history *The Family, Sex and Marriage in England*, argues that the ideology of sentimental love and "well-tried personal affection" as the basis of marriage spread from the aristocracy to the bourgeoisie in Europe in the latter part of the eighteenth century (the move was marked by the rise of the romantic novel) and moved gradually down the social scale during the nineteenth century. But this was neither a natural nor an uncomplicated change of ideas. Youthful courtship carried dangers—the threat of sexual disorder, a challenge to parental authority.

These dangers seemed to be multiplied by the emergence of working-class adolescents. From early in the nineteenth century, the feature of the industrial revolution that most concerned middle-class moralists was its apparent effect on the working-class family, as girls worked in the new factories alongside boys, achieving with them an "unnatural" independence from their parents. The bourgeoisie themselves were slowly adopting the ideology of romantic love as a way of regulating adolescent sexuality and guaranteeing their children's orderly transition to adult respectability. Romantic love was idealized in bourgeois fiction, in love songs, stories, and poetry, and routinized in the suburbs, in middle-class clubs and sports and dances where girls could meet boys who would be guaranteed to be suitable partners for love and marriage. Peer groups began to take over from parents as the arbiters of correct sexual behavior.

By the end of the nineteenth century middle-class reformers were beginning to apply the romantic approach to the problem of working-class adolescence too—in England and France, for example, romance was promoted as a replacement for community control of working-class sexuality, and young workers were encouraged to join their own "rational" peergroup leisure associations—youth clubs, cycle clubs, sports clubs, and so forth. In the USA the most important institution for the control of adolescent sexuality was, at least after 1918, the high school. Paula Fass suggests that the 1920s, in particular, were crucial for the development of American youth culture, because it was then that the ideology of sentimental love was fused with a new kind of advocacy of sexual pleasure. It was, in her words, the "dual process of the sexualization of love and the glorification of sex that helped to anchor the twentieth-century American marriage pattern, the horse-and-carriage ideal."

The "sexualization of love" was made possible by the spread of relatively efficient contraception. Delayed small families encouraged companionate marriages; sex itself, freed from conception, was reinterpreted as a form of emotional expression, a source of mutual pleasure—from the 1920s, middle-class marriage manuals recognized female sexuality. But the other side of this process was the domestication of sex. If sexual expression, for its own sake, became one of the pleasures and purposes of marriage, so marriage itself was defined as the necessary setting for the most pleasurable sex—necessary now not in terms of traditional morality but in terms of romance: love had become the reason for sex, and true love involved a commitment to marriage. First an engagement, later going steady, became the moment in youth culture when it was morally permissible to go all the way; and from the 1920s, middle-class girls, as prospective wives, could express their "sexual personalities" publicly, could use sexual devices, like makeup, that had previously been confined to prostitutes, to "loose women."

What made this ideology initially shocking was that it legitimated youthful sexual activity as an aspect of efficient mate selection; parents lost control not only over their children's marriage choices but also over their sexual behavior. Their place was taken, once more, by peer groups, which elaborated new rules of sexuality according to which some premarital pleasure was permissible, for girls and boys alike, but not such pleasure as would disrupt the romantic transition to marriage. Paula Fass quotes a female student from Ohio State University writing in 1922 in defense of her physical enjoyment of "smoking, dancing like voodoo devotees, dressing décolleté, petting and drinking." Her point was that although

> our tastes may appear riotous and unrestrained, the aspect of the situation is not alarming. The college girl—particularly the girl in the co-educational institution—is a plucky, coolheaded individual who thinks naturally. She doesn't lose her head— she knows her game and can play it dexterously. She is armed with sexual knowledge. . . . She is secure in the most critical situations—she knows the limits, and because of her safety in such knowledge she is able to run almost the complete gamut of experience. [2]

By the 1950s, knowledge of "the limits" was an aspect of teenage culture generally, but if the task of teenage peer groups was to control teenage sexuality, the issue was, really, girls' sexual behavior. It was female morality that was defined as chastity, female "trouble" that meant pregnancy. Adults worried about boys in terms of violence, the threat to order; they only worried about girls in terms of sex, the threat to the family. And they worried about all girls in these terms, their fears weren't confined to "delinquents."

Nineteen-fifties rock 'n' roll is usually described as a particularly sexual form of expression, a source of physical "liberation," but teenage culture was already sexualized by the time it appeared. The question we really have to examine concerns the use of music not in the general expression of sexuality but in its ordering. Sexuality is not a single phenomenon that is either expressed or repressed; the term refers, rather, to a range of pleasures and experiences, a range of ways in which people make sense of themselves as sexed subjects. Sexual discourses determine prohibitions as well as possibilities, what can't be expressed as well as what can. But the most important function of 1950s teenage culture wasn't to "repress" sexuality but to articulate it in a setting of love and marriage such that male and female sexuality were organized in quite different ways. And rock 'n' roll didn't change that sexual order. Elvis Presley's sexuality, for example, meant different things to his male and female fans. There was an obvious tension between his male appropriation as cock-rocker and his female appropriation as a teeny-bop idol. Rock 'n' roll was, say its historians significantly, "emasculated," but its "decline" (from crude, wild dance music to crafted romantic ballads and spruce idols) marked not a defused rebellion but a shift of sexual discourse as the music moved from the street to the bedroom. In neither place did it challenge the conventions of peer-group sex.

The youth culture that developed in the 1960s was, in sexual terms, more rebellious: the family was part of the system under attack. Domestic ideology was subverted, sexuality separated from marriage, romantic love intercut with fleeting hedonism. In Tom Hayden's words, there was "a generation of young whites with a new, less repressed attitude toward sex and pleasure, and music has been the means of their liberation."

Rock was experienced as a new sort of sexual articulation by women as well as men. The music was, in Sheila Rowbotham's words, "like a great release after all those super-consolation ballads." Rock, writes Karen Durbin, "provided me and a lot of women with a channel for saying 'want,' and for asserting our sexuality without apologies and without having to pretty up every passion with the traditionally 'feminine' desire for true love and marriage, and that was a useful step towards liberation." At a time when girls were still being encouraged from all directions to interpret their sexuality in terms of romance, to give priority to notions of love and commitment, rock performers like the Rolling Stones were exhilarating because of their antiromanticism, their concern for "the dark side of passion," their interest in sex as power and feeling. But the problem quickly became a different one: not whether rock stars were sexist, but whether women could enter their discourse, appropriate their music, without having to become "one of the boys."

## Rock and Sexual Liberation

Male sexuality is no more "naturally" aggressive, assertive, and urgent than female sexuality is "naturally" passive, meek, and sensitive. But the issue is not the nature of sex but its representations, and they work not by describing feelings, but by constructing them. The sexual content of rock can't be read off its texts unambiguously—lyrics are the sign of a voice, instrumental sounds don't have fixed connotations. The sexuality of music is usually referred to in terms of its rhythm—it is the beat that commands a directly physical response—but rock sexuality has other components too. The rock experience is a social experience, involves relationships among the listeners, refers to people's appreciation of other genres, other sound associations; and in sexual terms our musical response is, perhaps above all, to the grain of a voice, the "touch" someone has on an instrument, the sense of personality at play. The "pleasure of the text" is the pleasure of music production itself, and one reason for the dissolution of rock's liberating promises to the male routines of the 1970s was simply the inevitable translation of an open text into a closed formula: cock-rock, by definition, rules out the possibilities of surprise and delight. But the question remains: Why this formula? Nineteen-sixties rock was expressly opposed to the love and marriage ideology of traditional teenage culture; how then did it come to articulate an even more rigid sexual double standard?

The concept of youth developed in the 1960s by rock (among other media) involved the assumption that good sex meant spontaneity, free expression, an "honesty" that could only be judged in terms of immediate feelings. Sex was thus best experienced *outside* the restrictive sphere of marriage, with its distracting deceits of love and long-term commitment. This was, in principle, an ideology of sexual equality—men and women alike were entitled to set their own limits on their sexual experiences.

Such permissiveness reflected a number of shifts in the material situation of middle-class youth: an increasing number of them were at college for an increasing length of time (by the end of the 1960s more than a quarter of *all* twenty-one- to twenty-four-year-olds in the USA were in school), and they were enjoying new levels of affluence (a reflection of rising parental income), mobility, and independence. It was, therefore, increasingly possible to enjoy sex without any reference to marriage; and the pill, in particular, enabled women to manage their sex lives without reference to family, community, or peer group. Sex became just another form of leisure, and the ideology of leisure itself began to change. Free time was used increasingly impulsively, irrationally, unproductively, with reference to immediate gratification rather than to usefulness or respectability or sense of consequence. The expansion of sexual opportunity, in other words, occurred in the context of a new leisure stress on hedonism, and the result was that sex became an experience to be consumed, used up in the moment, like any other leisure good. Sex was now defined without reference to domestic ideology or romantic love, but it was still gender-bound: men were, by and large, the sexual consumers; women were, by and large, the sexual commodities, their charms laid out for customer approval in a never-ending supply of magazines and films and "spreads."

Rock sexuality developed in this permissive context, but defined itself (initially, at least) against such "plastic" consumer sex. Rock sex was bohemian sex—earthy, real, "free." The woman's place, though, remained subordinate.

Bohemian freedom, particularly in its young rebel version, is defined primarily against the family. It is from their families that the young must escape, it is through their family quarrels that they first recognize themselves as rebels, and it is their refusal to settle down to a respectable domestic life that makes their rebellion permanent. Youthful bohemia begins, then, as a revolt against women, who are identified with the home as mothers, sisters, potential domesticators. The young rebel has to be a loner, to move on, and female sexuality becomes, in itself, something repressive, confining, enveloping. In the Hollywood version of the young rebel's story (a story repeated in numerous films over the last thirty years, although James Dean remains the model for rock 'n' roll's rebellious style), the message is plain enough: the boy must get out, the girl tries to hold him back.

The original middle-class youth rebels in America, the bohemians drawn to big-city life and leisure at the turn of the century, were fascinated precisely by those proletarian institutions—gambling, drinking, sports like pool—which were, in Ned Polsky's words, aspects of a "bachelor subculture": they were institutions for men without women, and the only intimate relationships bohemians can have are with each other, as friends.

Even rebels need sexual and domestic female services, though (one 1960s result was the symbolic hippie woman, the fleet-footed earth mother), and, traditionally, the ideal bohemian woman is the "innocent" prostitute—antidomestic and a symbol of sex as transitory pleasure. The prostitute can be treated (as rock stars treat groupies) with a mixture of condescension and contempt, as someone without an autonomous sexuality. Sex as self-expression remains the prerogative of the man; the woman is the object of *his* needs and fantasies, admired, in a way, for her lack of romantic hypocrisy but despised for her anonymity.

Sexual relationships involve a number of necessary oppositions. These oppositions don't have to be divided between sexual partners, aren't gender defined, but mean constant negotiation, exploration, struggle, and experiment. These negotiations are the source of sexual pleasure as well as pain, and the issues at stake—independence/dependence, risk/security, activity/passivity, movement/stability, incident/routine, creation/consumption—inform the best rock music, which deals with the sexual *frisson* of relationships, the fact that all interesting affairs are alive. But, in general (and whatever the concerns of individual musicians like Neil Young or Van Morrison or Joni Mitchell), rock performers lay claim to sexual values—movement, independence, creativity, action, risk—in such a way that female sexuality is defined (just as in working-class street culture) by the opposite values—stability, dependence, inaction, security. Women are excluded from this "rebellion" by definition; rock's antidomestic ideology doesn't move women out of the home, but leaves them in it, as inadequates.

The issue here is sexual ideology, not sexual practice. The actual behavior of men and women is far more complicated than the ideology implies. . . . But there is one more practical point to be made. Nineteen-sixties youth culture opposed impulse to calculation, irrationality to rationality, the present to the future; but these values posed quite different problems for boys than for girls. Girls have to keep control. They can't get drunk or drugged with the same abandon as boys because to lose control *is* to face consequences—pregnancy most obviously ("I got drunk at a party . . ."), a bad reputation more generally ("She'll do *anything* . . ."). As long as female attraction is defined by the male gaze, girls are under constant pressure too to keep control of their appearance; they can't afford to let their performance go. A drunken, "raddled" woman remains a potent image of ugliness; a haggard Keith Richards retains a far more *glamorous* appeal than a haggard Janis Joplin or Grace Slick. The irrational elements of the counterculture—in other words, the sex and drugs and rock 'n' roll—could not be appropriated by girls as they were by boys without affecting their self-definitions, their relationships, their lives.

By the 1970s women were giving their own answers to the countercultural questions about sex and domesticity and love—the terms of male domination were challenged. One effect of the feminist rewriting of the sexual rule book has been a male movement to more irrational forms of sexual power—rape, violent fantasy, a neurotic inability to sustain any sexual relationship. As one male property right (as husband) is denied, another (as purchaser) is asserted; sex, and therefore women, have been commoditized. "I think," writes Lester Bangs about Debbie Harry at the end of the decade, "that if most guys in America could somehow get their fave-rave poster girl in bed and have total license to do whatever they wanted with this legendary body for one afternoon, at least 75 percent of the guys in the country would elect to beat her up." It is in this context that we have to analyze the musical forms of 1970s sexuality—punk and disco.

## Punk Sex and Disco Pleasure

Punks rejected both romantic and permissive conventions, and refused, in particular, to allow sexuality to be constructed as a commodity. They flaunted sex-shop goods in public, exposing the mass production of porno fantasy, dissolving its dehumanizing effects through shock—"Oh bondage! Up yours!" (not that this stopped the media from running numerous pictures of "punkettes" in corsets and fishnet tights). Punks denied that their sexuality had any significance at all—"My love lies limp," boasted Mark Perry of Alternative TV; "What is sex anyway?" asked Johnny Rotten. "Just thirty seconds of squelching noises."

Punk was the first form of youth music not to rest on love songs (romance remained the staple of rock lyrics throughout the countercultural 1960s), and one consequence of this was that new female voices were heard on record, stage, and radio—shrill, assertive, impure, individual voices, singer as subject not object. Punk's female musicians had a strident insistence that was far removed from the appeal of most postwar glamour girls (the only sexual surprise of a self-conscious siren like Debbie Harry, for example, was that she became a teeny-bop idol for a generation of young girls).

Punk interrupted the long-standing rock equation of sex and pleasure, though the implications of this interruption still remain unclear. British punk subculture itself hardly differed, in sexual terms, from any other working-class street movement—the boys led, the girls (fewer of them) hung on; and in the end it was probably punk's sexual effect on performers rather than on audiences that mattered—women were brought into a musical community from which they'd previously been excluded, and they brought with them new questions about sound and convention and image, about the sexuality of performance and the performance of sexuality. Whether these questions get answered we have yet to see, but at least punks opened the possibility that rock could be *against* sexism.

Disco, which between 1974 and 1978 became the dominant sound of mass music across the world, had different origins and different effects. The success of *Saturday Night Fever* simply confirmed the resonance of a genre that was already an $8-billion-per-year industry in the USA, already accounted for half the albums and singles in *Billboard*'s hot hundreds. Disco had changed the sound of radio, the organization of record companies, the status of club deejays, the meaning of a good night out, and all this has to be understood in the context of the 1970s' sexual mores. Disco was not a response (like punk) to rock itself, but challenged it indirectly, by the questions it asked about music and *dance*.

The dance floor is the most public setting for music as sexual expression and has been an important arena for youth culture since the dance crazes of the beginning of the century when Afro-American rhythms began to structure white middle-class leisure, to set new norms for physical display, contact, and movement. Dance has been, ever since, central to the meaning of popular music. Girls, in particular, have always flocked to dance halls, concerned not just about finding a husband, but also about pursuing their own pleasure. They may be attracting the lurking boys through their clothes, makeup, and appearance, but on the dance floor their energy and agility is their own affair. The most dedicated dancers in Britain, for example, the Northern soul fans, are completely self-absorbed, and even in *Saturday Night Fever* (in which dancing power was diluted by pop interests) John Travolta transcended Hollywood's clumsy choreography with the sheer quality of his commitment—from the opening shots of his strut through the streets, his gaze on himself never falters; the essence of dance floor sex is physical control, and, whatever happens, John Travolta is never going to let himself go.

Dancing as a way of life, an obsession, has a long American history. Shorty Snowden, the John Travolta of the Savoy Ballroom in the 1920s, suffered from "Sunday Night Fever": "We started getting ready for Sunday on Saturday. The ideal was to get our one sharp suit to the tailor to be pressed on Saturday afternoon. Then we'd meet at the poolroom and brag about what we were going to do on the dance floor the next night. . . ."[3]

The 1920s dance cult spread quickly to "hep" white teenagers who tried to dress, dance, move like these sharp black "dudes," and the Depression stimulated dancing among the nonhep too. Thousands of small, cheap bars with dance floors, used pianos, record players, radios, and jukeboxes to fill the weekends with noise. Such working-class dance halls were crucial to the culture of courtship, but dancing meant something else even more important: it was an escape, a suspension of real time, a way in which even the unemployed could enjoy their bodies, their physical skills, the sense of human power their lives otherwise denied. Such power does not need to be rooted in sexual competition (though it often enough is); parties, Friday and Saturday night bursts of physical pleasure, sex or no sex, have always been the most intense setting for working-class musics, from ragtime to punk.

A party matters most, of course, to those people who most need to party, and, whatever else happened to mass music in the 1950s and 1960s, there were many people (black working-class Americans, British working-class teenagers, using much the same music) who never stopped dancing—1970s disco itself emerged musically from black clubs, depended commercially on its continuing white youth appeal. But, sexually, disco was most important as a gay aesthetic, and what was surprising, socially, was the appropriation of this aesthetic by the mass middle class.

Disco is dance music in the abstract, its content determined by its form. Middle-class dance music in the past, even in the 1930s, was a form determined by its content—there were still influential dance hall instructors, sheet music salesmen, and band leaders who laid down rules of partnership, decorum, uplift, and grace. There are no such rules in disco, but, on the other hand, individual expression means nothing when there is nothing individual to express. Disco is not, despite its critics, anything like Muzak. Muzak's effect is subliminal; its purpose is to encourage its hearers to do anything but listen to it. Disco's effect is material; its purpose is to encourage its hearers to do nothing but listen to it.

What do they hear? An erotic appeal, most obviously—what Richard Dyer calls "whole body eroticism." All dancing means a commitment to physical sensation, but disco expanded the possibilities of sensation. Disco pleasure is not closed off, bound by the song structures, musical beginnings and ends, but is expressed, rather, through an open-ended series of repetitions, a shifting *intensity* of involvement. And disco, as Dyer suggests, shares rock's rhythmic pulse, while avoiding rock's phallocentrism: disco is committed to the 4:4 beat in all its implications. Disco dancing is sinuous, it avoids the jerk and grind and thrust of rock; disco dancers hustle and slide, they use all their bodies' erotic possibilities.

Dancing has always been a physical pleasure sufficiently intense to block out, for the moment, all other concerns, but disco pushed such enjoyment to new extremes: the disco experience is an overwhelming experience of *now-ness*, an experience intensified still further by drugs like amyl nitrite, an experience in which the dancer is, simultaneously, completely self-centered and quite selfless, completely sexualized and, in gender terms, quite sexless. On the disco floor there is no overt competition for partners, no isolation; and disco (unlike bohemia) signifies nothing, makes no expressive claims—if bohemia suggests a different way of life, disco simply offers a different experience of it.

The disco version of eroticism and ecstasy is not, in itself, homosexual, but the aesthetic uses of these experiences did reflect gay consciousness. They were imbued, for example, with gay romanticism: disco sensations were associated with the fleeting emotional contacts, the passing relationships of a culture in which everything in a love affair can happen in a night. Disco eroticism became, too, the sign of a sexuality that was always being constructed. It was the process of construction, the very artificiality of the disco experience, that made it erotic. Disco was a version of camp: the best disco records were those made with a sense of irony, an aggressive self-consciousness, a concern for appearances. There was an obvious link between the vocal styles of disco and 1930s torch songs: Billie Holiday and Donna Summer alike stylized feelings, distanced pain, opened up the texts of sexuality (and for this reason, disco, despised by punk-rockers on principle, had an immense appeal to the postpunk avant-garde).

Mainstream disco, the Saturday night fever of the teenage working class, continued to operate according to the traditional street party line; teenagers danced in different ways, to different sounds than gays. But it was the gay disco aesthetic that middle-class dancers began to appropriate from 1974 on. If 1960s "permissive" sexual ideology had reflected new leisure and sexual opportunities, then 1970s disco culture reflected their emotional consequences. Disco was music for singles bars, sexual mobility, heterosexual cruising, weekend flings, and transitory fantasies. Gay culture reflected, in its own way, the problems and possibilities of sex without domesticity, love without the conventional distinctions of male and female. These problems and possibilities had become important now for heterosexuals too.

Disco was about eroticism and ecstasy as material goods, produced not by spiritual or emotional work, God or love, but by technology, chemistry, wealth. The disco experience (the music and the mood, the poppers and the lights) revealed the artificiality and transience of sexual feelings—they were produced to be consumed; and disco pleasure, as it moved into the commercial mainstream, became the pleasure of consumption itself. This was obvious enough in the chic appeal of Studio 54, but was just as important for the strut of the factory girls, equally chic, up the steps of Tiffany's in provincial Britain. Disco made no claims to folk status; there was no creative disco community. The music was, rather, the new international symbol of American consumer society. Chic discos sprang up around the world, each offering the secret of eternal American youth; the pleasures of consumption and the pleasures of sex became, in such settings, the same thing.

The problem with escapism is not the escape itself, but what's still there when it's over—the rain still falls when Monday morning dawns. Once something's been consumed it's gone; new goods are necessary, new experiences, new highs, new sex. As many observers commented, by the end of the 1970s disco had become a drug, but it was leisure itself that had a new desperation. In Andrew Holleran's disco novel, *Dancer from the Dance,* the most dedicated disco-goers are the most eager to escape:

> They seldom looked happy. They passed one another without a word in the elevator, like silent shades in hell, hell-bent on their next look from a handsome stranger. Their next rush from a popper. The next song that turned their bones to jelly and left them all on the dance floor with heads back, eyes nearly closed, in the ecstasy of saints receiving the stigmata. They pursued these things with such devotion that they acquired, after a few seasons, a haggard look, a look of deadly seriousness. Some wiped everything they could off their faces and reduced themselves to blanks. Yet even these, when you entered the hallway where they stood waiting to go in, would turn toward you all at once in that one unpremeditated moment (as when we see ourselves in a mirror we didn't know was there), the same look on their faces: Take me away from this. [4]

## NOTES

[1] Rudi Blesh and Harriet Janis, *They All Played Ragtime* (New York, 1950), p. 33.

[2] Paula S. Fass, *The Damned and the Beautiful: American Youth in the 1920s* (New York: Oxford University Press, 1977), p. 307.

[3] Marshall and Jean Stearns, p. 322.

[4] Andrew Holleran, *Dancer from the Dance* (New York: Morrow, 1978), pp. 38–39.

. . . . . . . . . . .

## QUESTIONS FOR A SECOND READING

1. On page 227 Frith says, "The question we really have to examine concerns the use of music not in the general expression of sexuality but in its ordering." As Frith constructs his account of rock and sexuality, there are, then, real questions and false questions. As you reread the selection, try to piece out the key terms and assumptions of both positions. Who asks

the false questions? What are they? What terms would those asking these questions use to talk about rock and roll? Who asks the real questions? (that is, what are the interests, the beliefs, and the methods of this group?) What are these questions? What are the key terms of this discourse, as you see it being worked out in Frith's essay?

2. Frith is an Englishman writing primarily about the English experience of rock and roll. As you read back through the essay, mark those sections where, so far as you are concerned, the American experience would require different examples or a new twist to the argument.

3. One way of examining Frith's method is to examine the way he puts this essay together, to look to see just how he does it—how he makes his points, how he organizes his account of rock and sexuality (by historic period, through terms like "working class" and "middle class"), where he gets his examples. Behind it all is a general interpretative scheme—a tool Frith uses to interpret his material. As you read through a second time, mark those sections that best illustrate Frith at work with his material.

## ASSIGNMENTS FOR WRITING

1. Frith pays attention to the 1950s, 1960s, and 1970s, and he deals most immediately with the English experience of rock and roll. He is trying to "historicize" rock, to argue for its particular character or meaning in a particular culture at a particular point in time. The particulars of his account create a space for you to offer an account of your own, one that extends his discussion to the 1980s and to the United States (or your particular region of the United States).

   Write an essay in which you construct your own account of rock and sexuality. You can use this as the occasion to read with or against Frith (because you think he has something you can use or because you think he doesn't quite have it right). You should, however, begin your work by rereading the essay to get a sense of his method, of how he does what he does. (See the third "Question for a Second Reading.") Whether you work with or against the grain of Frith's essay, you will want to show that you understand not only his argument but his method—the procedures and assumptions, the terms and strategies, that enable him to say what he says. Be sure to quote and work from specific songs and MTV music videos.

2. At one point in the essay, Frith quotes a student at Ohio State University in 1922. He gives a special status, here and elsewhere, to first-person accounts by young people, the immediate audience for rock and roll. Write an essay in which you add your voice to those in Frith's essay and speak as precisely as you can about your experience with the representations of sex and gender in rock culture. You can think of this essay as primarily autobiographical—that is, its primary motive can be to tell your story, to

establish your point of view. You should imagine that you are writing your own musical autobiography, but you'll want to think of it as something that someone like Frith could use in an essay on culture.


## MAKING CONNECTIONS

1. Frith argues that "male sexuality is no more 'naturally' aggressive, assertive, and urgent than female sexuality is 'naturally' passive, meek, and sensitive. But the issue is not the nature of sex but its representations, and they work not by describing feelings, but by constructing them" (p. 228). It is not the nature of sexuality but its representations; sex roles are not naturally there but constructed. But constructed by whom, and reproduced by what mechanism? Adrienne Rich (p. 480) and Virginia Woolf (p. 639) make similar arguments about sex roles. Both Roland Barthes (p. 23) and John Berger (p. 65) offer arguments against those who would say that our cultural landscape is "naturally" there.

   Choose one (or any combination) of the authors listed and use her or his work as a way of beginning to explore the question of "agency" in these accounts of the shaping of culture—that is, who does what to whom, and how? How might you account for the source of rock's representations? If the "sexual discourses" of rock "organize" sexuality, whose interests are being served? How are they being served? How does the process work?

   One way of working closely on these questions is to look at the differences between essays that seem to take similar positions. As you look at Frith in the context of Rich, Woolf, Barthes, and/or Berger, ask how their accounts differ in their assumptions about the source of representations, the means by which they are transmitted and reproduced, and the ways they are received (or resisted) by their audiences. And ask, finally, what the differences mean to you, a person also interested in how a culture works on and with the people who participate in it.

2. Roland Barthes (p. 23), Mark Crispin Miller (p. 397), and Frith all write about popular culture. Barthes writes about "the myths of French daily life," Miller writes about TV, Frith about rock and roll. While they write about different cultural forms or objects, they all need to imagine the mind and response of the public—to theorize the spectator, reader, or listener.

   Write an essay in which you describe and examine the figure of the citizen (the common reader or viewer) and the figure of the critic (the uncommon reader or viewer) as represented in the work of these three writers. Use this inquiry as a way of placing and reflecting on what critics do—Who does this kind of work? What is it good for? What can't it accomplish?

# CARLOS
# FUENTES

$C$ARLOS FUENTES has been described as a "writer/diplomat, activist/profes-
sor, connoisseur/iconoclast," and "a left-wing utopian with an overlay of sentimental anarchism." He is a writer of extraordinary versatility, restricting himself
neither to any particular genre nor to a single, prominent theme. His published
work includes novels (among them, The Hydra Head, The Death of Artemio
Cruz, and Christopher Unborn), a recent collection of essays entitled Myself
with Others, and numerous plays, screenplays, political essays, short stories, and
works of literary and art criticism. He is considered, along with Juan Rulfo and
Agustín Yáñez, to be one of the three major novelists of contemporary Mexico.
Novelist William Styron, author of Sophie's Choice and a personal friend of
Fuentes, has said, "No one writes more eloquently about Latin America, its peculiarity, its revolutionary nature, its hopeless perplexities, or paradoxically, perceives it with such a North American eye."

Fuentes was born in Mexico City in 1928. He first came to the United States
before he was six, accompanying his father, who was then counselor of the Mexican
embassy. He studied at the Colegio Frances Morelos in Mexico, the National University of Mexico, and the Institut des Hautes Études Internationales in Geneva.
In the 1950s Fuentes held various positions with the Mexican government, and he

was the Mexican ambassador to France from 1974 to 1977. He has acted as editor for a number of Mexican journals and has taught at Columbia University in New York, Harvard University, the University of Pennsylvania, Barnard College, and Cambridge University in England.

Fuentes's relationship with the U.S. government has often been an uneasy one, because of his criticism of U.S. intervention in Central America and elsewhere. In the 1960s he was barred from entering the United States because he had spoken out against U.S. policy in Vietnam and the Dominican Republic. He continues to be an outspoken critic of U.S. military intervention in Central America; his most recent statement on the subject was a speech at Bard College in New York in May of 1988, a portion of which was later published under the title "Uncle Sam Stay Home."

In 1988 Fuentes won three international prizes for his work, the Cervantes Prize from Spain, the U.S. National Arts Club's gold medal for literature, and Nicaragua's highest cultural award, the Rubén Darío prize. Fuentes is currently researching a novel on Emiliano Zapata, the Mexican peasant revolutionary. "The Son of Andrés Aparicio," the story reproduced here, comes from Fuentes's collection of stories, Burnt Water, and presents us with a cross-section of the lives of a small group of people in a barrio, a nameless place, "a temporary place, like the cardboard and corrugated tin shacks" for the confused and displaced.

# The Son of Andrés Aparicio

To the memory of Pablo Neruda

### The Place

It had no name and so it didn't exist as a place. Other districts on the outskirts of Mexico City had names. Not this one. As if by oversight. As if a child had grown up without being baptized. Or worse: without even being given a name. It was as if by general agreement. Why name such a barrio? Perhaps someone had said, not really thinking, that no one would stay here very long. It was a temporary place, like the cardboard and corrugated tin shacks. Wind sifted through the badly fitting fiber walls; the sun camped on the tin roofs. Those were the true residents of the place. People came here confused, half dazed, not knowing why, maybe because this was better than nothing, because this flat landscape of scrub and pigweed and greasewood was the next frontier, one that came after the most recent place, a place that had a name. Here no name, no sewers, and the only light was an occasional light bulb where someone had tapped into the city power lines. No one had named the place because everyone pretended they were there temporarily. No one built on his own land. They were squatters, and though no one ever said it, they'd agreed among themselves that they wouldn't offer resistance to whoever came to run them off. They'd simply move on to the next frontier of the city. At least the time they spent here without paying rent would be time gained, time to catch their breath. Many of them had come from more comfortable districts with names like San Rafael, Balbuena, Canal del Norte, even Netzahualcóytl, where already two million people were living, want to or not, with its cement church and a supermarket or two. They came because not even in those lost cities could they make ends meet, but they refused to give up the last vestiges of decency, refused to go the way of the scavengers who picked over the dump or the paupers who sold stolen sand from Las Lomas. Bernabé had an idea. That this place had no name because it was like the huge sprawling city itself, that here they had everything that was bad about the city but maybe the best too, he wanted to say, and that's why it couldn't have a name of its own. But he couldn't say it, because words always came so hard to him. His mother still had a treasured old mirror and often gazed at herself in it. Ask her, Bernabé, whether she sees the place, the lost city with its scabrous winter crust, its spring dust devils, and in the summer the quagmires inevitably blending with the streams of excrement that run the entire year seeking an exit they never find. Where does the water come from, Mama? Where does all the shit go, Papa? Bernabé learned to breathe more slowly so he could swallow the black air trapped beneath the cold clouds, imprisoned within the encircling mountains. A defeated air that barely managed to drag itself to its feet and stagger across the plain, seeking mouths to enter. He never told anyone his idea because he couldn't get the words out. Every single one was locked inside him. Words were hard for him because nothing his mother said ever had any relation to reality, because his uncles laughed and whooped it up as if they felt an obligation to enjoy themselves once a week before returning to the bank and the gasoline station, but especially because he couldn't remember his father's voice. They'd been living here eleven years. No one had bothered them, no one had run them off. They hadn't had to offer resistance to anyone. Even the old blind man who'd serenaded the power lines had died, he'd strummed his guitar and sung the old ballad, *Oh, splendid, luminous electricity* . . . Why, Bernabé? Uncle Rosendo said it was a bad joke. They'd come temporarily and stayed eleven years. And if they'd been there eleven years they'd be there forever.

"Your papa's the only one who got out in time, Bernabé."

## *The Father*

Everyone remembered his suspenders. He always wore them, as if his salvation depended on them. They said he hung on to life by his suspenders, and oh, if only he'd been more like them he might have lasted a little longer. They watched his clothes get old and worn, but not his suspenders; they were always new, with shiny gilded clasps. The old people who still used such words said that like his gentility the suspenders were proverbial. No, his Uncle Richi told him, stubborn as an old mule and fooling himself, that was your father. At school Bernabé had to fight a big bully who asked him about his papa, and when Bernabé said he'd died, the bully laughed and said, That's what they all say, everyone knows no papa never dies, no, what happened was that your papa left you or worse never even said you were his, he laid your mama and ran off on her before you were even born. Stubborn but a good man, Uncle Rosendo said, do you remember? when he wasn't smiling he looked old and so he smiled the live-long day though he never had any reason to, oh, what a laugher Amparito's husband, laughing, always laughing, with nothing to laugh about, and all that bitterness inside because they'd sent him, a young agriculture student, a green kid, to be in charge of a co-op in a village in the state of Guerrero, just after he'd married your mama, Bernabé. When he got there he found the place burned out, many of the members of the co-op had been murdered and their crops stolen by the local political boss and the shippers. Your father wanted to file claims, he swore he was going to take it to the authorities in Mexico City and to the Supreme Court, what didn't he say, what didn't he promise, what didn't he intend to do? It was his first job and he went down there breathing fire. Well, what happened was that they no more than caught wind of the fact that outsiders were going to poke in and try to right all the injustices and crimes than they banded together, the victims the same as the criminals, to deny your father's charges and lay it all on him. Meddling outsider, come from Mexico City with his head filled with ideas about justice, the road to hell was paved by men like him, what all they didn't call him. They were bound together by years of quarrels and rivalries and by their dead. After all, time would work things out. Justice was rooted in families, in their honor and pride, and not in some butt-in agronomist. When the federal officials came, even the brothers and widows of the murdered blamed your papa. They laughed: let the government officials fight it out with the government agronomist. He never recovered from that defeat, you know. In the bureaucracy they were suspicious of him because he was an idealist and incompetent to boot, and he never got ahead there. Quite the opposite, he got stuck in a piddling desk job with no promotions and no raises and with his debts piling up, all because something had broken inside, a little flame had gone out in his heart is the way he told it, but he kept on smiling, hooking his thumbs in those suspenders. Who asked him to poke his nose in? Justice doesn't make good bedfellows with love, he used to say, those people loved one another even though they'd been wronged, their love was stronger than my promise of justice. It was as if you offered them a marble statue of a beautiful Greek goddess when they already had their ugly but oh, so warm and loving dark-skinned woman warming their covers. Why come to him? Your father Andrés Aparicio, smiling all the time, never forgot those mountains to the south and a lost village with no highway or telephone, where time was measured by the stars and news was transmitted only through memory and the one sure thing was that everyone would be buried in the same parcel of land guarded over by rose-colored angels and the withered yellow blossoms of the *cempazuchiles,* the flower of the dead, and they knew it. That village banded together and defeated him, you see, because passion unites more than justice, and what about you, Bernabé, who beat you up? where did you get that split lip and black eye? But Bernabé wasn't going to tell his uncles what he'd said to the big bully at school, or how they'd waded into each other because Bernabé hadn't known how to explain to the bully who his father Andrés Aparicio was, the words just wouldn't come and for the first time he knew vaguely, even though he didn't want to think about it too much, that if you weren't able to come up with words then you'd better be able to fight. But, oh, how he wished he could have told that sonofabitching bully that his father had died because it was the only dignified thing left to do, because a dead man has a kind of power over the living, even if he's a godforsaken corpse. Shit, you have to respect a dead man, don't you?

## The Mother

She struggled to keep her speech refined, her at once sentimental and cold, dreamy and unyielding character might have been molded in her manner of speech, as if to make credible the language that no one spoke any longer in this lost barrio. Only a few old people, the ones who'd spoken of the proverbial gentility of her husband Andrés Aparicio, called on her, and she insisted on setting a proper table with a tablecloth and knives and forks and spoons, demanding that no one begin until everyone was served and that no one leave the table until she the wife, the señora, the lady of the house, rose to leave. She always said "please" when she asked for something and reminded others to do the same. She was always hospitable and made her guests welcome, when there had been guests still, and birthdays and saint's days and Christmas and even a crèche with pilgrims and candles and a piñata. But that was when her husband Andrés Aparicio was living and bringing home a salary from the Department of Agriculture. Now, without a pension, she couldn't manage, now only the old people came and chatted with her, using words like meticulous and punctual, with your permission and allow me, courtesy and thoughtlessness. But the old people were dying out. They'd come in huge enormous groups, three and sometimes four generations strung together like beads on a necklace, but in fewer than ten years all you saw were young people and children and looking for old people who spoke genteelly was like looking for a needle in the proverbial haystack. What would she have to say if all her old friends kept dying, she thought, gazing at herself in the baroque mirror she'd inherited from her mother when they all still lived on República de Guatemala before the rent freeze had been lifted and their landlord, Don Federico Silva, had mercilessly raised their rent. She hadn't believed his message, that his mother insisted, that Doña Felícitas was tyrannical and greedy, because later their neighbor Doña Lourdes told them that Señor Silva's mother had died and still he didn't lower the rents, what did you expect? When Bernabé was old enough to think for himself, he tried to associate his mother's manners, the delicacy of the way she spoke in public, with tenderness, but he couldn't. The only times she became sentimental was when she spoke about poverty or about his father; but she was never more cold than when she spoke about those same subjects. Bernabé didn't know what his mother's theatrics meant but he did know that what she seemed to be saying had nothing to do with him, as if there were a great chasm between her acts and her words, don't ever forget Bernabé that you're well brought up, try not to mix with those ruffians at school, stay away from them, remember that you have a treasure beyond price, good family and good upbringing. Only twice did he remember his mother Amparo acting differently. Once when for the first time she heard Bernabé shout, You motherfucker, at another child in the street and when her son came into their hovel she collapsed against her dressing table, pressed her hands to her temples, and dropped the mirror to the floor, saying, Bernabé, I haven't given you what I wanted for you, you deserved better, look how you've had to grow up and where you've had to live, it isn't right, Bernabé. But the mirror didn't break. Bernabé never asked her what she meant. He knew that every time she sat before her dressing table with the mirror in her hand and cast sidelong glances at herself, stroking her chin, silently tracing the line of an eyebrow with a finger, erasing the tears of time from her eyes with the palm of her hand, his mother would speak, and this was more important to him than what she said, because for Bernabé speech was something miraculous, it took more courage to speak than to take a beating, because physical combat was merely a substitute for words. The day he came home after his fight with the bully at school he didn't know whether his mother was talking to herself or whether she knew he was creeping around behind one of the coarse cotton curtains the uncles had hung to mark off the rooms of the house that little by little every Sunday they were improving, replacing cardboard with adobe and adobe with brick until the place had a certain air of respectability, like the house they had when their father was the aide-de-camp to General Vicente Vergara, the famous the legendary Old General Iron Balls who often invited them to breakfast on the anniversary of the Revolution, on a cold morning toward the end of November. Not any longer; Amparito was right, the old people were dying off and all the young had sad faces. Not Andrés Aparicio, no, he was always smiling so he wouldn't look old. His proverbial gentility. He stopped smiling only once. A man from the barrio said something nasty to him and your father kicked him to death, Bernabé. We never saw him again. Oh, my child, look what they've done to you, Doña Amparo said finally, my poor child, my son, look how you've had to fight, and she stopped looking at herself in the mirror to look at her son my little sweetheart my dearest oh why do they pick on you my little saint and the mirror fell to the new brick floor and this time it shattered. Bernabé stared at her, unsurprised by the tenderness she so infrequently displayed. She looked at him as if she understood that he understood that he shouldn't be surprised by something he always deserved or that Doña Amparo's tenderness was as temporary as the lost city where they'd lived the last eleven years without anyone coming with an eviction notice, a fact that so encouraged the uncles that they were replacing cardboard with adobe and adobe with brick. The boy asked his mother whether his father was really dead. She told him that she never dreamed about him. She answered with precision, letting him know that the cold and calculating side of her nature had not been overcome by tenderness. As long as she didn't dream about her dead husband, she didn't have to accept his death, she told him. That made all the difference, she let herself go, she wanted to be lucid and emotional at the same time, come give me a hug, Bernabé I love you, my little doll, listen carefully to what I say. Don't ever kill anyone for money. Never kill unless you know what you're doing. But if you do kill someone, do it with reason, with passion. It will make you clean and strong. Never kill anyone, my son, unless you buy a little life for yourself, my precious.

## *The Uncles*

They were his mother's brothers and she called them the boys, though they were between thirty-eight and fifty years old. Uncle Rosendo was the oldest and he worked in a bank counting the old bank notes that were returned to the government to be burned. Romano and Richi, the youngest, worked in a gasoline station, but they looked older than Rosendo, because he spent most of the day on his feet and although they moved around a lot waiting on customers, lubricating cars, and cleaning windshields, they passed their time swilling soft drinks that swelled up their bellies. During all the spare time in the station located in a cloud of dust in the barrio of Ixtapalpa where you couldn't see anything clearly, not people not houses nothing but grimy cars and the hands of people paying, Romano drank Pepsis and read the sports pages while Richi played the flute, coaxing beautiful warm sounds from it and sipping from time to time on his Pepsi. They drank beer only on Sundays, before and after they went out to the barren field with their pistols to shoot rabbits and toads behind the shacks. They spent every Sunday this way, and Bernabé sitting on a pile of broken roof tiles watched from the back of the house. They laughed with a kind of slobbering glee, wiping their mustaches on their sleeves after every draught of beer, elbowing one another, howling like coyotes if they got a rabbit bigger than the rest. Then he watched them hug each other, clap each other on the back, and return dragging the bloody rabbits by the ears and Richi with a dead toad in each hand. While Amparo fanned the charcoal brazier and served them ears of corn sprinkled with chili pepper and rice cooked with tomatoes the brothers argued because Richi said that he was getting on toward forty and didn't want to die a big-bellied bastard, Amparito should forgive him, in some gas station even if it did belong to Licenciado Tín Vergara who did them the favor because the old General had ordered it and in a cabaret on San Juan de Letrán they were going to audition him to play flute in their dance band. Rosendo angrily picked up an ear of corn and Bernabé looked at his fingers leprous from counting all those filthy bank notes. He said that playing the flute was a queer's job, Amparito should forgive him, and Richi replied if he was so macho why hadn't he ever married and Romano rapped Richi's head half affectionately and half angrily because he wanted to get away from the station where Richi was his only company and Rosendo said it was because among the three of them they kept this household going, their sister Amparo and the boy Bernabé, that's why they never got married, they couldn't afford to feed any more than five mouths with what the three brothers earned and now only two if Richi went off with some dance band. They kept arguing and Richi said he'd earn more in the band and Romano said he'd blow it all on women just to prove something to the marimba players, and Rosendo said that no matter how small it was, with Amparo's permission, Andrés Aparicio's pension would help a little, all they had to do was declare him dead and Amparo wept and said it was her fault of course and would they forgive her. They all consoled her except Richi, who walked to the door and stood silently staring into the darkening dusk over the plain, ignoring Rosendo, who was again speaking as the head of the family. It isn't your fault Amparito but your husband could at least let us know whether or not he's dead. We've all worked at whatever we could, look at my hands, Amparito, do you think I enjoy it? but it was your husband who wanted to be something better (that was my fault, said Bernabé's mother) because a street sweeper or an elevator operator earns more than an office worker but your husband wanted to have a career so he could earn a pension (that was my fault, said Bernabé's mother), but to earn a pension you have to be dead and your husband just went up in smoke,

Amparito. Outside it's all dark and gray said Richi from the door and Amparito said her husband had struggled to be a gentleman so we wouldn't sink so low. What's low about work, Richi asked with irritation, and Bernabé followed him out onto the quiet and sleeping plain into a dusk smelling of dried shit and smoking tortillas and a hint of the green, squat greasewood. Uncle Richi hummed Agustín Lara's bolero, *caballera de plata: hair of silver, hair of snow, skein of tenderness with one tress daring . . .* as airplanes descended in their approach to the international airport, the only lights those on a distant runway. God, I wish they'd hire me for the band, Richi said to Bernabé, staring at the yellowish fog, in September they're going to Acapulco to play for the national fiesta and you can come with me, Bernabé. We're not going to die without seeing the sea, Bernabé.

## Bernabé

When he was twelve he stopped going to school, but didn't tell anyone. He hung around the station where his uncles worked and they let him clean the windshields as a part of the service; no matter if you only earn a few centavos, it's better than nothing. His absence went unnoticed at school, it didn't concern them. The classrooms were jammed with sometimes as many as a hundred children, and one fewer was a relief for everyone, even if no one noticed. They turned down Richi for the band and he told Bernabé flatly, at least come earn a few centavos, don't waste any more time or you're going to end up like your goddamn papa. He gave up playing the flute and signed Bernabé's grade cards so Amparo would think he was still in school and so a pact was sealed between the two that was the first secret relationship in Bernabé's life, because in school he was always too divided between what he saw and heard at home, where his mother always spoke of decency and good family and bad times, as if they'd known times that weren't bad, and when he tried to tell any of this at school he met hard, unseeing gazes. One of his teachers noticed and she told him that here no one offered or asked for pity because pity was a little like contempt. Here no one complained and no one was better than anyone else. Bernabé didn't understand but it made him mad that the teacher acted as if she understood better than anyone what only he could understand. Richi understood, come on Bernabé earn your coppers, just take a good look at what you can have if you're rich, look at that Jaguar coming into the station, jeez usually we get nothing here but rattletraps ah it's our boss the Honorable Tín passing by to see how business is and look at this magazine Bernabé wouldn't you like a babe like that all for yourself and I'll bet lawyer Tín's women look like that, look at those terrific tits Bernabé imagine lifting up her skirt and sliding between those thighs warm as milk Bernabé God I always get the short end of the stick look at this ad of Acapulco we're always shit on Bernabé look at the rich bastards in their Alfa Romeos, Bernabé, think how they must have lived when they were kids, think how they live now and how they'll live when they're old men, everything on a silver platter but you, Bernabé, you and me shit on from the day we're born, old men the day we're born, isn't that right? He envied his Uncle Richi, such a smooth talker, words came so hard for him and he'd already learned that when you don't have the words you get hard knocks, he left school to knock around in the city, which at least was dumb like him, isn't it true, Bernabé, that the big bully's words hurt more than his blows? Even if the city knocks you around, at least it doesn't talk. Why don't you read a book, Bernabé, the teacher who'd made him so mad asked, do you feel inferior to your classmates? He couldn't tell her that he felt uncomfortable when he read because books spoke the way his mother spoke. He didn't understand why but, from wanting it so much, tenderness was painful to him. In contrast, the city let itself be seen and loved and wanted, though in the end racing along Reforma and Insurgentes and Revolución and Universidad at rush hour, wiping windshields, hurling himself against the cars, playing them like bulls, hanging out with the other jobless kids and playing soccer with balls of wadded newspaper on a flat piece of ground like the one he'd grown up on, sweating the stench of gasoline fumes and pissing streams of sludge and stealing soft drinks on one corner and fried pork rind on another and sneaking into the movies drove him from his uncles and his mother, he became more independent and clever and greedy for all the things he was beginning to see, and everything beginning to speak to him, the damned words again, there was no way to escape them, buy me, take me, you need me, in every shop window, in the hand the woman extended from her car window to give him twenty centavos without a word of thanks for the swift and professional cleaning of her windshield, on the face of the rich young man who didn't even look at him as he said, keep your hands off my windshield, punk, in the wordless television programs he could see from the street through the glass of the show window, mute, intoxicating him with desires, as he stood as tall as he could and thought how he wasn't earning any more at fifteen than he had at twelve, cleaning windshields with an old rag on Reforma, Insurgentes, Universidad, and Revolución at the hour of the heaviest traffic and how he wasn't getting any closer to any of the things the songs and ads offered him and that his helplessness was stretching longer and longer and would never come to anything like his Uncle Richi's desire to play the flute in a dance band and spend the month of September in Acapulco skimming on water skis across a Technicolor bay, swooping from an orange hang glider above the fairytale palaces of the Hilton Marriott Holiday Inn Acapulco Princess. His mother, when she found out, was philosophical, she didn't scold him about anything any more, and she resigned herself to growing old. Her few remaining priggish friends, a widower pharmacist, a Carmelite nun, a forgotten cousin of former President Ruiz Cortines, saw in her gaze the tranquillity of a lesson well taught, of words well spoken. She could give no more of herself. She spent hours gazing down the empty road toward the horizon.

"I hear the wind and the world creaks."

"Beautifully stated, Doña Amparito."

## Sunday Afternoon Rodeo

He came to hate his Uncle Richi because leaving school and cleaning windshields along the broad avenues hadn't made him rich or given him what everybody else had, if anything he was worse off than ever. That's why when Bernabé was sixteen his Uncles Rosendo and Romano decided to give him a very special present. Where do you think we've gone for a good time all these years without women of our own? they asked him, licking their mustaches. Where do you think we went after shooting rabbits and eating dinner with your mother and you? Bernabé said he guessed with whores, but his uncles laughed and said that only dumb shits paid for a woman. They took him to an empty factory on the abandoned silent road to Azcapotzalco with its putrid smell of gasoline where for a peso a head the watchman let them enter and his Uncle Rosendo and Uncle Romano pushed him before them into a dark room and closed the door. All Bernabé could see was a flash of dark flesh and then he had to feel. He took the first one he touched, each of them standing, her back against the wall and he leaning against her, desperate Bernabé, trying to understand, not daring to speak because what was happening didn't need words, he was sure that this desperate pleasure was called life and he seized it with open hands, moving from the hard and scratchy wool of a sweater to the softness of shoulders and the creaminess of breasts, from the stiff cotton of a skirt to the wet spider between the legs, from the thick laddered stockings to cotton-candy buttocks. He was distracted by his uncles' bellowings, their hurried and vanquished labors, but he realized that because he was distracted everything lasted longer, and finally he could speak, amazing himself, as he thrust his penis into this soft, melting, creamy girl who clung to him twice with her arms about his neck and her legs locked around his waist. What's your name, mine's Bernabé. Love me, she said, be sweet, be good, she said, be a doll, the same thing his mother said when she felt tender, oh, baby, oh, handsome, what a cock you've got there. Later they sat for a while on the floor but his uncles began whistling the way they did in the station, like a mule driver, hey, come on, kid, let's go, put your sword away, leave a little something for next Sunday, don't let these bull-doggers sap your strength, oooheee they're castrators, they'll eat you alive and spit out the pieces, by-eee by-eee now, who are you anyway, María Felix? Bernabé jerked the medal from the girl's neck and she screamed, but the nephew and the two uncles had already hurried from the Sunday-afternoon rodeo.

## *Martincita*

The following Sunday he came early and leaned against the fence by the factory entrance to wait for her. The girls arrived sedately, sometimes exaggerating their charade by wearing veils as if for Mass or carrying shopping baskets, some were more natural, dressed like today's servant girls in turtleneck sweaters and checked slacks. She was wearing the same cotton skirt and woolly sweater, rubbing her eyes, which smarted from the heavy yellow air of the Azcapotzalco refinery. He knew it was she, he'd kept playing with the little medal of the Virgin of Guadalupe, dangling it from his wrist, twirling it so the sun would flash into the eyes of his Lupe and her eyes would glint in return and she would stop and look and look at him and reveal, with a betraying gesture of hand to throat, that she was the one. She was ugly. Really ugly. But Bernabé couldn't turn back now. He kept swinging the medal and she walked over to him and took it without a word. She was repulsive, she had the flattened face of an Otomí Indian, her hair was frizzled by cheap permanents and the gold of her badly capped teeth mirrored the glitter of Our Lady of Guadalupe. Bernabé managed to ask her if she wouldn't like to go for a little walk but he couldn't say, It's true, isn't it, that you don't do it for money? She said her name was Martina but that everyone called her Martincita. Bernabé took her elbow and they walked along the path toward the Spanish Cemetery, which is the only pretty place in the whole area, with its huge funeral wreaths and white marble angels. Cemeteries are so pretty, said Martincita, and Bernabé imagined the two of them making it in one of the chapels where the rich buried their dead. They sat on a tomb slab with gilded letters and she took a lily from a flower holder, smelled it, and covered the tip of her snub nose with orange pollen, she laughed and then teased him with the white bloom, tickling her nose and then Bernabé's, who burst into sneezes. She laughed, flashing teeth like eternal noonday, and said that since he didn't talk much she was going to tell him the whole story, they all went to the factory for fun, there were all kinds, girls from the country like Martina and girls who'd lived a long time in Mexico City, that didn't have anything to do with it, what mattered was that everyone came to the factory because they enjoyed it, it was the only place they could be free for a while from servant-chasing bosses or their sons or the barrio Romeos who took advantage of a girl and then said, Why, I never laid eyes on you, and that's why there were so many fatherless babies, but there in the dark where you never knew each other, where there weren't any complications, it was nice to have their moment of love every week, no? honest, they all thought it was wonderful to make love in the dark, where no one could see their faces or know what happened or with who, but one thing she was sure of was that what interested the men who came there was the feeling that they were getting it from someone weak. In her village that's what always happens to the women of the priests, who were passed off as nieces or servants, any man could lay them saying, If you don't come through I'll tell that bastard priest. They say the same thing used to happen to the nuns when the big estate owners went to the convents and screwed the sisters, because who was going to keep them from it? That night when he was sixteen Bernabé couldn't sleep, he could think of only one thing: how well Martincita spoke, she didn't lack for words, how well she fucked too, she had everything except looks, what a shame she was such a pig. They made a date to meet in the Spanish Cemetery every Sunday and make love in the Gothic mausoleum of a well-known industrial family and she said there was something funny about him, he still seemed like a little boy and she thought there must be something about his home that didn't jibe with his being so poor and so tongue-tied, she didn't understand what it could be, even before she left home she'd known that only rich kids had a right to be little boys and grow up to be big, people like Martincita and Bernabé were born grown up, the cards are stacked against us, Bernabé, from the minute we're born, except you're different, I think you want to be different, I don't know. At first they did the things all poor young couples do. They went to anything free like watching the *charro* cowboys ride and rope in Chapultepec Park on Sundays and they went to all the parades during the first months they were lovers, first the patriotic parade on Independence Day in September, when Uncle Richi had wanted to be in Acapulco with his flute, then the sports parade on Revolution Day, and in December they went to see the Christmas lights and the old Christmas crèches in Bernabé's old house in the tenements on Guatemala Street, where his crippled friend Luisito lived. They barely said hello because it was the first time Bernabé had taken Martincita to meet anyone he knew and who knew his mother, Doña Amparito, and Doña Lourdes, the mother of Luis, and Rosa María didn't even speak to them and the crippled boy stared at them through eyes without a future. Then Martina said she'd like to meet Bernabé's other friends, Luisito frightened her because he was just like an old man in her village but he was never going to grow old. So they looked up the boys who played soccer with Bernabé and cleaned windshields and sold Chiclets and Kleenex and sometimes even American cigarettes on Universidad, Insurgentes, Reforma, and Revolución but it was one thing to run through the broad avenues joking and insulting one another and fighting over business and then spending their remaining energy on a field with a paper soccer ball and it was something else to go out with girls and talk like regular people, sitting in a cheap café facing a few silent pork rolls and pineapple pop. Bernabé looked at them there in the little café, they were envious of Martina because he was really getting it and not just in wet dreams or jerking off but they didn't envy him because she was such a dog. Either to get back at him or to show off or just to set themselves apart from him the boys told them that some politician who drove down Constituyentes every day on his way to the presidential offices on Los Pinos had wanted to impress a watching presidential guard and had with a great flourish given two of them tickets for the soccer match and the rest of them had scraped together enough money to go on Sunday and they were inviting him, but it would have to be without her because the money wouldn't stretch that far and Bernabé said no, he wasn't going to leave her all by herself on a Sunday. They went with the boys as far as the entrance of the Azteca Stadium and Martincita said why didn't they go to the Spanish Cemetery, but Bernabé just shook his head, he bought Martina a soft drink and began to pace back and forth in front of the stadium like a caged tiger, kicking the lampposts every time he heard the shouting inside and the roar of *Goal!* So there was Bernabé kicking lampposts and muttering, This fucking life is beginning to get to me, when am I going to begin to live, when?

## Words

Martina asked him what they were going to do, she was very truthful and told him she could deceive him and let herself get pregnant but what good would that do if they didn't come to an agreement first about their future. She hinted around a lot like the time he suggested they hook a ride to Puebla to the fifth of May parade and managed to get a supply truck to take them as far as the Church of San Francisco Acatepec glittering like a thimble and from there they walked toward the city of shining tiles and caramel candies, still blissful from their adventure together and the clear landscape of pines and cool breezes from the volcanoes that was something new for Bernabé. She had come from the Indian plains of the state of Hidalgo and she knew what poor country looked like, but clean, too, not like the city filth, and watching the parade of the Zouaves and the Zacapoaxtlas, the troops of Napoleon and those of the Honorable Don Benito Juárez, she told him that she'd like to see him marching in a uniform, with a band and everything. His turn might come up in the lottery for the draft and everyone knew, said Martina with an air of being very much in the know, that they gave the draftees whatever education they needed and a career in the army wasn't a bad deal for someone who didn't even have a pot to pee in. Bernabé's words stuck in his throat because he felt he was different from Martincita but she didn't realize it, and looking at a display of sweets in a shop window he compared himself to her in the reflection and he thought he was handsomer, slimmer, even lighter of complexion, and his eyes had a kind of green spark, they weren't impenetrable like his sweetheart's black eyes, in which no white was visible. But since he didn't know how to tell her this, he took her to meet his mother. Martincita took it all to heart, she was thrilled and thought it was almost as good as a formal proposal. But all Bernabé wanted was to show her how different they were. Doña Amparito must have been waiting a long time for a day like this, an occasion that would make her feel young again. She took out her best clothes, a wide-shouldered tailored suit, her precious nylons and sharptoed patent-leather shoes, she hung up some old photographs that proved the existence of ancestors, they hadn't sprung from nowhere, johnny-come latelys, why certainly not, señorita, you see what kind of family you're hoping to get into and a photograph with President Calles in the center and to the left General Vergara and in the background the General's head groom, the father of Amparito, Romano, Rosendo, and Richi. But one look at Martincita, and Doña Amparo was speechless. Bernabé's mother could handle women like herself, women insecure of their place in the world, but Martincita showed no sign of insecurity. She was a country girl and had never pretended to be anything different. Doña Amparo glanced desolately at the table set for tea and the mocha tea cakes she'd asked Richi to bring from a distant bakery. But she didn't know how to offer tea to this servant girl, not only a servant but ugly ugly ugly, God help her but she was ugly, she could even contend with a girl of that class if she were pretty, but a servant and a scarecrow besides, what words could deal with that? how could she say, Have a seat, señorita, please forgive the circumstances but decency is something one carries inside, something seen in one's manners, the next time you come we can compare our family albums if you would like, now wouldn't you like a drop of tea? lemon or cream? a mocha tea cake, señorita? Bernabé loves French pastry more than anything, he is a young man with refined tastes, you know. She didn't offer her hand. She didn't rise. She didn't speak. Bernabé pleaded in silence, Speak, Mama, you know what words to say, you're like Martincita that way, you both know how to talk, I just plain can't get the words out. Let's go, Bernabé, Martina said pridefully after five minutes of strained silence. Stay and have your tea with me, I know how much you like it, Doña Amparo said, good afternoon, young lady. Martina waited a couple of seconds, then wrapped herself in her woolly sweater and hurried from the house. They saw each other again, they spent one of their Sundays together all close and cuddling, and Martincita's words, pretty and teasing but now with a hard and cutting edge.

"Ever since I was a little girl I knew I couldn't be a little girl. But not you, Bernabé, not you, I see that now."

## *Partings*

Bernabé tried once again, this time with the uncles, so many *r-r-r*'s Martina laughed, showing her gold teeth, Rosendo and Romano and Richi sitting with their pistols between their legs after a Sunday morning shooting rabbits and toads and then cutting pigweed leaves on the plain where the squat green greasewood grew. Richi said that the leaves of the pigweed were good for stomach cramps and frights and he elbowed his brother Rosendo and looked at Martincita, who was smiling, holding his nephew Bernabé's hand, and Romano told Bernabé that he was going to need some pigweed tea to get over his fright. The three uncles laughed maliciously and this time Martincita covered her face with her hands and ran from the house with Bernabé behind her, Wait for me, Martina, what's the matter? The uncles yelped like coyotes, licked their mustaches, hugged one another and clapped each other's shoulders weak with laughter: Listen, Bernabé, where'd you pick up the little stray? she looks like something you'd throw to the lions, our nephew with a reject like that? you shouldn't be screwing with her, let us get you something better, where'd you scare her up, kid? don't tell us from the Sunday-afternoon rodeo? Oh, what a blockhead you are, nephew, no wonder your mother's been so upset. But Bernabé didn't know how to tell them how well she spoke and that she was loving besides, that she had everything except beauty, he wanted to tell them that but he couldn't, I'll miss her, he watched her run across the flat ground, stop, look back, wait for the last time, decide, Bernabé, I don't give you a bellyache or haunt your dreams, I cuddle you, I fondle you, I give you all my sweetness, decide, Bernabé, Bernabé my love. A real asshole, nephew; it's one thing to get a free lay from some servant girl on Sundays just to get your hard off but it's something else again who you show to the world and that's the very reason you're going to need money, Bernabé, stay here, don't be stupid, let her go, you don't marry the first little bitch you go to bed with, certainly not a pig with a dish face like your Martincita, my God, what an ass you are, Bernabé, it's about time for you to grow up and be a man and earn yourself a wad so you can take girls out, we've never had any children, we've given everything to you, we're counting on you, Bernabé, what do you need? a car, money, clothes? how are you going to buy clothes? what are you going to say to the hot mommas, nephew? how are you going to attract them? be bold as a bullfighter, Bernabé, remember they're the heifers, you're the torero and you have to make them charge, you need style, Bernabé, class like the song says, come on, Bernabé, learn how to fire the pistol, it's time now, come along with your old uncles, we've sacrificed ourselves for you and your mother, don't fight it, forget her, Bernabé, do it for us, it's time for you to get ahead, kid, you were spinning your wheels with that dog, boy, don't tell us we sacrificed ourselves for nothing, look at my hands peeling like a scabby old mutt, look at your Uncle Romano's big belly and he's got a matching spare tire of grease and fumes in his head, what does he have to look forward to? and look at your Uncle Richi's glazed eyes who never got to go to Acapulco he's bleary-eyed from dreaming, you want to be like that, kid? You need to go your own way, claw your way up, Bernabé, I'm an old man now and I'm telling you whether you like it or not we're growing apart, the way you just parted from your sweetheart you're going to have to part from your mother and us, with some pain a little more a little less but you get used to everything, after a while partings will seem normal, that's life, life is just one parting after another, it's not what you keep but what you leave behind that's life, you'll see, Bernabé. He spent that afternoon alone without Martina for the first time in ten months, wandering through the streets of the Zona Rosa, staring at the cars, the suits, the restaurant entrances, the shoes of the people going in, the neckties of the people coming out, his gaze flashing from one thing to another without really focusing on anything or anyone, fearing the bitterness the bile in his guts and balls that would make him kick out at the well-dressed young men and hip-swinging girls going in and out of the bars and restaurants on Hamburgo and Genova and Niza the way he'd kicked the lampposts outside the stadium. He tramped up and down Insurgentes that Sunday, a street jammed with automobiles returning from Cuernavaca, bumpers crashing, balloon vendors, sandwich shops jammed too, he fantasized he could kick the whole city until there was nothing left but pieces of neon light and then grind up the pieces and swallow them and I'll be seeing you, Bernabé. That was when his Uncle Richi with whom he'd been angry even before he made fun of Martincita, waved excitedly from an open-air oyster stand near the bridge on Insurgentes.

"I've got it made, nephew. They've hired me as flute player and I'm off to Acapulco with the band. To prove I keep my word I want you to go with me. To tell you the truth, I think I owe it all to you. My boss wants to meet you."

## El Güero

He didn't have to go to Acapulco with his Uncle Richi because the Chief gave him a job on the spot. Bernabé didn't meet him immediately, he only heard a deep and unctuous voice, like on the radio, from behind the glass office doors. Tell the boys to take care of him. In the dressing rooms they looked him up and down, some thumbed their noses at him, some gestured up yours and continued dressing, carefully arranging their testicles in close-fitting undershorts. A tall dark-skinned youth with a long face and stiff eyelashes brayed at him and Bernabé was about to take a swing at him but another man they called El Güero because of his light hair came over and asked him what he would like to wear, the Chief offered a new wardrobe to new arrivals and he told him too that he shouldn't pay any attention to the Burro, the poor thing only brayed to say his name, not to insult anyone. Bernabé remembered what Martina had said in Puebla, Join the army, Bernabé, they'll give you an education, you'll learn to take orders, then they'll promote you and if they discharge you, you buy a gun and go into business for yourself, she joked. He told El Güero that a uniform would be fine, he didn't know how to dress, a uniform was fine. El Güero said it looked as if he was going to have to look after him and he picked out a leather jacket, some jeans still stiff from the factory, and a couple of checked shirts. He promised that as soon as he got a girl he'd get him a dress suit, but this would do for now and for the workouts a white T-shirt and watch out for your balls, eggs in a basket because sometimes the blows fell hot and heavy. They took him to a kind of military camp that didn't look like a camp from the outside, with a lot of gray trucks always waiting in front and sometimes men dressed in civilian clothes who tied a white handkerchief on their arm as they entered and removed it when they came out. They slept on campaign cots and from the crack of dawn went through training exercises in a gym that smelled of eucalyptus drifting through the broken windowpanes. First were the rings and parallel bars, the horizontal bar and box horse, the weights and the horse. Then came poles, rope climbing, tree trunks across barrancas and sharpshooting, and only at the end of the training, bludgeons, rubber hoses, and brass knuckles. He looked at himself naked in the full-length mirror in the dressing room, as if sketched with an iron nib, hair that curled naturally not with curling irons like poor straight-haired Martincita's, fine bony mestizo features with a real profile, not like Martincita's pushed-in face, a profile to his face and his belly and a profile between his legs and a green pride in his eyes that hadn't been there before. The Burro went by braying and laughing at the same time, with a lasso longer than his, and both things angered Bernabé. Again El Güero held him back and reminded him that the Burro didn't know any other way to laugh, that he announced himself with his braying the way that he, El Güero, announced his presence with his transistor, with the music that always preceded him, when you hear music, that's where your Güero is. One day Bernabé felt the earth change beneath his sneakers. It was no longer the soft earth of Las Lomas de Chapultepec, sandy and sprinkled with pine needles. Now all the training exercises were held in a huge handball court, where they learned to run hard, fight hard, move on hard pavement. Bernabé concentrated on the Burro to work up his anger, to turn nimbly and land a karate chop on the nape of the enemy's neck. He jammed a knee into the tall lanky youth with stiff eyelashes, which put him down for the count, but after ten minutes the Burro came to, brayed, and continued as if nothing had happened. Bernabé felt as if the moment for action was near. El Güero said no, he'd done well in training, worked like all get-out and he deserved a vacation. He sat him in a coppery Thunderbird and said have a good time with the cassettes, you can choose the music and if you get bored turn on this small TV, we're off to Acapulco, Bernabé, I'm going to give you a taste of what life's all about, *I was born to dance the rumba, down in Veracruz, I was born in silv'ry moonlight, I play it fast and loose,* choose anything you want. Not really, he said to himself later, I didn't choose anything, they chose for me, the blond American girl was waiting for me in that big bed with the glittery bedspread, the bellboy dressed like an organ grinder's monkey was waiting to carry my suitcases, and another just like him to bring my breakfast to my room and fill my refrigerator, the only thing they didn't give me were the sun and the sea, because they were already there. He looked at himself in the hotel mirrors but he didn't know whether they looked back. Other than Martincita, he didn't know whether or not women liked him. El Güero told him if he wanted to pay he'd have to make a lot of money so it wouldn't feel like he was receiving a tip; look at this Thunderbird, Bernabé, it may be secondhand but it's mine, I bought it with my own dough, he laughed and told him that they wouldn't be seeing so much of each other now, it was time to turn him over to Ureñita, old Dr. Ureñita himself, what a drag he was with a face like a sour old maid and ugly as a constipated monkey, he wasn't like El Güero, who knew how to enjoy life, hey, baby, *ciao*, he said, spitting on each hand and then slapping the saliva on the hood bright as a new coin before he roared off in his Thunderbird.

### Ureñita

"What rank did you reach young man?"

"I don't seem to remember."

"Don't be asinine. Second? Third?"

"Whatever you say, Señor Ureña."

"Oh yes, Bernabé, I'll be having plenty to say. That's why I'm here. We get knuckleheads like you by the ton here. Well, never mind. That's our raw material. We'll see what we can do to refine it, to make an exportable product."

"Whatever you say, Señor Ureña."

"Presentable, I mean. Dialectics. Our friends think we have no history and no ideas because they see dolts like you and they laugh at us. So much the better. Let them believe what they will. That way we will occupy all the history they vacate. Do you understand what I'm saying?"

"No, maestro."

"They've filled our country's history with lies in order to weaken it, in order to make it putty, then they tear off a little piece and then another and at first no one notices. But one day you wake up and you no longer have the great, free, unified nation you dreamed of, Bernabé."

"I dreamed of?"

"Yes, even you, though you don't know it. Why do you think you're here with me?"

"El Güero told me to come. I don't know anything."

"Well, I'm going to make you understand, you simpleton. You are here to assist at the birth of a new world. And a new world can only be born of tumultuous, hate-filled beginnings. Do you understand? Violence is the midwife of history."

"If you say so, Señor Ureñita."

"Don't use the diminutive. Diminutives diminish. Who told you to call me Ureñita?"

"No one, I swear."

"Poor muddlehead. If I wanted I could analyze you blindfolded. This is what they send us. We owe that to John Dewey and Moisés Sáenz. Tell me, Bernabé, do you have a fear of getting buried in poverty?"

"I'm already there, Señor Ureña."

"You are mistaken. There are worse things. Imagine your poor old mother scrubbing floors, still worse, imagine her streetwalking."

"You imagine yours, prof."

"You do not offend me. I know who I am and what my worth is. And I know who you are, shitty *lumpen*. Do you think I don't know your kind? When I was a student I went to the factories, to try to organize the workers, to awaken their radical consciousness. Do you think they paid me any heed?"

"All the way, maestro."

"They turned their backs on me. They refused to hear my message. They didn't want to face reality. And there you have it. Reality punished them, it avenged itself on them, on all of you, poor devils. You haven't wanted to face reality, that's the problem, you've tried to punish reality with dreams and you've failed as a revolutionary class. And yet here I am trying to form you, Bernabé. I warn you; I don't give up easily. Well, I've said what I had to say. They've vilified me."

"They?"

"Our enemies. But I want to be your friend. Tell me everything about yourself. Where do you come from?"

"Oh, around."

"Do you have a family?"

"That depends."

"Don't be so reticent. I want to help you."

"Right, prof."

"Do you have a sweetheart?"

"Could be."

"What are your ambitions, Bernabé? Trust me. I trust you, don't I?"

"That depends."

"It may be that the atmosphere here in the camp is too cold. Would you prefer to continue this conversation elsewhere?"

"It's all the same to me."

"We could go to a movie together, would you like that?"

"Maybe."

"Remember one thing. I can help you humiliate those who humiliate you."

"I like that fine."

"I have books in my home. No, not just books on theory, I have less arid books, all kinds of books for young men."

"Swell."

"Are you coming then, you doll?"

"Let's shake on it, Señor Ureñita."

## Licenciado Mariano

They took him to meet him after he bit Ureña's hand, they said the Chief fell out of his chair laughing and wanted to meet Bernabé. He received him in a leather-and-oak office with matched sets of red leather-bound books and statues and paintings of erupting volcanoes. He told him to call him Licenciado, the Honorable Mariano Carreón, it sounded a little pretentious to call him Chief the way they did in the camp, didn't he agree? Yes, Chief, Bernabé said, and thought to himself that the Licenciado looked exactly like the janitor at his school, a janitor who wore spectacles, and had a head like an olive with carefully combed hair and lenses thick as bottle glass and a mousy little mustache. He told him he liked how he'd reacted to that obnoxious Ureña, he was an old pinko who was working for them now because the other leaders in the movement said a varnishing of theory was important. He hadn't thought so and now he was going to see. He summoned Ureña and the theorist entered with bowed head, his hand bandaged where Bernabé had sunk his teeth. The chief ordered him to take a book from the shelf, any book at all, the one he liked most, and to read it aloud. Yes, sir, at your pleasure, sir, said Ureña, and read with a trembling voice *I could not love within each man a tree / with its remaindered autumns on its back,* do you understand any of that, Bernabé? No, said Bernabé, keep reading, Ureñita, as you wish, sir, *till in the last of hovels, lacking all light and fire, / bread, stone and silence, I paced at last alone, / dying of my own death,* keep going, Ureñita, don't swoon, I want the boy to understand what the fuck this culture thing is all about, *Stone within stone, and man, where was he? / Air within air, and man, where was he? / Time within time . . .* Ureña coughed, oh, I'm so sorry, *Were you also the shattered fragment / of indecision . . . ?* That's enough Ureñita, did you understand anything, boy? Bernabé shook his head. The Chief ordered Ureña to place the book in a huge blown-glass ashtray from Tlaquepaque as thick as his spectacles, put it right there and set fire to it, right now, double time, Licenciado Carreón said with a dry severe laugh, and while the pages blazed he said I didn't have to read any of that stuff to get where I am, who needs it, it would have got in my way, Ureñita, so why would this kid need it? He said the boy had been right to bite him, and if you ask me why I have this library, I'll tell you that it's to remember every minute that there are many books still to be burned. Look here, son, he said to Bernabé staring at him with all the intensity he was capable of behind his eight layers of congealed glass, any dumb shit can put a bullet through the most intelligent head in the world, don't forget that. He told him he was all right, that he liked him, that he reminded him of himself when he was young, that he perked up his spirits and oh, how he wished, he said as he invited him to accompany him in a Galaxy black as a hearse with all the windows darkened so you could look out without being seen, someone years ago had taken an interest in him, someone like himself, they stole the election from General Almazán, synarchism would have taken care of people like them, as they were doing now, don't you worry, if you had had us your life and your parents' lives would have been different. Better. But you have us now, Bernabé my friend. He told the chauffeur to come back about five and told Bernabé to come eat with him, they went into one of the restaurants in the Zona Rosa that a furious Bernabé had seen only from the outside one Sunday, all the majordomos and waiters bowed to them like acolytes during Mass, Señor Licenciado, your private table is ready, this way, what can we do for you, señor, anything at all, I'm putting the Señor Licenciado in your hands, Jesús Florencio. Bernabé realized that the Chief liked talking about his life, how he'd come from the very asshole of the city and with persistence and without books but with an idea of the greatness of the nation, yes that, had got where he was. They ate seafood au gratin and drank beer until El Güero came in with a message and the Chief listened and said bring that sonofabitch here and told Bernabé to keep calm and go on eating. A very cool chief went on recounting anecdotes and when El Güero returned with a well-dressed paper-skinned man, the Chief simply said good afternoon, Señor Secretary, El Güerito is going to tell you what you need to know. The Chief went on circumspectly eating his lobster thermidor as El Güero seized the Secretary by his tie and mouthed a string of curses, he'd better learn how to treat Licenciado Carreón, he shouldn't get independent and go see the president on his own, everything went through Licenciado Carreón first, didn't the Secretary owe him his job, see? The Chief simply ignored El Güero and the Secretary, he looked instead at Bernabé, and in his eyes at that moment Bernabé read what he was supposed to read, what the Chief intended him to read, you can be like me, you can treat the big shots this way and have no fear, Bernabé. The Chief ordered the remains of the lobster removed and the waiter Jesús Florencio bowed with alacrity when he saw the Secretary but when he saw Licenciado Carreón's face he decided not to speak to the Secretary but instead busied himself with removing the dishes. As they couldn't look at anyone else, Bernabé and Jesús Florencio exchanged glances. Bernabé liked the waiter. He felt as if this was someone he could talk to because they shared a secret. Though he had to ass-kiss the same as anyone, he earned his living and his life was his own. He found out all this because they decided to meet, Jesús Florencio took a liking to Bernabé and warned him, watch out, if you want to come to work as a waiter I'll help you, politics has its ups and downs and the Secretary's not going to forget that you saw him humiliated by the Licenciado and the Licenciado's not going to forget that you saw him humiliate someone the day they humiliate him.

"But congratulations just the same. I think you've bought yourself a winning ticket, buddy."

"You think so?"

"Just don't forget me." Jesús Florencio smiled.

## Pedregal

Bernabé felt that this was really a place with a name. The Chief took him to his house in Pedregal and said, Make yourself at home, as if I've adopted you, go wherever you want and get to know the boys in the kitchen and in administration. He wandered in and out of the house, which started at the service area on the ground level but then instead of rising descended along scarlet-colored cement ramps through a kind of crater toward the bedrooms and finally to the open rooms surrounding a swimming pool sunk into the very center of the house and illuminated from below by underwater lights and from above by a roof of celestial-blue lead tiles that capped the mansion. Licenciado Carreón's wife was a small fat woman with tight black curls and religious medals jangling beneath her double chin, on her breasts, and on her wrists, who when she saw him asked if he was a terrorist or a bodyguard, if he'd come to kidnap them or protect them—they all look alike, the brown scum. The señora was highly amused by her own joke. You could hear her coming a long way off, like El Güero and his transistor and the Burro and his braying. Bernabé heard her often the first two or three days he wandered around the house feeling like a fool, expecting the Chief to call him and give him some job to do, fingering the porcelain knickknacks, the glass display cabinets and large vases and at every turn bumping into a señora who smiled as endlessly as his father, Andrés Aparicio. One afternoon he heard music, sentimental boleros playing during the siesta hour and he felt languorous and handsome as he had when he looked at himself in the hotel mirrors in Acapulco, he was drawn by the soft sad music but when he reached the second floor he lost his way and walked through one of the bathrooms into a dressing room with dozens of kimonos and rubber-soled beach sandals and a half-open door. He saw a bed as large as the one in the Acapulco hotel covered with tiger skins and on the headboard he saw a shelf with votive candles and religious images, and beneath that a tape deck like the one El Güero had in his secondhand Thunderbird and lying on the skins Señora Carreón stark naked except for her religious medals, especially one in the shape of a seashell with a superimposed gold image of the virgin of Guadalupe that the señora held over her sex while Chief Mariano tried to lift it with his tongue and the señora laughed a high coquettish schoolgirl laugh and said, Oh no my Lord, no my King, respect your little virgin, and he naked on all fours his balls purple with cold trying to reach the medal in the shape of a seashell, oh my sexy plump beauty, oh my saintly little bitch, my perfumed whore, my mother-of-pearl ringleted goddess, let your own little Pope bless your Guadalupe, oh my love, and all the time the bolero on the tape, *I know I shall never kiss your lips, your lips of burning crimson, I know I shall never sip from your wild and passionate fountain . . .* Later the boys in the office and the kitchen told him, you can see the Chief's taken a liking to you, friend, don't do anything to blow it because he'll protect you against whatever comes. Get out of the brigade if you can, that's dangerous work, you'll see. On the other hand here in the kitchen and the office we've got the world by the tail. El Güero walked through the office to answer the telephone and invited Bernabé to go for a ride in the Jaguar that belonged to the Carreóns' daughter, she was in a Canadian finishing school with the nuns and the car had to be driven from time to time to keep it in good shape. He said the boys in the office were right, the Chief sees something in you to adopt you this way. Don't muff the chance, Bernabé. If you get to be one of his personal guard you're set up for life, said El Güero, driving the girl's Jaguar the way a jockey exercises a horse for a race, I give you my word, you'll be set up. The deal is to learn every little thing that's going on and then whatever shit they try to pull you've got a stranglehold on them, you can take any shit they try to pull, unless they shut you up forever. But if you play your cards right, just look, you've got it all, money, girls, cars, you even eat the same food they eat. But the Chief had to study, Bernabé replied, he had to get his degree before he made it big. El Güero hooted at that and said the Chief hadn't gone past grade school, they'd stuck on the Licenciado because that's what you call anyone important in Mexico even though he wouldn't recognize a law book if it fell on him, don't be a jerk, Bernabé. All you need to know is that every day a millionaire is born who someday is going to want you to protect his life, his kids, his cash, his ass. And you know why, Bernabé? Because every day a thousand bastards like you are born ready to tear the guts out of the rich man born the same day. One against a thousand, Bernabé. Don't tell me it isn't easy to choose. If we don't get away from where we were born we go right down the goddamn tubes. We have to get on the side of the ones who're born to screw us, as sure as seven and seven make heaven, right? The Chief called Bernabé to the bar beside the pool and told him to come with him, he wanted him to see the tinted photograph of his daughter Mirabella, wasn't she pretty? You bet she was and that's because she was made with love and feeling and passion and if you don't have those there's nothing, right, Bernabé? He said in Bernabé he saw himself when he didn't have a centavo or a roof over his head, but with the whole world to conquer. He envied him that, he said, his eyeglasses fogged with steam, because the first thing you know you have everything and you begin to hate yourself, you hate yourself because you can't stand the boredom and the exhaustion that comes of having reached the top, you see? On the one hand you're afraid of falling back where you came from but on the other hand you miss the struggle to reach the top. He asked him, wouldn't he like to marry a girl like Mirabella someday, didn't he have a sweetheart? and Bernabé compared the photograph of the girl surrounded by rose-colored clouds with Martincita, who was plain born for misfortune, but he didn't know what to say to Licenciado Mariano, because either way whether he said yes he did or no he didn't, it was an insult and besides the Chief wasn't listening to Bernabé, he was listening to himself thinking he was listening to Bernabé.

"The pain you go through, you have the right to make others suffer, my boy. That's the honest truth, I swear by all that's holy."

## The Brigade

They're planning to meet on Puente de Alvarado and march down Rosales toward the statue of Carlos IV. We're going to be in the gray trucks farther north at the corner of Héroes and Mina, and to the south at Ponciano Arriaga and Basilio Badillo, so we can cut them off from any direction. All of you are to wear your white armbands and white cotton neck bands and have vinegar-soaked handkerchiefs ready to protect yourselves against the tear gas when the police arrive. When the demonstration is a block and a half from the Carlos IV statue you who're on Héroes come down Rosales and attack from the rear. Shout, Viva Che Guevara! over and over, yell so loud that no one can doubt where your sentiments lie. Yell *Fascists* at the demonstrators. I repeat, *Fash-ists*. Get that straight, you must create total confusion, real pandemonium, and then lay into them, don't hold anything back, use your clubs and brass knuckles and yell anything you want, let yourselves go, boys, have a ball, those coming from the south will be yelling Viva Mao! but you send them flying, they won't give you any trouble, the whole thing's a breeze, let 'er rip, you're members of the Hawk Brigade and the moment's come to prove yourselves in the field, my boys, in the street, on the hard pavement, against posts and steel shutters, break as many windows as you can, that stirs up a lot of resentment against the students, but the main thing is that when you overtake them you go at it heart and soul, have no mercy for the bastards, kick and punch and knee and you, just you two, ice picks for you and see what happens and if you put out the eye of some Red bastard so what, it will be a lesson to them and we'll protect you here, you know that, get that in your thick heads, you bastards, we'll protect you here, so do God's will and do it well and the street is yours, you, where were you born? and you, where are you from? Azcapotzalco? Balbuena? Xochimilco? Canal del Norte? Atlampa? the Tránsito district? Mártires de Tacubaya? Panteones? Well today, my Hawks, you get your own back, just think about that, today the street where you've been fucked good is yours and you'll have your chance to fuck them back and go scot-free, it's like the conquest of Mexico, the man who wins wins, today you're going out in the street, my Hawks, and get your revenge for every sonofabitch who made you feel like a dog, for the abuse you've taken all your miserable lives, for every insult you couldn't return, for all the meals you didn't eat and all the women you didn't screw, you're going out to get even against the landlord who raised your rent and the shyster who ran you out of your rooms and the sawbones who wouldn't operate on your mother unless he had his five thousand in advance, you're going to beat up on the sons of the men who've exploited you, right? the students are spoiled young shits who one day will be landlords and pen-pushers and quacks like their papas but you're going to get even, you're going to give blow for blow, my Hawk Brigade, you know that, so go quietly in the gray trucks, then stalk like wild animals, then the fun, lash out, have the time of your lives, think about your little sister had against her will, your poor old mother on her knees washing and scrubbing, your father screwed all his life, his hands misshapen from grubbing in shit, today's the day to get your revenge, Hawks, today won't come again, don't miss it, don't worry, the police will recognize you by your white neck bands and armbands, they'll act like they're attacking you, play along with them, they'll pretend to shove a few of you in the Black Maria, but it's all a fake to put off the press because it's all-important that tomorrow's papers report a clash among leftist students, subversive disturbance in the heart of the city, the Communist conspiracy rears its ugly head, off with its head! save the republic from anarchy, and you, my hawks, just remember that others may be repressed but not you, no way, I promise you, and now, can't you hear the running feet on the pavement? the street is yours, conquer the street, step hard, go out into the smoke, don't be afraid of the smoke, the city is lost in smoke. No escape from it.

## A New Bernabé

His mother, Doña Amparo, didn't want to come because she was ashamed, his Uncles Rosendo and Romano told him, she didn't want to admit that a son of hers was in the clink; Richi now had a more or less permanent job with the Acapulco dance band, and from time to time he sent a hundred pesos to Bernabé's mother; she was dying of shame and didn't know this new Bernabé and Romano said that after all her husband, Andrés Aparicio, had kicked a man to death. Yes, she replied, but he never ended up behind bars, that's the difference, Bernabé is the first jailbird in the family. As far as you know, woman. But the uncles looked at Bernabé differently too, hardly recognizing him; he wasn't any longer the dumb little kid who'd sat on the roof tiles while they shot rabbits and toads on the plain where the greasewood grew. Bernabé had killed a man, he went at him with an ice pick during the fracas on Puente de Alvarado, he buried the pick deep in his chest and he felt how the wounded boy's guts were mightier than the cold iron of his weapon but in spite of it all the ice pick vanquished the viscera, the viscera sucked in the ice pick the way a lover sucks a beloved. The boy stopped laughing and braying and lay staring at the arches of neon light through stiff eyelashes. El Güero came to the prison to tell Bernabé not to worry, they had to put on an act, he understood, after a few days they'd let him go, meanwhile they were working things out and giving the appearance of law and order. But El Güero didn't recognize this new Bernabé either and for the first time he stammered and his eyes even filled with tears, if you had to stab someone, Bernabé, why did it have to be one of us? You should have been more careful. You knew the Burro, poor old Burro, he was a stupid fart but not a bad guy underneath, why, Bernabé? On the other hand the waiter Jesús Florencio came as a friend and told him that when he got out he should work in the restaurant, he could arrange everything with the owner, and he wanted to tell him why. Licenciado Mariano Carreón had got drunk in the restaurant the day of the row in the city, he was very excited and spilled the beans to his friends about how there was this one kid that reminded him of a lot of things, first what Don Mariano himself had been like as a boy and then of a man he'd known twenty years ago in a co-op in the state of Guerrero, a crazy agricultural student who wouldn't give in, who brought what he called justice to the state and wanted to impose it without so much as a fuck-you. Licenciado Mariano told how he'd organized the resistance against this agronomist Aparicio, playing on the unity of the village families, rich and poor, against a meddlesome outsider. It's so easy to exploit provincial ways for your own good. You have to keep the local bosses strong because where there's no law the boss will enforce order and without order you can't have property and wealth and how else can a man get rich fast, he asked his friends. That agronomist had the fanaticism of a saint, a crusading zeal that got under Licenciado Carreón's skin. For the next ten years he tried to corrupt him, offering him one thing after another, promotions, houses, money, voyages and virgins, protection. No dice. Aparicio the agronomist became an obsession with him and since he couldn't buy him he tried to ruin him, to make problems for him, to prevent his promotions, even evict him from the tenement on Guatemala Street and force him into the lost cities in Mexico City's poverty belt. Licenciado Mariano's obsession was so total that he bought all the land in the area where Andrés Aparicio and his family and other squatter families had gone to live, so no one could run them off, no, he said, let them stay here, the old people will die, no one can live on honor alone and dignity doesn't come with marrow-bone broth, it's good to have a breeding ground for angry kids so I can set them on the right track when they grow up, a nest for my Hawks. He told how every day he savored the fact that the agronomist who wouldn't be corrupted lived with his wife and son and bastard brothers-in-law on land that belonged to Licenciado Mariano, and because he allowed it. But the richest part of the joke was to tell the agronomist. So the Licenciado sent one of his musclemen to tell your father, Bernabé, you've been living on the Chief's bounty, you dirty beggar, ten years of charity, you think you're so pure, and your father, who never stopped smiling so he wouldn't look old, attacked Licenciado Carreón's bodyguard and kicked him to death and then disappeared forever because all he had left was the dignity of death, he didn't want to be buried in jail like you, even for a few days, Bernabé. It's better for you to know, said Jesús Florencio, you see what they offer you isn't as great as they make out. One day you'll run into a man, a real man, who'll knock your protection into a cocked hat. It's not much of a life to live under someone's protection, telling yourself, without the Chief I'm not worth a shit. Bernabé fell asleep on his cot, protecting even the crown of his head with the thin wool cover, talking in his sleep to the fucking Chief, you didn't dare look my father in the face, you had to send a hired killer after him and he killed your killer, you asshole. But then he had a dream in which he was tumbling in silence, dying, tumbling like a shattered fragment of indecision, what? what man? He dreamed, unable to separate his dream from a vague but driving desire that everything that exists be for all the earth, for everyone, water, air, gardens, stone, time.

"And man, where was he?"

## The Chief

He came out of jail hating him for everything, what he'd done to his father, what he'd done to him. El Güero picked him up at the exit of the Black Palace and he climbed into the red Thunderbird, *so give your heart in sweet surrender*, hey baby, where there's music and fun there's your Güerito. He told Bernabé that the Chief would be waiting in his house in Pedregal anytime the kid wanted to stop by and see him. The Chief was sorry Bernabé had been locked up ten days in Lecumberri. But a lot worse had happened to the Chief. Bernabé hadn't known, he hadn't read the newspapers or anything. Well, a real storm broke loose against the Chief, they said he was an agent provocateur and they threatened to send him as governor to Yucatán, which was roughly like being a ditchdigger on the moon, but he says he'll get even with his political enemies and he needs you. He said you were the best man in the brigade. You may have stiffed poor old Burro but the Chief says he understands that you're hotheaded and it's okay with him. Bernabé started sobbing like a baby, it all seemed so lousy, and El Güero didn't know what to do except stop the cassette music out of respect and Bernabé asked him to drop him on the road to Azcapotzalco near the Spanish Panteon but El Güero was worried about him and followed in the car as Bernabé walked along the dusty sidewalks where flower vendors were fashioning huge funeral wreaths of gardenias and stonecutters were chiseling tombstones, names, dates, the beginning and end of every man and woman, and where had they been, Bernabé kept asking himself, remembering the book burned by orders of Licenciado Carreón. El Güero decided to be patient and was waiting for him when an hour later he walked through the wrought-iron cemetery gate, that's the second time you've come through an iron gate today, kid, he joked, better watch your step. Bernabé, still hating the Chief, entered the house in Pedregal, but the minute he saw that nearsighted janitor's face he felt sorry for the man clinging to an oversized tumbler of whiskey as though it were a life belt. It made him sad to remember him on all fours stark naked his balls freezing trying to win his wife's cruel teasing game. Hell, didn't Mirabella have the right, after all, to go to finishing school rather than live in a tin-and-cardboard shack in some lost city? He walked into the house in Pedregal, he saw the Chief cut down to size and felt sorry for him, but now felt sure of himself, nothing bad could happen to him here, no one would abandon him here, the Chief wouldn't make him bust his ass cleaning windshields because the Chief had no intention of taking justice to the state of Guerrero, he wasn't about to die of hunger just to feel pure as the Host, the Chief wasn't a fuckup like his Chief, his Chief Mariano Carreón his Chief Andrés Aparicio, oh Father, do not forsake me. The Licenciado told El Güero to serve the kid his whiskey, he'd been brave and never mind, politics is nothing more than a lot of patience, it's like religion that way, and before you knew it the moment would arrive to get even with the men who were plotting against him and trying to exile him to Yucatán. He wanted Bernabé, who'd been with him in the hour of combat, to be with him in the hour of revenge. They'd change the name of the brigade, it had become too notorious, one day it would reappear bleached clean, bleached by the sun of revenge against the crypto-Communists who'd infiltrated the government, only six years, thank God for the one-term presidency, then those Reds would be out in the street and they'd see, they'd swing back in like a pendulum because they knew how to wait a long long long time like the stone idols in the museum, right? there's no one can stop us. He said to Bernabé, his arm around his neck, that there was no destiny that couldn't be overturned by contempt and he told El Güero that he didn't want to see any of them, not him, not the kid Bernabé, not any of the young toughs in the house while his daughter Mirabella was there, she'd be returning the next day from Canada. They went to the training camp and El Güero gave Bernabé a pistol so he could defend himself and told him not to worry, the Chief was right, there was no way to stop them once they got rolling, *look at that rock, how it keeps rolling,* shit, said El Güero with a shrewd and malicious expression Bernabé hadn't seen before, they could even slip out of the Chief's hands if they wanted, didn't he know everything there was to know? how to set things up, how to go to a barrio and round up the young kids, begin with slingshots if they had to, then chains, then ice picks like the one you killed the Burro with, Bernabé. It was so easy it was a laugh, all you had to do was create a kind of unseen but shared terror, we're terrified of always living under someone's protection, they're terrified of living without it. Choose, kid. But Bernabé didn't answer, he'd stopped listening. He was remembering his visit to the cemetery that morning, the Sundays he'd spent making love with Martincita in the crypt of a wealthy family, remembering a ragged old man urinating behind a cypress, bald, smiling like an idiot, smiling ceaselessly, who with his fly open walked away beneath that Azcapotzalco noonday sun hot as a great yellow chili pepper. Bernabé felt a surge of shame. But don't let it return. A vague memory, a kind of unknowing would be enough for this new

Bernabé. He went to see his mother when he had a new suit and a Mustang, secondhand but all his, and he told her that next year he'd have a sunny clean house for her in a respectable neighborhood. She tried to talk to him as he had when he was a boy, My little sweetheart, you're such a good boy, my little doll, you're not a ruffian like the others, she tried to say what she'd once said about his father, *I never dreamed you were dead,* but to Bernabé his mother's words now were neither tender nor demanding, they merely meant the opposite of what they said. On the other hand, he was grateful that she gave him his father's most handsome suspenders, the red ones with the gilded clasps that had been the pride of Andrés Aparicio.

. . . . . . . . . . . .

### QUESTIONS FOR A SECOND READING

1. The story begins with attention to names and words: Bernabé's barrio is nameless, and Bernabé himself appears inarticulate—"He never told anyone his idea because he couldn't get the words out." Bernabé's mother is well mannered and speaks with great delicacy in public, "with tenderness, but he couldn't associate her tenderness with her manners." Later on in the story the Chief, the Honorable Mariano Carreón, berates Ureñita in front of Bernabé for his attachment to language and ideas and goes on to make it clear that he favors burning books. And while Fuentes has given us a story with all this attention to language, he has also cast the story in political terms—there is the possibility of a revolution in the air, and Carreón wants to create unrest in the streets so that he can eventually take charge of the government.

   What does the story offer as possible explanations for this puzzling relationship between language and politics? How do the various characters—especially Andrés Aparicio, Bernabé, his mother, Martina, El Güero, and the Chief—enact this relationship between language and politics? The relationship doesn't seem at all straightforward or easily pinned down; Fuentes appears to have created a web intertwining language and politics. How can you begin to unravel it, to trace the connections with these various characters? What do you understand to be the relationship between being articulate or inarticulate and political understanding or political action?

2. What attitudes do you suppose Fuentes intends you to take toward Bernabé? (How, for example, do you read the references to the change in Bernabé after he kills the Burro? Are they ironic, or does he change? Is he like the Chief, whom he hates, or is he like something else, something differ-

ent, as Martina tells him? Does he love Martina, or is he just in love with sex, with the opportunity she represents?)

As you read back through the story, mark those passages that best represent the narrator's attitude (or attitudes) toward Bernabé. What attitudes do you expect Fuentes would like you to take toward Bernabé in each of these cases? What attitudes do you take, and how do these attitudes change or develop as you read the story from the beginning to the end?

## ASSIGNMENTS FOR WRITING

1. Is Bernabé like his parents? What parts of his father and his mother does he carry with him? What part of the barrio does he inherit? Write an essay in which you discuss what Bernabé inherits from the people around him and from his life in the barrio. How do his various inheritances come forward in his actions and in the course he finds himself on?

2. There is a way in which this story could be said to be about maleness, about male beliefs and codes of conduct—those primarily unspoken rules and assumptions that govern behavior and beliefs—and the various ways those beliefs and codes are enacted through relationships and politics (which might be said to represent relationships). What male codes would you say are enacted through the men's relationships (not all of them—just the two or three that strike you as the most interesting) with other men and women? How might these codes be related to social class, to life in the barrio or out of the barrio?

    Write an essay in which you discuss what you consider the two or three most significant moments in the story when male codes of conduct come into play, identify these codes (including however you might name them), and explain how they are enacted in specific behaviors toward others.

## MAKING CONNECTIONS

1. Like this Fuentes story, "A Silver Dish" by Saul Bellow (p. 39) might be said to be about male codes of conduct (those unspoken rules and assumptions that govern beliefs and behavior) and how those codes influence the relationships men and women share. Write an essay in which you examine what you consider the codes of conduct that affect the main characters in both these stories. Sketch out the codes by considering how you might read them from specific passages in the story. Then go on to explain, as best you can, their possible origins in specific relationships, including the men's relationships to their social class. What do you find out? What are the similarities and differences between the codes in these two stories? How might you explain these similarities and differences?

2. Clifford Geertz, in his essay "Deep Play: Notes on the Balinese Cockfight"

(p. 272), says that "the culture of a people is an ensemble of texts, themselves ensembles, which the anthropologist strains to read over the shoulders of those to whom they properly belong." Write an essay in which you do a Geertzian reading of the "play"—those moments when the characters are literally or metaphorically playing—in the Fuentes story. What does their play reveal about the characters' values and the social order around them? What, for example, might you say about the three uncles and their shooting games, or their visits to the factory, or the serious play of the Hawks' training and fighting on the streets? What values might Geertz see in the moments of play here, and how might he read their statements about the social order of the barrio or the city?

# CLIFFORD

# GEERTZ

*C* LIFFORD GEERTZ *was born in San Francisco in 1929. After two years in
the U.S. Navy Reserve, he earned a B.A. from Antioch College and a Ph.D.
from Harvard. A Fellow of the National Academy of Science, the American Academy of Arts and Sciences, and the American Philosophical Society, Geertz has been
a professor in the department of social science of the Institute for Advanced Study
in Princeton, New Jersey, since 1970. He has written several books (mostly anthropological studies of Third World cultures) and published two collections of essays,* Interpretation of Cultures *and* Local Knowledge. Interpretation of Cultures, *from which the following essay is drawn, became a classic and won for Geertz
the rare distinction of being an academic whose scholarly work is eagerly read by
people outside his academic discipline, even outside the academic community altogether. His most recent book is titled* Works and Lives: The Anthropologist as
Author.

*"Deep Play" was first presented at a Paris conference organized by Geertz, the
literary critic Paul de Man, and the American Academy of Arts and Sciences. The
purpose of the conference was to bring together scholars from various academic de-
partments (in the humanities, the social sciences, and the natural sciences) to see*

*if they could find a way of talking to each other and, in doing so, find a common ground to their work. The conference planners believed that there was a common ground, that all of these scholars were bound together by their participation in what they called the "systematic study of meaningful forms." This is a grand phrase, but Geertz's essay clearly demonstrates what work of this sort requires of an anthropologist. The essay begins with a story, an anecdote, and the story Geertz tells is as open to your interpretation as it is to anyone else's. What follows, however, are Geertz's attempts to interpret the story he has told, first this way and then that. As you watch him work—finding patterns, making comparisons, drawing on the theories of experts, proposing theories of his own—you are offered a demonstration of how he finds meaningful forms and then sets out to study them systematically.*

*"Deep Play," in fact, was sent out as a model for all prospective conference participants, since it was a paper that showed not only what its author knew about his subject (cockfights in Bali) but what he knew about the methods and procedures that gave him access to his subject. It is a witty and sometimes dazzling essay with a wonderful story to tell—a story of both a Balinese cockfight and an anthropologist trying to write about and understand people whose culture seems, at first, so very different from his own.*

# Deep Play: Notes on the Balinese Cockfight

## The Raid

Early in April of 1958, my wife and I arrived, malarial and diffident, in a Balinese village we intended, as anthropologists, to study. A small place, about five hundred people, and relatively remote, it was its own world. We were intruders, professional ones, and the villagers dealt with us as Balinese seem always to deal with people not part of their life who yet press themselves upon them: as though we were not there. For them, and to a degree for ourselves, we were nonpersons, specters, invisible men.

We moved into an extended family compound (that had been arranged before through the provincial government) belonging to one of the four major factions in village life. But except for our landlord and the village chief, whose cousin and brother-in-law he was, everyone ignored us in a way only a Balinese can do. As we wandered around, uncertain, wistful, eager to please, people seemed to look right through us with a gaze focused several yards behind us on some more actual stone or tree. Almost nobody greeted us; but nobody scowled or said anything unpleasant to us either, which would have been almost as satisfactory. If we ventured to approach someone (something one is powerfully inhibited from doing in such an atmosphere), he moved, negligently but definitively, away. If, seated or leaning against a wall, we had him trapped, he said nothing at all, or mumbled what for the Balinese is the ultimate nonword—"yes." The indifference, of course, was studied; the villagers were watching every move we made and they had an enormous amount of quite accurate information about who we were and what we were going to be doing. But they acted as if we simply did not exist, which, in fact, as this behavior was designed to inform us, we did not, or anyway not yet.

This is, as I say, general in Bali. Everywhere else I have been in Indonesia, and more latterly in Morocco, when I have gone into a new village people have poured out from all sides to take a very close look at me, and, often, an all-too-probing feel as well. In Balinese villages, at least those away from the tourist circuit, nothing happens at all. People go on pounding, chatting, making offerings, staring into space, carrying baskets about while one drifts around feeling vaguely disembodied. And the same thing is true on the individual level. When you first meet a Balinese, he seems virtually not to relate to you at all; he is, in the term Gregory Bateson and Margaret Mead made famous, "away." [1] Then—in a day, a week, a month (with some people the magic moment never comes)—he decides, for reasons I have never been quite able to fathom, that you *are* real, and then he becomes a warm, gay, sensitive, sympathetic, though, being Balinese, always precisely controlled person. You have crossed, somehow, some moral or metaphysical shadow line. Though you are not exactly taken as a Balinese (one has to be born to that), you are at least regarded as a human being rather than a cloud or a gust of wind. The whole complexion of your relationship dramatically changes to, in the majority of cases, a gentle, almost affectionate one—a low-keyed, rather playful, rather mannered, rather bemused geniality.

My wife and I were still very much in the gust of wind stage, a most frustrating, and even, as you soon begin to doubt whether you are really real after all, unnerving one, when, ten days or so after our arrival, a large cockfight was held in the public square to raise money for a new school.

Now, a few special occasions aside, cockfights are illegal in Bali under the Republic (as, for not altogether unrelated reasons, they were under the Dutch), largely as a result of the pretensions to puritanism radical nationalism tends to bring with it. The elite, which is not itself so very puritan, worries about the poor, ignorant peasant gambling all his money away, about what foreigners will think, about the waste of time better devoted to building up the country. It sees cockfighting as "primitive," "backward," "unprogressive," and generally unbecoming an ambitious nation. And, as with those other embarrassments—opium smoking, begging, or uncovered breasts—it seeks, rather unsystematically, to put a stop to it.

Of course, like drinking during prohibition or, today, smoking marihuana, cockfights, being a part of "The Balinese Way of Life," nonetheless go on happening, and with extraordinary frequency. And, like prohibition or marihuana, from time to time the police (who, in 1958 at least, were almost all not Balinese but Javanese) feel called upon to make a raid, confiscate the cocks and spurs, fine a few people, and even now and then expose some of them in the tropical sun for a day as object lessons which never, somehow, get learned, even though occasionally, quite occasionally, the object dies.

As a result, the fights are usually held in a secluded corner of a village in semisecrecy, a fact which tends to slow the action a little—not very much, but the Balinese do not care to have it slowed at all. In this case, however, perhaps because they were raising money for a school that the government was unable to give them, perhaps because raids had been few recently, perhaps, as I gathered from subsequent discussion, there was a notion that the necessary bribes had been paid, they thought they could take a chance on the central square and draw a larger and more enthusiastic crowd without attracting the attention of the law.

They were wrong. In the midst of the third match, with hundreds of people, including, still transparent, myself and my wife, fused into a single body around the ring, a superorganism in the literal sense, a truck full of policemen armed with machine guns roared up. Amid great screeching cries of "pulisi! pulisi!" from the crowd, the policemen jumped out, and, springing into the center of the ring, began to swing their guns around like gangsters in a motion picture, though not going so far as actually to fire them. The superorganism came instantly apart as its components scattered in all directions. People raced down the road, disappeared head first over walls, scrambled under platforms, folded themselves behind wicker screens, scuttled up coconut trees. Cocks armed with steel spurs sharp enough to cut off a finger or run a hole through a foot were running wildly around. Everything was dust and panic.

On the established anthropological principle, When in Rome, my wife and I decided, only slightly less instantaneously than everyone else, that the thing to do was run too. We ran down the main village street, northward, away from where we were living, for we were on that side of the ring. About half-way down another fugitive ducked suddenly into a compound—his own, it turned out—and we, seeing nothing ahead of us but rice fields, open country, and a very high volcano, followed him. As the three of us came tumbling into the courtyard, his wife, who had apparently been through this sort of thing before, whipped out a table, a tablecloth, three chairs, and three cups of tea, and we all, without any explicit communication whatsoever, sat down, commenced to sip tea, and sought to compose ourselves.

A few moments later, one of the policemen marched importantly into the yard, looking for the village chief. (The chief had not only been at the fight, he had arranged it. When the truck drove up he ran to the river, stripped off his sarong, and plunged in so he could say, when at length they found him sitting there pouring water over his head, that he had been away bathing when the whole affair had occurred and was ignorant of it. They did not believe him and fined him three hundred rupiah, which the village raised collectively.) Seeing my wife and I, "White Men," there in the yard, the policeman performed a classic double take. When he found his voice again he asked, approximately, what in the devil did we think we were doing there. Our host of five minutes leaped instantly to our defense, producing an impassioned description of who and what we were, so detailed and so accurate that it was my turn, having barely communicated with a living human being save my landlord and the village chief for more than a week, to be astonished. We had a perfect right to be there, he said, looking the Javanese upstart in the eye. We were American professors; the government had cleared us; we were there to study culture; we were going to write a book to tell Americans about Bali. And we had all been there drinking tea and talking about cultural matters all afternoon and did not know anything about any cockfight. Moreover, we had not seen the village chief all day, he must have gone to town. The policeman retreated in rather total disarray. And, after a decent interval, bewildered but relieved to have survived and stayed out of jail, so did we.

The next morning the village was a completely different world for us. Not only were we no longer invisible, we were suddenly the center of all attention, the object of a great outpouring of warmth, interest, and, most especially, amusement. Everyone in the village knew we had fled like everyone else. They asked us about it again and again (I must have told the story, small detail by small detail, fifty times by the end of the day), gently, affectionately, but quite insistently teasing us: "Why didn't you just stand there and tell the police who you were?" "Why didn't you just say you were only watching and not betting?" "Were you really afraid of those little guns?" As always, kinesthetically minded and, even when fleeing for their lives (or, as happened eight years later, surrendering them), the world's most poised people, they gleefully mimicked, also over and over again, our graceless style of running and what they claimed were our panic-stricken facial expressions. But above all, everyone was extremely pleased and even more surprised that we had not simply "pulled out our papers" (they knew about those too) and asserted our Distinguished Visitor status, but had instead demonstrated our solidarity with what were now our covillagers. (What we had actually demonstrated was our cowardice, but there is fellowship in that too.) Even the Brahmana priest, an old, grave, half-way-to-Heaven type who because of its associations with the underworld would never be involved, even distantly, in a cockfight, and was difficult to approach even to other Balinese, had us called into his courtyard to ask us about what had happened, chuckling happily at the sheer extraordinariness of it all.

In Bali, to be teased is to be accepted. It was the turning point so far as our relationship to the community was concerned, and we were quite literally "in." The whole village opened up to us, probably more than it ever would have otherwise (I might actually never have gotten to that priest, and our accidental host became one of my best informants), and certainly very much faster. Getting caught, or almost caught, in a vice raid is perhaps not a very generalizable recipe for achieving that mysterious necessity of anthropological field work, rapport, but for me it worked very well. It led to a sudden and unusually complete acceptance into a society extremely difficult for outsiders to penetrate. It gave me the kind of immediate, inside-view grasp of an aspect of "peasant mentality" that anthropologists not fortunate enough to flee headlong with their subjects from armed authorities normally do not get. And, perhaps most important of all, for the other things might have come in other ways, it put me very quickly on to a combination emotional explosion, status war, and philosophical drama of central significance to the society whose inner nature I desired to understand. By the time I left I had spent about as much time looking into cockfights as into witchcraft, irrigation, caste, or marriage.

## Of Cocks and Men

Bali, mainly because it is Bali, is a well-studied place. Its mythology, art, ritual, social organization, patterns of child rearing, forms of law, even styles of trance, have all been microscopically examined for traces of that elusive substance Jane Belo called "The Balinese Temper." [2] But, aside from a few passing remarks, the cockfight has barely been noticed, although as a popular obsession of consuming power it is at least as important a revelation of what being a Balinese "is really like" as these more celebrated phenomena. [3] As much of America surfaces in a ball park, on a golf links, at a race track, or around a poker table, much of Bali surfaces in a cock ring. For it is only apparently cocks that are fighting there. Actually, it is men.

To anyone who has been in Bali any length of time, the deep psychological identification of Balinese men with their cocks is unmistakable. The double entendre here is deliberate. It works in exactly the same way in Balinese as it does in English, even to producing the same tired jokes, strained puns, and uninventive obscenities. Bateson and Mead have even suggested that, in line with the Balinese conception of the body as a set of separately animated parts, cocks are viewed as detachable, self-operating penises, ambulant genitals with a life of their own. [4] And while I do not have the kind of unconscious material either to confirm or disconfirm this intriguing notion, the fact that they are masculine symbols *par excellence* is about as indubitable, and to the Balinese about as evident, as the fact that water runs downhill.

The language of everyday moralism is shot through, on the male side of it, with roosterish imagery. *Sabung,* the word for cock (and one which appears in inscriptions as early as A.D. 922), is used metaphorically to mean "hero," "warrior," "champion," "man of parts," "political candidate," "bachelor," "dandy," "lady-killer," or "tough guy." A pompous man whose behavior presumes above his station is compared to a tailless cock who struts about as though he had a large, spectacular one. A desperate man who makes a last, irrational effort to extricate himself from an impossible situation is likened to a dying cock who makes one final lunge at his tormentor to drag him along to a common destruction. A stingy man, who promises much, gives little, and begrudges that is compared to a cock which, held by the tail, leaps at another without in fact engaging him. A marriageable young man still shy with the opposite sex or someone in a new job anxious to make a good impression is called "a fighting cock caged for the first time." [5] Court trials, wars, political contests, inheritance disputes, and street arguments are all compared to cockfights. [6] Even the very island itself is perceived from its shape as a small, proud cock, poised, neck extended, back taut, tail raised, in eternal challenge to large, feckless, shapeless Java. [7]

But the intimacy of men with their cocks is more than metaphorical. Balinese men, or anyway a large majority of Balinese men, spend an enormous amount of time with their favorites, grooming them, feeding them, discussing them, trying them out against one another, or just gazing at them with a mixture of rapt admiration and dreamy self-absorbtion. Whenever you see a group of Balinese men squatting idly in the council shed or along the road in their hips down, shoulders forward, knees up fashion, half or more of them will have a rooster in his hands, holding it between his thighs, bouncing it gently up and down to strengthen its legs, ruffling its feathers with abstract sensuality, pushing it out against a neighbor's rooster to rouse its spirit, withdrawing it toward his loins to calm it again. Now and then, to get a feel for another bird, a man will fiddle this way with someone else's cock for a while, but usually by moving around to squat in place behind it, rather than just having it passed across to him as though it were merely an animal.

In the houseyard, the high-walled enclosures where the people live, fighting cocks are kept in wicker cages, moved frequently about so as to maintain the optimum balance of sun and shade. They are fed a special diet, which varies somewhat according to individual theories but which is mostly maize, sifted for impurities with far more care than it is when mere humans are going to eat it and offered to the animal kernel by kernel. Red pepper is stuffed down their beaks and up their anuses to give them spirit. They are bathed in the same ceremonial preparation of tepid water, medicinal herbs, flowers, and onions in which infants are bathed, and for a prize cock just about as often. Their combs are cropped, their plumage dressed, their spurs trimmed, their legs massaged, and they are inspected for flaws with the squinted concentration of a diamond merchant. A man who has a passion for cocks, an enthusiast in the literal sense of the term, can spend most of his life with them, and even those, the overwhelming majority, whose passion though intense has not entirely run away with them, can and do spend what seems not only to an outsider, but also to themselves, an inordinate amount of time with them. "I am cock crazy," my landlord, a quite ordinary *afficionado* by Balinese standards, used to moan as he went to move another cage, give another bath, or conduct another feeding. "We're all cock crazy."

The madness has some less visible dimensions, however, because although it is true that cocks are symbolic expressions or magnifications of their owner's self, the narcissistic male ego writ out in Aesopian terms, they are also expressions—and rather more immediate ones—of what the Balinese regard as the direct inversion, aesthetically, morally, and metaphysically, of human status: animality.

The Balinese revulsion against any behavior regarded as animal-like can hardly be overstressed. Babies are not allowed to crawl for that reason. Incest, though hardly approved, is a much less horrifying crime than bestiality. (The appropriate punishment for the second is death by drowning, for the first being forced to live like an animal.) [8] Most demons are represented—in sculpture, dance, ritual, myth—in some real or fantastic animal form. The main puberty rite consists in filing the child's teeth so they will not look like animal fangs. Not only defecation but eating is regarded as a disgusting, almost obscene activity, to be conducted hurriedly and privately, because of its association with animality. Even falling down or any form of clumsiness is considered to be bad for these reasons. Aside from cocks and a few domestic animals—oxen, ducks—of no emotional significance, the Balinese are aversive to animals, and treat their large number of dogs not merely callously but with a phobic cruelty. In identifying with his cock, the Balinese man is identifying not just with his ideal self, or even his penis, but also, and at the same time, with what he most fears, hates, and ambivalence being what it is, is fascinated by—The Powers of Darkness.

The connection of cocks and cockfighting with such Powers, with the animalistic demons that threaten constantly to invade the small, cleared off space in which the Balinese have so carefully built their lives and devour its inhabitants, is quite explicit. A cockfight, any cockfight, is in the first instance a blood sacrifice offered, with the appropriate chants and oblations, to the demons in order to pacify their ravenous, cannibal hunger. No temple festival should be conducted until one is made. (If it is omitted someone will inevitably fall into a trance and command with the voice of an angered spirit that the oversight be immediately corrected.) Collective responses to natural evils—illness, crop failure, volcanic eruptions—almost always involve them. And that famous holiday in Bali, The Day of Silence (*Njepi*), when everyone sits silent and immobile all day long in order to avoid contact with a sudden influx of demons chased momentarily out of hell, is preceded the previous day by large-scale cockfights (in this case legal) in almost every village on the island.

In the cockfight, man and beast, good and evil, ego and id, the creative power of aroused masculinity and the destructive power of loosened animality fuse in a bloody drama of hatred, cruelty, violence, and death. It is little wonder that when, as is the invariable rule, the owner of the winning cock takes the carcass of the loser—often torn limb from limb by its enraged owner—home to eat, he does so with a mixture of social embarrassment, moral satisfaction, aesthetic disgust, and cannibal joy. Or that a man who has lost an important fight is sometimes driven to wreck his family shrines and curse the gods, an act of metaphysical (and social) suicide. Or that in seeking earthly analogues for heaven and hell the Balinese compare the former to the mood of a man whose cock has just won, the latter to that of a man whose cock has just lost.

## The Fight

Cockfights (*tetadjen; sabungan*) are held in a ring about fifty feet square. Usually they begin toward late afternoon and run three of four hours until sunset. About nine or ten separate matches (*sehet*) comprise a program. Each match is precisely like the others in general pattern: there is no main match, no connection between individual matches, no variation in their format, and each is arranged on a completely ad hoc basis. After a fight has ended and the emotional debris is cleaned away—the bets paid, the curses cursed, the carcasses possessed—seven, eight, perhaps even a dozen men slop negligently into the ring with a cock and seek to find there a logical opponent for it. This process, which rarely takes less than ten minutes and often a good deal longer, is conducted in a very subdued, oblique, even dissembling manner. Those not immediately involved give it at best but disguised, sidelong attention; those who, embarrassedly, are, attempt to pretend somehow that the whole thing is not really happening.

A match made, the other hopefuls retire with the same deliberate indifference, and the selected cocks have their spurs (*tadji*) affixed—razor-sharp, pointed steel swords, four or five inches long. This is a delicate job which only a small portion of men, a half-dozen or so in most villages, know how to do properly. The man who attaches the spurs also provides them, and if the rooster he assists wins its owner awards him the spur-leg of the victim. The spurs are affixed by winding a long length of string around the foot of the spur and the leg of the cock. For reasons I shall come to presently, it is done somewhat differently from case to case, and is an obsessively deliberate affair. The lore about spurs is extensive—they are sharpened only at eclipses and the dark of the moon, should be kept out of the sight of women, and so forth. And they are handled, both in use and out, with the same curious combination of fussiness and sensuality the Balinese direct toward ritual objects generally.

The spurs affixed, the two cocks are placed by their handlers (who may or may not be their owners) facing one another in the center of the ring. [9] A coconut pierced with a small hole is placed in a pail of water, in which it takes about twenty-one seconds to sink, a period known as a *tjeng* and marked at beginning and end by the beating of a slit gong. During these twenty-one seconds the handlers (*pengangkeb*) are not permitted to touch their roosters. If, as sometimes happens, the animals have not fought during this time, they are picked up, fluffed, pulled, prodded, and otherwise insulted, and put back in the center of the ring and the process begins again. Sometimes they refuse to fight at all, or one keeps running away, in which case they are imprisoned together under a wicker cage, which usually gets them engaged.

Most of the time, in any case, the cocks fly almost immediately at one another in a wing-beating, head-thrusting, leg-kicking explosion of animal fury so pure, so absolute, and in its own way so beautiful, as to be almost abstract, a Platonic concept of hate. Within moments one or the other drives home a solid blow with his spur. The handler whose cock has delivered the blow immediately picks it up so that it will not get a return blow, for if he does not the match is likely to end in a mutually mortal tie as the two birds wildly hack each other to pieces. This is particularly true if, as often happens, the spur sticks in its victim's body, for then the aggressor is at the mercy of his wounded foe.

With the birds again in the hands of their handlers, the coconut is now sunk three times after which the cock which has landed the blow must be set down to show that he is firm, a fact he demonstrates by wandering idly around the ring for a coconut sink. The coconut is then sunk twice more and the fight must recommence.

During this interval, slightly over two minutes, the handler of the wounded cock has been working frantically over it, like a trainer patching a mauled boxer between rounds, to get it in shape for a last, desperate try for victory. He blows in its mouth, putting the whole chicken head in his own mouth and sucking and blowing, fluffs it, stuffs its wounds with various sorts of medicines, and generally tries anything he can think of to arouse the last ounce of spirit which may be hidden somewhere within it. By the time he is forced to put it back down he is usually drenched in chicken blood, but, as in prize fighting, a good handler is worth his weight in gold. Some of them can virtually make the dead walk, at least long enough for the second and final round.

In the climactic battle (if there is one; sometimes the wounded cock simply expires in the handler's hands or immediately as it is placed down again), the cock who landed the first blow usually proceeds to finish off his weakened opponent. But this is far from an inevitable outcome, for if a cock can walk he can fight, and if he can fight, he can kill, and what counts is which cock expires first. If the wounded one can get a stab in and stagger on until the other drops, he is the official winner, even if he himself topples over an instant later.

Surrounding all this melodrama—which the crowd packed tight around the ring follows in near silence, moving their bodies in kinesthetic sympathy with the movement of the animals, cheering their champions on with wordless hand motions, shiftings of the shoulders, turnings of the head, falling back *en masse* as the cock with the murderous spurs careens toward one side of the ring (it is said that spectators sometimes lose eyes and fingers from being too attentive), surging forward again as they glance off toward another—is a vast body of extraordinarily elaborate and precisely detailed rules.

These rules, together with the developed lore of cocks and cockfighting which accompanies them, are written down in palm leaf manuscripts (*lontar; rontal*) passed on from generation to generation as part of the general legal and cultural tradition of the villages. At a fight, the umpire (*saja komong; djuru kembar*)—the man who manages the coconut—is in charge of their application and his authority is absolute. I have never seen an umpire's judgment questioned on any subject, even by the more despondent losers, nor have I ever heard, even in private, a charge of unfairness directed against one, or, for that matter, complaints about umpires in general. Only exceptionally well-trusted, solid, and, given the complexity of the code, knowledgeable citizens perform this job, and in fact men will bring their cocks only to fights presided over by such men. It is also the umpire to whom accusations of cheating, which, though rare in the extreme, occasionally arise, are referred; and it is he who in the not infrequent cases where the cocks expire virtually together decides which (if either, for, though the Balinese do not care for such an outcome, there can be ties) went first. Likened to a judge, a king, a priest, and a policeman, he is all of these, and under his assured direction the animal passion of the fight proceeds within the civic certainty of the law. In the dozens of cockfights I saw in Bali, I never once saw an altercation about rules. Indeed, I never saw an open altercation, other than those between cocks, at all.

This crosswise doubleness of an event which, taken as a fact of nature, is rage untrammeled and, taken as a fact of culture, is form perfected, defines the cockfight as a sociological entity. A cockfight is what, searching for a name for something not vertebrate enough to be called a group and not structureless enough to be called a crowd, Erving Goffman has called a "focused gathering"—a set of persons engrossed in a common flow of activity and relating to one another in terms of that flow. [10] Such gatherings meet and disperse; the participants in them fluctuate; the activity that focuses them is discreet—a particulate process that reoccurs rather than a continuous one that endures. They take their form from the situation that evokes them, the floor on which they are placed, as Goffman puts it; but it is a form, and an articulate one, nonetheless. For the situation, the floor is itself created, in jury deliberations, surgical operations, block meetings, sit-ins, cockfights, by the cultural preoccupations—here, as we shall see, the celebration of status rivalry—which not only specify the focus but, assembling actors and arranging scenery, bring it actually into being.

In classical times (that is to say, prior to the Dutch invasion of 1908), when there were no bureaucrats around to improve popular morality, the staging of a cockfight was an explicitly societal matter. Bringing a cock to an important fight was, for an adult male, a compulsory duty of citizenship; taxation of fights, which were usually held on market day, was a major source of public revenue; patronage of the art was a stated responsibility of princes; and the cock ring, or *wantilan*, stood in the center of the village near those other monuments of Balinese civility—the council house, the origin temple, the marketplace, the signal tower, and the banyan tree. Today, a few special occasions aside, the newer rectitude makes so open a statement of the connection between the excitements of collective life and those of blood sport impossible, but, less directly expressed, the connection itself remains intimate and intact. To expose it, however, it is necessary to turn to the aspect of cockfighting around which all the others pivot, and through which they exercise their force, an aspect I have thus far studiously ignored. I mean, of course, the gambling.

## Odds and Even Money

The Balinese never do anything in a simple way that they can contrive to do in a complicated one, and to this generalization cockfight wagering is no exception.

In the first place, there are two sorts of bets, or *toh*. [11] There is the single axial bet on the center between the principals (*toh ketengah*), and there is the cloud of peripheral ones around the ring between members of the audience (*toh kesasi*). The first is typically large; the second typically small. The first is collective, involving coalitions of bettors clustering around the owner; the second is individual, man to man. The first is a matter of deliberate, very quiet, almost furtive arrangement by the coalition members and the umpire huddled like conspirators in the center of the ring; the second is a matter of impulsive shouting, public offers, and public acceptances by the excited throng around its edges. And most curiously, and as we shall see most revealingly, *where the first is always, without exception, even money, the second, equally without exception, is never such.* What is a fair coin in the center is a biased one on the side.

The center bet is the official one, hedged in again with a webwork of rules, and is made between the two cock owners, with the umpire as overseer and public witness. [12] This bet, which, as I say, is always relatively and sometimes very large, is never raised simply by the owner in whose name it is made, but by him together with four or five, sometimes seven or eight, allies—kin, village mates, neighbors, close friends. He may, if he is not especially well-to-do, not even be the major contributor, though, if only to show that he is not involved in any chicanery, he must be a significant one.

Of the fifty-seven matches for which I have exact and reliable data on the center bet, the range is from fifteen ringgits to five hundred, with a mean at eighty-five and with the distribution being rather noticeably trimodal: small fights (15 ringgits either side of 35) accounting for about 45 percent of the total number; medium ones (20 ringgits either side of 70) for about 25 percent; and large (75 ringgits either side of 175) for about 20 percent, with a few very small and very large ones out at the extremes. In a society where the normal daily wage of a manual laborer—a brickmaker, an ordinary farmworker, a market porter—was about three ringgits a day, and considering the fact that fights were held on the average about every two-and-a-half days in the immediate area I studied, this is clearly serious gambling, even if the bets are pooled rather than individual efforts.

The side bets are, however, something else altogether. Rather than the solemn, legalistic pactmaking of the center, wagering takes place rather in the fashion in which the stock exchange used to work when it was out on the curb. There is a fixed and known odds paradigm which runs in a continuous series from ten-to-nine at the short end to two-to-one at the long: 10-9, 9-8, 8-7, 7-6, 6-5, 5-4, 4-3, 3-2, 2-1. The man who wishes to back the *underdog cock* (leaving aside how favorites, *kebut*, and underdogs, *ngai*, are established for the moment) shouts the short-side number indicating the odds he wants *to be given*. That is, if he shouts *gasal*, "five," he wants the underdog at five-to-four (or, for him, four-to-five); if he shouts "four," he wants it at four-to-three (again, he putting up the "three"), if "nine," at nine-to-eight, and so on. A man backing the favorite, and thus considering giving odds if he can get them short enough, indicates the fact by crying out the color-type of that cock—"brown," "speckled," or whatever. [13]

As odds-takers (backers of the underdog) and odds-givers (backers of the favorite) sweep the crowd with their shouts, they begin to focus in on one another as potential betting pairs, often from far across the ring. The taker tries to shout the giver into longer odds, the giver to shout the taker into shorter ones. [14] The taker, who is the wooer in this situation, will signal how large a bet he wishes to make at the odds he is shouting by holding a number of fingers up in front of his face and vigorously waving them. If the giver, the wooed, replies in kind, the bet is made; if he does not, they unlock gazes and the search goes on.

The side betting, which takes place after the center bet has been made and its size announced, consists then in a rising crescendo of shouts as backers of the underdog offer their propositions to anyone who will accept them, while those who are backing the favorite but do not like the price being offered, shout equally frenetically the color of the cock to show they too are desperate to bet but want shorter odds.

Almost always odds-calling, which tends to be very consensual in that at any one time almost all callers are calling the same thing, starts off toward the long end of the range—five-to-four or four-to-three—and then moves, also consensually, toward the short end with greater or lesser speed and to a greater or lesser degree. Men crying "five" and finding themselves answered only with cries of "brown" start crying "six," either drawing the other callers fairly quickly with them or retiring from the scene as their too-generous offers are snapped up. If the change is made and partners are still scarce, the procedure is repeated in a move to "seven," and so on, only rarely, and in the very largest fights, reaching the ultimate "nine" or "ten" levels. Occasionally, if the cocks are clearly mismatched, there may be no upward movement at all, or even a movement down the scale to four-to-three, three-to-two, very, very rarely two-to-one, a shift which is accompanied by a declining number of bets as a shift upward is accompanied by an increasing number. But the general pattern is for the betting to move a shorter or longer distance up the scale toward the, for sidebets, nonexistent pole of even money, with the overwhelming majority of bets falling in the four-to-three to eight-to-seven range. [15]

As the moment for the release of the cocks by the handlers approaches, the screaming, at least in a match where the center bet is large, reaches almost frenzied proportions as the remaining unfulfilled bettors try desperately to find a last minute partner at a price they can live with. (Where the center bet is small, the opposite tends to occur: betting dies off, trailing into silence, as odds lengthen and people lose interest.) In a large-bet, well-made match—the kind of match the Balinese regard as "real cockfight-ing"—the mob scene quality, the sense that sheer chaos is about to break loose, with all those waving, shouting, pushing, clambering men is quite strong, an effect which is only heightened by the intense stillness that falls with instant suddenness, rather as if someone had turned off the current, when the slit gong sounds, the cocks are put down, and the battle begins.

When it ends, anywhere from fifteen seconds to five minutes later, *all bets are immediately paid*. There are absolutely no IOU's, at least to a betting opponent. One may, of course, borrow from a friend before offering or accepting a wager, but to offer or accept it you must have the money already in hand and, if you lose, you must pay it on the spot, before the next match begins. This is an iron rule, and as I have never heard of a disputed umpire's decision (though doubtless there must sometimes be some), I have also never heard of a welshed bet, perhaps because in a worked-up cockfight crowd the consequences might be, as they are re-ported to be sometimes for cheaters, drastic and immediate.

It is, in any case, this formal asymmetry between balanced center bets and unbalanced side ones that poses the critical analytical problem for a theory which sees cockfight wagering as the link connecting the fight to the wider world of Balinese culture. It also suggests the way to go about solving it and demonstrating the link.

The first point that needs to be made in this connection is that the higher the center bet, the more likely the match will in actual fact be an even one. Simple considerations of rationality suggest that. If you are bet-ting fifteen ringgits on a cock, you might be willing to go along with even money even if you feel your animal somewhat the less promising. But if you are betting five hundred you are very, very likely to be loathe to do so. Thus, in large-bet fights, which of course involve the better animals, tremendous care is taken to see that the cocks are about as evenly matched as to size, general condition, pugnacity, and so on as is humanly possible. The different ways of adjusting the spurs of the animals are often em-ployed to secure this. If one cock seems stronger, an agreement will be made to position his spur at a slightly less advantageous angle—a kind of handicapping, at which spur affixers are, so it is said, extremely skilled. More care will be taken, too, to employ skillful handlers and to match them exactly as to abilities.

In short, in a large-bet fight the pressure to make the match a genuinely fifty-fifty proposition is enormous, and is consciously felt as such. For me-dium fights the pressure is somewhat less, and for small ones less yet, though there is always an effort to make things at least approximately equal, for even at fifteen ringgits (five days work) no one wants to make an even money bet in a clearly unfavorable situation. And, again, what statistics I have tend to bear this out. In my fifty-seven matches, the favorite won thirty-three times over-all, the underdog twenty-four, a 1.4 to 1 ratio. But if one splits the figures at sixty ringgits center bets, the ratios turn out to be 1.1 to 1 (twelve favorites, eleven underdogs) for those above this line, and 1.6 to 1 (twenty-one and thirteen) for those below it. Or, if you take the extremes, for very large fights, those with center bets over a hundred ringgits the ratio is 1 to 1 (seven and seven); for very small fights, those under forty ringgits, it is 1.9 to 1 (nineteen and ten). [16]

Now, from this proposition—that the higher the center bet the more exactly a fifty-fifty proposition the cockfight is—two things more or less immediately follow: (1) the higher the center bet, the greater is the pull on the side betting toward the short-odds end of the wagering spectrum and vice versa; (2) the higher the center bet, the greater the volume of side betting and vice versa.

The logic is similar in both cases. The closer the fight is in fact to even money, the less attractive the long end of the odds will appear and, therefore, the shorter it must be if there are to be takers. That this is the case is apparent from mere inspection, from the Balinese's own analysis of the matter, and from what more systematic observations I was able to collect. Given the difficulty of making precise and complete recordings of side betting, this argument is hard to cast in numerical form, but in all my cases the odds-giver, odds-taker consensual point, a quite pronounced minimax saddle where the bulk (at a guess, two-thirds to three-quarters in most cases) of the bets are actually made, was three or four points further along the scale toward the shorter end for the large-center-bet fights than for the small ones, with medium ones generally in between. In detail, the fit is not, of course, exact, but the general pattern is quite consistent: the power of the center bet to pull the side bets toward its own even-money pattern is directly proportional to its size, because its size is directly proportional to the degree to which the cocks are in fact evenly matched. As for the volume question, total wagering is greater in large-center-bet fights because such fights are considered more "interesting" not only in the sense that they are less predictable, but, more crucially, that more is at stake in them—in terms of money, in terms of the quality of the cocks, and consequently, as we shall see, in terms of social prestige. [17]

The paradox of fair coin in the middle, biased coin on the outside is thus a merely apparent one. The two betting systems, though formally incongruent, are not really contradictory to one another, but part of a single larger system in which the center bet is, so to speak, the "center of gravity," drawing, the larger it is the more so, the outside bets toward the short-odds end of the scale. The center bet thus "makes the game," or perhaps better, defines it, signals what, following a notion of Jeremy Bentham's, I am going to call its "depth."

The Balinese attempt to create an interesting, if you will, "deep," match by making the center bet as large as possible so that the cocks matched will be as equal and as fine as possible, and the outcome, thus, as unpredictable as possible. They do not always succeed. Nearly half the matches are relatively trivial, relatively uninteresting—in my borrowed terminology, "shallow"—affairs. But that fact no more argues against my interpretation than the fact that most painters, poets, and playwrights are mediocre argues against the view that artistic effort is directed toward profundity and, with a certain frequency, approximates it. The image of artistic technique is indeed exact: the center bet is a means, a device, for creating "interesting," "deep" matches, *not* the reason, or at least not the main reason, *why* they are interesting, the source of their fascination, the substance of their depth. The question why such matches are interesting—indeed, for the Balinese, exquisitely absorbing—takes us out of the realm of formal concerns into more broadly sociological and social-psychological ones, and to a less purely economic idea of what "depth" in gaming amounts to. [18]

## Playing with Fire

Bentham's concept of "deep play" is found in his *The Theory of Legislation*. [19] By it he means play in which the stakes are so high that it is, from his utilitarian standpoint, irrational for men to engage in it at all. If a man whose fortune is a thousand pounds (or ringgits) wages five hundred of it on an even bet, the marginal utility of the pound he stands to win is clearly less than the marginal disutility of the one he stands to lose. In genuine deep play, this is the case for both parties. They are both in over their heads. Having come together in search of pleasure they have entered into a relationship which will bring the participants, considered collectively, net pain rather than net pleasure. Bentham's conclusion was, therefore, that deep play was immoral from the first principles and, a typical step for him, should be prevented legally.

But more interesting than the ethical problem, at least for our concerns here, is that despite the logical force of Bentham's analysis men do engage in such play, both passionately and often, and even in the face of law's revenge. For Bentham and those who think as he does (nowadays mainly lawyers, economists, and a few psychiatrists), the explanation is, as I have said, that such men are irrational—addicts, fetishists, children, fools, savages, who need only to be protected against themselves. But for the Balinese, though naturally they do not formulate it in so many words, the explanation lies in the fact that in such play money is less a measure of utility, had or expected, than it is a symbol of moral import, perceived or imposed.

It is, in fact, in shallow games, ones in which smaller amounts of money are involved, that increments and decrements of cash are more nearly synonyms for utility and disutility, in the ordinary, unexpanded sense—for pleasure and pain, happiness and unhappiness. In deep ones, where the amounts of money are great, much more is at stake than material gain: namely, esteem, honor, dignity, respect—in a word, though in Bali a profoundly freighted word, status. [20] It is at stake symbolically, for (a few cases of ruined addict gamblers aside) no one's status is actually altered by the outcome of a cockfight; it is only, and that momentarily, affirmed or insulted. But for the Balinese, for whom nothing is more pleasurable than an affront obliquely delivered or more painful than one obliquely received—particularly when mutual acquaintances, undeceived by surfaces, are watching—such appraisive drama is deep indeed.

This, I must stress immediately, is *not* to say that the money does not matter, or that the Balinese is no more concerned about losing five hundred ringgits than fifteen. Such a conclusion would be absurd. It is because money *does*, in this hardly unmaterialistic society, matter and matter very much that the more of it one risks the more of a lot of other things, such as one's pride, one's poise, one's dispassion, one's masculinity, one also risks, again only momentarily but again very publicly as well. In deep cockfights an owner and his collaborators, and, as we shall see, to a lesser but still quite real extent also their backers on the outside, put their money where their status is.

It is in large part *because* the marginal disutility of loss is so great at the higher levels of betting that to engage in such betting is to lay one's public self, allusively and metaphorically, through the medium of one's cock, on the line. And though to a Benthamite this might seem merely to increase the irrationality of the enterprise that much further, to the Balinese what it mainly increases is the meaningfulness of it all. And as (to follow Weber rather than Bentham) the imposition of meaning on life is the major end and primary condition of human existence, that access of significance more than compensates for the economic costs involved. [21] Actually, given the even-money quality of the larger matches, important changes in material fortune among those who regularly participate in them seem virtually nonexistent, because matters more or less even out over the long run. It is, actually, in the smaller, shallow fights, where one finds the handful of more pure, addict-type gamblers involved—those who *are* in it mainly for the money—that "real" changes in social position, largely downward, are affected. Men of this sort, plungers, are highly dispraised by "true cockfighters" as fools who do not understand what the sport is all about, vulgarians who simply miss the point of it all. They are, these addicts, regarded as fair game for the genuine enthusiasts, those who do understand, to take a little money away from, something that is easy enough to do by luring them, through the force of their greed, into irrational bets on mismatched cocks. Most of them do indeed manage to ruin themselves in a remarkably short time, but there always seems to be one or two of them around, pawning their land and selling their clothes in order to bet, at any particular time. [22]

This graduated correlation of "status gambling" with deeper fights and, inversely, "money gambling" with shallower ones is in fact quite general. Bettors themselves form a sociomoral hierarchy in these terms. As noted earlier, at most cockfights there are, around the very edges of the cockfight area, a large number of mindless, sheer-chance type gambling games (roulette, dice throw, coin-spin, pea-under-the-shell) operated by concessionaires. Only women, children, adolescents, and various other sorts of people who do not (or not yet) fight cocks—the extremely poor, the socially despised, the personally idiosyncratic—play at these games, at, of course, penny ante levels. Cockfighting men would be ashamed to go anywhere near them. Slightly above these people in standing are those who, though they do not themselves fight cocks, bet on the smaller matches around the edges. Next, there are those who fight cocks in small, or occasionally medium matches, but have not the status to join in the large ones, though they may bet from time to time on the side in those. And finally, there are those, the really substantial members of the community, the solid citizenry around whom local life revolves, who fight in the larger fights and bet on them around the side. The focusing element in these focused gatherings, these men generally dominate and define the sport as they dominate and define the society. When a Balinese male talks, in that almost venerative way, about "the true cockfighter," the *bebatoh* ("bettor") or *djuru kurung* ("cage keeper"), it is this sort of person, not those who bring the mentality of the pea-and-shell game into the quite different, inappropriate context of the cockfight, the driven gambler (*potét*, a word which has the secondary meaning of thief or reprobate), and the wistful hanger-on, that they mean. For such a man, what is really going on in a match is something rather close to an *affaire d'honneur* (though, with the Balinese talent for practical fantasy, the blood that is spilled is only figuratively human) than to the stupid, mechanical crank of a slot machine.

What makes Balinese cockfighting deep is thus not money in itself, but what, the more of it that is involved the more so, money causes to happen: the migration of the Balinese status hierarchy into the body of the cockfight. Psychologically an Aesopian representation of the ideal/demonic, rather narcissistic, male self, sociologically it is an equally Aesopian representation of the complex fields of tension set up by the controlled, muted, ceremonial, but for all that deeply felt, interaction of those selves in the context of everyday life. The cocks may be surrogates for their owners' personalities, animal mirrors of psychic form, but the cockfight is— or more exactly, deliberately is made to be—a simulation of the social matrix, the involved system of crosscutting, overlapping, highly corporate groups—villages, kingroups, irrigation societies, temple congregations, "castes"—in which its devotees live. [23] And as prestige, the necessity to affirm it, defend it, celebrate it, justify it, and just plain bask in it (but not, given the strongly ascriptive character of Balinese stratification, to seek it), is perhaps the central driving force in the society, so also—ambulant penises, blood sacrifices, and monetary exchanges aside—is it of the cockfight. This apparent amusement and seeming sport is, to take another phrase from Erving Goffman, "a status bloodbath." [24]

The easiest way to make this clear, and at least to some degree to demonstrate it, is to invoke the village whose cockfighting activities I observed the closest—the one in which the raid occurred and from which my statistical data are taken.

As all Balinese villages, this one—Tihingan, in the Klungkung region of southeast Bali—is intricately organized, a labyrinth of alliances and oppositions. But, unlike many, two sorts of corporate groups, which are also status groups, particularly stand out, and we may concentrate on them, in a part-for-whole way, without undue distortion.

First, the village is dominated by four large, patrilineal, partly endogamous descent groups which are constantly vying with one another and form the major factions in the village. Sometimes they group two and two, or rather the two larger ones versus the two smaller ones plus all the unaffiliated people; sometimes they operate independently. There are also subfactions within them, subfactions within the subfactions, and so on to rather fine levels of distinction. And second, there is the village itself, almost entirely endogamous, which is opposed to all the other villages round about in its cockfight circuit (which, as explained, is the market region), but which also forms alliances with certain of these neighbors against certain others in various supra-village political and social contexts. The exact situation is thus, as everywhere in Bali, quite distinctive; but the general pattern of a tiered hierarchy of status rivalries between highly corporate but various based groupings (and, thus, between the members of them) is entirely general.

Consider, then, as support of the general thesis that the cockfight, and especially the deep cockfight, is fundamentally a dramatization of status concerns, the following facts, which to avoid extended ethnographic description I will simply pronounce to be facts—though the concrete evidence—examples, statements, and numbers that could be brought to bear in support of them is both extensive and unmistakable:

1. A man virtually never bets against a cock owned by a member of his own kingroup. Usually he will feel obliged to bet for it, the more so the closer the kin tie and the deeper the fight. If he is certain in his

mind that it will not win, he may just not bet at all, particularly if it is only a second cousin's bird or if the fight is a shallow one. But as a rule he will feel he must support it and, in deep games, nearly always does. Thus the great majority of the people calling "five" or "speckled" so demonstratively are expressing their allegiance to their kinsman, not their evaluation of his bird, their understanding of probability theory, or even their hopes of unearned income.

2. This principle is extended logically. If your kingroup is not involved you will support an allied kingroup against an unallied one in the same way, and so on through the very involved networks of alliances which, as I say, make up this, as any other, Balinese village.

3. So, too, for the village as a whole. If an outsider cock is fighting any cock from your village, you will tend to support the local one. If, what is a rare circumstance but occurs every now and then, a cock from outside your cockfight circuit is fighting one inside it you will also tend to support the "home bird."

4. Cocks which come from any distance are almost always favorites, for the theory is the man would not have dared to bring it if it was not a good cock, the more so the further he has come. His followers are, of course, obliged to support him, and when the more grand-scale legal cockfights are held (on holidays, and so on) the people of the village take what they regard to be the best cocks in the village, regardless of ownership, and go off to support them, although they will almost certainly have to give odds on them and to make large bets to show that they are not a cheapskate village. Actually, such "away games," though infrequent, tend to mend the ruptures between village members that the constantly occurring "home games," where village factions are opposed rather than united, exacerbate.

5. Almost all matches are sociologically relevant. You seldom get two outsider cocks fighting, or two cocks with no particular group backing, or with group backing which is mutually unrelated in any clear way. When you do get them, the game is very shallow, betting very slow, and the whole thing very dull, with no one save the immediate principals and an addict gambler or two at all interested.

6. By the same token, you rarely get two cocks from the same group, even more rarely from the same subfaction, and virtually never from the same sub-subfaction (which would be in most cases one extended family) fighting. Similarly, in outside village fights two members of the village will rarely fight against one another, even though, as bitter rivals, they would do so with enthusiasm on their home grounds.

7. On the individual level, people involved in an institutionalized hostility relationship, called *puik*, in which they do not speak or otherwise have

anything to do with each other (the causes of this formal breaking of relations are many: wife-capture, inheritance arguments, political differences) will bet very heavily, sometimes almost maniacally, against one another in what is a frank and direct attack on the very masculinity, the ultimate ground of his status, of the opponent.

8. The center bet coalition is, in all but the shallowest games, *always* made up by structural allies—no "outside money" is involved. What is "outside" depends upon the context, of course, but given it, no outside money is mixed in with the main bet; if the principals cannot raise it, it is not made. The center bet, again especially in deeper games, is thus the most direct and open expression of social opposition, which is one of the reasons why both it and match making are surrounded by such an air of unease, furtiveness, embarrassment, and so on.

9. The rule about borrowing money—that you may borrow *for* a bet but not *in* one—stems (and the Balinese are quite conscious of this) from similar considerations: you are never at the *economic* mercy of your enemy that way. Gambling debts, which can get quite large on a rather short-term basis, are always to friends, never to enemies, structurally speaking.

10. When two cocks are structurally irrelevant or neutral so far as *you* are concerned (though, as mentioned, they almost never are to each other) you do not even ask a relative or a friend whom he is betting on, because if you know how he is betting and he knows you know, and you go the other way, it will lead to strain. This rule is explicit and rigid; fairly elaborate, even rather artificial precautions are taken to avoid breaking it. At the very least you must pretend not to notice what he is doing, and he what you are doing.

11. There is a special word for betting against the grain, which is also the word for "pardon me" (*mpura*). It is considered a bad thing to do, though if the center bet is small it is sometimes all right as long as you do not do it too often. But the larger the bet and the more frequently you do it, the more the "pardon me" tack will lead to social disruption.

12. In fact, the institutionalized hostility relation, *puik,* is often formally initiated (though its causes always lie elsewhere) by such a "pardon me" bet in a deep fight, putting the symbolic fat in the fire. Similarly, the end of such a relationship and resumption of normal social intercourse is often signalized (but, again, not actually brought about) by one or the other of the enemies supporting the other's bird.

13. In sticky, cross-loyalty situations, of which in this extraordinarily complex social system there are of course many, where a man is caught between two more or less equally balanced loyalties, he tends to wander off for a cup of coffee or something to avoid having to bet, a form

of behavior reminiscent of that of American voters in similar situations. [25]

14. The people involved in the center bet are, especially in deep fights, virtually always leading members of their group—kinship, village, or whatever. Further, those who bet on the side (including these people) are, as I have already remarked, the more established members of the village—the solid citizens. Cockfighting is for those who are involved in the everyday politics of prestige as well, not for youth, women, subordinates, and so forth.

15. So far as money is concerned, the explicitly expressed attitude toward it is that it is a secondary matter. It is not, as I have said, of no importance; Balinese are no happier to lose several weeks' income than anyone else. But they mainly look on the monetary aspects of the cockfight as self-balancing, a matter of just moving money around, circulating it among a fairly well-defined group of serious cockfighters. The really important wins and losses are seen mostly in other terms, and the general attitude toward wagering is not any hope of cleaning up, of making a killing (addict gamblers again excepted), but that of the horseplayer's prayer: "O, God, please let me break even." In prestige terms, however, you do not want to break even, but, in a momentary, punctuate sort of way, win utterly. The talk (which goes on all the time) is about fights against such-and-such a cock of So-and-So which your cock demolished, not on how much you won, a fact people, even for large bets, rarely remember for any length of time, though they will remember the day they did in Pan Loh's finest cock for years.

16. You must bet on cocks of your own group aside from mere loyalty considerations, for if you do not people generally will say, "What! Is he too proud for the likes of us? Does he have to go to Java or Den Pasar [the capital town] to bet, he is such an important man?" Thus there is a general pressure to bet not only to show that you are important locally, but that you are not so important that you look down on everyone else as unfit even to be rivals. Similarly, home team people must bet against outside cocks or the outsiders will accuse it—a serious charge—of just collecting entry fees and not really being interested in cockfighting, as well as again being arrogant and insulting.

17. Finally, the Balinese peasants themselves are quite aware of all this and can and, at least to an ethnographer, do state most of it in approximately the same terms as I have. Fighting cocks, almost every Balinese I have ever discussed the subject with has said, is like playing with fire only not getting burned. You activate village and kingroup rivalries and hostilities, but in "play" form, coming dangerously and entrancingly close to the expression of open and direct interpersonal and in-

tergroup aggression (something which, again, almost never happens in the normal course of ordinary life), but not quite, because, after all, it is "only a cockfight."

More observations of this sort could be advanced, but perhaps the general point is, if not made, at least well-delineated, and the whole argument thus far can be usefully summarized in a formal paradigm:

THE MORE A MATCH IS . . .

1. Between near status equals (and/or personal enemies)
2. Between high status individuals

THE DEEPER THE MATCH.

THE DEEPER THE MATCH . . .

1. The closer the identification of cock and man (or: more properly, the deeper the match the more the man will advance his best, most closely-identified-with cock).
2. The finer the cocks involved and the more exactly they will be matched.
3. The greater the emotion that will be involved and the more the general absorbtion in the match.
4. The higher the individual bets center and outside, the shorter the outside bet odds will tend to be, and the more betting there will be overall.
5. The less an "economic" and the more a "status" view of gaming will be involved, and the "solider" the citizens who will be gaming.[26]

Inverse arguments hold for the shallower the fight, culminating, in a reversed-signs sense, in the coin-spinning and dice-throwing amusements. For deep fights there are no absolute upper limits, though there are of course practical ones, and there are a great many legend-like tales of great Duel-in-the-Sun combats between lords and princes in classical times (for cockfighting has always been as much an elite concern as a popular one), far deeper than anything anyone, even aristocrats, could produce today anywhere in Bali.

Indeed, one of the great culture heroes of Bali is a prince, called after his passion for the sport, "The Cockfighter," who happened to be away at a very deep cockfight with a neighboring prince when the whole of his family—father, brothers, wives, sisters—were assassinated by commoner usurpers. Thus spared, he returned to dispatch the upstarts, regain the throne, reconstitute the Balinese high tradition, and build its most powerful, glorious, and prosperous state. Along with everything else that the

Balinese see in fighting cocks—themselves, their social order, abstract hatred, masculinity, demonic power—they also see the archetype of status virtue, the arrogant, resolute, honor-mad player with real fire, the ksatria prince. [27]

## Feathers, Blood, Crowds, and Money

"Poetry makes nothing happen," Auden says in his elegy of Yeats, "it survives in the valley of its saying . . . a way of happening, a mouth." The cockfight too, in this colloquial sense, makes nothing happen. Men go on allegorically humiliating one another and being allegorically humiliated by one another, day after day, glorying quietly in the experience if they have triumphed, crushed only slightly more openly by it if they have not. *But no one's status really changes.* You cannot ascend the status ladder by winning cockfights; you cannot, as an individual, really ascend it at all. Nor can you descend it that way. [28] All you can do is enjoy and savor, or suffer and withstand, the concocted sensation of drastic and momentary movement along an aesthetic semblance of that ladder, a kind of behind-the-mirror status jump which has the look of mobility without its actuality.

As any art form—for that, finally, is what we are dealing with—the cockfight renders ordinary, everyday experience comprehensible by presenting it in terms of acts and objects which have had their practical consequences removed and been reduced (or, if you prefer, raised) to the level of sheer appearances, where their meaning can be more powerfully articulated and more exactly perceived. The cockfight is "really real" only to the cocks—it does not kill anyone, castrate anyone, reduce anyone to animal status, alter the hierarchical relations among people, nor refashion the hierarchy; it does not even redistribute income in any significant way. What it does is what, for other peoples with other temperaments and other conventions, *Lear* and *Crime and Punishment* do; it catches up these themes—death, masculinity, rage, pride, loss, beneficence, chance—and, ordering them into an encompassing structure, presents them in such a way as to throw into relief a particular view of their essential nature. It puts a construction on them, makes them, to those historically positioned to appreciate the construction, meaningful—visible, tangible, graspable—"real," in an ideational sense. An image, fiction, a model, a metaphor, the cockfight is a means of expression; its function is neither to assuage social passions nor to heighten them (though, in its play-with-fire way, it does a bit of both), but, in a medium of feathers, blood, crowds, and money, to display them.

The question of how it is that we perceive qualities in things—paintings, books, melodies, plays—that we do not feel we can assert literally to be there has come, in recent years, into the very center of aesthetic theory. [29]

Neither the sentiments of the artist, which remain his, nor those of the audience, which remains theirs, can account for the agitation of one painting or the serenity of another. We attribute grandeur, wit, despair, exuberance to strings of sounds; lightness, energy, violence, fluidity to blocks of stone. Novels are said to have strength, buildings eloquence, plays momentum, ballets repose. In this realm of eccentric predicates, to say that the cockfight, in its perfected cases at least, is "disquietful" does not seem at all unnatural, merely, as I have just denied it practical consequence, somewhat puzzling.

The disquietfulness arises, "somehow," out of a conjunction of three attributes of the fight: its immediate dramatic shape; its metaphoric content; and its social context. A cultural figure against a social ground, the fight is at once a convulsive surge of animal hatred, a mock war of symbolical selves, and a formal simulation of status tensions, and its aesthetic power derives from its capacity to force together these diverse realities. The reason it is disquietful is not that it has material effects (it has some, but they are minor); the reason that it is disquietful is that, joining pride to selfhood, selfhood to cocks, and cocks to destruction, it brings to imaginative realization a dimension of Balinese experience normally well-obscured from view. The transfer of a sense of gravity into what is in itself a rather blank and unvarious spectacle, a commotion of beating wings and throbbing legs, is effected by interpreting it as expressive of something unsettling in the way its authors and audience live, or, even more ominously, what they are.

As a dramatic shape, the fight displays a characteristic that does not seem so remarkable until one realizes that it does not have to be there: a radically atomistical structure. [30] Each match is a world unto itself, a particulate burst of form. There is the match making, there is the betting, there is the fight, there is the result—utter triumph and utter defeat—and there is the hurried, embarrassed passing of money. The loser is not consoled. People drift away from him, look through him, leave him to assimilate his momentary descent into nonbeing, reset his face, and return, scarless and intact, to the fray. Nor are winners congratulated, or events rehashed; once a match is ended the crowd's attention turns totally to the next, with no looking back. A shadow of the experience no doubt remains with the principals, perhaps even with some of the witnesses, of a deep fight, as it remains with us when we leave the theater after seeing a powerful play well-performed; but it quite soon fades to become at most a schematic memory—a diffuse glow or an abstract shudder—and usually not even that. Any expressive form lives only in its own present—the one it itself creates. But, here, that present is severed into a string of flashes, some more bright than others, but all of them disconnected, aesthetic quanta. Whatever the cockfight says, it says in spurts.

But, as I have argued lengthily elsewhere, the Balinese live in spurts. [31] Their life, as they arrange it and perceive it, is less a flow, a directional movement out of the past, through the present, toward the future than an on-off pulsation of meaning and vacuity, an arhythmic alternation of short periods when "something" (that is, something significant) is happening and equally short ones where "nothing" (that is, nothing much) is—between what they themselves call "full" and "empty" times, or, in another idiom, "junctures" and "holes." In focusing activity down to a burning-glass dot, the cockfight is merely being Balinese in the same way in which everything from the monadic encounters of everyday life, through the changing pointillism of *gamelan* music, to the visiting-day-of-the-gods temple celebrations are. It is not an imitation of the punctuateness of Balinese social life, nor a depiction of it, nor even an expression of it; it is an example of it, carefully prepared. [32]

If one dimension of the cockfight's structure, its lack of temporal directionality, makes it seem a typical segment of the general social life, however, the other, its flat-out, head-to-head (or spur-to-spur) aggressiveness, makes it seem a contradiction, a reversal, even a subversion of it. In the normal course of things, the Balinese are shy to the point of obsessiveness of open conflict. Oblique, cautious, subdued, controlled, masters of indirection and dissimulation—what they call *alus*, "polished," "smooth,"—they rarely face what they can turn away from, rarely resist what they can evade. But here they portray themselves as wild and murderous, manic explosions of instinctual cruelty. A powerful rendering of life as the Balinese most deeply do not want it (to adapt a phrase Frye has used of Gloucester's blinding) is set in the context of a sample of it as they do in fact have it. [33] And, because the context suggests that the rendering, if less than a straightforward description is nonetheless more than an idle fancy, it is here that the disquietfulness—the disquietfulness of the *fight*, not (or, anyway, not necessarily) its patrons, who seem in fact rather thoroughly to enjoy it—emerges. The slaughter in the cock ring is not a depiction of how things literally are among men, but, what is almost worse, of how, from a particular angle, they imaginatively are. [34]

The angle, of course, is stratificatory. What, as we have already seen, the cockfight talks most forcibly about is status relationships, and what it says about them is that they are matters of life and death. That prestige is a profoundly serious business is apparent everywhere one looks in Bali—in the village, the family, the economy, the state. A peculiar fusion of Polynesian title ranks and Hindu castes, the hierarchy of pride is the moral backbone of the society. But only in the cockfight are the sentiments upon which that hierarchy rests revealed in their natural colors. Enveloped elsewhere in a haze of etiquette, a thick cloud of euphemism and ceremony, gesture and allusion, they are here expressed in only the thinnest disguise of an animal mask, a mask which in fact demonstrates them far more effectively than it conceals them. Jealousy is as much a part of Bali as poise, envy as grace, brutality as charm; but without the cockfight the Balinese would have a much less certain understanding of them, which is, presumably, why they value it so highly.

Any expressive form works (when it works) by disarranging semantic contexts in such a way that properties conventionally ascribed to certain things are unconventionally ascribed to others, which are then seen actually to possess them. To call the wind a cripple, as Stevens does, to fix tone and manipulate timbre, as Schoenberg does, or, closer to our case, to picture an art critic as a dissolute bear, as Hogarth does, is to cross conceptual wires; the established conjunctions between objects and their qualities are altered and phenomena—fall weather, melodic shape, or cultural journalism—are clothed in signifiers which normally point to other referents. [35] Similarly, to connect—and connect, and connect—the collision of roosters with the devisiveness of status is to invite a transfer of perceptions from the former to the latter, a transfer which is at once a description and a judgment. (Logically, the transfer could, of course, as well go the other way; but, like most of the rest of us, the Balinese are a great deal more interested in understanding men than they are in understanding cocks.)

What sets the cockfight apart from the ordinary course of life, lifts it from the realm of everyday practical affairs, and surrounds it with an aura of enlarged importance is not, as functionalist sociology would have it, that it reinforces status discriminations (such reinforcement is hardly necessary in a society where every act proclaims them), but that it provides a metasocial commentary upon the whole matter of assorting human beings into fixed hierarchical ranks and then organizing the major part of collective existence around that assortment. Its function, if you want to call it that, is interpretive: it is a Balinese reading of Balinese experience; a story they tell themselves about themselves.

## Saying Something of Something

To put the matter this way is to engage in a bit of metaphorical refocusing of one's own, for it shifts the analysis of cultural forms from an endeavor in general parallel to dissecting an organism, diagnosing a symptom, deciphering a code, or ordering a system—the dominant analogies in contemporary anthropology—to one in general parallel with penetrating a literary text. If one takes the cockfight, or any other collectively sustained symbolic structure, as a means of "saying something of something" (to invoke a famous Aristotelian tag), then one is faced with a problem not in social mechanics but social semantics. [36] For the anthropologist, whose concern is with formulating sociological principles, not with promoting or appreciating cockfights, the question is, what does one learn about such principles from examining culture as an assemblage of texts?

Such an extension of the notion of a text beyond written material, and even beyond verbal, is, though metaphorical, not, of course, all that novel. The *interpretatio naturae* tradition of the middle ages, which, culminating in Spinoza, attempted to read nature as Scripture, the Nietszchean effort to treat value systems as glosses on the will to power (or the Marxian one to treat them as glosses on property relations), and the Freudian replacement of the enigmatic text of the manifest dream with the plain one of the latent, all offer precedents, if not equally recommendable ones. [37] But the idea remains theoretically undeveloped; and the more profound corollary, so far as anthropology is concerned, that cultural forms can be treated as texts, as imaginative works built out of social materials, has yet to be systematically exploited. [38]

In the case at hand, to treat the cockfight as a text is to bring out a feature of it (in my opinion, the central feature of it) that treating it as a rite or a pastime, the two most obvious alternatives, would tend to obscure: its use of emotion for cognitive ends. What the cockfight says it says in a vocabulary of sentiment—the thrill of risk, the despair of loss, the pleasure of triumph. Yet what it says is not merely that risk is exciting, loss depressing, or triumph gratifying, banal tautologies of affect, but that it is of these emotions, thus exampled, that society is built and individuals put together. Attending cockfights and participating in them is, for the Balinese, a kind of sentimental education. What he learns there is what his culture's ethos and his private sensibility (or, anyway, certain aspects of them) look like when spelled out externally in a collective text; that the two are near enough alike to be articulated in the symbolics of a single such text; and—the disquieting part—that the text in which this revelation is accomplished consists of a chicken hacking another mindlessly to bits.

Every people, the proverb has it, loves its own form of violence. The cockfight is the Balinese reflection on theirs: on its look, its uses, its force, its fascination. Drawing on almost every level of Balinese experience, it brings together themes—animal savagery, male narcissism, opponent gambling, status rivalry, mass excitement, blood sacrifice—whose main connection is their involvement with rage and the fear of rage, and, binding them into a set of rules which at once contains them and allows them play, builds a symbolic structure in which, over and over again, the reality of their inner affiliation can be intelligibly felt. If, to quote Northrop Frye again, we go to see *Macbeth* to learn what a man feels like after he has gained a kingdom and lost his soul, Balinese go to cockfights to find out what a man, usually composed, aloof, almost obsessively self-absorbed, a kind of moral autocosm, feels like when, attacked, tormented, challenged, insulted, and driven in result to the extremes of fury, he has totally triumphed or been brought totally low. The whole passage, as it takes us back to Aristotle (though to the *Poetics* rather than the *Hermeneutics*), is worth quotation:

> But the poet [as opposed to the historian], Aristotle says, never makes any real statements at all, certainly no particular or specific ones. The poet's job is not to tell you what happened, but what happens: not what did take place, but the kind of thing that always does take place. He gives you the typical, recurring, or what Aristotle calls universal event. You wouldn't go to *Macbeth* to learn about the history of Scotland—you go to it to learn what man feels like after he's gained a kingdom and lost his soul. When you meet such a character as Micawber in Dickens, you don't feel that there must have been a man Dickens knew who was exactly like this: you feel that there's a bit of Micawber in almost everybody you know, including yourself. Our impressions of human life are picked up one by one, and remain for most of us loose and disorganized. But we constantly find things in literature that suddenly co-ordinate and bring into focus a great many such impressions, and this is part of what Aristotle means by the typical or universal human event. [39]

It is this kind of bringing of assorted experiences of everyday life to focus that the cockfight, set aside from that life as "only a game" and reconnected to it as "more than a game," accomplishes, and so creates what, better than typical or universal, could be called a paradigmatic human event—that is, one that tells us less what happens than the kind of thing that would happen if, as is not the case, life were art and could be as freely shaped by styles of feeling as *Macbeth* and *David Copperfield* are.

Enacted and reenacted, so far without end, the cockfight enables the Balinese, as, read and reread, *Macbeth* enables us, to see a dimension of his own subjectivity. As he watches fight after fight, with the active watching of an owner and a bettor (for cockfighting has no more interest as a pure spectator sport than croquet or dog racing do), he grows familiar with it and what it has to say to him, much as the attentive listener to string quartets or the absorbed viewer of still lifes grows slowly more familiar with them in a way which opens his subjectivity to himself. [40]

Yet, because—in another of those paradoxes, along with painted feelings and unconsequenced acts, which haunt aesthetics—that subjectivity does not properly exist until it is thus organized, art forms generate and regenerate the very subjectivity they pretend only to display. Quartets, still lifes, and cockfights are not merely reflections of a preexisting sensibility analogically represented; they are positive agents in the creation and maintenance of such a sensibility. If we see ourselves as a pack of Micawbers it is from reading too much Dickens (if we see ourselves as unillusioned realists, it is from reading too little); and similarly for Balinese, cocks, and cockfights. It is in such a way, coloring experience with the light they cast it in, rather than through whatever material effects they may have, that the arts play their role, as arts, in social life. [41]

In the cockfight, then, the Balinese forms and discovers his temperament and his society's temper at the same time. Or, more exactly, he forms and discovers a particular face of them. Not only are there a great many other cultural texts providing commentaries on status hierarchy and self-regard in Bali, but there are a great many other critical sectors of Balinese life besides the stratificatory and the agonistic that receive such commentary. The ceremony consecrating a Brahmana priest, a matter of breath control, postural immobility, and vacant concentration upon the depths of being, displays a radically different, but to the Balinese equally real, property of social hierarchy—its reach toward the numinous transcendent. Set not in the matrix of the kinetic emotionality of animals, but in that of the static passionlessness of divine mentality, it expresses tranquility not disquiet. The mass festivals at the village temples, which mobilize the whole local population in elaborate hostings of visiting gods—songs, dances, compliments, gifts—assert the spiritual unity of village mates against their status inequality and project a mood of amity and trust. [42] The cockfight is not the master key to Balinese life, any more than bullfighting is to Spanish. What it says about that life is not unqualified nor even unchallenged by what other equally eloquent cultural statements say about it. But there is nothing more surprising in this than in the fact that Racine and Molière were contemporaries, or that the same people who arrange chrysanthemums cast swords. [43]

The culture of a people is an ensemble of texts, themselves ensembles, which the anthropologist strains to read over the shoulders of those to whom they properly belong. There are enormous difficulties in such an enterprise, methodological pitfalls to make a Freudian quake, and some moral perplexities as well. Nor is it the only way that symbolic forms can be sociologically handled. Functionalism lives, and so does psychologism. But to regard such forms as "saying something of something," and saying it to somebody, is at least to open up the possibility of an analysis which attends to their substance rather than to reductive formulas professing to account for them.

As in more familiar exercises in close reading, one can start anywhere in a culture's repertoire of forms and end up anywhere else. One can stay, as I have here, within a single, more or less bounded form and circle steadily within it. One can move between forms in search of broader unities or informing contrasts. One can even compare forms from different cultures to define their character in reciprocal relief. But whatever the level at which one operates, and however intricately, the guiding principle is the same: societies, like lives, contain their own interpretations. One has only to learn how to gain access to them.

## References

[1] Gregory Bateson and Margaret Mead, *Balinese Character: A Photographic Analysis* (New York: New York Academy of Sciences, 1942), p. 68.

[2] Jane Belo, "The Balinese Temper," in Jane Belo, ed., *Traditional Balinese Culture* (New York: Columbia University Press, 1970; originally published in 1935), pp. 85–110.

[3] The best discussion of cockfighting is again Bateson and Mead's (*Balinese Character*, pp. 24–25, 140), but it, too, is general and abbreviated.

[4] *Ibid.*, pp. 25–26. The cockfight is unusual within Balinese culture in being a single-sex public activity from which the other sex is totally and expressly excluded. Sexual differentiation is culturally extremely played down in Bali and most activities, formal and informal, involve the participation of men and women on equal ground, commonly as linked couples. From religion, to politics, to economics, to kinship, to dress, Bali is a rather "uni-sex" society, a fact both its customs and its symbolism clearly express. Even in contexts where women do not in fact play much of a role—music, painting, certain agricultural activities—their absence, which is only relative in any case, is more a mere matter of fact than socially enforced. To this general pattern, the cockfight, entirely of, by, and for men (women—at least *Balinese* women—do not even watch), is the most striking exception.

[5] Christiaan Hooykaas, *The Lay of the Jaya Prana* (London, 1958), p. 39. The lay has a stanza (no. 17) with the reluctant bridegroom use. Jaya Prana, the subject of a Balinese Uriah myth, responds to the lord who has offered him the loveliest of six hundred servant girls: "Godly King, my Lord and Master / I beg you, give me leave to go / such things are not yet in my mind; / like a fighting cock encaged / indeed I am on my mettle / I am alone / as yet the flame has not been fanned."

[6] For these, see V. E. Korn, *Het Adatrecht van Bali*, 2d ed. ('S-Gravenhage: G. Naeff, 1932), index under *toh*.

[7] There is indeed a legend to the effect that the separation of Java and Bali is due to the action of a powerful Javanese religious figure who wished to protect himself against a Balinese culture hero (the ancestor of two Ksatria castes) who was a passionate cockfighting gambler. See Christiaan Hooykaas, *Agama Tirtha* (Amsterdam: Noord-Hollandsche, 1964), p. 184.

[8] An incestuous couple is forced to wear pig yokes over their necks and crawl to a pig trough and eat with their mouths there. On this, see Jane Belo, "Customs Pertaining to Twins in Bali," in Belo, ed., *Traditional Balinese Culture*, p. 49; on the abhorrence of animality generally, Bateson and Mead, *Balinese Character*, p. 22.

[9] Except for unimportant, small-bet fights (on the question of fight "importance," see below) spur affixing is usually done by someone other than the owner. Whether the owner handles his own cock or not more or less depends on how skilled he is at it, a consideration whose importance is again relative to the importance of the fight. When spur affixers and cock handlers are someone other than the owner, they are almost always a close relative—a brother or cousin—or a very intimate friend of his. They are thus almost extensions of his personality, as the fact that all three will refer to the cock as "mine," say "I" fought So-and-So, and so on, demonstrates. Also, owner-handler-affixer

triads tend to be fairly fixed, though individuals may participate in several and often exchange roles within a given one.

[10] Erving Goffman, *Encounters: Two Studies in the Sociology of Interaction* (Indianapolis: Bobbs-Merrill, 1961), pp. 9–10.

[11] This word, which literally means an indelible stain or mark, as in a birthmark or a vein in a stone, is used as well for a deposit in a court case, for a pawn, for security offered in a loan, for a stand-in for someone else in a legal or ceremonial context, for an earnest advanced in a business deal, for a sign placed in a field to indicate its ownership is in dispute, and for the status of an unfaithful wife from whose lover her husband must gain satisfaction or surrender her to him. See Korn, *Het Adatrecht van Bali*; Theodoor Pigeaud, *Javaans-Nederlands Handwoordenbock* (Groningen: Wolters, 1938); H. H. Juynboll, *Oudjavaansche-Nederlandsche Woordenlijst* (Leiden: Brill, 1923).

[12] The center bet must be advanced in cash by both parties prior to the actual fight. The umpire holds the stakes until the decision is rendered and then awards them to the winner, avoiding, among other things, the intense embarrassment both winner and loser would feel if the latter had to pay off personally following his defeat. About 10 per cent of the winner's receipts are subtracted for the umpire's share and that of the fight sponsors.

[13] Actually, the typing of cocks, which is extremely elaborate (I have collected more than twenty classes, certainly not a complete list), is not based on color alone, but on a series of independent, interacting, dimensions, which include, beside color, size, bone thickness, plumage, and temperament. (But *not* pedigree. The Balinese do not breed cocks to any significant extent, nor, so far as I have been able to discover, have they ever done so. The *asil*, or jungle cock, which is the basic fighting strain everywhere the sport is found, is native to southern Asia, and one can buy a good example in the chicken section of almost any Balinese market for anywhere from four or five ringgits up to fifty or more.) The color element is merely the one normally used as the type name, except when the two cocks of different types—as on principle they must be—have the same color, in which case a secondary indication from one of the other dimensions ("large speckled" v. "small speckled," etc.) is added. The types are coordinated with various cosmological ideas which help shape the making of matches, so that, for example, you fight a small, headstrong, speckled brown-on-white cock with flat-lying feathers and thin legs from the east side of the ring on a certain day of the complex Balinese calendar, and a large, cautious, all-black cock with tufted feathers and stubby legs from the north side on another day, and so on. All this is again recorded in palm-leaf manuscripts and endlessly discussed by the Balinese (who do not all have identical systems), and full-scale componential-cum-symbolic analysis of cock classifications would be extremely valuable both as an adjunct to the description of the cockfight and in itself. But my data on the subject, though extensive and varied, do not seem to be complete and systematic enough to attempt such an analysis here. For Balinese cosmological ideas more generally see Belo, ed., *Traditional Balinese Culture*, and J. L. Swellengrebel, ed., *Bali: Studies in Life, Thought, and Ritual* (The Hague: W. van Hoeve, 1960); for calendrical ones, Clifford Geertz, *Person, Time, and Conduct in Bali: An Essay in Cultural Analysis* (New Haven: Southeast Asia Studies, Yale University, 1966), pp. 45–53.

[14] For purposes of ethnographic completeness, it should be noted that it is possible for the man backing the favorite—the odds-giver—to make a bet in which he wins if his cock wins or there is a tie, a slight shortening of the odds (I do not have enough cases to be exact, but ties seem to occur about once every fifteen or twenty matches). He indicates his wish to do this by shouting *sapih* ("tie") rather than the cock-type, but such bets are in fact infrequent.

[15] The precise dynamics of the movement of the betting is one of the most intriguing,

most complicated, and, given the hectic conditions under which it occurs, most difficult to study, aspects of the fight. Motion picture recording plus multiple observers would probably be necessary to deal with it effectively. Even impressionistically—the only approach open to a lone ethnographer caught in the middle of all this—it is clear that certain men lead both in determining the favorite (that is, making the opening cock-type calls which always initiate the process) and in directing the movement of the odds, these "opinion leaders" being the more accomplished cockfighters-cum-solid-citizens to be discussed below. If these men begin to change their calls, others follow; if they begin to make bets, so do others and—though there is always a large number of frustrated bettors crying for shorter or longer odds to the end—the movement more or less ceases. But a detailed understanding of the whole process awaits what, alas, it is not very likely ever to get: a decision theorist armed with precise observations of individual behavior.

[16] Assuming only binominal variability, the departure from a fifty-fifty expectation in the sixty ringgits and below case is 1.38 standard deviations, or (in a one direction test) an eight in one hundred possibility by chance alone; for the below forty ringgits case it is 1.65 standard deviations, or about five in one hundred. The fact that these departures though real are not extreme merely indicates, again, that even in the smaller fights the tendency to match cocks at least reasonably evenly persists. It is a matter of relative relaxation of the pressures toward equalization, not their elimination. The tendency for high-bet contests to be coin-flip propositions is, of course, even more striking, and suggests the Balinese know quite well what they are about.

[17] The reduction in wagering in smaller fights (which, of course, feeds on itself; one of the reasons people find small fights uninteresting is that there is less wagering in them, and contrariwise for large ones) takes place in three mutually reinforcing ways. First, there is a simple withdrawal of interest as people wander off to have a cup of coffee or chat with a friend. Second, the Balinese do not mathematically reduce odds, but bet directly in terms of stated odds as such. Thus, for a nine-to-eight bet, one man wagers nine ringgits, the other eight; for five-to-four, one wagers five, the other four. For any given currency unit, like the ringgit, therefore, 6.3 times as much money is involved in a ten-to-nine bet as in a two-to-one bet, for example, and, as noted, in small fights betting settles toward the longer end. Finally, the bets which are made tend to be one- rather than two-, three-, or in some of the very largest fights, four- or five-finger ones. (The fingers indicate the *multiples* of the stated bet odds at issue, not absolute figures. Two fingers in a six-to-five situation means a man wants to wager ten ringgits on the underdog against twelve, three in an eight-to-seven situation, twenty-one against twenty-four, and so on.)

[18] Besides wagering there are other economic aspects of the cockfight, especially its very close connection with the local market system which, though secondary both to its motivation and to its function, are not without importance. Cockfights are open events to which anyone who wishes may come, sometimes from quite distant areas, but well over 90 per cent, probably over 95, are very local affairs, and the locality concerned is defined not by the village, nor even by the administrative district, but by the rural market system. Bali has a three-day market week with the familiar "solar-system" type rotation. Though the markets themselves have never been very highly developed, small morning affairs in a village square, it is the microregion such rotation rather generally marks out—ten or twenty square miles, seven or eight neighboring villages (which in contemporary Bali is usually going to mean anywhere from five to ten to eleven thousand people) from which the core of any cockfight audience, indeed virtually all of it, will come. Most of the fights are in fact organized and sponsored by small combines of petty rural merchants under the general premise, very strongly held by them and indeed by all Balinese, that

cockfights are good for trade because "they get money out of the house, they make it circulate." Stalls selling various sorts of things as well as assorted sheer-chance gambling games (see below) are set up around the edge of the area so that this even takes on the quality of a small fair. This connection of cockfighting with markets and market sellers is very old, as, among other things, their conjunction in inscriptions (Roelof Goris, *Prasasti Bali*, 2 vols. [Bandung: N. V. Masa Baru, 1954]) indicates. Trade has followed the cock for centuries in rural Bali and the sport has been one of the main agencies of the island's monetization.

[19] The phrase is found in the Hildreth translation, *International Liberty of Psychology*, 1931, note to p. 106; see L. L. Fuller, *The Morality of Law* (New Haven: Yale University Press, 1964), pp. 6ff.

[20] Of course, even in Bentham, utility is not normally confined as a concept to monetary losses and gains, and my argument here might be more carefully put in terms of a denial that for the Balinese, as for any people, utility (pleasure, happiness . . . ) is merely identifiable with wealth. But such terminological problems are in any case secondary to the essential point: the cockfight is not roulette.

[21] Max Weber, *The Sociology of Religion* (Boston: Beacon Press, 1963). There is nothing specifically Balinese, of course, about deepening significance with money, as Whyte's description of corner boys in a working-class district of Boston demonstrates: "Gambling plays an important role in the lives of Cornerville people. Whatever game the corner boys play, they nearly always bet on the outcome. When there is nothing at stake, the game is not considered a real contest. This does not mean that the financial element is all-important. I have frequently heard men say that the honor of winning was much more important than the money at stake. The corner boys consider playing for money the real test of skill and, unless a man performs well when money is at stake, he is not considered a good competitor." W. F. Whyte, *Street Corner Society*, 2d ed. (Chicago: University of Chicago Press, 1955), p. 140.

[22] The extremes to which this madness is conceived on occasion to go—and the fact that it is considered madness—is demonstrated by the Balinese folktale *I Tuhung Kuning*. A gambler becomes so deranged by his passion that, leaving on a trip, he orders his pregnant wife to take care of the prospective newborn if it is a boy but to feed it as meat to his fighting cocks if it is a girl. The mother gives birth to a girl, but rather than giving the child to the cocks she gives them a large rat and conceals the girl with her own mother. When the husband returns the cocks, crowing a jingle, inform him of the deception and, furious, he sets out to kill the child. A goddess descends from heaven and takes the girl up to the skies with her. The cocks die from the food given them, the owner's sanity is restored, the goddess brings the girl back to the father who reunites him with his wife. The story is given as "Geel Komkommertje" in Jacoba Hooykaas-van Leeuwen Boomkamp, *Sprookjes en Verhalen van Bali* ('S-Gravenhage: Van Hoeve, 1956), pp. 19–25.

[23] For a fuller description of Balinese rural social structure, see Clifford Geertz, "Form and Variation in Balinese Village Structure," *American Anthropologist*, 61 (1959), 94–108; "Tihingan, A Balinese Village," in R. M. Koentjaraningrat, *Villages in Indonesia* (Ithaca: Cornell University Press, 1967), pp. 210–243; and, though it is a bit off the norm as Balinese villages go, V. E. Korn, *De Dorpsrepubliek tnganan Pagringsingan* (Santpoort [Netherlands]: C. A. Mees, 1933).

[24] Goffman, *Encounters*, p. 78.

[25] B. R. Berelson, P. F. Lazersfeld, and W. N. McPhee, *Voting: A Study of Opinion Formation in a Presidential Campaign* (Chicago: University of Chicago Press, 1954).

[26] As this is a formal paradigm, it is intended to display the logical, not the causal, structure of cockfighting. Just which of these considerations leads to which, in what or-

der, and by what mechanisms, is another matter—one I have attempted to shed some light on in the general discussion.

[27] In another of Hooykaas-van Leeuwen Boomkamp's folk tales ("De Gast," *Sprookjes en Verhalen van Bali*, pp. 172–180), a low caste *Sudra*, a generous, pious, and carefree man who is also an accomplished cock fighter, loses, despite his accomplishment, fight after fight until he is not only out of money but down to his last cock. He does not despair, however—"I bet," he says, "upon the Unseen World."

His wife, a good and hard-working woman, knowing how much he enjoys cock-fighting, gives him her last "rainy day" money to go and bet. But, filled with misgivings due to his run of ill luck, he leaves his own cock at home and bets merely on the side. He soon loses all but a coin or two and repairs to a food stand for a snack, where he meets a decrepit, odorous, and generally unappetizing older beggar leaning on a staff. The old man asks for food, and the hero spends his last coins to buy him some. The old man then asks to pass the night with the hero, which the hero gladly invites him to do. As there is no food in the house, however, the hero tells his wife to kill the last cock for dinner. When the old man discovers this fact, he tells the hero he has three cocks in his own mountain hut and says the hero may have one of them for fighting. He also asks for the hero's son to accompany him as a servant, and, after the son agrees, this is done.

The old man turns out to be Siva and, thus, to live in a great palace in the sky, though the hero does not know this. In time, the hero decides to visit his son and collect the promised cock. Lifted up into Siva's presence, he is given the choice of three cocks. The first crows: "I have beaten fifteen opponents." The second crows, "I have beaten twenty-five opponents." The third crows, "I have beaten the King." "That one, the third, is my choice," says the hero, and returns with it to earth.

When he arrives at the cockfight, he is asked for an entry fee and replies, "I have no money; I will pay after my cock has won." As he is known never to win, he is let in because the king, who is there fighting, dislikes him and hopes to enslave him when he loses and cannot pay off. In order to insure that this happens, the king matches his finest cock against the hero's. When the cocks are placed down, the hero's flees, and the crowd, led by the arrogant king, hoots in laughter. The hero's cock then flies at the king himself, killing him with a spur stab in the throat. The hero flees. His house is encircled by the king's men. The cock changes into a Garuda, the great mythic bird of Indic legend, and carries the hero and his wife to safety in the heavens.

When the people see this, they make the hero king and his wife queen and they return as such to earth. Later his son, released by Siva, also returns and the hero-king announces his intention to enter a hermitage. ("I will fight no more cock-fights. I have bet on the Unseen and won.") He enters the hermitage and his son becomes king.

[28] Addict gamblers are really less declassed (for their status is, as everyone else's, inherited) than merely impoverished and personally disgraced. The most prominent addict gambler in my cockfight circuit was actually a very high caste *satria* who sold off most of his considerable lands to support his habit. Though everyone privately regarded him as a fool and worse (some, more charitable, regarded him as sick), he was publicly treated with the elaborate deference and politeness due his rank. On the independence of personal reputation and public status in Bali, see Geertz, *Person, Time, and Conduct,* pp. 28–35.

[29] For four, somewhat variant treatments, see Susanne Langer, *Feeling and Form* (New York: Scribners, 1953); Richard Wollheim, *Art and Its Objects* (New York: Harper and Row, 1968); Nelson Goodman, *Languages of Art* (Indianapolis: Bobbs-Merrill, 1968); Maurice Merleau-Ponty, "The Eye and the Mind," in his, *The Primacy of Perception* (Evanston: Northwestern University Press, 1964), pp. 159–190.

[30] British cockfights (the sport was banned there in 1840) indeed seem to have lacked it, and to have generated, therefore, a quite different family of shapes. Most British fights were "mains," in which a preagreed number of cocks were aligned into two teams and fought serially. Score was kept and wagering took place both on the individual matches and on the main as a whole. There were also "battle Royales," both in England and on the Continent, in which a large number of cocks were let loose at once with the one left standing at the end the victor. And in Wales, the so-called "Welsh main" followed an elimination pattern, along the lines of a present-day tennis tournament, winners proceeding to the next round. As a genre, the cockfight has perhaps less compositional flexibility than, say, Latin comedy, but it is not entirely without any. On cockfighting more generally, see Arch Ruport, *The Act of Cockfighting* (New York: Devin-Adair, 1949); G. R. Scott, *History of Cockfighting* (1957); and Lawrence Fitz-Barnard, *Fighting Sports* (London: Odhams Press, 1921).

[31] *Person, Time, and Conduct*, esp. pp. 42ff. I am, however, not the first person to have argued it: see G. Bateson, "Bali, the Value System of a Steady State," and "An Old Temple and a New Myth," in Belo, ed., *Traditional Balinese Culture*, pp. 384–402 and 111–136.

[32] For the necessity of distinguishing among "description," "representation," "exemplification," and "expression" (and the irrelevance of "imitation" to all of them), as modes of symbolic reference, see Goodman, *Languages of Art*, pp. 6–10, 45–91, 225–241.

[33] Northrop Frye, *The Educated Imagination* (Bloomington: University of Indiana Press, 1964), p. 99.

[34] There are two other Balinese values and disvalues which, connected with punctuate temporality on the one hand and unbridled aggressiveness on the other, reinforce the sense that the cockfight is at once continuous with ordinary social life and a direct negation of it: what the Balinese call *ramé*, and what they call *paling*. *Ramé* means crowded, noisy, and active, and is a highly sought after social state: crowded markets, mass festivals, busy streets are all *ramé*, as, of course, is, in the extreme, a cockfight. *Ramé* is what happens in the "full" times (its opposite, *sepi*, "quiet," is what happens in the "empty" ones). *Paling* is social vertigo, the dizzy, disoriented, lost, turned around feeling one gets when one's place in the coordinates of social space is not clear, and it is a tremendously disfavored, immensely anxiety-producing state. Balinese regard the exact maintenance of spatial orientation ("not to know where north is" is to be crazy), balance, decorum, status relationships, and so forth, as fundamental to ordered life (*krama*) and *paling*, the sort of whirling confusion of position the scrambling cocks exemplify as its profoundest enemy and contradiction. On *ramé*, see Bateson and Mead, *Balinese Character*, pp. 3, 64; on *paling*, *ibid.*, p. 11, and Belo, ed., *Traditional Balinese Culture*, p. 90ff.

[35] The Stevens reference is to his "The Motive for Metaphor" ("You like it under the trees in autumn, / Because everything is half dead. / The wind moves like a cripple among the leaves / And repeats words without meaning"); the Schoenberg reference is to the third of his *Five Orchestral Pieces* (Opus 16), and is borrowed from H. H. Drager, "The Concept of 'Tonal Body,'" in Susanne Langer, ed., *Reflections of Art* (New York: Oxford University Press, 1961), p. 174. On Hogarth, and on this whole problem—there called "multiple matrix matching"—see E. H. Gombrich, "The Use of Art for the Study of Symbols," in James Hogg, ed., *Psychology and the Visual Arts* (Baltimore: Penguin Books, 1969), pp. 149–170. The more usual term for this sort of semantic alchemy is "metaphorical transfer," and good technical discussions of it can be found in M. Black, *Models and Metaphors* (Ithaca: Cornell University Press, 1962), pp. 25ff; Goodman, *Languages of Art*, pp. 44ff; and W. Percy, "Metaphor as Mistake," *Sewanee Review*, 66 (1958), 78–99.

[36] The tag is from the second book of the *Organon*, *On Interpretation*. For a discussion of it, and for the whole argument for freeing "the notion of text . . . from the notion of

scripture or writing," and constructing, thus, a general hermeneutics, see Paul Ricoeur, *Freud and Philosophy* (New Haven: Yale University Press, 1970), pp. 20ff.

[37] *Ibid.*

[38] Lévi-Strauss's "structuralism" might seem an exception. But it is only an apparent one, for, rather than taking myths, totem rites, marriage rules, or whatever as texts to interpret, Lévi-Strauss takes them as ciphers to solve, which is very much not the same thing. He does not seek to understand symbolic forms in terms of how they function in concrete situations to organize perceptions (meanings, emotions, concepts, attitudes); he seeks to understand them entirely in terms of their internal structure, *indépendent de tout sujet, de tout objet, et de toute contexte.* For my own view of this approach—that is suggestive and indefensible—see Clifford Geertz, "The Cerebral Savage: On the Work of Lévi-Strauss," *Encounter*, 48 (1967), 25–32.

[39] Frye, *The Educated Imagination*, pp. 63–64.

[40] The use of the, to Europeans, "natural" visual idiom for perception—"see," "watches," and so forth—is more than usually misleading here, for the fact that, as mentioned earlier, Balinese follow the progress of the fight as much (perhaps, as fighting cocks are actually rather hard to see except as blurs of motion, more) with their bodies as with their eyes, moving their limbs, heads, and trunks in gestural mimicry of the cocks' maneuvers, means that much of the individual's experience of the fight is kinesthetic rather than visual. If ever there was an example of Kenneth Burke's definition of a symbolic act as "the dancing of an attitude" (*The Philosophy of Literary Form*, rev. ed. [New York: Vintage Books, 1957], p. 9) the cockfight is it. On the enormous role of kinesthetic perception in Balinese life, Bateson and Mead, *Balinese Character*, pp. 84–88; on the active nature of aesthetic perception in general, Goodman, *Languages of Art*, pp. 241–244.

[41] All this coupling of the occidental great with the oriental lowly will doubtless disturb certain sorts of aestheticians as the earlier effort of anthropologists to speak of Christianity and totemism in the same breath disturbed certain sorts of theologians. But as ontological questions are (or should be) bracketed in the sociology of religion, judgmental ones are (or should be) bracketed in the sociology of art. In any case, the attempt to deprovincialize the concept of art is but part of the general anthropological conspiracy to deprovincialize all important social concepts—marriage, religion, law, rationality—and though this is a threat to aesthetic theories which regard certain works of art as beyond the reach of sociological analysis, it is no threat to the conviction, for which Robert Graves claims to have been reprimanded at his Cambridge tripos, that some poems are better than others.

[42] For the consecration ceremony, see V. E. Korn, "The Consecration of the Priest," in Swellengrebel, ed., *Bali*, pp. 131–154; for (somewhat exaggerated) village communion, Roelof Goris, "The Religious Character of the Balinese Village," *ibid.*, pp. 79–100.

[43] That what the cockfight has to say about Bali is not altogether without perception and the disquiet it expresses about the general pattern of Balinese life is not wholly without reason is attested by the fact that in two weeks of December, 1965, during the upheavals following the unsuccessful coup in Djakarta, between forty and eighty thousand Balinese (in a population of about two million) were killed, largely by one another—the worst outburst in the country. (John Hughes, *Indonesian Upheaval* [New York: McKay, 1967], pp. 173–183. Hughes's figures are, of course, rather casual estimates, but they are not the most extreme.) This is not to say, of course, that the killings were caused by the cockfight, could have been predicted on the basis of it, or were some sort of enlarged version of it with real people in the place of the cocks—all of which is nonsense. It is merely to say that if one looks at Bali not just through the medium of its dances, its shadowplays, its sculpture, and its girls, but—as the Balinese themselves do—also

through the medium of its cockfight, the fact that the massacre occurred seems, if no less appealing, less like a contradiction to the laws of nature. As more than one real Gloucester has discovered, sometimes people actually get life precisely as they most deeply do not want it.

. . . . . . . . . . . .

## QUESTIONS FOR A SECOND READING

1. Geertz says that the cockfight provides a "commentary upon the whole matter of sorting human beings into fixed hierarchical ranks and then organizing the major parts of collective existence around that assortment." The cockfights don't reinforce the patterns of Balinese life; they comment on them. Perhaps the first question to ask as you go back to the essay is, "What is that commentary?" What do the cockfights say? And what don't they say?

2. "Deep Play: Notes on the Balinese Cockfight" is divided into seven sections. As you reread the essay, pay attention to the connections between these sections and the differences in the way they are written and in what they propose to do (some, for example, tell stories, some use numbers, some have more footnotes than others).

   What is the logic or system that makes one section follow another? Do you see the subtitles as seven headings on a topic outline? The last two sections are perhaps the most difficult to read and understand. They also make repeated reference to literary texts. Why? What is Geertz doing here?

   If you look at the differences in the style or method of each section, what might they be said to represent? If each is evident of something Geertz, as an anthropologist, knows how to do, what, in each case, is he doing? What is his expertise? And why, in each case, would it require this particular style of writing?

3. It could be argued that "Deep Play" tells again the story of how white Western men have taken possession of the Third World, here with Geertz performing an act of intellectual colonization. In the opening section, for example, Geertz as author quickly turns both his wife and the Balinese people into stock characters, characters in a story designed to make him a hero. And, in the service of this story, he pushes aside the difficult political realities of Bali—the later killing of Balinese by the police is put in parentheses (so as not to disturb the flow of the happy story of how an anthropologist wins his way into the community). The remaining sections turn Balinese culture into numbers and theories, reducing the irreducible detail of people's lives into material for the production of goods (an essay furthering his career). And, one could argue, the piece ends by turning to Shakespeare and Dickens to "explain" the Balinese, completing the displacement of Balinese culture by Western culture.

This, anyway, is how such an argument might be constructed. As you reread the essay, mark passages you could use, as the author, to argue both for and against Geertz and his relationship to this story of colonization. To what extent can one say that Geertz is, finally, one more white man taking possession of the Third World; and to what extent can one argue that Geertz, as a writer, is struggling against this dominant, conventional narrative, working to revise it or to distance himself from it.

4. Throughout the essay Geertz is working very hard to *do* something with what he observed in Bali. (There are "enormous difficulties in such an enterprise," he says.) He is also, however, working hard *not* to do some things. (He doesn't want to be a "formalist," for example.) As you read the essay for the second time, look for passages that help you specifically define what it is Geertz wants to do and what it is he wants to be sure not to do.

### ASSIGNMENTS FOR WRITING

1. If this essay were your only evidence, how might you describe the work of an anthropologist? What do anthropologists do and how do they do what they do? Write an essay in which you look at "Deep Play" section by section, describing on the basis of each what it is that an anthropologist must be able to do. In each case, you have the chance to watch Geertz at work. (Your essay, then, might well have sections that correspond to Geertz's.) When you have worked through them all, write a final section that discusses how these various skills or arts fit together to define the expertise of someone like Geertz.

2. Geertz says that "the culture of a people is an ensemble of texts, themselves ensembles, which the anthropologist strains to read over the shoulders of those to whom they properly belong." Anthropologists are expert at "reading" in this way. One of the interesting things about being a student is that you get to (or you have to) act like an expert even though, properly speaking, you are not. Write an essay in which you prepare a Geertzian "reading" of some part of our culture you know well (sorority rush, window-shopping in a shopping mall, studying in the library, decorating a dorm room, whatever). Ideally, you should go out and observe the behavior you are studying, examining it and taking notes with your project in mind. You should imagine that you are working in Geertz's spirit, imitating his method and style and carrying out work that he has begun.

3. This is really a variation on the first assignment. This assignment, however, invites you to read against the grain of Geertz's essay. Imagine that someone has made the argument outlined briefly in the third "Question for a Second Reading"—that "Deep Play" is just one more version of a familiar story, a story of a white man taking possession of everything that is not already made in his own image. If you were going to respond to this ar-

gument—to extend it or to answer it—to what in the essay would you turn for evidence? And what might you say about what you find?

Write an essay, then, in which you respond to the argument that says "Deep Play" is one more version of the familiar story of a white man taking possession of that which is not his.

## MAKING CONNECTIONS

1. Geertz was trained as an anthropologist, and Robert Coles (p. 93) was trained as a child psychiatrist. Both, however, went off to foreign territory (and you should work with the assumption that the world of wealthy children was foreign to Coles) to study the people and to learn what they could about who they were, how they saw the world, and why they acted as they did.

   Write an essay in which you explore and describe the different methods of these two scholars. What do they notice? What do they do with what they notice? And what can you say, then, about the possibilities and limitations of each method of analysis?

2. In "The Loss of the Creature" (p. 462), Walker Percy writes about tourists (actually several different kinds of tourists) and the difficulty they have seeing what lies before them. Properly speaking, anthropologists are not tourists. There is a scholarly purpose to their travel, and presumably they have learned or developed the strategies necessary to get beyond the preformed "symbolic complexes" which would keep them from seeing the place or the people they have traveled to study. Geertz is an expert, in other words, not just any "layman seer of sights."

   In his travels to Bali, Geertz seems to get just what he wants. He gets both the authentic experience and a complex understanding of that experience. If you read "Deep Play" from the perspective of Percy's essay, however, it is interesting to ask whether Percy would say that this was the case, and to ask how Percy would characterize the "strategies" that define Geertz's approach to his subject.

   Write an essay in which you place Geertz in the context of Percy's tourists—not all of them, but the two or three whose stories seem most interesting when placed alongside Geertz's. The purpose of your essay should be to determine whether or not Geertz has solved the problem Percy defines for the tourist in "The Loss of the Creature."

# HARRIET
# JACOBS

*H*ARRIET JACOBS° *was born in North Carolina in or around 1815. The se-*
*lection that follows reproduces the opening chapters of her autobiography,*
Incidents in the Life of a Slave Girl, *and tells the story of her life from childhood*
*to early adulthood, through the birth of her first child. In these chapters Jacobs*
*describes how she came to understand her identity as men's property—as a slave*
*and as a woman—as that identity was determined by her particular situation (her*
*appearance, her education, the psychology of her owner, the values of her family)*
*and by the codes governing slavery in the South.*

*In the remaining chapters of her book, Jacobs tells of the birth of a second child,*
*of her escape from her owner, Dr. Flint, and of seven years spent hiding in a crawl*
*space under the roof of her grandmother's house. The father of her children, Mr.*
*Sands, did not, as she thought he might, purchase and free her, although he even-*
*tually did purchase her children and allowed them to live with her grandmother.*
*He did not free the children, and they never bore his name.*

*Around 1842 Jacobs fled to New York, where she made contact with her children*

---

**Harriet Jacobs** is the name of the author. Linda Brent is a pseudonym that she used.

*and found work as a nursemaid in the family of Nathaniel P. Willis, a magazine editor who with his wife helped hide Jacobs from southern slaveholders and eventually purchased Jacobs and her children and gave them their freedom.*

*This is the end of Jacobs's story as it is reported in* Incidents. *Recent research, however, enables us to tell the story of the production of this autobiography, the text that represents its author's early life. Through her contact with the Willises, Jacobs met both black and white abolitionists and became active in the antislavery movement. She told her story to Amy Post, a feminist and abolitionist, and Post encouraged her to record it, which she did by writing in the evenings between 1853 and 1858. After unsuccessfully seeking publication in England, and with the help of the white abolitionist writer L. Maria Child, who read the manuscript and served as an editor (by rearranging sections and suggesting that certain incidents be expanded into chapters), Jacobs published* Incidents *in Boston in 1861 under the pseudonym "Linda Brent," along with Child's introduction, which is also reproduced here. During the Civil War, Jacobs left the Willises to be a nurse for black troops. She remained active, working with freed slaves for the next thirty years, and died in Washington, D.C., in 1897.*

*For years scholars questioned the authenticity of this autobiography, arguing that it seemed too skillfully written to have been written by a slave, and that more likely it had been written by white abolitionists as propaganda for their cause. The recent discovery, however, of a cache of letters and the research of Jean Fagan Yellin have established Jacobs's authorship and demonstrated that Child made only minor changes and assisted primarily by helping Jacobs find a publisher and an audience.*

*Still, the issue of authorship remains a complicated one, even if we can be confident that the writing belongs to Jacobs and records her struggles and achievements. The issue of authorship becomes complicated if we think of the dilemma facing Jacobs as a writer, telling a story that defied description to an audience who could never completely understand. There is, finally, a precarious relationship between the story of a slave's life, the story Jacobs had to tell, and the stories available to her and to her readers as models—stories of privileged, white, middle-class life: conventional narratives of family and childhood, love and marriage.*

*Houston Baker, one of our leading scholars of black culture, has described the situation of the slave narrator this way:*

> *But the slave narrator must also accomplish the almost unthinkable (since thought and language are inseparable) task of transmuting an authentic, unwritten self—a self that exists outside the conventional literary discourse structures of a white reading public—into a literary representation. . . . The voice of the unwritten self, once it is subjected to the linguistic codes, literary conventions, and audience expectations of a literate population, is perhaps never again the authentic voice of black American slavery. It is, rather, the voice of a self transformed by an autobiographical act into a sharer in the general public discourse about slavery.*

*The author of* Incidents *could be said to stand outside "the general public discourse," both because she was a slave and because she was a woman. The story she has to tell does not fit easily into the usual stories of courtship and marriage or the dominant attitudes toward sexuality and female "virtue." When you read Jacobs's concerns about her "competence" about her status as a woman or as a writer, concerns that seem strange in the face of this powerful text; when you hear her addressing her readers, sometimes instructing them, sometimes apologizing, trying to bridge the gap between her experience and theirs, you should not only think of the trials she faced as a woman and a mother but also of her work as a writer. Here, too, she is struggling to take possession of her life.*

# Incidents in the Life of a Slave Girl

## Written by Herself

Northerners know nothing at all about Slavery. They think it is perpetual bondage only. They have no conception of the depth of *degradation* involved in that word, SLAVERY; if they had, they would never cease their efforts until so horrible a system was overthrown.
— A WOMAN OF NORTH CAROLINA

Rise up, ye women that are at ease! Hear my voice, ye careless daughters! Give ear unto my speech.
— *Isaiah xxxii.9*

## Preface by the Author

### Linda Brent

Reader, be assured this narrative is no fiction. I am aware that some of my adventures may seem incredible; but they are, nevertheless, strictly true. I have not exaggerated the wrongs inflicted by Slavery; on the contrary, my descriptions fall far short of the facts. I have concealed the names of places, and given persons fictitious names. I had no motive for secrecy on my own account, but I deemed it kind and considerate towards others to pursue this course.

---

Edited by L. Maria Child.

I wish I were more competent to the task I have undertaken. But I trust my readers will excuse deficiencies in consideration of circumstances. I was born and reared in Slavery; and I remained in a Slave State twenty-seven years. Since I have been at the North, it has been necessary for me to work diligently for my own support, and the education of my children. This has not left me much leisure to make up for the loss of early opportunities to improve myself; and it has compelled me to write these pages at irregular intervals, whenever I could snatch an hour from household duties.

When I first arrived in Philadelphia, Bishop Paine advised me to publish a sketch of my life, but I told him I was altogether incompetent to such an undertaking. Though I have improved my mind somewhat since that time, I still remain of the same opinion; but I trust my motives will excuse what might otherwise seem presumptuous. I have not written my experiences in order to attract attention to myself; on the contrary, it would have been more pleasant to me to have been silent about my own history. Neither do I care to excite sympathy for my own sufferings. But I do earnestly desire to arouse the women of the North to a realizing sense of the condition of two millions of women at the South, still in bondage, suffering what I suffered, and most of them far worse. I want to add my testimony to that of abler pens to convince the people of the Free States what Slavery really is. Only by experience can any one realize how deep, and dark, and foul is that pit of abominations. May the blessing of God rest on this imperfect effort in behalf of my persecuted people!

## Introduction by the Editor

### L. Maria Child

The author of the following autobiography is personally known to me, and her conversation and manners inspire me with confidence. During the last seventeen years, she has lived the greater part of the time with a distinguished family in New York, and has so deported herself as to be highly esteemed by them. This fact is sufficient, without further credentials of her character. I believe those who know her will not be disposed to doubt her veracity, though some incidents in her story are more romantic than fiction.

At her request, I have revised her manuscript; but such changes as I have made have been mainly for purposes of condensation and orderly arrangement. I have not added any thing to the incidents, or changed the import of her very pertinent remarks. With trifling exceptions, both the ideas and the language are her own. I pruned excrescences a little, but otherwise I had no reason for changing her lively and dramatic way of telling her own story. The names of both persons and places are known to me; but for good reasons I suppress them.

It will naturally excite surprise that a woman reared in Slavery should be able to write so well. But circumstances will explain this. In the first place, nature endowed her with quick perceptions. Secondly, the mistress, with whom she lived till she was twelve years old, was a kind, considerate friend, who taught her to read and spell. Thirdly, she was placed in favorable circumstances after she came to the North; having frequent intercourse with intelligent persons, who felt a friendly interest in her welfare, and were disposed to give her opportunities for self-improvement.

I am well aware that many will accuse me of indecorum for presenting these pages to the public; for the experiences of this intelligent and much-injured woman belong to a class which some call delicate subjects, and others indelicate. This peculiar phase of Slavery has generally been kept veiled; but the public ought to be made acquainted with its monstrous features, and I willingly take the responsibility of presenting them with the veil withdrawn. I do this for the sake of my sisters in bondage, who are suffering wrongs so foul, that our ears are too delicate to listen to them. I do it with the hope of arousing conscientious and reflecting women at the North to a sense of their duty in the exertion of moral influence on the question of Slavery, on all possible occasions. I do it with the hope that every man who reads this narrative will swear solemnly before God that, so far as he has power to prevent it, no fugitive from Slavery shall ever be sent back to suffer in that loathsome den of corruption and cruelty.

## Incidents in the Life of a Slave Girl, Seven Years Concealed

### I
### Childhood

I was born a slave; but I never knew it till six years of happy childhood had passed away. My father was a carpenter, and considered so intelligent and skilful in his trade, that, when buildings out of the common line were to be erected, he was sent for from long distances, to be head workman. On condition of paying his mistress two hundred dollars a year, and supporting himself, he was allowed to work at his trade, and manage his own affairs. His strongest wish was to purchase his children; but, though he several times offered his hard earnings for that purpose, he never succeeded. In complexion my parents were a light shade of brownish yellow, and were termed mulattoes. They lived together in a comfortable home; and, though we were all slaves, I was so fondly shielded that I never dreamed I was a piece of merchandise, trusted to them for safe keeping, and liable to be demanded of them at any moment. I had one brother, William, who was two years younger than myself—a bright, affectionate child. I had also a great treasure in my maternal grandmother, who was a remarkable woman in many respects. She was the daughter of a planter in South Carolina, who, at his death, left her mother and his three children free, with money to go to St. Augustine, where they had relatives. It was during the Revolutionary War; and they were captured on their passage, carried back, and sold to different purchasers. Such was the story my grandmother used to tell me; but I do not remember all the particulars. She was a little girl when she was captured and sold to the keeper of a large hotel. I have often heard her tell how hard she fared during childhood. But as she grew older she evinced so much intelligence, and was so faithful, that her master and mistress could not help seeing it was for their interest to take care of such a valuable piece of property. She became an indispensable personage in the household, officiating in all capacities, from cook and wet nurse to seamstress. She was much praised for her cooking; and her nice crackers became so famous in the neighborhood that many people were desirous of obtaining them. In consequence of numerous requests of this kind, she asked permission of her mistress to bake crackers at night, after all the household work was done; and she obtained leave to do it, provided she would clothe herself and her children from the profits. Upon these terms, after working hard all day for her mistress, she began her midnight bakings, assisted by her two oldest children. The business proved profitable; and each year she laid by a little, which was saved for a fund to purchase her children. Her master died, and the property was divided among his heirs. The widow had her dower in the hotel, which she continued to keep open. My grandmother remained in her service as a slave; but her children were divided among her master's children. As she had five, Benjamin, the youngest one, was sold, in order that each heir might have an equal portion of dollars and cents. There was so little difference in our ages that he seemed more like my brother than my uncle. He was a bright, handsome lad, nearly white; for he inherited the complexion my grandmother had derived from Anglo-Saxon ancestors. Though only ten years old, seven hundred and twenty dollars were paid for him. His sale was a terrible blow to my grandmother; but she was naturally hopeful, and she went to work with renewed energy, trusting in time to be able to purchase some of her children. She had laid up three hundred dollars, which her mistress one day begged as a loan, promising to pay her soon. The reader probably knows that no promise or writing given to a slave is legally binding; for, according to Southern laws, a slave, *being* property, can *hold* no property. When my grandmother lent her hard earnings to her mistress, she trusted solely to her honor. The honor of a slaveholder to a slave!

To this good grandmother I was indebted for many comforts. My brother Willie and I often received portions of the crackers, cakes, and preserves, she made to sell; and after we ceased to be children we were indebted to her for many more important services.

Such were the unusually fortunate circumstances of my early childhood. When I was six years old, my mother died; and then, for the first time, I learned, by the talk around me, that I was a slave. My mother's mistress was the daughter of my grandmother's mistress. She was the foster sister of my mother; they were both nourished at my grandmother's breast. In fact, my mother had been weaned at three months old, that the babe of the mistress might obtain sufficient food. They played together as children; and, when they became women, my mother was a most faithful servant to her whiter foster sister. On her death-bed her mistress promised that her children should never suffer for any thing; and during her lifetime she kept her word. They all spoke kindly of my dead mother, who had been a slave merely in name, but in nature was noble and womanly. I grieved for her, and my young mind was troubled with the thought who would now take care of me and my little brother. I was told that my home was now to be with her mistress; and I found it a happy one. No toilsome or disagreeable duties were imposed upon me. My mistress was so kind to me that I was always glad to do her bidding, and proud to labor for her as much as my young years would permit. I would sit by her side for hours, sewing diligently, with a heart as free from care as that of any freeborn white child. When she thought I was tired, she would send me out to run and jump; and away I bounded, to gather berries or flowers to decorate her room. Those were happy days—too happy to last. The slave child had no thought for the morrow; but there came that blight, which too surely waits on every human being born to be a chattel.

When I was nearly twelve years old, my kind mistress sickened and died. As I saw the cheek grow paler, and the eye more glassy, how earnestly I prayed in my heart that she might live! I loved her; for she had been almost like a mother to me. My prayers were not answered. She died, and they buried her in the little churchyard, where, day after day, my tears fell upon her grave.

I was sent to spend a week with my grandmother. I was now old enough to begin to think of the future; and again and again I asked myself what they would do with me. I felt sure I should never find another mistress so kind as the one who was gone. She had promised my dying mother that her children should never suffer for any thing; and when I remembered that, and recalled her many proofs of attachment to me, I could not help having some hopes that she had left me free. My friends were almost certain it would be so. They thought she would be sure to do it, on account of my mother's love and faithful service. But, alas! we all know that the memory of a faithful slave does not avail much to save her children from the auction block.

After a brief period of suspense, the will of my mistress was read, and we learned that she had bequeathed me to her sister's daughter, a child of five years old. So vanished our hopes. My mistress had taught me the precepts of God's Word: "Thou shalt love thy neighbor as thyself." "Whatsoever ye would that men should do unto you, do ye even so unto them." But I was her slave, and I suppose she did not recognize me as her neighbor. I would give much to blot out from my memory that one great wrong. As a child, I loved my mistress; and, looking back on the happy days I spent with her, I try to think with less bitterness of this act of injustice. While I was with her, she taught me to read and spell; and for this privilege, which so rarely falls to the lot of a slave, I bless her memory.

She possessed but few slaves; and at her death those were all distributed among her relatives. Five of them were my grandmother's children, and had shared the same milk that nourished her mother's children. Notwithstanding my grandmother's long and faithful service to her owners, not one of her children escaped the auction block. These God-breathing machines are no more, in the sight of their masters, than the cotton they plant, or the horses they tend.

## II
### The New Master and Mistress

Dr. Flint, a physician in the neighborhood, had married the sister of my mistress, and I was now the property of their little daughter. It was not without murmuring that I prepared for my new home; and what added to my unhappiness, was the fact that my brother William was purchased by the same family. My father, by his nature, as well as by the habit of transacting business as a skilful mechanic, had more of the feelings of a freeman than is common among slaves. My brother was a spirited boy; and being brought up under such influences, he early detested the name of master and mistress. One day, when his father and his mistress both happened to call him at the same time, he hesitated between the two; being perplexed to know which had the strongest claim upon his obedience. He finally concluded to go to his mistress. When my father reproved him for it, he said, "You both called me, and I didn't know which I ought to go to first."

"You are *my* child," replied our father, "and when I call you, you should come immediately, if you have to pass through fire and water."

Poor Willie! He was now to learn his first lesson of obedience to a master. Grandmother tried to cheer us with hopeful words, and they found an echo in the credulous hearts of youth.

When we entered our new home we encountered cold looks, cold words, and cold treatment. We were glad when the night came. On my narrow bed I moaned and wept, I felt so desolate and alone.

I had been there nearly a year, when a dear little friend of mine was buried. I heard her mother sob, as the clods fell on the coffin of her only child, and I turned away from the grave, feeling thankful that I still had something left to love. I met my grandmother, who said, "Come with me, Linda"; and from her tone I knew that something sad had happened. She led me apart from the people, and then said, "My child, your father is dead." Dead! How could I believe it? He had died so suddenly I had not even heard that he was sick. I went home with my grandmother. My heart rebelled against God, who had taken from me mother, father, mistress, and friend. The good grandmother tried to comfort me. "Who knows the ways of God?" said she. "Perhaps they have been kindly taken from the evil days to come." Years afterwards I often thought of this. She promised to be a mother to her grandchildren, so far as she might be permitted to do so; and strengthened by her love, I returned to my master's. I thought I should be allowed to go to my father's house the next morning; but I was ordered to go for flowers, that my mistress's house might be decorated for an evening party. I spent the day gathering flowers and weaving them into festoons, while the dead body of my father was lying within a mile of me. What cared my owners for that? he was merely a piece of property. Moreover, they thought he had spoiled his children, by teaching them to feel that they were human beings. This was blasphemous doctrine for a slave to teach; presumptuous in him, and dangerous to the masters.

The next day I followed his remains to a humble grave beside that of my dear mother. There were those who knew my father's worth, and respected his memory.

My home now seemed more dreary than ever. The laugh of the little slave-children sounded harsh and cruel. It was selfish to feel so about the joy of others. My brother moved about with a very grave face. I tried to comfort him, by saying, "Take courage, Willie; brighter days will come by and by."

"You don't know any thing about it, Linda," he replied. "We shall have to stay here all our days; we shall never be free."

I argued that we were growing older and stronger, and that perhaps we might, before long, be allowed to hire our own time, and then we could earn money to buy our freedom. William declared this was much easier to say than to do; moreover, he did not intend to *buy* his freedom. We held daily controversies upon this subject.

Little attention was paid to the slaves' meals in Dr. Flint's house. If they could catch a bit of food while it was going, well and good. I gave myself no trouble on that score, for on my various errands I passed my grandmother's house, where there was always something to spare for me. I was frequently threatened with punishment if I stopped there; and my grandmother, to avoid detaining me, often stood at the gate with something for my breakfast or dinner. I was indebted to *her* for all my comforts, spiritual or temporal. It was *her* labor that supplied my scanty wardrobe. I have a vivid recollection of the linsey-woolsey dress given me every winter by Mrs. Flint. How I hated it! It was one of the badges of slavery.

While my grandmother was thus helping to support me from her hard earnings, the three hundred dollars she had lent her mistress was never repaid. When her mistress died, her son-in-law, Dr. Flint, was appointed executor. When grandmother applied to him for payment, he said the estate was insolvent, and the law prohibited payment. It did not, however, prohibit him from retaining the silver candelabra, which had been purchased with that money. I presume they will be handed down in the family, from generation to generation.

My grandmother's mistress had always promised her that, at her death, she should be free; and it was said that in her will she made good the promise. But when the estate was settled, Dr. Flint told the faithful old servant that, under existing circumstances, it was necessary she should be sold.

On the appointed day, the customary advertisement was posted up, proclaiming that there would be a "public sale of negroes, horses, &c." Dr. Flint called to tell my grandmother that he was unwilling to wound her feelings by putting her up at auction, and that he would prefer to dispose of her at private sale. My grandmother saw through his hypocrisy; she understood very well that he was ashamed of the job. She was a very spirited woman, and if he was base enough to sell her, when her mistress intended she should be free, she was determined the public should know it. She had for a long time supplied many families with crackers and preserves; consequently, "Aunt Marthy," as she was called, was generally known, and every body who knew her respected her intelligence and good character. Her long and faithful service in the family was also well known, and the intention of her mistress to leave her free. When the day of sale came, she took her place among the chattels, and at the first call she sprang upon the auction-block. Many voices called out, "Shame! Shame! Who is going to sell *you*, Marthy? Don't stand there! That is no place for *you*." Without saying a word she quietly awaited her fate. No one bid for her. At last, a feeble voice, said, "Fifty dollars." It came from a maiden lady, seventy years old, the sister of my grandmother's deceased mistress. She had lived forty years under the same roof with my grandmother; she knew how faithfully she had served her owners, and how cruelly she had been defrauded of her rights; and she resolved to protect her. The auctioneer waited for a higher bid; but her wishes were respected; no one bid above her. She could neither read nor write; and when the bill of sale was made out, she signed it with a cross. But what consequence was that, when she had a big heart overflowing with human kindness? She gave the old servant her freedom.

At that time, my grandmother was just fifty years old. Laborious years had passed since then; and now my brother and I were slaves to the man who had defrauded her of her money, and tried to defraud her of her freedom. One of my mother's sisters, called Aunt Nancy, was also a slave in his family. She was a kind, good aunt to me; and supplied the place of both housekeeper and waiting maid to her mistress. She was, in fact, at the beginning and end of every thing.

Mrs. Flint, like many southern women, was totally deficient in energy. She had not strength to superintend her household affairs; but her nerves were so strong, that she could sit in her easy chair and see a woman whipped, till the blood trickled from every stroke of the lash. She was a member of the church; but partaking of the Lord's supper did not seem to put her in a Christian frame of mind. If dinner was not served at the exact time on that particular Sunday, she would station herself in the kitchen, and wait till it was dished, and then spit in all the kettles and pans that had been used for cooking. She did this to prevent the cook and her children from eking out their meagre fare with the remains of the gravy and other scrapings. The slaves could get nothing to eat except what she chose to give them. Provisions were weighed out by the pound and ounce, three times a day. I can assure you she gave them no chance to eat wheat bread from her flour barrel. She knew how many biscuits a quart of flour would make, and exactly what size they ought to be.

Dr. Flint was an epicure. The cook never sent a dinner to his table without fear and trembling; for if there happened to be a dish not to his liking, he would either order her to be whipped, or compel her to eat every mouthful of it in his presence. The poor, hungry creature might not have objected to eating it; but she did object to having her master cram it down her throat till she choked.

They had a pet dog, that was a nuisance in the house. The cook was ordered to make some Indian mush for him. He refused to eat, and when his head was held over it, the froth flowed from his mouth into the basin. He died a few minutes after. When Dr. Flint came in, he said the mush had not been well cooked, and that was the reason the animal would not eat it. He sent for the cook, and compelled her to eat it. He thought that the woman's stomach was stronger than the dog's; but her sufferings afterwards proved that he was mistaken. This poor woman endured many cruelties from her master and mistress; sometimes she was locked up, away from her nursing baby, for a whole day and night.

When I had been in the family a few weeks, one of the plantation slaves was brought to town, by order of his master. It was near night when he arrived, and Dr. Flint ordered him to be taken to the work house, and tied up to the joist, so that his feet would just escape the ground. In that situation he was to wait till the doctor had taken his tea. I shall never forget that night. Never before, in my life, had I heard hundreds of blows fall, in succession, on a human being. His piteous groans, and his "O, pray don't, massa," rang in my ear for months afterwards. There were many conjectures as to the cause of this terrible punishment. Some said master accused him of stealing corn; others said the slave had quarrelled with his wife, in presence of the overseer, and had accused his master of being the father of her child. They were both black, and the child was very fair.

I went into the work house next morning, and saw the cowhide still wet with blood, and the boards all covered with gore. The poor man lived, and continued to quarrel with his wife. A few months afterwards Dr. Flint handed them both over to a slave-trader. The guilty man put their value into his pocket, and had the satisfaction of knowing that they were out of sight and hearing. When the mother was delivered into the trader's hands, she said, "You *promised* to treat me well." To which he replied, "You have let your tongue run too far; damn you!" She had forgotten that it was a crime for a slave to tell who was the father of her child.

From others than the master persecution also comes in such cases. I once saw a young slave girl dying soon after the birth of a child nearly white. In her agony she cried out, "O Lord, come and take me!" Her mistress stood by, and mocked at her like an incarnate fiend. "You suffer, do you?" she exclaimed. "I am glad of it. You deserve it all, and more too."

The girl's mother said, "The baby is dead, thank God; and I hope my poor child will soon be in heaven, too."

"Heaven!" retorted the mistress. "There is no such place for the like of her and her bastard."

The poor mother turned away, sobbing. Her dying daughter called her, feebly, and as she bent over her, I heard her say, "Don't grieve so, mother; God knows all about it; and HE will have mercy upon me."

Her sufferings, afterwards, became so intense, that her mistress felt unable to stay; but when she left the room, the scornful smile was still on her lips. Seven children called her mother. The poor black woman had but the one child, whose eyes she saw closing in death, while she thanked God for taking her away from the greater bitterness of life.

### III
### The Slaves' New Year's Day

Dr. Flint owned a fine residence in town, several farms, and about fifty slaves, besides hiring a number by the year.

Hiring-day at the south takes place on the 1st of January. On the 2d, the slaves are expected to go to their new masters. On a farm, they work until the corn and cotton are laid. They then have two holidays. Some masters give them a good dinner under the trees. This over, they work until Christmas eve. If no heavy charges are meantime brought against them, they are given four or five holidays, whichever the master or overseer may think proper. Then comes New Year's eve; and they gather together their little alls, or more properly speaking, their little nothings, and wait anxiously for the dawning of day. At the appointed hour the grounds are thronged with men, women, and children, waiting, like criminals, to hear their doom pronounced. The slave is sure to know who is the most humane, or cruel master, within forty miles of him.

It is easy to find out, on that day, who clothes and feeds his slaves well; for he is surrounded by a crowd, begging, "Please, massa, hire me this year. I will work *very* hard, massa."

If a slave is unwilling to go with his new master, he is whipped, or locked up in jail, until he consents to go, and promises not to run away during the year. Should he chance to change his mind, thinking it justifiable to violate an extorted promise, woe unto him if he is caught! The whip is used till the blood flows at his feet; and his stiffened limbs are put in chains, to be dragged in the field for days and days!

If he lives until the next year, perhaps the same man will hire him again, without even giving him an opportunity of going to the hiring-ground. After those for hire are disposed of, those for sale are called up.

O, you happy free women, contrast *your* New Year's day with that of the poor bond-woman! With you it is a pleasant season, and the light of the day is blessed. Friendly wishes meet you every where, and gifts are showered upon you. Even hearts that have been estranged from you soften at this season, and lips that have been silent echo back, "I wish you a happy New Year." Children bring their little offerings, and raise their rosy lips for a caress. They are your own, and no hand but that of death can take them from you.

But to the slave mother New Year's day comes laden with peculiar sorrows. She sits on her cold cabin floor, watching the children who may all be torn from her the next morning; and often does she wish that she and they might die before the day dawns. She may be an ignorant creature, degraded by the system that has brutalized her from childhood; but she has a mother's instincts, and is capable of feeling a mother's agonies.

On one of these sale days, I saw a mother lead seven children to the auction-block. She knew that *some* of them would be taken from her; but they took *all*. The children were sold to a slave-trader, and their mother was bought by a man in her own town. Before night her children were all far away. She begged the trader to tell her where he intended to take them; this he refused to do. How *could* he, when he knew he would sell them, one by one, wherever he could command the highest price? I met that mother in the street, and her wild, haggard face lives to-day in my mind. She wrung her hands in anguish, and exclaimed, "Gone! All gone! Why *don't* God kill me?" I had no words wherewith to comfort her. Instances of this kind are of daily, yea, of hourly occurrence.

Slaveholders have a method, peculiar to their institution, of getting rid of *old* slaves, whose lives have been worn out in their service. I knew an old woman, who for seventy years faithfully served her master. She had become almost helpless, from hard labor and disease. Her owners moved to Alabama, and the old black woman was left to be sold to any body who would give twenty dollars for her.

## IV
## The Slave Who Dared to Feel Like a Man

Two years had passed since I entered Dr. Flint's family, and those years had brought much of the knowledge that comes from experience, though they had afforded little opportunity for any other kinds of knowledge.

My grandmother had, as much as possible, been a mother to her orphan grandchildren. By perseverance and unwearied industry, she was now mistress of a snug little home, surrounded with the necessaries of life. She would have been happy could her children have shared them with her. There remained but three children and two grandchildren, all slaves. Most earnestly did she strive to make us feel that it was the will of God: that He had seen fit to place us under such circumstances; and though it seemed hard, we ought to pray for contentment.

It was a beautiful faith, coming from a mother who could not call her children her own. But I, and Benjamin, her youngest boy, condemned it. We reasoned that it was much more the will of God that we should be situated as she was. We longed for a home like hers. There we always found sweet balsam for our troubles. She was so loving, so sympathizing! She always met us with a smile, and listened with patience to all our sorrows. She spoke so hopefully, that unconsciously the clouds gave place to sunshine. There was a grand big oven there, too, that baked bread and nice things for the town, and we knew there was always a choice bit in store for us.

But, alas! even the charms of the old oven failed to reconcile us to our hard lot. Benjamin was now a tall, handsome lad, strongly and gracefully made, and with a spirit too bold and daring for a slave. My brother William, now twelve years old, had the same aversion to the word master that he had when he was an urchin of seven years. I was his confidant. He came to me with all his troubles. I remember one instance in particular. It was on a lovely spring morning, and when I marked the sunlight dancing here and there, its beauty seemed to mock my sadness. For my master, whose restless, craving, vicious nature roved about day and night, seeking whom to devour, had just left me, with stinging, scorching words; words that scathed ear and brain like fire. O, how I despised him! I thought how glad I should be, if some day when he walked the earth, it would open and swallow him up, and disencumber the world of a plague.

When he told me that I was made for his use, made to obey his command in *every* thing; that I was nothing but a slave, whose will must and should surrender to his, never before had my puny arm felt half so strong.

So deeply was I absorbed in painful reflections afterwards, that I neither saw nor heard the entrance of any one, till the voice of William sounded close beside me. "Linda," said he, "what makes you look so sad? I love you. O, Linda, isn't this a bad world? Every body seems so cross and unhappy. I wish I had died when poor father did."

I told him that every body was *not* cross, or unhappy; that those who had pleasant homes, and kind friends, and who were not afraid to love them, were happy. But we, who were slave-children, without father or mother, could not expect to be happy. We must be good; perhaps that would bring us contentment.

"Yes," he said, "I try to be good; but what's the use? They are all the time troubling me." Then he proceeded to relate his afternoon's difficulty with young master Nicholas. It seemed that the brother of master Nicholas had pleased himself with making up stories about William. Master Nicholas said he should be flogged, and he would do it. Whereupon he went to work; but William fought bravely, and the young master, finding he was getting the better of him, undertook to tie his hands behind him. He failed in that likewise. By dint of kicking and fisting, William came out of the skirmish none the worse for a few scratches.

He continued to discourse on his young master's *meanness;* how he whipped the *little* boys, but was a perfect coward when a tussle ensued between him and white boys of his own size. On such occasions he always took to his legs. William had other charges to make against him. One was his rubbing up pennies with quicksilver, and passing them off for quarters of a dollar on an old man who kept a fruit stall. William was often sent to buy fruit, and he earnestly inquired of me what he ought to do under such circumstances. I told him it was certainly wrong to deceive the old man, and that it was his duty to tell him of the impositions practised by his young master. I assured him the old man would not be slow to comprehend the whole, and there the matter would end. William thought it might with the old man, but not with *him.* He said he did not mind the smart of the whip, but he did not like the *idea* of being whipped.

While I advised him to be good and forgiving I was not unconscious of the beam in my own eye. It was the very knowledge of my own shortcomings that urged me to retain, if possible, some sparks of my brother's God-given nature. I had not lived fourteen years in slavery for nothing. I had felt, seen, and heard enough, to read the characters, and question the motives, of those around me. The war of my life had begun; and though one of God's most powerless creatures, I resolved never to be conquered. Alas, for me!

If there was one pure, sunny spot for me, I believed it to be in Benjamin's heart, and in another's, whom I loved with all the ardor of a girl's first love. My owner knew of it, and sought in every way to render me miserable. He did not resort to corporal punishment, but to all the petty, tyrannical ways that human ingenuity could devise.

I remember the first time I was punished. It was in the month of February. My grandmother had taken my old shoes, and replaced them with a new pair. I needed them; for several inches of snow had fallen, and it still continued to fall. When I walked through Mrs. Flint's room, their creaking grated harshly on her refined nerves. She called me to her, and asked what I had about me that made such a horrid noise. I told her it was my new shoes. "Take them off," said she; "and if you put them on again, I'll throw them into the fire."

I took them off, and my stockings also. She then sent me a long distance, on an errand. As I went through the snow, my bare feet tingled. That night I was very hoarse; and I went to bed thinking the next day would find me sick, perhaps dead. What was my grief on waking to find myself quite well!

I had imagined if I died, or was laid up for some time, that my mistress would feel a twinge of remorse that she had so hated "the little imp," as she styled me. It was my ignorance of that mistress that gave rise to such extravagant imaginings.

Dr. Flint occasionally had high prices offered for me; but he always said, "She don't belong to me. She is my daughter's property, and I have no right to sell her." Good, honest man! My young mistress was still a child, and I could look for no protection from her. I loved her, and she returned my affection. I once heard her father allude to her attachment to me; and his wife promptly replied that it proceeded from fear. This put unpleasant doubts into my mind. Did the child feign what she did not feel? or was her mother jealous of the mite of love she bestowed on me? I concluded it must be the latter. I said to myself, "Surely, little children are true."

One afternoon I sat at my sewing, feeling unusual depression of spirits. My mistress had been accusing me of an offence, of which I assured her I was perfectly innocent; but I saw, by the contemptuous curl of her lip, that she believed I was telling a lie.

I wondered for what wise purpose God was leading me through such thorny paths, and whether still darker days were in store for me. As I sat musing thus, the door opened softly, and William came in. "Well, brother," said I, "what is the matter this time?"

"O Linda, Ben and his master have had a dreadful time!" said he.

My first thought was that Benjamin was killed. "Don't be frightened, Linda," said William; "I will tell you all about it."

It appeared that Benjamin's master had sent for him, and he did not immediately obey the summons. When he did, his master was angry, and began to whip him. He resisted. Master and slave fought, and finally the master was thrown. Benjamin had cause to tremble; for he had thrown to the ground his master—one of the richest men in town. I anxiously awaited the result.

That night I stole to my grandmother's house, and Benjamin also stole thither from his master's. My grandmother had gone to spend a day or two with an old friend living in the country.

"I have come," said Benjamin, "to tell you good by. I am going away."

I inquired where.

"To the north," he replied.

I looked at him to see whether he was in earnest. I saw it all in his firm, set mouth. I implored him not to go, but he paid no heed to my words. He said he was no longer a boy, and every day made his yoke more galling. He had raised his hand against his master, and was to be publicly whipped for the offence. I reminded him of the poverty and hardships he must encounter among strangers. I told him he might be caught and brought back; and that was terrible to think of.

He grew vexed, and asked if poverty and hardships with freedom, were not preferable to our treatment in slavery. "Linda," he continued, "we are dogs here; foot-balls, cattle, every thing that's mean. No, I will not stay. Let them bring me back. We don't die but once."

He was right; but it was hard to give him up. "Go," said I, "and break your mother's heart."

I repented of my words ere they were out.

"Linda," said he, speaking as I had not heard him speak that evening, "how *could* you say that? Poor mother! be kind to her, Linda; and you, too, cousin Fanny."

Cousin Fanny was a friend who had lived some years with us.

Farewells were exchanged, and the bright, kind boy, endeared to us by so many acts of love, vanished from our sight.

It is not necessary to state how he made his escape. Suffice it to say, he was on his way to New York when a violent storm overtook the vessel. The captain said he must put into the nearest port. This alarmed Benjamin, who was aware that he would be advertised in every port near his own town. His embarrassment was noticed by the captain. To port they went.

There the advertisement met the captain's eye. Benjamin so exactly answered its description, that the captain laid hold on him, and bound him in chains. The storm passed, and they proceeded to New York. Before reaching that port Benjamin managed to get off his chains and throw them overboard. He escaped from the vessel, but was pursued, captured, and carried back to his master.

When my grandmother returned home and found her youngest child had fled, great was her sorrow; but, with characteristic piety, she said, "God's will be done." Each morning, she inquired if any news had been heard from her boy. Yes, news *was* heard. The master was rejoicing over a letter, announcing the capture of his human chattel.

That day seems but as yesterday, so well do I remember it. I saw him led through the streets in chains, to jail. His face was ghastly pale, yet full of determination. He had begged one of the sailors to go to his mother's house and ask her not to meet him. He said the sight of her distress would take from him all self-control. She yearned to see him, and she went; but she screened herself in the crowd, that it might be as her child had said.

We were not allowed to visit him; but we had known the jailer for years, and he was a kind-hearted man. At midnight he opened the jail door for my grandmother and myself to enter, in disguise. When we entered the cell not a sound broke the stillness. "Benjamin, Benjamin!" whispered my grandmother. No answer. "Benjamin!" she again faltered. There was a jingle of chains. The moon had just risen, and cast an uncertain light through the bars of the window. We knelt down and took Benjamin's cold hands in ours. We did not speak. Sobs were heard, and Benjamin's lips were unsealed; for his mother was weeping on his neck. How vividly does memory bring back that sad night! Mother and son talked together. He asked her pardon for the suffering he had caused her. She said she had nothing to forgive; she could not blame his desire for freedom. He told her that when he was captured, he broke away, and was about casting himself into the river, when thoughts of *her* came over him, and he desisted. She asked if he did not also think of God. I fancied I saw his face grow fierce in the moonlight. He answered, "No, I did not think of him. When a man is hunted like a wild beast he forgets there is a God, a heaven. He forgets every thing in his struggle to get beyond the reach of the bloodhounds."

"Don't talk so, Benjamin," said she. "Put your trust in God. Be humble, my child, and your master will forgive you."

"Forgive me for *what,* mother? For not letting him treat me like a dog? No! I will never humble myself to him. I have worked for him for nothing all my life, and I am repaid with stripes and imprisonment. Here I will stay till I die, or till he sells me."

The poor mother shuddered at his words. I think he felt it; for when he next spoke, his voice was calmer. "Don't fret about me, mother. I ain't worth it," said he. "I wish I had some of your goodness. You bear every thing patiently, just as though you thought it was all right. I wish I could."

She told him she had not always been so; once, she was like him; but when sore troubles came upon her, and she had no arm to lean upon, she learned to call on God, and he lightened her burdens. She besought him to do likewise.

We overstaid our time, and were obliged to hurry from the jail.

Benjamin had been imprisoned three weeks, when my grandmother went to intercede for him with his master. He was immovable. He said Benjamin should serve as an example to the rest of his slaves; he should be kept in jail till he was subdued, or be sold if he got but one dollar for him. However, he afterwards relented in some degree. The chains were taken off, and we were allowed to visit him.

As his food was of the coarsest kind, we carried him as often as possible a warm supper, accompanied with some little luxury for the jailer.

Three months elapsed, and there was no prospect of release or of a purchaser. One day he was heard to sing and laugh. This piece of indecorum was told to his master, and the overseer was ordered to re-chain him. He was now confined in an apartment with other prisoners, who were covered with filthy rags. Benjamin was chained near them, and was soon covered with vermin. He worked at his chains till he succeeded in getting out of them. He passed them through the bars of the window, with a request that they should be taken to his master, and he should be informed that he was covered with vermin.

This audacity was punished with heavier chains, and prohibition of our visits.

My grandmother continued to send him fresh changes of clothes. The old ones were burned up. The last night we saw him in jail his mother still begged him to send for his master, and beg his pardon. Neither persuasion nor argument could turn him from his purpose. He calmly answered, "I am waiting his time."

Those chains were mournful to hear.

Another three months passed, and Benjamin left his prison walls. We that loved him waited to bid him a long and last farewell. A slave-trader had bought him. You remember, I told you what price he brought when ten years of age. Now he was more than twenty years old, and sold for three hundred dollars. The master had been blind to his own interest. Long confinement had made his face too pale, his form too thin; moreover, the trader had heard something of his character, and it did not strike him as suitable for a slave. He said he would give any price if the handsome lad was a girl. We thanked God that he was not.

Could you have seen that mother clinging to her child, when they fastened the irons upon his wrists; could you have heard her heart-rending groans, and seen her bloodshot eyes wander wildly from face to face, vainly pleading for mercy; could you have witnessed that scene as I saw it, you would exclaim, *Slavery is damnable!*

Benjamin, her youngest, her pet, was forever gone! She could not realize it. She had had an interview with the trader for the purpose of ascertaining if Benjamin could be purchased. She was told it was impossible, as he had given bonds not to sell him till he was out of the state. He promised that he would not sell him till he reached New Orleans.

With a strong arm and unvaried trust, my grandmother began her work of love. Benjamin must be free. If she succeeded, she knew they would still be separated; but the sacrifice was not too great. Day and night she labored. The trader's price would treble that he gave; but she was not discouraged.

She employed a lawyer to write to a gentleman, whom she knew, in New Orleans. She begged him to interest himself for Benjamin, and he willingly favored her request. When he saw Benjamin, and stated his business, he thanked him; but said he preferred to wait a while before making the trader an offer. He knew he had tried to obtain a high price for him, and had invariably failed. This encouraged him to make another effort for freedom. So one morning, long before day, Benjamin was missing. He was riding over the blue billows, bound for Baltimore.

For once his white face did him a kindly service. They had no suspicion that it belonged to a slave; otherwise, the law would have been followed out to the letter, and the *thing* rendered back to slavery. The brightest skies are often overshadowed by the darkest clouds. Benjamin was taken sick, and compelled to remain in Baltimore three weeks. His strength was slow in returning; and his desire to continue his journey seemed to retard his recovery. How could he get strength without air and exercise? He resolved to venture on a short walk. A by-street was selected, where he thought himself secure of not being met by any one that knew him; but a voice called out, "Halloo, Ben, my boy! what are you doing *here*?"

His first impulse was to run; but his legs trembled so that he could not stir. He turned to confront his antagonist, and behold, there stood his old master's next door neighbor! He thought it was all over with him now; but it proved otherwise. That man was a miracle. He possessed a goodly number of slaves, and yet was not quite deaf to that mystic clock, whose ticking is rarely heard in the slaveholder's breast.

"Ben, you are sick," said he. "Why, you look like a ghost. I guess I gave you something of a start. Never mind, Ben, I am not going to touch you. You had a pretty tough time of it, and you may go on your way rejoicing for all men. But I would advise you to get out of this place plaguy quick, for there are several gentlemen here from our town." He described the nearest and safest route to New York, and added, "I shall be glad to tell your mother I have seen you. Good by, Ben."

Benjamin turned away, filled with gratitude, and surprised that the town he hated contained such a gem—a gem worthy of a purer setting.

This gentleman was a Northerner by birth, and had married a southern lady. On his return, he told my grandmother that he had seen her son, and of the service he had rendered him.

Benjamin reached New York safely, and concluded to stop there until he had gained strength enough to proceed further. It happened that my grandmother's only remaining son had sailed for the same city on business for his mistress. Through God's providence, the brothers met. You may be sure it was a happy meeting. "O Phil," exclaimed Benjamin, "I am here at last." Then he told him how near he came to dying, almost in sight of free land, and how he prayed that he might live to get one breath of free air. He said life was worth something now, and it would be hard to die. In the old jail he had not valued it; once, he was tempted to destroy it; but something, he did not know what, had prevented him; perhaps it was fear. He had heard those who profess to be religious declare there was no heaven for self-murderers; and as his life had been pretty hot here, he did not desire a continuation of the same in another world. "If I die now," he exclaimed, "thank God, I shall die a freeman!"

He begged my uncle Phillip not to return south; but stay and work with him, till they earned enough to buy those at home. His brother told him it would kill their mother if he deserted her in her trouble. She had pledged her house, and with difficulty had raised money to buy him. Would he be bought?

"No, never!" he replied. "Do you suppose, Phil, when I have got so far out of their clutches, I will give them one red cent? No! And do you suppose I would turn mother out of her home in her old age? That I would let her pay all those hard-earned dollars for me, and never to see me? For you know she will stay south as long as her other children are slaves. What a good mother! Tell her to buy *you*, Phil. You have been a comfort to her, and I have been a trouble. And Linda, poor Linda; what'll become of her? Phil, you don't know what a life they lead her. She has told me something about it, and I wish old Flint was dead, or a better man. When I was in jail, he asked her if she didn't want *him* to ask my master to forgive me, and take me home again. She told him, No; that I didn't want to go back. He got mad, and said we were all alike. I never despised my own master half as much as I do that man. There is many a worse slaveholder than my master; but for all that I would not be his slave."

While Benjamin was sick, he had parted with nearly all his clothes to pay necessary expenses. But he did not part with a little pin I fastened in his bosom when we parted. It was the most valuable thing I owned, and I thought none more worthy to wear it. He had it still.

His brother furnished him with clothes, and gave him what money he had.

They parted with moistened eyes; and as Benjamin turned away, he said, "Phil, I part with all my kindred." And so it proved. We never heard from him again.

Uncle Phillip came home; and the first words he uttered when he entered the house were, "Mother, Ben is free! I have seen him in New York." She stood looking at him with a bewildered air. "Mother, don't you believe it?" he said, laying his hand softly upon her shoulder. She raised her hands, and exclaimed, "God be praised! Let us thank him." She dropped on her knees, and poured forth her heart in prayer. Then Phillip must sit down and repeat to her every word Benjamin had said. He told her all; only he forbore to mention how sick and pale her darling looked. Why should he distress her when she could do him no good?

The brave old woman still toiled on, hoping to rescue some of her other children. After a while she succeeded in buying Phillip. She paid eight hundred dollars, and came home with the precious document that secured his freedom. The happy mother and son sat together by the old hearthstone that night, telling how proud they were of each other, and how they would prove to the world that they could take care of themselves, as they had long taken care of others. We all concluded by saying, "He that is *willing* to be a slave, let him be a slave."

## V
## The Trials of Girlhood

During the first years of my service in Dr. Flint's family, I was accustomed to share some indulgences with the children of my mistress. Though this seemed to me no more than right, I was grateful for it, and tried to merit the kindness by the faithful discharge of my duties. But I now entered on my fifteenth year—a sad epoch in the life of a slave girl. My master began to whisper foul words in my ear. Young as I was, I could not remain ignorant of their import. I tried to treat them with indifference or contempt. The master's age, my extreme youth, and the fear that his conduct would be reported to my grandmother, made me bear this treatment for many months. He was a crafty man, and resorted to many means to accomplish his purposes. Sometimes he had stormy, terrific ways, that made his victims tremble; sometimes he assumed a gentleness that he thought must surely subdue. Of the two, I preferred his stormy moods, although they left me trembling. He tried his utmost to corrupt the pure principles my grandmother had instilled. He peopled my young mind with unclean images, such as only a vile monster could think of. I turned from him with disgust and hatred. But he was my master. I was compelled to live under the same roof with him—where I saw a man forty years my senior daily violating the most sacred commandments of nature. He told me I was his property; that I must be subject to his will in all things. My soul revolted against the mean tyranny. But where could I turn for protection? No matter whether the slave girl be as black as ebony or as fair as her mistress. In either case, there is no shadow of law to protect her from insult, from violence, or even from death; all these are inflicted by fiends who bear the shape of men. The mistress, who ought to protect the helpless victim, has no other feelings towards her but those of jealousy and rage. The degradation, the wrongs, the vices, that grow out of slavery, are more than I can describe. They are greater than you would willingly believe. Surely, if you credited one half the truths that are told you concerning the helpless millions suffering in this cruel bondage, you at the north would not help to tighten the yoke. You surely would refuse to do for the master, on your own soil, the mean and cruel work which trained bloodhounds and the lowest class of whites do for him at the south.

Every where the years bring to all enough of sin and sorrow; but in slavery the very dawn of life is darkened by these shadows. Even the little child, who is accustomed to wait on her mistress and her children, will learn, before she is twelve years old, why it is that her mistress hates such and such a one among the slaves. Perhaps the child's own mother is among those hated ones. She listens to violent outbreaks of jealous passion, and cannot help understanding what is the cause. She will become prematurely knowing in evil things. Soon she will learn to tremble when she hears her master's footfall. She will be compelled to realize that she is no longer a child. If God has bestowed beauty upon her, it will prove her greatest curse. That which commands admiration in the white woman only hastens the degradation of the female slave. I know that some are too much brutalized by slavery to feel the humiliation of their position; but many slaves feel it most acutely, and shrink from the memory of it. I cannot tell how much I suffered in the presence of these wrongs, nor how I am still pained by the retrospect. My master met me at every turn, reminding me that I belonged to him, and swearing by heaven and earth that he would compel me to submit to him. If I went out for a breath of fresh air, after a day of unwearied toil, his footsteps dogged me. If I knelt by my mother's grave, his dark shadow fell on me even there. The light heart which nature had given me became heavy with sad forebodings. The other slaves in my master's house noticed the change. Many of them pitied me; but none dared to ask the cause. They had no need to inquire. They knew too well the guilty practices under that roof; and they were aware that to speak of them was an offence that never went unpunished.

I longed for some one to confide in. I would have given the world to have laid my head on my grandmother's faithful bosom, and told her all my troubles. But Dr. Flint swore he would kill me, if I was not as silent as the grave. Then, although my grandmother was all in all to me, I feared her as well as loved her. I had been accustomed to look up to her with a respect bordering upon awe. I was very young, and felt shamefaced about telling her such impure things, especially as I knew her to be very strict on such subjects. Moreover, she was a woman of a high spirit. She was usually very quiet in her demeanor; but if her indignation was once roused, it was not very easily quelled. I had been told that she once chased a white gentleman with a loaded pistol, because he insulted one of her daughters. I dreaded the consequences of a violent outbreak; and both pride and fear kept me silent. But though I did not confide in my grandmother, and even evaded her vigilant watchfulness and inquiry, her presence in the neighborhood was some protection to me. Though she had been a slave, Dr. Flint was afraid of her. He dreaded her scorching rebukes. Moreover, she was known and patronized by many people; and he did not wish to have his villany made public. It was lucky for me that I did not live on a distant plantation, but in a town not so large that the inhabitants were ignorant of each other's affairs. Bad as are the laws and customs in a slaveholding community, the doctor, as a professional man, deemed it prudent to keep up some outward show of decency.

O, what days and nights of fear and sorrow that man caused me! Reader, it is not to awaken sympathy for myself that I am telling you truthfully what I suffered in slavery. I do it to kindle a flame of compassion in your hearts for my sisters who are still in bondage, suffering as I once suffered.

I once saw two beautiful children playing together. One was a fair white child; the other was her slave, and also her sister. When I saw them embracing each other, and heard their joyous laughter, I turned sadly away from the lovely sight. I foresaw the inevitable blight that would fall on the little slave's heart. I knew how soon her laughter would be changed to sighs. The fair child grew up to be a still fairer woman. From childhood to womanhood her pathway was blooming with flowers, and overarched by a sunny sky. Scarcely one day of her life had been clouded when the sun rose on her happy bridal morning.

How had those years dealt with her slave sister, the little playmate of her childhood? She, also, was very beautiful; but the flowers and sunshine of love were not for her. She drank the cup of sin, and shame, and misery, whereof her persecuted race are compelled to drink.

In view of these things, why are ye silent, ye free men and women of the north? Why do your tongues falter in maintenance of the right? Would that I had more ability! But my heart is so full, and my pen is so weak! There are noble men and women who plead for us, striving to help those who cannot help themselves. God bless them! God give them strength and courage to go on! God bless those, every where, who are laboring to advance the cause of humanity!

# VI
## The Jealous Mistress

I would ten thousand times rather that my children should be the half-starved paupers of Ireland than to be the most pampered among the slaves of America. I would rather drudge out my life on a cotton plantation, till the grave opened to give me rest, than to live with an unprincipled master and a jealous mistress. The felon's home in a penitentiary is preferable. He may repent, and turn from the error of his ways, and so find peace; but it is not so with a favorite slave. She is not allowed to have any pride of character. It is deemed a crime in her to wish to be virtuous.

Mrs. Flint possessed the key to her husband's character before I was born. She might have used this knowledge to counsel and to screen the young and the innocent among her slaves; but for them she had no sympathy. They were the objects of her constant suspicion and malevolence. She watched her husband with unceasing vigilance; but he was well practised in means to evade it. What he could not find opportunity to say in words he manifested in signs. He invented more than were ever thought of in a deaf and dumb asylum. I let them pass, as if I did not understand what he meant; and many were the curses and threats bestowed on me for my stupidity. One day he caught me teaching myself to write. He frowned, as if he was not well pleased; but I suppose he came to the conclusion that such an accomplishment might help to advance his favorite scheme. Before long, notes were often slipped into my hand. I would return them, saying, "I can't read them, sir." "Can't you?" he replied; "then I must read them to you." He always finished the reading by asking, "Do you understand?" Sometimes he would complain of the heat of the tea room, and order his supper to be placed on a small table in the piazza. He would seat himself there with a well-satisfied smile, and tell me to stand by and brush aways the flies. He would eat very slowly, pausing between the mouthfuls. These intervals were employed in describing the happiness I was so foolishly throwing away, and in threatening me with the penalty that finally awaited my stubborn disobedience. He boasted much of the forbearance he had exercised towards me, and reminded me that there was a limit to his patience. When I succeeded in avoiding opportunities for him to talk to me at home, I was ordered to come to his office, to do some errand. When there, I was obliged to stand and listen to such language as he saw fit to address to me. Sometimes I so openly expressed my contempt for him that he would become violently enraged, and I wondered why he did not strike me. Circumstanced as he was, he probably thought it was better policy to be forbearing. But the state of things grew worse and worse daily. In desperation I told him that I must and would apply to my grandmother for protection. He threatened me with death, and worse than death, if I made any complaint to her. Strange to say, I did not despair. I was naturally of a buoyant disposition, and always I had a hope of somehow getting out of his clutches. Like many a poor, simple slave before me, I trusted that some threads of joy would yet be woven into my dark destiny.

I had entered my sixteenth year, and every day it became more apparent that my presence was intolerable to Mrs. Flint. Angry words frequently passed between her and her husband. He had never punished me himself, and he would not allow any body else to punish me. In that respect, she was never satisfied; but, in her angry moods, no terms were too vile for her to bestow upon me. Yet I, whom she detested so bitterly, had far more pity for her than he had, whose duty it was to make her life happy. I never wronged her, or wished to wrong her; and one word of kindness from her would have brought me to her feet.

After repeated quarrels between the doctor and his wife, he announced his intention to take his youngest daughter, then four years old, to sleep in his apartment. It was necessary that a servant should sleep in the same room, to be on hand if the child stirred. I was selected for that office, and informed for what purpose that arrangement had been made. By managing to keep within sight of people, as much as possible, during the day time, I had hitherto succeeded in eluding my master, though a [razor] was often held to my throat to force me to change this line of policy. At night I slept by the side of my great aunt, where I felt safe. He was too prudent to come into her room. She was an old woman, and had been in the family many years. Moreover, as a married man, and a professional man, he deemed it necessary to save appearances in some degree. But he resolved to remove the obstacle in the way of his scheme; and he thought he had planned it so that he should evade suspicion. He was well aware how much I prized my refuge by the side of my old aunt, and he determined to dispossess me of it. The first night the doctor had the little child in his room alone. The next morning, I was ordered to take my station as nurse the following night. A kind Providence interposed in my favor. During the day Mrs. Flint heard of this new arrangement, and a storm followed. I rejoiced to hear it rage.

After a while my mistress sent for me to come to her room. Her first question was, "Did you know you were to sleep in the doctor's room?"

"Yes, ma'am."

"Who told you?"

"My master."

"Will you answer truly all the questions I ask?"

"Yes, ma'am."

"Tell me, then, as you hope to be forgiven, are you innocent of what I have accused you?"

"I am."

She handed me a Bible, and said, "Lay your hand on your heart, kiss this holy book, and swear before God that you tell me the truth."

I took the oath she required, and I did it with a clear conscience.

"You have taken God's holy word to testify your innocence," said she. "If you have deceived me, beware! Now take this stool, sit down, look me directly in the face, and tell me all that has passed between your master and you."

I did as she ordered. As I went on with my account her color changed frequently, she wept, and sometimes groaned. She spoke in tones so sad, that I was touched by her grief. The tears came to my eyes; but I was soon convinced that her emotions arose from anger and wounded pride. She felt that her marriage vows were desecrated, her dignity insulted; but she had no compassion for the poor victim of her husband's perfidy. She pitied herself as a martyr; but she was incapable of feeling for the condition of shame and misery in which her unfortunate, helpless slave was placed.

Yet perhaps she had some touch of feeling for me; for when the conference was ended, she spoke kindly, and promised to protect me. I should have been much comforted by this assurance if I could have had confidence in it; but my experiences in slavery had filled me with distrust. She was not a very refined woman, and had not much control over her passions. I was an object of her jealousy, and, consequently, of her hatred; and I knew I could not expect kindness or confidence from her under the circumstances in which I was placed. I could not blame her. Slaveholders' wives feel as other women would under similar circumstances. The fire of her temper kindled from small sparks, and now the flame became so intense that the doctor was obliged to give up his intended arrangement.

I knew I had ignited the torch, and I expected to suffer for it afterwards; but I felt too thankful to my mistress for the timely aid she rendered me to care much about that. She now took me to sleep in a room adjoining her own. There I was an object of her especial care, though not of her especial comfort, for she spent many a sleepless night to watch over me. Sometimes I woke up, and found her bending over me. At other times she whispered in my ear, as though it was her husband who was speaking to me, and listened to hear what I would answer. If she startled me, on such occasions, she would glide stealthily away; and the next morning she would tell me I had been talking in my sleep, and ask who I was talking to. At last, I began to be fearful for my life. It had been often threatened; and you can imagine, better than I can describe, what an unpleasant sensation it must produce to wake up in the dead of night and find a jealous woman bending over you. Terrible as this experience was, I had fears that it would give place to one more terrible.

My mistress grew weary of her vigils; they did not prove satisfactory. She changed her tactics. She now tried the trick of accusing my master of crime, in my presence, and gave my name as the author of the accusation. To my utter astonishment, he replied, "I don't believe it; but if she did acknowledge it, you tortured her into exposing me." Tortured into exposing him! Truly, Satan had no difficulty in distinguishing the color of his soul! I understood his object in making this false representation. It was to show me that I gained nothing by seeking the protection of my mistress; that the power was still all in his own hands. I pitied Mrs. Flint. She was a second wife, many years the junior of her husband; and the hoary-headed miscreant was enough to try the patience of a wiser and better woman. She was completely foiled, and knew not how to proceed. She would gladly have had me flogged for my supposed false oath; but, as I have already stated, the doctor never allowed any one to whip me. The old sinner was politic. The application of the lash might have led to remarks that would have exposed him in the eyes of his children and grandchildren. How often did I rejoice that I lived in a town where all the inhabitants knew each other! If I had been on a remote plantation, or lost among the multitude of a crowded city, I should not be a living woman at this day.

The secrets of slavery are concealed like those of the Inquisition. My master was, to my knowledge, the father of eleven slaves. But did the mothers dare to tell who was the father of their children? Did the other slaves dare to allude to it, except in whispers among themselves? No, indeed! They knew too well the terrible consequences.

My grandmother could not avoid seeing things which excited her suspicions. She was uneasy about me, and tried various ways to buy me; but the never-changing answer was always repeated: "Linda does not belong to *me*. She is my daughter's property, and I have no legal right to sell her." The conscientious man! He was too scrupulous to *sell* me; but he had no scruples whatever about committing a much greater wrong against the helpless young girl placed under his guardianship, as his daughter's property. Sometimes my persecutor would ask me whether I would like to be sold. I told him I would rather be sold to any body than to lead such a life as I did. On such occasions he would assume the air of a very injured individual, and reproach me for my ingratitude. "Did I not take you into the house, and make you the companion of my own children?" he would say. "Have I ever treated you like a negro? I have never allowed you to be punished, not even to please your mistress. And this is the recompense I get, you ungrateful girl!" I answered that he had reasons of his own for screening me from punishment, and that the course he pursued made my mistress hate me and persecute me. If I wept, he would say, "Poor child! Don't cry! don't cry! I will make peace for you with your mistress. Only let me arrange matters in my own way. Poor, foolish girl! you don't know what is for your own good. I would cherish you. I would make a lady of you. Now go, and think of all I have promised you."

I did think of it.

Reader, I draw no imaginary pictures of southern homes. I am telling you the plain truth. Yet when victims make their escape from this wild beast of Slavery, northerners consent to act the part of bloodhounds, and hunt the poor fugitive back into his den, "full of dead men's bones, and all uncleanness." Nay, more, they are not only willing, but proud, to give their daughters in marriage to slaveholders. The poor girls have romantic notions of a sunny clime, and of the flowering vines that all the year round shade a happy home. To what disappointments are they destined! The young wife soon learns that the husband in whose hands she has placed her happiness pays no regard to his marriage vows. Children of every shade of complexion play with her own fair babies, and too well she knows that they are born unto him of his own household. Jealousy and hatred enter the flowery home, and it is ravaged of its loveliness.

Southern women often marry a man knowing that he is the father of many little slaves. They do not trouble themselves about it. They regard such children as property, as marketable as the pigs on the plantation; and it is seldom that they do not make them aware of this by passing them into the slave-trader's hands as soon as possible, and thus getting them out of their sight. I am glad to say there are some honorable exceptions.

I have myself known two southern wives who exhorted their husbands to free those slaves towards whom they stood in a "parental relation"; and their request was granted. These husbands blushed before the superior nobleness of their wives' natures. Though they had only counselled them to do that which it was their duty to do, it commanded their respect, and rendered their conduct more exemplary. Concealment was at an end, and confidence took the place of distrust.

Though this bad institution deadens the moral sense, even in white women, to a fearful extent, it is not altogether extinct. I have heard southern ladies say of Mr. Such a one, "He not only thinks it no disgrace to be the father of those little niggers, but he is not ashamed to call himself their master. I declare, such things ought not to be tolerated, in any decent society!"

## VII
## The Lover

Why does the slave ever love? Why allow the tendrils of the heart to twine around objects which may at any moment be wrenched away by the hand of violence? When separations come by the hand of death, the pious soul can bow in resignation, and say, "Not my will, but thine be done, O Lord!" But when the ruthless hand of man strikes the blow, regardless of the misery he causes, it is hard to be submissive. I did not reason thus when I was a young girl. Youth will be youth. I loved, and I indulged the hope that the dark clouds around me would turn out a bright lining. I forgot that in the land of my birth the shadows are too dense for light to penetrate. A land

> Where laughter is not mirth; nor thought the mind;
> Nor words a language; nor e'en men mankind.
> Where cries reply to curses, shrieks to blows,
> And each is tortured in his separate hell.

There was in the neighborhood a young colored carpenter; a free-born man. We had been well acquainted in childhood, and frequently met together afterwards. We became mutually attached, and he proposed to marry me. I loved him with all the ardor of a young girl's first love. But when I reflected that I was a slave, and that the laws gave no sanction to the marriage of such, my heart sank within me. My lover wanted to buy me; but I knew that Dr. Flint was too wilful and arbitrary a man to consent to that arrangement. From him, I was sure of experiencing all sorts of opposition, and I had nothing to hope from my mistress. She would have been delighted to have got rid of me, but not in that way. It would have relieved her mind of a burden if she could have seen me sold to some distant state, but if I was married near home I should be just as much in her husband's power as I had previously been,—for the husband of a slave has no power to protect her. Moreover, my mistress, like many others, seemed to think that slaves had no right to any family ties of their own; that they were created merely to wait upon the family of the mistress. I once heard her abuse a young slave girl, who told her that a colored man wanted to make her his wife. "I will have you peeled and pickled, my lady," said she, "if I ever hear you mention that subject again. Do you suppose that I will have you tending *my* children with the children of that nigger?" The girl to whom she said this had a mulatto child, of course not acknowledged by its father. The poor black man who loved her would have been proud to acknowledge his helpless offspring.

Many and anxious were the thoughts I revolved in my mind. I was at a loss what to do. Above all things, I was desirous to spare my lover the insults that had cut so deeply into my own soul. I talked with my grandmother about it, and partly told her my fears. I did not dare to tell her the worst. She had long suspected all was not right, and if I confirmed her suspicions I knew a storm would rise that would prove the overthrow of all my hopes.

This love-dream had been my support through many trials; and I could not bear to run the risk of having it suddenly dissipated. There was a lady in the neighborhood, a particular friend of Dr. Flint's, who often visited the house. I had a great respect for her, and she had always manifested a friendly interest in me. Grandmother thought she would have great influence with the doctor. I went to this lady, and told her my story. I told her I was aware that my lover's being a free-born man would prove a great objection; but he wanted to buy me; and if Dr. Flint would consent to that arrangement, I felt sure he would be willing to pay any reasonable price. She knew that Mrs. Flint disliked me; therefore, I ventured to suggest that perhaps my mistress would approve of my being sold, as that would rid her of me. The lady listened with kindly sympathy, and promised to do her utmost to promote my wishes. She had an interview with the doctor, and I believe she pleaded my cause earnestly; but it was all to no purpose.

How I dreaded my master now! Every minute I expected to be summoned to his presence; but the day passed, and I heard nothing from him. The next morning, a message was brought to me: "Master wants you in his study." I found the door ajar, and I stood a moment gazing at the hateful man who claimed a right to rule me, body and soul. I entered, and tried to appear calm. I did not want him to know how my heart was bleeding. He looked fixedly at me, with an expression which seemed to say, "I have half a mind to kill you on the spot." At last he broke the silence, and that was a relief to both of us.

"So you want to be married, do you?" said he, "and to a free nigger."

"Yes, sir."

"Well, I'll soon convince you whether I am your master, or the nigger fellow you honor so highly. If you *must* have a husband, you may take up with one of my slaves."

What a situation I should be in, as the wife of one of *his* slaves, even if my heart had been interested!

I replied, "Don't you suppose, sir, that a slave can have some preference about marrying? Do you suppose that all men are alike to her?"

"Do you love this nigger?" said he, abruptly.

"Yes, sir."

"How dare you tell me so!" he exclaimed, in great wrath. After a slight pause, he added, "I supposed you thought more of yourself; that you felt above the insults of such puppies."

I replied, "If he is a puppy I am a puppy, for we are both of the negro race. It is right and honorable for us to love each other. The man you call a puppy never insulted me, sir; and he would not love me if he did not believe me to be a virtuous woman."

He sprang upon me like a tiger, and gave me a stunning blow. It was the first time he had ever struck me; and fear did not enable me to control my anger. When I had recovered a little from the effects, I exclaimed, "You have struck me for answering you honestly. How I despise you!"

There was silence for some minutes. Perhaps he was deciding what should be my punishment; or, perhaps, he wanted to give me time to reflect on what I had said, and to whom I had said it. Finally, he asked, "Do you know what you have said?"

"Yes, sir; but your treatment drove me to it."

"Do you know that I have a right to do as I like with you,—that I can kill you, if I please?"

"You have tried to kill me, and I wish you had; but you have no right to do as you like with me."

"Silence!" he exclaimed, in a thundering voice. "By heavens, girl, you forget yourself too far! Are you mad? If you are, I will soon bring you to your senses. Do you think any other master would bear what I have borne from you this morning? Many masters would have killed you on the spot. How would you like to be sent to jail for your insolence?"

"I know I have been disrespectful, sir," I replied; "but you drove me to it; I couldn't help it. As for the jail, there would be more peace for me there than there is here."

"You deserve to go there," said he, "and to be under such treatment, that you would forget the meaning of the word *peace*. It would do you good. It would take some of your high notions out of you. But I am not ready to send you there yet, notwithstanding your ingratitude for all my kindness and forbearance. You have been the plague of my life. I have wanted to make you happy, and I have been repaid with the basest ingratitude; but though you have proved yourself incapable of appreciating my kindness, I will be lenient towards you, Linda. I will give you one more chance to redeem your character. If you behave yourself and do as I require, I will forgive you and treat you as I always have done; but if you disobey me, I will punish you as I would the meanest slave on my plantation. Never let me hear that fellow's name mentioned again. If I ever know of your speaking to him, I will cowhide you both; and if I catch him lurking about my premises, I will shoot him as soon as I would a dog. Do you hear what I say? I'll teach you a lesson about marriage and free niggers!"

Now go, and let this be the last time I have occasion to speak to you on this subject."

Reader, did you ever hate? I hope not. I never did but once; and I trust I never shall again. Somebody has called it "the atmosphere of hell"; and I believe it is so.

For a fortnight the doctor did not speak to me. He thought to mortify me; to make me feel that I had disgraced myself by receiving the honorable addresses of a respectable colored man, in preference to the base proposals of a white man. But though his lips disdained to address me, his eyes were very loquacious. No animal ever watched its prey more narrowly than he watched me. He knew that I could write, though he had failed to make me read his letters; and he was now troubled lest I should exchange letters with another man. After a while he became weary of silence; and I was sorry for it. One morning, as he passed through the hall, to leave the house, he contrived to thrust a note into my hand. I thought I had better read it, and spare myself the vexation of having him read it to me. It expressed regret for the blow he had given me, and reminded me that I myself was wholly to blame for it. He hoped I had become convinced of the injury I was doing myself by incurring his displeasure. He wrote that he had made up his mind to go to Louisiana; that he should take several slaves with him, and intended I should be one of the number. My mistress would remain where she was; therefore I should have nothing to fear from that quarter. If I merited kindness from him, he assured me that it would be lavishly bestowed. He begged me to think over the matter, and answer the following day.

The next morning I was called to carry a pair of scissors to his room. I laid them on the table, with the letter beside them. He thought it was my answer, and did not call me back. I went as usual to attend my young mistress to and from school. He met me in the street, and ordered me to stop at his office on my way back. When I entered, he showed me his letter, and asked me why I had not answered it. I replied, "I am your daughter's property, and it is in your power to send me, or take me, wherever you please." He said he was very glad to find me so willing to go, and that we should start early in the autumn. He had a large practice in the town, and I rather thought he had made up the story merely to frighten me. However that might be, I was determined that I would never go to Louisiana with him.

Summer passed away, and early in the autumn Dr. Flint's eldest son was sent to Louisiana to examine the country, with a view to emigrating. That news did not disturb me. I knew very well that I should not be sent with *him*. That I had not been taken to the plantation before this time, was owing to the fact that his son was there. He was jealous of his son; and jealousy of the overseer had kept him from punishing me by sending me into the fields to work. Is it strange that I was not proud of these protectors? As for the overseer, he was a man for whom I had less respect than I had for a bloodhound.

Young Mr. Flint did not bring back a favorable report of Louisiana, and I heard no more of that scheme. Soon after this, my lover met me at the corner of the street, and I stopped to speak to him. Looking up, I saw my master watching us from his window. I hurried home, trembling with fear. I was sent for, immediately, to go to his room. He met me with a blow. "When is mistress to be married?" said he, in a sneering tone. A shower of oaths and imprecations followed. How thankful I was that my lover was a free man! that my tyrant had no power to flog him for speaking to me in the street!

Again and again I revolved in my mind how all this would end. There was no hope that the doctor would consent to sell me on any terms. He had an iron will, and was determined to keep me, and to conquer me. My lover was an intelligent and religious man. Even if he could have obtained permission to marry me while I was a slave, the marriage would give him no power to protect me from my master. It would have made him miserable to witness the insults I should have been subjected to. And then, if we had children, I knew they must "follow the condition of the mother." What a terrible blight that would be on the heart of a free, intelligent father! For *his* sake, I felt that I ought not to link his fate with my own unhappy destiny. He was going to Savannah to see about a little property left him by an uncle; and hard as it was to bring my feelings to it, I earnestly entreated him not to come back. I advised him to go to the Free States, where his tongue would not be tied, and where his intelligence would be of more avail to him. He left me, still hoping the day would come when I could be bought. With me the lamp of hope had gone out. The dream of my girlhood was over. I felt lonely and desolate.

Still I was not stripped of all. I still had my good grandmother, and my affectionate brother. When he put his arms round my neck, and looked into my eyes, as if to read there the troubles I dared not tell, I felt that I still had something to love. But even that pleasant emotion was chilled by the reflection that he might be torn from me at any moment, by some sudden freak of my master. If he had known how we loved each other, I think he would have exulted in separating us. We often planned together how we could get to the north. But, as William remarked, such things are easier said than done. My movements were very closely watched, and we had no means of getting any money to defray our expenses. As for grandmother, she was strongly opposed to her children's undertaking any such project. She had not forgotten poor Benjamin's sufferings, and she was afraid that if another child tried to escape, he would have a similar or a worse fate. To me, nothing seemed more dreadful than my present life. I said to myself, "William *must* be free. He shall go to the north, and I will follow him." Many a slave sister has formed the same plans. . . .

## X

## A Perilous Passage in the Slave Girl's Life

After my lover went away, Dr. Flint contrived a new plan. He seemed to have an idea that my fear of my mistress was his greatest obstacle. In the blandest tones, he told me that he was going to build a small house for me, in a secluded place, four miles away from the town. I shuddered; but I was constrained to listen, while he talked of his intention to give me a home of my own, and to make a lady of me. Hitherto, I had escaped my dreaded fate, by being in the midst of people. My grandmother had already had high words with my master about me. She had told him pretty plainly what she thought of his character, and there was considerable gossip in the neighborhood about our affairs, to which the open-mouthed jealousy of Mrs. Flint contributed not a little. When my master said he was going to build a house for me, and that he could do it with little trouble and expense, I was in hopes something would happen to frustrate his scheme; but I soon heard that the house was actually begun. I vowed before my Maker that I would never enter it. I had rather toil on the plantation from dawn till dark; I had rather live and die in jail, than drag on, from day to day, through such a living death. I was determined that the master, whom I so hated and loathed, who had blighted the prospects of my youth, and made my life a desert, should not, after my long struggle with him, succeed at last in trampling his victim under his feet. I would do any thing, every thing, for the sake of defeating him. What *could* I do? I thought and thought, till I became desperate, and made a plunge into the abyss.

And now, reader, I come to a period in my unhappy life, which I would gladly forget if I could. The remembrance fills me with sorrow and shame. It pains me to tell you of it; but I have promised to tell you the truth, and I will do it honestly, let it cost me what it may. I will not try to screen myself behind the plea of compulsion from a master; for it was not so. Neither can I plead ignorance or thoughtlessness. For years, my master had done his utmost to pollute my mind with foul images, and to destroy the pure principles inculcated by my grandmother, and the good mistress of my childhood. The influences of slavery had had the same effect on me that they had on other young girls; they had made me prematurely knowing, concerning the evil ways of the world. I knew what I did, and I did it with deliberate calculation.

But, O, ye happy women, whose purity has been sheltered from childhood, who have been free to choose the objects of your affection, whose homes are protected by law, do not judge the poor desolate slave girl too severely! If slavery had been abolished, I, also, could have married the man of my choice; I could have had a home shielded by the laws; and I should have been spared the painful task of confessing what I am now about to relate; but all my prospects had been blighted by slavery. I wanted to keep myself pure; and, under the most adverse circumstances, I tried hard to preserve my self-respect; but I was struggling alone in the powerful grasp of the demon Slavery; and the monster proved too strong for me. I felt as if I was forsaken by God and man; as if all my efforts must be frustrated; and I became reckless in my despair.

I have told you that Dr. Flint's persecutions and his wife's jealousy had given rise to some gossip in the neighborhood. Among others, it chanced that a white unmarried gentleman had obtained some knowledge of the circumstances in which I was placed. He knew my grandmother, and often spoke to me in the street. He became interested for me, and asked questions about my master, which I answered in part. He expressed a great deal of sympathy, and a wish to aid me. He constantly sought opportunities to see me, and wrote to me frequently. I was a poor slave girl, only fifteen years old.

So much attention from a superior person was, of course, flattering; for human nature is the same in all. I also felt grateful for his sympathy, and encouraged by his kind words. It seemed to me a great thing to have such a friend. By degrees, a more tender feeling crept into my heart. He was an educated and eloquent gentleman; too eloquent, alas, for the poor slave girl who trusted in him. Of course I saw whither all this was tending. I knew the impassable gulf between us; but to be an object of interest to a man who is not married, and who is not her master, is agreeable to the pride and feelings of a slave, if her miserable situation has left her any pride or sentiment. It seems less degrading to give one's self, than to submit to compulsion. There is something akin to freedom in having a lover who has no control over you, except that which he gains by kindness and attachment. A master may treat you as rudely as he pleases, and you dare not speak; moreover, the wrong does not seem so great with an unmarried man, as with one who has a wife to be made unhappy. There may be sophistry in all this; but the condition of a slave confuses all principles of morality, and, in fact, renders the practice of them impossible.

When I found that my master had actually begun to build the lonely cottage, other feelings mixed with those I have described. Revenge, and calculations of interest, were added to flattered vanity and sincere gratitude for kindness. I knew nothing would enrage Dr. Flint so much as to know that I favored another; and it was something to triumph over my tyrant even in that small way. I thought he would revenge himself by selling me, and I was sure my friend, Mr. Sands, would buy me. He was a man of more generosity and feeling than my master, and I thought my freedom could be easily obtained from him. The crisis of my fate now came so near that I was desperate. I shuddered to think of being the mother of children that should be owned by my old tyrant. I knew that as soon as a new fancy took him, his victims were sold far off to get rid of them; especially if they had children. I had seen several women sold, with his babies at the breast. He never allowed his offspring by slaves to remain long in sight of himself and his wife. Of a man who was not my master I could ask to have my children well supported; and in this case, I felt confident I should obtain the boon. I also felt quite sure that they would be made free. With all these thoughts revolving in my mind, and seeing no other way of escaping the doom I so much dreaded, I made a headlong plunge. Pity me, and pardon me, O virtuous reader! You never knew what it is to be a slave; to be entirely unprotected by law or custom; to have the laws reduce you to the condition of a chattel, entirely subject to the will of another. You never exhausted your ingenuity in avoiding the snares, and eluding the power of a hated tyrant; you never shuddered at the sound of his footsteps, and trembled within hearing of his voice. I know I did wrong. No one can feel it more sensibly than I do. The painful and humiliating memory will haunt me to my dying day. Still, in looking back, calmly, on the events of my life, I feel that the slave woman ought not to be judged by the same standard as others.

The months passed on. I had many unhappy hours. I secretly mourned over the sorrow I was bringing on my grandmother, who had so tried to shield me from harm. I knew that I was the greatest comfort of her old age, and that it was a source of pride to her that I had not degraded myself, like most of the slaves. I wanted to confess to her that I was no longer worthy of her love; but I could not utter the dreaded words.

As for Dr. Flint, I had a feeling of satisfaction and triumph in the thought of telling *him*. From time to time he told me of his intended arrangements, and I was silent. At last, he came and told me the cottage was completed, and ordered me to go to it. I told him I would never enter it. He said, "I have heard enough of such talk as that. You shall go, if you are carried by force; and you shall remain there."

I replied, "I will never go there. In a few months I shall be a mother."

He stood and looked at me in dumb amazement, and left the house without a word. I thought I should be happy in my triumph over him. But now that the truth was out, and my relatives would hear of it, I felt wretched. Humble as were their circumstances, they had pride in my good character. Now, how could I look them in the face? My self-respect was gone! I had resolved that I would be virtuous, though I was a slave. I had said, "Let the storm beat! I will brave it till I die." And now, how humiliated I felt!

I went to my grandmother. My lips moved to make confession, but the words stuck in my throat. I sat down in the shade of a tree at her door and began to sew. I think she saw something unusual was the matter with me. The mother of slaves is very watchful. She knows there is no security for her children. After they have entered their teens she lives in daily expectation of trouble. This leads to many questions. If the girl is of a sensitive nature, timidity keeps her from answering truthfully, and this well-meant course has a tendency to drive her from maternal counsels. Presently, in came my mistress, like a mad woman, and accused me concerning her husband. My grandmother, whose suspicions had been previously awakened, believed what she said. She exclaimed, "O Linda! has it come to this? I had rather see you dead than to see you as you now are. You are a disgrace to your dead mother." She tore from my fingers my mother's wedding ring and her silver thimble. "Go away!" she exclaimed, "and never come to my house, again." Her reproaches fell so hot and heavy, that they left me no chance to answer. Bitter tears, such as the eyes never shed but once, were my only answer. I rose from my seat, but fell back again, sobbing. She did not speak to me; but the tears were running down her furrowed cheeks, and they scorched me like fire. She has always been so kind to me! *So* kind! How I longed to throw myself at her feet, and tell her all the truth! But she had ordered me to go, and never to come there again. After a few minutes, I mustered strength, and started to obey her. With what feelings did I now close that little gate, which I used to open with such an eager hand in my childhood! It closed upon me with a sound I never heard before.

Where could I go? I was afraid to return to my master's. I walked on recklessly, not caring where I went, or what would become of me. When I had gone four or five miles, fatigue compelled me to stop. I sat down on the stump of an old tree. The stars were shining through the boughs above me. How they mocked me, with their bright, calm light! The hours passed by, and as I sat there alone a chilliness and deadly sickness came over me. I sank on the ground. My mind was full of horrid thoughts. I prayed to die; but the prayer was not answered. At last, with great effort I roused myself, and walked some distance further, to the house of a woman who had been a friend of my mother. When I told her why I was there, she spoke soothingly to me; but I could not be comforted. I thought I could bear my shame if I could only be reconciled to my grandmother. I longed to open my heart to her. I thought if she could know the real state of the case, and all I had been bearing for years, she would perhaps judge me less harshly. My friend advised me to send for her. I did so; but days of agonizing suspense passed before she came. Had she utterly forsaken me? No. She came at last. I knelt before her, and told her the things that had poisoned my life; how long I had been persecuted; that I saw no way of escape; and in an hour of extremity I had become desperate. She listened in silence. I told her I would bear any thing and do any thing, if in time I had hopes of obtaining her forgiveness. I begged of her to pity me, for my dead mother's sake. And she did pity me. She did not say, "I forgive you"; but she looked at me lovingly, with her eyes full of tears. She laid her old hand gently on my head, and murmured, "Poor child! Poor child!"

# XI
## The New Tie to Life

I returned to my good grandmother's house. She had an interview with Mr. Sands. When she asked him why he could not have left her one ewe lamb,—whether there were not plenty of slaves who did not care about character,—he made no answer; but he spoke kind and encouraging words. He promised to care for my child, and to buy me, be the conditions what they might.

I had not seen Dr. Flint for five days. I had never seen him since I made the avowal to him. He talked of the disgrace I had brought on myself; how I had sinned against my master, and mortified my old grandmother. He intimated that if I had accepted his proposals, he, as a physician, could have saved me from exposure. He even condescended to pity me. Could he have offered wormwood more bitter? He, whose persecutions had been the cause of my sin!

"Linda," said he, "though you have been criminal towards me, I feel for you, and I can pardon you if you obey my wishes. Tell me whether the fellow you wanted to marry is the father of your child. If you deceive me, you shall feel the fires of hell."

I did not feel as proud as I had done. My strongest weapon with him was gone. I was lowered in my own estimation, and had resolved to bear his abuse in silence. But when he spoke contemptuously of the lover who had always treated me honorably; when I remembered that but for *him* I might have been a virtuous, free, and happy wife, I lost my patience. "I have sinned against God and myself," I replied; "but not against you."

He clinched his teeth, and muttered, "Curse you!" He came towards me, with ill-suppressed rage, and exclaimed, "You obstinate girl! I could grind your bones to powder! You have thrown yourself away on some worthless rascal. You are weak-minded, and have been easily persuaded by those who don't care a straw for you. The future will settle accounts between us. You are blinded now; but hereafter you will be convinced that your master was your best friend. My lenity towards you is a proof of it. I might have punished you in many ways. I might have had you whipped till you fell dead under the lash. But I wanted you to live; I would have bettered your condition. Others cannot do it. You are my slave. Your mistress, disgusted by your conduct, forbids you to return to the house; therefore I leave you here for the present; but I shall see you often. I will call tomorrow."

He came with frowning brows, that showed a dissatisfied state of mind. After asking about my health, he inquired whether my board was paid, and who visited me. He then went on to say that he had neglected his duty; that as a physician there were certain things that he ought to have explained to me. Then followed talk such as would have made the most shameless blush. He ordered me to stand up before him. I obeyed. "I command you," said he, "to tell me whether the father of your child is white or black." I hesitated. "Answer me this instant!" he exclaimed. I did answer. He sprang upon me like a wolf, and grabbed my arm as if he would have broken it. "Do you love him?" said he, in a hissing tone.

"I am thankful that I do not despise him," I replied.

He raised his hand to strike me; but it fell again. I don't know what arrested the blow. He sat down, with lips tightly compressed. At last he spoke. "I came here," said he, "to make you a friendly proposition; but your ingratitude chafes me beyond endurance. You turn aside all my good intentions towards you. I don't know what it is that keeps me from killing you." Again he rose, as if he had a mind to strike me.

But he resumed. "On one condition I will forgive your insolence and crime. You must henceforth have no communication of any kind with the father of your child. You must not ask any thing from him, or receive any thing from him. I will take care of you and your child. You had better promise this at once, and not wait till you are deserted by him. This is the last act of mercy I shall show towards you."

I said something about being unwilling to have my child supported by a man who had cursed it and me also. He rejoined, that a woman who had sunk to my level had no right to expect any thing else. He asked, for the last time, would I accept his kindness? I answered that I would not.

"Very well," said he; "then take the consequences of your wayward course. Never look to me for help. You are my slave, and shall always be my slave. I will never sell you, that you may depend upon."

Hope died away in my heart as he closed the door after him. I had calculated that in his rage he would sell me to a slave-trader; and I knew the father of my child was on the watch to buy me.

About this time my uncle Phillip was expected to return from a voyage. The day before his departure I had officiated as bridesmaid to a young friend. My heart was then ill at ease, but my smiling countenance did not betray it. Only a year had passed; but what fearful changes it had wrought! My heart had grown gray in misery. Lives that flash in sunshine, and lives that are born in tears, receive their hue from circumstances. None of us know what a year may bring forth.

I felt no joy when they told me my uncle had come. He wanted to see me, though he knew what had happened. I shrank from him at first; but at last consented that he should come to my room. He received me as he always had done. O, how my heart smote me when I felt his tears on my burning cheeks! The words of my grandmother came to my mind,—"Perhaps your mother and father are taken from the evil days to come." My disappointed heart could now praise God that it was so. But why, thought I, did my relatives ever cherish hopes for me? What was there to save me from the usual fate of slave girls? Many more beautiful and more intelligent than I had experienced a similar fate, or a far worse one. How could they hope that I should escape?

My uncle's stay was short, and I was not sorry for it. I was too ill in mind and body to enjoy my friends as I had done. For some weeks I was unable to leave my bed. I could not have any doctor but my master, and I would not have him sent for. At last, alarmed by my increasing illness, they sent for him. I was very weak and nervous; and as soon as he entered the room, I began to scream. They told him my state was very critical. He had no wish to hasten me out of the world, and he withdrew.

When my babe was born, they said it was premature. It weighed only four pounds; but God let it live. I heard the doctor say I could not survive till morning. I had often prayed for death; but now I did not want to die, unless my child could die too. Many weeks passed before I was able to leave my bed. I was a mere wreck of my former self. For a year there was scarcely a day when I was free from chills and fever. My babe also was sickly. His little limbs were often racked with pain. Dr. Flint continued his visits, to look after my health; and he did not fail to remind me that my child was an addition to his stock of slaves.

I felt too feeble to dispute with him, and listened to his remarks in silence. His visits were less frequent; but his busy spirit could not remain quiet. He employed my brother in his office, and he was made the medium of frequent notes and messages to me. William was a bright lad, and of much use to the doctor. He had learned to put up medicines, to leech, cup, and bleed. He had taught himself to read and spell. I was proud of my brother; and the old doctor suspected as much. One day, when I had not seen him for several weeks, I heard his steps approaching the door. I dreaded the encounter, and hid myself. He inquired for me, of course; but I was nowhere to be found. He went to his office, and despatched William with a note. The color mounted to my brother's face when he gave it to me; and he said, "Don't you hate me, Linda, for bringing you these things?" I told him I could not blame him; he was a slave, and obliged to obey his master's will. The note ordered me to come to his office. I went. He demanded to know where I was when he called. I told him I was at home. He flew into a passion, and said he knew better. Then he launched out upon his usual themes,—my crimes against him, and my ingratitude for his forbearance. The laws were laid down to me anew, and I was dismissed. I felt humiliated that my brother should stand by, and listen to such language as would be addressed only to a slave. Poor boy! He was powerless to defend me; but I saw the tears, which he vainly strove to keep back. This manifestation of feeling irritated the doctor. William could do nothing to please him. One morning he did not arrive at the office so early as usual; and that circumstance afforded his master an opportunity to vent his spleen. He was put in jail. The next day my brother sent a trader to the doctor, with a request to be sold. His master was greatly incensed at what he called his insolence. He said he had put him there to reflect upon his bad conduct, and he certainly was not giving any evidence of repentance. For two days he harassed himself to find somebody to do his office work; but every thing went wrong without William. He was released, and ordered to take his old stand, with many threats, if he was not careful about his future behavior.

As the months passed on, my boy improved in health. When he was a year old, they called him beautiful. The little vine was taking deep root in my existence, though its clinging fondness excited a mixture of love and pain. When I was most sorely oppressed I found a solace in his smiles. I loved to watch his infant slumbers; but always there was a dark cloud over my enjoyment. I could never forget that he was a slave. Sometimes I wished that he might die in infancy. God tried me. My darling became very ill. The bright eyes grew dull, and the little feet and hands were so icy cold that I thought death had already touched them. I had prayed for his death, but never so earnestly as I now prayed for his life; and my prayer was heard. Alas, what mockery it is for a slave mother to try to pray back her dying child to life! Death is better than slavery. It was a sad thought that I had no name to give my child. His father caressed him and treated him kindly, whenever he had a chance to see him. He was not unwilling that he should bear his name; but he had no legal claim to it; and if I had bestowed it upon him, my master would have regarded it as a new crime, a new piece of insolence, and would, perhaps, revenge it on the boy. O, the serpent of Slavery has many and poisonous fangs!

∙ ∙ ∙ ∙ ∙ ∙ ∙ ∙ ∙ ∙ ∙ ∙

## QUESTIONS FOR A SECOND READING

1. In her preface, Jacobs says that she doesn't care to excite sympathy for her suffering but to "arouse the women of the North to a realizing sense of the

condition of two millions of women at the South." As you reread this selection, pay attention to the ways Jacobs addresses (and tries to influence)
her readers. Why would she be suspicious of sympathy? What do you suppose she might have meant by "a realizing sense"? What kind of reader
does she want? Why does she address women?

Be sure to mark those sections that address the reader directly, and also
those that seem to give evidence of Jacobs as a writer, working on the material, highlighting some incidents and passing over others (why do we get
"incidents" and not the full story?), organizing our experience of the text,
shaping scenes and sentences, organizing chapters. What is Jacobs doing
in this text? What might her work as a writer have to do with her position
(as a female slave) in relation to the world of her readers?

2. The emotional and family relations between people are difficult to chart in
this book, partly because they defy easy categorization. Can we, for example, assume that blacks and whites lived separately? that blacks were in
bondage and whites were free? that family lines and color lines were distinct markers? that lovers were lovers and enemies were enemies? As you
reread, pay close attention to the ways people are organized by family,
love, community, and color. See what you can determine about the codes
that govern relations in this representation of slave culture. And ask where
and how Jacobs places herself in these various networks.

## ASSIGNMENTS FOR WRITING

1. In an essay titled "The Voice of the Southern Slave," Houston Baker says,

> The voice of the unwritten self, once it is subjected to the linguistic
> codes, literary conventions, and audience expectations of a literate
> population, is perhaps never again the authentic voice of black Amer-
> ican slavery. It is, rather, the voice of a self transformed by an au-
> tobiographical act into a sharer in the general public discourse about
> slavery.

This voice shares in the general public discourse about slavery and also in
the general public discourse representing family, growing up, love, marriage, and childbirth, the discourse representing "normal" life—that is, life
outside of slavery. For a slave the self and its relations to others has a
different public construction. A slave is property. A mother doesn't own
her own children. These relations, and others, are governed by a different
code.

The passage from Baker's essay allows us to highlight the difference
between a life and a narrative, a person (Harriet Jacobs) and a person rendered on the page (Linda Brent, the "I" of the narrative), between the experience of slavery and the conventional ways of telling the story of a life,
between experience and the ways experience is shaped by a writer, readers,
and a culture.

In other words, Jacobs's situation as a writer reproduces her position as a slave, cast as a member of the community but not as a person. Write an essay in which you examine Jacobs's work as a writer. Consider the ways she works on her reader (a figure she both imagines and constructs) and also the ways she works on her material (a set of experiences, a language, and the conventional ways of telling the story of one's life). To do this, you will need to reread the text as something constructed (see the first "Question for a Second Reading").

2. We can take these opening chapters of *Incidents in the Life of a Slave Girl* as an account of a girl's coming of age, particularly in the sense that coming of age is a cultural (and not simply a biological) process. The chapters represent the ways in which Jacobs comes to be positioned as a woman in the community, and they represent her understanding of that process (and the necessary limits to her understanding, since no person can stand completely outside her culture and what it desires her to believe or to take as natural).

Read back through *Incidents*, paying particular attention to what Jacobs sees as the imposed structure of slave culture and what she takes as part of human nature. Remember that there are different ways of reading the codes that govern human relations. What Jacobs takes to be unnatural may well seem natural to Dr. Flint. Jacobs could be said to be reading "against" what Flint, or the Slave Owner as a generic type, would understand as naturally there.

Now read through again, this time reading against Jacobs, to see how her view of relationships could be said to be shaped also by a set of beliefs and interests. Look for a system governing Jacobs's understanding. You might ask, for instance, what system leads her to see Dr. Flint and Mr. Sands as different, since they could also be said to be similar—both slave owners, both after the same thing. How does Jacobs place herself in relation to other slaves? other blacks? Jacobs is light skinned. How does she fit into a system governed by color? Both Mrs. Flint and her grandmother react strongly to Jacobs. What system governs Jacobs's sense of the difference between these two women?

Write an essay in which you try to explain the codes that govern the relations between people in slave culture, at least as that culture is represented in *Incidents*.

## MAKING CONNECTIONS

1. In her essay "In Search of Our Mother's Gardens" (p. 584), Alice Walker says,

> Our mothers and grandmothers, some of them: moving to music not yet written. And they waited.
> They waited for a day when the unknown thing that was in them would be made known; but guessed, somehow in their darkness, that on the day of their revelation they would be long dead.

Jacobs did not write as someone whose story would be lost. And she is no longer a forgotten figure. Yet she does not figure in Walker's litany of examples. What do you suppose Walker might find in Jacobs's story? What could she find here that she could not find in Virginia Woolf's "A Room of One's Own" (p. 641), a text she discovers she has to rewrite? What is there in Jacobs's text that Walker would miss? not see? or fail to appreciate? or wish were there but is not? Where or how might *Incidents* fit into Walker's essay? Write an essay in which you imagine how Walker might read (or misread) Jacobs's story.

2. In "When We Dead Awaken: Writing as Re-vision" (p. 482), Adrienne Rich says, "Re-vision—the act of looking back, of seeing with fresh eyes, of entering an old text from a new critical direction—is for women more than a chapter in cultural history: it is an act of survival. Until we can understand the assumptions in which we are drenched we cannot know ourselves."

Let's imagine that one of the difficulties we have in reading *Incidents* is that we approach it drenched in assumptions; we look with old eyes (or the wrong eyes). In honor of the challenge Rich sets for a reader—or, for that matter, in honor of Harriet Jacobs and the challenge she sets for a reader—write an essay in which you show what it would mean to revise your reading (or what you take to be most people's reading, the "common" reading) of *Incidents*. You will want to show both how the text would be read from this new critical direction and what effort (or method) would be involved in pushing against the old ways of reading.

3. Jean Franco, in "Killing Priests, Nuns, Women, Children" (p. 195), provides a demonstration of how spaces can be said to have gender—to be male or female—and of the ways these fundamental representations of space relate to political struggle, often a struggle to occupy or control the space of others. Following Franco's lead, how would you read the distribution of space in slave culture, particularly those spaces that Jacobs fears or desires, imagines as either safe and free or dangerous and limiting? Write an essay in which you apply this kind of analysis in a close reading of *Incidents*, to see what you can learn about the "imaginary topography" of slave culture.

# JULIA
# KRISTEVA

*J*ULIA KRISTEVA, *like her colleague and teacher, Roland Barthes, produces work that is difficult to classify. Kristeva has written on a wide variety of subjects, including literary history, linguistics, social theory, psychoanalysis, feminism, and semiotics. What makes Kristeva's intellectual project so difficult to define is the fact that, in each of these cases, she has not simply reproduced what Thomas Kuhn has called the "paradigm," or commonly accepted set of procedures, in each of these fields. Rather, she has vigorously and radically challenged the way work in these fields is undertaken.*

*For example, Kristeva does not merely "do" psychoanalysis, replicating commonly accepted methods or writing in an established vocabulary. Instead, she enacts a tradition, in the act of her writing, that questions what it means to study psychoanalysis. This tradition of challenging and questioning paradigms, which is especially characteristic of Kristeva's work in psychoanalysis, feminism, and semiotics, makes reading her work both exciting and difficult; it requires her readers to learn to read differently. When we read Kristeva, we must suspend many of our previous ideas about reading, and pay careful and close attention to the specific ways her essays are asking to be read.*

Born in Bulgaria in 1941, Kristeva received a degree from the Literary Institute of Sofia before traveling to Paris in 1966 as a doctoral-fellowship holder. She has remained in France ever since, traveling abroad occasionally to teach. She has taught at Columbia University in New York and at the University of Paris.

In the 1970s Kristeva became a member of the editorial board of Tel Quel, a French literary journal which argued for the careful analysis of the relationship of language to history, politics, and the human subject. Other members of the Tel Quel group included Roland Barthes and Philippe Sollers, a French novelist and theorist whom Kristeva eventually married. In 1979 Kristeva started her own psychoanalytic practice. She and Sollers remained with Tel Quel until 1983, when the journal disbanded.

Kristeva has written a number of books which have been translated into English, including Desire in Language: A Semiotic Approach to Literature and Art (1980) and About Chinese Women (1985). Her work over the past few years has moved from a consideration of linguistics and semiotics toward a more psychoanalytically oriented examination of the problems of femininity and motherhood.

The title of her essay, "Stabat Mater," refers to the Latin hymn depicting Mary, the mother of Christ, standing at the foot of the cross. The opening words, "Stabat Mater dolorosa," translate as "Stood the mother, full of grief." Kristeva's study of the myth and cult of the Virgin Mary is written with a countertext that records her own reflections on her experience as a mother. One of the purposes of the essay is to answer the standard feminist critique of motherhood without resorting to the predictable counterarguments (that women should be able to do it all or that women should prefer motherhood to any other role). Kristeva argues for an understanding of motherhood as a "locus of vulnerability," a place from which women can call into question the governing procedures and languages of a sexist culture.

This is a difficult essay. You should know this before you begin and at some point you should ask the question, "Why?" Why must this argument be presented in so unusual a form, a form that demands so much of its readers? Before that, however, you will need to find a way of working through the essay. You will need to be patient and to put aside any desire to understand at every moment what is being said. This is not the sort of text that asks a reader to be a master; it is not a text that wants to be possessed, owned, summed up, and turned to the usual use.

The essay is divided into sections—sections that follow one after another and sections that stand one against another, actually running side by side. You should work section by section, looking for passages that speak to you and taking time to put them into your own words. From this point of departure, you can begin to think about how the essay works as a whole. The essay opens by speculating that "it is not possible to say of a woman what she is." If you read with Kristeva, you should feel that the work you are doing is set against the direct statement of how or what things are. It is work that resists limited, habitual ways of thinking and, in particular, thinking about women.

# Stabat Mater

## [Introduction]

*First published as "Hérethique de l'amour" in* Tel Quel, 74 *(Winter 1977, pp. 30–49), this essay on the cult of the Virgin Mary and its implication for the Catholic understanding of motherhood and femininity was reprinted as "Stabat Mater" in* Histoires d'amour *(Paris: Denoël) in 1983. A slightly edited translation also entitled "Stabat Mater" by Arthur Goldhammer appeared in* Poetics Today, 6, 1–2 *(1985), pp. 135–52. The present translation is taken from the forthcoming American edition of* Histoires d'amour, *to be published by Columbia University Press. The title "Stabat Mater" refers to the Latin hymn on the agony of the Virgin Mary at the Crucifixion, set to music by many famous composers, not least Pergolesi. The opening words of the hymn, "Stabat mater dolorosa . . . ," literally mean "Stood the Mother, full of grief. . . ." At the time of its first publication this text was unique among Kristeva's essays not only for its free, easy, and personal style, but also for its deliberate typographical fragmentation of the page.*

*Kristeva's study of the Virgin Mother coincides with her own experience of maternity, recorded and reflected in the personal observations which break up the main body of the text. The first part of her essay summarizes the historical development of the cult of the Virgin, drawing on Marina Warner's* Alone of All Her Sex: The Myth and the Cult of the Virgin Mary *(London: Weidenfeld, 1976), a book well known to English-speaking readers. Her main concern, however, is to point out that today, due to the demise of the cult of the Virgin, and of religion in general, we are left without a satisfactory discourse on motherhood. Where the cult of the Virgin traditionally offered a solution to what Kristeva calls the problem of feminine paranoia, the decline of religion has left women with nothing to put in its place. Freud's contribution to this particular problem is more or less nil, she argues, and the feminist critique of the traditional representation of motherhood has still not produced a new understanding of women's continued desire to have children. Listing the various psychosocial functions of the cult of the Virgin, Kristeva asks what it is that subtle, but now necessarily crumbling edifice ignores or represses in modern women's experience of motherhood. In reply to her own question, she points to the need for a new understanding of the mother's body; the physical and psychological suffering of childbirth and of the need to raise the child in accordance with the Law; the mother–daughter relationship; and finally, the female foreclosure of masculinity. There is, then, an urgent need for a "postvirginal" discourse on maternity, one which ultimately would provide both women and men with a new ethics: a "herethics" encompassing both reproduction and death.*

---

Introduction by Toril Moi. Translated by León S. Roudiez.

*Opening up a fascinating field of investigation, this essay is of particular interest to feminists. So far, Kristeva herself has not really followed up her own "program" for research into maternity, although* Histoires d'amour *as a whole does contain many valuable observations on the topic.*

## The Paradox: Mother or Primary Narcissism

If it is not possible to say of a *woman* she *is* (without running the risk of abolishing her difference), would it perhaps be different concerning the *mother*, since that is the only function of the "other sex" to which we can definitely attribute existence? And yet, there too, we are caught in a paradox. First, we live in a civilization where the *consecrated* (religious or secular) representation of femininity is absorbed by motherhood. If, however, one looks at it more closely, this motherhood is the *fantasy* that is nurtured by the adult, man or woman, of a lost territory; what is more, it involves less an idealized archaic mother than the idealization of the *relationship* that binds us to her, one that cannot be localized—an idealization of primary narcissism. Now, when feminism demands a new representation of femininity, it seems to identify motherhood with that idealized misconception and, because it rejects the image and its misuse, feminism circumvents the real experience that fantasy overshadows. The result?—A negation or rejection of motherhood by some avant-garde feminist groups. Or else an acceptance—conscious or not—of its traditional representations by the great mass of people, women and men.

Christianity is doubtless the most refined symbolic construct in which femininity, to the extent that it transpires through it—and it does so incessantly—is focused on *Maternality*. [1]

FLASH—instant of time or of dream without time; inordinately swollen atoms of a bond, a vision, a shiver, a yet formless, unnameable embryo. Epiphanies. Photos of what is not yet visible and that language necessarily skims over from afar, allusively. Words that are always too distant, too abstract for this underground swarming of seconds, folding in unimaginable spaces. Writing them down is an ordeal of discourse, like love. What is loving, for a woman, the same

Let us call "maternal" the ambivalent principle that is bound to the species, on the one hand, and on the other stems from an identity catastrophe that causes the Name to topple over into the unnameable that one imagines as femininity, nonlanguage, or body. Thus Christ, the Son of man, when all is said and done is "human" only through his mother—as if Christly or Christian humanism could only be a materialism (this is, besides, what some secularizing trends within its orbit do not cease claiming in their esotericism). And yet, the humanity of the Virgin mother is not always obvious,

360

thing as writing. Laugh. Impossible. Flash on the unnameable, weavings of abstractions to be torn. Let a body venture at last out of its shelter, take a chance with meaning under a veil of words. WORD FLESH. From one to the other, eternally, broken up visions, metaphors of the invisible.

and we shall see how, in her being cleared of sin, for instance, Mary distinguishes herself from mankind. But at the same time the most intense revelation of God, which occurs in mysticism, is given only to a person who assumes himself as "maternal." Augustine, Bernard of Clairvaux, Meister Eckhart, to mention but a few, played the part of the Father's virgin spouses, or even, like Bernard, received drops of virginal milk directly on their lips. Freedom with respect to the maternal territory then becomes the pedestal upon which love of God is erected. As a consequence, mystics, those "happy Schrebers" (Sollers) throw a bizarre light on the psychotic sore of modernity: it appears as the incapability of contemporary codes to tame the maternal, that is, primary narcissism. Uncommon and "literary," their present-day counterparts are always somewhat oriental, if not tragical—Henry Miller who says he is pregnant, Artaud who sees himself as "his daughters" or "his mother." . . . It is the orthodox constituent of Christianity, through John Chrysostom's golden mouth, among others, that sanctioned the transitional function of the Maternal by calling the Virgin a "bond," a "middle," or an "interval," thus opening the door to more or less heretical identifications with the Holy Ghost.

This resorption of femininity within the Maternal is specific to many civilizations, but Christianity, in its own fashion, brings it to its peak. Could it be that such a reduction represents no more than a masculine appropriation of the Maternal, which, in line with our hypothesis, is only a fantasy masking primary narcissism? Or else, might one detect in it, in other respects, the workings of enigmatic sublimation? These are perhaps the workings of masculine sublimation, a sublimation just the same, if it be true that for Freud picturing Da Vinci, and even for Da Vinci himself, the taming of that economy (of the Maternal or of primary narcissism) is a requirement for artistic, literary, or painterly accomplishment?

Within that perspective, however, there are two questions, among others, that remain unanswered. What is there, in the portrayal of the Maternal in general and particularly in its Christian, virginal, one, that reduces social anguish and gratifies a male being; what is there that also satisfies a woman so that a commonality of the sexes is set up, beyond and in spite of their glaring incompatibility and permanent warfare? Beyond social and political demands, this takes the well-known "discontents" of our civilization to a level where Freud would not follow—the discontents of the species.

JULIA KRISTEVA

## A Triumph of the Unconscious in Monotheism

It would seem that the "virgin" attribute for Mary is a translation error, the translator having substituted for the Semitic term that indicates the sociolegal status of a young unmarried woman the Greek word *parthenos*, which on the other hand specifies a physiological and psychological condition: virginity. One might read into this the Indo-European fascination (which Dumezil analyzed) [2] with the virgin daughter as guardian of paternal power; one might also detect an ambivalent conspiracy, through excessive spiritualization, of the mother-goddess and the underlying matriarchy with which Greek culture and Jewish monotheism kept struggling. The fact remains that Western Christianity has organized that "translation error," projected its own fantasies into it, and produced one of the most powerful imaginary constructs known in the history of civilizations.

The story of the virginal cult in Christianity amounts in fact to the imposition of pagan-rooted beliefs on, and often against, dogmas of the official Church. It is true that the Gospels already posit Mary's existence. But they suggest only very discreetly the immaculate conception of Christ's mother, they say nothing concerning Mary's own background and speak of her only seldom at the side of her son or during crucifixion. Thus Matthew 1:20 (". . . the angel of the Lord appeared to him in a dream and said, 'Joseph, son of David, do not be afraid to take Mary home as your wife, because she has conceived what is in her by the Holy Spirit'"), and Luke 1:34 ("Mary said to the angel, 'But how can this come about since I do not know man?'"), open a door, a narrow opening for all that, but one that would soon widen thanks to apocryphal additions, on impregnation without sexuality; according to this notion a woman, preserved from masculine intervention, conceives alone with a "third party," a nonperson, the Spirit. In the rare instances when the Mother of Jesus appears in the Gospels, she is informed that filial relationship rests not with the flesh but with the name or, in other words, that any possible matrilinearism is to be repudiated and the symbolic link alone is to last. We thus have Luke 2:48–49 (". . . his mother said to him, 'My child, why have you done this to us? See how worried your father and I have been, looking for you.' 'Why were you looking for me?' he replied. 'Did you not know that I must be busy with my father's affairs?'"), and also John 2:3–5 (". . . the mother of Jesus said to him, 'They have no wine.' Jesus said, 'Woman, why turn to me? [3] My hour has not come yet.'"), and 19:26–27 ("Seeing his mother and the disciple he loved standing near her, Jesus said to his mother, 'Woman, this is your son.' Then to the disciple he said, 'This is your mother.' And from that moment the disciple made a place for her in his home.").

Starting from this programmatic material, rather skimpy nevertheless, a compelling imaginary construct proliferated in essentially three directions. In the first place, there was the matter of drawing a parallel between Mother and Son by expanding the theme of the immaculate conception, inventing a biography of Mary similar to that of Jesus and, by depriving her of sin, to deprive her of death: Mary leaves by way of Dormition or Assumption. Next, she needed letters patent of nobility, a power that, even though exercised in the beyond, is none the less political, since Mary was to be proclaimed queen, given the attributes and paraphernalia of royalty, and, in parallel fashion, declared Mother of the divine institution on earth, the Church. Finally, the relationship with Mary and from Mary was to be revealed as the prototype of love relationships and followed two fundamental aspects of Western love: courtly love and child love, thus fitting the entire range that goes from sublimation to asceticism and masochism.

### Neither Sex nor Death

Mary's life, devised on the model of the life of Jesus, seems to be the fruit of apocryphal literature. The story of her own miraculous conception, called "immaculate conception," by Anne and Joachim, after a long, barren marriage, together with her biography as a pious maiden, show up in apocryphal sources as early as the end of the first century. Their entirety may be found in the *Secret Book of James* and also in one of pseudoepigrapha, the Gospel according to the Hebrews (which inspired Giotto's frescos, for instance). Those "facts" were quoted by Clement of Alexandria and Origen but not officially accepted; even though the Eastern Church tolerated them readily, they were translated into Latin only in the sixteenth century. Yet the West was not long before glorifying the life of Mary on its own but always under orthodox guidance. The first Latin poem, "Maria," on the birth of Mary was written by the nun Hrotswith von Gandersheim (who died before 1002), a playwright and poet.

Fourth-century asceticism, developed by the Fathers of the Church, was grafted on that apocryphal shoot in order to bring out and rationalize the immaculate conception postulate. The demonstration was based on a simple logical relation: the intertwining of sexuality and death. Since they are mutually implicated with each other, one cannot avoid the one without fleeing the other. This asceticism, applicable to both sexes, was vigorously expressed by John Chrysostom (*On Virginity*: "For where there is death there is also sexual copulation, and where there is no death there is no sexual copulation either"); even though he was attacked by Augustine and Aquinas, he none the less fueled Christian doctrine. Thus, Augustine condemned "concupiscence" (*epithumia*) and posited that Mary's virginity is in fact only a logical precondition of Christ's chastity. The Orthodox Church, heir no doubt to a matriarchy that was more intense in Eastern European societies, emphasized Mary's virginity more boldly. Mary was contrasted with Eve, life with death (Jerome, *Letter 22*, "Death came through Eve but life came through Mary"; Irenaeus, "Through Mary the snake becomes a dove and we are freed from the chains of death"). People even got involved in tortuous arguments in order to demonstrate that Mary remained a virgin after childbirth (thus the second Constantinople council, in 381, under Arianistic influence, emphasized the Virgin's role in comparison to official dogma and asserted Mary's perpetual virginity; the 451 council called her *Aeiparthenos*—ever virgin). Once this was established, Mary, instead of being referred to as Mother of man or Mother of Christ, would be proclaimed Mother of God: *Theotokos*. Nestorius, patriarch of Constantinople, refused to go along; Nestorianism, however, for all practical purposes died with the patriarch's own death in 451, and the path that would lead to Mary's deification was then clear.

**Head reclining, nape finally relaxed, skin, blood, nerves warmed up, luminous flow: stream of hair made of ebony, of nectar, smooth darkness through her fingers, gleaming honey under the wings of bees, sparkling strands burning bright . . . silk, mercury, ductile copper: frozen light warmed under fingers. Mane of beast—squirrel, horse, and the happiness of a faceless head, Narcissuslike touching without eyes, slight dissolving in muscles, hair, deep, smooth, peaceful colors. Mamma: anamnesis.**

**Taut eardrum, tearing sound out of muted silence. Wind among grasses, a seagull's faraway call, echoes of waves, auto horns, voices, or nothing? Or his own tears, my newborn, spasm of syncopated void. I no longer hear anything, but the eardrum keeps transmitting this resonant vertigo to my skull,**

Very soon, within the complex relationship between Christ and his Mother where relations of God to mankind, man to woman, son to mother, etc. are hatched, the problematics of *time* similar to that of cause loomed up. If Mary preceded Christ and he originated in her if only from the standpoint of his humanity, should not the conception of Mary herself have been immaculate? For, if that were not the case, how could a being conceived in sin and harboring it in herself produce a God? Some apocryphal writers had not hesitated, without too much caution, to suggest such an absence of sin in Mary's conception, but the Fathers of the Church were more careful. Bernard of Clairvaux is reluctant to extol the conception of Mary by Anne, and thus he tries to check the homologation of Mary with Christ. But it fell upon Duns Scotus to change the hesitation over the promotion of a mother goddess within Christianity into a logical problem, thus saving them both, the Great Mother as well as logic. He viewed Mary's birth as a *praeredemptio*, as a matter of congruency: if it be true

the hair. My body is no longer mine, it doubles up, suffers, bleeds, catches cold, puts its teeth in, slobbers, coughs, is covered with pimples, and it laughs. And yet, when its own joy, my child's, returns, its smile washes only my eyes. But the pain, its pain—it comes from inside, never remains apart, other, it inflames me at once, without a second's respite. As if that was what I had given birth to and, not willing to part from me, insisted on coming back, dwelled in me permanently. One does not give birth in pain, one gives birth to pain: the child represents it and henceforth it settles in, it is continuous. Obviously you may close your eyes, cover up your ears, teach courses, run errands, tidy up the house, think about objects, subjects. But a mother is always branded by pain, she yields to it. "And a sword will pierce your own soul too. . . ."

Dream without glow, without sound, dream of brawn. Dark twisting, pain in the back, the arms, the thighs—pincers turned into fibers, infernos bursting veins, stones breaking bones: grinders of volumes, expanses, spaces, lines, points. All those words, now, ever visible things to register the roar of a silence that hurts all over. As if a geometry ghost could suffer when collapsing in a noiseless tumult. . . . Yet the eye picked

that Christ alone saves us through his redemption on the cross, the Virgin who bore him can but be preserved from sin in "recursive" fashion, from the time of her own conception up to that redemption.

For or against, with dogma or logical shrewdness, the battle around the Virgin intensified between Jesuits and Dominicans, but the Counter-Reformation, as is well known, finally ended the resistance: henceforth, Catholics venerated Mary in herself. The Society of Jesus succeeded in completing a process of popular pressure distilled by patristic asceticism, and in reducing, with neither explicit hostility nor brutal rejection, the share of the Maternal (in the sense given above) useful to a certain balance between the two sexes. Curiously and necessarily, when that balance began to be seriously threatened in the nineteenth century, the Catholic Church—more dialectical and subtle here than the Protestants who were already spawning the first suffragettes—raised the Immaculate Conception to dogma status in 1854. It is often suggested that the blossoming of feminism in Protestant countries is due, among other things, to the greater initiative allowed women on the social and ritual plane. One might wonder if, in addition, such a flowering is not the result of a *lack* in the Protestant religious structure with respect to the Maternal, which, on the contrary, was elaborated within Catholicism with a refinement to which the Jesuits gave the final touch, and which still makes Catholicism very difficult to analyze.

The fulfillment, under the name of

up nothing, the ear remained deaf. But everything swarmed, and crumbled, and twisted, and broke—the grinding continued. . . . Then, slowly, a shadowy shape gathered, became detached, darkened, stood out: seen from what must be the true place of my head, it was the right side of my pelvis. Just bony, sleek, yellow, misshapen, a piece of my body jutting out unnaturally, unsymmetrically, but slit: severed scaly surface, revealing under this disproportionate pointed limb the fibers of a marrow. . . . Frozen placenta, live limb of a skeleton, monstrous graft of life on myself, a living dead. Life . . . death . . . undecidable. During delivery it went to the left with the afterbirth. . . . My removed marrow, which nevertheless acts as a graft, which wounds but increases me. Paradox: deprivation and benefit of childbirth. But calm finally hovers over pain, over the terror of this dried branch that comes back to life, cut off, wounded, deprived of its sparkling bark. The calm of another life, the life of that other who wends his way while I remain henceforth like a framework. Still life. There is him, however, his own flesh, which was mine yesterday. Death, then, how could I yield to it?

Mary, of a totality made of woman and God is finally accomplished through the avoidance of death. The Virgin Mary experiences a fate more radiant than her son's: she undergoes no Calvary, she has no tomb, she doesn't die and hence has no need to rise from the dead. Mary doesn't die but, as if to echo oriental beliefs, Taoist among others, according to which human bodies pass from one place to another in an eternal flow that constitutes a carbon copy of the maternal receptacle—she is transported.

Her transition is more passive in the Eastern Church: it is a Dormition (*Koimesis*) during which, according to a number of iconographic representations, Mary can be seen changed into a little girl in the arms of her son who henceforth becomes her father; she thus reverses her role as Mother into a Daughter's role for the greater pleasure of those who enjoy Freud's "Theme of the Three Caskets."

Indeed, *mother* of her son and his *daughter* as well, Mary is also, and besides, his *wife*: she therefore actualizes the threefold metamorphosis of a woman in the tightest parenthood structure. From 1135 on, transposing the Song of Songs, Bernard of Clairvaux glorifies Mary in her role of beloved and wife. But Catherine of Alexandria (said to have been martyred in 307) already pictured herself as receiving the wedding ring from Christ, with the Virgin's help, while Catherine of Siena (1347–1380) goes through a mystical wedding with him. Is it the impact of Mary's function as Christ's beloved and wife that is responsible for the blossoming out of the Marian cult in the West after Bernard and thanks to the Cistercians? *"Vergine*

Madre, figlia del tuo Figlio," Dante exclaims, thus probably best condensing the gathering of the three feminine functions (daughter-wife-mother) within a totality where they vanish as specific corporealities while retaining their psychological functions. Their bond makes up the basis of unchanging and timeless spirituality; "the set time limit of an eternal design" [Termine fisso d'eterno consiglio], as Dante masterfully points out in his Divine Comedy.

The transition is more active in the West, with Mary rising body and soul towards the other world in an Assumption. That feast, honored in Byzantium as early as the fourth century, reaches Gaul in the seventh under the influence of the Eastern Church; but the earliest Western visions of the Virgin's assumption, women's visions (particularly that of Elizabeth von Schonau who died in 1164), date only from the twelfth century. For the Vatican, the Assumption became dogma only in 1950. What death anguish was it intended to soothe after the conclusion of the deadliest of wars?

## Image of Power

On the side of "power," Maria Regina appears in imagery as early as the sixth century in the church of Santa Maria Antiqua in Rome. Interestingly enough, it is she, woman and mother, who is called upon to represent supreme earthly power. Christ is king but neither he nor his father are pictured wearing crowns, diadems, costly paraphernalia and other external signs of abundant material goods. That opulent infringement to Christian idealism is centered on the Virgin Mother. Later, when she assumed the title of Our Lady, this will also be in analogy to the earthly power of the noble feudal lady of medieval courts. Mary's function as guardian of power, later checked when the Church became wary of it, nevertheless persisted in popular and pictural representation, witness Piero della Francesca's impressive painting, Madonna della Misericordia, which was disavowed by Catholic authorities at the time. And yet, not only did the papacy revere more and more the Christly mother as the Vatican's power over cities and municipalities was strengthened, it also openly identified its own institution with the Virgin: Mary was officially proclaimed Queen by Pius XII in 1954 and Mater Ecclesiae in 1964.

## Eia Mater, Fons Amoris!

Fundamental aspects of Western love finally converged on Mary. In a first step, it indeed appears that the Marian cult homologizing Mary with Jesus and carrying asceticism to the extreme was opposed to courtly love for the noble lady, which, while representing social transgression, was not at all a physical or moral sin. And yet, at the very dawn of a "courtliness" that was still very carnal, Mary and the Lady shared one common trait: they are the focal point of men's desires and aspirations. Moreover, because they were unique and thus excluded all other women, both the Lady and the Virgin embodied an absolute authority the more attractive as it appeared removed from paternal sternness. This feminine power must have been experienced as denied power, more pleasant to seize because it was both archaic and secondary, a kind of substitute for effective power in the family and the city but no less authoritarian, the underhand double of explicit phallic power. As early as the thirteenth century, thanks to the implantation of ascetic Christianity and especially, as early as 1328, to the promulgation of Salic laws, which excluded daughters from the inheritance and thus made the loved one very vulnerable and colored one's love for her with all the hues of the impossible, the Marian and courtly streams came together. Around Blanche of Castile (who died in 1252) the Virgin explicitly became the focus of courtly love, thus gathering the attributes of the desired woman and of the holy mother in a totality as accomplished as it was inaccessible. Enough to make any woman suffer, any man dream. One finds indeed in a *Miracle de Notre Dame* the story of a young man who abandons his fiancée for the Virgin: the latter came to him in a dream and reproached him for having left her for an "earthly woman."

Nevertheless, besides that ideal totality that no individual woman could possibly embody, the Virgin also became the fulcrum of the humanization of the West in general and of love in particular. It is again about the thirteenth century, with Francis of Assisi, that this tendency takes shape with the representation of Mary as poor, modest, and humble—madonna of humility at the same time as a devoted, fond mother. The famous nativity of Piero della Francesca in London, in which Simone de Beauvoir too hastily saw a feminine defeat because the mother kneeled before her barely born son, in fact consolidates the new cult of humanistic sensitivity. It replaces the high spirituality that assimilated the Virgin to Christ with an earthly conception of a wholly human mother. As a source for the most popularized pious images, such maternal humility comes closer to "lived" feminine experience than the earlier representations did. Beyond this, however, it is

**Scent of milk, dewed greenery, acid and clear, recall of wind, air, seaweed (as if a body lived without waste): it slides under the skin, does not remain in the mouth or nose but fondles the veins, detaches skin from bones, inflates me like an ozone balloon, and I hover with feet firmly planted on the ground in order to carry him, sure, stable, ineradicable, while he dances in my neck, flutters with my hair, seeks a smooth shoulder on the right, on the left, slips on the breast, swingles, silver vivid blossom of my belly, and finally flies away on my navel in his dream carried by my hands. My son.**

Nights of wakefulness, scattered sleep, sweetness of the child, warm mercury in my arms, cajolery, affection, defenseless body, his or mine, sheltered, protected. A wave swells again, when he goes to sleep, under my skin—tummy, thighs, legs: sleep of the muscles, not of the brain, sleep of the flesh. The wakeful tongue quietly remembers another withdrawal, mine: a blossoming heaviness in the middle of the bed, of a hollow, of the sea. . . . Recovered childhood, dreamed peace restored, in sparks, flash of cells, instants of laughter, smiles in the blackness of dreams, at night, opaque joy that roots me in her bed, my mother's, and projects him, a son, a butterfly soaking up dew from her hand, there, nearby, in the night. Alone: she, I, and he.

He returns from the depths of the nose, the vocal cords, the lungs, the ears, pierces their smothering stopping sickness swab, and awakens in his eyes. Gentleness of the sleeping face, contours of pinkish jade—forehead, eyebrows, nostrils, cheeks, parted features of the mouth, delicate, hard, pointed chin. Without fold or shadow, neither being nor unborn, neither present nor absent, but real, real inaccessible innocence, engaging weight and seraphic lightness. A child?—An angel, a glow on an Italian painting, impassive, peaceful

true that it integrates a certain feminine masochism but also displays its counterpart in gratification and *jouissance*. The truth of it is that the lowered head of the mother before her son is accompanied by the immeasurable pride of the one who knows she is also his wife and daughter. She knows she is destined to that eternity (of the spirit or of the species), of which every mother is unconsciously aware, and with regard to which maternal devotion or even sacrifice is but an insignificant price to pay. A price that is borne all the more easily since, contrasted with the love that binds a mother to her son, all other "human relationships" burst like blatant shams. The Franciscan representation of the Mother conveys many essential aspects of maternal psychology, thus leading up to an influx of common people to the churches and also a tremendous increase in the Marian cult— witness the building of many churches dedicated to her ("Notre Dame"). Such a humanization of Christianity through the cult of the mother also led to an interest in the humanity of the father-man: the celebration of "family life" showed Joseph to advantage as early as the fifteenth century.

## What Body?

We are entitled only to the ear of the virginal body, the tears and the breast. With the female sexual organ changed into an innocent shell, holder of sound, there arises a possible tendency to eroticize hearing, voice, or even understanding. By the same token, however, sexuality is brought down to the level of innuendo. Femi-

dream—dragnet of Mediterranean fishermen. And then, the mother-of-pearl bead awakens: quicksilver. Shiver of the eyelashes, imperceptible twitch of the eyebrows, quivering skin, anxious reflections, seeking, knowing, casting their knowledge aside in the face of my nonknowledge: fleeting irony of childhood gentleness that awakens to meaning, surpasses it, goes past it, causes me to soar in music, in dance. Impossible refinement, subtle rape of inherited genes: before what has been learned comes to pelt him, harden him, ripen him. Hard, mischievous gentleness of the first ailment overcome, innocent wisdom of the first ordeal undergone, yet hopeful blame on account of the suffering I put you through, by calling for you, desiring, creating. . . . Gentleness, wisdom, blame: your face is already human, sickness has caused you to join our species, you speak without words but your throat no longer gurgles—it harkens with me to the silence of your born meaning that draws my tears toward a smile.

The lover gone, forgetfulness comes, but the pleasure of the sexes remains, and there is nothing lacking. No representation, sensation, or recall. Inferno of vice. Later, forgetfulness returns but this time as a fall—leaden—gray, dull, opaque. Forgetfulness: blind-

nine sexual experience is thus rooted in the universality of sound, since it is distributed *equally* among all men, all women. A woman will only have the choice to live her life either *hyperabstractly* ("immediately universal," Hegel said) in order thus to earn divine grace and homologation with symbolic order; or merely *different*, other, fallen ("immediately particular," Hegel said). But she will not be able to accede to the complexity of being divided, of heterogeneity, of the catastrophic-fold-of-"being" ("never singular," Hegel said).

Under a full blue dress, the maternal, virginal body allowed only the breast to show, while the face, with the stiffness of Byzantine icons gradually softened, was covered with tears. Milk and tears became the privileged signs of the *Mater Dolorosa* who invaded the west beginning with the eleventh century, reaching the peak of its influx in the fourteenth. But it never ceased to fill the Marian visions of those, men or women (often children), who were racked by the anguish of a maternal frustration. Even though orality—threshold of infantile regression—is displayed in the area of the breast, while the spasm at the slipping away of eroticism is translated into tears, this should not conceal what milk and tears have in common: they are the metaphors of nonspeech, of a "semiotics" that linguistic communication does not account for. The Mother and her attributes, evoking sorrowful humanity, thus become representatives of a "return of the repressed" in monotheism. They reestablish what is nonverbal and show up as the receptacle of a signifying dising, smothering foam, but on the quiet. Like the fog that devours the park, wolfs down the branches, erases the green, rusty ground, and mists up my eyes.

Absence, inferno, forgetfulness. Rhythm of our loves.

A hunger remains, in place of the heart. A spasm that spreads, runs through the blood vessels to the tips of the breasts, to the tips of the fingers. It throbs, pierces the void, erases it, and gradually settles in. My heart: a tremendous pounding wound. A thirst.

Anguished, guilty. Freud's *Vaterkomplex* on the Acropolis? The impossibility of being without repeated legitimation (without books, man, family). Impossibility—depressing possibility—of "transgression."

Either repression in which I hand the other what I want from others.

Or this squalling of the void, open wound in my heart, which allows me to be only in purgatory.

I yearn for the Law. And since it is not made for me alone, I venture to desire outside the law. Then, narcissism thus awakened—the narcissism that wants to be sex—roams, astonished. In sensual rapture I am distraught. Nothing reassures, for only the law sets anything down. Who calls such a suffering *jouissance*? It is the pleasure of the damned.

position that is closer to so-called primary processes. Without them the complexity of the Holy Ghost would have been mutilated. On the other hand, as they return by way of the Virgin Mother, they find their outlet in the arts—painting and music—of which the Virgin necessarily becomes both patron saint and privileged object.

The function of this "Virginal Maternal" may thus be seen taking shape in the Western symbolic economy. Starting with the high Christly sublimation for which it yearns and occasionally exceeds, and extending to the extralinguistic regions of the unnameable, the Virgin Mother occupied the tremendous territory hither and yon of the parenthesis of language. She adds to the Christian trinity and to the Word that delineates their coherence the heterogeneity they salvage.

The ordering of the maternal libido reached its apotheosis when centered in the theme of death. The *Mater Dolorosa* knows no masculine body save that of her dead son, and her only pathos (which contrasts with the somewhat vacant, gentle serenity of the nursing Madonnas) is her shedding tears over a corpse. Since resurrection there is, and, as Mother of God, she must know this, nothing justifies Mary's outburst of pain at the foot of the cross, unless it be the desire to experience within her own body the death of a human being, which her feminine fate of being the source of life spares her. Could it be that the love, as puzzling as it is ancient, of mourners for corpses relates to the same longing of a woman whom nothing fulfills—the longing to experience the wholly masculine pain of a man who expires at every moment on account of *jouissance* due to obsession with his own death? And yet, Marian pain is in no way connected with tragic outburst: joy and even a kind of triumph follow upon tears, as if the conviction that death does not exist were an irrational but unshakable maternal certainty, on which the principle of resurrection had to rest. The brilliant illustration of the wrenching between desire for the masculine corpse and negation of death, a wrenching whose paranoid logic cannot be overlooked, is masterfully presented by the famous *Stabat Mater.*

**Belief in the mother is rooted in fear, fascinated with a weakness—the weakness of language. If language is powerless to locate myself for and state myself to the other, I assume—I want to believe—that there is someone who makes up for that weakness. Someone, of either sex, *before* the id speaks, before language, who might make me be by means of borders, separations, vertigos. In asserting that "in the beginning was the Word," Christians must have found such a postulate sufficiently hard to believe and, for whatever it was worth, they added its compensation, its permanent lining: the maternal receptacle, purified as it might be by the virginal fantasy. Archaic maternal love would be an incorporation of my suffering that is unfailing, unlike what often happens with the lacunary network of signs. In that sense, any belief, anguished by definition, is upheld by the fascinated fear of language's impotence. Every God, even including the God of the Word, relies on a mother Goddess. Christianity is perhaps also the**

It is likely that all beliefs in resurrections are rooted in mythologies marked by the strong dominance of a mother goddess. Christianity, it is true, finds its calling in the displacement of that biomaternal determinism through the postulate that immortality is mainly that of the name of the Father. But it does not succeed in imposing *its* symbolic revolution without relying on the feminine representation of an immortal biology. Mary defying death is the theme that has been conveyed to us by the numerous variations of the *Stabat Mater,* which, in the text attributed to Jacopone da Todi, enthralls us today through the music of Palestrina, Pergolesi, Haydn, and Rossini.

Let us listen to the baroque style of the young Pergolesi (1710–1736) who was dying of tuberculosis when he wrote his immortal *Stabat Mater.* His musical inventiveness, which, through Haydn, later reverberated in the work of Mozart, probably constitutes his one and only claim to immortality. But when this cry burst forth, referring to Mary facing her son's death, *"Eia Mater, fons amoris!"* ("Hail mother, source of love!")—was it merely a remnant of the period? Man overcomes the unthinkable of death by postulating maternal love in its place—in the place and stead of death and thought. This last of the religions to have displayed in broad daylight the bipolar structure of belief: on the one hand, the difficult experience of the Word—a passion; on the other, the reassuring wrapping in the proverbial mirage of the mother—a love. For that reason, it seems to me that there is only one way to go through the religion of the Word, or its counterpart, the more or less discreet cult of the Mother; it is the "artists'" way, those who make up for the vertigo of language weakness with the oversaturation of sign-systems. By this token, all art is a kind of counterreformation, an accepted baroqueness. For is it not true that if the Jesuits finally did persuade the official Church to accept the cult of the Virgin, following the puritanical wave of the Reformation, that dogma was in fact no more than a pretext, and its efficacy lay elsewhere? It did not become the opposite of the cult of the mother but its inversion through expenditure in the wealth of signs that constitutes the baroque. The latter renders belief in the Mother useless by overwhelming the symbolic weakness where she takes refuge, withdrawn from history, with an overabundance of discourse.

The immeasurable, unconfinable maternal body.

First there is the separation, love, of which divine love is merely a not always convincing derivation, psychologically is perhaps a recall, on the near side of early identifications, of the primal shelter that ensured the survival of the newborn. Such a love is in fact, logically speaking, a surge of anguish at the very moment when the identity of thought and living body collapses. The possibilities of communication having been swept away, only the subtle gamut of sound, touch, and visual traces, older than language and newly worked out, are preserved as an ultimate shield against death. It is only "normal" for a maternal representation to set itself up at the place of this subdued anguish called love. No one escapes it. Except perhaps the saint, the mystic, or the writer who, through the power of language, nevertheless succeeds in doing no better than to take apart the fiction of the mother as mainstay of love, and to identify with love itself and what he is in fact—*a fire of tongues,* an exit from representation. Might not modern art then be, for the few who are attached to it, the implementation of that maternal love—a veil of death, in death's very site and with full knowledge of the facts? A sublimated celebration of incest . . .

## Alone of Her Sex

Freud collected, among other objects of art and archaeology, countless statuettes representing mother goddesses. And yet his interest in them comes to light only in discreet fashion in his work. It shows up when Freud examines artistic creation and homosexuality in connection with Leonardo

previous to pregnancy, but which pregnancy brings to light and imposes without remedy.

On the one hand—the pelvis: center of gravity, unchanging ground, solid pedestal, heaviness and weight to which the thighs adhere, with no promise of agility on that score. On the other—the torso, arms, neck, head, face, calves, feet: unbounded liveliness, rhythm, and mask, which furiously attempt to compensate for the immutability of the central tree. We live on that border, crossroads beings, crucified beings. A woman is neither nomadic nor a male body that considers itself earthly only in erotic passion. A mother is a continuous separation, a division of the very flesh. And consequently a division of language—and it has always been so.

Then there is this other abyss that opens up between the body and what had been its inside: there is the abyss between the mother and the child. What connection is there between myself, or even more unassumingly between my body and this internal graft and fold, which, once the umbilical cord has been severed, is an inaccessible other? My body and . . . him. No connection. Nothing to do with it. And this, as early as the first gestures, cries, steps, long before *its* personality has become my opponent. The child, whether *he* or *she* is

da Vinci and deciphers there the ascendancy of an archaic mother, seen therefore from the standpoint of her effects on man and particularly on this strange function of his sometimes to change languages. Moreover, when Freud analyzes the advent and transformations of monotheism, he emphasizes that Christianity comes closer to pagan myths by integrating, through and against Judaic rigour, a preconscious acknowledgment of a maternal feminine. And yet, among the patients analyzed by Freud, one seeks in vain for mothers and their problems. One might be led to think that motherhood was a solution to neurosis and, by its very nature, ruled out psychoanalysis as a possible other solution. Or might psychoanalysis, at this point, make way for religion? In simplified fashion, the only thing Freud tells us concerning motherhood is that the desire for a child is a transformation of either penis envy or anal drive, and this allows her to discover the neurotic equation child-penis-feces. We are thus enlightened concerning an essential aspect of male phantasmatics with respect to childbirth, and female phantasmatics as well to the extent that it embraces, in large part and in its hysterical labyrinths, the male one. The fact remains, as far as the complexities and pitfalls of maternal experience are involved, that Freud offers only a massive *nothing*, which, for those who might care to analyze it, is punctuated with this or that remark on the part of Freud's mother, proving to him in the kitchen that his own body is anything but immortal and will crumble away like dough; or the sour photograph of Marthe Freud, irremediably an other. To say that there are no sexual relationships constitutes a skimpy assertion when confronting the flash that bedazzles me when I confront the abyss between what was mine and is henceforth but irreparably alien. Trying to think through that abyss: staggering vertigo. No identity holds up. A mother's identity is maintained only through the well-known closure of consciousness within the indolence of habit, when a woman protects herself from the borderline that severs her body and expatriates it from her child. Lucidity, on the contrary, would restore her as cut in half, alien to its other—and a ground favorable to delirium. But also and for that very reason, motherhood destines us to a demented *jouissance* that is answered, by chance, by the nursling's laughter in the sunny waters of the ocean. What connection is there between it and myself? No connection, except for that overflowing laughter where one senses the collapse of some ringing, subtle, fluid identity or other, softly buoyed by the waves.

Concerning that stage of my childhood, scented, warm, and soft to the touch, I have only a spatial memory. No time at all. Fragrance of honey, roundness of forms, silk and velvet under my fingers, on my cheeks.

the wife, a whole mute story. . . . There thus remained for his followers an entire continent to explore, a black one indeed, where Jung was the first to rush in, getting all his esoteric fingers burnt, but not without calling attention to some sore points of the imagination with regard to motherhood, points that are still resisting analytical rationality. [4]

There might doubtless be a way to approach the dark area that motherhood constitutes for a woman; one needs to listen, more carefully than ever, to what mothers are saying today, through their economic difficulties and, beyond the guilt that a too existentialist feminism handed down, through their discomforts, insomnias, joys, angers, desires, pains, and pleasures. . . . One might, in similar fashion, try better to understand the incredible construct of the Maternal that the West elaborated by means of the Virgin, and of which I have just mentioned a few episodes in a never-ending history.

What is it then in this maternal representation that, alone of her sex, goes against both of the two sexes, [5] and was able to attract women's wishes for identification as well as the very precise interposition of those who assumed to keep watch over the symbolic and social order?

Let me suggest, by way of hypothesis, that the virginal maternal is a way (not among the less effective ones) of dealing with feminine paranoia.

- The Virgin assumes her feminine denial of the other sex (of man) but overcomes him by setting up a third person: *I* do not conceive

Mummy. Almost no sight—a shadow that darkens, soaks me up, or vanishes amid flashes. Almost no voice in her placid presence. Except, perhaps, and more belatedly, the echo of quarrels: her exasperation, her being fed up, her hatred. Never straightforward, always held back, as if, although the unmanageable child deserved it, the daughter could not accept the mother's hatred—it was not meant for her. A hatred without recipient or rather whose recipient was not "I" and which, perturbed by such a lack of recipience, was toned down into irony or collapsed into remorse before reaching its destination. With others, this maternal aversion may be worked up to a spasm that is held like a delayed orgasm. Women doubtless reproduce among themselves the strange gamut of forgotten body relationships with their mothers. Complicity in the unspoken, connivance of the inexpressible, of a wink, a tone of voice, a gesture, a tinge, a scent. We are in it, set free of our identification papers and names, on an ocean of preciseness, a computerization of the unnameable. No communication between individuals but connections between atoms, molecules, wisps of words, droplets of sentences. The community of women is a community of dolphins. Conversely, when the other woman posits

with *you* but with *Him*. The result is an immaculate conception (therefore with neither man nor sex), conception of a God with whose existence a woman has indeed something to do, on condition that she acknowledge being subjected to it.

- The Virgin assumes the paranoid lust for power by changing a woman into a Queen in heaven and a Mother of the earthly institutions (of the Church). But she succeeds in stifling that megalomania by putting it on its knees before the child-god.
- The Virgin obstructs the desire for murder or devoration by means of a strong oral cathexis (the breast), valorization of pain (the sob), and incitement to replace the sexed body with the ear of understanding.
- The Virgin assumes the paranoid fantasy of being excluded from time and death through the very flattering representation of Dormition or Assumption.
- The Virgin especially agrees with the repudiation of the other woman (which doubtless amounts basically to a repudiation of the woman's mother) by suggesting the image of A Unique Woman: alone among women, alone among mothers, alone among humans since she is without sin. But the acknowledgment of a longing for uniqueness is immediately checked by the postulate according to which uniqueness is attained only through an exacerbated masochism: a concrete

herself as such, that is, as singular and inevitably in opposition, "I" am startled, so much that "I" no longer know what is going on. There are then two paths left open to the rejection that bespeaks the recognition of the other woman as such. Either, not wanting to experience her, I ignore her and, "alone of my sex," I turn my back on her in friendly fashion. It is a hatred that, lacking a recipient worthy enough of its power, changes to unconcerned complacency. Or else, outraged by her own stubbornness, by that other's belief that she is singular, I unrelentingly let go at her claim to address me and find respite only in the eternal return of power strokes, bursts of hatred—blind and dull but obstinate. I do not see her as herself but beyond her I aim at the claim to singularity, the unacceptable ambition to be something other than a child or a fold in the plasma that constitutes us, an echo of the cosmos that unifies us. What an inconceivable ambition it is to aspire to singularity, it is not natural, hence it is inhuman; the mania smitten with Oneness ("There is only One woman") can only impugn it by condemning it as "masculine." . . . Within this strange feminine seesaw that makes "me" swing from the unnameable community of women over to the war of individual singularities, it is unset-

woman, worthy of the feminine ideal embodied by the Virgin as an inaccessible goal, could only be a nun, a martyr or, if she is married, one who leads a life that would remove her from the "earthly" condition and dedicate her to the highest sublimation alien to her body. A bonus, however: the promised *jouissance.*

A skillful balance of concessions and constraints involving feminine paranoia, the representation of virgin motherhood appears to crown the efforts of a society to reconcile the social remnants of matrilinearism and the unconscious needs of primary narcissism on the one hand, and on the other the requirements of a new society based on exchange and before long on increased production, which require the contribution of the superego and rely on the symbolic paternal agency.

While that clever balanced architecture today appears to be crumbling, one is led to ask the following: what are the aspects of the feminine psyche for which that representation of motherhood does not provide a solution or else provides one that is felt as too coercive by twentieth-century women?

The unspoken doubtless weighs first on the maternal body: as no signifier can uplift it without leaving a remainder, for the signifier is always meaning, communication, or structure, whereas a woman as mother would be, instead, a strange fold that changes culture into nature, the speaking into biology. Although it concerns every woman's body, the heterogeneity that cannot be subsumed in the sig-

tling to say "I." The languages of the great formerly matriarchal civilizations must avoid, do avoid, personal pronouns: they leave to the context the burden of distinguishing protagonists and take refuge in tones to recover an underwater, transverbal communication between bodies. It is a music from which so-called oriental civility tears away suddenly through violence, murder, blood baths. A woman's discourse, would that be it? Did not Christianity attempt, among other things, to freeze that seesaw? To stop it, tear women away from its rhythm, settle them permanently in the spirit? Too permanently . . .

nifier nevertheless explodes violently with pregnancy (the threshold of culture and nature) and the child's arrival (which extracts woman out of her oneness and gives her the possibility—but not the certainty—of reaching out to the other, the ethical). Those particularities of the maternal body compose woman into a being of folds, a catastrophe of being that the dialectics of the trinity and its supplements would be unable to subsume.

Silence weighs heavily none the less on the corporeal and psychological suffering of childbirth and especially the self-sacrifice involved in becoming anonymous in order to pass on the social norm, which one might repudiate for one's own sake but within which *one must* include the child in order to educate it along the chain of generations. A suffering lined with jubilation—ambivalence of masochism—on account of which a woman, rather refractory to perversion, in fact allows herself a coded, fundamental, perverse behavior, ultimate guarantee of society, without which society will not reproduce and will not maintain a constancy of standardized household. Feminine perversion does not reside in the parceling or the Don Juan–like multiplying of objects of desire; it is at once legalized, if not rendered paranoid, through the agency of masochism: all sexual "dissoluteness" will be accepted and hence become insignificant, provided a child seals up such outpours. Feminine perversion [*père-version*] is coiled up in the desire for law as desire for reproduction and continuity, it promotes feminine masochism to the rank of structure stabilizer (against its deviations); by assuring the mother that she may thus enter into an order that is above that of human will it gives her her reward of pleasure. Such coded perversion, such close combat between maternal masochism and the law have been utilized by totalitarian powers of all times to bring women to their side, and, of course, they succeed easily. And yet, it is not enough to "declaim against" the reactionary role of mothers in the service of "male dominating power." One would need to examine to what extent that role corresponds to the biosymbolic latencies of motherhood and, on that basis, to try to understand, since the myth of the Virgin does not subsume them, or no longer does, how their surge lays women open to the most fearsome manipulations, not to mention blinding, or pure and simple rejection by progressive activists who refuse to take a close look.

Among things left out of the virginal myth there is the war between mother and daughter, a war masterfully but too quickly settled by promoting Mary as universal and particular, but never singular—as "alone of her sex." The relation to the other woman has presented our culture, in massive fashion during the past century, with the necessity to reformulate its representations of love and hatred—inherited from Plato's *Symposium*, the troubadours, or Our Lady. On that level, too, motherhood opens out a vista: a woman seldom (although not necessarily) experiences her passion (love and hatred) for another woman without having taken her own mother's place—without having herself become a mother, and especially without slowly learning to differentiate between same beings—as being face to face with her daughter forces her to do.

Finally, repudiation of the other sex (the masculine) no longer seems possible under the aegis of the third person, hypostatized in the child as go-between: "neither me, nor you, but him, the child, the third person, the nonperson, God, which I still am in the final analysis. . . ." Since there is repudiation, and if the feminine being that struggles within it is to remain there, it henceforth calls for, not the deification of the third party, but countercathexes in strong values, in strong *equivalents of power*. Feminine psychosis today is sustained and absorbed through passion for politics, science, art. . . . The variant that accompanies motherhood might be analyzed perhaps more readily than the others from the standpoint of the rejection of the other sex that it compromises. To allow what? Surely not some understanding or other on the part of "sexual partners" within the preestablished harmony of primal androgyny. Rather, to lead to an acknowledgment of what is irreducible, of the irreconcilable interest of both sexes in asserting their differences, in the quest of each one—and of women, after all—for an appropriate fulfillment.

**The love of God and for God resides in a gap: the broken space made explicit by sin on the one side, the beyond on the other. Discontinuity, lack, and arbitrariness: topography of the sign, of the symbolic relation that posits my otherness as impossible. Love, here, is only for the impossible.**

**For a mother, on the other hand, strangely so, the other as arbitrary (the child) is taken for granted. As far as she is concerned—impossible, that is just the way it is: it is reduced to the implacable. The other is inevitable, she seems to say, turn**

These, then, are a few questions among others concerning a motherhood that today remains, after the Virgin, without a discourse. They suggest, all in all, the need of an ethics for

it into a God if you wish, it is nevertheless natural, for such an other has come out of myself, which is yet not myself but a flow of unending germinations, an eternal cosmos. The other goes much without saying and without my saying that, at the limit, it does not exist for itself. The "just the same" of motherly peace of mind, more persistent than philosophical doubt, gnaws, on account of its basic disbelief, at the symbolic's allmightiness. It bypasses perverse negation ("I know, but just the same") and constitutes the basis of the social bond in its generality, in the sense of "resembling others and eventually the species." Such an attitude is frightening when one imagines that it can crush everything the other (the child) has that is specifically irreducible: rooted in that disposition of motherly love, besides, we find the leaden strap it can become, smothering any different individuality. But it is there, too, that the speaking being finds a refuge when his/her symbolic shell cracks and a crest emerges where speech causes biology to show through: I am thinking of the time of illness, of sexual-intellectual-physical passion, of death . . .

this "second" sex, which, as one asserts it, is reawakening.

Nothing, however, suggests that a feminine ethics is possible, and Spinoza excluded women from his (along with children and the insane). Now, if a contemporary ethics is no longer seen as being the same as morality; if ethics amounts to not avoiding the embarrassing and inevitable problematics of the law but giving it flesh, language, and *jouissance*—in that case its reformulation demands the contribution of women. Of women who harbor the desire to reproduce (to have stability). Of women who are available so that our speaking species, which knows it is moral, might withstand death. Of mothers. For an heretical ethics separated from morality, an *herethics*, is perhaps no more than that which in life makes bonds, thoughts, and therefore the thought of death, bearable: herethics is undeath [*a-mort*], love . . . *Eia Mater, fons amoris* . . . So let us again listen to the *Stabat Mater*, and the music, all' the music . . . it swallows up the goddesses and removes their necessity.

NOTES

[1] Between the lines of this section one should be able to detect the presence of Marina Warner, *Alone of All Her Sex: The Myth and Cult of the Virgin Mary* (New York: Knopf,

1976), and Ilse Barande, *Le Maternel singulier* (Paris: Aubier-Montaigne, 1977), which underlay my reflections.

² Georges Dumezil, *La Religion romaine archaïque* (Paris: Payot, 1974).

³ [The French version quoted by Kristeva ("Woman, what is there in common between you and me?") is even stronger than the King James's translation, "Woman, what have I to do with thee?"—Trans.]

⁴ Jung thus noted the "hierogamous" relationship between Mary and Christ as well as the overprotection given the Virgin with respect to original sin, which places her on the margin of mankind; finally, he insisted very much on the Vatican's adoption of the Assumption as dogma, seeing it as one of the considerable merits of Catholicism as opposed to Protestantism (C. J. Jung, *Answer to Job*, Princeton: Princeton University Press, 1969).

⁵ As Caelius Sedulius wrote, "She . . . had no peer / Either in our first mother or in all women / Who were to come. But alone of all her sex / She pleased the Lord" ("Paschalis Carminis," Book II, ll. 68ff. of *Opera Omnia*, Vienna, 1885). Epigraph to Marina Warner, *Alone of All Her Sex*.

* * * * * * * * * * * *

## QUESTIONS FOR A SECOND READING

1. One of the reasons Kristeva's essay is interesting (and challenging) is the way she situates two texts together on the same pages. How did you choose to read these two texts? Did you read one section all the way through first, then the other, did you bounce back and forth page by page or section by section, or did you read another way? Why did you choose this way of reading? What did your strategy allow you to do with the essay? As you read back through, take note of how you first read these texts, and pay particular attention to two or three moments when you could say that the parallel texts speak to each other. How would you explain that conversation? What is being said by one text to the other in those moments? And why do you imagine that Kristeva chose to speak about motherhood in Western culture in this double form?

2. Kristeva refers to a nonspeech, a *semiotics* of milk and tears. As you reread the three or four pages before and after this section (p. 370), pay particular attention to those passages where she discusses both language and "the metaphors of nonspeech." How does she connect this nonlanguage to language? How, in other words, does she relate the actual experiences of birth and motherhood to language? And, finally, how would you explain her thinking about the "subtle gamut of sound, touch, and visual traces" that "are preserved as an ultimate shield against death." Why does she include death in this relationship?

## ASSIGNMENTS FOR WRITING

1. Kristeva is writing about the myth of the Virgin Mary as Stabat Mater in

Western Culture. In doing this, she traces and refers to the whole Judeo-Christian myth (and tradition), which also includes Christ as Mary's son and upholds the idea that "in the beginning was the Word." This is an ambitious and difficult essay that proceeds from Kristeva's reading of a complicated religious myth. Her reading is a construction, a set of understandings that rests on her beliefs and experiences.

Write an essay in which you identify a key belief of Kristeva's that strikes you as important, troubling, or problematic, and use that belief as a way into her essay. What does she have to say about this belief? How does it work into her arguments? What does she find compelling or troubling about it? And what do you find compelling or troubling about it?

2. Early on in this essay, Kristeva poses two questions that prompt her work. "What is there," she asks, "in the portrayal of the Maternal in general and particularly in its Christian, virginal, one, that reduces social anguish and gratifies a male being; what is there that also satisfies a woman so that a commonality of the sexes is set up, beyond and in spite of their glaring incompatibility and permanent warfare?" She is asking, in other words, how the Judeo-Christian myth of the Virgin Mary satisfies both the men and the women who believe it. What "anguish" does it relieve, and how does it set up "a commonality of the sexes"?

Write an essay in which you discuss how, according to Kristeva, this myth "gratifies" the men and "satisfies" the women who subscribe to it. Then discuss what such gratification and satisfaction might say about men and women.

## MAKING CONNECTIONS

1. On page 375, after Kristeva has presented her reading of the Virgin myth, she begins to discuss motherhood in current terms and asks for an awakening to the voices of mothers. "One needs to listen," she says, "more carefully than ever, to what mothers are saying today, through their economic difficulties and, beyond the guilt that a too existentialist feminism handed down, through their discomforts, insomnias, joys, angers, desires, pains, and pleasures."

In this passage Kristeva touches on an issue that Gloria Steinem speaks to in her essay, "Ruth's Song (Because She Could Not Sing It)" (p. 542), when she discusses her awakening to the forces arrayed against her mother, forces that she regards as responsible for her mother's transformation from an "energetic, fun-loving, book-loving woman . . . into someone who was afraid to be alone, who could not hang on to reality long enough to hold a job, and who could rarely concentrate enough to read a book." Steinem feels that many of the forces that affected her mother are patterns women share and that what happened to her mother "was not all personal or accidental."

Later on in her essay (page 377), Kristeva asks, "What are the aspects of the feminine psyche for which that representation of motherhood does not provide a solution or else provides one that is felt as too coercive by twentieth-century women?" Write an essay in which you discuss how you think Kristeva might explain the transformation of Steinem's mother. How might she interpret the forces arrayed against Ruth? How might she, in other words, read these forces in terms of motherly expectations—Ruth's own, Ruth's mother's, and those of the men in Ruth's life? What would Kristeva say about the aspects of Ruth's life for which motherhood did not provide a solution? How might she discuss the commingling of the expectations of motherhood and those expectations outside it?

2. Adrienne Rich in her essay, "When We Dead Awaken: Writing as Re-Vision" (p. 482), argues that old forms of language are traps and that women must learn to develop new forms to better serve their experiences. Toward the end of her essay, she says,

> And today, much poetry by women—and prose for that matter—is charged with anger. I think we need to go through that anger, and we will betray our own reality if we try, as Virginia Woolf was trying, for an objectivity, a detachment, that would make us sound more like Jane Austen or Shakespeare.

Later on she says that "both the victimization and the anger experienced by women" are "built into society, language, the structures of thought."

Write a paper in which you read Kristeva's essay through Rich's. As you reread Kristeva's essay, look for places that might allow you to discuss her anger or victimization or freedom. Would Rich say that Kristeva is trapped, as she was, by the language available to her? If so, what might she identify as evidence of this? If not, what might Rich point to as signs of Kristeva's freedom?

# THOMAS
# KUHN

*T*HOMAS KUHN *was once referred to by Clifford Geertz as an "all-purpose subversive," a man responsible for one of the "shaking originalities" of our century. It is an apt description. His work has not only revised our way of understanding scientific progress, it has given us a new way of looking at progress in any academic discipline or communal enterprise.*

*The key term in Kuhn's theory (and the most controversial term) is "paradigm." According to Kuhn, scientists work within a common paradigm when they work with a shared storehouse of examples, a shared set of theories to explain those examples, and a shared set of procedures to look at new ones. Essentially, these scientists have all had the same training; they all read the same journals, share the same goals, adhere to the same principles, and conduct their work in a similar fashion.*

*Kuhn argues that scientists can happily and profitably work within a paradigm (astronomers can go to the observatory and assume that it is their job to look at the stars in pretty much the same way as all other astronomers). Something significant and dramatic occurs, however, when a scientist steps or stumbles outside the paradigm, when the old examples and explanations no longer hold, and scientists sud-*

*denly see the world in a fundamentally different way (as when the sun, rather than the earth, was recognized as the center of our planetary system). Kuhn presents this argument in his book* The Structure of Scientific Revolutions, *but part of the argument is nicely summarized in an earlier paper of his, "The Historical Structure of Scientific Discovery," first published in the journal* Science.

*Kuhn was born in 1922 in Cincinnati and attended Harvard University, graduating summa cum laude in physics in 1943. He earned his Ph.D., also at Harvard, six years later. A Guggenheim fellow in 1954–55, Kuhn worked for the U.S. Office of Scientific Research and Development before teaching at the University of California at Berkeley, at Princeton, and at MIT. Kuhn was trained as a physicist but now works in the history of science, a field that originally attracted him when he noticed how different science looked to an historian, someone looking in from the outside.*

# The Historical Structure of Scientific Discovery

My object in this article is to isolate and illuminate one small part of what I take to be a continuing historiographic revolution in the study of science. The structure of scientific discovery is my particular topic, and I can best approach it by pointing out that the subject itself may well seem extraordinarily odd. Both scientists and, until quite recently, historians have ordinarily viewed discovery as the sort of event which, though it may have preconditions and surely has consequences, is itself without internal structure. Rather than being seen as a complex development extended both in space and time, discovering something has usually seemed to be a unitary event, one which, like seeing something, happens to an individual at a specific time and place.

This view of the nature of discovery has, I suspect, deep roots in the nature of the scientific community. One of the few historical elements recurrent in the textbooks from which the prospective scientist learns his field is the attribution of particular natural phenomena to the historical personages who first discovered them. As a result of this and other aspects of their training, discovery becomes for many scientists an important goal. To make a discovery is to achieve one of the closest approximations to a property right that the scientific career affords. Professional prestige is often closely associated with these acquisitions. [1] Small wonder, then, that acrimonious disputes about priority and independence in discovery have often marred the normally placid tenor of scientific communication. Even less wonder that many historians of science have seen the individual discovery as an appropriate unit with which to measure scientific progress and have devoted much time and skill to determining what man made which discovery at what point in time. If the study of discovery has a surprise to offer, it is only that, despite the immense energy and ingenuity expended upon it, neither polemic nor painstaking scholarship has often succeeded in pinpointing the time and place at which a given discovery could properly be said to have "been made."

That failure, both of argument and of research, suggests the thesis that I now wish to develop. Many scientific discoveries, particularly the most interesting and important, are not the sort of event about which the questions "Where?" and, more particularly, "When?" can appropriately be asked. Even if all conceivable data were at hand, those questions would not regularly possess answers. That we are persistently driven to ask them nonetheless is symptomatic of a fundamental inappropriateness in our image of discovery. That inappropriateness is here my main concern, but I approach it by considering first the historical problem presented by the attempt to date and to place a major class of fundamental discoveries.

The troublesome class consists of those discoveries—including oxygen, the electric current, X rays, and the electron—which could not be predicted from accepted theory in advance and which therefore caught the assembled profession by surprise. That kind of discovery will shortly be my exclusive concern, but it will help first to note that there is another sort and one which presents very few of the same problems. Into this second class of discoveries fall the neutrino, radio waves, and the elements which filled empty places in the periodic table. The existence of all these objects had been predicted from theory before they were discovered, and the men who made the discoveries therefore knew from the start what to look for. That foreknowledge did not make their task less demanding or less interesting, but it did provide criteria which told them when their goal had been reached. [2] As a result, there have been few priority debates over discoveries of this second sort, and only a paucity of data can prevent the historian from ascribing them to a particular time and place. Those facts help to isolate the difficulties we encounter as we return to the troublesome discoveries of the first class. In the cases that most concern us here there are no benchmarks to inform either the scientist or the historian when the job of discovery has been done.

As an illustration of this fundamental problem and its consequences, consider first the discovery of oxygen. Because it has repeatedly been studied, often with exemplary care and skill, that discovery is unlikely to offer any purely factual surprises. Therefore it is particularly well suited to clarify points of principle. [3] At least three scientists—Carl Scheele, Joseph Priestley, and Antoine Lavoisier—have a legitimate claim to this discovery, and polemicists have occasionally entered the same claim for Pierre Bayen. [4] Scheele's work, though it was almost certainly completed before the relevant researches of Priestley and Lavoisier, was not made public until their work was well known. [5] Therefore it had no apparent causal role, and I shall simplify my story by omitting it. [6] Instead, I pick up the main route to the discovery of oxygen with the work of Bayen, who, sometime before March 1774, discovered that red precipitate of mercury ($HgO$) could, by heating, be made to yield a gas. That aeriform product Bayen identified as fixed air ($CO_2$), a substance made familiar to most pneumatic chemists by the earlier work of Joseph Black. [7] A variety of other substances were known to yield the same gas.

At the beginning of August 1774, a few months after Bayen's work had appeared, Joseph Priestley, repeated the experiment, though probably independently. Priestley, however, observed that the gaseous product would support combustion and therefore changed the identification. For him the gas obtained on heating red precipitate was nitrous air ($N_2O$), a substance that he had himself discovered more than two years before. [8] Later in the same month Priestley made a trip to Paris and there informed Lavoisier of the new reaction. The latter repeated the experiment once more, both in November 1775 and in February 1774. But, because he used tests somewhat more elaborate than Priestley's, Lavoisier again changed the identification. For him, as of May 1775, the gas released by red precipitate was neither fixed air nor nitrous air. Instead, it was "[atmospheric] air itself entire without alteration . . . even to the point that . . . it comes out more pure." [9] Meanwhile, however, Priestley had also been at work, and, before the beginning of March 1775, he, too, had concluded that the gas must be "common air." Until this point all of the men who had produced a gas from red precipitate of mercury had identified it with some previously known species. [10]

The remainder of this story of discovery is briefly told. During March 1775 Priestley discovered that his gas was in several respects very much "better" than common air, and he therefore reidentified the gas once more, this time calling it "dephlogisticated air," that is, atmospheric air deprived of its normal complement of phlogiston. ° This conclusion Priestley published in the *Philosophical Transactions*, and it was apparently that publication which led Lavoisier to reexamine his own results. [11] The reexamination began during February 1776 and within a year had led Lavoisier to the conclusion that the gas was actually a separable component of the atmos-

---

**Phlogiston**   Was once believed to be the element that caused combustion and that was given off by anything burning.

pheric air which both he and Priestley had previously thought of as homogeneous. With this point reached, with the gas recognized as an irreducibly distinct species, we may conclude that the discovery of oxygen had been completed.

But to return to my initial question, when shall we say that oxygen was discovered and what criteria shall we use in answering that question? If discovering oxygen is simply holding an impure sample in one's hands, then the gas had been "discovered" in antiquity by the first man who ever bottled atmospheric air. Undoubtedly, for an experimental criterion, we must at least require a relatively pure sample like that obtained by Priestley in August 1774. But during 1774 Priestley was unaware that he had discovered anything except a new way to produce a relatively familiar species. Throughout that year his "discovery" is scarcely distinguishable from the one made earlier by Bayen, and neither case is quite distinct from that of the Reverend Stephen Hales, who had obtained the same gas more than forty years before. [12] Apparently to discover something one must also be aware of the discovery and know as well what it is that one has discovered.

But, that being the case, how much must one know? Had Priestley come close enough when he identified the gas as nitrous air? If not, was either he or Lavoisier significantly closer when he changed the identification to common air? And what are we to say about Priestley's next identification, the one made in March 1775? Dephlogisticated air is still not oxygen or even, for the phlogistic chemist, a quite unexpected sort of gas. Rather it is a particularly pure atmospheric air. Presumably, then, we wait for Lavoisier's work in 1776 and 1777, work which led him not merely to isolate the gas but to see what it was. Yet even that decision can be questioned, for in 1777 and to the end of his life Lavoisier insisted that oxygen was an atomic "principle of acidity" and that oxygen *gas* was formed only when that "principle" united with caloric, the matter of heat. [13] Shall we therefore say that oxygen had not yet been discovered in 1777? Some may be tempted to do so. But the principle of acidity was not banished from chemistry until after 1810 and caloric lingered on until the 1860s. Oxygen had, however, become a standard chemical substance long before either of those dates. Furthermore, what is perhaps the key point, it would probably have gained that status on the basis of Priestley's work alone without benefit of Lavoisier's still partial reinterpretation.

I conclude that we need a new vocabulary and new concepts for analyzing events like the discovery of oxygen. Though undoubtedly correct, the sentence "Oxygen was discovered" misleads by suggesting that discovering something is a single simple act unequivocally attributable, if only we knew enough, to an individual and an instant in time. When the discovery is unexpected, however, the latter attribution is always impossible and the former often is as well. Ignoring Scheele, we can, for example, safely say that oxygen had not been discovered before 1774; probably we would also insist that it had been discovered by 1777 or shortly thereafter. But within those limits any attempt to date the discovery or to attribute it to an individual must inevitably be arbitrary. Furthermore, it must be arbitrary just because discovering a new sort of phenomenon is necessarily a complex process which involves recognizing both *that* something is and *what* it is. Observation and conceptualization, fact and the assimilation of fact to theory, are inseparably linked in the discovery of scientific novelty. Inevitably, that process extends over time and may often involve a number of people. Only for discoveries in my second category—those whose nature is known in advance—can discovering *that* and discovering *what* occur together and in an instant.

Two last, simpler, and far briefer examples will simultaneously show how typical the case of oxygen is and also prepare the way for a somewhat more precise conclusion. On the night of 13 March 1781, the astronomer William Herschel made the following entry in his journal: "In the quartile near Zeta Tauri . . . is a curious either nebulous star or perhaps a comet." [14] That entry is generally said to record the discovery of the planet Uranus, but it cannot quite have done that. Between 1690 and Herschel's observation in 1781 the same object had been seen and recorded at least seventeen times by men who took it to be a star. Herschel differed from them only in supposing that, because in his telescope it appeared especially large, it might actually be a *comet!* Two additional observations on 17 and 19 March confirmed that suspicion by showing that the object he had observed moved among the stars. As a result, astronomers throughout Europe were informed of the discovery, and the mathematicians among them began to compute the new comet's orbit. Only several months later, after all those attempts had repeatedly failed to square with observation, did the astronomer Lexell suggest that the object observed by Herschel might be a planet. And only when additional computations, using a planet's rather than a comet's orbit, proved reconcilable with observation was that suggestion generally accepted. At what point during 1781 do we want to say that the planet Uranus was discovered? And are we entirely and unequivocally clear that it was Herschel rather than Lexell who discovered it?

Or consider still more briefly the story of the discovery of X rays, a story which opens on the day in 1895 when the physicist Roentgen interrupted a well-precedented investigation of cathode rays because he noticed that a barium platinocyanide screen far from his shielded apparatus glowed when the discharge was in process. [15] Additional investigations—they required seven hectic weeks during which Roentgen rarely left the laboratory—indicated that the cause of the glow traveled in straight lines from the cathode ray tube, that the radiation cast shadows, that it could not be deflected by a magnet, and much else besides. Before announcing his discovery Roentgen had convinced himself that his effect was not due to cathode rays themselves but to a new form of radiation with at least some similarity to light. Once again the question suggests itself: When shall we say that X rays were actually discovered? Not, in any case, at the first instant, when all that had been noted was a glowing screen. At least one other investigator had seen that glow and, to his subsequent chagrin, discovered nothing at all. Nor, it is almost as clear, can the moment of discovery be pushed back to a point during the last week of investigation. By that time Roentgen was exploring the properties of the new radiation he had *already* discovered. We may have to settle for the remark that X rays emerged in Würzburg between 8 November and 28 December 1895.

The characteristics shared by these examples are, I think, common to all the episodes by which unanticipated novelties become subjects for scientific attention. I therefore conclude these brief remarks by discussing three such common characteristics, one which may help to provide a framework for the further study of the extended episodes we customarily call "discoveries."

In the first place, notice that all three of our discoveries—oxygen, Uranus, and X rays—began with the experimental or observational isolation of an anomaly, that is, with nature's failure to conform entirely to expectation. Notice, further, that the process by which that anomaly was educed displays simultaneously the apparently incompatible characteristics of the inevitable and the accidental. In the case of X rays, the anomalous glow which provided Roentgen's first clue was clearly the result of an accidental disposition of his apparatus. But by 1895 cathode rays were a normal subject for research all over Europe; that research quite regularly juxtaposed cathode-rays tubes with sensitive screens and films; as a result, Roentgen's accident was almost certain to occur elsewhere, as in fact it had. Those remarks, however, should make Roentgen's case look very much like those of Herschel and Priestley. Herschel first observed his oversized and thus anomalous star in the course of a prolonged survey of the northern heavens. That survey was, except for the magnification provided by Herschel's instruments, precisely of the sort that had repeatedly been carried through before and that had occasionally resulted in prior observations of Uranus. And Priestley, too—when he isolated the gas that behaved almost but not quite like nitrous air and then almost but not quite like common air—was seeing something unintended and wrong in the outcome of a sort of experiment for which there was much European precedent and which had more than once before led to the production of the new gas.

These features suggest the existence of two normal requisites for the beginning of an episode of discovery. The first, which throughout this paper I have largely taken for granted, is the individual skill, wit, or genius to recognize that something has gone wrong in ways that may prove consequential. Not any and every scientist would have noted that no unrecorded star should be so large, that the screen ought not to have glowed, that nitrous air should not have supported life. But that requisite presupposes another which is less frequently taken for granted. Whatever the level of genius available to observe them, anomalies do not emerge from the normal course of scientific research until both instruments and concepts have developed sufficiently to make their emergence likely and to make the anomaly which results recognizable as a violation of expectation. [16] To say that an unexpected discovery begins only when something goes wrong is to say that it begins only when scientists know well both how their instruments and how nature should behave. What distinguished Priestley, who saw an anomaly, from Hales, who did not, is largely the considerable articulation of pneumatic techniques and expectations that had come into being during the four decades which separate their two isolations of oxygen. [17] The very number of claimants indicates that after 1770 the discovery could not have been postponed for long.

The role of anomaly is the first of the characteristics shared by our three examples. A second can be considered more briefly, for it has provided the main theme for the body of my text. Though awareness of anomaly marks the beginning of a discovery, it marks only the beginning. What necessarily follows, if anything at all is to be discovered, is a more or less extended period during which the individual and often many members of his group struggle to make the anomaly lawlike. Invariably that period demands additional observation or experimentation as well as repeated cogitation. While it continues, scientists repeatedly revise their expectations, usually their instrumental standards, and sometimes their most fundamental theories as well. In this sense discoveries have a proper internal history as well as prehistory and a posthistory. Furthermore, within the rather vaguely delimited interval of internal history, there is no single moment or day which the historian, however complete his data, can identify as the point at which the discovery was made. Often, when several individuals are involved, it is even impossible unequivocally to identify any one of them as the discoverer.

Finally, turning to the third of these selected common characteristics, note briefly what happens as the period of discovery draws to a close. A full discussion of that question would require additional evidence and a separate paper, for I have had little to say about the aftermath of discovery in the body of my text. Nevertheless, the topic must not be entirely neglected, for it is in part a corollary of what has already been said.

Discoveries are often described as mere additions or increments to the growing stockpile of scientific knowledge, and that description has helped make the unit discovery seem a significant measure of progress. I suggest, however, that it is fully appropriate only to those discoveries which, like the elements that filled missing places in the periodic table, were anticipated and sought in advance and which therefore demanded no adjustment, adaptation, and assimilation from the profession. Though the sorts of discoveries we have here been examining are undoubtedly additions to scientific knowledge, they are also something more. In a sense that I can now develop only in part, they also react back upon what has previously been known, providing a new view of some previously familiar objects and simultaneously changing the way in which even some traditional parts of science are practiced. Those in whose area of special competence the new phenomenon falls often see both the world and their work differently as they emerge from the extended struggle with anomaly which constitutes the discovery of that phenomenon.

William Herschel, for example, when he increased by one the time-honored number of planetary bodies, taught astronomers to see new things when they looked at the familiar heavens even with instruments more traditional than his own. That change in the vision of astronomers must be a principal reason why, in the half century after the discovery of Uranus, twenty additional circumsolar bodies were added to the traditional seven. [18] A similar transformation is even clearer in the aftermath of Roentgen's work. In the first place, established techniques for cathode-ray research had to be changed, for scientists found they had failed to control a relevant variable. Those changes included both the redesign of old apparatus and revised ways of asking old questions. In addition, those scientists most concerned experienced the same transformation of vision that we have just noted in the aftermath of the discovery of Uranus. X rays were the first new sort of radiation discovered since infrared and ultraviolet at the beginning of the century. But within less than a decade after Roentgen's work, four more were disclosed by the new scientific sensitivity (for example, to fogged photographic plates) and by some of the new instrumental techniques that had resulted from Roentgen's work and its assimilation. [19]

Very often these transformations in the established techniques of scientific practice prove even more important than the incremental knowledge provided by the discovery itself. That could at least be argued in the cases of Uranus and of X rays; in the case of my third example, oxygen, it is categorically clear. Like the work of Herschel and Roentgen, that of Priestley and Lavoisier taught scientists to view old situations in new ways. Therefore, as we might anticipate, oxygen was not the only new chemical species to be identified in the aftermath of their work. But, in the case of oxygen, the readjustments demanded by assimilation were so profound that they played an integral and essential role—though they were not by themselves the cause—in the gigantic upheaval of chemical theory and practice which has since been known as the chemical revolution. I do not suggest that every unanticipated discovery has consequences for science so deep and so far-reaching as those which followed the discovery of oxygen. But I do suggest that every such discovery demands, from those most concerned, the sorts of readjustment that, when they are more obvious, we equate with scientific revolution. It is, I believe, just because they demand readjustments like these that the process of discovery is necessarily and inevitably one that shows structure and that therefore extends in time.

## NOTES

[1] For a brilliant discussion of these points, see R. K. Merton, "Priorities in Scientific Discovery: A Chapter in the Sociology of Science," *American Sociological Review* 22 (1957): 635. Also very relevant, though it did not appear until this article had been prepared, is F. Reif, "The Competitive World of the Pure Scientist," *Science* 134 (1961): 1957.

[2] Not all discoveries fall so neatly as the preceding into one or the other of my two classes. For example, Anderson's work on the positron was done in complete ignorance of Dirac's theory from which the new particle's existence had already been very nearly predicted. On the other hand, the immediately succeeding work by Blackett and Occhialini made full use of Dirac's theory and therefore exploited experiment more fully and constructed a more forceful case for the positron's existence than Anderson had been able to do. On this subject see N. R. Hanson, "Discovering the Positron," *British Journal for the Philosophy of Science* 12 (1961): 194; 12 (1962): 299. Hanson suggests several of the points developed here. I am much indebted to Professor Hanson for a preprint of this material.

[3] I have adapted a less familiar example from the same viewpoint in "The Caloric Theory of Adiabatic Compression," *Isis* 49 (1958): 132. A closely similar analysis of the emergence of a new theory is included in the early pages of my essay "Energy Conservation as an Example of Simultaneous Discovery," in *Critical Problems in the History of Science*, ed. M. Clagett (Madison: University of Wisconsin Press, 1959), pp. 321–56. . . . Reference to these papers may add depth and detail to the following discussion.

[4] The still classic discussion of the discovery of oxygen is A. N. Meldrum, *The Eighteenth Century Revolution in Science: The First Phase* (Calcutta, 1930), chap. 5. A more convenient and generally quite reliable discussion is included in J. B. Conant, *The Overthrow of the Phlogiston Theory: The Chemical Revolution of 1775–1789*, Harvard Case Histories in Experimental Science, case 2 (Cambridge: Harvard University Press, 1950). A recent and indispensable review which includes an account of the development of the priority controversy, is M. Daumas, *Lavoisier, théoricien et expérimentateur* (Paris, 1955), chaps. 2 and 3. H. Guerlac has added much significant detail to our knowledge of the early relations between Priestley and Lavoisier in his "Joseph Priestley's First Papers on Gases and Their Reception in France," *Journal of the History of Medicine* 12 (1957): 1 and in his very recent monograph, *Lavoisier: The Crucial Year* (Ithaca: Cornell University Press, 1961). For Scheele see J. R. Partington, *A Short History of Chemistry*, 2d ed. (London, 1951), pp. 104–09.

[5] For the dating of Scheele's work, see A. E. Nordenskjöld, *Carl Wilhelm Scheele, Nachgelassene Briefe und Aufzeichnungen* (Stockholm, 1892).

[6] U. Bocklund ("A Lost Letter from Scheele to Lavoisier," *Lychnos*, 1957–58, pp. 39–62) argues that Scheele communicated his discovery of oxygen to Lavoisier in a letter of 30 Sept. 1774. Certainly the letter is important, and it clearly demonstrates that Scheele was ahead of both Priestley and Lavoisier at the time it was written. But I think the letter is not quite so candid as Bocklund supposes, and I fail to see how Lavoisier could have drawn the discovery of oxygen from it. Scheele describes a procedure for reconstituting common air, not for producing a new gas, and that, as we shall see, is almost the same information that Lavoisier received from Priestley at about the same time. In any case, there is no evidence that Lavoisier performed the sort of experiment that Scheele suggested.

[7] P. Bayen, "Essai d'expériences chymiques, faites sur quelques précipités de mer-

cure, dans la vue de découvrir leur nature, Seconde partie," *Observations sur la physique* 3 (1774): 280–95, particularly pp. 289–91.

[8] J. B. Conant, *The Overthrow of the Phlogiston Theory*, pp. 34–40.

[9] Ibid., p. 23. A useful translation of the full text is available in Conant.

[10] For simplicity I use the term *red precipitate* throughout. Actually, Bayen used the precipitate; Priestley used both the precipitate and the oxide produced by direct calcination of mercury; and Lavoisier used only the latter. The difference is not without importance, for it was not unequivocally clear to chemists that the two substances were identical.

[11] There has been some doubt about Priestley's having influenced Lavoisier's thinking at this point, but, when the latter returned to experimenting with the gas in February 1776, he recorded in his notebooks that he had obtained "l'air dephlogistique de M. Priestley" (M. Daumas, *Lavoisier*, p. 36).

[12] J. R. Partington, *A Short History of Chemistry*, p. 91.

[13] For the traditional elements in Lavoisier's interpretations of chemical reactions, see H. Metzger, *La philosophie de la matière chez Lavoisier* (Paris, 1935), and Daumas, *Lavoisier*, chap. 7.

[14] P. Doig, *A Concise History of Astronomy* (London: Chapman, 1950), pp. 115–16.

[15] L. W. Taylor, *Physics, the Pioneer Science* (Boston: Houghton Mifflin Co., 1941), p. 790.

[16] Though the point cannot be argued here, the conditions which make the emergence of anomaly likely and those which make anomaly recognizable are to a very great extent the same. That fact may help us understand the extraordinarily large amount of simultaneous discovery in the sciences.

[17] A useful sketch of the development of pneumatic chemistry is included in Partington, *A Short History of Chemistry*, chap. 6.

[18] R. Wolf, *Geschichte der Astronomie* (Munich, 1877), pp. 513–15, 683–93. The prephotographic discoveries of the asteroids is often seen as an effect of the invention of Bode's law. But that law cannot be the full explanation and may not even have played a large part. Piazzi's discovery of Ceres, in 1801, was made in ignorance of the current speculation about a missing planet in the "hole" between Mars and Jupiter. Instead, like Herschel, Piazzi was engaged on a star survey. More important, Bode's law was old by 1800 (ibid., p. 683), but only one man before that date seems to have thought it worthwhile to look for another planet. Finally, Bode's law, by itself, could only suggest the utility of looking for additional planets; it did not tell astronomers where to look. Clearly, however, the drive to look for additional planets dates from Herschel's work on Uranus.

[19] For α-,β-, and γ-radiation, discovery of which dates from 1896, see Taylor, *Physics*, pp. 800–804. For the fourth new form of radiation, N rays, see D. J. S. Price, *Science Since Babylon* (New Haven: Yale University Press, 1961), pp. 84–89. That N rays were ultimately the source of a scientific scandal does not make them less revealing of the scientific community's state of mind.

. . . . . . . . . . .

## QUESTIONS FOR A SECOND READING

1. In his essay, Kuhn says that "we need a new vocabulary and new concepts for analyzing events like the discovery of oxygen." As you read back

through the essay, what might be the key terms of this "new vocabulary," and what the key concepts?

2. Kuhn says that the sentence "Oxygen was discovered," though undoubtedly correct, "misleads by suggesting that discovering something is a single simple act unequivocally attributable, if only we knew enough, to an individual and an instant in time." The phrase "if only we knew enough" calls attention to the kind of knowledge historians of the old school used to think they had to aspire to in order to write the history of science. What did those historians believe they had to know? How would you characterize that kind of knowledge? And what kind of knowledge, then, do Kuhn and historians of his school believe they should have? As you reread the essay, look for passages that will help you to distinguish between these two schools of historians.

### ASSIGNMENTS FOR WRITING

1. Kuhn's essay presents some interesting problems for a general reader. It's not a particularly difficult essay to understand—the examples are not overly technical or arcane, and the terms, with few exceptions, are drawn from the general language of academic discussion. It would take considerable effort and training, however, to be able to look critically at Kuhn's examples—to look at what he does with the discovery of oxygen, to see what else he might have done or what he was unable to do. Furthermore, few of us have ready access to instances of advanced scientific experimentation and discovery that we could use to test or to apply Kuhn's theory of the "internal structure" of scientific discovery.

If you can't work with Kuhn's examples, however, you can work with his terms, terms that can be put to use to examine discoveries drawn from your own immediate repertoire of examples. Write an essay that describes and analyzes a discovery whose "history" you know well. This need not be a scientific discovery, but it should be a discovery of some consequence to you personally. In Kuhn's terms, it should be a discovery that gave you a "new view" of something familiar, something you had taken for granted, and that caused you to readjust your way of thinking. This discovery may have occurred in school (even in the science lab), but it may also have occurred at home, on the streets, or in sports. The point of your essay should be to describe this event and then, as though you were doing a Kuhnian analysis, to analyze its "historical structure."

2. Kuhn says that all three of the discoveries he studied began with an anomaly, with "nature's failure to conform entirely to expectation." Phrases like this are often used to describe the experience of reading, where a reader moves along expecting to hear the sorts of things one usually hears but then is surprised by what a writer does and has to readjust his view of what the author is saying. Texts, or sections of texts, that might be called "difficult" or "obscure" or "boring" might also, that is, be called "anoma-

lous," and, as a consequence, the story of reading could be plotted differently.

Write an essay in which you tell a story of reading, the history of your experience as a reader with this essay or with one of the other essays in this book. Your primary responsibility is to be a good historian—to tell a story that is rich in detail and in understanding. This is your story. You are one of the characters, if not the main character. And so you want to bring forward the features that make it a story—suspense, action, context, drama. You are also writing, however, to see the degree to which Kuhn's approach to understanding scientific discovery can be usefully applied to the study of the process of reading. You should use his terms and methods where you can, and where they do not seem appropriate, think about why they don't work and what you need to put in their place.

## MAKING CONNECTIONS

1. In his essay, Kuhn talks about William Herschel and the discovery of Uranus. In "When We Dead Awaken" (p. 482), and in the poem "Planetarium" contained in that essay, Adrienne Rich writes about Caroline Herschel, his sister. Both Rich and Kuhn, we could say, are writing histories of these figures. Write an essay in which you discuss what you see to be the interesting difference (or differences) between the goals and methods of these two historians. Both Rich and Kuhn have explicitly stated goals, to be sure, but you should work as well from the evidence of what they actually do when they write about these figures (and you should say what you can about *why* they do what they do). You want to be sure to draw examples, that is, from the *actual* practice.

2. Kuhn provides a way of seeing and describing the "internal structure" of a discovery. He also provides a way of seeing and talking about the relation of a scientist to the community within which he or she works—the community of scientists who share a particular way of seeing and talking about the subjects they study.

   Kuhn's terms and methods could be used to study Clifford Geertz's essay, "Deep Play: Notes on the Balinese Cockfight" (p. 272). While it would be hard to say that Geertz "discovered" the Balinese cockfight, it is possible to say that he discovered a way of describing and interpreting it. Geertz also places his work in the context of the work of others, some of whom are working anthropologists, but some of whom are not. He does this through references in the essay itself, but also in his footnotes. There is an ample record, in other words, of the scholarly community within which Geertz was working.

   Write an essay in which you give a Kuhnian reading of Geertz's essay. What, in other words, might Kuhn say if he were studying and describing Geertz's work with the Balinese cockfight? How might he describe the historical structure of Geertz's discovery?

# MARK CRISPIN
# MILLER

*M*ARK CRISPIN MILLER *(b. 1949) is one of the most interesting and persuasive critics of American popular culture at work today. He was educated at Johns Hopkins and Northwestern universities. After serving on the faculty at the University of Pennsylvania, he returned to Baltimore, where he teaches in the Writing Seminars at Johns Hopkins while maintaining a career as a journalist. Miller has written on cinema, rock and roll, television, and advertising in magazines such as* The Nation, Mother Jones, *the* Georgia Review, *and the* New York Review of Books. *The essays that follow appeared originally in* The New Republic *(where Miller worked as a regular columnist) and an anthology,* Watching Television *(1987; ed. Todd Gitlin). Both essays are collected in Miller's recent book,* Boxed In: The Culture of TV *(1988). In preparing the book, Miller added a brief afterword to each selection.*

*Like Simon Frith, Miller has written about the unesasy fit between his two careers. Miller began as a specialist in English Renaissance literature and a professor in an English department. Even then, however, he was writing regularly about popular culture. As a consequence of his two preoccupations, Miller reached a point early in his professional life at which his list of publications, as he said,* had "*a certain jaunty schizophrenic air, associating 'Welcome Back, Kotter' with The Faerie Queene, or Castiglione's notion of* sprezzatura *with Elvis Presley's weight problem.*" After a while, "*It was not easy to sustain this dual project. In fact, it soon turned out to be impossible, because of numerous subtle pressures. For one thing, most of my superiors could see little excuse for the public writing, which struck them as unseemly, trivial, too 'journalistic' an enterprise for one trained to be a scholar/critic.*"

*Miller's work argues, however, why a scholar's training both can and should be focused on the material of our common culture—TV, for example. For one thing, television is powerfully* there *at the center of contemporary life; it is the culture that defines the experience of millions. Television simply touches many more than does the "high" culture of the Renaissance, and it would be foolish to assume that this is not a matter of national importance or that "low" commercial culture is not worth careful, disciplined attention. But Miller makes another argument as well:*

> *Those who have grown up watching television are not, because of all that gaping, now automatically adept at visual interpretation. That spectatorial "experience" is passive, mesmeric, undiscriminating, and therefore not conducive to the refinement of the critical faculties: logic and imagination, linguistic precision, historical awareness, and a capacity for long, intense absorption. These—and not the abilities to compute, apply, or memorize—are the true desiderata of any higher education, and it is critical thinking that can best realize them.*

*In his essay "The Imaginary Signifier," the French film theorist Christian Metz describes the relationship of the film critic to film as marked by ambivalence. To write convincingly about film, Metz argues, one must love and hate it simultaneously: love it enough to watch with pleasure and attention, and hate it enough to reveal its unpleasant assumptions and effects. In a similar vein, Miller describes his work as a critic this way, "To read is not just to undo. Critical analysis can just as easily reclaim a marvel, reveal—in all humility—some excellence obscured by time or preconception, as it can devastate a lie." But to read is still a matter of "undoing." "Such a project . . . demands that we not simply snicker at TV, presuming its stupidity and our own superiority. Rather we need a critical approach that would take TV seriously (without extolling it), a method of deciphering TV's component images, requiring both a meticulous attention to concrete detail, and a sense of TV's historical situation. Genuinely seen through, those details illuminate that larger context, and vice versa, so that the reading of TV contains and necessitates a reading of our own moment and its past."*

*The two essays that follow represent Miller's attempts, as he said, to set such a critical example. "They constitute the record of my discovery, begun down in the library, that there was also a lot of reading to be done outside. To look and look again into the glowering features of a Winston smoker ('I like the box'), or into a thirty-second ad for Shield ('I do feel cleaner!'), or into a certain three minutes of convention coverage ('Mr. Mayor, I work with my colleagues'), or at Bill Cosby's pseudoimpish grin, . . . has been to train the New Critical attentiveness on some of the ephemeral details of a spectacle approaching total closure, yet at the same time pointing some way out."*

# Getting Dirty

We are outside a house, looking in the window, and this is what we see: a young man, apparently nude and half-crazed with anxiety, lunging toward the glass. "Gail!" he screams, as he throws the window open and leans outside, over a flower box full of geraniums: "The most important shower of my life, and you switch deodorant soap!" He is, we now see, only half-naked, wearing a towel around his waist; and he shakes a packaged bar of soap—"Shield"—in one accusing hand. Gail, wearing a blue man-tailored shirt, stands outside, below the window, clipping a hedge. She handles this reproach with an ease that suggests years of contempt. "Shield is better," she explains patiently, in a voice somewhat deeper than her husband's. "It's extra strength." (Close-up of the package in the husband's hand, Gail's efficient finger gliding along beneath the legend, THE EXTRA STRENGTH DEODORANT SOAP.) "Yeah," whimpers Mr. Gail, "but my first call on J. J. Siss [sic], the company's *toughest customer*, and now *this*!" Gail nods with broad mock-sympathy, and stands firm: "Shield fights odor better, so you'll feel *cleaner*," she assures her husband, who darts away with a jerk of panic, as Gail rolls her eyes heavenward and gently shakes her head, as if to say, "What a half-wit!"

Cut to our hero, as he takes his important shower. No longer frantic, he now grins down at himself, apparently delighted to be caked with Shield, which, in its detergent state, has the consistency of wet cement. He then goes out of focus, as if glimpsed through a shower door. "Clinical tests prove," proclaims an eager baritone, "Shield fights odor better than the *leading* deodorant soap!" A bar of Shield (green) and a bar of that other soap (yellow) zip up the screen with a festive toot, forming a sort of graph which demonstrates that Shield does, indeed, "fight odor better, so you'll feel *cleaner*!"

This particular contest having been settled, we return to the major one, which has yet to be resolved. Our hero reappears, almost transformed: calmed down, dressed up, his voice at least an octave lower. "I *do* feel cleaner!" he announces cheerily, leaning into the doorway of a room where Gail is arranging flowers. She pretends to be ecstatic at this news, and he comes toward her, setting himself up for a profound humiliation by putting on a playful air of suave command. Adjusting his tie like a real man of the world, he saunters over to his wife and her flower bowl, where he plucks a dainty purple flower and lifts it to his lapel: "And," he boasts throughout all this, trying to make his voice sound even deeper, "with old J. J.'s business and my brains—" "—you'll . . . *clean up again*?" Gail asks with suggestive irony, subverting his authoritative pose by leaning against him, draping one hand over his shoulder to dangle a big yellow daisy down his chest. Taken aback, he shoots her a distrustful look, and she titters at him.

Finally, the word SHIELD appears in extreme close-up and the camera pulls back, showing two bars of the soap, one packaged and one not, on display amidst an array of steely bubbles. "Shield fights odor better, so you'll feel *cleaner!*" the baritone reminds us, and then our hero's face appears once more, in a little square over the unpackaged bar of soap: "I feel *cleaner* than *ever before!*" he insists, sounding faintly unconvinced.

Is all this as stupid as it seems at first? Or is there, just beneath the surface of this moronic narrative, some noteworthy design, intended to appeal to (and to worsen) some of the anxieties of modern life? A serious look at this particular trifle might lead us to some strange discoveries.

We are struck, first of all, by the commercial's pseudofeminism, an advertising ploy with a long history, and one ubiquitous on television nowadays. Although the whole subject deserves more extended treatment, this commercial offers us an especially rich example of the strategy. Typically, it woos its female viewers—i.e., those who choose the soap in most households—with a fantasy of dominance; and it does so by inverting the actualities of woman's lot through a number of imperceptible details. For instance, in this marriage it is the wife, and not the husband, who gets to keep her name; and Gail's name, moreover, is a potent one, because of its brevity and its homonymic connotation. (If this housewife were more delicately named, called "Lillian" or Cecilia," it would lessen her illusory strength.) She is also equipped in more noticeable ways: she's the one who wears the button-down shirt in this family, she's the one who's competent both outdoors and in the house, and it is she, and only she, who wields the tool.

These visual details imply that Gail is quite a powerful housewife, whereas her nameless mate is a figure of embarrassing impotence. This "man," in fact, is actually Gail's *wife*: he is utterly feminized, striking a posture and displaying attributes which men have long deplored in women. In other words, this commercial, which apparently takes the woman's side, is really the expression (and reflection) of misogyny. Gail's husband is dependent and hysterical, entirely without that self-possession which we expect from solid, manly types, like Gail. This is partly the result of his demeanor: in the opening scene, his voice sometimes cracks ludicrously, and he otherwise betrays the shrill desperation of a man who can't remember where he left his scrotum. The comic effect of this frenzy, moreover, is subtly enhanced by the mise-en-scène, which puts the man in a conventionally feminine position—in dishabille, looking down from a window. Thus we infer that he is sheltered and housebound, a modern Juliet calling for his/her Romeo; or—more appropriately—the image suggests a scene in some suburban red-light district, presenting this husband as an item on display, like the flowers just below his stomach, available for anyone's enjoyment, at a certain price. Although in one way contradictory, these implications are actually quite congruous, for they both serve to emasculate the husband, so that the wife might take his place, or play his part.

Such details, some might argue, need not have been the conscious work of this commercial's makers. The authors, that is, might have worked by instinct rather than design, and so would have been no more aware of their work's psychosocial import than we ourselves: they just wanted to make the guy look like a wimp, merely for the purposes of domestic comedy. While such an argument certainly does apply to many ads, in this case it is unlikely. Advertising agencies do plenty of research, by which we can assume that they don't select their tactics arbitrarily. They take pains to analyze the culture which they help to sicken, and then, with much wit and cynicism, use their insights in devising their small dramas. This commercial is a subtle and meticulous endorsement of castration, meant to play on certain widespread guilts and insecurities; and all we need to do to demonstrate this fact is to subject the two main scenes to the kind of visual analysis which commercials, so brief and broad, tend to resist (understandably). The ad's visual implications are too carefully achieved to have been merely accidental or unconscious.

The crucial object in the opening shot is that flower box with its bright geraniums, which is placed directly in front of the husband's groin. This clever stroke of composition has the immediate effect of equating our hero's manhood with a bunch of flowers. This is an exquisitely perverse suggestion, rather like using a cigar to represent the Eternal Feminine: flowers are frail, sweet, and largely ornamental, hardly an appropriate phallic symbol, but (of course) a venerable symbol of *maidenhood*. The geraniums stand, then, not for the husband's virility, but for its absence.

More than a clever instance of inversion, furthermore, these phallic blossoms tell us something odd about this marital relationship. As Gail, clippers in hand, turns from the hedge to calm her agitated man, she appears entirely capable of calming him quite drastically, if she hasn't done so already (which might explain his hairless chest and high-pitched voice). She has the power, that is, to take away whatever slender potency he may possess, and uses the power repeatedly, trimming her husband (we infer) as diligently as she prunes her foliage. And, as she can snip his manhood, so too can she restore it, which is what the second scene implies. Now the flower bowl has replaced the flower box as the visual crux, dominating the bottom center of the frame with a crowd of blooms. As the husband, cleaned and dressed, comes to stand beside his wife, straining to affect a new authority, the flower bowl too appears directly at his lower center; so that Gail, briskly adding flowers to the bouquet, appears to be replenishing his vacant groin with extra stalks. He has a lot to thank her for, it seems: she is his helpmate, confidante, adviser, she keeps his house and grounds in order, and she is clearly the custodian of the family jewels.

Of course, her restoration of his potency cannot be complete, or he might shatter her mastery by growing a bit too masterful himself. He could start choosing his own soap, or take her shears away, or—worst of all— walk out for good. Therefore, she punctures his momentary confidence by taunting him with that big limp daisy, countering his lordly gesture with the boutonniere by flaunting that symbol of his floral status. He can put on whatever airs he likes, but she still has his fragile vigor firmly in her hand.

Now what, precisely, motivates this sexless battle of the sexes? That is, what really underlies this tense and hateful marriage, making the man so weak, the woman so contemptuously helpful? The script, seemingly nothing more than a series of inanities, contains the answer to these questions, conveying, as it does, a concern with cleanliness that amounts to an obsession: "Shield fights odor better, so you'll feel cleaner!" "I *do* feel cleaner!" "Shield fights odor better, so you'll feel *cleaner!*" "I feel *cleaner* than *ever before!*" Indeed, the commercial emphasizes the feeling of cleanliness even more pointedly than the name of the product, implying, by its very insistence, a feeling of dirtiness, an apprehension of deep filth.

And yet there is not a trace of dirt in the vivid world of this commercial. Unlike many ads for other soaps, this one shows no sloppy children, no sweat-soaked working men with blackened hands, not even a bleary housewife in need of her morning shower. We never even glimpse the ground in Gail's world, nor is her husband even faintly smudged. In fact, the filth which Shield supposedly "fights" is not physical but psychological besmirchment: Gail's husband feels soiled because of what he has to do for a living, in order to keep Gail in that nice big house, happily supplied with shirts and shears.

"My first call on J. J. Siss, the company's *toughest customer*, and now *this!*" The man's anxiety is yet another feminizing trait, for it is generally women, and not men, who are consumed by doubts about the sweetness of their bodies, which must never be offensive to the guys who run the world. (This real anxiety is itself aggravated by commercials.) Gail's husband must play the female to the mighty J. J. Siss, a name whose oxymoronic character implies perversion: "J. J." is a stereotypic nickname for the potent boss, while "Sis" is a term of endearment, short for "sister" (and perhaps implying "sissy," too, in this case). Gail's husband must do his boyish best to please the voracious J. J. Siss, just as a prostitute must satisfy a demanding trick, or "tough customer." It is therefore perfectly fitting that this employee refer to the encounter, not as a "meeting" or "appointment," but as a "call" and his demeaning posture in the window—half dressed and bent over—conveys, we now see, a definitive implication.

Gail's job as the "understanding wife" is not to rescue her husband from these sordid obligations, but to help him meet them successfully. She may seem coolly self-sufficient, but she actually depends on her husband's attractiveness, just as a pimp relies on the charm of his whore. And, also like a pimp, she has to keep her girl in line with occasional reminders of who's boss. When her husband starts getting uppity *après la douche*, she jars him from the very self-assurance which she had helped him to discover, piercing that "shield" which was her gift.

"And, with old J. J.'s business and my brains—" "—you'll . . . *clean up again?*" He means, of course, that he'll work fiscal wonders with old J. J.'s account, but his fragmentary boast contains a deeper significance, upon which Gail plays with sadistic cleverness. "Old J. J.'s business and my brains" implies a feminine self-description, since it suggests a variation on the old commonplace of "brains vs. brawn": J. J.'s money, in the world of this commercial (as in ours), amounts to brute strength, which the flexible husband intends to complement with his mother wit. Gail's retort broadens this unconscious hint of homosexuality: "—you'll . . . *clean up again?*" Given the monetary nature of her husband's truncated remark, the retort must mean primarily, "You'll make a lot of money." If this were all it meant, however, it would not be a joke, nor would the husband find it so upsetting. Moreover, we have no evidence that Gail's husband ever "cleaned up"—i.e., made a sudden fortune—in the past. Rather, the ad's milieu and *dramatis personae* suggest upward mobility, gradual savings and a yearly raise, rather than one prior killing. What Gail is referring to, in fact, with that "again," is her husband's shower: she implies that what he'll have to do, after his "call" on J. J. Siss, is, quite literally, wash himself off. Like any other tidy hooker, this man will have to clean up after taking on a tough customer, so that he might be ready to take on someone else.

These suggestions of pederasty are intended, not as a literal characterization of the husband's job, but as a metaphor for what it takes to get ahead: Gail's husband, like most white-collar workers, must debase himself to make a good impression, toadying to his superiors, offering himself, body and soul, to the corporation. Maybe, therefore, it isn't really Gail who has neutered him; it may be his way of life that has wrought the ugly change. How, then, are women represented here? The commerical does deliberately appeal to women, offering them a sad fantasy of control; but it also, perhaps inadvertently, illuminates the unhappiness which makes that fantasy attractive.

The husband's status, it would seem, should make Gail happy, since it makes her physically comfortable, and yet Gail can't help loathing her husband for the degradations which she helps him undergo. For her part of the bargain is, ultimately, no less painful than his. She has to do more than put up with him; she has to prepare him for his world of affairs, and then must help him to conceal the shame. Of course, it's all quite hopeless. She clearly despises the man whom she would bolster; and the thing which she provides to help him "feel cleaner than ever before" is precisely what has helped him to do the job that's always made him feel so dirty. "A little water clears us of this deed" is her promise, which is false, for she is just as soiled as her doomed husband, however fresh and well-ironed she may look.

Of course, the ad not only illuminates this mess, but helps perpetuate it, by obliquely gratifying the guilts, terrors, and resentments that underlie it and arise from it. The strategy is not meant to be noticed, but works through the apparent comedy, which must therefore be studied carefully, not passively received. Thus, thirty seconds of ingenious advertising, which we can barely stand to watch, tell us something more than we might want to know about the souls of men and women under corporate capitalism.

## *Afterword*

*Advertising Age* came back at this essay with an edifying two-pronged put-down. In the issue for 7 June 1982 Fred Danzig (now the magazine's editor) devoted his weekly column to the Shield analysis: "The professor prunes a television trifle," ran the headline. After a genial paraphrase of my argument, Danzig reported a few of the things I'd told him in a telephone conversation, and then finally got down to the necessary business of dismissive chuckling: "[Miller's] confession that he had watched the Shield spot more than 15 times quickly enabled me to diagnose his problem: Self-inflicted acute soap storyboard sickness. This condition inevitably leads to a mind spasm, to hallucination." The column featured the ad's crucial frames, over a caption quoting an unnamed "Lever executive": "We can hardly wait for Mr. Miller to get his hands on the Old Testament. His comments merit no comment from us; the Shield commercial speaks for itself."

Leaving aside (with difficulty) that naive crack about the Bible, I point here to the exemplary suppressiveness of his seeming "trifle" in *Advertising*

*Age.* Indeed, "the Shield commercial speaks for itself," but the guardians of the spectacle try to talk over it permitting it no significance beyond the superficial pitch: "—so you'll feel *cleaner!*" Through managerial scorn ("no comment") and journalistic ridicule ("mind spasm . . . hallucination"), they would shut down all discussion. (J. Walter Thompson later refused to send anyone to debate the matter with me on a radio program.) Thus was a divergent reading written off as the perversity of yet another cracked "professor"—when in fact it was the ad itself that was perverse.

Although that campaign did not appeal to its TV audience (J. Walter Thompson ultimately lost the Shield account), such belligerent "common sense" does have a most receptive public. While the admakers—and others—insist that "people today are adwise," in fact most Americans still perceive the media image as transparent, a sign that simply says what it means and means what it says. They therefore tend to dismiss any intensive explication as a case of "reading too much into it"—an objection that is philosophically dubious, albeit useful to the admakers and their allies. It is now, perhaps, one obligation of the academic humanists, empowered, as they are, by critical theory, to demonstrate at large the faultiness—and the dangers—of that objection.

A historical note on the Shield commercial's pseudofeminism. Since 1982, the contemptuous housewife has all but vanished from the antiseptic scene of advertising. Gail was among the last of an endangered species. By now, the housewife/mother is a despised figure—most despised by actual housewife/mothers, who make up 60% of the prime-time audience. Since these viewers now prefer to see themselves represented as execu-

tives, or at least as mothers with beepers and attaché cases, the *hausfrau* of the past, whether beaming or sneering, has largely been obliterated by the advertisers. In 1985, Advertising to Women Inc., a New York advertising agency, found that, out of 250 current TV ads, only nine showed recognizable Moms.

This is a triumph not for women's liberation, but for advertising; for, now that Mom is missing from the ads, presumably off knocking heads together in the boardroom, it is the commodity that seems to warm her home and tuck her children in at night.

In any case, the Shield strategy itself certainly outlasted the wry and/ or perky Mommy-imagoes of yesteryear. Indeed, because the sexes are now at war within the scene of advertising (and elsewhere), the nasty visual metaphors have become ubiquitous. For example, note how "Amy," in the ad taken from *Good Housekeeping*, February 1988 (p. 406), appears to topple her wincing boyfriend with a shapely knee right to the tulips ("Ohh . . . ")

# *Cosby Knows Best*

Bill Cosby is today's quintessential TV Dad—at once the nation's best-liked sitcom character and the most successful and ubiquitous of celebrity pitchmen. Indeed, Cosby himself ascribes his huge following to his appearances in the ads: "I think my popularity came from doing solid thirty-second commercials. They can cause people to love you and see more of you than in a full thirty-minute show." Like its star, "The Cosby Show" must owe much of its immense success to advertising, for this sitcom is especially well attuned to the commercials, offering a full-scale confirmation of their vision.

On the face of it, the Huxtables' milieu is as upbeat and well stocked as a window display at Bloomingdale's, or any of those visions of domestic happiness that graced the billboards during the Great Depression. Everything within this spacious brownstone is luminously clean and new, as if it had all been set up by the state to make a good impression on a group of visiting foreign dignitaries. Here are all the right commodities—lots of bright sportswear, plants and paintings, gorgeous bedding, plenty of copperware, portable tape players, thick carpeting, innumerable knickknacks, and, throughout the house, big, burnished dressers, tables, couches, chairs, and cabinets (Early American yet looking factory-new). Each week, the happy Huxtables nearly vanish amid the porcelain, stainless steel, ma-

hogany, and fabric of their lives. In every scene, each character appears in some fresh designer outfit that positively glows with newness, never to be seen a second time.

Like all this pricey clutter, the plots and subplots, the dialogue and even many of the individual shots reflect in some way on consumption as a way of life: Cliff's new juicer is the leitmotif of one episode; Cliff does a monologue on his son Theo's costly sweatshirt; Cliff kids daughter Rudy for wearing a dozen wooden necklaces. Each Huxtable, in fact, is hardly more than a mobile display case for his/her momentary possessions. In the show's first year, the credit sequence was a series of vivid stills presenting Cliff alongside a shiny Dodge Caravan, out of which the lesser Huxtables each emerged in shining playclothes, as if the van were their true parent, with Cliff serving as the genial midwife to this antiseptic birth. Each is routinely upstaged by what he/she eats or wears or lugs around: in a billowing blouse imprinted with gigantic blossoms, daughter Denise appears, carrying a tape player as big as a suitcase; Theo enters to get himself a can of Coke from the refrigerator, and we notice that he's wearing both a smart beige belt *and* a pair of lavender suspenders; Rudy munches cutely on a piece of pizza roughly twice the size of her own head.

As in the advertising vision, life among the Huxtables is not only well supplied, but remarkable for its surface harmony. Relations between these five pretty kids and their cute parents are rarely complicated by the slightest serious discord. Here affluence is magically undisturbed by the pressures that ordinarily enable it. Cliff and Clair, although both employed, somehow enjoy the leisure to devote themselves full-time to the trivial and comfortable concerns that loosely determine each episode: a funeral for Rudy's goldfish, a birthday surprise for Cliff, the kids' preparations for their first day of school. And daily life in this bright house is just as easy on the viewer as it is (apparently) for Cliff's dependents: "The Cosby Show" is devoid of any dramatic tension whatsoever. Nothing happens, nothing changes, there is no suspense or ambiguity or disappointment. In one episode, Cliff accepts a challenge to race once more against a runner who, years before, had beaten him at a major track meet. At the end, the race is run, and—it's a tie!

Of course, "The Cosby Show" is by no means the first sitcom to present us with a big, blissful family whose members never collide with one another, or with anything else; "Eight is Enough," "The Brady Bunch," and "The Partridge Family" are just a few examples of earlier prime-time idylls. There are, however, some crucial differences between those older shows and this one. First of all, "The Cosby Show" is far more popular than any of its predecessors. It is (as of this writing) the top-rated show in the United States and elsewhere, attracting an audience that is not only vast, but often near fanatical in its devotion. Second, and stranger still, this show and its immense success are universally applauded as an exhilarating sign of progress. Newspaper columnists and telejournalists routinely deem "The Cosby Show" a "breakthrough" into an unprecedented *realism,* because it uses none of the broad plot devices or rapid-fire gags that define the standard sitcom. Despite its fantastic ambience of calm and plenty, "The Cosby Show" is widely regarded as a rare glimpse of truth, whereas "The Brady Bunch" et al., though just as cheery, were never extolled in this way. And there is a third difference between this show and its predecessors that may help explain the new show's greater popularity and peculiar reputation for progressivism: Cliff Huxtable and his dependents are not only fabulously comfortable and mild, but also noticeably black.

Cliff's blackness serves an affirmative purpose within the ad that is "The Cosby Show." At the center of his ample tableau, Cliff is himself an ad, implicitly proclaiming the fairness of the American system: "Look!" he shows us. "Even *I* can have all this!" Cliff is clearly meant to stand for Cosby himself, whose name appears in the opening credits as "Dr. William E. Cosby, Jr., Ed.D."—a testament both to Cosby's lifelong effort at self-improvement, and to his sense of brotherhood with Cliff. And, indeed, Dr. Huxtable is merely the latest version of the same statement that Dr. Cosby has been making for years as a talk show guest and stand-up comic: "I got mine!" The comic has always been quick to raise the subject of his own success. "What do I care what some ten-thousand-dollar-a-year writer says about me?" he once asked Dick Cavett. And on "The Tonight Show" a few years ago, Cosby told of how his father, years before, had warned him that he'd never make a dime in show business, "and then he walked slowly back to the projects . . . Well, I just lent him forty thousand dollars!"

That anecdote got a big hand, just like "The Cosby Show" but despite the many plaudits for Cosby's continuing tale of self-help, it is not quite convincing. Cliff's brownstone is too crammed, its contents too lustrous, to seem like his—or anyone's—own personal achievement. It suggests instead the corporate showcase which, in fact, it is. "The Cosby Show" attests to the power, not of Dr. Cosby/Huxtable, but of a consumer society that has produced such a tantalizing vision of reality. As Cosby himself admits, it was not his own Algeresque efforts that "caused people to love" him, but those ads put out by Coca-Cola, Ford, and General Foods—those ads in which he looks and acts precisely as he looks and acts in his own show.

Cosby's image is divided in a way that both facilitates the corporate project and conceals its true character. On the face of it, the Cosby style is pure impishness. Forever mugging and cavorting, throwing mock tantrums or beaming hugely to himself or doing funny little dances with his stomach pushed out, Cosby carries on a ceaseless parody of some euphoric eight-year-old. His delivery suggests the same childish spontaneity, for in the high, coy gabble of his harangues and monologues there is a disarming quality of baby talk. And yet all this artful goofiness barely conceals an intimidating hardness—the same uncompromising willfulness that we learn to tolerate in actual children (however cute they may be), but which can seem a little threatening in a grown-up. And Cosby is indeed a most imposing figure, in spite of all his antics: a big man boasting of his wealth, and often handling an immense cigar.

It is a disorienting blend of affects, but it works perfectly whenever he confronts us on behalf of Ford or Coca-Cola. With a massive car or Coke machine behind him, or with a calculator at his fingertips, he hunches toward us, wearing a bright sweater and an insinuating grin, and makes his playful pitch, cajoling us to buy whichever thing he's selling, his face and words, his voice and posture all suggesting this implicit and familiar come-on: "Kitchy-koo!" It is not so much that Cosby makes his mammoth bureaucratic masters seem as nice and cuddly as himself (although such a strategy is typical of corporate advertising); rather, he implicitly assures us that *we* are nice and cuddly, like little children. At once solicitous and overbearing, he personifies the corporate force that owns him. Like it, he comes across as an easygoing parent, and yet, also like it, he cannot help betraying the impulse to coerce. We see that he is bigger than we are, better known, better off, and far more powerfully sponsored. Thus we find ourselves ambiguously courted, just like those tots who eat up lots of Jell-O pudding under his playful supervision.

Dr. Huxtable controls his family with the same enlightened deviousness. As widely lauded for its "warmth" as for its "realism," "The Cosby Show" has frequently been dubbed "the 'Father Knows Best' of the eighties." Here again (the columnists agree) is a good strong Dad maintaining the old "family values." This equation, however, blurs a crucial difference between Cliff and the early fathers. Like them, Cliff always wins; but this modern Dad subverts his kids not by evincing the sort of calm power that once made Jim Anderson so daunting, but by seeming to subvert himself at the same time. His is the executive style, in other words not of the small businessman as evoked in the fifties, but of the corporate manager, skilled at keeping his subordinates in line while half concealing his authority through various disarming moves: Cliff rules the roost through teasing put-downs, clever mockery, and amiable shows of helpless bafflement. [1] This dad is no straightforward tyrant, then, but the playful type who strikes his children as a peach, until they realize, years later, and after lots of psychotherapy, what a subtle thug he really was.

An intrusive kidder, Cliff never fails to get his way; and yet there is more to his manipulativeness than simple egomania. Obsessively, Cliff sees to it, through his takes and teasing, that his children always keep things light. As in the corporate culture and on TV generally, so on this show there is no negativity allowed. This is a conscious policy: Dr. Alvin F. Poussaint, a professor of psychiatry at Harvard, reads through each script as a "consultant," censoring any line or bit that might somehow tarnish the show's "positive images." And the show's upscale mise-en-scène has also been deliberately contrived to glow, like a fixed smile: "When you look at the artwork [on the walls], there is a positive feeling, an up feeling," Cosby says. "You don't see downtrodden, negative, I-can't-do-I-won't-do."

Cliff's function, then, is to police the corporate playground, always on the lookout for any downbeat tendencies. In one episode, for instance, Denise sets herself up by reading Cliff some somber verses that she's written for the school choir. The mood is despairing; the refrain, "I walk alone . . . I walk alone." It is clear that the girl does not take the effort very seriously, and yet Cliff merrily overreacts against this slight and artificial plaint, as if it were a crime. First, while she recites, he wears a clownish look of deadpan bewilderment, then laughs out loud as soon as she has finished, and ends by snidely mooing the refrain in outright parody. The studio audience roars, and Denise takes the hint. At the end of the episode, she reappears with a new version, which she reads sweetly, blushingly, while Cliff and Clair, sitting side by side in their high-priced pajamas, beam with tenderness and pride on her act of self-correction:

> My mother and my father are my best friends.
> When I'm all alone, I don't have to be.
> It's because of me that I'm all alone, you see.
> Their love is real. . . .
>
> Never have they lied to me, never connived me,
> talked behind my back.
> Never have they cheated me.
> Their love is real, their love is real

Clair, choked up, gives the girl a big warm hug, and Cliff then takes her little face between his hands and kisses it, as the studio audience bursts into applause.

Thus, this episode ends with a paean to the show itself (for "their love" is *not* "real," but a feature of the fiction), a moment that, for all its mawkishness, attests to Cliff's managerial adeptness. Yet Cliff is hardly a mere enforcer; he is also an underling, even as he seems to run things. This subservient status is manifest in his blackness. Cosby's blackness is indeed a major reason for the show's popularity, despite his frequent claims, and the journalistic consensus, that "The Cosby Show" is somehow "color-blind," simply appealing in some general "human" way. Although whitened by their status and commodities, the Huxtables are still unmistakably black. However, it would be quite inaccurate to hail their popularity as evidence of a new and rising amity between the races in America. On the contrary, "The Cosby Show" is such a hit with whites in part because whites are just as worried about blacks as they have always been—not blacks like Bill Cosby, or Lena Horne, or Eddie Murphy, but poor blacks, and the poor in general, whose existence is a well-kept secret on prime-time TV.

And yet TV betrays the very fears that it denies. In thousands of high-security buildings, and in suburbs reassuringly remote from the cities' "bad neighborhoods," whites may, unconsciously, be further reassured by watching not just Cosby, but a whole set of TV shows that negate the possibility of black violence with lunatic fantasies of containment: "Diff'rent Strokes" and "Webster," starring Gary Coleman and Emmanuel Lewis, respectively, each an overcute, miniaturized black person, each playing the adopted son of good white parents. In seeming contrast to these tabletop models, there is the oversized and growling Mr. T, complete with bangles, mohawk, and other primitivizing touches. Even this behemoth is a comforting joke, the dangerous ex-slave turned comic and therefore innocuous by campy excess; and he too is kept in line by a casual white father: Hannibal Smith, the commander of the A-Team, who employs Mr. T exclusively for his brawn.

As a willing advertisement for the system that pays him well, Cliff Huxtable also represents a threat contained. Although dark-skinned and physically imposing, he ingratiates us with his childlike mien and enviable lifestyle, a surrender that must offer some deep solace to a white public terrified that, one day, blacks might come with guns to steal the copperware, the juicer, the microwave, the VCR, even the TV itself. On "The Cosby Show," it appears as if blacks in general can have, or do have, what many whites enjoy, and that such material equality need not entail a single break-in. And there are no hard feelings, none at all, now that the old injustice has been so easily rectified. Cosby's definitive funny face, flashed at the show's opening credits and reproduced on countless magazine covers, is a strained denial of all animosity. With its little smile, the lips pursed tight, eyes opened wide, eyebrows raised high, that dark face shines toward us like the white flag of surrender—a desperate look that no suburban TV Dad of yesteryear would ever have put on, and one that millions of Americans today find indispensable.

By and large, American whites need such reassurance because they are now further removed than ever, both spatially and psychologically, from the masses of the black poor. And yet the show's appeal cannot be explained merely as a symptom of class and racial uneasiness, because there are, in our consumer culture, anxieties still more complicated and pervasive. Thus, Cliff is not just an image of the dark Other capitulating to the white establishment, but also the reflection of any constant viewer, who, whatever his/her race, must also feel like an outsider, lucky to be tolerated by the distant powers that be. There is no negativity allowed, not anywhere; and so Cliff serves both as our guide and as our double. His look of tense playfulness is more than just a sign that blacks won't hurt us; it is an expression that we too would each be wise to adopt, lest we betray some devastating sign of anger or dissatisfaction. If we stay cool and cheerful, white like him, and learn to get by with his sort of managerial acumen, we too, perhaps, can be protected from the world by a barrier of new appliances, and learn to put down others as each of us has, somehow, been put down.

## Afterword

I have a reason for juxtaposing this essay with the next. ° Dr. Cosby has much in common with the presidential image. In 1987, Video Storyboard

---

The "next" essay (not included here, titled "Virtù, Inc.") examines former President Ronald Reagan's popularity. [Editor's note.]

Tests Inc., a polling outfit, named Cosby as "the most 'believable' celebrity endorser"—the same believability that, for a term and a half, made Reagan hugely popular, against every claim of morality and reason. As Cosby could get away with fronting for a firm like E. F. Hutton, Reagan once could get away with nearly anything—and through the very medium that, its champions claim, has made the national audience very knowing.

Like the celebrants of "Hill Street Blues," of pseudofeminist spectacle, and of TV's images of war, the authors of "The Cosby Show" are incapable of seeing any difference between the real world and their own enlightened bias. Presumably fighting evil "stereotypes," they feel free to proffer, and to deem as "realism," fictions far more fantastic than the most dated depictions—more fantastic, because the newer depictions do not seem dated.

Interviewed by *Harvard Magazine* in 1987, Tom Werner, producer of "The Cosby Show," recalled that "we saw unreal things on TV—atypical families, children constantly talking back. We wanted to make a show where people watching would say, 'How did they get inside my house?'" And, interviewed in *The Christian Science Monitor* the same year, Alvin F. Poussaint, the Harvard professor of psychiatry whose job it is to censor all the "stereotypes" in each week's script, proclaims—correctly—that "television can do a lot better in more truly mirroring, or being a mirror of society in its diversity," while boasting of the show's relentless "positive images"—as if the Huxtables "truly mirror" most, or any, of the households watching them.

Perhaps Harvard's alumni and faculty can look at that preposterous scene of affluence and murmur, "How did they get inside my house?" Most people cannot, however—and that inability explains, in part, the show's success. But the point about such fantasy is not just that it is "unrealistic"—that children do "talk back," for instance, or that there is criminality among blacks, or that warfare gratifies some of its participants.

Rather, the point is, first, that TV, whose only purpose is to push consumption, should not dictate anyone's self-image, however right-minded a given program's censors. And—more important—it is surely not the case that all those "positive images" infuse the audience with the pride and vigor that you need to get ahead. "Everywhere I go," says Poussaint, "people in the black community feel proud that the show is doing so well and that it has positive role models." However, it takes far more than a spectacle of affluence to end poverty or end discrimination; and in fact such advertising idylls do not motivate their viewers to go out and claim the world, but only make the world seem drab and disappointing by comparison. A psychiatrist writing in *TV Guide* quotes a woman who is "a devotee of 'The Cosby Show.' She told me, 'I always compare how my husband deals with a situation with what Bill Cosby would do.' When her husband is crabby or nasty, or can't defuse an argument with a warm, Cosbyesque joke, she ends up feeling angry, even cheated." It is just such unhappiness that TV and its sponsors both require and reinforce, even as they promise our fulfillment.

NOTES

<sup></sup>[1] Cliff's managerial style is, evidently, also Cosby's. According to Tempestt Bledsoe, who plays Cliff's daughter Vanessa, Cosby "can make kids behave without telling them to do so." (Quoted in *People*, 10 December 1984.)

. . . . . . . . . . .

## QUESTIONS FOR A SECOND READING

In the introductory essay to *Boxed In*, Miller said, "We need a critical approach that would take TV seriously . . . , a method of deciphering TV's component images, requiring both a meticulous attention to concrete detail, and a sense of TV's historical situation. Genuinely seen through, those details illuminate that larger context, and vice versa, so that the reading of TV contains and necessitates a reading of our own moment and its past."

1. While Miller's readings of the Shield ad and "The Cosby Show" are smart, surprising, and not difficult to follow, it is often hard to see the "larger context," to get a sense of who is doing what to whom, where, and why. As you reread the essays, look for what more Miller may be doing other than offering a clever reading of two moments on recent TV. What, generally, does he assume about the experience of the viewer? Who is this viewer? Does this assumption ring true to you?

2. What, generally, is Miller saying about how TV "works"? What are its strategies? If there is something of a conspiracy against the viewer, who is behind it? It seems often as if the ad or the show were the primary agent— that is, Miller talks about the ad or the show *doing* or *saying something*, but of course the ad or the show aren't responsible for their own creation. What do these essays allow you to understand about the forces behind or beyond these two presentations?

3. The afterwords to both these brief essays provide an additional context to Miller's work. They allow him to invoke other points of view. Who are the other interested parties he cites? What do they have to say? In what ways aren't they anticipated?

## ASSIGNMENTS FOR WRITING

1. Miller is an example of a critic who works against the grain of the material he studies (in this case TV) and against the grain of what he assumes to

be a common misreading of that material. He reads against the way "The Cosby Show" or the Shield ad want to be read; he writes against what he assumes to be the viewers' blindness to motive and detail.

It seems that this takes considerable effort. Television (and for Miller this is both a culture and an industry) is very sophisticated in diverting our attention. As he said in the essay that introduces *Boxed In*: "Hectic, ironic, and seemingly unintended, the ads do not stand out—and so TV has all but boxed us in. Whereas, out on the walls and billboards, the ads were once overt and recognizable, TV has resubmerged them, by overwhelming the mind that would perceive them, making it only half-aware—as every adman knows: 'People don't watch television like they're taking notes for an exam,' says Lou Centlivre, Executive Creative Director at Foote Cone Belding." And from the very beginning, Miller argues, TV has developed strategies to counter criticism. The most recent is TV's own version of irony—there is no achievement in arguing that a TV show is banal if it never presents itself as serious in the first place. This is how Miller accounts for the impact of figures such as Bruce Willis, David Letterman, or Mariette Hartley. "The generation that once laughed off TV, in short, is trying still to laugh it off while disappearing into it."

Write an essay in which you try your hand at Miller's kind of criticism, developing a close reading of a particular show or ad currently on TV. Like Miller, you will need to present your material carefully and to show how it might be read. The questions you ask should include these: How does it work? What does it assume of its audience? What is its hidden logic? What are its intentions? How and why are these intentions hidden or hard to see? Whose interests might these intentions be said to represent?

Note: This last question is the hardest one. It is possible to talk about the TV ad or show simply as though it were the agent *doing* something (as when Miller says that the Shield ad offers women a fantasy of power and control). But there is, of course, some force behind the ad or show. You could think about the goals of a particular industry—the soap maker or the TV producer. Miller invites you to think as well about culture (the culture of TV) and history (the history of American TV and American consumerism).

2. You've seen Miller's "reading" of both a Shield ad and "The Cosby Show." Behind both are certain assumptions about how TV works and how viewers typically respond (both consciously and subconsciously). Let's assume (for the sake of the exercise) that Miller has only sort of got it right, that something about the nature of TV (including its "concrete detail," "its historical situation") and something about a viewer's experience of TV is missing or hidden, displaced or skewed or lost in his reading.

Write an essay in which you respond to Miller as though you were going to show him where and how his account is wrong or incomplete. As the ground for your response, use a particular ad or show (something similar to Miller's material), something you could put up next to his readings of the Shield ad or "The Cosby Show."

### MAKING CONNECTIONS

Here are three passages from Simon Frith's essay, "Rock and Sexuality" (p. 224):

> Sexual discourses determine prohibitions as well as possibilities, what can't be expressed as well as what can. But the most important function of 1950s teenage culture wasn't to "repress" sexuality but to articulate it in a setting of love and marriage such that male and female sexuality were organized in quite different ways.

> Male sexuality is no more "naturally" aggressive, assertive, and urgent than female sexuality is "naturally" passive, meek, and sensitive. But the issue is not the nature of sex but its representations, and they work not by describing feelings but by constructing them.

> Disco was about eroticism and ecstasy as material goods, produced not by spiritual or emotional work, God or love, but by technology, chemistry, wealth. The disco experience (the music and the mood, the poppers and the lights) revealed the artificiality and transience of sexual feelings—they were produced to be consumed; and disco pleasure, as it moved into the commercial mainstream, became the pleasure of consumption itself.

Frith—like Miller, John Barthes (p. 23), John Berger (p. 65), Adrienne Rich (p. 480)—is trying to find a way of talking about how culture "works" in the life of the individual. He is not making a simple argument—that listening to rock songs makes people do things (be promiscuous or monogamous, passive or violent). Yet he wants to argue that culture does something—that it is an agent, a shaping force in our lives, that it is more than an expression of thoughts and feelings, that it does more than express what is already, naturally, inevitably *there*. This is a difficult argument to make for two reasons: It requires a language different from the usual language of cause and effect (in which people are presumed to act by reasoned decision or obvious intent). And it requires that we imagine a shaping force beyond the individual (the force of culture or history, for example) which is better seen in its effect on groups.

1. Choose selections written by one or two of the authors cited, compare them with Miller, and write an essay about how these leading culture critics have tried to account for the ways culture "works." You will want to begin with specific passages that describe or address a particular cultural event or phenomenon: how it works, how it is reproduced or altered, and how its effects can be seen. You might best think of yourself here as translating a difficult concept to an audience not familiar with these critics and their work. You will need to work with your authors' ideas but with your own examples and other devices (such as metaphor) that you can use to convey challenging concepts to a naive audience.

2. Or, after rereading Miller and one or two of the authors suggested above, write an autobiographical essay telling your story, a story to reflect or illustrate (and then, perhaps, to challenge) the arguments of these critics. Your essay will be, in a sense, a chapter from your autobiography, a chapter on your experience as a participant or consumer in some areas of contemporary American culture. Your story should be rich and detailed—a good story, that is. But a careful reader should also be able to see echoes and allusions to more formal arguments by the critics to whom you are responding.

# JOYCE CAROL
# OATES

*JOYCE CAROL OATES (b. 1938) began publishing her fiction as an under-
graduate at Syracuse University, winning the* Mademoiselle *college fiction
award for her story "In the Old World" in 1959. She has since published over forty
books of fiction, poetry, and literary criticism—an extraordinary record. Along the
way, she completed an M.A. at the University of Wisconsin and began a career as
a teacher, teaching at the University of Detroit, the University of Windsor, Ontario,
and Princeton, among others. She once said, "I'm always working. . . . Writing
is much more interesting to me than eating or sleeping." In Oates's case, one is
inclined to believe that this may be true.*

*Even though the evidence might indicate that writing comes naturally to her,
Oates has said that failure is what writing continually teaches: "The writer, however battered a veteran, can't have any real faith . . . in his stamina (let alone his
theoretical 'gift') to get through the ordeal. . . . One is frequently asked whether
the process becomes easier with the passage of time, and the reply is obvious—
Nothing gets easier with the passage of time, not even the passing of time." Oates
writes, she says, in "flurries" and then works and reworks her stories into shape.*

*This process of revision sometimes goes on even after a work has been published. The version of "Theft" Oates offered for this volume, for example, differs from the version we first read in* Northwest Review. *And the story reappears, with minor additional changes, as Chapter 6 of her novel* Marya: A Life (1986). *"The pleasure is the rewriting," Oates has said. "The first sentence can't be written until the final sentence is written. . . . The completion of any work automatically necessitates its revisioning. The same is true with reading, of course." About the revision of* Marya, *Oates has written, "It was not until I wrote the sentence 'Marya this is going to cut your life in two' on the novel's final page that I fully understood Marya's story, and was then in a position to begin again and to recast it as a single work of prose fiction. As I recall now how obsessively certain pages of the novel were written and rewritten, it seems to me miraculous that the novel was ever completed at all."*

*Oates is currently Roger S. Berlind Distinguished Professor in the Humanities at Princeton University. Her recent work includes* On Boxing (1987), *a book-length essay on the sport;* (Woman) Writer: Occasions and Opportunities (1988), *her fifth collection of essays; and* American Appetites (1989), *a novel.*

# *Theft*

The semester Marya became acquainted with Imogene Skillman, a thief suddenly appeared in Maynard House, where Marya was rooming in her sophomore year at Port Oriskany: striking at odd, inspired, daring hours, sometimes in the early morning when a girl was out of her room and showering in the bathroom just down the corridor, sometimes late at night when some of the girls sat in the kitchen, drinking coffee, their voices kept low so that the resident adviser would not hear. (The kitchen was supposed to close officially at midnight. Maynard House itself "closed" at midnight—there were curfews in those days, in the women's residences.) A wristwatch stolen from one room, seven dollars from another, a physics textbook from yet another . . . the thief was clearly one of the residents, one of the twenty-six girls who roomed in the house, but no one knew who it was; no one wanted to speculate too freely. Naturally there were wild rumors, cruel rumors. Marya once heard the tail end of a conversation in which her own name—"Knauer"—was mentioned. She had brushed by, her expression neutral, stony. She wanted the girls to know she had heard—she scorned even confronting them.

One Saturday morning in November Marya returned to her room after having been gone less than five minutes—she'd run downstairs to check the mail, though she rarely received letters—to see, with a sickening pang, that the door was ajar.

Her wallet had been taken from her leather bag, which she'd left carelessly in sight, tossed on top of her bed.

Her lips shaped empty, angry prayers—Oh God please *no*—but of course it was too late. She felt faint, sickened. She had just cashed a check for forty-five dollars—a week's part-time wages from the university library—and she'd had time to spend only a few dollars; she needed the money badly. "No," she said aloud, baffled, chagrined. "God damn it, *no*."

Someone stood in the opened doorway behind her saying Marya? Is something wrong? but Marya paid her no notice. She was opening the drawers of her bureau one by one; she saw, disgusted, frightened, that the thief had been there too—rooting around in Marya's woollen socks and sweaters and frayed underwear. And her fountain pen was gone. She kept it in the top drawer of the bureau, a prize of her own, a handsome black Parker pen with a thick nub . . . now it was gone.

She had to resist the impulse to yank the drawer out and throw it to the floor—to yank all the drawers out—to give herself up to rage. A flame seemed to pass through her, white-hot, scalding. It was so unfair: she needed that money, every penny of that money, she'd worked in the library in that flickering fluorescent light until she staggered with exhaustion, and even then she'd been forced to beg her supervisor to allow her a few more hours. Her scholarships were only for tuition; she needed that money. And the pen—she could never replace the pen.

It was too much: something in her chest gave way: she burst into tears like an overgrown child. She had never heard such great gulping ugly sobs. And the girl in the doorway—Phyllis, whose room was across the hall— shy, timid, sweet-faced Phyllis—actually tried to hold her in her arms and comfort her. It's so unfair, it's so unfair, Marya wept, what am I going to *do*. . . .

Eventually the wallet was returned to Marya, having been found in a trash can up the street. Nothing was missing but the money, as it turned out: nothing but the money! Marya thought savagely. The wallet itself— simulated crocodile, black, with a fancy brass snap—now looked despoiled, worn, contemptible. It had been a present from Emmett two years before and she supposed she'd had it long enough.

She examined it critically inside and out. She wondered what the thief had thought. Marya Knauer's things, Marya Knauer's "personal" possessions: were they worth stealing, really?

For weeks afterward Marya dreaded returning to her room. Though she was careful to lock the door all the time now it always seemed, when she stepped inside, that someone had been there . . . that something was out of place. Sometimes when she was halfway up the long steep hill to Stafford Hall she turned impulsively and ran back to her dormitory seven blocks away, to see if she'd remembered to lock the door. You're breaking down, aren't you, she mocked herself as she ran, her heart pumping, perspiration itching beneath her arms,—this is how it begins, isn't it: cracking up.

In the early years of the century Maynard House must have been impressive: a small Victorian mansion with high handsome windows, a wide veranda rimmed with elaborate fretwork, a cupola, a half-dozen fireplaces, walnut paneling in several of the downstairs rooms. But now it had become dim and shabby. The outside needed painting; the wallpaper in most of the rooms was discolored. Because it was so far from the main campus, and because its rooms were so cramped (Marya could stand at her full height on only one side of her room, the ceiling on the other slanted so steeply) it was one of the lowest priced residences for women. The girls who roomed there were all scholarship students like Marya, and, like Marya, uneasily preoccupied with studies, grades, part-time employment, finances of a minute and degrading nature. They were perhaps not so humorless and unattractive as Maynard House's reputation would have it, but they did share a superficial family resemblance—they might have been cousins, grimly energetic, easily distracted, a little vain (for they *were* scholarship winners after all, competition for these scholarships was intense throughout the state), badly frightened at the prospect of failure. They were susceptible to tears at odd unprovoked moments, to eating binges, to outbursts of temper; several, including Marya, were capable of keeping their doors closed for days on end and speaking to no one when they did appear.

Before the theft Marya had rather liked Maynard House; she prized her cubbyhole of a room because it was *hers*; because in fact she could lock the door for days on end. The standard university furniture didn't displease her—the same minimal bed, desk, chair, bureau, bedside table, lamp in each room—and the sloped ceiling gave the room a cavelike, warmly intimate air, especially at night when only her desk lamp was burning. Though she couldn't really afford it Marya had bought a woven rug for the floor—Aztec colors, even more fierce than those in hers and Alice's rug at home—and a new lampshade edged with a festive gold braid; she had bought a Chagall print for ninety-eight cents (marked down because it was slightly shopworn) at the University Store. The walls were decorated with unframed charcoal drawings she had done, sketches of imaginary people, a few glowering self-portraits: when she was too tense or excited to sleep after hours of studying, or after having taken an exam, she took up a stick of charcoal and did whatever it seemed to wish to do—her fingers empowered with a curious sort of energy, twitchy, sporadic, often quite surprising. From the room's walls smudged and shadowy variants of her own sober face contemplated her. Strong cheekbones, dark eyes, thick dark censorious brows. . . . She had made the portraits uglier than she supposed she really was; that provided some comfort, it might be said to have been a reverse vanity. Who is *that*? one of the girls on the floor once asked, staring at Marya's own image,—is it a man?—a woman?

Marya prized her aloneness, her monastic isolation at the top of the house, tucked away in a corner. She could stay up all night if she wished, she could skip breakfast if she wished, she could fall into bed after her morning classes and sleep a heavy drugged sleep for much of the afternoon; and no one knew or cared. It seemed extraordinary to her now that for so many years—for all of her lifetime, in fact—she had had to submit to the routine schedule of Wilma's household: going to bed when she wasn't sleepy, getting up when the others did, eating meals with them, living her life as if it were nothing more than an extension of theirs. She loved to read for pleasure once her own assignments were completed: the reading she did late at night acquired an aura, a value, a mysterious sort of enchantment, that did not usually belong to daylight. It was illicit, precious beyond estimation. It seemed to her at such times that she was capable of slipping out of her own consciousness and into that of the writer's . . . into the very rhythms of another's prose. Bodiless, weightless, utterly absorbed, she traversed the landscape of another's mind and found it like her own yet totally unlike—surprising and jarring her, enticing her, leading her on. It was a secret process yet it was not criminal or forbidden—she made her way with the stealth of the thief, elated, subdued, through another's imagination, risking no harm, no punishment. The later the hour and the more exhausted she was, the greater, oddly, her powers of concentration; nothing in her resisted, nothing stood aside to doubt or ridicule; the books she read greedily seemed to take life through her, by way of her, with virtually no exertion of her own. It scarcely seemed to matter what she read, or whom—Nietzsche, William James, the Brontës, Wallace Stevens, Virginia Woolf, Stendhal, the early Greek philosophers—the experience of reading was electrifying, utterly mesmerizing, beyond anything she could recall from the past. She'd been, she thought severely, a superficial person in the past—how could anything that belonged to Innisfail, to those years, matter?

A writer's authentic self, she thought, lay in his writing and not in his life; it was the landscape of the imagination that endured, that was really real. Mere life was the husk, the actor's performance, negligible in the long run. . . . How could it be anything more than the vehicle by which certain works of art were transcribed . . . ? The thought frightened her, exhilarated her. She climbed out of her bed and leaned out her window as far as she could, her hair whipping in the wind. For long vacant minutes she stared at the sky; her vision absorbed without recording the illuminated water tower two miles north of the campus, the flickering red lights of a radio station, the passage of clouds blown livid across the moon. Standing in her bare feet, shivering, her head fairly ringing with fatigue and her eyes filling with tears, she thought her happiness almost too exquisite to be borne.

The first time Imogene Skillman climbed, uninvited, to Marya's room at the top of the old mansion, she stood in the doorway and exclaimed in her low throaty amused voice, "So *this* is where you hide out! . . . this depressing little hole."

Imogene was standing with her hands on her hips, her cheeks flushed, her eyes moving restlessly about. Why, Marya's room was a former maid's room, wasn't it, partitioned off from the others on the floor; and it had only that one window—no wonder the air was stale and close; and that insufferable Chagall print!—wasn't Marya aware that everyone on campus had one? And it was a poor reproduction at that. Then Imogene noticed the charcoal sketches; she came closer to investigate; she said, after a long moment, "At least these are interesting, I wouldn't mind owning one or two of them myself."

Marya had been taken by surprise, sitting at her desk, a book opened before her; she hadn't the presence of mind to invite Imogene in, or to tell her to go away.

"So this is where Marya Knauer lives," Imogene said slowly. Her eyes were a pellucid blue, blank and innocent as china. "All alone, of course. Who would *you* have roomed with—?"

The loss of the money and the Parker fountain pen was so upsetting to Marya, and so bitterly ironic, partly because Marya herself had become a casual thief.

She thought, I deserve this.

She thought, I will never steal anything again.

Alice had led her on silly little shoplifting expeditions in Woolworth's: plastic combs, spools of thread, lipsticks, useless items (hairnets, thumb-tacks) pilfered for the sheer fun of it. Once, years ago, when she was visiting Bonnie Michalak, she made her way stealthily into Mrs. Michalak's bedroom and took—what had it been?—a button, a thimble, two or three pennies?—from the top of her dresser. A tube of much-used scarlet lipstick from the locker of a high school friend; a card-sized plastic calendar (an advertisement from a stationer's in town) from Mr. Schwilk's desk; stray nickels and dimes, quarters, fifty-cent pieces. . . . One of her prizes, ac-quired with great daring and trepidation, was a (fake) ruby ring belonging to someone's older sister, which Marya had found beneath carelessly folded clothing in a stall in the women's bathroom at Wolf's Head Lake, but had never dared to wear. The thefts were always impulsive and rather pointless. Marya saw her trembling hand dart out, saw the fingers close . . . and in that instant, wasn't the object hers?

There was a moment when an item passed over from belonging to another person to belonging to Marya; that moment interested her greatly. She felt excitement, near-panic, elation. A sense of having triumphed, in however petty a fashion.

(It had come to seem to her in retrospect that she'd stolen Father Shearing's wristwatch. She seemed to recall . . . unless it was a particularly vivid dream . . . she seemed to recall slipping the watch from his table into her bookbag, that old worn soiled bookbag she'd had for years. Father Shearing was asleep in his cranked-up bed. Though perhaps not . . . perhaps he was watching her all along through his eyelashes. Marya? Dear Marya? A common thief?)

Since coming to Port Oriskany she felt the impulse more frequently but she knew enough to resist. It was a childish habit, she thought, disgusted,—it wasn't even genuine theft, intelligently committed. Presumably she wanted to transgress; even to be punished; she *wanted* to be sinful.

Odd, Marya thought uneasily, that no one has ever caught me. When I haven't seemed to care. When I haven't seemed to have *tried*.

It happened that, in her classes, she found herself gazing at certain individuals, and at their belongings, day after day, week after week. What began as simple curiosity gradually shaded into intense interest. She might find herself, for instance, staring at a boy's spiral notebook in a lecture class . . . plotting a way to getting it for herself, leafing through it, seeing what he'd written. (For this boy, like Marya, was a daydreamer; an elaborate and tireless doodler, not without talent.) There was an antique opal ring belonging to a girl in her English literature class: the girl herself had waist-long brown hair, straight and coarse, and Marya couldn't judge whether she was striking, and very good-looking, or really quite repulsive. (Marya's own hair was growing long again—long and wavy and unruly—but it would never be that length again; the ends simply broke off.) Many of the students at Port Oriskany were from well-to-do families, evidently, judging from their clothes and belongings: Marya's eye moved upon handtooled leather bags, and boots, and wristwatches, and earrings, and coats (suede, leather, fur-trimmed, camel's hair) half in scorn and half in envy. She did not want to steal these items, she did not *want* these items, yet, still, her gaze drifted onto them time and again, helplessly. . . .

She studied faces too, when she could. Profiles. That blonde girl in her political science class, for instance: smooth clear creamy skin, china-blue mocking eyes, a flawless nose, mouth: long hair falling over one shoulder.

Knee-high leather boots, kid gloves, a handsome camel's hair coat, a blue cashmere muffler that hadn't been cleaned in some time. An engagement ring with a large square-cut diamond. . . . But it was the girl's other pieces of jewelry that drew Marya's interest. Sometimes she wore a big silver ring with a turquoise stone; and a long sporty necklace made of copper coins; and a succession of earrings in her pierced ears—gold loops that swung and caught the light, tiny iridescent-black stones, ceramic disks in which gold-burnished reds and blues flashed. Marya stared and stared, her heart quickening with—was it envy?—but envy of precisely what? It could not have been these expensive trinkets she coveted.

Imogene Skillman was a theatre arts major; she belonged to one of the sororities on Masefield Avenue; Marya had even been able to discover that she was from Laurel Park, Long Island, and that she was engaged to a law student who had graduated from Port Oriskany several years ago. After she became acquainted with Imogene she would have been deeply humiliated if Imogene had known how much Marya knew of her beforehand. Not only her background, and her interest in acting, but that big leather bag, those boots, the silver ring, the ceramic earrings. . . .

It might have been Imogene's presence in class that inspired Marya to speak as she frequently did; answering their professor's questions in such detail, in such self-consciously structured sentences. (Marya thought of herself as shy, but, as it turned out, she could often speak at length if required—she became, suddenly, articulate and emphatic—even somewhat combative. The tenor of her voice caused people to turn around in their seats and often surprised, when it did not disconcert, her professors.) It wasn't that she spoke her mind—she rarely offered opinions—it seemed to her necessary to consider as many sides of an issue as possible, as many relevant points, presenting her case slowly and clearly and forcefully, showing no sign of the nervousness she felt. It was not simply that most of her professors solicited serious discussion—gave evidence, in fact, of being greatly dependent upon it to fill up fifty minutes of class time—or even that (so Marya reasoned, calculated) her precious grade might depend upon such contributions; she really became caught up in the subjects themselves. Conflicting theories of representative democracy, property rights, civil disobedience . . . the ethics of propaganda . . . revolution and counter-revolution . . . whether in fact terrorism might ever be justified. . . . Even when it seemed, as it sometimes did, that Marya's concern for these issues went beyond that of the professor's, she made her point; she felt a grudging approval throughout the room; and Imogene Skillman turned languidly in her seat to stare at her.

One afternoon Imogene left behind a little handwoven purse that must have slipped out of her leather bag. Marya snatched it up as if it were a prize. She followed after Imogene—followed her out of the building—that

426

tall blonde girl in the camel's hair coat—striding along, laughing, in a high-spirited conversation with her friends. Marya approached her and handed her the purse, saying only, "You dropped this," in a neutral voice; she turned away without waiting for Imogene's startled thanks.

Afterward she felt both elated and unaccountably fatigued. As if she had experienced some powerful drain on her energy. As if, having returned Imogene's little purse to her, she now regretted having done so; and wondered if she had been a fool.

Marya's friendship with Imogene Skillman began, as it was to end, with a puzzling abruptness.

One day Imogene simply appeared beside Marya on one of the campus paths, asking if she was walking this way?—and falling comfortably in step with her. It was done as easily and as effortlessly as if they were old friends; as if Imogene had been reading Marya's most secret thoughts.

She began by flattering her, telling her she said "interesting" things in class; that she seemed to be the only person their professor really listened to. Then, almost coyly: "I should confess that it's your voice that really intrigues me. What if—so I ask myself, I'm always trying things on other people!—what if *she* was playing Hedda—Hedda Gabler—with that remarkable voice—and not mine—*mine* is so reedy—I've heard myself on tape and can barely stop from gagging. And there's something about your manner too—also your chin—when you speak—it looks as if you're gritting your teeth but you *are* making yourself perfectly audible, don't be offended! The thing is, I'm doing Hedda myself, I can't help but be jealous of how you might do her in my place though it's all *my* imagination of course. Are you free for lunch? No? Yes? We could have it at my sorority—no, better out—it's not so claustrophobic, out. We'll have to hurry, though, Marya, is it?—I have a class at one I don't *dare* cut again."

It gave Marya a feeling of distinct uneasiness, afterward, to think that Imogene had pursued *her*. Or, rather, that Imogene must have imagined herself the pursuer; and kept up for weeks the more active, the more charitably outgoing and inquisitive, of their two roles. (During their first conversation, for instance, Marya found herself stammering and blushing as she tried to answer Imogene's questions—Where are you from, what are you studying, where do you live on campus, what do you *think* of this place, isn't it disappointing?—put in so candid and ingenuous a manner, with that wide blue-eyed stare, Marya felt compelled to reply. She also felt vaguely criminal, guilty—as if she'd somehow drawn Imogene to her by the very intensity of her own interest, without Imogene's conscious knowledge.)

If Imogene reached out in friendship, at the beginning, Marya naturally drew back. She shared the Knauers' peasant shrewdness, or was it mean-spiritedness: what does this person want from *me*, why on earth would this person seek out *me*? It was mysterious, puzzling, disconcerting. Imogene was so pretty, so popular and self-assured, a dominant campus personality; Marya had only a scattering of friends—friendly acquaintances, really. She hadn't, as she rather coolly explained to Imogene, time for "wasting" on people.

She also disapproved of Imogene's public manner, her air of flippancy, carelessness. In fact Imogene was quite intelligent—her swiftness of thought, her skill at repartee, made that clear—but she played at seeming otherwise, to Marya's surprise and annoyance. Imogene was always *Imogene*, always *on*. She was a master of sudden dramatic reversals: sunny warmth that shaded into chilling mockery; low-voiced serious conversations, on religion, perhaps (Imogene was an agnostic who feared, she said, lapsing into Anglicanism—it ran in her family), that deteriorated into wisecracks and bawdy jokes simply because one of her theatre friends appeared. While Marya was too reserved to ask Imogene about herself, Imogene was pitiless in her interrogation of Marya, once the formality of their first meeting was out of the way. Has your family *always* lived in that part of the state, do you mean your father was really a *miner*, how old were you when he died, how old were you when your mother died, do you keep in touch with your high school friends, are you happy here, are you in love with anyone, have you ever been in love, are you a virgin, do you have any plans for this summer, what will you do after graduation?—what do you think your *life* will be? Marya was dazed, disoriented. She answered as succinctly and curtly as she dared, never really telling the truth, yet not precisely lying; she had the idea that Imogene could detect a lie; she'd heard her challenge others when she doubted the sincerity of what they said. Half-truths went down very well, however. Half-truths, Marya had begun to think, were so much more reasonable—so much more convincing—than whole truths.

For surely brazen golden-haired Imogene Skillman didn't really want to know the truth about Marya's family—her father's death (of a heart attack, aged thirty-nine, wasn't that a possibility?—having had rheumatic fever, let's say, as a boy); her mother's disappearance that was, at least poetically, a kind of death too (automobile accident, Marya ten at the time, no one to blame). Marya was flattered, as who would not be, by Imogene's intense *interest* and *sympathy* ("You seem to have had such a hard life. . . .") but she was shrewd enough to know she must not push her friend's generosity of spirit too far: it was one thing to be moved, another thing to be repulsed.

So she was sparing with the truth. A little truth goes a long way, she thought, not knowing if the remark was an old folk saying, or something she'd coined herself.

She told herself that she resented Imogene's manner, her assumption of an easygoing informality that was all one-sided, or nearly; at the same time it couldn't be denied that Marya Knauer visibly brightened in Imogene Skillman's presence. She saw with satisfaction how Imogene's friends—meeting them in the student union, in the pub, in the restaurants and coffee shops along Fairfield Street—watched them with curiosity, and must have wondered who Imogene's new friend was.

Marya Knauer: but who is *she*?—where did Imogene pick up *her*?

Marya smiled cynically to herself, thinking that she understood at last the gratification a man must feel, in public, in the company of a beautiful woman. Better, really, than being the beautiful woman yourself.

They would have quarrelled, everything would have gone abrasive and sour immediately, if Marya hadn't chosen (consciously, deliberately) to admire Imogene's boldness, rather than to be insulted by it. (*Are you happy, are you lonely, have you even been in love, are you a virgin?*—no one had ever dared ask Marya such questions. The Knauers were reticent, prudish, about such things as personal feelings: Wilma might haul off and slap her, and call her a little shit, but she'd have been convulsed with embarrassment to ask Marya if she was happy or unhappy, if she loved anyone, if, maybe, she knew how Wilma loved *her*. Just as Lee and Everard might quarrel, and Lee might dare to tell his brawny hot-tempered father to go to hell, but he'd never have asked him—he'd never have even imagined asking him—how much money he made in a year, how much he had in the bank, what the property was worth, did he have a will, did he guess that, well, Lee sort of looked up to *him*, loved *him*, despite all these fights?)

Marya speculated that she'd come a great distance from Innisfail and the Canal Road—light-years, really, not two hundred miles—and she had to be careful, cautious, about speaking in the local idiom.

Imogene was nearly as tall as Marya, and her gold-gleaming hair and ebullient manner made her seem taller. Beside her, Marya knew herself shabby, undramatic, unattractive; it was not *her* prerogative to take offense, to recoil from her friend's extreme interest. After all—were so very many people interested in her, here in Port Oriskany? Did anyone really care if she lied, or told the truth, or invented ingenious half-truths . . . ? In any case, despite Imogene's high spirits, there was usually something harried about her. She hadn't studied enough for an exam, play rehearsals were going badly, she'd had an upsetting telephone call from home the night before, what in Christ's name was she to *do*? . . . Marya noted that beautiful white-toothed smile marred by tiny tics of vexation. Imogene was always turning the diamond ring round and round her finger, impatiently; she fussed with her earrings and hair; she was always late, always running—her coat unbuttoned and flapping about her, her tread heavy. Her eyes sometimes filled with tears that were, or were not, genuine.

Even her agitation, Marya saw, was enviable. There are certain modes of unhappiness with far more style than happiness.

Imogene insisted that Marya accompany her to a coffee shop on Fairfield—pretentiously called a coffee "house"—where all her friends gathered. These were her *real* friends, apart from her sorority sisters and her fraternity admirers. Marya steeled herself against their critical amused eyes; she didn't want to be one of their subjects for mimicry. (They did devastating imitations of their professors and even of one another—Marya had to admit, laughing, that they were really quite good. If only she'd known such people back in Innisfail!—in high school!—she might have been less singled out for disapproval; she might have been less lonely.)

Marya made certain that she gave her opinions in a quick flat unhesitating voice, since opinions tenuously offered were usually rejected. If she chose to talk with these people at all she made sure that she talked fast, so that she wouldn't be interrupted. (They were always interrupting one another, Imogene included.) With her excellent memory Marya could, if required, quote passages from the most difficult texts; her vocabulary blossomed wonderfully in the presence of a critical, slightly hostile audience she knew she *must* impress. (For Imogene prided herself on Marya Knauer's brilliance, Marya Knauer's knowledge and wit. Yes, that's right, she would murmur, laughing, nudging Marya in the ribs, go on, go *on*, you're absolutely right—you've got them now!) And Marya smoked cigarettes with the others, and drank endless cups of bitter black coffee, and flushed with pleasure when things went well . . . though she was wasting a great deal of time these days, wasn't she? . . . and wasn't time the precious element that would carry her along to her salvation?

The coffee shop was several blocks from the University's great stone archway, a tunnellike place devoid of obvious charm, where tables were crowded together and framed photographs of old, vanished athletes lined the walls. Everyone—Imogene's "everyone"—drifted there to escape from their living residences, and to sit for hours, talking loudly and importantly, about Strindberg, or Whitman, or Yeats, or the surrealists, or Prufrock, or Artaud, or *Ulysses*, or the Grand Inquisitor; or campus politics (who was in, who was out); or the theater department (comprised half of geniuses and saints, half of losers). Marya soon saw that several of the boys were in love with Imogene, however roughly they sometimes treated her. She didn't care to learn their names but of course she did anyway—Scott, and Andy, and Matthew (who took a nettlesome sort of dislike to Marya); there was a dark ferret-faced mathematics student named Brian whose manner was broadly theatrical and whose eyeglasses flashed with witty malice. The other girls in the group were attractive enough, in fact quite striking, but they were no match for Imogene when she was most herself.

Of course the love, even the puppyish affection, went unrequited. Imogene was engaged—the diamond ring was always in sight, glittering and winking; Imogene occasionally made reference to someone named Richard, whose opinion she seemed to value highly. (What is Imogene's fiancé like, Marya asked one of the girls, and was told he was "quiet"—"watchful"— that Imogene behaved a little differently around him; she was quieter herself.)

One wintry day when Marya should have been elsewhere she sat with Imogene's friends in a booth at the smoky rear of the coffee house, half-listening to their animated talk, wondering why Imogene cared so much for them. Her mind drifted loose; she found herself examining one of the photographs on the walls close by. It was sepia-tinted, and very old: the 1899 University rowing team. Beside it was a photograph of the 1902 football team. How young those smiling athletes must have felt, as the century turned, Marya thought. It must have seemed to them . . . *theirs.*

She was too lazy to excuse herself and leave. She was too jealous of Imogene. No, it was simply that her head ached; she hadn't slept well the night before and wouldn't sleep well tonight. . . . Another rowing team. Hopeful young men, standing so straight and tall; their costumes slightly comical; their haircuts bizarre. An air of team spirit, hearty optimism, doom. Marya swallowed hard, feeling suddenly strange. She really should leave . . . She really shouldn't be here. . . .

Time had been a nourishing stream, a veritable sea, for those young men. Like fish they'd swum in it without questioning it—without knowing it was the element that sustained them and gave them life. And then it had unaccountably withdrawn and left them exposed . . . Forever youthful in those old photographs, in their outdated costumes; long since aged, dead, disposed of.

Marya thought in a panic that she must leave; she must return to her room and lock the door.

But when she rose Imogene lay a hand on her arm and asked irritably what was wrong, why was she always jumping up and down: couldn't she for Christ's sake sit *still*?

The vehemence of Imogene's response struck them all, it was in such disproportion to Marya's behavior. Marya herself was too rushed, too frightened, to take offense. She murmured, "Good-bye, Imogene," without looking at her; and escaped.

It was that night, not long before curfew, that Imogene dropped by for the first time at Maynard House. She rapped on Marya's door, poked her head in, seemed to fill the doorway, chattering brightly as if nothing were wrong; as if they'd parted amiably. Of course she *was* rather rude about the room—Marya hadn't realized it must have been a maid's room, in the house's earliest incarnation—but her rudeness as always passed by rather casually, in a sort of golden blue. She looked so pretty, flushed with cold, her eyes inordinately damp. . . .

Tell me about these drawings, she said,—I didn't know you were an artist. These are *good*.

But Marya wasn't in a mood for idle conversation. She said indifferently that she *wasn't* an artist; she was a student.

But Imogene insisted she was an artist. Because the sketches were so rough, unfinished, yet they caught the eye, there was something unnerving about them. "Do you see yourself like this, though?—Marya?" Imogene asked almost wistfully. "So stern and ugly?—it *isn't* you, is it?"

"It isn't anyone," Marya said. "It's a few charcoal strokes on old paper."

She was highly excited that Imogene Skillman had come to her room: had anyone on the floor noticed?—had the girl downstairs at the desk, on telephone duty, noticed? At the same time she wished her gone, it was an intrusion into her privacy, insufferable. She had never invited Imogene to visit her—she never would.

"So this is where you live," Imogene said, drawing a deep breath. Her eyes darted mercilessly about; she would miss nothing, forget nothing. "You're alone and you don't mind, that's *just* like you. You have a whole other life, a sort of secret life, don't you," she said, with a queer pouting downward turn of her lips.

Friendship, Marya speculated in her journal,—the most enigmatic of all relationships.

In a sense it flourished unbidden; in another, it had to be cultivated, nurtured, sometimes even forced into existence. Though she was tirelessly active in most aspects of her life she'd always been quite passive when it came to friendship. She hadn't time, she told herself; she hadn't energy for something so . . . ephemeral.

Nothing was worthwhile, really worthwhile, except studying; getting high grades; and her own reading, her own work. Sometimes Marya found herself idly contemplating a young man—in one of her classes, in the library; sometimes, like most of her female classmates, she contemplated one or another of her male professors. But she didn't want a lover, not even a romance. To cultivate romance, Marya thought, you had to give over a great deal of time for daydreaming: she hadn't time to waste on *that*.

Since the first month of her freshman year Marya had acquired a reputation for being brilliant—the word wasn't hers but Imogene's: Do you know everyone thinks you're brilliant, everyone is afraid of you?—and it struck Marya as felicitous, a sort of glass barrier that would keep other people at a distance. . . . And then again she sometimes looked up from her reading, and noted that hours had passed; where was she and what was she doing to herself? (Had someone called her? Whispered her name? Marya, Marya. . . . You little savage, Marya. . . .) Suddenly she ached with the desire to see Wilma, and Everard; and her brothers; even Lee. She felt as if she must leave this airless little cubbyhole of a room—take a Greyhound bus to Innisfail—see that house on the Canal Road—sit at the kitchen table with the others—tell them she loved them, she loved them and couldn't help herself: what was happening?

Great handfuls of her life were being stolen from her and she would never be able to retrieve them.

To counteract Imogene Skillman's importance in her life, Marya made it a point to be friendly—if not, precisely, to *become friends*—with a number of Maynard House girls. She frequently ate meals with them in the dining hall a few blocks away, though she was inclined (yes, it was rude) to bring along a book or two just in case. And if the conversation went nowhere Marya would murmur, Do you mind?—I have so much reading to do.

Of course they didn't mind. Catherine or Phyllis or Sally or Diane. They too were scholarship students; they too were frightened, driven.

(Though Marya knew they discussed her behind her back. She was the only girl in the house with a straight-A average and they were waiting . . . were they perhaps hoping? . . . for her to slip down a notch or two. They were afraid of her sarcasm, her razorish wit. Then again, wasn't she sometimes very funny?—If you liked that sort of humor. As for the sorority girl Imogene Skillman: what did Marya see in *her*?—what did *she* see in Marya? It was also likely, wasn't it, that Marya was the house thief? For the thief still walked off with things sporadically. These were mean, pointless thefts—a letter from a mailbox, another textbook, a single angora glove, an inexpensive locket on a tarnished silver chain. Pack-rat sort of thievery, unworthy, in fact, of any girl who roomed in Maynard.)

When Marya told Imogene about the thief and the money she'd lost, Imogene said indifferently that there was a great deal of stealing on campus, and worse things too (this, with a sly twist of her lips), but no one wanted to talk about it; the student newspaper (the editors were all friends of hers, she knew such things) was forever being censored. For instance, last year a girl committed suicide by slashing her wrists in one of the off-campus senior houses and the paper wasn't allowed to publish the news, not even to *hint* at it, and the local newspaper didn't run anything either, it was all a sort of totalitarian kindergarten state, the university. As for theft: "*I've* never stolen anything in my life," Imogene said, smiling, brooding, "because why would I want anything that somebody else has already had?—something second-hand, used?"

Your friend Imogene, people began to say.

Your friend Imogene: she dropped by at noon, left this note for you.

Marya's pulses rang with pleasure, simple gratitude. She was flattered but—well, rather doubtful. Did she even *like* Imogene? Were they really friends? In a sense she liked one or two of the girls in Maynard better than she liked Imogene. Phyllis, for instance, a mathematics major, very sharp, very bright, though almost painfully shy; and a chunky farm girl named Diane from a tiny settlement north of Shaheen Falls, precociously matronly, with thick glasses and a heavy tread on the stairs and a perpetual odor of unwashed flesh, ill-laundered clothes. . . . But Diane was bright, very bright; Marya thought privately that here was her real competition at Port Oriskany, encased in baby fat, blinking through those thick lenses. (The residence buzzed with the rumor, however, that Diane was doing mysteriously poorly in her courses, had she a secret grief?—an unstated terror?) Marya certainly liked Phyllis and Diane, she recognized them as superior individuals, really much nicer, much kinder, than Imogene. Yet she had to admit it would not have deeply troubled her if she never saw them again. And the loss of Imogene would have been a powerful blow.

She went twice to see the production of *Hedda Gabler* in which Imogene starred. For she really did star, it was a one-woman show. That hard slightly drawling slightly nasal voice, that mercurial manner (cruel, seductive, mocksweet, languid, genuinely anguished by turns), certain odd tricks and mannerisms (the way she held her jaw, for instance: had she pilfered that from Marya?)—Imogene was *really* quite good; really a success. And they'd made her up to look even more beautiful on stage than she looked in life: her golden hair in a heavy Victorian twist, her cheeks subtly rouged, her eyes enormous. Only in the tense sparring scene with Judge Brack, when Hedda was forced to confront a personality as strong as her own, did Imogene's acting falter: her voice went strident, her manner became too broadly erotic.

Marya thought, slightly dazed,—Is she really talented? Is there some basis for her reputation, after all?

Backstage, Marya didn't care to compete for Imogene's attention; let the others hug and kiss her and shriek congratulations if they wished. It was all exaggerated, florid, embarrassing . . . so much emotion, such a *display*. . . . And Imogene looked wild, frenzied, her elaborate makeup now rather clownish, seen at close quarters. "Here's Marya," she announced, "— Marya will tell the truth—here's Marya—shut up, you idiots!—she'll tell the truth—*was* I any good, Marya?—*was* I really Hedda?" She pushed past her friends and gripped Marya's hands, staring at her with great shining painted eyes. She smelled of greasepaint and powder and perspiration; it seemed to Marya that Imogene towered over her.

"Of course you were good," Marya said flatly. "You know you were good."

Imogene gripped her hands tighter, her manner was feverish, outsized. "What are you saying?—you didn't care for the performance? It wasn't right? I failed?"

"Don't be ridiculous," Marya said, embarrassed, trying to pull away. "You don't need me to assess you, in any case. You *know* you were—"

"You didn't like it! Did you!"

"—you were perfect."

"*Perfect!*" Imogene said in hoarse stage voice, "—but that doesn't sound like one of your words, Marya—you don't *mean* it."

It was some seconds before Marya, her face burning with embarrassment and resentment, could extricate her hands from Imogene's desperate grip. No, she couldn't come to the cast party; she had to get back to work. And yes, yes, for Christ's sake, *yes*—Imogene had been "perfect": or nearly.

Friendship, Marya wrote in her journal, her heart pounding with rage,—play-acting of an amateur type.

Friendship, she wrote,—a puzzle that demands too much of the imagination.

So she withdrew from Imogene, tried even to stop thinking about her, looking for her on campus. (That blue muffler, that camel's hair coat. And she had a new coat too: Icelandic shearling, with a black fur collar.) She threw herself into her work with more passion than before. Exams were upon her, papers were due, she felt the challenge with a sort of eager dread, an actual greed, knowing she could do well even if she didn't work hard; and she intended to work very, very hard. Even if she got sick, even if her eyes went bad.

Hour after hour of reading, taking notes, writing, rewriting. In her room, the lamp burning through the night; in one or another of her secret places in the library; in a corner of an old brick mansion a quarter-mile away that had been converted into the music school, where she might read and scribble notes and daydream, her heartbeat underscored by the muffled sounds of pianos, horns, violins, cellos, flutes, from the rows of practice rooms. The sounds—the various musics—were all rather harmonious, heard like this, in secret. Marya thought, closing her eyes: If you could only *be* music.

At the same time she had her job in the library, her ill-paid job, a drain on her time and spirit, a terrible necessity. She explained that she'd lost her entire paycheck—the money had been stolen out of her wallet—she *must* be allowed to work a little longer, to clock a few more hours each week. She intended (so she explained to her supervisor) to make up the loss she'd suffered by disciplining herself severely, spending no extra money if she could avoid it. She *must* be allowed a few hours extra work. . . . (The Parker pen could never be replaced, of course. As for the money: Marya washed her hair now once a week, and reasoned that she did not really need toothpaste, why did anyone *need* toothpaste?—she was sparing with her toiletries in general, and, if she could, used other girls', left in the third floor bathroom. She was always coming upon lost ballpoint pens, lost notebooks, even loose change; she could appropriate—lovely word, "appropriate"—cheap mimeograph paper from a supply room in the library; sometimes she even found half-empty packs of cigarettes—though her newest resolution was to stop smoking, since she resented every penny spent on so foolish a habit. Her puritan spirit blazed; she thought it an emblem of her purity, that the waistbands of her skirts were now too loose, her underwear was a size too large.)

After an evening of working in the library—her pay was approximately $1 an hour—she hurried home to Maynard, exhausted, yet exhilarated, eager to get to her schoolwork. Once she nearly fainted running up the stairs and Diane, who happened to be nearby, insisted that she come into her room for a few minutes. You look terrible, she said in awe—almost as bad as I do. But Marya brushed her aside, Marya hadn't time. She was lightheaded from the stairs, that was all.

One night Imogene telephoned just before the switchboard was to close. What the hell was wrong, Imogene demanded, was Marya angry at her? She hurried out of class before Imogene could say two words to her—she never came down to Fairfield Street any longer—was she secretly in love?—was she working longer hours at the library?—would she like to come to dinner sometime this week, at the sorority?—or next week, before Christmas break?

Yes, thought Marya, bathed in gratitude, in golden splendor, "No," she said aloud, quietly, chastely, "—but thank you very much."

Schopenhauer, Dickens, Marx, Euripides. Oscar Wilde. Henry Adams. Sir Thomas More. Thomas Hobbes. And Shakespeare—of course. She read, she took notes, she daydreamed. It sometimes disturbed her that virtually nothing of what she read had been written by women (except Jane Austen, dear perennial Jane, *so* feminine!) but in her arrogance she told herself *she* would change all that.

Is this how it begins, she wondered, half-amused. Breaking down. Cracking up.

Why breaking *down* . . . but cracking *up* . . . ?

Her long periods of intense concentration began to be punctuated by bouts of directionless daydreaming, sudden explosions of *feeling*. At such times Shakespeare was too dangerous to be read closely—Hamlet whispered truths too cruel to be borne, every word in *Lear* hooked in flesh and could not be dislodged. As for Wilde, Hobbes, Schopenhauer . . . even cynicism, Marya saw, can't save you.

At such times she went for walks along Masefield Avenue, past the enormous sorority and fraternity houses. They too were converted mansions but had retained much of their original glamor and stateliness. Imogene's, for instance, boasted pretentious white columns, four of them, in mock-Southern Colonial style. The cryptic Greek letters on the portico struck an especially garish and irrelevant note. What did such symbols mean, what did it mean (so Marya wondered, not quite bitterly) to be *club-bable*—? In the winter twilight, in the cold, these outsized houses appeared especially warm and secretive; every window of their several storeys blazed. Marya thought, Why don't I feel anything, can't I even feel envy . . . ? But the sororities were crudely discriminatory (one was exclusively for Catholic girls, another exclusively for Jewish girls, the sixteen others had quotas for Catholics and blackballed all Jews who dared cross their threshold: the procedure was that blunt, that childish). Dues and fees were absurdly high, beyond the inflated price for room and board; the meetings involved pseudoreligious "Greek" rituals (handshakes, secret passwords, special prayers). Imogene complained constantly, was always cutting activities and being fined ($10 fine for missing a singing rehearsal!—the very thought made Marya shiver in disbelief), always mocking the alumns, those well-to-do matrons with too much time on their hands. Such assholes, all of them, Imogene said loftily, such *pretentious* assholes. It was part of Imogene's charm that she could be both contemptuous of pretension and marvelously—shamelessly—pretentious herself.

Time is the element in which we exist, Marya noted solemnly in her journal,—We are either borne along by it, or drowned in it.

It occurred to her with a chilling certitude that *every moment not consciously devoted to her work* was an error, a blunder. As if you can kill time, Thoreau said, without injuring Eternity.

Lying drowsily and luxuriously in bed after she'd wakened . . . conversations with most people, or, indeed *all* people . . . spending too long in the shower, or cleaning her room, or staring out the window, or eating three meals a day (unless of course she brought along a book to read) . . . daydreaming and brooding about Innisfail, or the Canal Road, or that wretched little tarpaper-roofed shanty near Shaheen Falls that had been her parents' house . . . crying over the past (though in fact she rarely cried these days) as if the past were somehow present. In high school she had been quite an athlete, especially at basketball and field hockey; in college she hadn't time, hadn't the slightest interest. It pleased her that she always received grades of A but at the same time she wondered,—Are these *really* significant grades, do I *really* know anything?—or is Port Oriskany one of the backwaters of the world, where nothing, even "excellence," greatly matters? She needed high grades in order to get into graduate school, however; beyond that she didn't allow herself to think. Though perhaps she wouldn't go to graduate school at all . . . perhaps she would try to write . . . her great problem being not that she hadn't anything to write about but that she had too much.

Unwisely, once, she confided in Imogene that she halfway feared to write anything that wasn't academic or scholarly or firmly rooted in the real world: once she began she wouldn't be able to stop: she was afraid of sinking too deep into her own head, cracking up, becoming lost.

Imogene said it once that Marya was just the type to be excessive, she needed reining in. "I know the symptoms," she said severely. Anyway, what good would academic success—or any kind of success—do her, if she destroyed her health?

"*You're* concerned about my health?" Marya asked increduously.

"Of course. Yes, I *am.* Why shouldn't I be," Imogene said, "—aren't I a friend of yours?"

Marya stared at her, unable to reply. It struck her as wildly incongruous that Imogene Skillman, with her own penchant for abusing her health (she drank too much at fraternity parties, she stayed up all night doing hectic last-minute work) should be worrying about Marya.

"Aren't I a friend of yours?" Imogene asked less certainly. "Don't I have the right . . . ?"

Marya turned away with an indifferent murmur, perhaps because she was so touched.

"My health isn't of any use to me," she said, "if I don't get anything accomplished. If I fail."

Of course it was possible, Marya saw, to ruin one's health and fail anyway.

Several of her fellow residents in Maynard House were doing poorly in their courses, despite their high intelligence and the goading terror that energized them. One of them was Phyllis, who was failing an advanced calculus class; another, a chronically withdrawn and depressed girl named Mary, a physics major, whose deeply shadowed eyes and pale grainy skin, as well as her very name, struck a superstitious chord of dread in Marya—she avoided her as much as possible, and had the idea that Mary avoided *her.*

The University piously preached an ethic of knowledge for its own sake—knowledge and beauty being identical—the "entire person" was to be educated, not simply the mind; but of course it acted swiftly and pragmatically upon another ethic entirely. Performance was all, the grade-point average *was* everything. Marya, no idealist, saw that this was sound and just; but she felt an impatient sort of pity for those who fell by the wayside, or who, like the scholarship girls, in not being *best*, were to be judged *worthless*, and sent back home. (Anything below a B was failing for them.) She wanted only to be best, to be outstanding, to be . . . defined to herself as extraordinary . . . for, apart from being extraordinary, had she any essence at all?

The second semester of her freshman year she had come close to losing her perfect grade-point average. Unwisely, she signed up for a course in religion, having been attracted to the books on the syllabus and the supplementary reading list (the *Upanishads*; the *Bhagavad-Gītā*; the *Bible*; the *Koran*; *Hymns of the Rigveda*; books on Gnosticism, and Taoism, and medieval Christianity, and the Christian heresies, and animism, magic, witchcraft, Renaissance ideas of Platonic love). It was all very promising, very heady stuff; quite the antidote to the catechismal Catholicism in which Marya no longer believed, and for which she had increasingly less tolerance. The professor, however turned out to be an ebullient balding popinjay who lectured from old notes in a florid and self-dramatizing style, presenting ideas in a melange clearly thrown together from others' books and articles. He wanted nothing more than these ideas (which were fairly simple, not at all metaphysical or troubling) given back to him on papers and examinations; and he did not encourage questions from the class. Marya would surely have done well—she transcribed notes faultlessly, even when contemptuous of their content—but she could not resist sitting in stony silence and refusing to laugh when the professor embarked upon one or another of his jocular anecdotes. It was a classroom mannerism of his, almost a sort of tic, that each time he alluded to something female he lowered his voice and added, as if off the cuff, a wry observation, meant not so much to be insulting as to be mildly teasing. He was a popular lecturer, well-liked by most, not taken seriously by the better students; even the girls laughed at his jokes, being grateful, as students are, for something—anything—to laugh at. Marya alone sat with her arms folded, her brow furrowed, staring. It was not until some years later that she realized, uncomfortably, how she must have appeared to that silly perspiring man—a sort of gorgon in the midst of his amiable little sea of admirers.

So it happened that, though Marya's grades for the course were all A's, the grade posted for her final examination was C; and the final grade for the course—a humiliating B+.

Marya was stunned, Marya was sickened—she would have had to reach back to her childhood—or to the night of that going-away party—for an episode of equal mortification. That it was petty made it all the more mortifying.

I can forget this insult and forget him, Marya instructed herself,—or I can go to him and protest. To forget it seemed in a way noble, even Christian; to go the man's office and humble herself in trying to get the grade raised (for she knew very well she hadn't written a C exam) somehow childish, degrading.

Of course she ran up to his office, made an appointment to see him; and, after a few minutes' clucking and fretting (he pretended she had failed to answer the last question, she hadn't handed in both examination booklets, but there the second booklet was, at the bottom of a heap of papers—ah, what a surprise!), he consented to raise the grade to A. And smiled roguishly at her, as if she had been caught out in mischief, or some sort of deception; for which he was forgiving her. "You seem like a rather grim young woman," he said, "you never smile—you look so *preoccupied*." Marya stared at his swinging foot. He was a satyrish middle-aged man, red-brown tufts of hair in his ears, a paunch straining against his shirt front, a strangely vulnerable smile; a totally mediocre personality in every way—vain, uncertain, vindictive—yet Marya could see why others liked him; he was predictable, safe, probably decent enough. But she hated him. She simply wished him dead.

He continued as if not wanting to release her, waiting for her smile of blushing gratitude and her meek *thank you*—which assuredly was not going to come; he said again, teasing, "Are you *always* such an ungiving young woman, Miss Knauer?"—and Marya swallowed hard, and fixed her dark loathing stare on him, and said: "My mother is sick. She's been sick all semester. I know I shouldn't think about it so much . . . I shouldn't depress other people . . . but sometimes I can't help it. She isn't expected to live much longer, the cancer has metastasized to the brain. . . . I'm sorry if I offended you."

He stared at her; then began to stammer his apologies, rising from his desk, flushing deeply—the very image of chagrin and repentance. In an instant the entire atmosphere between them changed. He was sorry, he murmured, so very sorry . . . of course he couldn't have known. . . .

A minute later Marya was striding down the corridor, her pulses beating hot, in triumph. In her coat pocket was the black fountain pen she had lifted from the man's cluttered desk.

An expensive pen, as it turned out. A Parker, with a squarish blunt nub, and the engraved initials E. W. S.


Marya used the pen to take notes in her journal, signing her name repeatedly, hypnotically: *Marya, Marya Knauer, Marya Marya Marya Marya Knauer,* a name that eventually seemed to have been signed by someone else, a stranger.

The shame of having humbled herself before the ignorant man had been erased by the shame—what should have been shame—of theft.

So Marya speculated, thinking of that curious episode in her life. Eventually the pen ran out of ink and she didn't indulge herself in buying more—it was so old-fashioned a practice, a luxury she couldn't afford.

Phyllis began staying out late, violating curfew, returning to the residence drunk, dishevelled, tearful, angry—she couldn't stand the four walls of her room any longer, she told Marya; she couldn't stand shutting the door upon herself.

One night she didn't return at all. It was said afterward that she had been picked up by Port Oriskany police, wandering downtown, miles away, dazed and only partly clothed in the bitter cold—the temperature had gone as low as −5°F. She was taken at once to the emergency room of the city hospital; her parents, who lived upstate, were called; they came immediately the next morning to take her back home. No one at Maynard House was ever to see her again.

All the girls in the residence talked of Phyllis, somewhat dazed themselves, frightened. How quickly it had happened—how quickly Phyllis had disappeared. Marya was plied with questions about Phyllis (how many subjects she was failing, who were the boys she'd gone out with) but Marya didn't know; Marya grew vague, sullen.

*And then the waters close over your head.*—This phrase ran through Marya's mind repeatedly.

They talked about Phyllis for two or three days, then forgot her.

The following Saturday, however, Phyllis's mother and older sister arrived to pack up her things, clean out her room, fill out a half-dozen university forms. The resident advisor accompanied them; they looked confused, nervous, rather lost. Both women had Phyllis's pale blond limp hair, her rather small, narrow face. How is Phyllis, some of the girls asked, smiling, cautious, and Mrs. Myer said without looking at anyone, Oh Phyllis is fine, resting and eating and sleeping right again, sleeping good hours, she said, half-reproachfully, as if sleeping right hadn't been possible in Maynard House; and they were all to blame. Marya asked whether she might be returning second semester. No, not that soon, Mrs. Myer said quickly. She and the silent older sister were emptying drawers, packing suitcases briskly. Marya helped with Phyllis's books and papers, which lay in an untidy heap on her desk and on the floor surrounding the desk. There were dust balls everywhere. A great cobweb in which the dessicated corpses of insects hung, including that of the spider itself. Stiffened crumpled Kleenex wadded into balls, everywhere underfoot. An odor of grime and despair. . . . Marya discovered a calculus bluebook slashed heavily in red with a grade of D.; a five-page paper on a subject that made no sense to her—Ring theory?—with a blunt red grade of F. It seemed to Marya that Phyllis was far more real now, more present, than she had been in the past . . . even when she'd tried to comfort Marya by taking her in her arms.

Marya supposed she had been Phyllis's closest friend at Port Oriskany. Yet Phyllis's mother and sister hadn't known her name, had no message for her . . . clearly Phyllis had never mentioned her to them at all. It was disappointing, sobering.

*And the waters close over your head,* Marya thought.

Then something remarkable happened: Marya rose from Phyllis's closet, a pile of books in her arms, her hair in her face, when she happened to see Mrs. Myer dumping loose items out of a drawer into a suitcase: a comb, ballpoint pens, coins, loose pieces of jewelry,—and her black fountain pen. *The* pen, unmistakable.

My God, Marya whispered.

No one heard. Marya stood rooted to the spot, staring, watching as her prize disappeared into Phyllis's suitcase, hidden now by a miscellany of socks and underwear. *The* pen—the emblem of her humiliation and triumph—disappearing forever.

It wasn't until months later that someone in Maynard made the observation that the thefts seemed to have stopped. . . . Since Phyllis moved out. . . . And the rest of the girls (they were at breakfast, eight or ten of them at a table) took it up, amazed, reluctant, wondering. Was it possible . . . *Phyllis* . . . ?

Marya said quietly that they shouldn't say such things since it couldn't be proved; that constituted slander.

Wednesday dinner, a "formal" dinner, in Imogene's sorority house, and Marya is seated beside Imogene, self-conscious, unnaturally shy, eating her food without tasting it. She *can* appreciate the thick slabs of roast beef, the small perfectly cooked parsley potatoes, the handsome gilt-edged china, the white linen tablecloth ("Oh it's Portuguese—from Portugal"), the crystal water goblets, the numerous tall candles, the silvery-green silk wallpaper, the house mother's poised social chatter at the head table . . . and the girls' stylized animation, their collective stylized beauty. For they *are* beautiful, without exception, as unlike the girls of Maynard House as one species is unlike another.

Imogene Skillman, in this dazzling context, isn't Marya's friend; she is clearly a sorority girl; even wearing her pin with its tiny diamonds and rubies just above her left breast. Her high delicate laughter echoes, that of the others', . . . she isn't going to laugh coarsely here, or say anything witty and obscene . . . she can be a little mischievous, just a little cutting, at best. Marya notes how refined her table manners have become for the occasion; how practiced she is at passing things about, summoning one of the houseboys for assistance without quite looking at him. (The houseboy in his white uniform!—one of a subdued and faintly embarrassed little squadron of four or five boys, he turns out to be an acquaintance of Marya's from her Shakespeare class, who resolutely avoids her eye throughout the prolonged meal.)

Marya makes little effort to take part in the table's conversation, which swings from campus topics to vacation plans—Miami Beach, Sarasota, Bermuda, the Barbados, Trinidad, Switzerland ("for skiing"). Where are you going, Imogene asks Marya brightly, and Marya, with a pinched little smile says she will spend a few days at home, then return to school; she has work to do that must be done here. And Imogene's friends gaze upon her with faint neutral smiles. Is this the one Imogene boasted of, who is so intelligent and so well-spoken . . . ? So *witty* . . . ?

For days Marya has been anticipating this dinner, half in dread and half in simple childish excitement. She feared being ravenous with hunger and eating too much out of anxiety; she feared having no appetite at all. But everything is remote, detached, impersonal. Everything is taking place at a little distance from her. A mistake, my coming here, she thinks, my being invited. But she doesn't feel any great nervousness or discomfort. Like the uniformed houseboys who stand with such unnatural stiffness near the doorway to the kitchen, Marya is simply waiting for the meal to end.

She finds herself thinking of friendship, in the past tense. Phyllis, and Diane, and one or two others at Maynard; and, back in Innisfail, Bonnie Michalak, Erma Dietz. She *might* have been a close friend to any of these girls but of course she wasn't, isn't. As for Imogene—she knows she is disappointing Imogene but she can't seem to force herself to care. She halfway resents Imogene for having invited her—for having made a fool out of *herself,* in bringing Marya Knauer to dinner.

How pretty you look, Imogene said, very nearly puzzled, when Marya arrived at six-thirty,—what have you *done* to yourself?

Marya flushed with annoyance; then laughed; with such exuberance that Imogene laughed with her. For it *was* amusing, wasn't it?—Marya Knauer with her hair attractively up in a sort of French twist; Marya Knauer with her lips reddened, and her eyebrows plucked ("pruned," she might have said), Marya Knauer in a green-striped jersey dress that fitted her almost perfectly. A formal dinner meant high heels and stockings, which Marya detested; but she was wearing them nonetheless. And all for Imogene.

Yet now, seated beside Imogene, she pays very little attention to her friend's chatter; she feels subdued, saddened; thinking instead of old friendships, old half-friendships, that year or so during which she'd imagined herself extraordinary, because it had seemed that Emmett Schroeder loved her. She had not loved him—she wasn't capable, she supposed, of loving anyone—but she had certainly basked in the sunny intensity of *his* love: she'd lapped it up eagerly, thirstily (so she very nearly saw herself, a dog lapping water) as if convinced that it had something to do with her. And now Imogene's friendship, which she knows she cannot keep for very long . . . Imogene who has a reputation for being as recklessly improvident with her female friends as with her male friends. . . . Why make the effort, Marya reasons, when all that matters in life is one's personal accomplishment? Work, success, that numbing grade-point average . . . that promise of a future, any future. . . .

While Imogene and several of the others are discussing (animatedly, severely) a sorority sister not present, Marya studies her face covertly; recalls an odd remark Imogene made some weeks ago. The measure of a person's love for you is the depth of his hurt at your betrayal; *that's* the only way you can know how much, or how little, you matter.

Imogene's face had fairly glowed in excited triumph, as she told Marya this bit of wisdom. Marya thought,—She knows from experience, the bitch. She knows her own value.

Imogene is telling a silly convoluted story about a dear friend of hers (it turns out to be Matthew, devoted Matthew) who "helped" her with her term paper on Chekhov: she'd given him a messy batch of notes, he was kind enough to "arrange" them and "expand upon them" and "shape them into an 'A' paper." He's a saint, Imogene says sighing, laughing,—so sweet and so patient; so pathetic, really. But now Imogene is worried ("terrified") that their professor will call her into his office and interrogate her on her own paper, which she hadn't the time to read in its entirety; it was thirty pages long and heavy with footnotes. The girls assure her that if he marked it "A" it *is* an "A"; he'd never ask to see it again. Yes, says Imogene, opening her eyes wide,—but wait until he reads my final exam, and I say these ridiculous things about Chekhov!

Part of this is play-acting, Marya knows, because Imogene is quite intelligent enough, on the subject of Chekhov or anything else connected with drama; so Marya says, though not loudly enough for the entire table to hear: "That wasn't a very kind thing for *you* to do, was it?—and not very honest either."

Imogene chooses not to hear the tone of Marya's remark; she says gaily: "Oh you mean leading poor Matt on? Making him think—? But otherwise he wouldn't have written so *well*, there wouldn't have been so many impressive *footnotes*."

Marya doesn't reply. Marya draws her thumbnail hard against the linen tablecloth, making a secret indentation.

Imogene says, making a joke of it: "Marya's such a puritan—I know better than to ask help of *her*."

Marya doesn't rise to the bait; the conversation shifts onto other topics; in another fifteen minutes the lengthy dinner is over.

"You aren't going home immediately, are you?" Imogene says, surprised. She is smiling but there are strain lines around her mouth. "Come upstairs to my room for a while. Come on, we haven't had a chance to talk."

"Thank you for everything," says Marya. "But I really have to leave. I'm pressed for time these days. . . . "

"You *are* angry?—about that silly Matthew?" Imogene says.

Marya shrugs her shoulders, turns indifferently away.

"Well—are *you* so honest?" Imogene cries.

Marya get her coat from the closet, her face burning. (Are *you* so honest! *You!*) Imogene is apologizing, talking of other things, laughing, while Marya thinks calmly that she will never see Imogene Skillman again.


"There's no reason why you shouldn't take this coat, it's a perfectly good coat," Imogene said in her "serious" voice—frank, level, unemphatic. "I don't want it any longer because I have so many coats, I never get to wear it and it *is* perfectly lovely, it shouldn't just hang in the closet. . . . Anyway here it is; I think it would look wonderful on you."

Marya stared at the coat. It was the camel's hair she had long admired. Pleasantly scratchy beneath her fingers, belted in back, with a beautiful silky-beige lining: she estimated it would have cost $250 or more, new. And it was almost new.

(Marya's coat, bought two or three years before in Innisfail, had cost $45 on sale.)

Imogene insisted, and Marya tried on the coat, flicking her hair out from inside the collar, studying herself critically in Imogene's full-length mirror. Imogene was saying, "If you're worrying that people will know it's my coat—it *was* my coat—don't: camel's hair coats all look alike. Except they don't look like wool imitations."

Marya met Imogene's frank blue gaze in the mirror. "What about your parents, your mother?—won't someone wonder where the coat has gone?"

Imogene puckered her forehead quizzically. "What business is it of theirs?" she asked. "It's *my* coat. My things are mine, I do what I want with them."

Marya muttered that she just couldn't *take* the coat, and Imogene scolded her for talking with her jaw clenched, and Marya protested in a louder voice, yet still faintly, weakly. . . . "It's a beautiful coat," she said.

She was thinking: It's too good for me, I can't accept and I can't refuse and I hate Imogene for this humiliation.

Imogene brought the episode to an end by saying rather coldly: "You'll hurt my feelings, Knauer, if you refuse it. If you're weighing your pride against mine, don't bother—mine is far, far more of a burden."


"So you are—Marya," Mrs. Skillman said in an ambiguous voice (warm? amused? doubtful?) in the drab front parlor of Maynard House, as Marya approached. She and Mr. Skillman and Imogene were taking Marya out to dinner, downtown at the Statler Chop House, one of the area's legendary good restaurants. "We've heard so much about you from Imogene," Mrs. Skillman said, "I think we were expecting someone more. . . . "

"Oh Mother, what on earth—!" Imogene laughed sharply.

". . . I was going to say *taller*, perhaps *older*," Mrs. Skillman said, clearly annoyed by her daughter's interruption.

Marya shook hands with both the Skillmans and saw to her relief that they appeared to be friendly well-intentioned people, attractive enough, surely, and very well-dressed, but nothing like their striking daughter. *She* might have been their daughter, brunette and subdued. (Except she hadn't dared wear the camel's hair coat, as Imogene had wanted. She was wearing her old plaid wool and her serviceable rubberized boots.)

In their presence Imogene was a subtly different person. Rather more disingenuous, childlike, sweet. Now and then at dinner Marya heard a certain self-mocking tone in her friend's voice ("am I playing this scene correctly?—how is it going down?") but neither of the Skillmans took notice; and perhaps it was Marya's imagination anyway.

Then, near the end of the meal, Imogene got suddenly high on white wine and said of her father's business: "It's a sophisticated form of theft."

She giggled, no one else laughed; Marya kept her expression carefully blank.

". . . I mean it *is*, you know . . . it's indirect. . . . 'Savings and Loans' . . . and half the clients blacks who want their Dee-troit cars financed," Imogene said.

"Imogene, you aren't funny," Mrs. Skillman said.

"She's just teasing," Mr. Skillman said. "My little girl likes to tease."

"I do like to tease, don't I?—Marya knows." Imogene said, nudging her. Then, as if returning to her earlier sobriety, she said: "*I never mean a word of what I say and everybody knows it.*"

The subject leapt to Imogene's negligence about writing letters, or even telephoning home. "If we try to call," Mrs. Skillman said, "the line at the residence is busy for hours; and when we finally get through you aren't in; you're *never* in. And you never return our calls. . . . "

Imogene said carelessly that her sorority sisters were bad at taking down messages. Most of them were assholes, actually—

"Imogene!" Mrs. Skillman said.

"Oh Mother you know they *are*," Imogene said in a childlike voice.

After an awkward pause Mr. Skillman asked about Richard: Richard had evidently telephoned *them,* asking if something was wrong with Imogene because he couldn't get through to her either. "Your mother and I were hoping there wasn't some sort of . . . misunderstanding between you."

Imogene murmured that there weren't any misunderstandings at all between them.

"He seemed to think . . . to wonder . . . " Mrs. Skillman said. "That is, as long as we were driving up to visit. . . . "

Imogene finished off her glass of white wine and closed here eyes ecstatically. She said: "I really don't care to discuss my private matters in a restaurant. —Anyway Marya is here: why don't we talk about something lofty and intellectual? *She's* taking a philosophy course—if she can't tell us the meaning of life no one can."

"You and Richard haven't quarrelled, have you?" Mrs. Skillman said.

Imogene raised her left hand and showed the diamond ring to her mother, saying, "*Please* don't worry, I haven't given it back, it's safe." To Marya she said lightly: "Mother would be mortified if Dickie demanded it back. It's somebody's old dead socialite *grandmother's.*"

"Imogene," Mr. Skillman said, his voice edged with impatience, "you really shouldn't tease so much. I've just read that teasing is a form of aggression . . . did you know that?"

"Not that I'd give it back if Dickie *did* demand it," Imogene laughed. "It's mine, I've earned it, let him *sue* to get it back—right, Marya?—he's going to be a hotshot lawyer after all. Let him *practice.*"

Everyone, including Marya, laughed as if Imogene had said something unusually witty; and Imogene, in the cool voice she used to summon the houseboys at her sorority, asked a passing waiter for more wine.

Richard.

"Dickie."

Am I jealous of someone called "Dickie," Marya wondered, lying sprawled and slovenly across her bed. She was doing rough, impatient charcoal sketches of imaginary faces—beetle-browed, glowering, defiantly ugly—that inevitably turned out to be forms of her own.

In Imogene's cluttered room on the second floor of the baronial sorority house Marya had come upon, to her astonishment, copies of *Bride* magazine. She leafed through them, jeering, while Imogene hid her face in laughing protestation. Wedding gowns! Satin and pearls! Veils made of antique lace! Orange blossoms! Shoes covered in white silk! And what is this, Marya said, flapping the pages in Imogene's direction,—a wedding-cake bridegroom to go with it all?—standing a little out of the range of the camera's focus, amiable and blurred.

"Ah, but you'll have to be a bridesmaid," Imogene said dryly. "Or a maid of honor."

Imogene showed her snapshots of the legendary Richard, flicking them like playing cards. Marya saw that, yes, Richard was a handsome young man—dark strong features, a slightly heavy chin, intelligent eyes. He was demanding, perhaps; an excellent match for Imogene. But it was difficult, Marya thought, to believe that the person in the snapshots—*this* person, standing with his hands on his hips, his hair lifting in the wind—would be capable of loving Imogene as much as she required being loved.

Imogene threw herself across her bed, lay on her back, let her long hair dangle to the floor. Her belly was stretched flat; her pelvic bones protruded. She smoothed her shirt across her abdomen with long nervous fingers. ". . . The first time I came with him," she said hesitantly, but with a breathy laugh, "it wasn't . . . you know . . . it wasn't with him inside me, the way you're supposed to . . . I was afraid of that then, I thought I might get pregnant. And he was so big, I thought he'd hurt me, they're *very* big compared to . . . compared to us. The first time it worked for me he was, well, you know, kissing me there . . . he'd gotten all crazy and wild and I couldn't stop him, and I never thought I would let anyone do that . . . I'd *heard* about that . . . because . . . oh Marya, am I embarrassing you? . . . because afterward," she said, laughing shrilly, "they only want to kiss you: and it's disgusting."

She rolled over amidst the tumble of things strewn on her bed and hid her face from Marya.

After a long time she said, her breath labored, her face still turned away: "Am I embarrassing you?"

Marya's throat and chest were so constricted, she couldn't reply.


A Marya Knauer anecdote, told by Imogene with peals of cruel ribald laughter. . . .

Imogene insisted that Marya accompany her on a date, yes a "date," and actual "date" (though it was generally thought that Marya shunned men because she imagined they weren't *serious* enough). Her escort was Matthew Fein, of all people—Matthew who had seemed to dislike Marya but who in fact (so Imogene revealed) had simply been afraid of her.

"Afraid of me?—you're being ridiculous," Marya said. She hardly knew whether to be hurt or flattered.

"Of course he's afraid of you, or was," Imogene said. "And my poor sorority sisters!—they told me afterward they'd never seen such eyes as yours—taking them all in and condemning them! *Those assholes!"*

It would be an ordinary evening, Imogene promised, no need to dress up, no *need* for the high-heels-stockings routine, though it was perfectly all right (so Imogene said innocently) if Marya wanted to comb her hair. Imogene's date for the evening was a senior in business administration and advertising whose name Marya never caught, or purposefully declined to hear. They drove out to a suburban mall to see a movie—in fact it was a pretentious French "film"—and then they went to a local Italian restaurant where everyone, excepting of course Marya, drank too much; and then they drove to the water-tower hill where numerous other cars were parked, their headlights off. Marya stiffened. Matthew had not yet touched her but she knew that he would be kissing her in another minute; and she had no idea of how to escape gracefully.

". . . Few minutes?" Imogene murmured from the front seat.

She was sending them away!—Marya saw with disbelief that, by the time she and Matthew climbed out of the car, Imogene and her date were locked in a ravenous embrace. One would have thought the two of them lovers; one would have thought them at least fond of each other. Marya's heart was beating frantically. That bitch! That bitch! Marya worried that she might suffocate—she couldn't seem to catch her breath.

Matthew took her cold unresisting hand. He slipped his arm around her shoulders.

They were meant to stroll for a few minutes along the darkened path, to contemplate, perhaps, the view of Port Oriskany below, all sparkling winking lights. A romantic sight, no doubt. Beautiful in its way. Matthew was saying something rather forced—making a joke of some kind—about the French movie?—about Imogene's reckless behavior?—but Marya interrupted. "Isn't she supposed to be engaged?" she asked. "Yes, I suppose so," Matthew said in resignation, "but she does this all the time. It's just Imogene." "She does this all the *time*?" Marya said, "but why—?" Matthew laughed uncomfortably. He was not quite Marya's height and his dark eyes shied away from hers. "I don't know," he said defensively, "—as I said, it's just Imogene, it's her business. Why shouldn't she do what she wants to do? Don't be angry with *me.*"

He was nervous yet keenly excited; Marya sensed his sexual agitation. Behind them, parked along the gravelled drive, were lovers' cars, one after another; from this distance, the car in which Imogene and her "date" were pawing at each other was undistinguishable from the others.

"You might not approve," Matthew said, his voice edged now with an air of authority, "—but Imogene is a free soul, she does what she wants, I don't suppose she actually *lies* to her fiancé. He'd have to allow her some freedom, you know, or she'd break off the engagement."

"You know a lot about her," Marya said.

"Imogene is a close friend of mine, we've worked together . . . I was stage manager for *Hedda Gabler*, don't you remember?"

"It's all so . . . trivial," Marya said slowly. "So degrading."

"What do you mean?"

"Oh—this."

"This—?"

Marya indicated the cars parked along the drive. Her expression was contemptuous.

"You take an awfully superior attitude, don't you," Matthew said, with an attempt at jocular irony. He tightened his arm around her shoulders; he drew nearer. Marya could hear his quickened breathing.

Is this idiot really going to kiss me, Marya wondered. Her heart was still beating heavily; she could see Imogene's profile, the cameo-clear outline of her face, illuminated for an instant as the headlights were extinguished. Then she moved into the young man's embrace, she kissed him, slid her arms around his neck. . . .

"Does she make love with them?" Marya asked.

"Them—?"

"Different boys. Men. One week after another."

"I don't know," Matthew said resentfully. "I suppose so—if she wants to."

"I thought *you* were in love with her," Marya said mockingly.

"We're just friends," Matthew said, offended.

"Oh no," said Marya, "—everyone knows you're in *love* with her."

Matthew drew away from Marya and walked beside her without speaking. There was nothing for them to do, suddenly; not a thing left to say. It was still March and quite cold. Their footsteps sounded dully on the crusted snow. Marya thought, The various ways we seek out our humiliations. . . .

After a few minutes Matthew said something conciliatory about the night, the stars, the city lights, "infinity," certain remarks of Pascal's; but Marya made no effort to listen. She kept seeing Imogene kissing that near-stranger, Imogene locking her arms about his neck *as if he mattered. As if they were lovers.*

She was going to observe aloud, cynically, that making love was as good a way as any of passing the time, if you hadn't anything better to do, when Matthew, brave Matthew, turned to her and took hold of her shoulders and tried to kiss her. It was desperate gesture—his breath smelled of sweet red wine—but Marya would have none of it. She shoved him roughly in the chest.

"Marya, for Christ's sake grow up," Matthew said angrily. "You're a big girl now—"

"Why should you *kiss* me?" Marya said, equally angry, "—when you don't even *like* me? When you know I don't like you in the slightest, when we haven't anything to say to each other, when we're just waiting for the evening to get finished!—in fact we've been made fools of, both of us. And now you want to kiss me," she said, jeering, "—just for something to do."

He began to protest but Marya dismissed him with a derisory wave of her hand. She was going to walk back to the residence, she said; she was through with them all. Especially Imogene.

Matthew followed along behind her for a few minutes, trying to talk her into coming back to the car. It was almost midnight, he said; the campus was two miles away; what if something happened to her. . . . Marya ignored him and walked faster, descending the hill past a slow stream of cars that were ascending it, their headlights blinding her eyes. She lowered her head, tried to hide her face, her hands thrust deep in the pockets of her camel's hair coat. At first she was furious—almost sick with fury—her head rang with accusations against Imogene—but the cold still night air was so invigorating, so wonderfully cleansing, she felt quite good by the time she got to Maynard House, not very long after midnight. She felt *very* good.

Next day, Sunday, Imogene stood at the downstairs desk ringing Marya's buzzer repeatedly, one two three four, one two three four, and then one long rude ring, until Marya appeared at the top of the stairs, her hair in a towel. "Who the hell—?" she called down. She and Imogene stared at each other. Then Imogene said contemptuously, "Here's your purse, you left your purse in the car, Knauer. D'you know, Knauer, your behavior is getting eccentric; it isn't even amusing, just what if something had happened to you last night—walking back here all alone—a college girl, in some of those neighborhoods!—don't you think Lyle and Matt and I would feel responsible? But *you*," she said, her voice rising, "—*you* haven't the slightest sense of—of responsibility to other people—"

"Just leave the purse," Marya said, leaning over the bannister. "Leave it and go back to screwing what's-his-name—that's *your* responsibility—"

"Go screw yourself!" Imogene shouted. "Go fuck yourself!"

"Go fuck *yourself!*" Marya shouted.

As the stories sifted back to Marya, over a period of a week or ten days, they became increasingly disturbing, ugly.

In one version Marya Knauer had been almost attacked—that is, raped—in a black neighborhood near the foot of Tower Hill; and had run back to her residence hall, hysterical and sobbing. It was an even graver insult that her purse had been taken from her—her purse and all her money.

In another version, Marya was so panicked at being simply touched by her date (she was a virgin, she was frigid, she'd never been kissed before) that she ran from the car, hysterical and panting . . . ran all the way back to campus. The boy was a blind date, someone in drama, or maybe business administration, it was all a total surprise to him that Marya Knauer was so . . . crazy.

In a third improbable version it was Imogene Skillman's fiancé who offered to take Marya back to the residence, because she was so upset—having a breakdown of some kind—and when they were halfway there she threw herself on him in the car *while he was actually driving*. And then, ashamed, she opened the car door and jumped out *while the car was still in motion*.

"It's Imogene," Marya said, licking her numbed lips. "She's making these things up . . . Why is she *doing* this to me . . . !"

There were vague rumors too that Marya had borrowed small sums of money from Imogene. And items of clothing as well—the camel's hair coat, for instance. (Because she hadn't a coat of her own. Because her coat had literally gone to shreds. Because she was so *poor*, a scholarship student from the hills, practically a *hillbilly*. . . . ) As far as she was concerned, Imogene was reported saying, Marya Knauer could keep the coat if she was that desperate. Imogene no longer wanted it back.

Marya telephoned Imogene and accused her of telling lies, of telling slanderous tales. "Do you think I don't know who's behind this?" Marya cried. But Imogene hung up at once: Imogene was too wise to reply.

Marya began to see how people watched her . . . smiling covertly as she passed. They were pitying her, yet merciless. They knew. Marya Knauer with all her pretensions, Marya Knauer who had made a fool of herself with another girl's fiancé, Marya Knauer who was cracking up. . . .

In the fluorescent-lit dining hall she sat alone in an alcove, eating quickly, her head bowed; it was too much trouble to remove her plates and glass of water from the tray. Two boys passed near and she heard them laugh softly. . . . *That* the one? There? one of them whispered. She turned back to her book ( . . . *the thought of suicide is a strong consolation, one can get through many a bad night with it*) but the print danced crazily in her eyes.

"Do you think I don't know who's behind this,—who's responsible?" Marya asked aloud, in anguish, in the privacy of her room. She tried to lock her door from the inside—as if there were any danger of being interrupted, invaded—but the doors in Maynard, as in university housing generally, did not lock in that direction.

At about this time Marya was notified that a short story she had submitted to a national competition had placed first; and, not long afterward—

within a week or ten days, in fact—she learned that another story, sent out blindly and naively to a distinguished literary magazine, was accepted for publication.

She thought of telephoning Wilma and Everard . . . she thought of telephoning Imogene . . . running along the corridors of Maynard House, knocking on doors, sharing her good news. But her elation was tempered almost at once by a kind of sickened dread—she was going to be unequal to the task of whatever it was (so her panicked thoughts raced, veered) she might be expected to do.

Lately her "serious" writing frightened her. Not just the content itself—though the content was often wild, disturbing, unanticipated—but the emotional and psychological strain it involved. She could write all night long, sprawled across her bed, taking notes, drafting out sketches and scenes, narrating a story she seemed to be hearing in a kind of trance; she could write until her hand ached and her eyes filled with tears and she felt that another pulsebeat would push her over the brink—into despair, into madness, into sheer extinction. Nothing is worth this, she told herself very early one morning, nothing can be worth this, she thought, staring at herself in the mirror of the third floor bathroom,—a ghastly hollowed-eyed death's head of a face, hardly recognizable as Marya, as a girl of nineteen.

Give up. Don't risk it. *Don't* risk it.

So she cautioned herself, so she gave and took warning. There was another kind of writing—highly conscious, cerebral, critical, discursive—which she found far easier; far less dangerous. She was praised for it lavishly, given the highest grades, the most splendid sort of encouragement. She should plan, her professors said, to go on to graduate school . . . they would advise her, help her get placed, help her make her way. . . . Don't risk this, she told herself, the waters will suck you down and close over your head: I know the symptoms.

And she did, she did. As if she had lived a previous life and could recall vividly the anguish of . . . whatever it was that might happen.

One windy morning at the end of March she saw Imogene Skillman walking with several of her friends. Imogene in sunglasses, her hair blowing wild, her laughter shrill and childish, Imogene in tight-fitting jeans and a bulky white ski sweater, overlong in the sleeves. That slatternly waifish affect. . . . Marya stood watching. Staring. Poor Marya Knauer, staring. Why did you lie about me! she wanted to cry. Why did you betray me! But she stood silent, paralyzed, watching. No doubt a figure of pathos—or of comedy—her snarled black hair blowing wild as Imogene's, her skin grainy and sallow.

Of course Imogene saw her; but Imogene's eyes were discreetly hidden by the dark-tinted glasses. No need for her to give any sign of recognition. No need.

Marya wrote Imogene a muddled little note, the first week in April.

*Things aren't going well for me, I missed a philosophy exam & have no excuse & can't make myself lie. I don't know . . . am I unhappy (is it that simple?) Why don't you drop by & see me sometime . . . or I could come over there & see you. . . .*

Yet she felt a revulsion for Imogene; she *really* disliked her. That lazy drunken dip of her head, her lipstick smeared across her face, sliding her arms around the neck of . . . whoever it had been: kissing open-mouthed, simulating passion. Would you two let us alone for a few minutes, Imogene drawled,—Would you two like to go for a stroll, for a few minutes?

*I'll come over there,* Marya wrote, *and strangle you with that pretentious braid of yours.*

In all she wrote a dozen notes, some by hand and some on the type-writer. But she sent only the first ("why don't you drop by & see me some-time . . . or I could come over there & see you"), not expecting, and not receiving, an answer.

What is fictitious in a friendship, Marya pondered, and what is "real": the world outside the head, the world *inside*: but whose world?—from whose point of view?

If Imogene died. . . .

If Imogene were dying. . . .

She wouldn't lift a hand to prevent that death!—so she thought.

At the same time she quizzed herself about how to respond, should Imogene really ask her to be a bridesmaid. (She had declined being a bridesmaid at Alice's wedding; but then she had the excuse of schoolwork, distance.) Imogene's wedding was going to be a costly affair held in Long Beach, New York sometime the following year. The bridesmaid's dress, the shoes . . . the shoes alone . . . would be staggeringly expensive.

I can't afford it, Marya would say.

I can't afford *you.*

Though they hadn't any classes together this semester Marya learned that Imogene had been absent from one of her lectures for three days run-ning. So she simply went, one rainy April afternoon, to Imogene's resi-dence—to that absurd white-columned "house" on Masefield Avenue—and rapped hard on Imogene's door; and let herself in before Imogene could call out sleepily, who is it . . . ?

The shades were crookedly drawn. Clothes and towels and books were strewn about. Imogene lay half-undressed on the bed with the quilted spread pulled over her; the room smelled of something acrid and medicinal.

"Oh Marya," Imogene said guiltily.

"Are you sick?" Marya asked.

They had both spoken at the same time.

". . . a headache, cramps, nothing worth mentioning," Imogene said hoarsely. ". . . the tail-end of this shitty flu that's been going around."

Marya stood with her hands on her hips, regarding Imogene in bed. Imogene's skin looked oddly coarse, her hair lay in spent greasy tangles on the pillow, spilling off the edge of the bed; her body was flat, curiously immobile. Without makeup she looked both young and rather ravaged. "If you're really sick, if you need a doctor, your sorority sisters will see to it," Marya said half-mockingly.

"I'm not really sick," said Imogene at once. "I'm resting."

After a long pause Marya said, as if incidentally: "You told so many lies about me."

Imogene coughed feebly. "They weren't exactly *lies*, there was an essence. . . . "

"They were lies," Marya said. "I wanted to strangle you."

Imogene lay without moving, her hands flat on her stomach. She said in a childish vague voice: "Oh nobody believed anything, it was just . . . talk . . . spinning tales. . . . You know, thinking "What if" . . . that sort of thing. Anyway there was an *essence* that was true."

Marya was pacing about the room, the balls of her feet springy, the tendons of her calves strained. "I don't intend to let you destroy me," she said softly. "I don't even intend to do poorly in my courses." She brushed her hair out of her face and half-smiled at Imogene—a flash of hatred. "You won't make me lose my perfect record," she said.

"Won't I," said Imogene.

Marya laughed. She said: "But why did you concoct a story about your fiancé and me?—you know I've never even met him; I don't have any interest in meeting him."

"Yes you do," Imogene said, a little sharply. "You're jealous of him—of him and me."

"You're angry that I'm not jealous *enough*," Marya said. "Do you think I'd want to sleep with your precious, 'Dickie'?"

"You think so goddam fucking highly of yourself, don't you," Imogene said, sitting up, adjusting a pillow impatiently behind her. "*You* can't be cracked open, can you?—a nut that can't be cracked," she said, laughing, yawning. "A tight little virgin, I suppose. And Catholic too!—what a joke! Very very proud of yourself."

"Why didn't you talk to me on the phone, why didn't you answer my note?" Marya asked quietly.

"Why did you avoid me on campus?"

"Avoid you when?"

"Why do you always look the other way?"

"Look the other way *when*—?"

*"All the time."*

Marya was striking her hands, her fists, lightly together. She drew a deep shaky breath. "As for the coat—you *gave* me the coat. Your precious Salvation Army gesture. You *gave* me the coat, you *forced* it on me."

"Oh Knauer, noboby forces anything on *you*," Imogene said, sneering. "What bullshit—!"

"I want to know why you've been spreading lies about me and ridiculing me behind my back," Marya said levelly.

Imogene pulled at her hair in a lazy, mawkishly theatrical gesture. "Hey. Did I tell you. I'm transferring out of here next year," she said. "I'm going to school somewhere in New York, N.Y.U. probably. The drama courses are too *restrained* here, there's too much crap about *tradition*. . . . "

"I said I want to know *why*."

"Oh for Christ's sweet sake what are you talking about!" Imogene cried. "I'm sick, my head is spinning, if you don't leave me alone I'm going to puke all over everything. I haven't been to a class in two weeks and I don't give a damn but I refuse to give *you* the satisfaction. . . . Transfer to New York, Marya, why don't you: you know you think you're too good for us *here*."

Marya stared at her, trembling. She had a vision of running at her friend and pummelling her with her fists—the two of them fighting, clawing, grunting in silence.

"Your jealousy, your morbid possessiveness. . . . " Imogene was saying wildly, her eyes wide, ". . . the way you sat in judgment of my parents . . . my poor father trying so hard to be *nice* to you, to be *kind*, because he felt *sorry* for you . . . and my mother too. . . . 'Is she one of your strays and misfits?' Mother said, 'another one of that gang that will turn on you'. . . . As for my sorority sisters. . . . "

Marya said slowly, groping: "And what about you? You're spoiled, you're vicious. . . . And you don't even act that well: people here baby you, lie to you, tell you the kind of crap you want to hear."

At this Imogene threw herself back against the flattened pillows, laughing, half-sobbing. "Yes," she said. "Good. Now leave me alone."

"Do you think they tell you anything else?—anything else but crap?" Marya said carelessly, "—people who are in love with you? People who don't even know who you *are*?"

Imogene pawed at the bedspread and pulled it roughly over herself. She lay very still but Marya could hear her labored breath. ". . . I took some aspirin before you came in, I want to sleep, maybe you'd better let me alone. I think you'd better let me alone."

She closed her eyes, she waved Marya away with a languid gesture. "Good-bye, Marya!" she whispered.

On the sidewalk outside the house Marya took out the earrings boldly to examine them.

The Aztec ones, the barbarian-princess ones, bronze and red and blue, burnished, gleaming. . . . Marya had seen her hand reach out to take them but she did not remember *taking* them from the room.

She tossed them in the palm of her hand as she strode along Masefield Avenue, smiling, grinning. No one, she thought in triumph, can keep me from my perfect record.

She went that day to an earring shop down on Fairfield Street; asked to have her ears pierced and Imogene's splendid earrings inserted. But the proprietor told her that wasn't the procedure; first, gold studs are inserted . . . then, after a few weeks, when the wounds are healed. . . .

No, Marya insisted, put in *these*. I don't have time to waste.

But there was the danger of infection, she was told. Everything has to be germ-free, antiseptic. . . .

"I don't give a damn about that," Marya said fiercely. "These earrings *are* gold. Put antiseptic on *them*. . . . Just pierce my ears and put them in and I'll pay you and that's all."

"Do you have five dollars?" the young man said curtly.

Crossing the quadrangle between Stafford Hall and the chapel one cold May afternoon, Marya caught sight of Imogene approaching her. It had been approximately two weeks since the theft of the earrings—two weeks during which Marya had worn the earrings everywhere, for everyone to see, to comment upon, to admire. She and Imogene had frequently noticed each other, usually at a distance, though once in rather close quarters on a crowded stairway; and Marya had been amused at Imogene's shocked expression; and the clumsy way she'd turned aside, pretending she hadn't seen Marya and Marya's new earrings.

Not a very good actress after all, Marya thought.

Now, however, Imogene was approaching her head-on, though her movements were rather forced, wooden. Marya didn't slacken her pace; she was headed for the library. She wore her raincoat half-unbuttoned, her head was bare, her hair loose, the earrings swung heavily as she walked, tugged at her earlobes. (Yes, her earlobes *were* sore. Probably infected, Marya thought indifferently, waking in the night to small stabs of pain.)

Imogene's face was dead white, and not very attractive. Something horsy about that face, after all, Marya thought. Her mouth was strained, and the tendons in her neck were clearly visible as, suddenly, she ran at Marya. She was screaming something about "hillbilly bitch"—"thief"—She grabbed at Marya's left ear, she would have ripped the earring out of Marya's flesh, but Marya was too quick for her: she knew instinctively what Imogene would try to do.

She struck Imogene's hand aside, and gave her a violent shove; Imogene slapped her hard across the face; Marya slapped *her*. "You bitch!" Imogene cried. "You won't get away with this! *I know you!*"

All their books had fallen to the sidewalk, Imogene's leather bag was tripping her up, passers-by stopped to stare, incredulous. What a sight, Imogene Skillman and Marya Knauer fighting, in front of the chapel,—both in blue jeans, both livid with rage. Marya was shouting, "Don't you touch me, you! What do you mean, touching *me!*" She was the better fighter, crouching with her knees bent, like a man, swinging at Imogene, striking her on the jaw. Not a slap but an actual punch: Marya's fist was unerring.

The blow was a powerful one, for Marya struck from the shoulder. Imogene's head snapped back—blood appeared on her mouth—she staggered backward and swayed, almost lost her balance. "Oh, Marya," she said.

Marya snatched up her things and turned away. Her long fast stride and the set of her shoulders, the set of her head, must have indicated confidence; angry assurance; but in fact she was badly shaken . . . it was some time before she could catch her breath. When she turned to look back Imogene was sitting on the ground and a small crowd had gathered around her. You'll be all right, Marya thought, someone will always take care of *you*.


After that, very little happened.

Marya kept the earrings, though her ears *were* infected and she had to give up wearing them; Imogene Skillman never approached her again, never pressed charges; nor did anyone dare bring the subject up to either of the girls.

Marya's record remained perfect but Imogene did poorly at the end of the semester, failing two subjects; and, in place of transferring to another university she quit college altogether.

That fall, Marya learned that Imogene was living in New York City. She had broken off her engagement over the summer; she had joined a troupe of semiprofessional actors, and lived in an apartment off St. Mark's Square. It was said that she had a small role in an off-Broadway play scheduled to open sometime that winter but Marya never learned the title of the play, or when, precisely, it opened; or how successful it was.

. . . . . . . . . . . .

## QUESTIONS FOR A SECOND READING

1. Go back over the variety of thefts in this story (and not all of them Marya's): outright thefts, supposed or imagined thefts, and metaphorical thefts (where something other than property could be said to be "stolen"). If we are getting Marya's view of the world in this story, what is it? Why would "theft" be a good term for describing what goes on in that world? What can you conclude from this about Marya's sense of her relations to other people? about the way she sees the connections between people and things?

2. How would you explain the relationship between Marya and Imogene? Is there a difference between how you would explain it and how the story *would have you* explain it? That is, what does Oates offer as the key terms and key moments in the story, and what do *you* see as the key terms and key moments?

## ASSIGNMENTS FOR WRITING

1. The narrator of this story says, "There was a moment when an item passed over from belonging to another person to belonging to Marya; that moment interested her greatly." Why do you suppose this moment interests Marya? How does this fit with your sense of her personality? And how, then, would you explain why she steals? For this assignment, write an essay explaining why you think Marya steals. What's her problem, and how might you account for it?

2. Reading, for Marya, at times was "a secret process yet it was not criminal or forbidden—she made her way with the stealth of the thief, elated, subdued, through another's imagination, risking no harm, no punishment." Look back over the sections of the story that give you access to Marya's intellectual life and her success as a student. What connections can you make between her academic life and her life as a thief? In an essay, explore how her successful intellectual performance as a student could be related to her thievery. As you read the story, what are the points of the comparison?

## MAKING CONNECTIONS

1. The stories by Bellow ("A Silver Dish," p. 39) and Oates deal with theft. People take things, and things are taken from them. For this assignment, you need to think about theft as something more than the act of stealing.

Ask yourself what the thefts in the Bellow and Oates stories might stand for, what they might represent. How, in other words, might one use the *metaphor* of theft to talk about people, their pasts and presents, and the culture they live in? Write an essay in which you discuss "Theft" and "A Silver Dish" and what the thefts in these stories allow you to understand about the people involved and their relationships to each other. (Don't misunderstand—stealing is bad, but that's not the point. This question isn't about actual acts of stealing but what stealing—as something people do and have done to them—might represent.)

2. Richard Rodriguez, in "The Achievement of Desire" (p. 500), talks about his schooling as the process of becoming a "scholarship boy." He borrows the term (or takes it, as he takes many things, from his teachers) and uses it to analyze his experience as a student. If you look at Marya the way Rodriguez looks at himself, do you think the term (or its equivalent, "scholarship girl") applies to her? If you consider Rodriguez as a student like Marya, as a person fascinated with that "moment when an item passed over from belonging to another person to belonging" to him, a person not beyond stealing but not quite a thief either, what can you say to explain his relationship to others? to the culture around him? Write an essay in which you discuss Rodriguez and Marya as examples of people who have a similar response to the experience of growing up, entering the world, and becoming educated.

# WALKER
# PERCY



*W*ALKER PERCY, *in his mid-forties, after a life of relative obscurity and after a career as, he said, a "failed physician," wrote his first novel,* The Movie-goer. *It won the National Book Award for fiction in 1962, and Percy emerged as one of this country's leading novelists. Little in his background would have predicted such a career.*

*After graduating from Columbia University's medical school in 1941, Percy (b. 1916) went to work at Bellevue Hospital in New York City. He soon contracted tuberculosis from performing autopsies on derelicts and was sent to a sanitorium to recover, where, as he said, "I was in bed so much, alone so much, that I had nothing to do but read and think. I began to question everything I had once believed." He returned to medicine briefly but suffered a relapse and during his long recovery began "to make reading a full-time occupation." He left medicine, but not until 1954, almost a decade later, did he publish his first essay, "Symbol as Need."*

*The essays that followed, including "The Loss of the Creature," all dealt with the relationships between language and understanding or belief, and they were all published in obscure academic journals. In the later essays, Percy seemed to turn away from academic forms of argument and to depend more and more on stories or anecdotes from daily life—to write, in fact, as a storyteller and to be wary of abstraction or explanation. Robert Coles has said that it was Percy's failure to find a form that would reach a larger audience that led him to try his hand at a novel. You will notice in the essay that follows that Percy delights in piling example upon example; he never seems to settle down to a topic sentence, or any sentence for that matter that sums everything up and makes the examples superfluous.*

*In addition to* The Moviegoer, *Percy has written five other novels, including* Lancelot *(1977) and* Love in the Ruins *(1971). He has published two books of essays,* The Message in the Bottle: How Queer Man Is, How Queer Language Is, and What One Has to Do with the Other *(1975, from which "The Loss of the Creature" is taken), and* Lost in the Cosmos: The Last Self-help Book *(1983). His most recent novel,* The Thanatos Syndrome *(1984), was dedicated to his friend Robert Coles.*

# The Loss of the Creature

## I

Every explorer names his island Formosa, beautiful. To him it is beautiful because, being first, he has access to it and can see it for what it is. But to no one else is it ever as beautiful—except the rare man who manages to recover it, who knows that it has to be recovered.

Garcia López de Cárdenas discovered the Grand Canyon and was amazed at the sight. It can be imagined: One crosses miles of desert, breaks through the mesquite, and there it is at one's feet. Later the government set the place aside as a national park, hoping to pass along to millions the experience of Cárdenas. Does not one see the same sight from the Bright Angel Lodge that Cárdenas saw?

The assumption is that the Grand Canyon is a remarkably interesting and beautiful place and that if it had a certain value $P$ for Cárdenas, the same value $P$ may be transmitted to any number of sightseers—just as Banting's discovery of insulin can be transmitted to any number of diabetics. A counterinfluence is at work, however, and it would be nearer the truth to say that if the place is seen by a million sightseers, a single sightseer does not receive value $P$ but a millionth part of value $P$.

It is assumed that since the Grand Canyon has the fixed interest value $P$, tours can be organized for any number of people. A man in Boston decides to spend his vacation at the Grand Canyon. He visits his travel bureau, looks at the folder, signs up for a two-week tour. He and his family take the tour, see the Grand Canyon, and return to Boston. May we say that this man has seen the Grand Canyon? Possibly he has. But it is more likely that what he has done is the one sure way not to see the canyon.

Why is it almost impossible to gaze directly at the Grand Canyon under these circumstances and see it for what it is—as one picks up a strange object from one's back yard and gazes directly at it? It is almost impossible because the Grand Canyon, the thing as it is, has been appropriated by the symbolic complex which has already been formed in the sightseer's mind. Seeing the canyon under approved circumstances is seeing the symbolic complex head on. The thing is no longer the thing as it confronted the Spaniard; it is rather that which has already been formulated—by picture postcard, geography book, tourist folders, and the words *Grand Canyon*. As a result of this preformulation, the source of the sightseer's pleasure undergoes a shift. Where the wonder and delight of the Spaniard arose from his penetration of the thing itself, from a progressive discovery of depths, patterns, colors, shadows, etc., now the sightseer measures his satisfaction *by the degree to which the canyon conforms to the preformed complex.* If it does so, if it looks just like the postcard, he is pleased; he might even say, "Why it is every bit as beautiful as a picture postcard!" He feels he has not been cheated. But if it does not conform, if the colors are somber, he will not be able to see it directly; he will only be conscious of the disparity between what it is and what it is supposed to be. He will say later that he was unlucky in not being there at the right time. The highest point, the term of the sightseer's satisfaction, is not the sovereign discovery of the thing before him; it is rather the measuring up of the thing to the criterion of the preformed symbolic complex.

Seeing the canyon is made even more difficult by what the sightseer does when the moment arrives, when sovereign knower confronts the thing to be known. Instead of looking at it, he photographs it. There is no confrontation at all. At the end of forty years of preformulation and with the Grand Canyon yawning at his feet, what does he do? He waives his right of seeing and knowing and records symbols for the next forty years. For him there is no present; there is only the past of what has been formulated and seen and the future of what has been formulated and not seen. The present is surrendered to the past and the future.

The sightseer may be aware that something is wrong. He may simply be bored; or he may be conscious of the difficulty: that the great thing yawning at his feet somehow eludes him. The harder he looks at it, the less he can see. It eludes everybody. The tourist cannot see it; the bellboy at the Bright Angel Lodge cannot see it: for him it is only one side of the space he lives in, like one wall of a room; to the ranger it is a tissue of everyday signs relevant to his own prospects—the blue haze down there means that he will probably get rained on during the donkey ride.

How can the sightseer recover the Grand Canyon? He can recover it in any number of ways, all sharing in common the stratagem of avoiding the approved confrontation of the tour and the Park Service.

It may be recovered by leaving the beaten track. The tourist leaves the tour, camps in the back country. He arises before dawn and approaches the South Rim through a wild terrain where there are no trails and no railed-in lookout points. In other words, he sees the canyon by avoiding all the facilities for seeing the canyon. If the benevolent Park Service hears about this fellow and thinks he has a good idea and places the following notice in the Bright Angel Lodge: *Consult ranger for information on getting off the beaten track*—the end result will only be the closing of another access to the canyon.

It may be recovered by a dialectical movement which brings one back to the beaten track but at a level above it. For example, after a lifetime of avoiding the beaten track and guided tours, a man may deliberately seek out the most beaten track of all, the most commonplace tour imaginable: he may visit the canyon by a Greyhound tour in the company of a party from Terre Haute—just as a man who has lived in New York all his life may visit the Statue of Liberty. (Such dialectical savorings of the familiar as the familiar are, of course, a favorite stratagem of *The New Yorker* magazine.) The thing is recovered from familiarity by means of an exercise in familiarity. Our complex friend stands behind the fellow tourists at the Bright Angel Lodge and sees the canyon through them and their predicament, their picture taking and busy disregard. In a sense, he exploits his fellow tourists; he stands on their shoulders to see the canyon.

Such a man is far more advanced in the dialectic than the sightseer who is trying to get off the beaten track—getting up at dawn and approaching the canyon through the mesquite. This stratagem is, in fact, for our complex man the weariest, most beaten track of all.

It may be recovered as a consequence of a breakdown of the symbolic machinery by which the experts present the experience to the consumer. A family visits the canyon in the usual way. But shortly after their arrival, the park is closed by an outbreak of typhus in the south. They have the canyon to themselves. What do they mean when they tell the home folks of their good luck: "We had the whole place to ourselves"? How does one see the thing better when the others are absent? Is looking like sucking: the more lookers, the less there is to see? They could hardly answer, but by saying this they testify to a state of affairs which is considerably more complex than the simple statement of the schoolbook about the Spaniard and the millions who followed him. It is a state in which there is a complex distribution of sovereignty, of zoning.

It may be recovered in a time of national disaster. The Bright Angel Lodge is converted into a rest home, a function that has nothing to do with the canyon a few yards away. A wounded man is brought in. He regains consciousness; there outside his window is the canyon.

The most extreme case of access by privilege conferred by disaster is the Huxleyan novel of the adventures of the surviving remnant after the great wars of the twentieth century. An expedition from Australia lands in Southern California and heads east. They stumble across the Bright Angel Lodge, now fallen into ruins. The trails are grown over, the guard rails fallen away, the dime telescope at Battleship Point rusted. But there is the canyon, exposed at last. Exposed by what? By the decay of those facilities which were designed to help the sightseer.

This dialectic of sightseeing cannot be taken into account by planners, for the object of the dialectic is nothing other than the subversion of the efforts of the planners.

The dialectic is not known to objective theorists, psychologists, and the like. Yet it is quite well known in the fantasy-consciousness of the popular arts. The devices by which the museum exhibit, the Grand Canyon, the ordinary thing, is recovered have long since been stumbled upon. A movie shows a man visiting the Grand Canyon. But the moviemaker knows something the planner does not know. He knows that one cannot take the sight frontally. The canyon must be approached by the stratagems we have mentioned: the Inside Track, the Familiar Revisited, the Accidental Encounter. Who is the stranger at the Bright Angel Lodge? Is he the ordinary tourist from Terre Haute that he makes himself out to be? He is not. He has another objective in mind, to revenge his wronged brother, counter-espionage, etc. By virtue of the fact that he has other fish to fry, he may take a stroll along the rim after supper and then we can see the canyon through him. The movie accomplishes its purpose by concealing it. Overtly the characters (the American family marooned by typhus) and we the onlookers experience pity for the sufferers, and the family experience anxiety for themselves; covertly and in truth they are the happiest of people and we are happy through them, for we have the canyon to ourselves. The movie cashes in on the recovery of sovereignty through disaster. Not only is the canyon now accessible to the remnant: the members of the remnant are now accessible to each other, a whole new ensemble of relations becomes possible—friendship, love, hatred, clandestine sexual adventures. In a movie when a man sits next to a woman on a bus, it is necessary either that the bus break down or that the woman lose her memory. (The question occurs to one: Do you imagine there are sightseers who see sights just as they are supposed to? a family who live in Terre Haute, who decide to take the canyon tour, who go there, see it, enjoy it immensely, and go home content? a family who are entirely innocent of all the barriers, zones, losses of sovereignty I have been talking about? Wouldn't most people be sorry if Battleship Point fell into the canyon, carrying all one's fellow passengers to their death, leaving one alone on the South Rim? I cannot answer this. Perhaps there are such people. Certainly a great many American families would swear they had no such problems, that they came, saw, and went away happy. Yet it is just these families who would be happiest if they had gotten the Inside Track and been among the surviving remnant.)

It is now apparent that as between the many measures which may be taken to overcome the opacity, the boredom, of the direct confrontation of the thing or creature in its citadel of symbolic investiture, some are less authentic than others. That is to say, some stratagems obviously serve other purposes than that of providing access to being—for example, various unconscious motivations which it is not necessary to go into here.

Let us take an example in which the recovery of being is ambiguous, where it may under the same circumstances contain both authentic and unauthentic components. An American couple, we will say, drives down into Mexico. They see the usual sights and have a fair time of it. Yet they are never without the sense of missing something. Although Taxco and Cuernavaca are interesting and picturesque as advertised, they fall short of "it." What do the couple have in mind by "it"? What do they really hope for? What sort of experience could they have in Mexico so that upon their return, they would feel that "it" had happened? We have a clue: Their hope has something to do with their own role as tourists in a foreign country and the way in which they conceive this role. It has something to do with other American tourists. Certainly they feel that they are very far from "it" when, after traveling five thousand miles, they arrive at the plaza in Guanajuato only to find themselves surrounded by a dozen other couples from the Midwest.

Already we may distinguish authentic and unauthentic elements. First, we see the problem the couple faces and we understand their efforts to surmount it. The problem is to find an "unspoiled" place. "Unspoiled" does not mean only that a place is left physically intact; it means also that it is not encrusted by renown and by the familiar (as in Taxco), that it has not been discovered by others. We understand that the couple really want to get at the place and enjoy it. Yet at the same time we wonder if there is not something wrong in their dislike of their compatriots. Does access to the place require the exclusion of others?

Let us see what happens.

The couple decide to drive from Guanajuato to Mexico City. On the way they get lost. After hours on a rocky mountain road, they find themselves in a tiny valley not even marked on the map. There they discover an Indian village. Some sort of religious festival is going on. It is apparently a corn dance in supplication of the rain god.

The couple know at once that this is "it." They are entranced. They spend several days in the village, observing the Indians and being themselves observed with friendly curiosity.

Now may we not say that the sightseers have at last come face to face with an authentic sight, a sight which is charming, quaint, picturesque, unspoiled, and that they see the sight and come away rewarded? Possibly this may occur. Yet is is more likely that what happens is a far cry indeed from an immediate encounter with being, that the experience, while masquerading as such, is in truth a rather desperate impersonation. I use the word *desperate* advisedly to signify an actual loss of hope.

The clue to the spuriousness of their enjoyment of the village and the festival is a certain restiveness in the sightseers themselves. It is given expression by their repeated exclamations that "this is too good to be true," and by their anxiety that it may not prove to be so perfect, and finally by their downright relief at leaving the valley and having the experience in the bag, so to speak—that is, safely enbalmed in memory and movie film.

What is the source of their anxiety during the visit? Does it not mean that the couple are looking at the place with a certain standard of performance in mind? Are they like Fabre, who gazed at the world about him with wonder, letting it be what it is; or are they not like the overanxious mother who sees her child as one performing, now doing badly, now doing well? The village is their child and their love for it is an anxious love because they are afraid that at any moment it might fail them.

We have another clue in their subsequent remark to an ethnologist friend. "How we wished you had been there with us! What a perfect goldmine of folkways! Every minute we would say to each other, if only you were here! You must return with us." This surely testifies to a generosity of spirit, a willingness to share their experience with others, not at all like their feelings toward their fellow Iowans on the plaza at Guanajuato!

I am afraid this is not the case at all. It is true that they longed for their ethnologist friend, but it was for an entirely different reason. They wanted him, not to share their experience, but to certify their experience as genuine.

"This is it" and "Now we are really living" do not necessarily refer to the sovereign encounter of the person with the sight that enlivens the mind and gladdens the heart. It means that now at last we are having the acceptable experience. The present experience is always measured by a prototype, the "it" of their dreams. "Now I am really living" means that now I am filling the role of sightseer and the sight is living up to the prototype

467

of sights. This quaint and picturesque village is measured by a Platonic ideal of the Quaint and the Picturesque.

Hence their anxiety during the encounter. For at any minute something could go wrong. A fellow Iowan might emerge from a 'dobe hut; the chief might show them his Sears catalogue. (If the failures are "wrong" enough, as these are, they might still be turned to account as rueful conversation pieces. "There we were expecting the chief to bring us a churinga and he shows up with a Sears catalogue!") They have snatched victory from disaster, but their experience always runs the danger of failure.

They need the ethnologist to certify their experience as genuine. This is borne out by their behavior when the three of them return for the next corn dance. During the dance, the couple do not watch the goings-on; instead they watch the ethnologist! Their highest hope is that their friend should find the dance interesting. And if he should show signs of true absorption, an interest in the goings-on so powerful that he becomes oblivious of his friends—then their cup is full. "Didn't we tell you?" they say at last. What they want from him is not ethnological explanations; all they want is his approval.

What has taken place is a radical loss of sovereignty over that which is as much theirs as it is the ethnologist's. The fault does not lie with the ethnologist. He has no wish to stake a claim to the village; in fact, he desires the opposite: he will bore his friends to death by telling them about the village and the meaning of the folkways. A degree of sovereignty has been surrendered by the couple. It is the nature of the loss, moreover, that they are not aware of the loss, beyond a certain uneasiness. (Even if they read this and admitted it, it would be very difficult for them to bridge the gap in their confrontation of the world. Their consciousness of the corn dance cannot escape their consciousness of their consciousness, so that with the onset of the first direct enjoyment, their higher consciousness pounces and certifies: "Now you are doing it! Now you are really living!" and, in certifying the experience, sets it at nought.)

Their basic placement in the world is such that they recognize a priority of title of the expert over his particular department of being. The whole horizon of being is staked out by "them," the experts. The highest satisfaction of the sightseer (not merely the tourist but any layman seer of sights) is that his sight should be certified as genuine. The worst of this impoverishment is that there is no sense of impoverishment. The surrender of title is so complete that it never even occurs to one to reassert title. A poor man may envy the rich man, but the sightseer does not envy the expert. When a caste system becomes absolute, envy disappears. Yet the caste of layman-expert is not the fault of the expert. It is due altogether to the eager surrender of sovereignty by the layman so that he may take up the role not of the person but of the consumer.

I do not refer only to the special relation of layman to theorist. I refer to the general situation in which sovereignty is surrendered to a class of privileged knowers, whether these be theorists or artists. A reader may surrender sovereignty over that which has been theorized about. The consumer is content to receive an experience just as it has been presented to him by theorists and planners. The reader may also be content to judge life by whether it has or has not been formulated by those who know and write about life. A young man goes to France. He too has a fair time of it, sees the sights, enjoys the food. On his last day, in fact as he sits in a restaurant in Le Havre waiting for his boat, something happens. A group of French students in the restaurant get into an impassioned argument over a recent play. A riot takes place. Madame la concierge joins in, swinging her mop at the rioters. Our young American is transported. This is "it." And he had almost left France without seeing "it"!

But the young man's delight is ambiguous. On the one hand, it is a pleasure for him to encounter the same Gallic temperament he had heard about from Puccini and Rolland. But on the other hand, the source of his pleasure testifies to a certain alienation. For the young man is actually barred from a direct encounter with anything French excepting only that which has been set forth, authenticated by Puccini and Rolland—those who know. If he had encountered the restaurant scene without reading Hemingway, without knowing that the performance was so typically, charmingly French, he would not have been delighted. He would only have been anxious at seeing things get out of hand. The source of his delight is the sanction of those who know.

This loss of sovereignty is not a marginal process, as might appear from my example of estranged sightseers. It is a generalized surrender of the horizon to those experts within whose competence a particular segment of the horizon is thought to lie. Kwakiutls are surrendered to Franz Boas; decaying Southern mansions are surrendered to Faulkner and Tennessee Williams. So that, although it is by no means the intention of the expert to expropriate sovereignty—in fact he would not even know what sovereignty meant in this context—the danger of theory and consumption is a seduction and deprivation of the consumer.

In the New Mexico desert, natives occasionally come across the strange-looking artifacts which have fallen from the skies and which are stenciled: *Return to U.S. Experimental Project, Alamogordo. Reward.* The finder returns the object and is rewarded. He knows nothing of the nature of the object he has found and does not care to know. The sole role of the native, the highest role he can play, is that of finder and returner of the mysterious equipment.

The same is true of the laymen's relation to *natural* objects in a modern technical society. No matter what the object or event is, whether it is a star, a swallow, a Kwakiutl, a "psychological phenomenon," the layman who confronts it does not confront it as a sovereign person, as Crusoe confronts a seashell he finds on the beach. The highest role he can conceive himself as playing is to be able to recognize the title of the object, to return it to the appropriate expert and have it certified as a genuine find. He does not even permit himself to see the thing—as Gerard Hopkins could see a rock or a cloud or a field. If anyone asks him why he doesn't look, he may reply that he didn't take that subject in college (or he hasn't read Faulkner).

This loss of sovereignty extends even to oneself. There is the neurotic who asks nothing more of his doctor than that his symptoms should prove interesting. When all else fails, the poor fellow has nothing to offer but his own neurosis. But even this is sufficient if only the doctor will show interest when he says, "Last night I had a curious sort of dream; perhaps it will be significant to one who knows about such things. It seems I was standing in a sort of alley—" (I have nothing else to offer you but my own unhappiness. Please say that it, at least, measures up, that it is a *proper* sort of unhappiness.)

## II

A young Falkland Islander walking along a beach and spying a dead dogfish and going to work on it with his jackknife has, in a fashion wholly unprovided in modern educational theory, a great advantage over the Scarsdale high-school pupil who finds the dogfish on his laboratory desk. Similarly the citizen of Huxley's *Brave New World* who stumbles across a volume of Shakespeare in some vine-grown ruins and squats on a potsherd to read it is in a fairer way of getting at a sonnet than the Harvard sophomore taking English Poetry II.

The educator whose business it is to teach students biology or poetry is unaware of a whole ensemble of relations which exist between the student and the dogfish and between the student and the Shakespeare sonnet. To put it bluntly: A student who has the desire to get at a dogfish or a Shakespeare sonnet may have the greatest difficulty in salvaging the creature itself from the educational package in which it is presented. The great difficulty is that he is not aware that there is a difficulty; surely, he thinks, in such a fine classroom, with such a fine textbook, the sonnet must come across! What's wrong with me?

The sonnet and the dogfish are obscured by two different processes. The sonnet is obscured by the symbolic package which is formulated not by the sonnet itself but by the *media* through which the sonnet is transmitted, the media which the educators believe for some reason to be transparent. The new textbook, the type, the smell of the page, the classroom, the aluminum windows and the winter sky, the personality of Miss Hawkins—these media which are supposed to transmit the sonnet may only succeed in transmitting themselves. It is only the hardiest and cleverest of students who can salvage the sonnet from this many-tissued package. It is only the rarest student who knows that the sonnet must be salvaged from the package. (The educator is well aware that something is wrong, that there is a fatal gap between the student's learning and the student's life: The student reads the poem, appears to understand it, and gives all the answers. But what does he recall if he should happen to read a Shakespeare sonnet twenty years later? Does he recall the poem or does he recall the smell of the page and the smell of Miss Hawkins?)

One might object, pointing out that Huxley's citizen reading his sonnet in the ruins and the Falkland Islander looking at his dogfish on the beach also receive them in a certain package. Yes, but the difference lies in the fundamental placement of the student in the world, a placement which makes it possible to extract the thing from the package. The pupil at Scarsdale High sees himself placed as a consumer receiving an experience-package; but the Falkland Islander exploring his dogfish is a person exercising the sovereign right of a person in his lordship and mastery of creation. He too could use an instructor and a book and a technique, but he would use them as his subordinates, just as he uses his jackknife. The biology student does not use his scalpel as an instrument, he uses it as a magic wand! Since it is a "scientific instrument," it should do "scientific things."

The dogfish is concealed in the same symbolic package as the sonnet. But the dogfish suffers an additional loss. As a consequence of this double deprivation, the Sarah Lawrence student who scores A in zoology is apt to know very little about a dogfish. She is twice removed from the dogfish, once by the symbolic complex by which the dogfish is concealed, once again by the spoliation of the dogfish by theory which renders it invisible. Through no fault of zoology instructors, it is nevertheless a fact that the zoology laboratory at Sarah Lawrence College is one of the few places in the world where it is all but impossible to see a dogfish.

The dogfish, the tree, the seashell, the American Negro, the dream, are rendered invisible by a shift of reality from concrete thing to theory which Whitehead has called the fallacy of misplaced concreteness. It is the mistaking of an idea, a principle, an abstraction, for the real. As a consequence of the shift, the "specimen" is seen as less real than the theory of the specimen. As Kierkegaard said, once a person is seen as a specimen of a race or a species, at that very moment he ceases to be an individual. Then there are no more individuals but only specimens.

To illustrate: A student enters a laboratory which, in the pragmatic view, offers the student the optimum conditions under which an educational experience may be had. In the existential view, however—that view of the student in which he is regarded not as a receptacle of experience but as a knowing being whose peculiar property it is to see himself as being in a certain situation—the modern laboratory could not have been more effectively designed to conceal the dogfish forever.

The student comes to his desk. On it, neatly arranged by his instructor, he finds his laboratory manual, a dissecting board, instruments, and a mimeographed list:

*Exercise 22: Materials*
1 dissecting board
1 scalpel
1 forceps
1 probe
1 bottle india ink and syringe
1 specimen of *Squalus acanthias*

The clue of the situation in which the student finds himself is to be found in the last item: 1 specimen of *Squalus acanthias*.

The phrase *specimen of* expresses in the most succinct way imaginable the radical character of the loss of being which has occurred under his very nose. To refer to the dogfish, the unique concrete existent before him, as a "specimen of *Squalas acanthias*" reveals by its grammar the spoliation of the dogfish by the theoretical method. This phrase, *specimen of,* example of, instance of, indicates the ontological status of the individual creature in the eyes of the theorist. The dogfish itself is seen as a rather shabby expression of an ideal reality, the species *Squalus acanthias*. The result is the radical devaluation of the individual dogfish. (The *reductio ad absurdum* of Whitehead's shift is Toynbee's employment of it in his historical method. If a gram of NaCl is referred to by the chemist as a "sample of" NaCl, one may think of it as such and not much is missed by the oversight of the act of being of this particular pinch of salt, but when the Jews and the Jewish religion are understood as—in Toynbee's favorite phrase—a "classical example of" such and such a kind of *Voelkerwanderung,* we begin to suspect that something is being left out.)

If we look into the ways in which the student can recover the dogfish (or the sonnet), we will see that they have in common the stratagem of avoiding the educator's direct presentation of the object as a lesson to be learned and restoring access to sonnet and dogfish as beings to be known, reasserting the sovereignty of knower over known.

In truth, the biography of scientists and poets is usually the story of the discovery of the indirect approach, the circumvention of the educator's presentation—the young man who was sent to the *Technikum* and on his way fell into the habit of loitering in book stores and reading poetry; or the young man dutifully attending law school who on the way became curious about the comings and goings of ants. One remembers the scene in *The Heart Is a Lonely Hunter* where the girl hides in the bushes to hear the Capehart in the big house play Beethoven. Perhaps she was the lucky one after all. Think of the unhappy souls inside, who see the record, worry about scratches, and most of all worry about whether they are *getting it*, whether they are bona fide music lovers. What is the best way to hear Beethoven: sitting in a proper silence around the Capehart or eavesdropping from an azalea bush?

However it may come about, we notice two traits of the second situation: (1) an openness of the thing before one—instead of being an exercise to be learned according to an approved mode, it is a garden of delights which beckons to one; (2) a sovereignty of the knower—instead of being a consumer of a prepared experience, I am a sovereign wayfarer, a wanderer in the neighborhood of being who stumbles into the garden.

One can think of two sorts of circumstances through which the thing may be restored to the person. (There is always, of course, the direct recovery: A student may simply be strong enough, brave enough, clever enough to take the dogfish and the sonnet by storm, to wrest control of it from the educators and the educational package.) First by ordeal: The Bomb falls; when the young man recovers consciousness in the shambles of the biology laboratory, there not ten inches from his nose lies the dogfish. Now all at once he can see it directly and without let, just as the exile or the prisoner or the sick man sees the sparrow at his window in all its inexhaustibility; just as the commuter who has had a heart attack sees his own hand for the first time. In these cases, the simulacrum of everydayness and of consumption has been destroyed by disaster; in the case of the bomb, literally destroyed. Secondly, by apprenticeship to a great man: One day a great biologist walks into the laboratory; he stops in front of our student's desk; he leans over, picks up the dogfish, and, ignoring instruments and procedure, probes with a broken fingernail into the little carcass. "Now here is a curious business," he says, ignoring also the proper jargon of the specialty. "Look here how this little duct reverses its direction and drops into the pelvis. Now if you would look into a coelacanth, you would see that it—" And all at once the student can see. The technician and the sophomore who loves his textbooks are always offended by the genuine research man because the latter is usually a little vague and always humble before the thing; he doesn't have much use for the equipment or the jargon. Whereas the technician is never vague and never humble before the thing; he holds the thing disposed of by the principle, the formula, the textbook outline; and he thinks a great deal of equipment and jargon.

But since neither of these methods of recovering the dogfish is pedagogically feasible—perhaps the great man even less so than the Bomb—I wish to propose the following educational technique which should prove equally effective for Harvard and Shreveport High School. I propose that English poetry and biology should be taught as usual, but that at irregular intervals, poetry students should find dogfishes on their desks and biology students should find Shakespeare sonnets on their dissection boards. I am serious in declaring that a Sarah Lawrence English major who began poking about in a dogfish with a bobby pin would learn more in thirty minutes than a biology major in a whole semester; and that the latter upon reading on her dissecting board

> That time of year Thou may'st in me behold
> When yellow leaves, or none, or few, do hang
> Upon those boughs which shake against the cold—
> Bare ruin'd choirs where late the sweet birds sang

might catch fire at the beauty of it.

The situation of the tourist at the Grand Canyon and the biology student are special cases of a predicament in which everyone finds himself in a modern technical society—a society, that is, in which there is a division between expert and layman, planner and consumer, in which experts and planners take special measures to teach and edify the consumer. The measures taken are measures appropriate to the consumer: The expert and the planner *know* and *plan*, but the consumer *needs* and *experiences*.

There is a double deprivation. First, the thing is lost through its packaging. The very means by which the thing is presented for consumption, the very techniques by which the thing is made available as an item of need-satisfaction, these very means operate to remove the thing from the sovereignty of the knower. A loss of title occurs. The measures which the museum curator takes to present the thing to the public are self-liquidating. The upshot of the curator's efforts are not that everyone can see the exhibit but that no one can see it. The curator protests: Why are they so indifferent? Why do they even deface the exhibit? Don't they know it is theirs? But it is not theirs. It is his, the curator's. By the most exclusive sort of zoning, the museum exhibit, the park oak tree, is part of an ensemble, a package, which is almost impenetrable to them. The archaeologist who puts his find in a museum so that everyone can see it accomplishes the reverse of his expectations. The result of his action is that no one can see it now but the archaeologist. He would have done better to keep it in his pocket and show it now and then to strangers.

The tourist who carves his initials in a public place, which is theoretically "his" in the first place, has good reasons for doing so, reasons which the exhibitor and planner know nothing about. He does so because in his role of consumer of an experience (a "recreational experience" to satisfy a "recreational need") he knows that he is disinherited. He is deprived of his title over being. He knows very well that he is in a very special sort of zone in which his only rights are the rights of a consumer. He moves like a ghost through schoolroom, city streets, trains, parks, movies. He carves his initials as a last desperate measure to escape his ghostly role of consumer. He is saying in effect: I am not a ghost after all; I am a sovereign person. And he establishes title the only way remaining to him, by staking his claim over one square inch of wood or stone.

Does this mean that we should get rid of museums? No, but it means that the sightseer should be prepared to enter into a struggle to recover a sight from a museum.

The second loss is the spoliation of the thing, the tree, the rock, the swallow, by the layman's misunderstanding of scientific theory. He believes that the thing is *disposed of* by theory, that it stands in the Platonic relation of being a *specimen of* such and such an underlying principle. In the transmission of scientific theory from theorist to layman, the expectation of the theorist is reversed. Instead of the marvels of the universe being made available to the public, the universe is disposed of by theory. The loss of sovereignty takes this form: As a result of the science of botany, trees are not made available to every man. On the contrary. The tree loses its proper density and mystery as a concrete existent and, as merely another *specimen of* a species, becomes itself nugatory.

Does this mean that there is no use taking biology at Harvard and Shreveport High? No, but it means that the student should know what a fight he has on his hands to rescue the specimen from the educational package. The educator is only partly to blame. For there is nothing the educator can do to provide for this need of the student. Everything the educator does only succeeds in becoming, for the student, part of the educational package. The highest role of the educator is the maieutic role of Socrates: to help the student come to himself not as a consumer of experience but as a sovereign individual.

The thing is twice lost to the consumer. First, sovereignty is lost: It is theirs, not his. Second, it is radically devalued by theory. This is a loss which has been brought about by science but through no fault of the scientist and through no fault of scientific theory. The loss has come about as a consequence of the seduction of the layman by science. The layman will be seduced as long as he regards beings as consumer items to be experienced rather than prizes to be won, and as long as he waives his sovereign rights as a person and accepts his role of consumer as the highest estate to which the layman can aspire.

As Mounier said, the person is not something one can study and provide for; he is something one struggles for. But unless he also struggles for himself, unless he knows that there is a struggle, he is going to be just what the planners think he is.

. . . . . . . . . . .

### QUESTIONS FOR A SECOND READING

1. Percy's essay proceeds by adding example to example, one after another. If all the examples were meant to illustrate the same thing, the same general point or idea, then one would most likely have been enough. The rest would have been redundant. It makes sense, then, to assume that each example gives a different view of what Percy is saying, that each modifies the others, or qualifies them, or adds a piece that was otherwise lacking. It's as though Percy needed one more to get it right or to figure out what was missing along the way. As you read back through the essay, pay particular attention to the *differences* between the examples (between the various tourists going to the Grand Canyon, or between the tourists at the Grand Canyon and the tourists in Mexico). Also note the logic or system that leads from one to the next. What progress of thought is represented by the movement from one example to another, or from tourists to students?

2. The essay is filled with talk about "loss"—the loss of sovereignty, the loss of the creature—but it is resolutely ambiguous about what it is that we have lost. As you work your way back through, note the passages that describe what we are missing and why we should care. Are we to believe, for example, that Cárdenas actually had it (whatever "it" is)—that he had no preconceived notions when he saw the Grand Canyon? Mightn't he have said, "I claim this for my queen" or "There I see the glory of God" or "This wilderness is not fit for man." To whom, or in the name of what, is this loss that Percy chronicles such a matter of concern? If this is not just Percy's peculiar prejudice, if we are asked to share his concerns, whose interests or what interests are represented here?

3. The essay is made up of stories or anecdotes, all of them fanciful. Percy did not, in other words, turn to first-person accounts of visitors to the Grand Canyon or to statements by actual students or teachers. Why not, do you suppose? What does this choice say about his "method"—about what it can and can't do? As you reread the essay, look for sections you could use to talk about the power and limits of Percy's method.

## ASSIGNMENTS FOR WRITING

1. Percy tells several stories—some of them quite good stories—but it is often hard to know just what he is getting at, just what point it is he is trying to make. If he's making an argument, it's not the sort of argument that is easy to summarize. And if the stories (or anecdotes) are meant to serve as examples, they are not the sort of examples that lead directly to a single, general conclusion or that serve to clarify a point or support an obvious thesis. In fact, at the very moment when you expect Percy to come forward and pull things together, he offers yet another story, as though another example, rather than any general statement, would get you closer to what he is saying.

   There are, at the same time, terms and phrases to suggest that this is an essay with a point to make. Percy talks, for example, about "the loss of sovereignty," "symbolic packages," "consumers of experience," and "dialectic," and it seems that these terms and phrases are meant to name or comment on key scenes, situations, or characters in the examples.

   For this assignment, tell a story of your own, one that is suggested by the stories Percy tells—perhaps a story about a time you went looking for something or at something, or about a time when you did or did not find a dogfish in your Shakespeare class. You should imagine that you are carrying out a project that Walker Percy has begun, a project that has you looking back at your own experience through the lens of "The Loss of the Creature," noticing what Percy would notice and following the paths that he would find interesting. Try to bring the terms that Percy uses—like "sovereign," "consumer," "expert," and "dialectic"—to bear on the story you have to tell. Feel free to imitate Percy's style and method in your essay.

2. Percy charts several routes to the Grand Canyon: you can take the packaged tour, you can get off the beaten track, you can wait for a disaster, you can follow the "dialectical movement which brings one back to the beaten track but at a level above it." This last path (or stratagem), he says, is for the complex traveler. "Our complex friend stands behind his fellow tourists at the Bright Angel Lodge and sees the canyon through them and their predicament, their picture taking and busy disregard. In a sense, he exploits his fellow tourists; he stands on their shoulders to see the canyon."

   The complex traveler sees the Grand Canyon through the example of the common tourists with "their predicament, their picture taking and busy disregard." He "stands on their shoulders" to see the canyon. The distinction between complex and common approaches is an important one in the essay. It is interesting to imagine how the distinction could be put to work to define ways of reading.

   Suppose that you read "The Loss of the Creature" as a common reader. What would you see? What would you identify as key sections of the text? What would you miss? What would you say about what you see?

If you think of yourself, now, as a complex reader, modeled after any of Percy's more complex tourists or students, what would you see? What would you identify as key sections of the text? What would you miss? What would you say about what you see?

For this assignment, write an essay with three sections. You may number them, if you choose. The first section should represent the work of a common reader with "The Loss of the Creature," and the second should represent the work of a complex reader. The third section should look back and comment on the previous two. In particular, you might address these questions: Why might a person prefer one reading over the other? What is to be gained or lost with both?

## MAKING CONNECTIONS

1. In "The Loss of the Creature," Percy writes about tourists and the difficulty they have seeing that which lies before them. In "Deep Play: Notes on the Balinese Cockfight" (p. 272), Clifford Geertz tells the story of his travels in Bali. Anthropologists, properly speaking, are not tourists. There is a scholarly purpose to their travel and, presumably, they have learned or developed the strategies necessary to get beyond the preformed "symbolic complex" that would keep them from seeing the place or the people they have traveled to study. They are experts, in other words, not common sightseers.

   In his travels to Bali, Geertz seems to get just what he wants. He gets both the authentic experience and a complex understanding of that experience. If you read "Deep Play" from the perspective of Percy's essay, however, it is interesting to ask whether Percy would say that this was the case (whether Percy might say that Geertz has gone as far as one can go after Cárdenas), and it is interesting to ask how Percy would characterize the "strategies" that define Geertz's approach to his subject.

   Write an essay in which you place Geertz in the context of Percy's tourists (not all of them, but two or three whose stories seem most interesting when placed alongside Geertz's). The purpose of your essay is offer a Percian reading of Geertz's essay—to study his text, that is, in light of the terms and methods Percy has established in "The Loss of the Creature."

2. But the difference lies in the fundamental placement of the student in the world (Walker Percy, p. 471).

   In short, to the list of made or constructed objects we must add ourselves, for we not less than the poems and assignments we see are the products of social and cultural patterns of thought (Stanley Fish, p. 187).

   Both Percy and Stanley Fish (in "How to Recognize a Poem When You See One," p. 179) write about students and how they are "placed" in the world by teachers and by schools' characteristic ways of representing knowledge, the novice, and the expert. And both tell stories to make their points, stories of characteristic students in characteristic situations. Write an essay in which you tell a story of your own, one meant to serve as a corrective or a supplement to the stories Percy and Fish tell. You will want both to tell your story and to use it as a way of returning to and commenting on Percy and Fish, and the arguments they make. Your authority can rest on the fact that you are a student and as a consequence have ways of understanding that position that they do not.

# ADRIENNE
RICH

*A* DRIENNE RICH *(b. 1929) once said that whatever she knows, she wants to*
*"know it in [her] own nerves." As a writer, Rich found it necessary to ac-*
*knowledge her anger at both the oppression of women and her immediate experience*
*of that oppression. She needed to find the "anger that is creative." "Until I could*
*tap into the very rich ocean," she said, "I think that my work was constrained in*
*certain ways. There's this fear of anger in women, which is partly because we've*
*been told it was always destructive, it was always unseemly, and unwomanly, and*
*monstrous."*

*Rich's poetry combines passion and anger with a "yen for order." She wrote*
*her first book of poems,* A Change of World, *while an undergraduate at Radcliffe*
*College. The book won the 1951 Yale Younger Poets Award and a generous intro-*
*duction from W. H. Auden who was one of the judges. Her subsequent works which*
*include* The Diamond Cutters *(1955),* Snapshots of a Daughter-in-Law *(1963,*
*1967),* Necessities of Life *(1966),* Leaflets *(1969),* The Will to Change *(1970),*
*and* Diving into the Wreck *(1973), show an increasing concern for the political*
*and psychological consequences of life in patriarchal society. When offered the Na-*
*tional Book Award for* Diving into the Wreck, *Rich refused the award as an*

*individual but accepted it, in a statement written with two other nominees—Audre Lorde and Alice Walker (whose essay "In Search of Our Mothers' Gardens" appears on p. 584)—in the name of all women:*

> *We . . . together accept this award in the name of all the women whose voices have gone and still go unheard in a patriarchal world, and in the name of those who, like us, have been tolerated as token women in this culture, often at great cost and in great pain. . . . We dedicate this occasion to the struggle for self-determination of all women, of every color, identification or derived class . . . the women who will understand what we are doing here and those who will not understand yet; the silent women whose voices have been denied us, the articulate women who have given us the strength to do our work.*

*After graduating from Radcliffe in 1951, Rich married and raised three sons. One of her prose collections,* Of Woman Born: Motherhood as Experience and Institution *(1976), treats her experience as both mother and daughter with eloquence, even as it calls for the destruction of motherhood as an institution. In 1970 Rich left her marriage, and six years later she published a book of poems which explore a lesbian relationship. But the term* lesbian *for Rich, referred to "nothing so simple and dismissible as the fact that two women might go to bed together." As she says in "It Is the Lesbian in Us," a speech reprinted in* On Lies, Secrets, and Silence: Selected Prose *(1979), it refers also to "a sense of desiring oneself, choosing oneself; it was also a primary intensity which in the world at large was trivialized, caricatured, or invested with evil. . . . It is the lesbian in us who drives us to feel imaginatively, render in language, grasp, the full connection between woman and woman."*

*Rich has published fourteen books of poetry and three collections of prose. In her most recent collection,* Blood, Bread and Poetry: Selected Prose *(1986), she offers a series of commencement speeches, reviews, lectures, and articles on feminism, gay and lesbian rights, racism, anti-Semitism, and the necessity for the artist, university, and state to find a commitment to social justice. Rich has taught at Columbia and Brandeis universities, Swarthmore College, and the City College of New York.*

# When We Dead Awaken:
# Writing as Re-Vision°

*The Modern Language Association is both marketplace and funeral parlor for the professional study of Western literature in North America. Like all gatherings of the professions, it has been and remains a "procession of the sons of educated men" (Virginia Woolf): a congeries of old-boys' networks, academicians rehearsing their numb canons in sessions dedicated to the literature of white males, junior scholars under the lash of "publish or perish" delivering papers in the bizarrely lit drawing-rooms of immense hotels: a ritual competition veering between cynicism and desperation.*

*However, in the interstices of these gentlemanly rites (or, in Mary Daly's words, on the boundaries of this patriarchal space), [1] some feminist scholars, teachers, and graduate students, joined by feminist writers, editors, and publishers, have for a decade been creating more subversive occasions, challenging the sacredness of the gentlemanly canon, sharing the rediscovery of buried works by women, asking women's questions, bringing literary history and criticism back to life in both senses. The Commission of the Status of Women in the Profession was formed in 1969, and held its first public event in 1970. In 1971 the Commission asked Ellen Peck Killoh, Tillie Olsen, Elaine Reuben, and myself, with Elaine Hedges as moderator, to talk on "The Woman Writer in the Twentieth Century." The essay that follows was written for that forum, and later published, along with the other papers from the forum and workshops, in an issue of* College English *edited by Elaine Hedges ("Women Writing and Teaching," vol. 34, no. 1, October 1972). With a few revisions, mainly updating, it was reprinted in* American Poets *in 1976, edited by William Heyen (New York: Bobbs-Merrill, 1976). That later text is the one published here.*

The challenge flung by feminists at the accepted literary canon, at the methods of teaching it, and at the biased and astigmatic view of male "literary scholarship," has not diminished in the decade since the first Women's Forum; it has become broadened and intensified more recently by the challenges of black and lesbian feminists pointing out that feminist literary criticism itself has overlooked or held back from examining the work of black women and lesbians. The dynamic between a political vision and the

---

As Rich explains, this essay—written in 1971—was first published in 1972 and then included in her volume *On Lies, Secrets, and Silence* (1978). At that time she added the introductory note reprinted here, as well as some notes, identified as "*A.R., 1978.*" [Editor's note in the Norton edition.]

demand for a fresh vision of literature is clear: without a gro'
movement, the first inroads of feminist scholarship could ·
made; without the sharpening of a black feminist consciousᵢ.
women's writing would have been left in limbo between misogynist ᴅ.
male critics and white feminists still struggling to unearth a white women's
tradition; without an articulate lesbian/feminist movement, lesbian writing
would still be lying in that closet where many of us used to sit reading
forbidden books "in a bad light."

Much, much more is yet to be done; and university curricula have of
course changed very little as a result of all this. What *is* changing is the
availability of knowledge, of vital texts, the visible effects on women's lives
of seeing, hearing our wordless or negated experience affirmed and pursued further in language.

Ibsen's *When We Dead Awaken* is a play about the use that the male artist
and thinker—in the process of creating culture as we know it—has made
of women, in his life and in his work; and about a woman's slow struggling
awakening to the use to which her life has been put. Bernard Shaw wrote
in 1900 of this play:

> [Ibsen] shows us that no degradation ever devized or per-
> mitted is as disastrous as this degradation; that through it
> women can die into luxuries for men and yet can kill them;
> that men and women are becoming conscious of this; and that
> what remains to be seen as perhaps the most interesting of
> all imminent social developments is what will happen "when
> we dead awaken." [2]

It's exhilarating to be alive in a time of awakening consciousness; it can
also be confusing, disorienting, and painful. This awakening of dead or
sleeping consciousness has already affected the lives of millions of women,
even those who don't know it yet. It is also affecting the lives of men, even
those who deny its claims upon them. The argument will go on whether
an oppressive economic class system is responsible for the oppressive nature of male/female relations, or whether, in fact, partriarchy—the domination of males—is the original model of oppression on which all others
are based. But in the last few years the women's movement has drawn
inescapable and illuminating connections between our sexual lives and our
political institutions. The sleepwalkers are coming awake, and for the first
time this awakening has a collective reality; it is no longer such a lonely
thing to open one's eyes.

Re-vision—the act of looking back, of seeing with fresh eyes, of entering
an old text from a new critical direction—is for women more than a chapter

in cultural history: it is an act of survival. Until we can understand the assumptions in which we are drenched we cannot know ourselves. And this drive to self-knowledge, for women, is more than a search for identity: it is part of our refusal of the self-destructiveness of male-dominated society. A radical critique of literature, feminist in its impulse, would take the work first of all as a clue to how we live, how we have been living, how we have been led to imagine ourselves, how our language has trapped as well as liberated us, how the very act of naming has been till now a male prerogative, and how we can begin to see and name—and therefore live—afresh. A change in the concept of sexual identity is essential if we are not going to see the old political order reassert itself in every new revolution. We need to know the writing of the past, and know it differently than we have ever known it; not to pass on a tradition but to break its hold over us.

For writers, and at this moment for women writers in particular, there is the challenge and promise of a whole new psychic geography to be explored. But there is also a difficult and dangerous walking on the ice, as we try to find language and images for the consciousness we are just coming into, and with little in the past to support us. I want to talk about some aspect of this difficulty and this danger.

Jane Harrison, the great classical anthropologist, wrote in 1914 in a letter to her friend Gilbert Murray:

> By and by, about "Women," it has bothered me often—why do women never want to write poetry about Man as a sex—why is Woman a dream and a terror to man and not the other way around? . . . Is it mere convention and propriety, or something deeper? [3]

I think Jane Harrison's question cuts deep into the myth-making tradition, the romantic tradition; deep into what women and men have been to each other; and deep into the psyche of the woman writer. Thinking about that question, I began thinking of the work of two twentieth-century women poets, Sylvia Plath and Diane Wakoski. It strikes me that in the work of both Man appears as, if not a dream, a fascination and a terror; and that the source of the fascination and the terror is, simply, Man's power—to dominate, tyrannize, choose, or reject the woman. The charisma of Man seems to come purely from his power over her and his control of the world by force, not from anything fertile or life-giving in him. And, in the work of both these poets, it is finally the woman's sense of *herself*—embattled, possessed—that gives the poetry its dynamic charge, its rhythms of struggle, need, will, and female energy. Until recently this female anger and this furious awareness of the Man's power over her were not available materials to the female poet, who tended to write of Love as the source of her suffering, and to view that victimization by Love as an almost inevitable fate. Or, like Marianne Moore and Elizabeth Bishop, she kept sexuality at a measured and chiseled distance in her poems.

One answer to Jane Harrison's question has to be that historically men and women have played very different parts in each others' lives. Where woman has been a luxury for man, and has served as the painter's model and the poet's muse, but also as comforter, nurse, cook, bearer of his seed, secretarial assistant, and copyist of manuscripts, man has played a quite different role for the female artist. Henry James repeats an incident which the writer Prosper Mérimée described, of how, while he was living with George Sand,

> he once opened his eyes, in the raw winter dawn, to see his companion, in a dressing-gown, on her knees before the domestic hearth, a candle-stick beside her and a red *madras* round her head, making bravely, with her own hands the fire that was to enable her to sit down betimes to urgent pen and paper. The story represents him as having felt that the spectacle chilled his ardor and tried his taste; her appearance was unfortunate, her occupation an inconsequence, and her industry a reproof—the result of all which was a lively irritation and an early rupture. [4]

The specter of this kind of male judgment, along with the misnaming and thwarting of her needs by a culture controlled by males, has created problems for the woman writer: problems of contact with herself, problems of language and style, problems of energy and survival.

In rereading Virginia Woolf's *A Room of One's Own* (1929) for the first time in some years, I was astonished at the sense of effort, of pains taken, of dogged tentativeness, in the tone of that essay. And I recognized that tone. I had heard it often enough, in myself and in other women. It is the tone of a woman almost in touch with her anger, who is determined not to appear angry, who is *willing* herself to be calm, detached, and even charming in a roomful of men where things have been said which are attacks on her very integrity. Virginia Woolf is addressing an audience of women, but she is acutely conscious—as she always was—of being overheard by men: by Morgan and Lytton and Maynard Keynes and for that matter by her father, Leslie Stephen. [5] She drew the language out into an exacerbated thread in her determination to have her own sensibility yet protect it from those masculine presences. Only at rare moments in that essay do you hear the passion in her voice; she was trying to sound as cool as Jane Austen, as Olympian as Shakespeare, because that is the way the men of the culture thought a writer should sound.

No male writer has written primarily or even largely for women, or with the sense of women's criticism as a consideration when he chooses his materials, his theme, his language. But to a lesser or greater extent, every woman writer has written for men even when, like Virginia Woolf, she was supposed to be addressing women. If we have come to the point when this balance might begin to change, when women can stop being haunted, not only by "convention and propriety" but by internalized fears of being and saying themselves, then it is an extraordinary moment for the woman writer—and reader.

I have hesitated to do what I am going to do now, which is to use myself as an illustration. For one thing, it's a lot easier and less dangerous to talk about other women writers. But there is something else. Like Virginia Woolf, I am aware of the women who are not with us here because they are washing the dishes and looking after the children. Nearly fifty years after she spoke, that fact remains largely unchanged. And I am thinking also of women whom she left out of the picture altogether—women who are washing other people's dishes and caring for other people's children, not to mention women who went on the streets last night in order to feed their children. We seem to be special women here, we have liked to think of ourselves as special, and we have known that men would tolerate, even romanticize us as special, as long as our words and actions didn't threaten their privilege of tolerating or rejecting us and our work according to *their* ideas of what a special woman ought to be. An important insight of the radical women's movement has been how divisive and how ultimately destructive is this myth of the special woman, who is also the token woman. Every one of us here in this room has had great luck—we are teachers, writers, academicians; our own gifts could not have been enough, for we all know women whose gifts are buried or aborted. Our struggles can have meaning and our privileges—however precarious under patriarchy—can be justified only if they can help to change the lives of women whose gifts—and whose very being—continue to be thwarted and silenced.

My own luck was being born white and middle-class into a house full of books, with a father who encouraged me to read and write. So for about twenty years I wrote for a particular man, who criticized and praised me and made me feel I was indeed "special." The obverse side of this, of course, was that I tried for a long time to please him, or rather, not to displease him. And then of course there were other men—writers, teachers—the Man, who was not a terror or a dream but a literary master and a master in other ways less easy to acknowledge. And there were all those poems about women, written by men: it seemed to be a given that men wrote poems and women frequently inhabited them. These women were almost always beautiful, but threatened with the loss of beauty, the loss of youth—the fate worse than death. Or, they were beautiful and died young, like Lucy and Lenore. Or, the woman was like Maud Gonne, cruel and disastrously mistaken, and the poem reproached her because she had refused to become a luxury for the poet.

A lot is being said today about the influence that the myths and images of women have on all of us who are products of culture. I think it has been a peculiar confusion to the girl or woman who tries to write because she is peculiarly susceptible to language. She goes to poetry or fiction looking for *her* way of being in the world, since she too has been putting words and images together; she is looking eagerly for guides, maps, possibilities; and over and over in the "words' masculine persuasive force" of literature she comes up against something that negates everything she is about: she meets the image of Woman in books written by men. She finds a terror and a dream, she finds a beautiful pale face, she finds La Belle Dame Sans Merci, she finds Juliet or Tess or Salomé, but precisely what she does not find is that absorbed, drudging, puzzled, sometimes inspired creature, herself, who sits at a desk trying to put words together.

So what does she do? What did I do? I read the older women poets with their peculiar keenness and ambivalence: Sappho, Christina Rossetti, Emily Dickinson, Elinor Wylie, Edna Millay, H. D. I discovered that the woman poet most admired at the time (by men) was Marianne Moore, who was maidenly, elegant, intellectual, discreet. But even in reading these women I was looking in them for the same things I had found in the poetry of men, because I wanted women poets to be the equals of men, and to be equal was still confused with sounding the same.

I know that my style was formed first by male poets: by the men I was reading as an undergraduate—Frost, Dylan Thomas, Donne, Auden, MacNeice, Stevens, Yeats. What I chiefly learned from them was craft. [6] But poems are like dreams: in them you put what you don't know you know. Looking back at poems I wrote before I was twenty-one, I'm startled because beneath the conscious craft are glimpses of the split I even then experienced between the girl who wrote poems, who defined herself in writing poems, and the girl who was to define herself by her relationships with men. "Aunt Jennifer's Tigers" (1951), written while I was a student, looks with deliberate detachment at this split.

> Aunt Jennifer's tigers stride across a screen,
> Bright topaz denizens of a world of green.
> They do not fear the men beneath the tree;
> They pace in sleek chivalric certainty.
>
> Aunt Jennifer's fingers fluttering through her wool
> Find even the ivory needle hard to pull.

The massive weight of Uncle's wedding band
Sits heavily upon Aunt Jennifer's hand.

When Aunt is dead, her terrified hands will lie
Still ringed with ordeals she was mastered by.
The tigers in the panel that she made
Will go on striding, proud and unafraid.

In writing this poem, composed and apparently cool as it is, I thought I
was creating a portrait of an imaginary woman. But this woman suffers
from the opposition of her imagination, worked out in tapestry, and her
lifestyle, "ringed with ordeals she was mastered by." It was important to
me that Aunt Jennifer was a person as distinct from myself as possible—
distanced by the formalism of the poem, by its objective, observant tone—
even by putting the woman in a different generation.

In those years formalism was part of the strategy—like asbestos gloves,
it allowed me to handle materials I couldn't pick up barehanded. A later
strategy was to use the persona of a man, as I did in "The Loser" (1958):

*A man thinks of the woman he once loved:*
*first, after her wedding, and then nearly a*
*decade later.*

I
I kissed you, bride and lost, and went
home from that bourgeois sacrament,
your cheek still tasting cold upon
my lips that gave you benison
with all the swagger that they knew—
as losers somehow learn to do.

Your wedding made my eyes ache; soon
the world would be worse off for one
more golden apple dropped to ground
without the least protesting sound,
and you would windfall lie, and we
forget your shimmer on the tree.

Beauty is always wasted: if
not Mignon's song sung to the deaf,
at all events to the unmoved.
A face like yours cannot be loved
long or seriously enough.
Almost, we seem to hold it off.

II
Well, you are tougher than I thought.
Now when the wash with ice hangs taut
this morning of St. Valentine,
I see you strip the squeaking line,

your body weighed against the load,
and all my groans can do no good.

Because you are still beautiful,
though squared and stiffened by the pull
of what nine windy years have done.
You have three daughters, lost a son.
I see all your intelligence
flung into that unwearied stance.

My envy is of no avail.
I turn my head and wish him well
who chafed your beauty into use
and lives forever in a house
lit by the friction of your mind.
You stagger in against the wind.

I finished college, published my first book by a fluke, as it seemed to me, and broke off a love affair. I took a job, lived alone, went on writing, fell in love. I was young, full of energy, and the book seemed to mean that others agreed I was a poet. Because I was also determined to prove that as a woman poet I could also have what was then defined as a "full" woman's life, I plunged in my early twenties into marriage and had three children before I was thirty. There was nothing overt in the environment to warn me: these were the fifties, and in reaction to the earlier wave of feminism, middle-class women were making careers of domestic perfection, working to send their husbands through professional schools, then retiring to raise large families. People were moving out to the suburbs, technology was going to be the answer to everything, even sex; the family was in its glory. Life was extremely private; women were isolated from each other by the loyalties of marriage. I have a sense that women didn't talk to each other much in the fifties—not about their secret emptinesses, their frustrations. I went on trying to write; my second book and first child appeared in the same month. But by the time that book came out I was already dissatisfied with those poems, which seemed to me mere exercises for poems I hadn't written. The book was praised, however, for its "gracefulness"; I had a marriage and a child. If there were doubts, if there were periods of null depression or active despairing, these could only mean that I was ungrateful, insatiable, perhaps a monster.

About the time my third child was born, I felt that I had either to consider myself a failed woman and a failed poet, or to try to find some synthesis by which to understand what was happening to me. What frightened me most was the sense of drift, of being pulled along a current which called itself my destiny, but in which I seemed to be losing touch with whoever I had been, with the girl who had experienced her own will and energy almost ecstatically at times, walking around a city or riding a train at night or typing in a student room. In a poem about my grandmother I wrote (of myself): "A young girl, thought sleeping, is certified dead" ("Halfway"). I was writing very little, partly from fatigue, that female fatigue of suppressed anger and loss of contact with my own being; partly from the discontinuity of female life with its attention to small chores, errands, work that others constantly undo, small children's constant needs. What I did write was unconvincing to me; my anger and frustration were hard to acknowledge in or out of poems because in fact I cared a great deal about my husband and my children. Trying to look back and understand that time I have tried to analyze the real nature of the conflict. Most, if not all, human lives are full of fantasy—passive day-dreaming which need not be acted on. But to write poetry or fiction, or even to think well, is not to fantasize, or to put fantasies on paper. For a poem to coalesce, for a character or an action to take shape, there has to be an imaginative transformation of reality which is no way passive. And a certain freedom of the mind is needed—freedom to press on, to enter the currents of your thought like a glider pilot, knowing that your motion can be sustained, that the buoyancy of your attention will not be suddenly snatched away. Moreover, if the imagination is to transcend and transform experience it has to question, to challenge, to conceive of alternatives, perhaps to the very life you are living at that moment. You have to be free to play around with the notion that day might be night, love might be hate; nothing can be too sacred for the imagination to turn into its opposite or to call experimentally by another name. For writing is renaming. Now, to be maternally with small children all day in the old way, to be with a man in the old way of marriage, requires a holding-back, a putting-aside of that imaginative activity, and demands instead a kind of conservatism. I want to make it clear that I am *not* saying that in order to write well, or think well, it is necessary to become unavailable to others, or to become a devouring ego. This has been the myth of the masculine artist and thinker; and I do not accept it. But to be a female human being trying to fulfill traditional female functions in a traditional way *is* in direct conflict with the subversive function of the imagination. The word traditional is important here. There must be ways, and we will be finding out more and more about them, in which the energy of creation and the energy of relation can be united. But in those years I always felt the conflict as a failure of love in myself. I had thought I was choosing a full life; the life available to most men, in which sexuality, work, and parenthood could coexist. But I felt, at twenty-nine, guilt toward the people closest to me, and guilty toward my own being.

I wanted, then, more than anything, the one thing of which there was never enough: time to think, time to write. The fifties and early sixties were years of rapid revelations: the sit-ins and marches in the South, the Bay of Pigs, the early antiwar movement, raised large questions—questions for which the masculine world of the academy around me seemed to have expert and fluent answers. But I needed to think for myself—about pacifism and dissent and violence, about poetry and society, and about my own relationship to all these things. For about ten years I was reading in fierce snatches, scribbling in notebooks, writing poetry in fragments; I was looking desperately for clues, because if there were no clues then I thought I might be insane. I wrote in a notebook about this time:

> Paralyzed by the sense that there exists a mesh of relation-
> ships—e.g., between my anger at the children, my sensual
> life, pacifism, sex (I mean sex in its broadest significance, not
> merely sexual desire)—an interconnectedness which, if I
> could see it, make it valid, would give me back myself, make
> it possible to function lucidly and passionately. Yet I grope in
> and out among these dark webs.

I think I began at this point to feel that politics was not something "out there" but something "in here" and of the essence of my condition.

In the late fifties I was able to write, for the first time, directly about experiencing myself as a woman. The poem was jotted in fragments during children's naps, brief hours in a library, or at 3:00 A.M. after rising with a wakeful child. I despaired of doing any continuous work at this time. Yet I began to feel that my fragments and scraps had a common consciousness and a common theme, one which I would have been very unwilling to put on paper at an earlier time because I had been taught that poetry should be "universal," which meant, of course, nonfemale. Until then I had tried very much *not* to identify myself as a female poet. Over two years I wrote a ten-part poem called "Snapshots of a Daughter-in-Law" (1958–1960), in a longer looser mode than I'd ever trusted myself with before. It was an extraordinary relief to write that poem. It strikes me now as too literary, too dependent on allusion; I hadn't found the courage yet to do without authorities, or even to use the pronoun "I"—the woman in the poem is always "she." One section of it, No. 2, concerns a woman who thinks she is going mad; she is haunted by voices telling her to resist and rebel, voices which she can hear but not obey.

> 2.
> Banging the coffee-pot into the sink
> she hears the angels chiding, and looks out
> past the raked gardens to the sloppy sky.
> Only a week since They said: *Have no patience.*
>
> The next time it was: *Be insatiable.*
> Then: *Save yourself; others you cannot save.*
> Sometimes she'd let the tapstream scald her arm,
> a match burn to her thumbnail,
>
> or held her hand above the kettle's snout
> right in the woolly steam. They are probably angels,

since nothing hurts her anymore, except
each morning's grit blowing into her eyes.

The poem "Orion," written five years later, is a poem of reconnection
with a part of myself I had felt I was losing—the active principle, the energetic imagination, the "half-brother" whom I projected, as I had for many
years, into the constellation Orion. It's no accident that the words "cold
and egotistical" appear in this poem, and are applied to myself.

Far back when I went zig-zagging
through tamarack pastures
you were my genius, you
my cast-iron Viking, my helmed
lion-heart king in prison.
Years later now you're young

my fierce half-brother, staring
down from that simplified west
your breast open, your belt dragged down
by an oldfashioned thing, a sword
the last bravado you won't give over
though it weighs you down as you stride

and the stars in it are dim
and maybe have stopped burning.
But you burn, and I know it;
as I throw back my head to take you in
an old transfusion happens again:
divine astronomy is nothing to it.

Indoors I bruise and blunder,
break faith, leave ill enough
alone, a dead child born in the dark.
Night cracks up over the chimney.
pieces of time, frozen geodes
coming showering down in the grate.

A man reaches behind my eyes
and finds them empty
a woman's head turns away
from my head in the mirror
children are dying my death
and eating crumbs of my life.

Pity is not your forte.
Calmly you ache up there
pinned aloft in your crow's nest,
my speechless pirate!
You take it all for granted
and when I look you back

it's with a starlike eye
shooting its cold and egotistical spear
where it can do least damage.
Breathe deep! No hurt, no pardon
out here in the cold with you
you with your back to the wall.

The choice still seemed to be between "love"—womanly, maternal love, altruistic love—a love defined and ruled by the weight of an entire culture; and egotism—a force directed by men into creation, achievement, ambition, often at the expense of others, but justifiably so. For weren't they men, and wasn't that their destiny as womanly, selfless love was ours? We know now that the alternatives are false ones—that the word "love" is itself in need of re-vision.

There is a companion poem to "Orion," written three years later, in which at last the woman in the poem and the woman writing the poem become the same person. It is called "Planetarium," and it was written after a visit to a real planetarium, where I read an account of the work of Caroline Herschel, the astronomer, who worked with her brother William, but whose name remained obscure, as his did not.

*Thinking of Caroline Herschel, 1750–1848,*
*astronomer, sister of William; and others*

A woman in the shape of a monster
a monster in the shape of a woman
the skies are full of them

a woman       "in the snow
among the Clocks and instruments
or measuring the ground with poles"

in her 98 years to discover
8 comets

she whom the moon ruled
like us
levitating into the night sky
riding the polished lenses

Galaxies of women, there
doing penance for impetuousness
ribs chilled
in those spaces       of the mind

An eye,
      "virile, precise and absolutely certain"
      from the mad webs of Uranisborg
                  encountering the NOVA

493

every impulse of light exploding
from the core
as life flies out of us

    Tycho whispering at last
    "Let me not seem to have lived in vain"

What we see, we see
and seeing is changing

the light that shrivels a mountain
and leaves a man alive

Heartbeat of the pulsar
heart sweating through my body

The radio impulse
pouring in from Taurus

    I am bombarded yet     I stand

I have been standing all my life in the
direct path of a battery of signals
the most accurately transmitted most
untranslateable language in the universe
I am a galactic cloud so deep    so invo-
luted that a light wave could take 15
years to travel through me    And has
taken    I am an instrument in the shape
of a woman trying to translate pulsations
into images    for the relief of the body
and the reconstruction of the mind.

In closing I want to tell you about a dream I had last summer. I dreamed I was asked to read my poetry at a mass women's meeting, but when I began to read, what came out were the lyrics of a blues song. I share this dream with you because it seemed to me to say something about the problems and the future of the woman writer, and probably of women in general. The awakening of consciousness is not like the crossing of a frontier—one step and you are in another country. Much of woman's poetry has been of the nature of the blues song: a cry of pain, of victimization, or a lyric of seduction. [7] And today, much poetry by women—and prose for that matter—is charged with anger. I think we need to go through that anger, and we will betray our own reality if we try, as Virginia Woolf was trying, for an objectivity, a detachment, that would make us sound more like Jane Austen or Shakespeare. We know more than Jane Austen or Shakespeare knew: more than Jane Austen because our lives are more complex, more than Shakespeare because we know more about the lives of women—Jane Austen and Virginia Woolf included.

Both the victimization and the anger experienced by women are real, and have real sources, everywhere in the environment, built into society, language, the structures of thought. They will go on being trapped and explored by poets, among others. We can neither deny them, nor will we rest there. A new generation of women poets is already working out of the psychic energy released when women begin to move out towards what the feminist philosopher Mary Daly has described as the "new space" on the boundaries of patriarchy. [8] Women are speaking to and of women in these poems, out of a newly released courage to name, to love each other, to share risk and grief and celebration.

To the eye of a feminist, the work of Western male poets now writing reveals a deep, fatalistic pessimism as to the possibilities of change, whether societal or personal, along with a familiar and threadbare use of women (and nature) as redemptive on the one hand, threatening on the other; and a new tide of phallocentric sadism and overt woman-hating which matches the sexual brutality of recent films. "Political" poetry by men remains stranded amid the struggles for power among male groups; in condemning U. S. imperialism or the Chilean junta the poet can claim to speak for the oppressed while remaining, as male, part of a system of sexual oppression. The enemy is always outside the self, the struggle somewhere else. The mood of isolation, self-pity, and self-imitation that pervades "nonpolitical" poetry suggests that a profound change in masculine consciousness will have to precede any new male poetic—or other—inspiration. The creative energy of patriarchy is fast running out; what remains is its self-generating energy for destruction. As women, we have our work cut out for us.

## NOTES

[1] Mary Daly, *Beyond God the Father* (Boston: Beacon, 1971), pp. 40–41.

[2] G. B. Shaw, *The Quintessence of Ibsenism* (New York: Hill & Wang, 1922), p. 139.

[3] J. G. Stewart, *Jane Ellen Harrison: A Portrait from Letters* (London: Merlin, 1959), p. 140.

[4] Henry James, "Notes on Novelists," in *Selected Literary Criticism of Henry James,* Morris Shapira, ed. (London: Heinemann, 1963), pp. 157–58.

[5] *A. R., 1978:* This intuition of mine was corroborated when, early in 1978, I read the correspondence between Woolf and Dame Ethel Smyth (Henry W. and Albert A. Berg Collection, The New York Public Library, Astor, Lenox and Tilden Foundations); in a letter dated June 8, 1933, Woolf speaks of having kept her own personality out of *A Room of One's Own* lest she not be taken seriously: ". . . how personal, so will they say, rubbing their hands with glee, women always are; *I even hear them as I write.*" (Italics mine.)

[6] *A. R., 1978:* Yet I spent months, at sixteen, memorizing and writing imitations of Millay's sonnets; and in notebooks of that period I find what are obviously attempts to imitate Dickinson's metrics and verbal compression. I knew H. D. only through anthologized lyrics; her epic poetry was not then available to me.

[7] *A. R., 1978:* When I dreamed that dream, was I wholly ignorant of the tradition of

Bessie Smith and other women's blues lyrics which transcended victimization to sing of resistance and independence?

[8] Mary Daly, *Beyond God the Father: Towards a Philosophy of Women's Liberation* (Boston: Beacon, 1973).

．．．．．．．．．．．

## QUESTIONS FOR A SECOND READING

1. Rich says, "We need to know the writing of the past, and know it differently than we have ever known it; not to pass on a tradition but to break its hold over us." In what ways does this essay, as an example of a woman writing, both reproduce and revise the genre? As she is writing here, what does Rich *do* with the writing of the past—with the conventions of the essay or the public lecture? As you reread the essay, mark sections that illustrate the ways Rich is either reproducing or revising the conventions of the essay or the public lecture. Where and how does she revise the genre? Where and how does she not? Where does Rich resist tradition? Where does she conform? How might you account for the differences?

2. It is a rare pleasure to hear a poet talk in detail about her work. As you read back through the essay, pay particular attention to what Rich notices in her poems. What *does* she notice? What does she say about what she notices? What does this allow you to say about poems or the making of poems? What does it allow you to say about the responsibilities of a reader?

## ASSIGNMENTS FOR WRITING

1. Rich says,

> For a poem to coalesce, for a character or an action to take shape, there has to be an imaginative transformation of reality which is no way passive. . . . Moreover, if the imagination is to transcend and transform experience it has to question, to challenge, to conceive of alternatives, perhaps to the very life you are living at that moment. You have to be free to play around with the notion that day might be night, love might be hate; nothing can be too sacred for the imagination to turn into its opposite or to call experimentally by another name. For writing is re-naming.

This is powerful language, and it is interesting to imagine how it might work for a person trying to read and understand one of Rich's poems. For this assignment, choose one of the poems Rich includes in the essay and write an essay of your own that considers the poem as an act of "re-naming." What is transformed into what? And to what end? Or to what consequence? What can you say about the poem as an act of imagination? as a form of political action?

2. In "When We Dead Awaken," Rich chooses several of her poems to represent stages in her history as a poet. Write an essay describing what you consider to be the most significant pattern of change in Rich's poems. When you are done, compare your account with Rich's account of the changes she sees in her own work. Does your account agree with hers? on what points?

   Note: You will need, in your essay, to make very careful and precise use of examples drawn from the poems and from Rich's discussion of those poems.

3.    I have hesitated to do what I am going to do now, which is to use myself as an illustration. For one thing, it's a lot easier and less dangerous to talk about other[s]. . . . (p. 486)

   Until we can understand the assumptions in which we are drenched we cannot know ourselves. (p. 484)

   Write an essay in which you, like Rich (and perhaps with similar hesitation), use your own experience as an illustration, as a way of investigating not just your situation but the situation of people like you. Tell a story of your own and use it to talk about the ways you might be said to have been shaped or named or positioned by an established and powerful culture. You should imagine that this assignment is a way for you to use (and put to the test) some of Rich's key terms, words like "re-vision," "re-naming," "structure," and "patriarchy."

4. Rich says, "We need to know the writing of the past, and know it differently than we have ever known it; not to pass on a tradition but to break its hold over us." That "us" includes you too. Look back over your own writing (perhaps the drafts and revisions you have written for this course), and think back over comments teachers have made, textbooks you've seen; think about what student writers do and what they are told to do, about the secrets students keep and the secrets teachers keep. You can assume, as Rich does, that there are ways of speaking about writing that are part of the culture of schooling and that they are designed to preserve certain ways of writing and thinking and to discourage others.

   One might argue, in other words, that there are traditions here. As you look at the evidence of the "past" in your own work, what are its significant features? What might you name this tradition (or these traditions)? How would you illustrate its hold on your work or the work of students generally? What might you have to do to begin to "know it differently," "to break its hold," or to revise? And, finally, why would someone want (or not want) to break its hold?

### MAKING CONNECTIONS

1. There are striking parallels between Rich's essay and Virginia Woolf's "A Room of One's Own" (p. 641) but also some striking differences. If you think of Rich's essay as a revision of Woolf's—that is, if you imagine that

Rich had, for whatever reason, to rewrite Woolf's essay for her own time and her own purposes—what would you notice in the differences between the two essays and what might you say about what you notice? Write an essay in which you discuss "When We Dead Awaken" as a demonstration of Rich's efforts to reread and rewrite the writing of the past.

2. Jean Franco's "Killing Priests, Nuns, Women, Children" (p. 195), Julia Kristeva's "Stabat Mater" (p. 359), Gloria Steinem's "Ruth's Song (Because She Could Not Sing It)" (p. 542), Alice Walker's "In Search of Our Mothers' Gardens" (p. 584), and Rich's "When We Dead Awaken" all make strong statements about the situation of women. The essays have certain similarities, but it is also interesting to consider their differences and what these differences might be said to represent. Choose one or two essays that you might compare with "When We Dead Awaken," and write an essay in which you examine the interesting differences among these essays. Consider the essays as different forms or schools of feminist thought, different ways of thinking critically about the situation of women. How might you account for these differences (if it is more than a case of different people with opinions that differ)? and what significance do you see in these differences?

# RICHARD
# RODRIGUEZ

*R* ICHARD RODRIGUEZ, *the son of Mexican immigrants, was born in San* Francisco in 1944. *He grew up in Sacramento, where he attended Catholic schools before going on to Stanford University, Columbia University, the Warburg Institute in London, and the University of California at Berkeley, eventually completing a Ph.D. in English Renaissance literature. His essays have been published in* Saturday Review, The American Scholar, Change, *and elsewhere. He now lives in San Francisco and works as a lecturer, educational consultant, and freelance writer.*

*In his book of autobiographical essays,* Hunger of Memory (1981)—*which the* Christian Science Monitor *called "beautifully written, wrung from a sore heart"— Rodriguez tells the story of his education, paying particular attention to both the meaning of his success as a student and, as he said, "its consequent price— the loss." Rodriguez's loss is represented most powerfully by his increased alienation from his parents and the decrease of intimate exchanges in family life. His parents' primary language was Spanish; his, once he became eager for success in school, was English. But the barrier was not only a language barrier. Rodriguez discovered that the interests he developed at school and through his reading were interests he did* not share with those at home—in fact, his desire to speak of them tended to threaten and humiliate his mother and father.

This separation, Rodriguez argues, is a necessary part of every person's development, even though not everyone experiences it so dramatically. We must leave home and familiar ways of speaking and understanding in order to participate in public life. On these grounds, Rodriguez has been a strong voice against bilingual education, arguing that classes conducted in Spanish will only reinforce Spanish-speaking students' separateness from mainstream American life. Rodriguez's book caused a great deal of controversy upon publication, particularly in the Hispanic community. As one critic argued, "It is indeed painful that Mr. Rodriguez has come to identify himself so completely with the majority culture that he must propagandize for a system of education which can only produce other deprived and impoverished souls like himself."

The selection that follows, Chapter 2 of Hunger of Memory, deals with Rodriguez's experiences in school. If, he said, "because of my schooling I had grown culturally separated from my parents, my education finally had given me ways of speaking and caring about that fact." This essay is a record of how he came to understand the changes in his life. A reviewer writing in the Atlantic Monthly concluded that Hunger of Memory will survive in our literature "not because of some forgotten public issues that once bisected Richard Rodriguez's life, but because his history of that life has something to say about what it means to be American . . . and what it means to be human." Rodriguez's second book is titled Mexico's Children (1989).

# The Achievement
# of Desire

I stand in the ghetto classroom—"the guest speaker"—attempting to lecture on the mystery of the sounds of our words to rows of diffident students. "Don't you hear it? Listen! The music of our words. 'Sumer is i-cumen in. . . .' And songs on the car radio. We need Aretha Franklin's voice to fill plain words with music—her life." In the face of their empty stares, I try to create an enthusiasm. But the girls in the back row turn to watch some boy passing outside. There are flutters of smiles, waves. And some-one's mouth elongates heavy, silent words through the barrier of glass. Silent words—the lips straining to shape each voiceless syllable: "*Meet meee late errr.*" By the door, the instructor smiles at me, apparently hoping that I will be able to spark some enthusiasm in the class. But only one student seems to be listening. A girl, maybe fourteen. In this gray room her eyes shine with ambition. She keeps nodding and nodding at all that I say; she even takes notes. And each time I ask a question, she jerks up and down in her desk like a marionette, while her hand waves over the bowed heads of her classmates. It is myself (as a boy) I see as she faces me now (a man in my thirties).

The boy who first entered a classroom barely able to speak English, twenty years later concluded his studies in the stately quiet of the reading room in the British Museum. Thus with one sentence I can summarize my academic career. It will be harder to summarize what sort of life connects the boy to the man.

With every award, each graduation from one level of education to the next, people I'd meet would congratulate me. Their refrain always the same: "Your parents must be very proud." Sometimes then they'd ask me how I managed it—my "success." (How?) After a while, I had several quick answers to give in reply. I'd admit, for one thing, that I went to an excellent grammar school. (My earliest teachers, the nuns, made my success their ambition.) And my brother and both my sisters were very good students. (They often brought home the shiny school trophies I came to want.) And my mother and father always encouraged me. (At every graduation they were behind the stunning flash of the camera when I turned to look at the crowd.)

As important as these factors were, however, they account inadequately for my academic advance. Nor do they suggest what an odd success I managed. For although I was a very good student, I was also a very bad student. I was a "scholarship boy," a certain kind of scholarship boy. Always successful, I was always unconfident. Exhilarated by my progress. Sad. I became the prized student—anxious and eager to learn. Too eager, too anxious—an imitative and unoriginal pupil. My brother and two sisters enjoyed the advantages I did, and they grew to be as successful as I, but none of them ever seemed so anxious about their schooling. A second-grade student, I was the one who came home and corrected the "simple" grammatical mistakes of our parents. ("Two negatives make a positive.") Proudly I announced—to my family's startled silence—that a teacher had said I was losing all trace of a Spanish accent. I was oddly annoyed when I was unable to get parental help with a homework assignment. The night my father tried to help me with an arithmetic exercise, he kept reading the instructions, each time more deliberately, until I pried the textbook out of his hands, saying, "I'll try to figure it out some more by myself."

When I reached the third grade, I outgrew such behavior. I became more tactful, careful to keep separate the two very different worlds of my day. But then, with ever-increasing intensity, I devoted myself to my studies. I became bookish, puzzling to all my family. Ambition set me apart.

When my brother saw me struggling home with stacks of library books, he would laugh, shouting: "Hey, Four Eyes!" My father opened a closet one day and was startled to find me inside, reading a novel. My mother would find me reading when I was supposed to be asleep or helping around the house or playing outside. In a voice angry or worried or just curious, she'd ask: "What do you see in your books?" It became the family's joke. When I was called and wouldn't reply, someone would say I must be hiding under my bed with a book.

(How did I manage my success?)

What I am about to say to you has taken me more than twenty years to admit: *A primary reason for my success in the classroom was that I couldn't forget that schooling was changing me and separating me from the life I enjoyed before becoming a student.* That simple realization! For years I never spoke to anyone about it. Never mentioned a thing to my family or my teachers or classmates. From a very early age, I understood enough, just enough about my classroom experiences to keep what I knew repressed, hidden beneath layers of embarrassment. Not until my last months as a graduate student, nearly thirty years old, was it possible for me to think much about the reasons for my academic success. Only then. At the end of my schooling, I needed to determine how far I had moved from my past. The adult finally confronted, and now must publicly say, what the child shuddered from knowing and could never admit to himself or to those many faces that smiled at his every success. ("Your parents must be very proud. . . .")

# I

At the end, in the British Museum (too distracted to finish my dissertation) for weeks I read, speed-read, books by modern educational theorists, only to find infrequent and slight mention of students like me. (Much more is written about the more typical case, the lower-class student who barely is helped by his schooling.) Then one day, leafing through Richard Hoggart's *The Uses of Literacy*, I found, in his description of the scholarship boy, myself. For the first time I realized that there were other students like me, and so I was able to frame the meaning of my academic success, its consequent price—the loss.

Hoggart's description is distinguished, at least initially, by deep understanding. What he grasps very well is that the scholarship boy must move between environments, his home and the classroom, which are at cultural extremes, opposed. With his family, the boy has the intense pleasure of intimacy, the family's consolation in feeling public alienation. Lavish emotions texture home life. *Then,* at school, the instruction bids him to trust lonely reason primarily. Immediate needs set the pace of his parents' lives. From his mother and father the boy learns to trust spontaneity and nonrational ways of knowing. *Then,* at school, there is mental calm. Teachers emphasize the value of a reflectiveness that opens a space between thinking and immediate action.

Years of schooling must pass before the boy will be able to sketch the cultural differences in his day as abstractly as this. But he senses those differences early. Perhaps as early as the night he brings home an assignment from school and finds the house too noisy for study.

> He has to be more and more alone, if he is going to "get on." He will have, probably unconsciously, to oppose the ethos of the hearth, the intense gregariousness of the working-class family group. Since everything centres upon the living-room, there is unlikely to be a room of his own; the bedrooms are cold and inhospitable, and to warm them or the front room, if there is one, would not only be expensive, but would require an imaginative leap—out of the tradition—which most families are not capable of making. There is a corner of the living room table. On the other side Mother is ironing, the wireless is on, someone is singing a snatch of song or Father says intermittently whatever comes into his head. The boy has to cut himself off mentally, so as to do his homework, as well as he can. [1]

The next day, the lesson is as apparent at school. There are even rows of desks. Discussion is ordered. The boy must rehearse his thoughts and raise his hand before speaking out in a loud voice to an audience of classmates. And there is time enough, and silence, to think about ideas (big ideas) never considered at home by his parents.

Not for the working-class child alone is adjustment to the classroom difficult. Good schooling requires that any student alter early childhood habits. But the working-class child is usually least prepared for the change. And, unlike many middle-class children, he goes home and sees in his parents a way of life not only different but starkly opposed to that of the classroom. (He enters the house and hears his parents talking in ways his teachers discourage.)

Without extraordinary determination and the great assistance of others—at home and at school—there is little chance for success. Typically most working-class children are barely changed by the classroom. The exception succeeds. The relative few become scholarship students. Of these, Richard Hoggart estimates, most manage a fairly graceful transition. Somehow they learn to live in the two very different worlds of their day. There are some others, however, those Hoggart pejoratively terms "scholarship boys," for whom success comes with special anxiety. Scholarship boy: good student, troubled son. The child is "moderately endowed," intellectually mediocre, Hoggart supposes—though it may be more pertinent to note the special qualities of temperament in the child. High-strung child. Brooding. Sensitive. Haunted by the knowledge that one *chooses* to become a student. (Education is not an inevitable or natural step in growing up.) Here is a child who cannot forget that his academic success distances him from a life he loved, even from his own memory of himself.

Initially, he wavers, balances allegiance. ("The boy is himself [until he reaches, say, the upper forms] very much of *both* the worlds of home and school. He is enormously obedient to the dictates of the world of school, but emotionally still strongly wants to continue as part of the family circle.") Gradually, necessarily, the balance is lost. The boy needs to spend more and more time studying, each night enclosing himself in the silence permitted and required by intense concentration. He takes his first step toward academic success, away from his family.

From the very first days, through the years following, it will be with his parents—the figures of lost authority, the persons toward whom he feels deepest love—that the change will be most powerfully measured. A separation will unravel between them. Advancing in his studies, the boy notices that his mother and father have not changed as much as he. Rather, when he sees them, they often remind him of the person he once was and the life he earlier shared with them. He realizes what some Romantics also know when they praise the working class for the capacity for human closeness, qualities of passion and spontaneity, that the rest of us experience in like measure only in the earliest part of our youth. For the Romantic, this doesn't make working-class life childish. Working-class life challenges precisely because it is an *adult* way of life.

The scholarship boy reaches a different conclusion. He cannot afford to admire his parents. (How could he and still pursue such a contrary life?) He permits himself embarrassment at their lack of education. And to evade nostalgia for the life he has lost, he concentrates on the benefits education will bestow upon him. He becomes especially ambitious. Without the support of old certainties and consolations, almost mechanically, he assumes the procedures and doctrines of the classroom. The kind of allegiance the young student might have given his mother and father only days earlier, he transfers to the teacher, the new figure of authority. "[The scholarship boy] tends to make a father-figure of his form-master," Hoggart observes.

But Hoggart's calm prose only makes me recall the urgency with which I came to idolize my grammar school teachers. I began by imitating their accents, using their diction, trusting their every direction. The very first facts they dispensed, I grasped with awe. Any book they told me to read, I read—then waited for them to tell me which books I enjoyed. Their every casual opinion I came to adopt and to trumpet when I returned home. I stayed after school "to help"—to get my teacher's undivided attention. It was the nun's encouragement that mattered most to me. (She understood exactly what—my parents never seemed to appraise so well—all my achievements entailed.) Memory gently caressed each word of praise bestowed in the classroom so that compliments teachers paid me years ago come quickly to mind even today.

The enthusiasm I felt in second-grade classes I flaunted before both my parents. The docile, obedient student came home a shrill and precocious son who insisted on correcting and teaching his parents with the remark: "My teacher told us. . . ."

I intended to hurt my mother and father. I was still angry at them for having encouraged me toward classroom English. But gradually this anger was exhausted, replaced by guilt as school grew more and more attractive to me. I grew increasingly successful, a talkative student. My hand was raised in the classroom; I yearned to answer any question. At home, life was less noisy than it had been. (I spoke to classmates and teachers more often each day than to family members.) Quiet at home, I sat with my papers for hours each night. I never forgot that schooling had irretrievably changed my family's life. That knowledge, however, did not weaken ambition. Instead, it strengthened resolve. Those times I remembered the loss of my past with regret, I quickly reminded myself of all the things my teachers could give me. (They could make me an educated man.) I tightened my grip on pencil and books. I evaded nostalgia. Tried hard to forget. But one does not forget by trying to forget. One only remembers. I remembered too well that education had changed my family's life. I would not have become a scholarship boy had I not so often remembered.

Once she was sure that her children knew English, my mother would tell us, "You should keep up your Spanish." Voices playfully groaned in response. "¡Pochos!" my mother would tease. I listened silently.

After a while, I grew more calm at home. I developed tact. A fourth-grade student, I was no longer the show-off in front of my parents. I became a conventionally dutiful son, politely affectionate, cheerful enough, even—for reasons beyond choosing—my father's favorite. And much about my family life was easy then, comfortable, happy in the rhythm of our living together: hearing my father getting ready for work; eating the breakfast my mother had made me; looking up from a novel to hear my brother or one of my sisters playing with friends in the backyard; in winter, coming upon the house all lighted up after dark.

But withheld from my mother and father was any mention of what most mattered to me: the extraordinary experience of first-learning. Late afternoon: In the midst of preparing dinner, my mother would come up behind me while I was trying to read. Her head just over mine, her breath warmly scented with food. "What are you reading?" Or, "Tell me all about your new courses." I would barely respond, "Just the usual things, nothing special." (A half smile, then silence. Her head moving back in the silence.

Silence! Instead of the flood of intimate sounds that had once flowed smoothly between us, there was this silence.) After dinner, I would rush to a bedroom with papers and books. As often as possible, I resisted parental pleas to "save lights" by coming to the kitchen to work. I kept so much, so often, to myself. Sad. Enthusiastic. Troubled by the excitement of coming upon new ideas. Eager. Fascinated by the promising texture of a brand-new book. I hoarded the pleasures of learning. Alone for hours. Enthralled. Nervous. I rarely looked away from my books—or back on my memories. Nights when relatives visited and the front rooms were warmed by Spanish sounds, I slipped quietly out of the house.

It mattered that education was changing me. It never ceased to matter. My brother and sisters would giggle at our mother's mispronounced words. They'd correct her gently. My mother laughed girlishly one night, trying not to pronounce *sheep* as *ship*. From a distance I listened sullenly. From that distance, pretending not to notice on another occasion, I saw my father looking at the title pages of my library books. That was the scene on my mind when I walked home with a fourth-grade companion and heard him say that his parents read to him every night. (A strange-sounding book—*Winnie the Pooh*.) Immediately, I wanted to know, "What is it like?" My companion, however, thought I wanted to know about the plot of the book. Another day, my mother surprised me by asking for a "nice" book to read. "Something not too hard you think I might like." Carefully I chose one, Willa Cather's *My Ántonia*. But when, several weeks later, I happened to see it next to her bed unread except for the first few pages, I was furious and suddenly wanted to cry. I grabbed up the book and took it back to my room and placed it in its place, alphabetically on my shelf.

"Your parents must be very proud of you." People began to say that to me about the time I was in sixth grade. To answer affirmatively, I'd smile. Shyly I'd smile, never betraying my sense of the irony: I was not proud of my mother and father. I was embarrassed by their lack of education. It was not that I ever thought they were stupid, though stupidly I took for granted their enormous native intelligence. Simply, what mattered to me was that they were not like my teachers.

But, "Why didn't you tell us about the award?" my mother demanded, her frown weakened by pride. At the grammar school ceremony several weeks after, her eyes were brighter than the trophy I'd won. Pushing back the hair from my forehead, she whispered that I had "shown" the *gringos*. A few minutes later, I heard my father speak to my teacher and felt ashamed of his labored, accented words. Then guilty for the shame. I felt such contrary feelings. (There is no simple road-map through the heart of the scholarship boy.) My teacher was so soft-spoken and her words were edged sharp and clean. I admired her until it seemed to me that she spoke too carefully. Sensing that she was condescending to them, I became nervous. Resentful. Protective. I tried to move my parents away. "You both must be very proud of Richard," the nun said. They responded quickly. (They were proud.) "We are proud of all our children." Then this afterthought: "They sure didn't get their brains from us." They all laughed. I smiled.

Tightening the irony into a knot was the knowledge that my parents were always behind me. They made success possible. They evened the path. They sent their children to parochial schools because the nuns "teach better." They paid a tuition they couldn't afford. They spoke English to us.

For their children my parents wanted chances they never had—an easier way. It saddened my mother to learn that some relatives forced their children to start working right after high school. To *her* children she would say, "Get all the education you can." In schooling she recognized the key to job advancement. And with the remark she remembered her past.

As a girl new to America my mother had been awarded a high school diploma by teachers too careless or busy to notice that she hardly spoke English. On her own, she determined to learn how to type. That skill got her jobs typing envelopes in letter shops, and it encouraged in her an optimism about the possibility of advancement. (Each morning when her sisters put on uniforms, she chose a bright-colored dress.) The years of young womanhood passed, and her typing speed increased. She also became an excellent speller of words she mispronounced. "And I've never been to college," she'd say, smiling, when her children asked her to spell words they were too lazy to look up in a dictionary.

Typing, however, was dead-end work. Finally frustrating. When her youngest child started high school, my mother got a full-time office job once again. (Her paycheck combined with my father's to make us—in fact—what we had already become in our imagination of ourselves—middle class.) She worked then for the (California) state government in numbered civil service positions secured by examinations. The old ambition of her youth was rekindled. During the lunch hour, she consulted bulletin boards for announcements of openings. One day she saw mention of something called an "anti-poverty agency." A typing job. A glamorous job, part of the governor's staff. "A knowledge of Spanish required." Without hesitation she applied and became nervous only when the job was suddenly hers.

"Everyone comes to work all dressed up," she reported at night. And didn't need to say more than that her co-workers wouldn't let her answer the phones. She was only a typist, after all, albeit a very fast typist. And an excellent speller. One morning there was a letter to be sent to a Washington cabinet officer. On the dictating tape, a voice referred to urban guerrillas. My mother typed (the wrong word, correctly): "gorillas." The mistake horrified the anti-poverty bureaucrats who shortly after arranged to have her returned to her previous position. She would go no further. So she willed her ambition to her children. "Get all the education you can; with an education you can do anything." (With a good education *she* could have done anything.)

When I was in high school, I admitted to my mother that I planned to become a teacher someday. That seemed to please her. But I never tried to explain that it was not the occupation of teaching I yearned for as much as it was something more elusive: I wanted to *be* like my teachers, to possess their knowledge, to assume their authority, their confidence, even to assume a teacher's persona.

In contrast to my mother, my father never verbally encouraged his children's academic success. Nor did he often praise us. My mother had to remind him to "say something" to one of his children who scored some academic success. But whereas my mother saw in education the opportunity for job advancement, my father recognized that education provided an even more startling possibility: It could enable a person to escape from a life of mere labor.

In Mexico, orphaned when he was eight, my father left school to work as an "apprentice" for an uncle. Twelve years later, he left Mexico in frustration and arrived in America. He had great expectations then of becoming an engineer. ("Work for my hands and my head.") He knew a Catholic priest who promised to get him money enough to study full time for a high school diploma. But the promises came to nothing. Instead there was a dark succession of warehouse, cannery, and factory jobs. After work he went to night school along with my mother. A year, two passed. Nothing much changed, except that fatigue worked its way into the bone; then everything changed. He didn't talk anymore of becoming an engineer. He stayed outside on the steps of the school while my mother went inside to learn typing and shorthand.

By the time I was born, my father worked at "clean" jobs. For a time he was a janitor at a fancy department store. ("Easy work; the machines do it all.") Later he became a dental technician. ("Simple.") But by then he was pessimistic about the ultimate meaning of work and the possibility of ever escaping its claims. In some of my earliest memories of him, my father already seems aged by fatigue. (He has never really grown old like my mother.) From boyhood to manhood, I have remembered him in a single image: seated, asleep on the sofa, his head thrown back in a hideous corpselike grin, the evening newspaper spread out before him. "But look at all you've accomplished," his best friend said to him once. My father said nothing. Only smiled.

It was my father who laughed when I claimed to be tired by reading and writing. It was he who teased me for having soft hands. (He seemed to sense that some great achievement of leisure was implied by my papers and books.) It was my father who became angry while watching on television some woman at the Miss America contest tell the announcer that she was going to college. ("Majoring in fine arts.") "College!" he snarled. He despised the trivialization of higher education, the inflated grades and cheapened diplomas, the half education that so often passed as mass education in my generation.

It was my father again who wondered why I didn't display my awards on the wall of my bedroom. He said he liked to go to doctors' offices and see their certificates and degrees on the wall. ("Nice.") My citations from school got left in closets at home. The gleaming figure astride one of my trophies was broken, wingless, after hitting the ground. My medals were placed in a jar of loose change. And when I lost my high school diploma, my father found it as it was about to be thrown out with the trash. Without telling me, he put it away with his own things for safekeeping.

These memories slammed together at the instant of hearing that refrain familiar to all scholarship students: "Your parents must be proud. . . ." Yes, my parents were proud. I knew it. But my parents regarded my progress with more than mere pride. They endured my early precocious behavior—but with what private anger and humiliation? As their children got older and would come home to challenge ideas both of them held, they argued before submitting to the force of logic or superior factual evidence with the disclaimer, "It's what we were taught in our time to believe." These discussions ended abruptly, though my mother remembered them on other occasions when she complained that our "big ideas" were going to our heads. More acute was her complaint that the family wasn't close anymore, like some others she knew. Why weren't we close, "more in the Mexican style"? Everyone is so private, she added. And she mimicked the yes and no answers she got in reply to her questions. Why didn't we talk more? (My father never asked.) I never said.

I was the first in my family who asked to leave home when it came time to go to college. I had been admitted to Stanford, one hundred miles away. My departure would only make physically apparent the separation that had occurred long before. But it was going too far. In the months preceding my leaving, I heard the question my mother never asked except indirectly. In the hot kitchen, tired at the end of her workday, she demanded to know, "Why aren't the colleges here in Sacramento good enough for you? They are for your brother and sister." In the middle of a car ride, not turning to face me, she wondered, "Why do you need to go so far away?" Late at night, ironing, she said with disgust, "Why do you have to put us through this big expense? You know your scholarship will never cover it all." But when September came there was a rush to get everything ready. In a bedroom that last night I packed the big brown valise, and my mother sat nearby sewing initials onto the clothes I would take. And she said no more about my leaving.

Months later, two weeks of Christmas vacation: The first hours home were the hardest. ("What's new?") My parents and I sat in the kitchen for a conversation. (But, lacking the same words to develop our sentences and to shape our interests, what was there to say? What could I tell them of the term paper I had just finished on the "universality of Shakespeare's appeal"?) I mentioned only small, obvious things: my dormitory life; weekend trips I had taken; random events. They responded with news of their own. (One was almost grateful for a family crisis about which there was much to discuss.) We tried to make our conversation seem like more than an interview.

## II

From an early age I knew that my mother and father could read and write both Spanish and English. I had observed my father making his way through what, I now suppose, must have been income tax forms. On other occasions I waited apprehensively while my mother read onion-paper letters airmailed from Mexico with news of a relative's illness or death. For both my parents, however, reading was something done out of necessity and as quickly as possible. Never did I see either of them read an entire book. Nor did I see them read for pleasure. Their reading consisted of work manuals, prayer books, newspaper, recipes.

Richard Hoggart imagines how, at home,

> . . . [The scholarship boy] sees strewn around, and reads regularly himself, magazines which are never mentioned at school, which seem not to belong to the world to which the school introduces him; at school he hears about and reads books never mentioned at home. When he brings those books into the house they do not take their place with other books which the family are reading, for often there are none or almost none; his books look, rather, like strange tools.

In our house each school year would begin with my mother's careful instruction: "Don't write in your books so we can sell them at the end of the year." The remark was echoed in public by my teachers, but only in part: "Boys and girls, don't write in your books. You must learn to treat them with great care and respect."

OPEN THE DOORS OF YOUR MIND WITH BOOKS, read the red and white poster over the nun's desk in early September. It soon was apparent to me that reading was the classroom's central activity. Each course had its own book. And the information gathered from a book was unquestioned. READ TO LEARN, the sign on the wall advised in December. I privately wondered: What was the connection between reading and learning? Did one learn something only by reading it? Was an idea only an idea if it could be written down? In June, CONSIDER BOOKS YOUR BEST FRIENDS. Friends? Reading was, at best, only a chore. I needed to look up whole paragraphs of words in a dictionary. Lines of type were dizzying, the eye having to move slowly across the page, then down, and across. . . . The sentences of the first books I read were cooly impersonal. Toned hard. What most bothered me, however, was the isolation reading required. To console myself for the loneliness I'd feel when I read, I tried reading in a very soft voice. Until: "Who is doing all that talking to his neighbor?" Shortly after, remedial reading classes were arranged for me with a very old nun.

At the end of each school day, for nearly six months, I would meet with her in the tiny room that served as the school's library but was actually only a storeroom for used textbooks and a vast collection of *National Geographics.* Everything about our sessions pleased me: the smallness of the room; the noise of the janitor's broom hitting the edge of the long hallway outside the door; the green of the sun, lighting the wall; and the old woman's face blurred white with a beard. Most of the time we took turns. I began with my elementary text. Sentences of astonishing simplicity seemed to me lifeless and drab: "The boys ran from the rain . . . She wanted to sing . . . The kite rose in the blue." Then the old nun would read from her favorite books, usually biographies of early American presidents. Playfully she ran through complex sentences, calling the words alive with her voice, making it seem that the author somehow was speaking directly to me. I smiled just to listen to her. I sat there and sensed for the very first time some possibility of fellowship between a reader and a writer, a communication, never *intimate* like that I heard spoken words at home convey, but one nonetheless *personal.*

One day the nun concluded a session by asking me why I was so reluctant to read by myself. I tried to explain; said something about the way written words made me feel all alone—almost, I wanted to add but didn't, as when I spoke to myself in a room just emptied of furniture. She studied my face as I spoke; she seemed to be watching more than listening. In an uneventful voice she replied that I had nothing to fear. Didn't I realize that reading would open up whole new worlds? A book could open doors for me. It could introduce me to people and show me places I never imagined existed. She gestured toward the bookshelves. (Bare-breasted African women danced, and the shiny hubcaps of automobiles on the back covers of the *Geographic* gleamed in my mind.) I listened with respect. But her words were not very influential. I was thinking then of another consequence of literacy, one I was too shy to admit but nonetheless trusted. Books were going to make me "educated." *That* confidence enabled me, several months later, to overcome my fear of the silence.

In fourth grade I embarked upon a grandiose reading program. "Give me the names of important books," I would say to startled teachers. They soon found out that I had in mind "adult books." I ignored their suggestion of anything I suspected was written for children. (Not until I was in college, as a result, did I read *Huckleberry Finn* or *Alice's Adventures in Wonderland.*) Instead, I read *The Scarlet Letter* and Franklin's *Autobiography.* And whatever I read I read for extra credit. Each time I finished a book, I reported the achievement to a teacher and basked in the praise my effort earned. Despite my best efforts, however, there seemed to be more and more books I needed to read. At the library I would literally tremble as I came upon whole shelves of books I hadn't read. So I read and I read and I read: *Great Expectations*; all the short stories of Kipling; *The Babe Ruth Story*; the entire first volume of the *Encyclopedia Britannica* (A–ANSTEY); the *Iliad*; *Moby Dick*; *Gone with the Wind*; *The Good Earth*; *Ramona*; *Forever Amber*; *The Lives of the Saints*; *Crime and Punishment*; *The Pearl.* . . . Librarians who initially frowned when I checked out the maximum ten books at a time started saving books they thought I might like. Teachers would say to the rest of the class, "I only wish the rest of you took reading as seriously as Richard obviously does."

But at home I would hear my mother wondering, "What do you see in your books?" (Was reading a hobby like her knitting? Was so much reading even healthy for a boy? Was it the sign of "brains"? Or was it just a convenient excuse for not helping about the house on Saturday mornings?) Always, "What do you see . . . ?"

What *did* I see in my books? I had the idea that they were crucial for my academic success, though I couldn't have said exactly how or why. In the sixth grade I simply concluded that what gave a book its value was some major idea or theme it contained. If that core essence could be mined and memorized, I would become learned like my teachers. I decided to record in a notebook the themes of the books that I read. After reading *Robinson Crusoe*, I wrote that its theme was "the value of learning to live by oneself." When I completed *Wuthering Heights,* I noted the danger of "letting emotions get out of control." Rereading these brief moralistic appraisals usually left me disheartened. I couldn't believe that they were really the source of reading's value. But for many more years, they constituted the only means I had of describing to myself the educational value of books.

In spite of my earnestness, I found reading a pleasurable activity. I came to enjoy the lonely good company of books. Early on weekday mornings,

I'd read in my bed. I'd feel a mysterious comfort then, reading in the dawn quiet—the blue-gray silence interrupted by the occasional churning of the refrigerator motor a few rooms away or the more distant sounds of a city bus beginning its run. On weekends I'd go to the public library to read, surrounded by old men and women. Or, if the weather was fine, I would take my books to the park and read in the shade of a tree. A warm summer evening was my favorite reading time. Neighbors would leave for vacation and I would water their lawns. I would sit through the twilight on the front porches or in backyards, reading to the cool, whirling sounds of the sprinklers.

I also had favorite writers. But often those writers I enjoyed most I was least able to value. When I read William Saroyan's *The Human Comedy*, I was immediately pleased by the narrator's warmth and the charm of his story. But as quickly I became suspicious. A book so enjoyable to read couldn't be very "important." Another summer I determined to read all the novels of Dickens. Reading his fat novels, I loved the feeling I got—after the first hundred pages—of being at home in a fictional world where I knew the names of the characters and cared about what was going to happen to them. And it bothered me that I was forced away at the conclusion, when the fiction closed tight, like a fortune-teller's fist—the futures of all the major characters neatly resolved. I never knew how to take such feelings seriously, however. Nor did I suspect that these experiences could be part of a novel's meaning. Still, there were pleasures to sustain me after I'd finish my books. Carrying a volume back to the library, I would be pleased by its weight. I'd run my fingers along the edge of the pages and marvel at the breadth of my achievement. Around my room, growing stacks of paperback books reenforced my assurance.

I entered high school having read hundreds of books. My habit of reading made me a confident speaker and writer of English. Reading also enabled me to sense something of the shape, the major concerns, of Western thought. (I was able to say something about Dante and Descartes and Engels and James Baldwin in my high school term papers.) In these various ways, books brought me academic success as I hoped that they would. But I was not a good reader. Merely bookish, I lacked a point of view when I read. Rather, I read in order to acquire a point of view. I vacuumed books for epigrams, scraps of information, ideas, themes—anything to fill the hollow within me and make me feel educated. When one of my teachers suggested to his drowsy tenth-grade English class that a person could not have a "complicated idea" until he had read at least two thousand books, I heard the remark without detecting either its irony or its very complicated truth. I merely determined to compile a list of all the books I had ever read. Harsh with myself, I included only once a title I might have read several times.

(How, after all, could one read a book more than once?) And I included only those books over a hundred pages in length. (Could anything shorter be a book?)

There was yet another high school list I compiled. One day I came across a newspaper article about the retirement of an English professor at a nearby state college. The article was accompanied by a list of the "hundred most important books of Western Civilization." "More than anything else in my life," the professor told the reporter with finality, "these books have made me all that I am." That was the kind of remark I couldn't ignore. I clipped out the list and kept it for the several months it took me to read all of the titles. Most books, of course, I barely understood. While reading Plato's *Republic*, for instance, I needed to keep looking at the book jacket comments to remind myself what the text was about. Nevertheless, with the special patience and superstition of a scholarship boy, I looked at every word of the text. And by the time I reached the last word, relieved, I convinced myself that I had read *The Republic*. In a ceremony of great pride, I solemnly crossed Plato off my list.

### III

The scholarship boy pleases most when he is young—the working-class child struggling for academic success. To his teachers, he offers great satisfaction; his success is their proudest achievement. Many other persons offer to help him. A businessman learns the boy's story and promises to underwrite part of the cost of his college education. A woman leaves him her entire library of several hundred books when she moves. His progress is featured in a newspaper article. Many people seem happy for him. They marvel. "How did you manage so fast?" From all sides, there is lavish praise and encouragement.

In his grammar school classroom, however, the boy already makes students around him uneasy. They scorn his desire to succeed. They scorn him for constantly wanting the teacher's attention and praise. "Kiss Ass," they call him when his hand swings up in response to every question he hears. Later, when he makes it to college, no one will mock him aloud. But he detects annoyance on the faces of some students and even some teachers who watch him. It puzzles him often. In college, then in graduate school, he behaves much as he always has. If anything is different about him it is that he dares to anticipate the successful conclusion of his studies. At last he feels that he belongs in the classroom, and this is exactly the source of the dissatisfaction he causes. To many persons around him, he appears too much the academic. There may be some things about him that recall his beginnings—his shabby clothes; his persistent poverty; or his dark skin (in those cases when it symbolizes his parents' disadvantaged condition)—but they only make clear how far he has moved from his past. He has used education to remake himself.

It bothers his fellow academics to face this. They will not say why exactly. (They sneer.) But their expectations become obvious when they are disappointed. They expect—they want—a student less changed by his schooling. If the scholarship boy, from a past so distant from the classroom, could remain in some basic way unchanged, he would be able to prove that it is possible for anyone to become educated without basically changing from the person one was.

Here is no fabulous hero, no idealized scholar-worker. The scholarship boy does not straddle, cannot reconcile, the two great opposing cultures of his life. His success is unromantic and plain. He sits in the classroom and offers those sitting beside him no calming reassurance about their own lives. He sits in the seminar room—a man with brown skin, the son of working-class Mexican immigrant parents. (Addressing the professor at the head of the table, his voice catches with nervousness.) There is no trace of his parents' in his speech. Instead he approximates the accents of teachers and classmates. Coming from *him* those sounds seem suddenly odd. Odd too is the effect produced when *he* uses academic jargon—bubbles at the tip of his tongue: "*Topos* . . . negative capability . . . vegetation imagery in Shakespearean comedy." He lifts an opinion from Coleridge, takes something else from Frye or Empson or Leavis. He even repeats exactly his professor's earlier comment. All his ideas are clearly borrowed. He seems to have no thought of his own. He chatters while his listeners smile—their look one of disdain.

When he is older and thus when so little of the person he was survives, the scholarship boy makes only too apparent his profound lack of *self*-confidence. This is the conventional assessment that even Richard Hoggart repeats:

> [The scholarship boy] tends to over-stress the importance of examinations, of the piling-up of knowledge and of received opinions. He discovers a technique of apparent learning, of the acquiring of facts rather than of the handling and use of facts. He learns how to receive a purely literate education, one using only a small part of the personality and challenging only a limited area of his being. He begins to see life as a ladder, as permanent examination with some praise and some further exhortation at each stage. He becomes an expert imbiber and doler-out; his competence will vary, but will rarely be accompanied by genuine enthusiasms. He rarely feels the

reality of knowledge, of other men's thoughts and imaginings, on his own pulses. . . . He has something of the blinkered pony about him. . . .

But this is criticism more accurate than fair. The scholarship boy is a very bad student. He is the great mimic; a collector of thoughts, not a thinker; the very last person in class who ever feels obliged to have an opinion of his own. In large part, however, the reason he is such a bad student is because he realizes more often and more acutely than most other students—than Hoggart himself—that education requires radical self-reformation. As a very young boy, regarding his parents, as he struggles with an early homework assignment, he knows this too well. That is why he lacks self-assurance. He does not forget that the classroom is responsible for remaking him. He relies on his teacher, depends on all that he hears in the classroom and reads in his books. He becomes in every obvious way the worst student, a dummy mouthing the opinions of others. But he would not be so bad—nor would he become so successful, a *scholarship boy*—if he did not accurately perceive that the best synonym for primary "education" is "imitation."

Those who would take seriously the boy's success—and his failure—would be forced to realize how great is the change any academic undergoes, how far one must move from one's past. It is easiest to ignore such considerations. So little is said about the scholarship boy in pages and pages of educational literature. Nothing is said of the silence that comes to separate the boy from his parents. Instead, one hears proposals for increasing the self-esteem of students and encouraging early intellectual independence. Paragraphs glitter with a constellation of terms like *creativity* and *originality*. (Ignored altogether is the function of imitation in a student's life.) Radical educationalists meanwhile complain that ghetto schools "oppress" students by trying to mold them, stifling native characteristics. The truer critique would be just the reverse: not that schools change ghetto students too much, but that while they might promote the occasional scholarship student, they change most students barely at all.

From the story of the scholarship boy there is no specific pedagogy to glean. There is, however, a much larger lesson. His story makes clear that education is a long, unglamorous, even demeaning process—*a nurturing never natural to the person one was before one entered a classroom.* At once different from most other students, the scholarship boy is also the archetypal "good student." He exaggerates the difficulty of being a student, but his exaggeration reveals a general predicament. Others are changed by their schooling as much as he. They too must re-form themselves. They must develop the skill of memory long before they become truly critical thinkers.

And when they read Plato for the first several times, it will be with awe more than deep comprehension.

The impact of schooling on the scholarship boy is only more apparent to the boy himself and to others. Finally, although he may be laughable—a blinkered pony—the boy will not let his critics forget their own change. He ends up too much like them. When he speaks, they hear themselves echoed. In his pedantry, they trace their own. His ambitions are theirs. If his failure were singular, they might readily pity him. But he is more troubling than that. They would not scorn him if this were not so.

## IV

Like me, Hoggart's imagined scholarship boy spends most of his years in the classroom afraid to long for his past. Only at the very end of his schooling does the boy-man become nostalgic. In this sudden change of heart, Richard Hoggart notes:

> He longs for the membership he lost, "he pines for some Nameless Eden where he never was." The nostalgia is the stronger and the more ambiguous because he is really "in quest of his own absconded self yet scared to find it." He both wants to go back and yet thinks he has gone beyond his class, feels himself weighted with knowledge of his own and their situation, which hereafter forbids him the simpler pleasures of his father and mother. . . .

According to Hoggart, the scholarship boy grows nostalgic because he remains the uncertain scholar, bright enough to have moved from his past, yet unable to feel easy, a part of a community of academics.

This analysis, however, only partially suggests what happened to me in my last year as a graduate student. When I traveled to London to write a dissertation on English Renaissance literature, I was finally confident of membership in a "community of scholars." But the pleasure that confidence gave me faded rapidly. After only two or three months in the reading room of the British Museum, it became clear that I had joined a lonely community. Around me each day were dour faces eclipsed by large piles of books. There were the regulars, like the old couple who arrived every morning, each holding a loop of the shopping bag which contained all their notes. And there was the historian who chattered madly to herself. ("Oh dear! Oh! Now, what's this? What? Oh, my!") There were also the faces of young men and women worn by long study. And everywhere eyes turned away the moment our glance accidentally met. Some persons I sat beside day after day, yet we passed silently at the end of the day, strangers. Still, we were united by a common respect for the written word and for scholarship. We did form a union, though one in which we remained distant from one another.

More profound and unsettling was the bond I recognized with those writers whose books I consulted. Whenever I opened a text that hadn't been used for years, I realized that my special interests and skills united me to a mere handful of academics. We formed an exclusive—eccentric!—society, separated from others who would never care or be able to share our concerns. (The pages I turned were stiff like layers of dead skin.) I began to wonder: Who, beside my dissertation director and a few faculty members, would ever read what I wrote? And: Was my dissertation much more than an act of social withdrawal? These questions went unanswered in the silence of the Museum reading room. They remained to trouble me after I'd leave the library each afternoon and feel myself shy—unsteady, speaking simple sentences at the grocer's or the butcher's on my way back to my bed-sitter.

Meanwhile my file cards accumulated. A professional, I knew exactly how to search a book for pertinent information. I could quickly assess and summarize the usability of the many books I consulted. But whenever I started to write, I knew too much (and not enough) to be able to write anything but sentences that were overly cautious, timid, strained brittle under the heavy weight of footnotes and qualifications. I seemed unable to dare a passionate statement. I felt drawn by professionalism to the edge of sterility, capable of no more than pedantic, lifeless, unassailable prose.

*Then* nostalgia began.

After years spent unwilling to admit its attractions, I gestured nostalgically toward the past. I yearned for that time when I had not been so alone. I became impatient with books. I wanted experience more immediate. I feared the library's silence. I silently scorned the gray, timid faces around me. I grew to hate the growing pages of my dissertation on genre and Renaissance literature. (In my mind I heard relatives laughing as they tried to make sense of its title.) I wanted something—I couldn't say exactly what. I told myself that I wanted a more passionate life. And a life less thoughtful. And above all, I wanted to be less alone. One day I heard some Spanish academics whispering back and forth to each other, and their sounds seemed ghostly voices recalling my life. Yearning became preoccupation then. Boyhood memories beckoned, flooded my mind. (Laughing intimate voices. Bounding up the front steps of the porch. A sudden embrace inside the door.)

For weeks after, I turned to books by educational experts. I needed to learn how far I had moved from my past—to determine how fast I would be able to recover something of it once again. But I found little. Only a chapter in a book by Richard Hoggart. . . . I left the reading room and the circle of faces.

I came home. After the year in England, I spent three summer months living with my mother and father, relieved by how easy it was to be home. It no longer seemed very important to me that we had little to say. I felt easy sitting and eating and walking with them. I watched them, nevertheless, looking for evidence of those elastic, sturdy strands that bind generations in a web of inheritance. I thought as I watched my mother one night: Of course a friend had been right when she told me that I gestured and laughed just like my mother. Another time I saw for myself: My father's eyes were much like my own, constantly watchful.

But after the early relief, this return, came suspicion, nagging until I realized that I had not neatly sidestepped the impact of schooling. My desire to do so was precisely the measure of how much I remained an academic. *Negatively* (for that is how this idea first occurred to me): My need to think so much and so abstractly about my parents and our relationship was in itself an indication of my long education. My father and mother did not pass their thinking about the cultural meanings of their experience. It was I who described their daily lives with airy ideas. And yet, *positively*: The ability to consider experience so abstractly allowed me to shape into desire what would otherwise have remained indefinite, meaningless longing in the British Museum. If, because of my schooling, I had grown culturally separated from my parents, my education finally had given me ways of speaking and caring about that fact.

My best teachers in college and graduate school, years before, had tried to prepare me for this conclusion, I think, when they discussed texts of aristocratic pastoral literature. Faithfully, I wrote down all that they said. I memorized it: "The praise of the unlettered by the highly educated is one of the primary themes of 'elitist' literature." But, "the importance of the praise given the unsolitary, richly passionate and spontaneous life is that it simultaneously reflects the value of a reflective life." I heard it all. But there was no way for any of it to mean very much to me. I was a scholarship boy at the time, busily laddering my way up the rungs of education. To pass an examination, I copied down exactly what my teachers told me. It would require many more years of schooling (an inevitable miseducation) in which I came to trust the silence of reading and the habit of abstracting from immediate experience—moving away from a life of closeness and immediacy I remembered with my parents, growing older—before I turned unafraid to desire the past, and thereby achieved what had eluded me for so long—the end of education.

519

NOTES

¹ All quotations in this essay are from Richard Hoggart, *The Uses of Literacy* (London: Chatto and Windus, 1957), chapter 10. [Author's note]

. . . . . . . . . . .

## QUESTIONS FOR A SECOND READING

1. In *Hunger of Memory,* the book from which "The Achievement of Desire" is drawn, Rodriguez says several times that the story he tells, although it is very much his story, is also a story of our common experience—growing up, leaving home, becoming educated, entering the world. When you re-read this essay, look particularly for sections or passages you might bring forward as evidence that this is, in fact, an essay which can give you a way of looking at your own life, and not just his. And look for sections that defy universal application. To what degree *is* his story the story of our common experience? Why might he (or his readers) want to insist that his story is everyone's story?

2. At the end of the essay, Rodriguez says

   > It would require many more years of schooling (an inevitable mis-
   > education) in which I came to trust the silence of reading and the
   > habit of abstracting from immediate experience—moving away from
   > a life of closeness and immediacy I remembered with my parents,
   > growing older—before I turned unafraid to desire the past, and
   > thereby achieved what had eluded me for so long—the end of edu-
   > cation.

   What, as you reread this essay is the "end of education"? And what does that end (that goal? stopping point?) have to do with "miseducation," "the silence of reading," "the habit of abstracting from immediate experience," and "desiring the past"?

## ASSIGNMENTS FOR WRITING

1. You could look at the relationship between Richard Rodriguez and Richard Hoggart as a case study of the relation of a reader to a writer or a student to a teacher. Look closely at Rodriguez's references to Hoggart's book, *The Uses of Literacy,* and at the way Rodriguez made use of that book to name and describe his own experience as a student. What did he find in the book? How did he use it? How does he use it in his own writing?

   Write an essay in which you discuss Rodriguez's use of Hoggart's *The Uses of Literacy.* How, for example, would you compare Rodriguez's version of the "scholarship boy" with Hoggart's? (At one point, Rodriguez says that Hoggart's account is "more accurate than fair." What might he have meant by that?) And what kind of reader is the Rodriguez who is writing "The Achievement of Desire"—is he still a "scholarship boy," or is that description no longer appropriate?

Note: You might begin your research with what may seem to be a purely technical matter, examining how Rodriguez handles quotations and works Hoggart's words into paragraphs of his own. On the basis of Rodriguez's use of quoted passages, how would you describe the relationship between Hoggart's words and Rodriguez's? Who has the greater authority? Who is the expert, and under what conditions? What "rules" might Rodriguez be said to follow or to break? Do you see any change in the course of the essay in how Rodriguez uses block quotations? in how he comments on them?

2. Rodriguez insists that his story is also everyone's story. Take an episode from your life, one that seems in some way similar to one of the episodes in "The Achievement of Desire," and cast it into a shorter version of Rodriguez's essay. Your job here is to look at your experience in Rodriguez's terms, which means thinking the way he does, noticing what he would notice, interpreting details in a similar fashion, using his key terms, seeing through his point of view; it could also mean imitating his style of writing, doing whatever it is you see him doing characteristically while he writes. Imitation, Rodriguez argues, is not necessarily a bad thing; it can, in fact, be one of the powerful ways in which a person learns.

Note: This assignment can also be used to read against "The Achievement of Desire." Rodriguez insists on the universality of his experience leaving home and community and joining the larger public life. You could highlight the differences between your experience and his. You should begin by imitating Rodriguez's method; you do not have to arrive at his conclusions, however.

## MAKING CONNECTIONS

1. Paulo Freire, in "The 'Banking' Concept of Education" (p. 206), discusses the political implications of the relations between teachers and students. Some forms of schooling, he says, can give students control over their lives, but most schooling teaches students only to submit to domination by others. If you look closely at the history of Rodriguez's schooling from the perspective of Freire's essay, what do you see? Write an essay describing how Freire might analyze Rodriguez's education. How would he see the process as it unfolds throughout Rodriguez's experience, as a student, from his early schooling (including the study he did on his own at home), through his college and graduate studies, to the position he takes, finally, as the writer of "The Achievement of Desire."

2. Stanley Fish, in "How to Recognize a Poem When You See One" (p. 178), argues that the students in his class could see the list of names on the board as a poem because "as members of a literary community they knew what

a poem was." Students generally behave as they do because they know how to "do school"; they have become part of a community that thinks and acts in certain predictable ways.

Membership in this community was never such an easy matter for Rodriguez, although the evidence in "The Achievement of Desire" suggests that it was not difficult for him to enter the community, and once inside he worked hard to stay there. He was a good student. He knew how to do school. In high school, he once read through a list of the "hundred most important books of Western Civilization."

Imagine that one of Fish's students in the class Fish describes in his essay is a student from a background like Rodriguez's. After attending the class, the student has a conversation with Rodriguez in which he or she tells the students' side of the story and speaks with pleasure of the class's ability to interpret that "poem" so convincingly in such a short period of time. How would Rodriguez respond? What advice would he give to the student about that course and about his or her education generally?

# JOHN
# RUSKIN

*J*OHN RUSKIN *was an important social critic and a leading critic of Victorian art. He acquired the passion for beauty that informs all his work from travels to the Continent with his father. This passion was doomed to frustration, however, in the industrial society in which he lived. Ruskin had a particular enthusiasm for Gothic architecture and wanted to revive the kind of culture that had made that style possible, one in which an individual worker—such as a stonemason—could express himself and thereby derive pleasure, as well as wages, from his work. Ruskin thought that industrial society, unless fundamentally changed, would never be capable of producing anything as grand, beautiful, or just as a gothic cathedral.*

*Ruskin was born in London in 1819 and died there in 1900, barely putting his foot into our century, yet his eccentric tastes and his vision of a better world back in a simpler past made their mark on both Victorian society and our own. He took B.A. and M.A. degrees (in 1842 and 1843) at Oxford University, where his skill in looking at buildings was sharpened and tested by the architecture of the many colleges and chapels in a university complex that today remains a gothic cloister in the midst of an industrial city. Ruskin's books include* Modern Painters *(5 vols., 1843–1860) and* The Stones of Venice *(3 vols., 1851–1853).*

*During the last thirty years of his life, Ruskin suffered a series of mental break-downs, which his biographers often attribute to his frustration about the course of English society. He was one of the first to recognize the dangers of "progress" to the environment, and he spoke eloquently throughout his life about the ugliness of modern urban life and its effect on the lives and spirit of those who live in cities. His influence can be seen in the work of William Morris, George Bernard Shaw, and D. H. Lawrence, but also in J. R. R. Tolkien's* Lord of the Rings, *in "Dungeons and Dragons," and in the special status we give to folk songs, local crafts, and handmade articles.*

*Ruskin was a writer who wanted to teach his readers to pay attention. He once wrote, "You might read all the books in the British Museum (if you could live long enough) and remain an utterly 'illiterate,' uneducated person, but . . . if you read ten pages of a good book, letter by letter—that is to say, with real accuracy—you are forevermore in some measure an educated person." We do not recommend that you read the following selection from* The Stones of Venice *letter by letter (whatever that might mean). His prose will take time and attention, however. You will have to give it a chance to teach you how it wants to be read. Ruskin's prose is partly the product of his age, partly the product of the rhythm and cadences of the King James Bible, and partly the product of his own peculiar way of thinking about things. Be patient with it. Don't give in to the temptation to be annoyed by those long sentences or strange, dramatic gestures. Think, rather, about why he might want to talk to you in this way and what, in return, you get if you become his listener.*

# The Nature of Gothic

VII. I. SAVAGENESS. I am not sure when the word "Gothic" was first generically applied to the architecture of the North; but I presume that, whatever the date of its original usage, it was intended to imply reproach, and express the barbaric character of the nations among whom that architecture arose. It never implied that they were literally of Gothic lineage, far less that their architecture had been originally invented by the Goths themselves; but it did imply that they and their buildings together exhibited a degree of sternness and rudeness, which, in contradistinction to the character of Southern and Eastern nations, appeared like a perpetual reflection of the contrast between the Goth and the Roman in their first encounter. And when that fallen Roman, in the utmost impotence of his luxury, and insolence of his guilt, became the model for the imitation of civilised Europe, at the close of the so-called Dark ages, the word Gothic became a term of unmitigated contempt, not unmixed with aversion. From that contempt, by the exertion of the antiquaries and architects of this century, Gothic architecture has been sufficiently vindicated; and perhaps some among us, in our admiration of the magnificent science of its structure, and sacredness of its expression, might desire that the term of ancient reproach should be withdrawn, and some other, of more apparent honourableness, adopted in its place. There is no chance, as there is no need, of such a substitution. As far as the epithet was used scornfully, it was used falsely; but there is no reproach in the word, rightly understood; on the contrary, there is a profound truth, which the instinct of mankind almost unconsciously recognises. It is true, greatly and deeply true, that the architecture of the North is rude and wild; but it is not true, that, for this reason, we are to condemn it, or despise. Far otherwise: I believe it is in this very character that it deserves our profoundest reverence.

VIII. The charts of the world which have been drawn up by modern science have thrown into a narrow space the expression of a vast amount of knowledge, but I have never yet seen any one pictorial enough to enable the spectator to imagine the kind of contrast in physical character which exists between Northern and Southern countries. We know the difference in detail, but we have not that broad glance and grasp which would enable us to feel them in their fulness. We know that gentians grow on the Alps, and olives on the Apennines; but we do not enough conceive for ourselves that variegated mosaic of the world's surface which a bird sees in its migration, that difference between the district of the gentian and of the olive which the stork and the swallow see far off, as they lean upon the sirocco wind. Let us, for a moment, try to raise ourselves even about the level of their flight, and imagine the Mediterranean lying beneath us like an irregular lake, and all its ancient promontories sleeping in the sun: here and there an angry spot of thunder, a grey stain of storm, moving upon the burning field; and here and there a fixed wreath of white volcano smoke, surrounded by its circle of ashes; but for the most part a great peacefulness of light, Syria and Greece, Italy and Spain, laid like pieces of a golden pavement into the sea-blue, chased, as we stoop nearer to them, with bossy beaten work of mountain chains, and glowing softly with terraced gardens, and flowers heavy with frankincense, mixed among masses of laurel, and orange, and plumy palm, that abate with their grey-green shadows the burning of the marble rocks, and of the ledges of porphyry sloping under lucent sand. Then let us pass farther towards the north, until we see the orient colours change gradually into a vast belt of rainy green, where the pastures of Switzerland, and poplar valleys of France, and dark forests of the Danube and Carpathians stretch from the mouths of the Loire to those of the Volga, seen through clefts in grey swirls of rain-cloud and flaky veils of the mist of the brooks, spreading low along the pasture lands: and then, farther north still, to see the earth heave into mighty masses of leaden rock and heathy moor, bordering with a broad waste of gloomy purple that belt of field and wood, and splintering into irregular and grisly islands amidst the northern seas, beaten by storm, and chilled by ice-drift, and tormented by furious pulses of contending tide, until the roots of the last forests fail from among the hill ravines, and the hunger of the north wind bites their peaks into barrenness; and, at last, the wall of ice, durable like iron, sets, deathlike, its white teeth against us out of the polar twilight. And, having once traversed in thought this gradation of the zoned iris of the earth in all its material vastness, let us go down nearer to it, and watch the parallel change in the belt of animal life: the multitudes of swift and brilliant creatures that glance in the air and sea, or tread the sands of the southern zone; striped zebras and spotted leopards, glistening serpents, and birds arrayed in purple and scarlet. Let us contrast their delicacy and brilliancy of colour, and swiftness of motion, with the frost-cramped strength, and shaggy covering, and dusky plumage of the northern tribes; contrast the Arabian horse with the Shetland, the tiger and leopard with the wolf and bear, the antelope with the elk, the bird of paradise with the osprey: and then, submissively acknowledging the great laws by which the earth and all that it bears are ruled throughout their being, let us not condemn, but rejoice in the expression by man of his own rest in the statutes of the lands that gave him birth. Let us watch him with reverence as he sets side by side the burning gems, and smooths with soft sculpture the jasper pillars, that are to reflect a ceaseless sunshine, and rise into a cloudless sky: but not with less reverence let us stand by him, when, with rough strength and hurried stroke, he smites an uncouth animation out of the rocks which he has torn from among the moss of the moorland, and heaves into the darkened air the pile of iron buttress and rugged wall, instinct with work of an imagination as wild and wayward as the northern sea; creations of ungainly shape and rigid limb, but full of wolfish life; fierce as the winds that beat, and changeful as the clouds that shade them.

There is, I repeat, no degradation, no reproach in this, but all dignity and honourableness: and we should err grievously in refusing either to recognise as an essential character of the existing architecture of the North, or to admit as a desirable character in that which it yet may be, this wildness of thought, and roughness of work; this look of mountain brotherhood between the cathedral and the Alp; this magnificence of sturdy power, put forth only the more energetically because the fine finger-touch was chilled away by the frosty wind, and the eye dimmed by the moormist, or blinded by the hail; this outspeaking of the strong spirit of men who may not gather redundant fruitage from the earth, nor bask in dreamy benignity of sunshine, but must break the rock for bread, and cleave the forest for fire, and show, even in what they did for their delight, some of the hard habits of the arm and heart that grew on them as they swung the axe or pressed the plough.

IX. If, however, the savageness of Gothic architecture, merely as an expression of its origin among Northern nations, may be considered, in some sort, a noble character, it possesses a higher nobility still, when considered as an index, not of climate, but of religious principle.

In the 13th and 14th paragraphs of Chapter XXI of the first volume of this work, it was noticed that the systems of architectural ornament, properly so called, might be divided into three:—1. Servile ornament, in which the execution or power of the inferior workman is entirely subjected to the intellect of the higher;—2. Constitutional ornament, in which the executive inferior power is, to a certain point, emancipated and indepedent, having a will of its own, yet confessing its inferiority and rendering obedience to higher powers;—and 3. Revolutionary ornament, in which no executive inferiority is admitted at all. I must here explain the nature of these divisions at somewhat greater length.

Of Servile ornament, the principal schools are the Greek, Ninevite, and Egyptian; but their servility is of different kinds. The Greek master-workman was far advanced in knowledge and power above the Assyrian or Egyptian. Neither he nor those for whom he worked could endure the appearance of imperfection in anything; and, therefore, what ornament he appointed to be done by those beneath him was composed of mere geometrical forms,—balls, ridges, and perfectly symmetrical foliage,—which could be executed with absolute precision by line and rule, and were as perfect in their way, when completed, as his own figure sculpture. The Assyrian and Egyptian, on the contrary, less cognisant of accurate form in anything, were content to allow their figure sculpture to be executed by inferior workmen, but lowered the method of its treatment to a standard which every workman could reach, and then trained him by discipline so rigid, that there was no chance of his falling beneath the standard appointed. The Greek gave to the lower workman no subject which he could not perfectly execute. The Assyrian gave him subjects which he could only execute imperfectly, but fixed a legal standard for his imperfection. The workman was, in both systems, a slave. [1]

X. But in the mediæval, or especially Christian, system of ornament, this slavery is done away with altogether; Christianity having recognised, in small things as well as great, the individual value of every soul. But it not only recognises its value; it confesses its imperfection, in only bestowing dignity upon the acknowledgment of unworthiness. That admission of lost power and fallen nature, which the Greek or Ninevite felt to be intensely painful, and, as far as might be, altogether refused, the Christian makes daily and hourly, contemplating the fact of it without fear, as tending, in the end, to God's greater glory. Therefore, to every spirit which Christianity summons to her service, her exhortation is: Do what you can, and confess frankly what you are unable to do; neither let your effort be shortened for fear of failure, nor your confession silenced for fear of shame. And it is, perhaps, the principal admirableness of the Gothic schools of architecture, that they thus receive the results of the labour of inferior minds: and out of fragments full of imperfection, and betraying that imperfection in every touch, indulgently raise up a stately and unaccusable whole.

XI. But the modern English mind has this much in common with that of the Greek, that it intensely desires, in all things, the utmost completion or perfection compatible with their nature. This is a noble character in the abstract, but becomes ignoble when it causes us to forget the relative dignities of that nature itself, and to prefer the perfectness of the lower nature to the imperfection of the higher; not considering that as, judged by such a rule, all the brute animals would be preferable to man, because more perfect in their functions and kind, and yet are always held inferior to him, so also in the works of man, those which are more perfect in their kind are always inferior to those which are, in their nature, liable to more faults and shortcomings. For the finer the nature, the more flaws it will show through the clearness of it; and it is a law of this universe, that the best things shall be seldomest seen in their best form. The wild grass grows well and strongly, one year with another; but the wheat is, according to the greater nobleness of its nature, liable to the bitterer blight. And therefore, while in all things that we see, or do, we are to desire perfection, and strive for it, we are nevertheless not to set the meaner thing, in its narrow accomplishment, above the nobler thing, in its mighty progress; not to esteem smooth minuteness above shattered majesty; not to prefer mean victory to honourable defeat; not to lower the level of our aim, that we may the more surely enjoy the complacency of success. But, above all, in our dealings with the souls of other men, we are to take care how we check, by severe requirement or narrow caution, efforts which might otherwise lead to a noble issue; and, still more, how we withhold our admiration from great excellencies, because they are mingled with rough faults. Now, in the make and nature of every man, however rude or simple, whom we employ in manual labour, there are some powers for better things: some tardy imagination, torpid capacity of emotion, tottering steps of thought, there are, even at the worst; and in most cases it is all our own fault that they *are* tardy or torpid. But they cannot be strengthened, unless we are content to take them in their feebleness, and unless we prize and honour them in their imperfection above the best and most perfect manual skill. And this is what we have to do with all our labourers; to look for the *thoughtful* part of them, and get that out of them, whatever we lose for it, whatever faults and errors we are obliged to take with it. For the best that is in them cannot manifest itself, but in company with much error. Understand this clearly: You can teach a man to draw a straight line, and to cut one; to strike a curved line, and to carve it; and to copy and carve any number of given lines or forms, with admirable speed and perfect precision; and you find his work perfect of its kind: but if you ask him to think about any of those forms, to consider if he cannot find any better in his own head, he stops; his execution becomes hesitating; he thinks, and ten to one he thinks wrong; ten to one he makes a mistake in the first touch he gives to his work as a thinking being. But you have made a man of him for all that. He was only a machine before, an animated tool.

XII. And observe, you are put to stern choice in this matter. You must either make a tool of the creature, or a man of him. You cannot make both. Men were not intended to work with the accuracy of tools, to be precise and perfect in all their actions. If you will have that precision out of them, and make their fingers measure degrees like cog-wheels, and their arms strike curves like compasses, you must unhumanise them. All the energy of their spirits must be given to make cogs and compasses of themselves. All their attention and strength must go to the accomplishment of the mean act. The eye of the soul must be bent upon the finger-point, and the soul's force must fill all the invisible nerves that guide it, ten hours a day, that it may not err from its steely precision, and so soul and sight be worn away, and the whole human being be lost at last—a heap of sawdust, so far as its intellectual work in this world is concerned; saved only by its Heart, which cannot go into the form of cogs and compasses, but expands, after the ten hours are over, into fireside humanity. On the other hand, if you will make a man of the working creature, you cannot make a tool. Let him but begin to imagine, to think, to try to do anything worth doing; and the engine-turned precision is lost at once. Out come all his roughness, all his dulness, all his incapability; shame upon shame, failure upon failure, pause after pause; but out comes the whole majesty of him also; and we know the height of it only, when we see the clouds settling upon him. And, whether the clouds be bright or dark, there will be transfiguration behind and within them.

XIII. And now, reader, look round this English room of yours, about which you have been proud so often, because the work of it was so good and strong, and the ornaments of it so finished. Examine again all those accurate mouldings, and perfect polishings, and unerring adjustments of the seasoned wood and tempered steel. Many a time you have exulted over them, and thought how great England was, because her slightest work was done so thoroughly. Alas! if read rightly, these perfectnesses are signs of a slavery in our England a thousand times more bitter and more degrading than that of the scourged African, or helot Greek. Men may be beaten, chained, tormented, yoked like cattle, slaughtered like summer flies, and yet remain in one sense, and the best sense, free. But to smother their souls within them, to blight and hew into rotting pollards the suckling branches of their human intelligence, to make the flesh and skin which, after the worm's work on it, is to see God, into leathern thongs to yoke machinery with,—this it is to be slave-masters indeed; and there might be more freedom in England, though her feudal lords' lightest words were worth men's lives, and though the blood of the vexed husbandman dropped in the furrows of her fields, than there is while the animation of her multitudes is sent like fuel to feed the factory smoke, and the strength of them is given daily to be wasted into the fineness of a web, or racked into the exactness of a line.

xiv. And, on the other hand, go forth again to gaze upon the old cathedral front, where you have smiled so often at the fantastic ignorance of the old sculptors: examine once more those ugly goblins, and formless monsters, and stern statues, anatomiless and rigid; but do not mock at them, for they are signs of the life and liberty of every workman who struck the stone; a freedom of thought, and rank in scale of being, such as no laws, no charters, no charities can secure; but which it must be the first aim of all Europe at this day to regain for her children.

xv. Let me not be thought to speak wildly or extravagantly. It is verily this degradation of the operative into a machine, which, more than any other evil of the times, is leading the mass of the nations everywhere into vain, incoherent, destructive struggling for a freedom of which they cannot explain the nature to themselves. Their universal outcry against wealth, and against nobility, is not forced from them either by the pressure of famine, or the sting of mortified pride. These do much, and have done much in all ages; but the foundations of society were never yet shaken as they are at this day. It is not that men are ill fed, but that they have no pleasure in the work by which they make their bread, and therefore look to wealth as the only means of pleasure. It is not that men are pained by the scorn of the upper classes, but they cannot endure their own; for they feel that the kind of labour to which they are condemned is verily a degrading one, and makes them less than men. Never had the upper classes so much sympathy with the lower, or charity for them, as they have at this day, and yet never were they so much hated by them: for, of old, the separation between the noble and the poor was merely a wall built by law; now it is a veritable difference in level of standing, a precipice between upper and lower grounds in the field of humanity, and there is pestilential air at the bottom of it. I know not if a day is ever to come when the nature of right freedom will be understood, and when men will see that to obey another man, to labour for him, yield reverence to him or to his place, is not slavery. It is often the best kind of liberty,—liberty from care. The man who says to one, Go, and he goeth, and to another, Come and he cometh, has, in most cases, more sense of restraint and difficulty than the man who obeys him. The movements of the one are hindered by the burden on his shoulder; of the other, by the bridle on his lips: there is no way by which the burden may be lightened; but we need not suffer from the bridle if we do not champ at it. To yield reverence to another, to hold ourselves and our lives at his disposal, is not slavery; often, it is the noblest state in which a man can live in this world. There is, indeed, a reverence which is servile, that is to say irrational or selfish: but there is also noble reverence, that is to say, reasonable and loving; and a man is never so noble as when he is reverent in this kind; nay, even if the feeling pass the bounds of mere reason, so that it be loving, man is raised by it. Which had, in reality, most of the serf nature in him—the Irish peasant who was lying in wait yesterday for his landlord, with his musket muzzle thrust through the ragged hedge; or that old mountain servant, who, two hundred years ago, at Inverkeithing, gave up his own life and the lives of his seven sons for his chief?—as each fell, calling forth his brother to the death, "Another for Hector!" And therefore, in all ages and all countries, reverence has been paid and sacrifice made by men to each other, not only without complaint, but rejoicingly; and famine, and peril, and sword, and all evil, and all shame, have been borne willingly in the causes of masters and kings; for all these gifts of the heart ennobled the men who gave, not less than the men who received them, and nature prompted, and God rewarded the sacrifice. But to feel their souls withering within them, unthanked, to find their whole being sunk into an unrecognised abyss, to be counted off into a heap of mechanism, numbered with its wheels, and weighed with its hammer strokes;—this nature bade not,—this God blesses not,—this humanity for no long time is able to endure.

xvi. We have much studied and much perfected, of late, the great civilised invention of the division of labour; only we give it a false name. It is not, truly speaking, the labour that is divided; but the men:—Divided into mere segments of men—broken into small fragments and crumbs of life; so that all the little piece of intelligence that is left in a man is not enough to make a pin, or a nail, but exhausts itself in making the point of a pin, or the head of a nail. Now it is a good and desirable thing, truly, to make many pins in a day; but if we could only see with what crystal sand their points were polished,—sand of human soul, much to be magnified before it can be discerned for what it is,—we should think there might be some loss in it also. And the great cry that rises from all our manufacturing cities, louder than their furnace blast, is all in very deed for this,—that we manufacture everything there except men; we blanch cotton, and strengthen steel, and refine sugar, and shape pottery; but to brighten, to strengthen, to refine, or to form a single living spirit, never enters into our estimate of advantages. And all the evil to which that cry is urging our myriads can be met only in one way: not by teaching nor preaching, for to teach them is but to show them their misery, and to preach to them, if we do nothing more than preach, is to mock at it. It can be met only by a right understanding, on the part of all classes, of what kinds of labour are good for men, raising them, and making them happy; by a determined sacrifice of such convenience, or beauty, or cheapness as is to be got only by the degradation of the workman; and by equally determined demand for the products and results of healthy and ennobling labour.

XVII. And how, it will be asked, are these products to be recognised, and this demand to be regulated? Easily: by the observance of three broad and simple rules:

1. Never encourage the manufacture of any article not absolutely necessary, in the production of which *Invention* has no share.
2. Never demand an exact finish for its own sake, but only for some practical or noble end.
3. Never encourage imitation or copying of any kind, except for the sake of preserving record of great works.

The second of these principles is the only one which directly rises out of the consideration of our immediate subject; but I shall briefly explain the meaning and extent of the first also, reserving the enforcement of the third for another place.

1. Never encourage the manufacture of anything not necessary, in the production of which invention has no share.

For instance. Glass beads are utterly unnecessary, and there is no design or thought employed in their manufacture. They are formed by first drawing out the glass into rods; these rods are chopped up into fragments of the size of beads by the human hand, and the fragments are then rounded in the furnace. The men who chop up the rods sit at their work all day, their hands vibrating with a perpetual and exquisitely timed palsy, and the beads dropping beneath their vibration like hail. Neither they, nor the men who draw out the rods or fuse the fragments, have the smallest occasion for the use of any single human faculty; and every young lady, therefore, who buys glass beads is engaged in the slave-trade, and in a much more cruel one than that which we have so long been endeavouring to put down.

But glass cups and vessels may become the subjects of exquisite invention; and if in buying these we pay for the invention, that is to say for the beautiful form, or colour, or engraving, and not for mere finish of execution, we are doing good to humanity.

XVIII. So, again, the cutting of precious stones, in all ordinary cases, requires little exertion of any mental faculty; some tact and judgment in avoiding flaws, and so on, but nothing to bring out the whole mind. Every person who wears cut jewels merely for the sake of their value is, therefore, a slave-driver.

But the working of the goldsmith, and the various designing of grouped jewellery and enamel-work, may become the subject of the most noble human intelligence. Therefore, money spent in the purchase of well-designed plate, of precious engraved vases, cameos, or enamels, does good to humanity; and, in work of this kind, jewels may be employed to heighten its splendour; and their cutting is then a price paid for the attainment of a noble end, and thus perfectly allowable.

xix. I shall perhaps press this law farther elsewhere, but our immediate concern is chiefly with the second, namely, never to demand an exact finish, when it does not lead to a noble end. For observe, I have only dwelt upon the rudeness of Gothic, or any other kind of imperfectness, as admirable, where it was impossible to get design or thought without it. If you are to have the thought of a rough and untaught man, you must have it in a rough and untaught way; but from an educated man, who can without effort express his thoughts in an educated way, take the graceful expression, and be thankful. Only *get* the thought, and do not silence the peasant because he cannot speak good grammar, or until you have taught him his grammar. Grammar and refinement are good things, both, only be sure of the better thing first. And thus in art, delicate finish is desirable from the greatest masters, and is always given by them. In some places Michael Angelo, Leonardo, Phidias, Perugino, Turner, all finished with the most exquisite care; and the finish they give always leads to the fuller accomplishment of their noble purposes. But lower men than these cannot finish, for it requires consummate knowledge to finish consummately, and then we must take their thoughts as they are able to give them. So the rule is simple: Always look for invention first, and after that, for such execution as will help the invention, and as the inventor is capable of without painful effort, and *no more*. Above all, demand no refinement of execution where there is no thought, for that is slaves' work, unredeemed. Rather choose rough work than smooth work, so only that the practical purpose be answered, and never imagine there is reason to be proud of anything that may be accomplished by patience and sand-paper.

xx. I shall only give one example, which however will show the reader what I mean, from the manufacture already alluded to, that of glass. Our modern glass is exquisitely clear in its substance, true in its form, accurate in its cutting. We are proud of this. We ought to be ashamed of it. The old Venice glass was muddy, inaccurate in all its forms, and clumsily cut, if at all. And the old Venetian was justly proud of it. For there is this difference between the English and Venetian workman, that the former thinks only of accurately matching his patterns, and getting his curves perfectly true and his edges perfectly sharp, and becomes a mere machine for rounding curves and sharpening edges, while the old Venetian cared not a whit whether his edges were sharp or not, but he invented a new design for every glass that he made, and never moulded a handle or a lip without a new fancy in it. And therefore, though some Venetian glass is ugly and clumsy enough, when made by clumsy and uninventive workmen, other Venetian glass is so lovely in its forms that no price is too great for it; and we never see the same form in it twice. Now you cannot have the finish and the varied form too. If the workman is thinking about his edges, he cannot be thinking of his design; if of his design, he cannot think of his edges. Choose whether you will pay for the lovely form or the perfect finish, and choose at the same moment whether you will make the worker a man or a grindstone.

xxi. Nay, but the reader interrupts me,—"If the workman can design beautifully, I would not have him kept at the furnace. Let him be taken away and made a gentleman, and have a studio, and design his glass there, and I will have it blown and cut for him by common workmen, and so I will have my design and my finish too."

All ideas of this kind are founded upon two mistaken suppositions: the first, that one man's thoughts can be, or ought to be, executed by another man's hands; the second, that manual labour is a degradation, when it is governed by intellect.

On a large scale, and in work determinable by line and rule, it is indeed both possible and necessary that the thoughts of one man should be carried out by the labour of others; in this sense I have already defined the best architecture to be the expression of the mind of manhood by the hands of childhood. But on a smaller scale, and in a design which cannot be mathematically defined, one man's thoughts can never be expressed by another: and the difference between the spirit of touch of the man who is inventing, and of the man who is obeying directions, is often all the difference between a great and a common work of art. How wide the separation is between original and second-hand execution, I shall endeavour to show elsewhere; it is not so much to our purpose here as to mark the other and more fatal error of despising manual labour when governed by intellect; for it is no less fatal an error to despise it when thus regulated by intellect, than to value it for its own sake. We are always in these days endeavouring to separate the two; we want one man to be always thinking, and another to be always working, and we call one a gentleman, and the other an operative; whereas the workman ought often to be thinking, and the thinker often to be working, and both should be gentlemen, in the best sense. As it is, we make both ungentle, the one envying, the other despising, his brother; and the mass of society is made up of morbid thinkers, and miserable workers. Now it is only by labour that thought can be made healthy, and only by thought that labour can be made happy, and the two cannot be separated with impunity. It would be well if all of us were good handicraftsmen in some kind, and the dishonour of manual labour done away with altogether; so that though there should still be a trenchant distinction of race between nobles and commoners, there should not, among the latter, be a trenchant distinction of employment, as between idle and working men, or between men of liberal and illiberal professions. All professions should be liberal, and there should be less pride felt in peculiarity of employment, and more in excellence of achievement. And yet more, in each several profession, no master should be too proud to do its hardest work. The painter should grind his own colours; the architect work in the mason's yard with his men; the master-manufacturer be himself a more skilful operative than any man in his mills; and the distinction between one man and another be only in experience and skill, and the authority and wealth which these must naturally and justly obtain.

xxii. I should be led far from the matter in hand, if I were to pursue this interesting subject. Enough, I trust, has been said to show the reader that the rudeness or imperfection which at first rendered the term "Gothic" one of reproach is indeed, when rightly understood, one of the most noble characters of Christian architecture, and not only a noble but an *essential* one. It seems a fantastic paradox, but it is nevertheless a most important truth, that no architecture can be truly noble which is *not* imperfect. And this is easily demonstrable. For since the architect, whom we will suppose capable of doing all in perfection, cannot execute the whole with his own hands, he must either make slaves of his workmen in the old Greek, and present English fashion, and level his work to a slave's capacities, which is to degrade it; or else he must take his workmen as he finds them, and let them show their weaknesses together with their strength, which will involve the Gothic imperfection, but render the whole work as noble as the intellect of the age can make it.

xxiii. But the principle may be stated more broadly still. I have confined the illustration of it to architecture, but I must not leave it as if true of architecture only. Hitherto I have used the words imperfect and perfect merely to distinguish between work grossly unskilful, and work executed with average precision and science; and I have been pleading that any degree of unskilfulness should be admitted, so only that the labourer's mind had room for expression. But, accurately speaking, no good work whatever can be perfect, and *the demand for perfection is always a sign of a misunderstanding of the ends of art.*

xxiv. This for two reasons, both based on everlasting laws. The first, that no great man ever stops working till he has reached his point of failure; that is to say, his mind is always far in advance of his powers of execution, and the latter will now and then give way in trying to follow it; besides that he will always give to the inferior portions of his work only such inferior attention as they require; and according to his greatness he becomes so accustomed to the feeling of dissatisfaction with the best he can do, that in moments of lassitude or anger with himself he will not care though the beholder be dissatisfied also. I believe there has only been one man who would not acknowledge this necessity, and strove always to reach perfection, Leonardo; the end of his vain effort being merely that he would take ten years to a picture, and leave it unfinished. And therefore, if we are to have great men working at all, or less men doing their best, the work will be imperfect, however beautiful. Of human work none but what is bad can be perfect, in its own bad way. [2]

xxv. The second reason is, that imperfection is in some sort essential to all that we know of life. It is the sign of life in a mortal body, that is to say, of a state of progress and change. Nothing that lives is, or can be, rigidly perfect; part of it is decaying, part nascent. The foxglove blossom,— a third part bud, a third part past, a third part in full bloom,—is a type of the life of this world. And in all things that live there are certain irregularities and deficiencies which are not only signs of life, but sources of beauty. No human face is exactly the same in its lines on each side, no leaf perfect in its lobes, no branch in its symmetry. All admit irregularity as they imply change; and to banish imperfection is to destroy expression, to check exertion, to paralyse vitality. All things are literally better, lovelier, and more beloved for the imperfections which have been divinely appointed, that the law of human life may be Effort, and the law of human judgment, Mercy.

Accept this then for a universal law, that neither architecture nor any other noble work of man can be good unless it be imperfect; and let us be prepared for the otherwise strange fact, which we shall discern clearly as we approach the period of the Renaissance, that the first cause of the fall of the arts of Europe was a relentless requirement of perfection, incapable alike either of being silenced by veneration for greatness, or softened into forgiveness of simplicity.

NOTES

[1] The third kind of ornament, the Renaissance, is that in which the inferior detail becomes principal, the executor of every minor portion being required to exhibit skill and possess knowledge as great as that which is possessed by the master of the design; and in the endeavour to endow him with this skill and knowledge, his own original power is overwhelmed, and the whole building becomes a wearisome exhibition of well-educated imbecility. We must fully inquire into the nature of this form of error, when we arrive at the examination of the Renaissance schools.

[2] The Elgin marbles are supposed by many persons to be "perfect." In the most important portions they indeed approach perfection, but only there. The draperies are unfinished, the hair and wool of the animals are unfinished, and the entire bas-reliefs of the frieze are roughly cut.

. . . . . . . . . . .

## QUESTIONS FOR A SECOND READING

1. On pages 537 and 538 you will find two photographs of the Gothic cathedral at Chartres, in France. The first one, on page 537, shows the view as

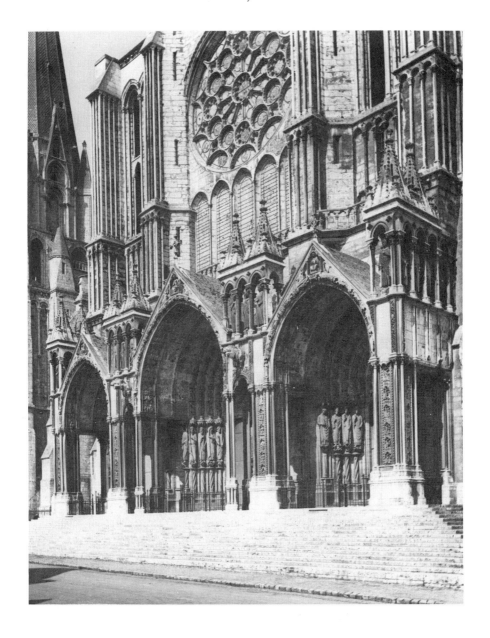

you approach the cathedral; the other, on page 538, shows detail from the carvings in the main entrance. Before you reread the essay, study these pictures carefully. What do you notice? What would Ruskin have you notice? If there is a difference, how would you explain it? What assumptions guide your vision or determine your point of view? And what about Ruskin—what leads him to notice one part of the facade but to ignore another?

Ruskin was writing to readers who, he felt, considered Gothic architecture ugly, savage, and crude. Can you imagine such a reader? What would be the expectations or prejudices of those who looked at a cathedral from this point of view? What might they consider beautiful or fine? What does Ruskin assume, in other words, about the tastes and prejudices of his readers?

2. Ruskin says,

> And it is, perhaps, the principal admirableness of the Gothic schools of architecture, that they thus receive the results of the labor of inferior minds; and out of fragments full of imperfection, and betraying that imperfection in every touch, indulgently raise up a stately and unaccusable whole.

Inferior, imperfect, betrayal, indulgence: these are strange terms to use to describe what is admirable (or, as Ruskin says, "unaccusable") in a work of art. As you reread the chapter, ask yourself what these terms come to represent in the essay. How, that is, does Ruskin use these terms in his argument, and what is required of a reader who is willing to follow it? What metaphors does he develop for the "healthy" life and "good" work, and, finally, what does a reader have to do to keep up with him, to keep believing that good work must be imperfect?

### ASSIGNMENTS FOR WRITING

1. On page 532, Ruskin offers three general rules we can use to ensure that we buy only products created through "healthy and ennobling labour." As you think of the things that are yours, particularly those that are important to you, what would you have to give up, or what changes would you have to make in your patterns of consumption, to follow Ruskin's guidelines? In an essay, describe these changes, explain why you would have to make them, and go on, then, to say what you can about the culture and society Ruskin would imagine as ideal in a modern, industrial setting. Would you be willing to live in such a world?

2. At one point in the essay, Ruskin offers two specific challenges to his readers: "And now, reader, look round this English room of yours, about which you have been proud so often, because the work of it was so good and strong, and the ornaments of it so finished"; and "go forth again to gaze upon the old cathedral front, where you have smiled so often at the fantastic ignorance of the old sculptors." Ruskin believed that the perfection of the English room, "if read rightly," was a sign of slavery and degradation, whereas the ugliness and imperfection of the cathedral facade were signs of freedom.

   See if you can extend this challenge to your own immediate surroundings. Look again at something that is part of your local environment—perhaps a building or a room. Look at it for what it says about the life and character of the persons who made it, and for what it says about the culture that values it (or fails to value it). Write an essay in which you explain what you see and how it might be read "rightly." Your job, then, is to extend Ruskin's method of analysis to your world, seen at this point in time. (You should not, however, feel that you have to share Ruskin's conclusions about how things should and should not be made.)

## MAKING CONNECTIONS

1. John Berger, in "Ways of Seeing" (p. 66), says, "The way we see things is affected by what we know or what we believe." He demonstrates this by showing how critics' perceptions of art are affected by their political beliefs; as a result, he says, they indulge in mystification, "the process of explaining away what might otherwise be evident." As you read Berger's essay, pay particular attention to what he says about history and the effects of "mystification" on our understanding of the past.

   What would Berger say about Ruskin's treatment of Gothic architecture? Would he, for example, say that Ruskin mystifies it or demystifies it? What would he choose as examples to test his contention? And how would he establish whether Ruskin was bringing forward or "explaining away" that which is "evident" in a Gothic cathedral? Write an essay in which you discuss Ruskin's treatment of Gothic architecture in the context of Berger's essay, "Ways of Seeing."

   Note: As you work on this essay, you might ask yourself whether Ruskin's political views determined his way of looking at buildings or whether looking at buildings determined his political views. How would you know?

2. Walker Percy, in his essay "The Loss of the Creature" (p. 462), offers several examples of people having difficulty seeing the things around them: tourists at the Grand Canyon, tourists in Mexico, a student at Sarah Lawrence College. And he talks about the various strategies people use to see what would otherwise remain hidden: "standing on the shoulders of others," getting off the beaten track, apprenticing themselves to a master, "dialectical savorings of the familiar."

   Write an essay in which you examine Ruskin through Percy's eyes. What would Percy notice in what Ruskin says and does? What strategy has Ruskin developed to recover what was lost or hidden? Which of Percy's examples does Ruskin most resemble? And, finally, what would Percy see as the limits and possibilities of Ruskin's work?

   Note: You might consider writing this essay in Percy's style—telling Ruskin's story, that is, as Percy might tell it.

# GLORIA
# STEINEM

*G* LORIA STEINEM, *one of the leading figures of the contemporary women's*
*movement, is the granddaughter of Pauline Steinem, who was president of*
*a women's suffrage group and representative to the 1908 International Council of*
*Women. Steinem dates her own involvement in feminism from a 1968 Redstockings*
*meeting she attended to gather material on the group for her column in* New York
*magazine. She has since become one of the most admired, and most controversial,*
*women of our time.*

*Steinem was born in 1934 in Toledo, Ohio. After graduating magna cum laude*
*from Smith College in 1956, Steinem served as Chester Bowles Asian Fellow at the*
*University of Delhi and the University of Calcutta, India; from 1956 to 1958. She*
*later became a writer for "That Was the Week That Was" (a weekly television show*
*of political satire), and a member of the National Women's Political Caucus, the*
*Women's Action Alliance, and the Student Non-Violent Coordinating Committee.*
*She was the founding editor of* Ms. *magazine and has worked as a writer since*
*1961, publishing articles in* Esquire, Vogue, Life, Cosmopolitan, Glamour, *and*
New York *magazines. She has also written three books, the most recent of which*
*is* Marilyn (1986). *"Ruth's Song" was drawn from her collection of essays,* Out-

rageous Acts and Everyday Rebellions *(1983). Part of the strength of her crit-icism of contemporary life is her fair yet passionate assessment of people and issues. In "Ruth's Song," however, Steinem turns from contemporary life to her own life; she writes about her mother and their relationship. The essay's remarkable achieve-ment lies in the balance of passion and clarity Steinem maintains while sorting through difficult memories.*

# Ruth's Song (Because She Could Not Sing It)

Happy or unhappy, families are all mysterious. We have only to imag-ine how differently we would be described—and will be, after our deaths—by each of the family members who believe they know us. The only ques-tion is, Why are some mysteries more important than others?

The fate of my Uncle Ed was a mystery of importance in our family. We lavished years of speculation on his transformation from a brilliant young electrical engineer to the town handyman. What could have changed this elegant, Lincolnesque student voted "Best Dressed" by his classmates to the gaunt, unshaven man I remember? Why did he leave a young son and a first wife of the "proper" class and religion, marry a much less educated woman of the "wrong" religion, and raise a second family in a house near an abandoned airstrip; a house whose walls were patched with metal signs to stop the wind? Why did he never talk about his trans-formation?

For years, I assumed that some secret and dramatic events of a year he spent in Alaska had made the difference. Then I discovered that the trip had come after his change and probably been made because of it. Strangers he worked for as a much-loved handyman talked about him as one more tragedy of the Depression, and it was true that Uncle Ed's father, my pa-ternal grandfather, had lost his money in the stockmarket Crash and died of (depending on who was telling the story) pneumonia or a broken heart. But the Crash of 1929 also had come long after Uncle Ed's transformation. Another theory was that he was afflicted with a mental problem that lasted most of his life, yet he was supremely competent at his work, led an in-dependent life, and asked for help from no one.

Perhaps he had fallen under the spell of a radical professor in the early days of the century, the height of this country's romance with socialism and anarchism. That was the theory of another uncle on my mother's side. I do remember that no matter how much Uncle Ed needed money, he would charge no more for his work than materials plus 10 percent, and I never saw him in anything other than ancient boots and overalls held up with strategic safety pins. Was he really trying to replace socialism-in-one-country with socialism-in-one-man? If so, why did my grandmother, a woman who herself had run for the school board in coalition with anarchists and socialists, mistrust his judgment so much that she left his share of her estate in trust, even though he was over fifty when she died? And why did Uncle Ed seem uninterested in all other political words and acts? Was it true instead that, as another relative insisted, Uncle Ed had chosen poverty to disprove the myths of Jews and money?

Years after my uncle's death, I asked a son in his second family if he had the key to this family mystery. No, he said. He had never known his father any other way. For that cousin, there had been no question. For the rest of us, there was to be no answer.

For many years I also never imagined my mother any way other than the person she had become before I was born. She was just a fact of life when I was growing up; someone to be worried about and cared for; an invalid who lay in bed with eyes closed and lips moving in occasional response to voices only she could hear; a woman to whom I brought an endless stream of toast and coffee, bologna sandwiches and dime pies, in a child's version of what meals should be. She was a loving, intelligent, terrorized woman who tried hard to clean our littered house whenever she emerged from her private world, but who could rarely be counted on to finish one task. In many ways, our roles were reversed: I was the mother and she was the child. Yet that didn't help her, for she still worried about me with all the intensity of a frightened mother, plus the special fears of her own world full of threats and hostile voices.

Even then I suppose I must have known that, years before she was thirty-five and I was born, she had been a spirited adventurous young woman who struggled out of a working-class family and into college, who found work she loved and continued to do, even after she was married and my older sister was there to be cared for. Certainly, our immediate family and nearby relatives, of whom I was by far the youngest, must have remembered her life as a whole and functioning person. She was thirty before she gave up her own career to help my father run the Michigan summer resort that was the most practical of his many dreams, and she worked hard there as everything from bookkeeper to bar manager. The family must have watched this energetic, fun-loving, book-loving woman turn into someone who was afraid to be alone, who could not hang on to reality long enough to hold a job, and who could rarely concentrate enough to read a book.

Yet I don't remember any family speculation about the mystery of my mother's transformation. To the kind ones and those who liked her, this new Ruth was simply a sad event, perhaps a mental case, a family problem to be accepted and cared for until some natural process made her better. To the less kind or those who had resented her earlier independence, she was a willful failure, someone who lived in a filthy house, a woman who simply would not pull herself together.

Unlike the case of my Uncle Ed, exterior events were never suggested as reason enough for her problems. Giving up her own career was never cited as her personal parallel of the Depression. (Nor was there discussion of the Depression itself, though my mother, like millions of others, had made potato soup and cut up blankets to make my sister's winter clothes.) Her fears of dependence and poverty were no match for my uncle's possible political beliefs. The real influence of newspaper editors who had praised her reporting was not taken as seriously as the possible influence of one radical professor.

Even the explanation of mental illness seemed to contain more personal fault when applied to my mother. She had suffered her first "nervous breakdown," as she and everyone else called it, before I was born and when my sister was about five. It followed years of trying to take care of a baby, be the wife of a kind but financially irresponsible man with show-business dreams, and still keep her much-loved job as reporter and newspaper editor. After many months in a sanatorium, she was pronounced recovered. That is, she was able to take care of my sister again, to move away from the city and the job she loved, and to work with my father at the isolated rural lake in Michigan he was trying to transform into a resort worthy of the big dance bands of the 1930s.

But she was never again completely without the spells of depression, anxiety, and visions into some other world that eventually were to turn her into the nonperson I remember. And she was never again without a bottle of dark, acrid-smelling liquid she called "Doc Howard's medicine": a solution of chloral hydrate that I later learned was the main ingredient of "Mickey Finns" or "knockout drops," and that probably made my mother and her doctor the pioneers of modern tranquilizers. Though friends and relatives saw this medicine as one more evidence of weakness and indulgence, to me it always seemed an embarrassing but necessary evil. It slurred her speech and slowed her coordination, making our neighbors and my school friends believe she was a drunk. But without it, she would not sleep for days, even a week at a time, and her feverish eyes began to see only that private world in which wars and hostile voices threatened the people she loved.

Because my parents had divorced and my sister was working in a far-away city, my mother and I were alone together then, living off the meager fixed income that my mother got from leasing her share of the remaining land in Michigan. I remember a long Thanksgiving weekend spent hanging on to her with one hand and holding my eighth-grade assignment of *Tale of Two Cities* in the other, because the war outside our house was so real to my mother that she had plunged her hand through a window, badly cutting her arm in an effort to help us escape. Only when she finally agreed to swallow the medicine could she sleep, and only then could I end the terrible calm that comes with crisis and admit to myself how afraid I had been.

No wonder that no relative in my memory challenged the doctor who prescribed this medicine, asked if some of her suffering and hallucinating might be due to overdose or withdrawal, or even consulted another doctor about its use. It was our relief as well as hers.

But why was she never returned even to that first sanatorium? Or to help that might come from other doctors? It's hard to say. Partly, it was her own fear of returning. Partly, it was too little money, and a family's not-unusual assumption that mental illness is an inevitable part of someone's personality. Or perhaps other family members had feared something like my experience when, one hot and desperate summer between the sixth and seventh grade, I finally persuaded her to let me take her to the only doctor from those sanatorium days whom she remembered without fear.

Yes, this brusque old man told me after talking to my abstracted, timid mother for twenty minutes: She definitely belongs in a state hospital. I should put her there right away. But even at that age, *Life* magazine and newspaper exposés had told me what horrors went on inside those hospitals. Assuming there to be no other alternative, I took her home and never tried again.

In retrospect, perhaps the biggest reason my mother was cared for but not helped for twenty years was the simplest: her functioning was not that necessary to the world. Like women alcoholics who drink in their kitchens while costly programs are constructed for executives who drink, or like the homemakers subdued with tranquilizers while male patients get therapy and personal attention instead, my mother was not an important worker. She was not even the caretaker of a very young child, as she had been when she was hospitalized the first time. My father had patiently brought home the groceries and kept our odd household going until I was eight or so and my sister went away to college. Two years later when wartime gas rationing closed his summer resort and he had to travel to buy and sell in summer as well as winter, he said: How can I travel and take care of your mother? How can I make a living? He was right. It was impossible to do both. I did not blame him for leaving once I was old enough to be the bringer of meals and answerer of my mother's questions. ("Has your sister been killed in a car crash?" "Are there German soldiers outside?") I replaced my father, my mother was left with one more way of maintaining a sad status quo, and the world went on undisturbed.

That's why our lives, my mother's from forty-six to fifty-three, and my own from ten to seventeen, were spent alone together. There was one sane winter in a house we rented to be near my sister's college in Massachusetts, then one bad summer spent house-sitting in suburbia while my mother hallucinated and my sister struggled to hold down a summer job in New York. But the rest of those years were lived in Toledo where both my mother and father had been born, and on whose city newspapers an earlier Ruth had worked.

First we moved into a basement apartment in a good neighborhood. In those rooms behind a furnace, I made one last stab at being a child. By pretending to be much sicker with a cold than I really was, I hoped my mother would suddenly turn into a sane and cheerful woman bringing me chicken soup à la Hollywood. Of course, she could not. It only made her feel worse that she could not. I stopped pretending.

But for most of those years, we lived in the upstairs of the house my mother had grown up in and her parents left her—a deteriorating farm house engulfed by the city, with poor but newer houses stacked against it and a major highway a few feet from its sagging front porch. For a while, we could rent the two downstairs apartments to a newlywed factory worker and a local butcher's family. Then the health department condemned our ancient furnace for the final time, sealing it so tight that even my resourceful Uncle Ed couldn't produce illegal heat.

In that house, I remember:

. . . lying in the bed my mother and I shared for warmth, listening on the early morning radio to the royal wedding of Princess Elizabeth and Prince Philip being broadcast live, while we tried to ignore and thus protect each other from the unmistakable sounds of the factory worker downstairs beating up and locking out his pregnant wife.

. . . hanging paper drapes I had bought in the dime store; stacking books and papers in the shape of two armchairs and covering them with blankets; evolving my own dishwashing system (I waited until all the dishes were dirty, then put them in the bathtub); and listening to my mother's high praise for these housekeeping efforts to bring order from chaos, though in retrospect I think they probably depressed her further.

. . . coming back from one of the Eagles' Club shows where I and other veterans of a local tap-dancing school made ten dollars a night for two shows, and finding my mother waiting with a flashlight and no coat in the dark cold of the bus stop, worried about my safety walking home.

. . . in a good period, when my mother's native adventurousness came through, answering a classified ad together for an amateur acting troupe that performed Biblical dramas in churches, and doing several very corny performances of *Noah's Ark* while my proud mother shook metal sheets backstage to make thunder.

. . . on a hot summer night, being bitten by one of the rats that shared our house and its back alley. It was a terrifying night that turned into a touching one when my mother, summoning courage from some unknown reservoir of love, became a calm, comforting parent who took me to a hospital emergency room despite her terror at leaving home.

. . . coming home from a local library with the three books a week into which I regularly escaped, and discovering that for once there was no need to escape. My mother was calmly planting hollyhocks in the vacant lot next door.

But there were also times when she woke in the early winter dark, too frightened and disoriented to remember that I was at my usual after-school job, and so called the police to find me. Humiliated in front of my friends by sirens and policemen, I would yell at her—and she would bow her head in fear and say "I'm sorry, I'm sorry, I'm sorry," just as she had done so often when my otherwise-kindhearted father had yelled at her in frustration. Perhaps the worst thing about suffering is that it finally hardens the hearts of those around it.

And there were many, many times when I badgered her until her shaking hands had written a small check to cash at the corner grocery and I could leave her alone while I escaped to the comfort of well-heated dime stores that smelled of fresh doughnuts, or to air-conditioned Saturday-afternoon movies that were windows on a very different world.

But my ultimate protection was this: I was just passing through, a guest in the house; perhaps this wasn't my mother at all. Though I knew very well that I was her daughter, I sometimes imagined that I had been adopted and that my real parents would find me, a fantasy I've since discovered is common. (If children wrote more and grownups less, being adopted might be seen not only as a fear but also as a hope.) Certainly, I didn't mourn the wasted life of this woman who was scarcely older than I am now. I worried only about the times when she got worse.

Pity takes distance and a certainty of surviving. It was only after our house was bought for demolition by the church next door, and after my sister had performed the miracle of persuading my father to give me a carefree time before college by taking my mother with him to California for a year, that I could afford to think about the sadness of her life. Suddenly, I was far away in Washington, living with my sister and sharing a house with several of her friends. While I finished high school and discovered to my surprise that my classmates felt sorry for me because my mother *wasn't* there, I also realized that my sister, at least in her early childhood, had known a very different person who lived inside our mother, an earlier Ruth.

She was a woman I met for the first time in a mental hospital near Baltimore, a humane place with gardens and trees where I visited her each weekend of the summer after my first year away in college. Fortunately, my sister hadn't been able to work and be our mother's caretaker, too. After my father's year was up, my sister had carefully researched hospitals and found the courage to break the family chain.

At first, this Ruth was the same abstracted, frightened woman I had lived with all those years, though now all the sadder for being approached through long hospital corridors and many locked doors. But gradually she began to talk about her past life, memories that doctors there must have been awakening. I began to meet a Ruth I had never known.

. . . A tall, spirited, auburn-haired high-school girl who loved basketball and reading; who tried to drive her uncle's Stanley Steamer when it was the first car in the neighborhood; who had a gift for gardening and who sometimes, in defiance of convention, wore her father's overalls; a girl with the courage to go to dances even though her church told her that music itself was sinful, and whose sense of adventure almost made up for feeling gawky and unpretty next to her daintier, dark-haired sister.

. . . A very little girl, just learning to walk, discovering the body places where touching was pleasurable, and being punished by her mother who slapped her hard across the kitchen floor.

. . . A daughter of a handsome railroad-engineer and a schoolteacher who felt she had married "beneath her"; the mother who took her two daughters on Christmas trips to faraway New York on an engineer's free railroad pass and showed them the restaurants and theaters they should aspire to—even though they could only stand outside them in the snow.

. . . A good student at Oberlin College, whose freethinking traditions she loved, where friends nicknamed her "Billy"; a student with a talent for both mathematics and poetry, who was not above putting an invisible film of Karo syrup on all the john seats in her dormitory the night of a big prom; a daughter who had to return to Toledo, live with her family, and go to a local university when her ambitious mother—who had scrimped and saved, ghostwritten a minister's sermons, and made her daughters' clothes in order to get them to college at all—ran out of money. At home, this Ruth became a part-time bookkeeper in a lingerie shop for the very rich, commuting to classes and listening to her mother's harsh lectures on the security of becoming a teacher; but also a young woman who was still rebellious enough to fall in love with my father, the editor of her university newspaper, a funny and charming young man who was a terrible student, had no intention of graduating, put on all the campus dances, and was unacceptably Jewish.

I knew from family lore that my mother had married my father twice: once secretly, after he invited her to become the literary editor of his campus newspaper, and once a year later in a public ceremony, which some members of both families refused to attend as the "mixed marriage" of its day.

And I knew that my mother had gone on to earn a teaching certificate. She had used it to scare away truant officers during the winters when, after my father closed the summer resort for the season, we lived in a house trailer and worked our way to Florida or California and back by buying and selling antiques.

But only during those increasingly adventurous weekend outings from the hospital—going shopping, to lunch, to the movies—did I realize that she had taught college calculus for a year in deference to her mother's insistence that she have teaching "to fall back on." And only then did I realize she had fallen in love with newspapers along with my father. After graduating from the university paper, she wrote a gossip column for a local tabloid, under the name "Duncan MacKenzie," since women weren't supposed to do such things, and soon had earned a job as society reporter on one of Toledo's two big dailies. By the time my sister was four or so, she had worked her way up to the coveted position of Sunday editor.

It was a strange experience to look into those brown eyes I had seen so often and realize suddenly how much they were like my own. For the first time, I realized that she might really be my mother.

I began to think about the many pressures that might have led up to that first nervous breakdown: leaving my sister who she loved very much with a grandmother whose values my mother didn't share; trying to hold on to a job she loved but was being asked to leave by her husband; wanting very much to go with a woman friend to pursue their own dreams in New York; falling in love with a co-worker at the newspaper who frightened her by being more sexually attractive, more supportive of her work than my father, and perhaps the man she should have married; and finally, nearly bleeding to death with a miscarriage because her own mother had little faith in doctors and refused to get help.

Did those months in the sanatorium brainwash her in some Freudian or very traditional way into making what were, for her, probably the wrong choices? I don't know. It almost doesn't matter. Without extraordinary support to the contrary, she was already convinced that divorce was unthinkable. A husband could not be left for another man, and certainly not for a reason as selfish as a career. A daughter could not be deprived of her father and certainly not be uprooted and taken off to an uncertain future in New

York. A bride was supposed to be virginal (not "shop-worn," as my euphemistic mother would have said), and if your husband turned out to be kind, but innocent of the possibility of a woman's pleasure, then just be thankful for kindness.

Of course, other women have torn themselves away from work and love and still survived. But a story my mother told me years later has always symbolized for me the formidable forces arrayed against her.

> It was early spring, nothing was open yet. There was nobody for miles around. We had stayed at the lake that winter, so I was alone a lot while your father took the car and traveled around on business. You were a baby. Your sister was in school, and there was no phone. The last straw was that the radio broke. Suddenly it seemed like forever since I'd been able to talk with anyone—or even hear the sound of another voice.
>
> I bundled you up, took the dog, and walked out to the Brooklyn road. I thought I'd walk the four or five miles to the grocery store, talk to some people, and find somebody to drive me back. I was walking along with Fritzie running up ahead in the empty road—when suddenly a car came out of nowhere and down the hill. It hit Fritzie head on and threw him over to the side of the road. I yelled and screamed at the driver, but he never slowed down. He never looked at us. He never even turned his head.
>
> Poor Fritzie was all broken and bleeding, but he was still alive. I carried him and sat down in the middle of the road, with his head cradled in my arms. I was going to *make* the next car stop and help.
>
> But no car ever came. I sat there for hours, I don't know how long, with you in my lap and holding Fritzie, who was whimpering and looking up at me for help. It was dark by the time he finally died. I pulled him over to the side of the road and walked back home with you and washed the blood out of my clothes.
>
> I don't know what it was about that one day—it was like a breaking point. When your father came home, I said: "From now on, I'm going with you. I won't bother you. I'll just sit in the car. But I can't bear to be alone again."

I think she told me that story to show she had tried to save herself, or perhaps she wanted to exorcise a painful memory by saying it out loud. But hearing it made me understand what could have turned her into the woman I remember: a solitary figure sitting in the car, perspiring through the summer, bundled up in winter, waiting for my father to come out of this or that antique shop, grateful just not to be alone. I was there, too, because I was too young to be left at home, and I loved helping my father wrap and unwrap the newspaper around the china and small objects he had bought at auctions and was selling to dealers. It made me feel necessary and grown-up. But sometimes it was hours before we came back to the car again and to my mother who was always patiently, silently waiting.

At the hospital and later when Ruth told me stories of her past, I used to say, "But why didn't you leave? Why didn't you take the job? Why didn't you marry the other man?" She would always insist it didn't matter, she was lucky to have my sister and me. If I pressed hard enough, she would add, "If I'd left you never would have been born."

I always thought but never had the courage to say: *But you might have been born instead.*

I'd like to tell you that this story has a happy ending. The best I can do is one that is happier than its beginning.

After many months in that Baltimore hospital, my mother lived on her own in a small apartment for two years while I was in college and my sister married and lived nearby. When she felt the old terrors coming back, she returned to the hospital at her own request. She was approaching sixty by the time she emerged from there and from a Quaker farm that served as a halfway house, but she confounded her psychiatrists' predictions that she would be able to live outside for shorter and shorter periods. In fact, she never returned. She lived more than another twenty years, and for six of them, she was well enough to stay in a rooming house that provided both privacy and company. Even after my sister and her husband moved to a larger house and generously made two rooms into an apartment for her, she continued to have some independent life and many friends. She worked part-time as a "salesgirl" in a china shop; went away with me on yearly vacations and took one trip to Europe with relatives; went to women's club meetings; found a multiracial church that she loved; took meditation courses; and enjoyed many books. She still could not bear to see a sad movie, to stay alone with any of her six grandchildren while they were babies, to live without many tranquilizers, or to talk about those bad years in Toledo. The old terrors were still in the back of her mind, and each day was a fight to keep them down.

It was the length of her illness that had made doctors pessimistic. In fact, they could not identify any serious mental problem and diagnosed her only as having "an anxiety neurosis": low self-esteem, a fear of being dependent, a terror of being alone, a constant worry about money. She also had spells of what now would be called agoraphobia, a problem almost entirely confined to dependent women: fear of going outside the house, and incapacitating anxiety attacks in unfamiliar or public places.

Would you say, I asked one of her doctors, that her spirit had been broken? "I guess that's as good a diagnosis as any," he said. "And it's hard to mend anything that's been broken for twenty years."

But once out of the hospital for good, she continued to show flashes of the different woman inside; one with a wry kind of humor, a sense of adventure, and a love of learning. Books on math, physics, and mysticism occupied a lot of her time. ("Religion," she used to say firmly, "begins in the laboratory.") When she visited me in New York during her sixties and seventies, she always told taxi drivers that she was eighty years old ("so they will tell me how young I look"), and convinced theater ticket sellers that she was deaf long before she really was ("so they'll give us seats in the front row"). She made friends easily, with the vulnerability and charm of a person who feels entirely dependent on the approval of others. After one of her visits, every shopkeeper within blocks of my apartment would say, "Oh yes, I know your mother!" At home, she complained that people her own age were too old and stodgy for her. Many of her friends were far younger than she. It was as if she were making up for her own lost years.

She was also overly appreciative of any presents given to her—and that made giving them irresistible. I loved to send her clothes, jewelry, exotic soaps, and additions to her collection of tarot cards. She loved receiving them, though we both knew they would end up stored in boxes and drawers. She carried on a correspondence in German with our European relatives, and exchanges with many other friends, all written in her painfully slow, shaky handwriting. She also loved giving gifts. Even as she worried about money and figured out how to save pennies, she would buy or make carefully chosen presents for grandchildren and friends.

Part of the price she paid for this much health was forgetting. A single reminder of those bad years in Toledo was enough to plunge her into days of depression. There were times when this fact created loneliness for me, too. Only two of us had lived most of my childhood. Now, only one of us remembered. But there were also times in later years when, no matter how much I pled with reporters *not* to interview our friends and neighbors in Toledo, *not* to say that my mother had been hospitalized, they published things that hurt her very much and sent her into a downhill slide.

On the other hand, she was also her mother's daughter, a person with a certain amount of social pride and pretension, and some of her objections had less to do with depression than false pride. She complained bitterly about one report that we had lived in a house trailer. She finally asked angrily: "Couldn't they at least say 'vacation mobile home'?" Divorce was still a shame to her. She might cheerfully tell friends, "I don't know *why*

Gloria says her father and I were divorced—we never were." I think she justified this to herself with the idea that they had gone through two marriage ceremonies, one in secret and one in public, but been divorced only once. In fact, they were definitely divorced, and my father had briefly married someone else.

She was very proud of my being a published writer, and we generally shared the same values. After her death, I found a mother-daughter morals quiz I once had written for a women's magazine. In her unmistakably shaky writing, she had recorded her own answers, her entirely accurate imagination of what my answers would be, and a score that concluded our differences were less than those "normal for women separated by twenty-odd years." Nonetheless, she was quite capable of putting a made-up name on her name tag when going to a conservative women's club where she feared our shared identity would bring controversy or even just questions. When I finally got up the nerve to tell her I was signing a 1972 petition of women who publicly said we had had abortions and were demanding the repeal of laws that made them illegal and dangerous, her only reply was sharp and aimed to hurt back. "Every starlet says she's had an abortion," she said. "It's just a way of getting publicity." I knew she agreed that abortion should be a legal choice, but I also knew she would never forgive me for embarrassing her in public.

In fact, her anger and a fairly imaginative ability to wound with words increased in her last years when she was most dependent, most focused on herself, and most likely to need the total attention of others. When my sister made a courageous decision to go to law school at the age of fifty, leaving my mother in a house that not only had many loving teenage grandchildren in it but a kindly older woman as a paid companion besides, my mother reduced her to frequent tears by insisting that this was a family with no love in it, no home-cooked food in the refrigerator; not a real family at all. Since arguments about home cooking wouldn't work on me, my punishment was creative and different. She was going to call up *The New York Times,* she said, and tell them that this was what feminism did: it left old sick women all alone.

Some of this bitterness brought on by failing faculties was eventually solved by a nursing home near my sister's house where my mother not only got the twenty-four-hour help her weakening body demanded, but the attention of affectionate nurses besides. She charmed them, they loved her, and she could still get out for an occasional family wedding. If I ever had any doubts about the debt we owe to nurses, those last months laid them to rest.

When my mother died just before her eighty-second birthday in a hospital room where my sister and I were alternating the hours in which her heart wound slowly down to its last sounds, we were alone together for a few hours while my sister slept. My mother seemed bewildered by her surroundings and the tubes that invaded her body, but her consciousness cleared long enough for her to say: "I want to go home. Please take me home." Lying to her one last time, I said I would. "Okay, honey," she said. "I trust you." Those were her last understandable words.

The nurses let my sister and me stay in the room long after there was no more breath. She had asked us to do that. One of her many fears came from a story she had been told as a child about a man whose coma was mistaken for death. She also had made out a living will requesting that no extraordinary measures be used to keep her alive, and that her ashes be sprinkled in the same stream as my father's.

Her memorial service was in the Episcopalian church that she loved because it fed the poor, let the homeless sleep in its pews, had members of almost every race, and had been sued by the Episcopalian hierarchy for having a woman priest. Most of all, she loved the affection with which its members had welcomed her, visited her at home, and driven her to services. I think she would have liked the Quaker-style informality with which people rose to tell their memories of her. I know she would have loved the presence of many friends. It was to this church that she had donated some of her remaining Michigan property in the hope that it could be used as a multiracial camp, thus getting even with those people in the tiny nearby town who had snubbed my father for being Jewish.

I think she also would have been pleased with her obituary. It emphasized her brief career as one of the early women journalists and asked for donations to Oberlin's scholarship fund so others could go to this college she loved so much but had to leave.

I know I will spend the next years figuring out what her life has left in me.

I realize that I've always been more touched by old people than by children. It's the talent and hopes locked up in a failing body that gets to me; a poignant contrast that reminds me of my mother, even when she was strong.

I've always been drawn to any story of a mother and a daughter on their own in the world. I saw *A Taste of Honey* several times as both a play and a film, and never stopped feeling it. Even *Gypsy* I saw over and over again, sneaking in backstage for the musical and going to the movies as well. I told myself that I was learning the tap-dance routines, but actually my eyes were full of tears.

I once fell in love with a man only because we both belonged to that large and secret club of children who had "crazy mothers." We traded stories of the shameful houses to which we could never invite our friends.

Before he was born, his mother had gone to jail for her pacifist convictions. Then she married the politically ambitious young lawyer who had defended her, stayed home and raised many sons. I fell out of love when he confessed that he wished I wouldn't smoke or swear, and he hoped I wouldn't go on working. His mother's plight had taught him self-pity—nothing else.

I'm no longer obsessed, as I was for many years, with the fear that I would end up in a house like that one in Toledo. Now, I'm obsessed instead with the things I could have done for my mother while she was alive, or the things I should have said.

I still don't understand why so many, many years passed before I saw my mother as a person and before I understood that many of the forces in her life are patterns women share. Like a lot of daughters, I suppose I couldn't afford to admit that what had happened to my mother was not all personal or accidental, and therefore could happen to me.

One mystery has finally cleared. I could never understand why my mother hadn't been helped by Pauline, her mother-in-law; a woman she seemed to love more than her own mother. This paternal grandmother had died when I was five, before my mother's real problems began but long after that "nervous breakdown," and I knew Pauline was once a suffragist who addressed Congress, marched for the vote, and was the first woman member of a school board in Ohio. She must have been a courageous and independent woman, yet I could find no evidence in my mother's reminiscences that Pauline had encouraged or helped my mother toward a life of her own.

I finally realized that my grandmother never changed the politics of her own life, either. She was a feminist who kept a neat house for a husband and four antifeminist sons, a vegetarian among five male meat eaters, and a woman who felt so strongly about the dangers of alcohol that she used only paste vanilla; yet she served both meat and wine to the men of the house and made sure their lives and comforts were continued undisturbed. After the vote was won, Pauline seems to have stopped all feminist activity. My mother greatly admired the fact that her mother-in-law kept a spotless house and prepared a week's meals at a time. Whatever her own internal torments, Pauline was to my mother a woman who seemed able to "do it all." "Whither thou goest, I shall go," my mother used to say to her much-loved mother-in-law, quoting the Ruth of the Bible. In the end, her mother-in-law may have added to my mother's burdens of guilt.

Perhaps like many later suffragists, my grandmother was a public feminist and a private isolationist. That may have been heroic in itself, the most she could be expected to do, but the vote and a legal right to work were not the only kind of help my mother needed.

The world still missed a unique person named Ruth. Though she longed to live in New York and in Europe, she became a woman who was afraid to take a bus across town. Though she drove the first Stanley Steamer, she married a man who never let her drive.

I can only guess what she might have become. The clues are in moments of spirit or humor.

After all the years of fear, she still came to Oberlin with me when I was giving a speech there. She remembered everything about its history as the first college to admit blacks and the first to admit women, and responded to students with the dignity of a professor, the accuracy of a journalist, and a charm that was all her own.

When she could still make trips to Washington's wealth of libraries, she became an expert genealogist, delighting especially in finding the rogues and rebels in our family tree.

Just before I was born, when she had cooked one more enormous meal for all the members of some famous dance band at my father's resort and they failed to clean their plates, she had taken a shotgun down from the kitchen wall and held it over their frightened heads until they had finished the last crumb of strawberry shortcake. Only then did she tell them the gun wasn't loaded. It was a story she told with great satisfaction.

Though sex was a subject she couldn't discuss directly, she had a great appreciation of sensuous men. When a friend I brought home tried to talk to her about cooking, she was furious. ("He came out in the kitchen and talked to me about *stew!*") But she forgave him when we went swimming. She whispered, "He has wonderful legs!"

On her seventy-fifth birthday, she played softball with her grandsons on the beach, and took pride in hitting home runs into the ocean.

Even in the last year of her life, when my sister took her to visit a neighbor's new and luxurious house, she looked at the vertical stripes of a very abstract painting in the hallway and said, tartly, "Is that the price code?"

She worried terribly about being socially accepted herself, but she never withheld her own approval for the wrong reasons. Poverty or style or lack of education couldn't stand between her and a new friend. Though she lived in a mostly white society and worried if I went out with a man of the "wrong" race, just as she had once married a man of the "wrong" religion, she always accepted each person as an individual.

"Is he *very* dark?" she once asked worriedly about a friend. But when she met this very dark person, she only said afterward, "What a kind and nice man!"

My father was the Jewish half of the family, yet it was my mother who taught me to have pride in that tradition. It was she who encouraged me to listen to a radio play about a concentration camp when I was little. "You should know that this can happen," she said. Yet she did it just enough to teach, never enough to frighten.

It was she who introduced me to books and a respect for them, to poetry that she knew by heart, and to the idea that you could never criticize someone unless you "walked miles in their shoes."

It was she who sold that Toledo house, the only home she had, with the determination that the money be used to start me in college. She gave both her daughters the encouragement to leave home for four years of independence that she herself had never had.

After her death, my sister and I found a journal she had kept of her one cherished and belated trip to Europe. It was a trip she had described very little when she came home: she always deplored people who talked boringly about their personal travels and showed slides. Nonetheless, she had written a descriptive essay called "Grandma Goes to Europe." She still must have thought of herself as a writer. Yet she showed this long journal to no one.

I miss her, but perhaps no more in death than I did in life. Dying seems less sad than having lived too little. But at least we're now asking questions about all the Ruths and all our family mysteries.

If her song inspires that, I think she would be the first to say: It was worth the singing.

. . . . . . . . . . .

## QUESTIONS FOR A SECOND READING

1. About a third of the way through the essay, Steinem tells a number of stories about her mother. Reread these stories, then ask yourself how each of them represents her mother. What does each story say about her mother's life and Steinem's relationship with her? How did Steinem's image of her mother change from the early set of stories to the later ones?

2. For Steinem, the story about the walk her mother took that ended with the death of her dog represented the "formidable forces" arrayed against her mother. Steinem says that this story shows how her mother tried to save herself. How does it show that? How does Steinem read the incident? What, in other words, does it mean to Steinem?

## ASSIGNMENTS FOR WRITING

1. Late in the essay, Steinem writes:

> I still don't understand why so many, many years passed before
> I saw my mother as a person and before I understood that many of

the forces in her life are patterns women share. Like a lot of daughters, I suppose I couldn't afford to admit that what had happened to my mother was not all personal or accidental, and therefore could happen to me.

Write an essay describing the forces arrayed against Steinem's mother—the forces Steinem regards as responsible for her mother's transformation—and explain how they affected her mother.

2. How was Steinem affected by her mother's life? Reread the stories she tells about her mother and then write an essay explaining how the circumstances they describe seem to have affected Steinem—both then, as a child, and now, as a writer recalling and reshaping the past. Steinem is careful and precise in telling her mother's story, avoiding the temptation for quick summary and happy endings. Be sure to show equal care and precision in telling Steinem's story.

3. Steinem is telling a personal story, and yet she draws on common materials, including all the stories we tell each other about mothers, children and families. She is telling her own story, in other words, but it is not *just* hers alone. She is part of a culture and that culture, in a sense, is writing her story; it wants her to speak in certain ways and, in some cases, to remain silent.

   Reread Steinem's account of her mother and try to mark the places where Steinem is telling a familiar story in a familiar mode, and try to mark those places where she resists or revises the familiar account. You will be reading to try to chart the ways Steinem, as a writer, is working with or against usual, conventional ways of writing.

   When you have completed your preliminary research, write an essay in which you describe Steinem's work as a writer. Look at the ways in which she works with her past and also works with the familiar materials of our culture—familiar phrases and metaphors, familiar stories with familiar characters, settings, and conclusions. As you discuss the ways in which she accepts or revises familiar material, be sure to take time to speculate on why she does what she does. To what degree (or in which cases) would you say that she is consciously making decisions as a writer? To what degree (and where and why) would you say that the choices are not entirely hers?

## MAKING CONNECTIONS

1. Steinem and John Edgar Wideman ("Our Time," p. 596) both tell stories of their mothers' changes. Steinem speaks in terms of the forces arrayed against her mother, and Wideman notices his mother's change when she tells him the story of his brother Robby's friend Garth. Later on Wideman says, "My mother realized her personal unhappiness and grief were inseparable from what was happening *out there*. . . . Garth's death and Robby's troubles were at the center of her new vision."

Write an essay in which you discuss the forces arrayed against both these women, Steinem's mother and Wideman's mother. Steinem introduces the idea of forces arrayed against her mother, and you'll need to discuss these and how Steinem thinks they affected Ruth, but you'll also need to imagine Wideman's understanding of "what was happening *out there*" in Steinem's terms, as forces responsible for his mother's change. How might you explain her transformation and the forces arrayed against her? What can you say about the similarities and differences in these women's transformations? To what would you attribute the similarities and differences?

2. Like Steinem, Richard Rodriguez, in "The Achievement of Desire" (p. 500), and Alice Walker, in "In Search of Our Mothers' Gardens" (p. 584), write about their families and the past. Consider Steinem and Rodriguez or Walker as cases in point, as writers working to recall and reshape (and thereby understand) the past. How are their essays different? How is the writing different? And to what would you attribute these differences?

# JANE

# TOMPKINS

*J ANE TOMPKINS (born in 1940) received her B.A. from Bryn Mawr and completed both an M.A. and a Ph.D. at Yale. She has taught at Temple University and Connecticut College, and is currently a professor of English at Duke University. Her most recent book is* Sensational Designs: The Cultural Work of American Fiction, 1790–1860 *(1985). She is also the editor of* Reader-Response Criticism: From Formalism to Post-Structuralism *(1980).*

*In* Sensational Designs *Tompkins suggests that novels and short stories ought to be studied "not because they manage to escape the limitations of their particular time and place, but because they offer powerful examples of the way a culture thinks about itself, articulating and proposing solutions for the problems that shape a particular historical moment." This perspective leads Tompkins to conclude that the study of literature ought to focus not merely on those texts we call masterpieces but also on the texts of popular or best-selling authors. By studying these popular texts, Tompkins believes we can learn more of the "work" of novels and short stories, the influence they exert over the society in which they have been produced.*

*"Indians" was first published in 1986 in the influential journal of literary criticism* Critical Inquiry. *It is an unusual essay in many ways, not the least of which*

*is the way it turns, as Tompkins's work often does, to anecdote and personal example. This is a surprising essay, perhaps even more surprising to faculty than to undergraduates. It is as though Tompkins was not willing to hide the "limitations of [her] particular time and place," limitations most scholars are more than happy to hide. In fact, Tompkins's selection could be said to take the reader behind the scenes of the respectable drama of academic research, offering a powerful example of how contemporary academic culture thinks about itself, articulating and proposing solutions for the problems that shape its particular historical moment. If individual interpretations are made and not found; if, for that matter, the "truths" of history or the background to American literature is something that is made and not found, then there is every reason to acknowledge the circumstances of their making. And this is what Tompkins does. "Indians" is both a report on Tompkins's research and a reflection on the ways knowledge is produced, defended, and revised in academic life.*

# *"Indians": Textualism, Morality, and the Problem of History*

When I was growing up in New York City, my parents used to take me to an event in Inwood Park at which Indians—real American Indians dressed in feathers and blankets—could be seen and touched by children like me. This event was always a disappointment. It was more fun to imagine that you *were* an Indian in one of the caves in Inwood Park than to shake the hand of an old man in a headdress who was not overwhelmed at the opportunity of meeting you. After staring at the Indians for a while, we would take a walk in the woods where the caves were, and once I asked my mother if the remains of a fire I had seen in one of them might have been left by the original inhabitants. After that, wandering up some stone steps cut into the side of the hill, I imagined I was a princess in a rude castle. My Indians, like my princesses, were creatures totally of the imagination, and I did not care to have any real exemplars interfering with what I already knew.

I already knew about Indians from having read about them in school. Over and over we were told the story of how Peter Minuit had bought Manhattan Island from the Indians for twenty-four dollars' worth of glass beads. And it was a story we didn't mind hearing because it gave us the rare pleasure of having someone to feel superior to, since the poor Indians had not known (as we eight-year-olds did) how valuable a piece of property Manhattan Island would become. Generally, much was made of the Indian presence in Manhattan; a poem in one of our readers began: "Where we walk to school today / Indian children used to play," and we were encouraged to write poetry on this topic ourselves. So I had a fairly rich relationship with Indians before I ever met the unprepossessing people in Inwood Park. I felt that I had a lot in common with them. They, too, liked animals (they were often named after animals); they, too, made mistakes—they liked the brightly colored trinkets of little value that the white men were always offering them; they were handsome, warlike, and brave and had led an exciting, romantic life in the forest long ago, a life such as I dreamed of leading myself. I felt lucky to be living in one of the places where they had definitely been. Never mind where they were or what they were doing now.

My story stands for the relationship most non-Indians have to the people who first populated this continent, a relationship characterized by narcissistic fantasies of freedom and adventure, of a life lived closer to nature and to spirit than the life we lead now. As Vine Deloria, Jr., has pointed out, the American Indian Movement in the early seventies couldn't get people to pay attention to what was happening to Indians who were alive in the present, so powerful was this country's infatuation with people who wore loincloths, lived in tepees, and roamed the plains and forests long ago. [1] The present essay, like these fantasies, doesn't have much to do with actual Indians, though its subject matter is the histories of European-Indian relations in seventeenth-century New England. In a sense, my encounter with Indians as an adult doing "research" replicates the childhood one, for while I started out to learn about Indians, I ended up preoccupied with a problem of my own.

This essay enacts a particular instance of the challenge poststructuralism poses to the study of history. In simpler language, it concerns the difference that point of view makes when people are giving accounts of events, whether at first or second hand. The problem is that if all accounts of events are determined through and through by the observer's frame of reference, then one will never know, in any given case, what really happened.

I encountered this problem in concrete terms while preparing to teach a course in colonial American literature. I'd set out to learn what I could about the Puritans' relations with American Indians. All I wanted was a general idea of what had happened between the English settlers and the natives in seventeenth-century New England; poststructuralism and its dilemmas were the furthest thing from my mind. I began, more or less automatically, with Perry Miller, who hardly mentions the Indians at all, then proceeded to the work of historians who had dealt exclusively with the

European-Indian encounter. At first, it was a question of deciding which of these authors to believe, for it quickly became apparent that there was no unanimity on the subject. As I read on, however, I discovered that the problem was more complicated than deciding whose version of events was correct. Some of the conflicting accounts were not simply contradictory, they were completely incommensurable, in that their assumptions about what counted as a valid approach to the subject, and what the subject itself was, diverged in fundamental ways. Faced with an array of mutually ir-reconcilable points of view, points of view which determined what was being discussed as well as the terms of the discussion, I decided to turn to primary sources for clarification, only to discover that the primary sources reproduced the problem all over again. I found myself, in other words, in an epistemological quandary, not only unable to decide among conflicting versions of events but also unable to believe that any such de-cision could, in principle, be made. It was a moral quandary as well. Knowledge of what really happened when the Europeans and the Indians first met seemed particularly important, since the result of that encounter was virtual genocide. This was the kind of past "mistake" which, presum-ably, we studied history in order to avoid repeating. If studying history couldn't put us in touch with actual events and their causes, then what was to prevent such atrocities from happening again?

For a while, I remained at this impasse. But through analyzing the proc-ess by which I had reached it, I eventually arrived at an understanding which seemed to offer a way out. This essay records the concrete experi-ence of meeting and solving the difficulty I have just described (as an ab-stract problem, I thought I had solved it long ago). My purpose is not to throw new light on antifoundationalist epistemology—the solution I reached is not a new one—but to dramatize and expose the troubles an-tifoundationalism gets you into when you meet it, so to speak, in the road.

My research began with Perry Miller. Early in the preface to *Errand into the Wilderness,* while explaining how he came to write his history of the New England mind, Miller writes a sentence that stopped me dead. He says that what fascinated him as a young man about his country's history was "the massive narrative of the movement of European culture into the vacant wilderness of America." [2] "Vacant?" Miller, writing in 1956, doesn't pause over the word "vacant," but to people who read his preface thirty years later, the word is shocking. In what circumstances could someone proposing to write a history of colonial New England *not* take account of the Indian presence there?

The rest of Miller's preface supplies an answer to this question, if one takes the trouble to piece together its details. Miller explains that as a young man, jealous of older compatriots who had had the luck to fight in

World War I, he had gone to Africa in search of adventure. "The adventures that Africa afforded," he writes, "were tawdry enough, but it became the setting for a sudden epiphany" (p. vii). "It was given to me," he writes, "disconsolate on the edge of a jungle of central Africa, to have thrust upon me the mission of expounding what I took to be the innermost propulsion of the United States, while supervising, in that barbaric tropic, the unloading of drums of case oil flowing out of the inexhaustible wilderness of America" (p. viii). Miller's picture of himself on the banks of the Congo furnishes a key to the kind of history he will write and to his mental image of a vacant wilderness; it explains why it was just there, under precisely these conditions, that he should have had his epiphany.

The fuel drums stand, in Miller's mind, for the popular misconception of what this country is about. They are "tangible symbols of [America's] appalling power," a power that everyone but Miller takes for the ultimate reality (p. ix). To Miller, "the mind of man is the basic factor in human history," and he will plead, all unaccommodated as he is among the fuel drums, for the intellect—the intellect for which his fellow historians, with their chapters on "stoves or bathtubs, or tax laws," "the Wilmot Proviso" and "the chain store," "have so little respect" (p. viii, ix). His preface seethes with a hatred of the merely physical and mechanical, and this hatred, which is really a form of moral outrage, explains not only the contempt with which he mentions the stoves and bathtubs but also the nature of his experience in Africa and its relationship to the "massive narrative" he will write.

Miller's experiences in Africa are "tawdry," his tropic is barbaric because the jungle he stands on the edge of means nothing to him, no more, indeed something less, than the case oil. It is the nothingness of Africa that precipitates his vision. It is the barbarity of the "dark continent," the obvious (but superficial) parallelism between the jungle at Matadi and America's "vacant wilderness" that releases in Miller the desire to define and vindicate his country's cultural identity. To the young Miller, colonial Africa and colonial America are—but for the history he will bring to light—mirror images of one another. And what he fails to see in the one landscape is the same thing he overlooks in the other: the human beings who people it. As Miller stood with his back to the jungle, thinking about the role of mind in human history, his failure to see that the land into which European culture had moved was not vacant but already occupied by a varied and numerous population, is of a piece with his failure, in his portrait of himself at Matadi, to notice *who* was carrying the fuel drums he was supervising the unloading of.

The point is crucial because it suggests that what is invisible to the historian in his own historical moment remains invisible when he turns his gaze to the past. It isn't that Miller didn't "see" the black men, in a literal sense, any more than it's the case that when he looked back he didn't "see" the Indians, in the sense of not realizing they were there. Rather, it's that neither the Indians nor the blacks *counted* for him, in a fundamental way. The way in which Indians can be seen but not counted is illustrated by an entry in Governor John Winthrop's journal, three hundred years before, when he recorded that there had been a great storm with high winds "yet through God's great mercy it did no hurt, but only killed one Indian with the fall of a tree." [3] The juxtaposition suggests that Miller shared with Winthrop a certain colonial point of view, a point of view from which Indians, though present, do not finally matter.

A book entitled *New England Frontier: Puritans and Indians, 1620–1675*, written by Alden Vaughan and published in 1965, promised to rectify Miller's omission. In the outpouring of work on the European-Indian encounter that began in the early sixties, this book is the first major landmark, and to a neophyte it seems definitive. Vaughan acknowledges the absence of Indian sources and emphasizes his use of materials which catch the Puritans "off guard." [4] His announced conclusion that "the New England Puritans followed a remarkably humane, considerate, and just policy in their dealings with the Indians" seems supported by the scope, documentation, and methodicalness of his project (*NEF*, p. vii). The author's fair-mindedness and equanimity seem everywhere apparent, so that when he asserts "the history of interracial relations from the arrival of the Pilgrims to the outbreak of King Philip's War is a credit to the integrity of both peoples," one is positively reassured (*NEF*, p. viii).

But these impressions do not survive an admission that comes late in the book, when, in the course of explaining why works like Helen Hunt Jackson's *Century of Dishonor* had spread misconceptions about Puritan treatment of the Indians, Vaughan finally lays his own cards on the table.

> The root of the misunderstanding [about Puritans and Indians] . . . lie[s] in a failure to recognize the nature of the two societies that met in seventeenth century New England. One was unified, visionary, disciplined, and dynamic. The other was divided, self-satisfied, undisciplined, and static. It would be unreasonable to expect that such societies could live side by side indefinitely with no penetration of the more fragmented and passive by the more consolidated and active. What resulted, then, was not—as many have held—a clash of dissimilar ways of life, but rather the expansion of one into the areas in which the other was lacking. [*NEF*, p. 323]

From our present vantage point, these remarks seem culturally biased to an incredible degree, not to mention inaccurate: Was Puritan society unified? If so, how does one account for its internal dissensions and obsessive need to cast out deviants? Is "unity" necessarily a positive culture trait? From what standpoint can one say that American Indians were neither disciplined nor visionary, when both these characteristics loom so large in the ethnographies? Is it an accident that ways of describing cultural strength and weakness coincide with gender stereotypes—active/passive, and so on? Why is one culture said to "penetrate" the other? Why is the "other" described in terms of "lack"?

Vaughan's fundamental categories of apprehension and judgment will not withstand even the most cursory inspection. For what looked like even-handedness when he was writing *New England Frontier* does not look that way anymore. In his introduction to *New Directions in American Intellectual History*, John Higham writes that by the end of the sixties

> the entire conceptual foundation on which [this sort of work] rested [had] crumbled away. . . . Simultaneously, in sociology, anthropology, and history, two working assumptions . . . came under withering attack: first, the assumption that societies tend to be integrated, and second, that a shared culture maintains that integration. . . . By the late 1960s all claims issued in the name of an "American mind" . . . were subject to drastic skepticism. [5]

"Clearly," Higham continues, "the sociocultural upheaval of the sixties created the occasion" for this reaction. [6] Vaughan's book, it seemed, could only have been written before the events of the sixties had sensitized scholars to questions of race and ethnicity. It came as no surprise, therefore, that ten years later there appeared a study of European-Indian relations which reflected the new awareness of social issues the sixties had engendered. And it offered an entirely different picture of the European-Indian encounter.

Francis Jennings's *The Invasion of America* (1975) rips wide open the idea that the Puritans were humane and considerate in their dealings with the Indians. In Jennings's account, even more massively documented than Vaughan's, the early settlers lied to the Indians, stole from them, murdered them, scalped them, captured them, tortured them, raped them, sold them into slavery, confiscated their land, destroyed their crops, burned their homes, scattered their possessions, gave them alcohol, undermined their systems of belief, and infected them with diseases that wiped out ninety percent of their numbers within the first hundred years after contact. [7]

Jennings mounts an all-out attack on the essential decency of the Puritan leadership and their apologists in the twentieth century. The Pequot War, which previous historians had described as an attempt on the part of Massachusetts Bay to protect itself from the fiercest of the New England tribes, becomes, in Jennings's painstakingly researched account, a deliberate war of extermination, waged by whites against Indians. It starts with trumped-up charges, is carried on through a series of increasingly bloody reprisals, and ends in the massacre of scores of Indian men, women, and children, all so that Massachusetts Bay could gain political and economic control of the southern Connecticut Valley. When one reads this and then turns over the page and sees a reproduction of the Bay Colony seal, which depicts an Indian from whose mouth issue the words "Come over and help us," the effect is shattering. [8]

But even so powerful an argument as Jennings's did not remain unshaken by subsequent work. Reading on, I discovered that if the events of the sixties had revolutionized the study of European-Indian relations, the events of the seventies produced yet another transformation. The American Indian Movement, and in particular the founding of the Native American Rights Fund in 1971 to finance Indian litigation, and a court decision in 1975 which gave the tribes the right to seek redress for past injustices in federal court, created a climate within which historians began to focus on the Indians themselves. "Almost simultaneously," writes James Axtell, "frontier and colonial historians began to discover the necessity of considering the American natives as real determinants of history and the utility of ethnohistory as a way of ensuring parity of focus and impartiality of judgment." [9] In Miller, Indians had been simply beneath notice; in Vaughan, they belonged to an inferior culture; and in Jennings, they were the more or less innocent prey of power-hungry whites. But in the most original and provocative of the ethnohistories, Calvin Martin's *Keepers of the Game*, Indians became complicated, purposeful human beings, whose lives were spiritually motivated to a high degree. [10] Their relationship to the animals they hunted, to the natural environment, and to the whites with whom they traded became intelligible within a system of beliefs that formed the basis for an entirely new perspective on the European-Indian encounter.

Within the broader question of why European contact had such a devastating effect on the Indians, Martin's specific aim is to determine why Indians participated in the fur trade which ultimately led them to the brink of annihilation. The standard answer to this question had always been that once the Indian was introduced to European guns, copper kettles, woolen blankets, and the like, he literally couldn't keep his hands off them. In order to acquire these coveted items, he decimated the animal populations on which his survival depended. In short, the Indian's motivation in participating in the fur trade was assumed to be the same as the white European's—a desire to accumulate material goods. In direct opposition to this thesis, Martin argues that the reason why Indians ruthlessly exploited their own resources had nothing to do with supply and demand, but stemmed rather from a breakdown of the cosmic worldview that tied them to the game they killed in a spiritual relationship of parity and mutual obligation.

The hunt, according to Martin, was conceived not primarily as a physical activity but as a spiritual quest, in which the spirit of the hunter must overmaster the spirit of the game animal before the kill can take place. The animal, in effect, *allows* itself to be found and killed, once the hunter has mastered its spirit. The hunter prepared himself through rituals of fasting, sweating, or dreaming which revealed the identity of his prey and where he can find it. The physical act of killing is the least important element in the process. Once the animal is killed, eaten, and its parts used for clothing or implements, its remains must be disposed of in ritually prescribed fashion, or the game boss, the "keeper" of that species, will not permit more animals to be killed. The relationship between Indians and animals, then, is contractual; each side must hold up its end of the bargain, or no further transactions can occur.

What happened, according to Martin, was that as a result of diseases introduced into the animal population by Europeans, the game suddenly disappeared, began to act in inexplicable ways, or sickened and died in plain view, and communicated their diseases to the Indians. The Indians, consequently, believed that their compact with the animals had been broken and that the keepers of the game, the tutelary spirits of each animal species whom they had been so careful to propitiate, had betrayed them. And when missionization, wars with the Europeans, and displacement from their tribal lands had further weakened Indian society and its belief structure, the Indians, no longer restrained by religious sanctions, in effect, turned on the animals in a holy war of revenge.

Whether or not Martin's specific claim about the "holy war" was correct, his analysis made it clear to me that, given the Indians' understanding of economic, religious, and physical processes, an Indian account of what transpired when the European settlers arrived here would look nothing like our own. Their (potential, unwritten) history of the conflict could bear only a marginal resemblance to Eurocentric views. I began to think that the key to understanding European-Indian relations was to see them as an encounter between wholly disparate cultures, and that therefore either defending or attacking the colonists was beside the point since, given the cultural disparity between the two groups, conflict was inevitable and in large part a product of mutual misunderstanding.

But three years after Martin's book appeared, Shepard Krech III edited a collection of seven essays called *Indians, Animals, and the Fur Trade*, attacking Martin's entire project. Here the authors argued that we don't need an ideological or religious explanation for the fur trade. As Charles Hudson writes,

> The Southeastern Indians slaughtered deer (and were
> prompted to enslave and kill each other) because of their po-
> sition on the outer fringes of an expanding modern world-
> system. . . . In the modern world-system there is a core re-
> gion which establishes *economic* relations with its colonial
> periphery. . . . If the Indians could not produce commodities,
> they were on the road to cultural extinction. . . . To maximize
> his chances for survival, an eighteenth-century Southeastern
> Indian had to . . . live in the interior, out of range of European
> cattle, forestry, and agriculture. . . . He had to produce a com-
> modity which was valuable enough to earn him some pro-
> tection from English slavers. [11]

Though we are talking here about Southeastern Indians, rather than the
subarctic and Northeastern tribes Martin studied, what really accounts for
these divergent explanations of why Indians slaughtered the game are the
assumptions that underlie them. Martin believes that the Indians acted on
the basis of perceptions made available to them by their own cosmology;
that is, he explains their behavior as the Indians themselves would have
explained it (insofar as he can), using a logic and a set of values that are
not Eurocentric but derived from within Amerindian culture. Hudson, on
the other hand, insists that the Indians' own beliefs are irrelevant to an
explanation of how they acted, which can only be understood, as far as he
is concerned, in the terms of a Western materialist economic and political
analysis. Martin and Hudson, in short, don't agree on what counts as an
explanation, and this disagreement sheds light on the preceding accounts
as well. From this standpoint, we can see that Vaughan, who thought that
the Puritans were superior to the Indians, and Jennings, who thought the
reverse, are both, like Hudson, using Eurocentric criteria of description and
evaluation. While all three critics (Vaughan, Jennings, and Hudson) acknowledge that Indians and Europeans behave differently from one another, the behavior differs, as it were, within the order of the same: all
three assume, though only Hudson makes the assumption explicit, that an
understanding of relations between the Europeans and the Indians must
be elaborated in European terms. In Martin's analysis, however, what we
have are not only two different sets of behavior but two incommensurable
ways of describing and assigning meaning to events. This difference at the
level of explanation calls into question the possibility of obtaining any the-
ory-independent account of interaction between Indians and Europeans.

At this point, dismayed and confused by the wildly divergent views of
colonial history the twentieth-century historians had provided, I decided
to look at some primary materials. I thought, perhaps, if I looked at some
firsthand accounts and at some scholars looking at those accounts, it would
be possible to decide which experts were right and which were wrong by

comparing their views with the evidence. Captivity narratives seemed a good place to begin, since it was logical to suppose that the records left by whites who had been captured by Indians would furnish the sort of first-hand information I wanted.

I began with two fascinating essays based on these materials written by the ethnohistorian James Axtell, "The White Indians of Colonial America" and "The Scholastic Philosophy of the Wilderness." [12] These essays suggest that it would have been a privilege to be captured by North American Indians and taken off to Canada to dwell in a wigwam for the rest of one's life. Axtell's reconstruction of the process by which Indians taught European captives to feel comfortable in the wilderness, first taking their shoes away and giving them moccasins, carrying the children on their backs, sharing the scanty food supply equally, ceremonially cleansing them of their old identities, giving them Indian clothes and jewelry, assiduously teaching them the Indian language, finally adopting them into their families, and even visiting them after many years if, as sometimes happened, they were restored to white society—all of this creates a compelling portrait of Indian culture and helps to explain the extraordinary attraction that Indian culture apparently exercised over Europeans.

But, as I had by now come to expect, this beguiling portrait of the Indians' superior humanity is called into question by other writings on Indian captivity—for example, Norman Heard's *White into Red*, whose summation of the comparative treatment of captive children east and west of the Mississippi seems to contradict some of Axtell's conclusions:

> The treatment of captive children seems to have been similar in initial stages. . . . Most children were treated brutally at the time of capture. Babies and toddlers usually were killed immediately and other small children would be dispatched during the rapid retreat to the Indian villages if they cried, failed to keep the pace, or otherwise indicated a lack of fortitude needed to become a worthy member of the tribe. Upon reaching the village, the child might face such ordeals as running the gauntlet or dancing in the center of a throng of threatening Indians. The prisoner might be so seriously injured at this time that he would no longer be acceptable for adoption. [13]

One account which Heard reprints is particularly arresting. A young girl captured by the Comanches who had not been adopted into a family but used as a slave had been peculiarly mistreated. When they wanted to wake her up the family she belonged to would take a burning brand from the fire and touch it to her nose. When she was returned to her parents, the flesh of her nose was completely burned away, exposing the bone. [14]

Since the pictures drawn by Heard and Axtell were in certain respects irreconcilable, it made sense to turn to a firsthand account to see how the Indians treated their captives in a particular instance. Mary Rowlandson's "The Soveraignty and Goodness of God," published in Boston around 1680, suggested itself because it was so widely read and had set the pattern for later narratives. Rowlandson interprets her captivity as God's punishment on her for failing to keep the Sabbath properly on several occasions. She sees everything that happens to her as a sign from God. When the Indians are kind to her, she attributes her good fortune to divine Providence; when they are cruel, she blames her captors. But beyond the question of how Rowlandson interprets events is the question of what she saw in the first place and what she considered worth reporting. The following passage, with its abrupt shifts of focus and peculiar emphases, makes it hard to see her testimony as evidence of anything other than the Puritan point of view:

> Then my heart began to fail: and I fell weeping, which was the first time to my remembrance, that I wept before them. Although I had met with so much Affliction, and my heart was many times ready to break, yet could I not shed one tear in their sight: but rather had been all this while in a maze, and like one astonished: but not I may say as, Psal. 137.1. *By the Rivers of Babylon, there we sate down; yea, we wept when we remembered Zion.* There one of them asked me, why I wept, I could hardly tell what to say: yet I answered, they would kill me: No, said he, none will hurt you. Then came one of them and gave me two spoon-fulls of Meal to comfort me, and another gave me half a pint of Pease; which was more worth than many Bushels at another time. Then I went to see King Philip, he bade me come in and sit down, and asked me whether I woold smoke it (a usual Complement nowadayes among Saints and Sinners) but this no way suited me. For though I had formerly used Tobacco, yet I had left it ever since I was first taken. It seems to be a Bait, the Devil layes to make men loose their precious time: I remember with shame, how formerly, when I had taken two or three pipes, I was presently ready for another, such a bewitching thing it is: But I thank God, he has now given me power over it; surely there are many who may be better imployed than to ly sucking a stinking Tobacco-pipe. [15]

Anyone who has ever tried to give up smoking has to sympathize with Rowlandson, but it is nonetheless remarkable, first, that a passage which begins with her weeping openly in front of her captors, and comparing herself to Israel in Babylon, should end with her railing against the vice of tobacco; and, second, that it has not a word to say about King Philip, the leader of the Indians who captured her and mastermind of the campaign that devastated the white population of the English colonies. The fact that Rowlandson has just been introduced to the chief of chiefs makes hardly any impression on her at all. What excites her is a moral issue which was being hotly debated in the seventeenth century: to smoke or not to smoke (Puritans frowned on it, apparently, because it wasted time and presented a fire hazard). What seem to us the peculiar emphases in Rowlandson's relation are not the result of her having *screened out* evidence she couldn't handle, but of her way of constructing the world. She saw what her seventeenth-century English Separatist background made visible. It is when one realizes that the biases of twentieth-century historians like Vaughan or Axtell cannot be corrected for simply by consulting the primary materials, since the primary materials are constructed according to *their* authors' biases, that one begins to envy Miller his vision at Matadi. Nor for what he didn't see—the Indian and the black—but for his epistemological confidence.

Since captivity narratives made a poor source of evidence for the nature of European-Indian relations in early New England because they were so relentlessly pietistic, my hope was that a better source of evidence might be writings designed simply to tell Englishmen what the American natives were like. These authors could be presumed to be less severely biased, since they hadn't seen their loved ones killed by Indians or been made to endure the hardships of captivity, and because they weren't writing propaganda calculated to prove that God had delivered his chosen people from the hands of Satan's emissaries.

The problem was that these texts were written with aims no less specific than those of the captivity narratives, though the aims were of a different sort. Here is a passage from William Wood's *New England's Prospect*, published in London in 1634.

> To enter into a serious discourse concerning the natural conditions of these Indians might procure admiration from the people of any civilized nations, in regard of their civility and good natures. . . . These Indians are of affable, courteous and well disposed natures, ready to communicate the best of their wealth to the mutual good of one another; . . . so . . . perspicuous is their love . . . that they are as willing to part with a mite in poverty as treasure in plenty. . . . If it were possible to recount the courtesies they have showed the English, since their first arrival in those parts, it would not only steady belief, that they are a loving people, but also win the

love of those that never saw them, and wipe off that needless
fear that is too deeply rooted in the conceits of many who
think them envious and of such rancorous and inhumane dis-
positions, that they will one day make an end of their English
inmates. [16]

However, in a pamphlet published twenty-one years earlier, Alexander
Whitaker of Virginia has this to say of the natives:

These naked slaves . . . serve the divell for feare, after a most
base manner, sacrificing sometimes (as I have heere heard)
their own Children to him. . . . They live naked in bodie, as
if their shame of their sinne deserved no covering: Their
names are as naked as their bodie: They esteem it a virtue to
lie, deceive and steale as their master the divell teacheth to
them. [17]

According to Robert Berkhofer in *The White Man's Indian*, these divergent reports can be explained by looking at the authors' motives. A favorable report like Wood's, intended to encourage new emigrants to America,
naturally represented Indians as loving and courteous, civilized and generous, in order to allay the fears of prospective colonists. Whitaker, on the
other hand, a minister who wishes to convince his readers that the Indians
are in need of conversion, paints them as benighted agents of the devil.
Berkhofer's commentary constantly implies that white men were to blame
for having represented the Indians in the image of their own desires and
needs. [18] But the evidence supplied by Rowlandson's narrative, and by the
accounts left by early reporters such as Wood and Whitaker, suggest something rather different. Though it is probably true that in certain cases Europeans did consciously tamper with the evidence, in most cases there is
no reason to suppose that they did not record faithfully what they saw.
And what they saw was not an illusion, was not determined by selfish
motives in any narrow sense, but was there by virtue of a *way* of seeing
which they could not more consciously manipulate than they could choose
not to have been born. At this point, it seemed to me, the ethnocentric
bias of the firsthand observers invited an investigation of the cultural situation they spoke from. Karen Kupperman's *Settling with the Indians* (1980)
supplied just such an analysis.

Kupperman argues that Englishmen inevitably looked at Indians in exactly the same way that they looked at other Englishmen. For instance, if
they looked down on Indians and saw them as people to be exploited, it
was not because of racial prejudice or antique notions about savagery, it
was because they looked down on ordinary English men and women and
saw them as subjects for exploitation as well. [19] According to Kupperman,
what concerned these writers most when they described the Indians were

the insignia of social class, of rank, and of prestige. Indian faces are virtually never described in the earliest accounts, but clothes and hairstyles, tattoos and jewelry, posture and skin color are. "Early modern Englishmen believed that people can create their own identity, and that therefore one communicates to the world through signals such as dress and other forms of decoration who one is, what group or category one belongs to." [20]

Kupperman's book marks a watershed in writings on European-Indian relations, for it reverses the strategy employed by Martin two years before. Whereas Martin had performed an ethnographic analysis of Indian cosmology in order to explain, from within, the Indians' motives for engaging in the fur trade, Kupperman performs an ethnographic study of seventeenth-century England in order to explain, from within, what motivated Englishmen's behavior. The sympathy and understanding that Martin, Axtell, and others extend to the Indians are extended in Kupperman's work to the English themselves. Rather than giving an account of "what happened" between Indians and Europeans, like Martin, she reconstructs the worldview that gave the experience of one group its content. With her study, scholarship on European-Indian relations comes full circle.

It may well seem to you at this point that, given the tremendous variation among the historical accounts, I had no choice but to end in relativism. If the experience of encountering conflicting versions of the "same" events suggests anything certain it is that the attitude a historian takes up in relation to a given event, the way in which he or she judges and even describes "it"—and the "it" has to go in quotation marks because, depending on the perspective, that event either did or did not occur—this stance, these judgments and descriptions are a function of the historian's position in relation to the subject. Miller, standing on the banks of the Congo, couldn't see the black men he was supervising because of his background, his assumptions, values, experiences, goals. Jennings, intent on exposing the distortions introduced into the historical record by Vaughan and his predecessors stretching all the way back to Winthrop, couldn't see that Winthrop and his peers were not racists but only Englishmen who looked at other cultures in the way their own culture had taught them to see one another. The historian can never escape the limitations of his or her own position in history and so inevitably gives an account that is an extension of the circumstances from which it springs. But it seems to me that when one is confronted with this particular succession of stories, cultural and historical relativism is not a position that one can comfortably assume. The phenomena to which these histories testify—conquest, massacre, and genocide, on the one hand; torture, slavery, and murder on the other—cry out for judgment. When faced with claims and counterclaims of this magnitude one feels obligated to reach an understanding of what actually did occur. The dilemma posed by the study of European-Indian relations in early America is that the highly charged nature of the materials demands a moral decisiveness which the succession of conflicting accounts effectively precludes. That is the dilemma I found myself in at the end of this course of reading, and which I eventually came to resolve as follows.

After a while it began to seem to me that there was something wrong with the way I had formulated the problem. The statement that the materials on European-Indian relations were so highly charged that they demanded moral judgment, but that the judgment couldn't be made because all possible descriptions of what happened were biased, seemed to contain an internal contradiction. The statement implied that in order to make a moral judgment about something, you have to know something else first— namely, the facts of the case you're being called upon to judge. My complaint was that their perspectival nature would disqualify any facts I might encounter and that therefore I couldn't judge. But to say as I did that the materials I had read were "highly charged" and therefore demanded judgment suggests both that I was reacting to something real—to some facts— *and* that I had judged them. Perhaps I wasn't so much in the lurch morally or epistemologically as I had thought. If you—or I—react with horror to the story of the girl captured and enslaved by Comanches who touched a firebrand to her nose every time they wanted to wake her up, it's because we read this as a story about cruelty and suffering, and not as a story about the conventions of prisoner exchange or the economics of Comanche life. The *seeing* of the story as a cause for alarm rather than as a droll anecdote or a piece of curious information is evidence of values we already hold, of judgments already made, of facts already perceived as facts.

My problem presupposed that I couldn't judge because I didn't know what the facts were. All I had, or could have, was a series of different perspectives, and so nothing that would count as an authoritative source on which moral judgments could be based. But, as I have just shown, I did judge, and that is because, as I now think, I did have some facts. I seemed to accept as facts that ninety percent of the native American population of New England died after the first hundred years of contact, that tribes in eastern Canada and the northeastern United States had a compact with the game they killed, that Comanches had subjected a captive girl to casual cruelty, that King Philip smoked a pipe, and so on. It was only where different versions of the same event came into conflict that I doubted the text was a record of something real. And even then, there was no question about certain major catastrophes. I believed that four hundred Pequots were killed near Saybrook, that Winthrop was the Governor of the Massachusetts Bay Colony when it happened, and so on. My sense that certain events, such as the Pequot War, did occur in no way reflected the indecisiveness that overtook me when I tried to choose among the various historical versions. In fact, the need I felt to make up my mind was impelled by the conviction that certain things *had* happened that shouldn't have happened. Hence it was never the case that "what happened" was completely unknowable or unavailable. It's rather that in the process of reading so many different approaches to the same phenomenon I became aware of the difference in the attitudes that informed these approaches. This awareness of the interests motivating each version cast suspicion over everything, in retrospect, and I ended by claiming that there was nothing I could know. This, I now see, was never really the case. But how did it happen?

Someone else, confronted with the same materials, could have decided that one of these historical accounts was correct. Still another person might have decided that more evidence was needed in order to decide among them. Why did I conclude that none of the accounts was accurate because they were all produced from some particular angle of vision? Presumably there was something in my background that enabled me to see the problem in this way. That something, very likely, was poststructuralist theory. I let my discovery that Vaughan was a product of the fifties, Jennings of the sixties, Rowlandson of a Puritan worldview, and so on lead me to the conclusion that all facts are theory dependent because that conclusion was already a thinkable one for me. My inability to come up with a true account was not the product of being situated nowhere; it was the product of certitude that existed *somewhere else*, namely, in contemporary literary theory. Hence, the level at which my indecision came into play was a function of particular beliefs I held. I was never in a position of epistemological indeterminacy, I was never *en abyme*. The idea that all accounts are perspectival seemed to me a superior standpoint from which to view all the versions of "what happened," and to regard with sympathetic condescension any person so old-fashioned and benighted as to believe that there really was some way of arriving at the truth. But this skeptical standpoint was just as firm as any other. The fact that it was also seriously disabling—it prevented me from coming to any conclusion about what I had read—did not render it any less definite.

At this point something is beginning to show itself that has up to now been hidden. The notion that all facts are only facts within a perspective has the effect of emptying statements of their content. Once I had Miller and Vaughan and Jennings, Martin and Hudson, Axtell and Heard, Rowlandson and Wood and Whitaker, and Kupperman; I had Europeans and Indians, ships and canoes, wigwams and log cabins, bows and arrows and muskets, wigs and tattoos, whisky and corn, rivers and forts, treaties and battles, fire and blood—and then suddenly all I had was a metastatement about perspectives. The effect of bringing perspectivism to bear on history was to wipe out completely the subject matter of history. And it follows that bringing perspectivism to bear in this way on any subject matter would have a similar effect; everything is wiped out and you are left with nothing but a single idea—perspectivism itself.

But—and it is a crucial but—all this is true only if you believe that there is an alternative. As long as you think that there are or should be facts that exist outside of any perspective, then the notion that facts are perspectival will have this disappearing effect on whatever it touches. But if you are convinced that the alternative does not exist, that there really are no facts except as they are embedded in some particular way of seeing the world, then the arguments that a set of facts derives from some particular world-view is no longer an argument against that set of facts. If all facts share this characteristic, to say that any one fact is perspectival doesn't change its factual nature in the slightest. It merely reiterates it.

This doesn't mean that you have to accept just anybody's facts. You can show that what someone else asserts to be a fact is false. But it does mean that you can't argue that someone else's facts are not facts *because they are only the product of a perspective,* since this will be true of the facts that you perceive as well. What this means then is that arguments about "what happened" have to proceed much as they did before poststructuralism broke in with all its talk about language-based reality and culturally produced knowledge. Reasons must be given, evidence adduced, authorities cited, analogies drawn. Being aware that all facts are motivated, believing that people are always operating inside some particular interpretive framework or other is a pertinent argument when what is under discussion is the way beliefs are grounded. But it doesn't give one any leverage on the facts of a particular case. [21]

What this means for the problem I've been addressing is that I must piece together the story of European-Indian relations as best I can, believing this version up to a point, that version not at all, another almost entirely, according to what seems reasonable and plausible, given everything else that I know. And this, as I've shown, is what I was already doing in the back of my mind without realizing it, because there was nothing else I *could* do. If the accounts don't fit together neatly, that is not a reason for rejecting them all in favor of a metadiscourse about epistemology; on the contrary, one encounters contradictory facts and divergent points of view in practically every phase of life, from deciding whom to marry to choosing the right brand of cat food, and one decides as best one can given the evidence available. It is only the nature of the academic situation which makes it appear that one can linger on the threshold of decision in the name of an epistemological principle. What has really happened in such a case is that the subject of debate has changed from the question of what happened in a particular instance to the question of how knowledge is arrived at. The absence of pressure to decide what happened creates the possibility for this change of venue.

The change of venue, however, is itself an action taken. In diverting attention from the original problem and placing it where Miller did, on "the mind of man," it once again ignores what happened and still is happening to American Indians. The moral problem that confronts me now is not that I can never have any facts to go on, but that the work I do is not directed toward solving the kinds of problems that studying the history of European-Indian relations has awakened me to.

## NOTES

[1] See Vine Deloria, Jr., *God is Red* (New York, 1973), pp. 39–56.

[2] Perry Miller, *Errand into the Wilderness* (Cambridge, Mass., 1964), p. vii; all further references will be included in the text.

[3] This passage from John Winthrop's *Journal* is excerpted by Perry Miller in his anthology *The American Puritans: Their Prose and Poetry* (Garden City, N.Y., 1956), p. 43. In his headnote to the selections from the *Journal*, Miller speaks of Winthrop's "characteristic objectivity" (p. 37).

[4] Alden T. Vaughan, *New England Frontier: Puritans and Indians, 1620–1675* (Boston, 1965), pp. vi–vii; all further references to this work, abbreviated *NEF*, will be included in the text.

[5] John Higham, intro. to *New Directions in American Intellectual History*, ed. Higham and Paul K. Conkin (Baltimore, 1979), p. xii.

[6] Ibid.

[7] See Francis Jennings, *The Invasion of America: Indians, Colonialism, and the Cant of Conquest* (New York, 1975), pp. 3–31. Jennings writes: "The so-called settlement of America was a *re*settlement, reoccupation of a land made waste by the diseases and demoralization introduced by the newcomers. Although the source data pertaining to populations have never been compiled, one careful scholar, Henry F. Dobyns, has provided a relatively conservative and meticulously reasoned estimate conforming to the known effects of conquest catastrophe. Dobyns has calculated a total aboriginal population for the western hemisphere within the range of 90 to 112 million, of which 10 to 12 million lived north of the Rio Grande" (p. 30).

[8] Jennings, fig. 7, p. 229; and see pp. 186–229.

[9] James Axtell, *The European and the Indian: Essays in the Ethnohistory of Colonial North America* (Oxford, 1981), p. viii.

[10] See Calvin Martin, *Keepers of the Game: Indian-Animal Relationships and the Fur Trade* (Berkeley and Los Angeles, 1978).

[11] See the essay by Charles Hudson in *Indians, Animals, and the Fur Trade: A Critique of "Keepers of the Game,"* ed. Shepard Krech III (Athens, Ga., 1981), pp. 167–69.

[12] See Axtell, "The White Indians of Colonial America" and "The Scholastic Philosophy of the Wilderness," *The European and the Indian*, pp. 168–206 and 131–67.

[13] J. Norman Heard, *White into Red: A Study of the Assimilation of White Persons Captured by Indians* (Metuchen, N.J., 1973), p. 97.

[14] See ibid., p. 98.

[15] Mary Rowlandson, "The Soveraignty and Goodness of God, Together with the Faithfulness of His Promises Displayed; Being a Narrative of the Captivity and Restauration of Mrs. Mary Rowlandson (1676)," in *Held Captive by Indians: Selected Narratives, 1642–1836*, ed. Richard VanDerBeets (Knoxville, Tenn., 1973), pp. 57–58.

[16] William Wood, *New England's Prospect*, ed. Vaughan (Amherst, Mass., 1977), pp. 88–89.

[17] Alexander Whitaker, *Goode Newes from Virginia* (1613), quoted in Robert F. Berkhofer, Jr., *The White Man's Indian: Images of the American Indian from Columbus to the Present* (New York, 1978), p. 19.

[18] See, for example, Berkhofer's discussion of the passages he quotes from Whitaker (*The White Man's Indian,* pp. 19, 20).

[19] See Karen Ordahl Kupperman, *Settling with the Indians: The Meeting of English and Indian Cultures in America, 1580–1640* (Totowa, N.J., 1980), pp. 3, 4.

[20] Ibid., p. 35.

[21] The position I've been outlining is a version of neopragmatism. For an exposition, see *Against Theory: Literary Studies and the New Pragmatism,* ed. W. J. T. Mitchell (Chicago, 1985).

. . . . . . . . . . .

## QUESTIONS FOR A SECOND READING

1. Tompkins's essay could be divided into three parts: the account of her childhood understanding of Indians (in Kuhn's terms, the "prehistory" of her later discoveries); the account of her research into scholarly and first-person accounts of the relations between the Indians and the settlers in New England; and a final conclusion (beginning, on p. 575). The conclusion, in many ways, is the hardest part of the essay to understand. Like the conclusion to Geertz's "Deep Play: Notes on the Balinese Cockfight" (p. 272), it assumes not only that you have followed a chain of reasoning but that you have access to the larger philosophical questions that have preoccupied the academic community. In this sense the conclusion presents special problems for a student reader. Why might one be dissatisfied with "metadiscourse"? What kind of work is Tompkins talking about, for example, when she says, "The moral problem that confronts me now is . . . that the work I do is not directed toward solving the kinds of problems that studying the history of European-Indian relations has awakened me to"?

   As you reread the essay, look to see how the first two sections might be seen as a preparation for the conclusion. And as you reread the concluding section (which you may have to do several times), try to imagine the larger, unspoken issues it poses for those who teach American literature or who are professionally involved in reading and researching the past.

2. One of the things to notice about Tompkins's essay is how neatly all the pieces fit together in her narrative. If you wanted to read against this essay, you might say that they fit together *too* neatly. The seemingly "natural" progression from book to book or step to step in this account of her research and her thinking could be said to reveal the degree to which the story was shaped or made, constructed for the occasion. Real experience is never quite so tidy.

   As you reread the essay, be aware of the narrative as something made and ask yourself, How does she do that? What is she leaving out? Where is she working hard to get her material to fit? This is partly a matter of watching how Tompkins does her work—looking at paragraphs, for instance, and seeing how they represent her material and her reading of that material. It is also a matter of looking for what is not there, for seams that indicate necessary or unconscious omissions (as though while writing this essay, too, she "did not care to have any real exemplars interfering with what I already knew").

## ASSIGNMENTS FOR WRITING

1. Tompkins's essay tells the story of a research project. It also, however, "reads" that narrative—that is, Tompkins not only describes what she did, or what other people said, but she reflects on what her actions or the work of others might be said to represent. She writes about "point of view" or "frame of reference" and the ways they might be said to determine how people act, what they write, and what they know.

   Write an essay that tells a similar story, one of your own, using Tompkins's essay as a model. There are two ways you might do this:

   1. You could tell the story of a research project, a paper (most likely a term paper) you prepared for school. This does not have to be a pious or dutiful account. Tompkins, after all, is writing against what she takes to be the predictable or expected account of research as the disinterested pursuit of truth—in which a student would go to the library to "find" the truth about the Indians and the settlers. And she writes in a style that is not solemnly academic. Like Tompkins, you can tell what you take to be the untold story of term-paper research, you can reflect on the "problem" of such research by turning to your own account.

      Your account should begin well before your work in the library—that is, you too will want to show the "prehistory" of your project, the possible connections between schoolwork and your life outside school. It should also tell the story of your work with other people's writing. The purpose of all this is to reflect on how knowledge is constructed and how you, as a student, have been expected to participate (and how you have, in fact, participated) in that process.

   2. You could tell the story of a discovery that did not involve reading or library research; in fact, you could tell the story of a discovery that did not involve school at all. In this sense you would be working in response to the first section of Tompkins's essay, where what she knows about Indians is constructed from a combination of cultural models and personal desire.

2. In her essay Tompkins offers her experience as a representative case. Her story is meant to highlight a problem central to teaching, learning, and research—central, that is, to academic life. As a student, you can read this essay as a way of looking in on the work and concerns of your faculty (a

group represented not only by Tompkins but by those against whom she is arguing). Write an essay directed to someone who has not read "Indians," someone who will be entering your school as a first-year student next semester. Your job is to introduce an incoming freshman to the academy, using Tompkins as your guide. You will need to present her argument and her conclusion in such a way as to make clear the consequences of what she says for someone about to begin an undergraduate education. Remember, you are writing to an incoming student; you will want to capture that audience's attention.

### MAKING CONNECTIONS

1. As Tompkins reviews the books she gathered in her project, she presents each in terms of its point of view, the "aims" with which it was written. She sees these books, that is, not as sources of truth but as representations of Indians and settlers, representations shaped by a theory, an agenda, or the cultural-historical situation of the scholar. The differences between the sources are not matters of right and wrong, nor are they simply matters of individual style.

   In a parallel way, take two essays from *Ways of Reading* that deal with a single subject and treat them as cases of different points of view or frames of reference. "When We Dead Awaken: Writing as Re-Vision" by Rich (p. 482) or "A Room of One's Own" by Virginia Woolf (p. 641) are particularly suggestive for a project like this. They both deal with the situation of women writers. In fact, Rich's essay makes specific reference to Woolf and her work. One sign of Rich's difference from Woolf, then, will be the way she reads Woolf.

   Write an essay in which you look at the differences between Rich's essay and Woolf's (or two others you might choose on your own) and speculate on how those differences might reflect different times (different frames of reference) and different agendas (different points of view), even though they deal with a common topic and could easily be said to make a similar argument.

2. Thomas Kuhn, in "The Historical Structure of Scientific Discovery" (p. 385), argues that discoveries have a "prehistory," a "posthistory," and an internal structure. Tompkins is not a scientist, and there are some significant differences between her discovery and the discoveries recorded in Kuhn's essay. But Kuhn's contribution to the history of science (and the history of knowledge) is the way he imagines a historical and cultural context for the work a scientist does, so to speak, "on his own."

   Write an essay in which you compare Tompkins's representation of how knowledge is constructed and reproduced from written texts with Kuhn's representation of the construction and reproduction of knowledge in science. On the basis of these two essays alone, what are the significant differences and similarities between the practice of science and the practice of history? What are the significant similarities and differences between Kuhn and Tompkins, both of whom could be said to be writing histories?

3. In "Our Time" (p. 596) John Edgar Wideman writes about the problems he has "knowing" and writing about his brother, Robby. In this sense, both "Our Time" and "Indians" are about the problems of understanding, about the difficult relationship between "real exemplars" and what we know. Write an essay in which you compare these two selections, looking in particular at the differences in the way each author represents this problem and its possible solutions. Although you are working from only two sources, you could imagine that your essay is a way of investigating the differences between the work of a "creative" writer and a scholar.

# ALICE
# WALKER

*A* LICE WALKER, *the youngest of eight children in a sharecropping family, was born in 1944 in Eatonton, Georgia. She is now one of the most widely read contemporary American novelists. In her work, she frequently returns to scenes of family life—some violent, some peaceful. "I was curious to know," she writes, "why people of families (specifically black families) are often cruel to each other and how much of this cruelty is caused by outside forces. . . . Family relationships are sacred. No amount of outside pressure and injustice should make us lose sight of that fact." In her nonfiction, Walker has helped to define a historical context for the contemporary black artist, a legacy that has had to be recovered from libraries and archives. The essay that follows, "In Search of Our Mothers' Gardens," defines black history as a family matter. It begins by charting the violence done to women who "died with their real gifts stifled within them" and concludes with Walker's recollection of her own mother, a recollection that enables her to imagine generations of black women handing on a "creative spark" to those who follow.*

*In addition to* In Search of Our Mothers' Gardens *(1983), Walker has written novels, including* The Third Life of Grange Copeland *(1970) and* The Color Purple *(1982), which won the Pultizer Prize; collections of poems, including* Revolutionary Petunias *(1973), and* Good Night, Willie Lee, I'll See You in the Morning *(1979); two collections of short stories,* In Love and Trouble *(1973) and* You Can't Keep a Good Woman Down *(1981), and a biography of Langston Hughes. She has also served as an editor at* Ms. *magazine. After graduating from Sarah Lawrence College in 1965, she taught at a number of colleges and universities, including Wellesley College and Yale University. She has held a Guggenheim Fellowship and a National Endowment for the Arts fellowship. She lives in San Francisco and teaches at the University of California, Berkeley.*

*While pursuing her own career as a writer, Walker has fought to win recognition for the work of Zora Neale Hurston, a black woman author and anthropologist whose best-known work is the novel* Their Eyes Were Watching God *(1937). Hurston died penniless in a Florida welfare home. Walker's most recent work includes* Living by the Word *(1988), a collection of essays, letters, journal entries, lectures, and poems on the themes of race, gender, sexuality, and political freedom;* To Hell with Dying *(1988), a children's picture book; and* The Temple of My Familiar *(1989), a novel.*

# In Search of
# Our Mothers' Gardens

I described her own nature and temperament. Told how they needed a larger life for their expression. . . . I pointed out that in lieu of proper channels, her emotions had overflowed into paths that dissipated them. I talked, beautifully I thought, about an art that would be born, an art that would open the way for women the likes of her. I asked her to hope, and build up an inner life against the coming of that day. . . . I sang, with a strange quiver in my voice, a promise song.

> – "AVEY," JEAN TOOMER, *Cane*
> *The poet speaking to a prostitute who falls
> asleep while he's talking*

When the poet Jean Toomer walked through the South in the early twenties, he discovered a curious thing: black women whose spirituality was so intense, so deep, so *unconscious*, they were themselves unaware of the richness they held. They stumbled blindly through their lives: creatures so abused and mutilated in body, so dimmed and confused by pain, that they considered themselves unworthy even of hope. In the selfless abstractions their bodies became to the men who used them, they became more than "sexual objects," more even than mere women: they became "Saints." Instead of being perceived as whole persons, their bodies became shrines: what was thought to be their minds became temples suitable for worship. These crazy Saints stared out at the world, wildly, like lunatics—or quietly, like suicides; and the "God" that was in their gaze was as mute as a great stone.

Who were these Saints? These crazy, loony, pitiful women?

Some of them, without a doubt, were our mothers and grandmothers.

In the still heat of the post-Reconstruction South, this is how they seemed to Jean Toomer: exquisite butterflies trapped in an evil honey, toiling away their lives in an era, a century, that did not acknowledge them, except as "the *mule* of the world." They dreamed dreams that no one knew—not even themselves, in any coherent fashion—and saw visions no one could understand. They wandered or sat about the countryside crooning lullabies to ghosts, and drawing the mother of Christ in charcoal on courthouse walls.

They forced their minds to desert their bodies and their striving spirits sought to rise, like frail whirlwinds from the hard red clay. And when those frail whirlwinds fell, in scattered particles, upon the ground, no one mourned. Instead, men lit candles to celebrate the emptiness that remained, as people do who enter a beautiful but vacant space to resurrect a God.

Our mothers and grandmothers, some of them: moving to music not yet written. And they waited.

They waited for a day when the unknown thing that was in them would be made known; but guessed, somehow in their darkness, that on the day of their revelation they would be long dead. Therefore to Toomer they walked, and even ran, in slow motion. For they were going nowhere immediate, and the future was not yet within their grasp. And men took our mothers and grandmothers, "but got no pleasure from it." So complex was their passion and their calm.

To Toomer, they lay vacant and fallow as autumn fields, with harvest time never in sight: and he saw them enter loveless marriages, without joy; and become prostitutes, without resistance; and become mothers of children, without fulfillment.

For these grandmothers and mothers of ours were not Saints, but Artists; driven to a numb and bleeding madness by the springs of creativity in them for which there was no release. They were Creators, who lived lives of spiritual waste, because they were so rich in spirituality—which is the basis of Art—that the strain of enduring their unused and unwanted talent drove them insane. Throwing away this spirituality was their pathetic attempt to lighten the soul to a weight their work-worn, sexually abused bodies could bear.

What did it mean for a black woman to be an artist in our grandmothers' time? In our great-grandmothers' day? It is a question with an answer cruel enough to stop the blood.

Did you have a genius of a great-great-grandmother who died under some ignorant and depraved white overseer's lash? Or was she required to bake biscuits for a lazy backwater tramp, when she cried out in her soul to paint watercolors of sunsets, or the rain falling on the green and peaceful pasturelands? Or was her body broken and forced to bear children (who were more often than not sold away from her)—eight, ten, fifteen, twenty children—when her one joy was the thought of modeling heroic figures of rebellion, in stone or clay?

How was the creativity of the black woman kept alive, year after year and century after century, when for most of the years black people have been in America, it was a punishable crime for a black person to read or write? And the freedom to paint, to sculpt, to expand the mind with action did not exist. Consider, if you can bear to imagine it, what might have been the result if singing, too, had been forbidden by law. Listen to the voices of Bessie Smith, Billie Holiday, Nina Simone, Roberta Flack, and Aretha Franklin, among others, and imagine those voices muzzled for life. Then you may begin to comprehend the lives of our "crazy," "Sainted" mothers and grandmothers. The agony of the lives of women who might have been Poets, Novelists, Essayists, and Short-Story Writers (over a period of centuries), who died with their real gifts stifled within them.

And, if this were the end of the story, we would have cause to cry out in my paraphrase of Okot p'Bitek's great poem:

> O, my clanswomen
> Let us all cry together!
> Come,
> Let us mourn the death of our mother,
> The death of a Queen
> The ash that was produced
> By a great fire!
> O, this homestead is utterly dead
> Close the gates
> With *lacari* thorns,
> For our mother
> The creator of the Stool is lost!
> And all the young men
> Have perished in the wilderness!

But this is not the end of the story, for all the young women—our mothers and grandmothers, *ourselves*—have not perished in the wilderness. And if we ask ourselves why, and search for and find the answer, we will know beyond all efforts to erase it from our minds, just exactly who, and of what, we black American women are.

One example, perhaps the most pathetic, most misunderstood one, can provide a backdrop for our mothers' work: Phillis Wheatley, a slave in the 1700s.

Virginia Woolf, in her book *A Room of One's Own,* wrote that in order for a woman to write fiction she must have two things, certainly: a room of her own (with key and lock) and enough money to support herself.

What then are we to make of Phillis Wheatley, a slave, who owned not even herself? This sickly, frail black girl who required a servant of her own at times—her health was so precarious—and who, had she been white, would have been easily considered the intellectual superior of all the women and most of the men in the society of her day.

Virginia Woolf wrote further, speaking of course not of our Phillis, that "any woman born with a great gift in the sixteenth century [insert "eighteenth century," insert "black woman," insert "born or made a slave"] would certainly have gone crazed, shot herself, or ended her days in some lonely cottage outside the village, half witch, half wizard [insert "Saint"], feared and mocked at. For it needs little skill and psychology to be sure that a highly gifted girl who had tried to use her gift of poetry would have been so thwarted and hindered by contrary instincts [add "chains, guns, the lash, the ownership of one's body by someone else, submission to an alien religion"], that she must have lost her health and sanity to a certainty."

The key words, as they relate to Phillis, are "contrary instincts." For when we read the poetry of Phillis Wheatley—as when we read the novels of Nella Larsen or the oddly false-sounding autobiography of that freest of all black women writers, Zora Hurston—evidence of "contrary instincts" is everywhere. Her loyalties were completely divided, as was, without question, her mind.

But how could this be otherwise? Captured at seven, a slave of wealthy, doting whites who instilled in her the "savagery" of the Africa they "rescued" her from . . . one wonders if she was even able to remember her homeland as she had known it, or as it really was.

Yet, because she did try to use her gift for poetry in a world that made her a slave, she was "so thwarted and hindered by . . . contrary instincts, that she . . . lost her health. . . ." In the last years of her brief life, burdened not only with the need to express her gift but also with a penniless, friendless "freedom" and several small children for whom she was forced to do strenuous work to feed, she lost her health, certainly. Suffering from malnutrition and neglect and who knows what mental agonies, Phillis Wheatley died.

So torn by "contrary instincts" was black, kidnapped, enslaved Phillis that her description of "the Goddess"—as she poetically called the Liberty she did not have—is ironically, cruelly humorous. And, in fact, has held Phillis up to ridicule for more than a century. It is usually read prior to hanging Phillis's memory as that of a fool. She wrote:

> The Goddess comes, she moves divinely fair,
> Olive and laurel binds her *golden* hair.
> Wherever shines this native of the skies,
> Unnumber'd charms and recent graces rise. [My italics]

It is obvious that Phillis, the slave, combed the "Goddess's" hair every morning; prior, perhaps, to bringing in the milk, or fixing her mistress's lunch. She took her imagery from the one thing she saw elevated above all others.

With the benefit of hindsight we ask, "How could she?"

But at last, Phillis, we understand. No more snickering when your stiff, struggling, ambivalent lines are forced on us. We know now that you were not an idiot or a traitor; only a sickly little black girl, snatched from your home and country and made a slave; a woman who still struggled to sing the song that was your gift, although in a land of barbarians who praised you for your bewildered tongue. It is not so much what you sang, as that you kept alive, in so many of our ancestors, *the notion of song.*

Black women are called, in the folklore that so aptly identified one's status society, "the *mule* of the world," because we have been handed the burdens that everyone else—*everyone* else—refused to carry. We have also been called "Matriarchs," "Superwomen," and "Mean and Evil Bitches." Not to mention "Castraters" and "Sapphire's Mama." When we have pleaded for understanding, our character has been distorted; when we have asked for simple caring, we have been handed empty inspirational appellations, then stuck in the farthest corner. When we have asked for love, we have been given children. In short, even our plainer gifts, our labors of fidelity and love, have been knocked down our throats. To be an artist and a black woman, even today, lowers our status in many respects, rather than raises it: and yet, artists we will be.

Therefore we must fearlessly pull out of ourselves and look at and identify with our lives the living creativity some of our great-grandmothers were not allowed to know. I stress *some* of them because it is well known that the majority of our great-grandmothers knew, even without "knowing" it, the reality of their spirituality, even if they didn't recognize it beyond what happened in the singing at church—and they never had any intention of giving it up.

How they did it—those millions of black women who were not Phillis Wheatley, or Lucy Terry or Frances Harper or Zora Hurston or Nella Larsen or Bessie Smith; or Elizabeth Catlett, or Katherine Dunham, either—brings me to the title of this essay, "In Search of Our Mothers' Gardens," which is a personal account that is yet shared, in its theme and its meaning, by all of us. I found, while thinking about the far-reaching world of the creative black woman, that often the truest answer to a question that really matters can be found very close.

In the late 1920s my mother ran away from home to marry my father. Marriage, if not running away, was expected of seventeen-year-old girls. By the time she was twenty, she had two children and was pregnant with a third. Five children later, I was born. And this is how I came to know my mother: she seemed a large, soft, loving-eyed woman who was rarely impatient in our home. Her quick, violent temper was on view only a few times a year, when she battled with the white landlord who had the misfortune to suggest to her that her children did not need to go to school.

She made all the clothes we wore, even my brothers' overalls. She made all the towels and sheets we used. She spent the summers canning vegetables and fruits. She spent the winter evenings making quilts enough to cover all our beds.

During the "working" day, she labored beside—not behind—my father in the fields. Her day began before sunup, and did not end until late at night. There was never a moment for her to sit down, undisturbed, to unravel her own private thoughts; never a time free from interruption—by work or the noisy inquiries of her many children. And yet, it is to my mother—and all our mothers who were not famous—that I went in search of the secret of what has fed that muzzled and often mutilated, but vibrant, creative spirit that the black woman has inherited, and that pops out in wild and unlikely places to this day.

But when, you will ask, did my overworked mother have time to know or care about feeding the creative spirit?

The answer is so simple that many of us have spent years discovering it. We have constantly looked high, when we should have looked high—and low.

For example: in the Smithsonian Institution in Washington, D.C., there hangs a quilt unlike any other in the world. In fanciful, inspired, and yet simple and identifiable figures, it portrays the story of the Crucifixion. It is considered rare, beyond price. Though it follows no known pattern of quilt-making, and though it is made of bits and pieces of worthless rags, it is obviously the work of a person of powerful imagination and deep spiritual feeling. Below this quilt I saw a note that says it was made by "an anonymous black woman in Alabama, a hundred years ago."

If we could locate this "anonymous" black woman from Alabama, she would turn out to be one of our grandmothers—an artist who left her mark in the only materials she could afford, and in the only medium her position in society allowed her to use.

As Virginia Woolf wrote further, in *A Room of One's Own*:

> Yet genius of a sort must have existed among women as it must have existed among the working class. [Change this to "slaves" and "the wives and daughters of sharecroppers."] Now and again an Emily Brontë or a Robert Burns [change this to "a Zora Hurston or a Richard Wright"] blazes out and proves its presence. But certainly it never got itself on to paper. When, however, one reads of a witch being ducked, of a woman possessed by devils [or "Sainthood"], of a wise woman selling herbs [our root workers], or even a very remarkable man who had a mother, then I think we are on the track of a lost novelist, a suppressed poet, or some mute and inglorious Jane Austen. . . . Indeed, I would venture to guess that Anon, who wrote so many poems without singing them, was often a woman. . . .

And so our mothers and grandmothers have, more often than not anonymously, handed on the creative spark, the seed of the flower they themselves never hoped to see: or like a sealed letter they could not plainly read.

And so it is, certainly, with my own mother. Unlike "Ma" Rainey's songs, which retained their creator's name even while blasting forth from Bessie Smith's mouth, no song or poem will bear my mother's name. Yet so many of the stories that I write, that we all write, are my mother's stories. Only recently did I fully realize this: that through years of listening to my mother's stories of her life, I have absorbed not only the stories themselves, but something of the manner in which she spoke, something of the urgency that involves the knowledge that her stories—like her life—must be recorded. It is probably for this reason that so much of what I have written is about characters whose counterparts in real life are so much older than I am.

But the telling of these stories, which came from my mother's lips as naturally as breathing, was not the only way my mother showed herself as an artist. For stories, too, were subject to being distracted, to dying without conclusion. Dinners must be started, and cotton must be gathered before the big rains. The artist that was and is my mother showed itself to me only after many years. This is what I finally noticed:

Like Mem, a character in *The Third Life of Grange Copeland*, my mother adorned with flowers whatever shabby house we were forced to live in. And not just your typical straggly country stand of zinnias, either. She planted ambitious gardens—and still does—with over fifty different varieties of plants that bloom profusely from early March until late November. Before she left home for the fields, she watered her flowers, chopped up the grass, and laid out new beds. When she returned from the fields she might divide clumps of bulbs, dig a cold pit, uproot and replant roses, or prune branches from her taller bushes or trees—until night came and it was too dark to see.

Whatever she planted grew as if by magic, and her fame as a grower of flowers spread over three counties. Because of her creativity with her flowers, even my memories of poverty are seen through a screen of blooms—sunflowers, petunias, roses, dahlias, forsythia, spirea, delphiniums, verbena . . . and on and on.

And I remember people coming to my mother's yard to be given cuttings from her flowers; I hear again the praise showered on her because whatever rocky soil she landed on, she turned into a garden. A garden so brilliant with colors, so original in its design, so magnificent with life and creativity, that to this day people drive by our house in Georgia—perfect strangers and imperfect strangers—and ask to stand or walk among my mother's art.

I notice that it is only when my mother is working in her flowers that she is radiant, almost to the point of being invisible—except as Creator: hand and eye. She is involved in work her soul must have. Ordering the universe in the image of her personal conception of Beauty.

Her face, as she prepares the Art that is her gift, is a legacy of respect she leaves to me, for all that illuminates and cherishes life. She has handed down respect for the possibilities—and the will to grasp them.

For her, so hindered and intruded upon in so many ways, being an artist has still been a daily part of her life. This ability to hold on, even in very simple ways, is work black women have done for a very long time.

This poem is not enough, but it is something, for the woman who literally covered the holes in our walls with sunflowers:

> They were women then
> My mama's generation
> Husky of voice—Stout of
> Step
> With fists as well as
> Hands
> How they battered down
> Doors
> And ironed
> Starched white
> Shirts
> How they led
> Armies

Headragged Generals
Across mined
Fields
Booby-trapped
Kitchens
To discover books
Desks
A place for us
How they knew what we
*Must* know
Without knowing a page
Of it
Themselves

Guided by my heritage of a love of beauty and a respect for strength—in search of my mother's garden, I found my own.

And perhaps in Africa over two hundred years ago, there was just such a mother; perhaps she painted vivid and daring decorations in oranges and yellows and greens on the walls of her hut; perhaps she sang—in a voice like Roberta Flack's—*sweetly* over the compounds of her village; perhaps she wove the most stunning mats or told the most ingenious stories of all the village storytellers. Perhaps she was herself a poet—though only her daughter's name is signed to the poems that we know.

Perhaps Phillis Wheatley's mother was also an artist.

Perhaps in more than Phillis Wheatley's biological life is her mother's signature made clear.

. . . . . . . . . . .

## QUESTIONS FOR A SECOND READING

1. In the essay, Walker develops the interesting notion of "contrary instincts," particularly when she discusses Phillis Wheatley. The problem for Walker (and others) is that Wheatley would idolize a fair-haired white woman as a goddess of liberty rather than turning to herself as a model, or to the black women who struggled mightily for their identities and liberty. Walker asks, "How could she?" As you reread the essay, pay particular attention to the sections where Walker discusses "contrary instincts." How would you define this term? What kind of answers does this essay make possible to the question "How could she?"

2. As you reread the essay, note particularly the sections where Walker talks about herself. How does she feel about her mother, the history of black

women in America, and "contrary instincts"? How would you describe Walker's feelings and attitudes toward herself, the past, and the pressures of living in a predominantly white culture? In considering these questions, don't settle for big words like "honest," "sensitive," or "compassionate." They are accurate, to be sure, but they are imprecise and don't do justice to Walker's seriousness and individuality.

### ASSIGNMENTS FOR WRITING

1. What do you consider the most significant passage in this essay? Why do you consider it important? Write an essay where you identify and explain what you see as the most significant passage in this essay. What can you say about it to demonstrate its importance?

2. Walker's essay poses a number of questions about the history of black women in America, including their "creative spirit" in the face of oppressive working and living conditions. At one point, Walker describes her mother's life in the late 1920s after she ran away from home to marry her father. Her mother's difficult life was filled with unrelenting work, yet she managed to keep a "vibrant, creative spirit" alive. Walker asks, "But when, you will ask, did my overworked mother have time to know or care about feeding the creative spirit?" She goes on to say that "the answer is so simple that many of us have spent years discovering it." Write an essay explaining what you think this "simple" answer might be and why it took Alice Walker—or why it would take anyone—so long to find it.

### MAKING CONNECTIONS

1. Throughout "Our Time" (p. 596) by John Edgar Wideman, Robby talks about his contrary instincts, his ambivalent feelings towards making it in the white world. How can you consider Robby in light of Walker's observations about contrary instincts and the way black women lived in the past? Write an essay in which you explore how Wideman's understanding of his brother Robby's contrary instincts are different from Walker's understanding of her mother's contrary instincts.

2. Gloria Steinem's mother, Ruth (in "Ruth's Song," p. 542), finds self-expression, at least for a while, in her job; but that ends, and she's left alone by a husband whose work involves a great deal of traveling. Even though she does travel with him for a time, her life changes to the point where Steinem calls it a "transformation"—a transformation, Steinem concludes, more the result of forces that affect all women than of personal or acci-

dental forces. On the basis of Walker's and Steinem's mothers' experiences, what can you conclude about the forces that affected their lives? Write an essay in which you discuss these forces. Are they the same for both women? If so, in what ways? If not, how do they differ? Finally, how were the lessons Walker and Steinem learned from their mothers' examples similar? different?

# JOHN EDGAR
# WIDEMAN

*J*OHN EDGAR WIDEMAN *was born in 1941 in Washington, D.C., but spent most of his youth in Homewood, a neighborhood in Pittsburgh. He earned a B.A. from the University of Pennsylvania, taught at the University of Wyoming, and is currently a professor of English at the University of Massachusetts, Amherst. In addition to the nonfiction work* Brothers and Keepers, *from which this selection is drawn, Wideman has published several critically acclaimed novels, including* Sent for You Yesterday, *which won the 1984 PEN/Faulkner Award, and* The Lynchers.

*Wideman's seventh work of fiction,* Reuben (1987), *tells the story of a lawyer who lives in Homewood. Wideman describes Reuben as a "kind of god or spirit" trying to "hold his community together, prop people up, keep them going." He is currently working on a book of short stories and a novel based on the bombing of the MOVE headquarters in Philadelphia in May 1985.*

*"Stories are letters," Wideman once wrote, "letters sent to anybody or everybody. But the best kind are meant to be read by a specific somebody. When you read that kind you know you are eavesdropping. You know a real person somewhere will read the same words you are reading and the story is that person's business and*

*you are a ghost listening in." Brothers and Keepers is a family story, about Wideman and his brother, Robby. John went to Oxford as a Rhodes scholar and Robby went to prison for his role in a robbery and a murder. The section that follows tells part of Robby's story and asks whose business it is to speak of such things and whose business it is to listen. In this account, you will hear the voices of Robby, John, and people from the neighborhood, but also the voice of the writer, speaking about the difficulty of writing and the dangers of explaining away the complexity of Robby's life.*

*In an article called "The Language of Home," Wideman says, "One of the earliest lessons I learned as a child was that if you looked away from something, it might not be there when you looked back. I feared loss, feared turning to speak to someone and finding no one there. . . . Writing forces me to risk ignoring the logic of this lesson. . . . I examine minutely the place I come from, repeat its stories, sing its songs, preserve its language and values, because they make me what I am and because if I don't, who will?"*

# *Our Time*

*You remember what we were saying about young black men in the street-world life. And trying to understand why the "square world" becomes completely unattractive to them. It has to do with the fact that their world is the GHETTO and in that world all the glamour, all the praise and attention is given to the slick guy, the gangster especially, the ones that get over in the "life." And it's because we can't help but feel some satisfaction seeing a brother, a black man, get over on these people, on their system without playing by their rules. No matter how much we have incorporated these rules as our own, we know that they were forced on us by people who did not have our best interests at heart. So this hip guy, this gangster or player or whatever label you give these brothers that we like to shun because of the poison that they spread, we, black people, still look at them with some sense of pride and admiration, our children openly, us adults somewhere deep inside. We know they represent rebellion—what little is left in us. Well, having lived in the "life," it becomes very hard—almost impossible—to find any contentment in joining the status quo. Too hard to go back to being nobody in a world that hates you. Even if I had struck it rich in the life, I would have managed to throw it down the fast lane. Or have lost it on a revolutionary whim. Hopefully the latter.*

*I have always burned up in my fervent passions of desire and want. My senses at times tingle and itch with my romantic, idealistic outlook on life, which has always made me keep my distance from reality, reality that was a constant insult to my world, to my dream of happiness and peace, to my people-for-people kind of world, my easy-cars-for-a-nickel-or-a-dime sorta world. And these driving passions, this sensitivity to the love and good in people, also turned on me because I used it to play on people and their feelings. These aspirations of love and desire turned on me when I wasn't able to live up to this sweet-self morality, so I began to self-destruct, burning up in my sensitivity, losing direction, because nowhere could I find this world of truth and love and harmony.*

*In the real world, the world left for me, it was unacceptable to be "good," it was square to be smart in school, it was jive to show respect to people outside the street world, it was cool to be cold to your woman and the people that loved you. The things we liked we called "bad." "Man, that was a bad girl." The world of the angry black kid growing up in the sixties was a world in which to be in was to be out—out of touch with the square world and all of its rules on what's right and wrong. The thing was to make your own rules, do your own thing, but make sure it's contrary to what society says or is.*

*I SHALL ALWAYS PRAY*

# I

Garth looked bad. Real bad. Ichabod Crane anyway, but now he was a skeleton. Lying there in the bed with his bones poking through his skin, it made you want to cry. Garth's barely able to talk, his smooth, medium-brown skin yellow as pee. Ichabod legs and long hands and long feet, Garth could make you laugh just walking down the street. On the set you'd see him coming a far way off. Three-quarters leg so you knew it had to be Garth the way he was split up higher in the crotch than anybody else. Wilt the Stilt with a lean bird body perched on top his high waist. Size-fifteen shoes. Hands could palm a basketball easy as holding a pool cue. Fingers long enough to wrap round a basketball, but Garth couldn't play a lick. Never could get all that lankiness together on the court. You'd look at him sometimes as he was trucking down Homewood Avenue and think that nigger ain't walking, he's trying to remember how to walk. Awkward as a pigeon on roller skates. Knobby joints out of whack, arms and legs flailing, going their separate ways, his body jerking to keep them from going too far. Moving down the street like that wouldn't work, didn't make sense if you stood back and watched, if you pretended you hadn't seen Garth get where he was going a million times before. Nothing funny now, though. White hospital sheets pulled to his chest. Garth's head always looked small as a tennis ball way up there on his shoulders. Now it's a yellow, shrunken skull.

Ever since Robby had entered the ward, he'd wanted to reach over and hide his friend's arm under the covers. For two weeks Gar had been wasting away in the bed. Bad enough knowing Gar was dying. Didn't need

597

that pitiful stick arm reminding him how close to nothing his main man had fallen. So fast. It could happen so fast. If Robby tried to raise that arm it would come off in his hand. As gentle as he could would not be gentle enough. The arm would disintegrate, like a long ash off the end of a cigarette.

Time to leave. No sense in sitting any longer. Garth not talking, no way of telling whether he was listening either. And Robby has nothing more to say. Choked up the way he gets inside hospitals. Hospital smell and quiet, the bare halls and bare floors, the echoes, something about all that he can't name, wouldn't try to name, rises in him and chills him. Like his teeth are chattering the whole time he's inside a hospital. Like his entire body is trembling uncontrollably, only nobody can see it or hear it but him. Shaking because he can't breathe the stuffy air. Hot and cold at the same time. He's been aching to leave since he entered the ward. Aching to get up and bust through the big glass front doors. Aching to pounce on that spidery arm flung back behind Gar's head. The arm too wasted to belong to his friend. He wants to grab it and hurl it away.

Robby pulls on tight white gloves the undertaker had dealt out to him and the rest of the pallbearers. His brown skin shows through the thin material, turns the white dingy. He's remembering that last time in Garth's ward. The hospital stink. Hot, chilly air. A bare arm protruding from the sleeve of the hospital gown, more dried-up toothpick than arm, a withered twig, with Garth's fingers like a bunch of skinny brown bananas drooping from the knobby tip.

Robby had studied the metal guts of the hospital bed, the black scuff marks swirling around the chair's legs. When he'd finally risen to go, his chair scraping against the vinyl floor broke a long silence. The noise must have roused Garth's attention. He'd spoken again.

You're good, man. Don't ever forget, Rob. You're the best.

Garth's first words since the little banter back and forth when Robby had entered the ward and dragged a chair to the side of Gar's bed. A whisper scarcely audible now that Robby was standing. Garth had tried to grin. The best he could manage was a pained adjustment of the bones of his face, no more than a shadow scudding across the yellow skull, but Robby had seen the famous smile. He hesitated, stopped rushing toward the door long enough to smile back. Because that was Gar. That was the way Gar was. He always had a smile and a good word for his cut buddies. Garth's grin was money in the bank. You could count on it like you could count on a good word from him. Something in his face would tell you you were alright, better than alright, that he believed in you, that you were, as he'd just whispered, "the best." You could depend on Garth to say something to make you feel good, even though you knew he was lying. With that grin greasing the lie you had to believe it, even though you knew better.

Garth was the gang's dreamer. When he talked, you could see his dreams. That's why Robby had believed it, seen the grin, the bright shadow lighting Garth's face an instant. Out of nothing, out of pain, fear, the certainty of death gripping them both, Garth's voice had manufactured the grin.

Now they had to bury Garth. A few days after the visit to the hospital the phone rang and it was Garth's mother with the news of her son's death. Not really news. Robby had known it was just a matter of time. Of waiting for the moment when somebody else's voice would pronounce the words he'd said to himself a hundred times. *He's gone. Gar's dead.* Long gone before the telephone rang. Gar was gone when they stuck him up in the hospital bed. By the time they'd figured out what ailed him and admitted him to the hospital, it was too late. The disease had turned him to a skeleton. Nothing left of Garth to treat. They hid his messy death under white sheets, perfumed it with disinfectant, pumped him full of drugs so he wouldn't disturb his neighbors.

The others had squeezed into their pallbearers' gloves. Cheap white cotton gloves so you could use them once and throw them away like the rubber ones doctors wear when they stick their fingers up your ass. Michael, Cecil, and Sowell were pallbearers, too. With Robby and two men from Garth's family they would carry the coffin from Gaines Funeral Parlor to the hearse. Garth had been the dreamer for the gang. Robby counted four black fingers in the white glove. Garth was the thumb. The hand would be clumsy, wouldn't work right without him. Garth was different. But everybody else was different, too. Mike, the ice man, supercool. Cecil indifferent, ready to do most anything or nothing and couldn't care less which it was. Sowell wasn't really part of the gang; he didn't hang with them, didn't like to take the risks that were part of the "life." Sowell kept a good job. The "life" for him was just a way to make quick money. He didn't shoot up; he thought of himself as a businessman, an investor not a partner in their schemes. They knew Sowell mostly through Garth. Perhaps things would change now. The four survivors closer after they shared the burden of Gar's coffin, after they hoisted it and slid it on steel rollers into the back of Gaines's Cadillac hearse.

Robby was grateful for the gloves. He'd never been able to touch anything dead. He'd taken a beating once from his father rather than touch the bloody mousetrap his mother had nudged to the back door with her toe and ordered him to empty. The brass handle of the coffin felt damp through the glove. He gripped tighter to stop the flow of blood or sweat, whatever it was leaking from him or seeping from the metal. Garth had melted down to nothing by the end so it couldn't be him nearly yanking off Robby's shoulder when the box shifted and its weight shot forward. Felt like a coffin full of bricks. Robby stared across at Mike but Mike was a soldier, eyes front, riveted to the yawning rear door of the hearse. Mike's eyes wouldn't admit it, but they'd almost lost the coffin. They were rookie pallbearers and maneuvering down the carpeted front steps of Gaines Funeral Parlor they'd almost let Garth fly out their hands. They needed somebody who knew what he was doing. An old, steady head to show them the way. They needed Garth. But Garth was long gone. Ashes inside the steel box.

They began drinking later that afternoon in Garth's people's house. Women and food in one room, men hitting the whiskey hard in another. It was a typical project apartment. The kind everybody had stayed in or visited one time or another. Small, shabby, featureless. Not a place to live. No matter what you did to it, how clean you kept it or what kind of furniture you loaded it with, the walls and ceilings were not meant to be home for anybody. A place you passed through. Not yours, because the people who'd been there before you left their indelible marks everywhere and you couldn't help adding your bruises and knots for the next tenants. You could rent a kitchen and bedroom and a bathroom and a living room, the project flats were laid out so you had a room for each of the things people did in houses. Problem was, every corner was cut. Living cramped is one thing and people can get cozy in the closest quarters. It's another thing to live in a place designed to be just a little less than adequate. No slack, no space to personalize, to stamp the flat with what's peculiar to your style. Like a man sitting on a toilet seat that's too small and the toilet too close to the bathtub so his knees shove against the enamel edge. He can move his bowels that way and plenty of people in the world have a lot less but he'll never enjoy sitting there, never feel the deep down comfort of belonging where he must squat.

Anyway, the whiskey started flowing in that little project apartment. Robby listened, for Garth's sake, as long as he could to old people reminiscing about funerals they'd attended, about all the friends and relatives they'd escorted to the edge of Jordan, old folks sipping good whiskey and moaning and groaning till it seemed a sin to be left behind on this side of the river after so many saints had crossed over. He listened to people express their grief, tell sad, familiar stories. As he got high he listened less closely to the words. Faces and gestures revealed more than enough. When he split with Mike and Cecil and their ladies, Sowell tagged along. By then the tacky, low-ceilinged rooms of the flat were packed. Loud talk, laughter, storytellers competing for audiences. Robby half expected the door he pushed shut behind himself to pop open again, waited for bottled-up noise to explode into the funky hallway.

Nobody thinking about cemeteries now. Nobody else needs to be buried today, so it was time to get it on. Some people had been getting close to rowdy. Some people had been getting mad. Mad at one of the guests in the apartment, mad at doctors and hospitals and whites in general who had the whole world in their hands but didn't have the slightest idea what to do with it. A short, dark man, bubble-eyed, immaculately dressed in a three-piece, wool, herringbone suit, had railed about the callousness, the ignorance of white witch doctors who, by misdiagnosing Garth's illness, had sealed his doom. His harangue had drawn a crowd. He wasn't just talking, he was testifying, and a hush had fallen over half the room as he dissected the dirty tricks of white folks. If somebody ran to the hospital and snatched a white-coated doctor and threw him into the circle surrounding the little fish-eyed man, the mourners would tear the pale-faced devil apart. Robby wished he could feed them one. Remembered Garth weak and helpless in the bed and the doctors and nurses flitting around in the halls, jiving the other patients, ignoring Gar like he wasn't there. Garth was dead because he had believed them. Dead because he had nowhere else to turn when the pain in his gut and the headaches grew worse and worse. Not that he trusted the doctors or believed they gave a flying fuck about him. He'd just run out of choices and had to put himself in their hands. They told him jaundice was his problem, and while his liver rotted away and pain cooked him dizzy Garth assured anyone who asked that it was just a matter of giving the medicine time to work. To kill the pain he blew weed as long as he had strength to hold a joint between his lips. Take a whole bunch of smoke to cool me out these days. Puffing like a chimney till he lost it and fell back and Robby scrambling to grab the joint before Garth torched hisself.

When you thought about it, Garth's dying made no sense. And the more you thought the more you dug that nothing else did neither. The world's a stone bitch. Nothing true if that's not true. The man had you coming and going. He owned everything worth owning and all you'd ever get was what he didn't want anymore, what he'd chewed and spit out and left in the gutter for niggers to fight over. Garth had pointed to the street and said, If we ever make it, it got to come from there, from the curb. We got to melt that rock till we get us some money. He grinned then, Ain't no big thing. We'll make it, brother man. We got what it takes. It's our time.

Something had crawled in Garth's belly. The man said it wasn't nothing. Sold him some aspirins and said he'd be alright in no time. The man killed Garth. Couldn't kill him no deader with a .357 magnum slug, but ain't no crime been committed. Just one those things. You know, everybody makes mistakes. And a dead nigger ain't really such a big mistake when you think about it. Matter of fact you mize well forget the whole thing. Nigger wasn't going nowhere, nohow. I mean he wasn't no brain surgeon or astronaut, no movie star or big-time athlete. Probably a dope fiend or gangster. Wind up killing some innocent person or wasting another nigger. Shucks. That doctor ought to get a medal.

Hey, man. Robby caught Mike's eye. Then Cecil and Sowell turned to him. They knew he was speaking to everybody. Late now. Ten, eleven, because it had been dark outside for hours. Quiet now. Too quiet in his pad. And too much smoke and drink since the funeral. From a bare bulb in the kitchen ceiling light seeped down the hallway and hovered dimly in the doorway of the room where they sat. Robby wondered if the others felt as bad as he did. If the cemetery clothes itched their skin. If they could smell grave dust on their shoes. He hoped they'd finish this last jug of wine and let the day be over. He needed sleep, downtime to get the terrible weight of Garth's death off his mind. He'd been grateful for the darkness. For the company of his cut buddies after the funeral. For the Sun Ra tape until it ended and plunged them into a deeper silence than any he'd ever known. Garth was gone. In a few days people would stop talking about him. He was in the ground. Stone-cold dead. Robby had held a chunk of crumbly ground in his white-gloved fingers and mashed it and dropped the dust into the hole. Now the ground had closed over Garth and what did it mean? Here one day and gone the next and that was that. They'd bury somebody else out of Gaines tomorrow. People would dress up and cry and get drunk and tell lies and next day it'd be somebody else's turn to die. Which one of the shadows in this black room would go first? What did it matter? Who cared? Who would remember their names; they were ghosts already. Dead as Garth already. Only difference was, Garth didn't have it to worry about no more. Garth didn't have to pretend he was going anywhere cause he was there. He'd made it to the place they all were headed fast as their legs could carry them. Every step was a step closer to the stone-cold ground, the pitch-black hole where they'd dropped Garth's body.

Hey, youall. We got to drink to Garth one last time.

They clinked glasses in the darkness. Robby searched for something to say. The right words wouldn't come. He knew there was something proper and precise that needed to be said. Because the exact words eluded him, because only the right words would do, he swallowed his gulp of heavy, sweet wine in silence.

He knew he'd let Garth down. If it had been one of the others dead, Michael or Cecil or Sowell or him, Garth wouldn't let it slide by like this, wouldn't let it end like so many other nights had ended, the fellows nodding off one by one, stupefied by smoke and drink, each one beginning to shop around in his mind, trying to figure whether or not he should turn in or if there was a lady somewhere who'd welcome him in her bed. No. Garth would have figured a way to make it special. They wouldn't be hiding in the bushes. They'd be knights in shining armor around a big table. They'd raise their giant, silver cups to honor the fallen comrade. Like in the olden days. Clean, brave dudes with gold rings and gold chains.

They'd draw their blades. Razor-edged swords that gleam in the light with jewels sparkling in the handles. They'd make a roof over the table when they stood and raised their swords and the points touched in the sky. A silver dagger on a satin pillow in the middle of the table. Everybody roll up their sleeves and prick a vein and go round, each one touching everybody else so the blood runs together and we're brothers forever, brothers as long as blood flows in anybody's arm. We'd ride off and do unbelievable shit. The dead one always with us cause we'd do it all for him. Swear we'd never let him down.

It's our time now. We can't let Garth down. Let's drink this last one for him and promise him we'll do what he said we could. We'll be the best. We'll make it to the top for him. We'll do it for Garth.

Glasses rattled together again. Robby empties his and thinks about smashing it against a wall. He'd seen it done that way in movies but it was late at night and these crazy niggers might not know when to stop throwing things. A battlefield of broken glass for him to creep through when he gets out of bed in the morning. He doesn't toss the empty glass. Can't see a solid place anyway where it would strike clean and shatter to a million points of light.

My brother had said something about a guy named Garth during one of my visits to the prison. Just a name mentioned in passing. *Garth* or *Gar*. I'd asked Robby to spell it for me. Garth had been a friend of Robby's, about Robby's age, who died one summer of a mysterious disease. Later when Robby chose to begin the story of the robbery and killing by saying, "It all started with Gar dying," I remembered that first casual mention and remembered a conversation with my mother. My mom and I were in the kitchen of the house on Tokay Street. My recollection of details was vague at first but something about the conversation had made a lasting impression because, six years later, hearing Robby say the name *Garth* brought back my mother's words.

My mother worried about Robby all the time. Whenever I visited home, sooner or later I'd find myself alone with Mom and she'd pour out her fears about Robby's *wildness,* the deep trouble he was bound for, the web of entanglements and intrigues and bad company he was weaving around himself with a maddening disregard for the inevitable consequences.

I don't know. I just don't know how to reach him. He won't listen. He's doing wrong and he knows it but nothing I say makes any difference. He's not like the rest of youall. You'd misbehave but I could talk to you or smack you if I had to and you'd straighten up. With Robby it's like talking to a wall.

I'd listen and get angry at my brother because I registered not so much the danger he was bringing on himself, but the effect of his escapades on the woman who'd brought us both into the world. After all, Robby was no baby. If he wanted to mess up, nobody could stop him. Also Robby was my brother, meaning that his wildness was just a stage, a chaotic phase of his life that would only last till he got his head together and decided to start doing right. Doing as the rest of us did. He was my brother. He couldn't fall too far. His brushes with the law (I'd had some, too), the time he'd spent in jail, were serious but temporary setbacks. I viewed his troubles, when I thought about them at all, as a form of protracted juvenile delinquency, and fully expected Robby would learn his lesson sooner or later and return to the fold, the prodigal son, chastened, perhaps a better person for the experience. In the meantime the most serious consequence of his wildness was Mom's devastating unhappiness. She couldn't sustain the detachment, the laissez-faire optimism I had talked myself into. Because I was two thousand miles away, in Wyoming, I didn't have to deal with the day-to-day evidence of Robby's trouble. The syringe Mom found under his bed. The twenty-dollar bill missing from her purse. The times he'd cruise in higher than a kite, his pupils reduced to pinpricks, with his crew and they'd raid the refrigerator and make a loud, sloppy feast, all of them feeling so good they couldn't imagine anybody not up there on cloud nine with them enjoying the time of their lives. Cruising in, then disappearing just as abruptly, leaving their dishes and pans and mess behind. Robby covering Mom with kisses and smiles and drowning her in babytalk hootchey-coo as he staggers through the front door. Her alone in the ravaged, silent kitchen, listening as doors slam and a car squeals off on the cobblestones of Tokay, wondering where they're headed next, wishing, praying Robby will return and eat and eat and eat till he falls asleep at the table so she can carry him upstairs and tuck him in and kiss his forehead and shut the door gently on his sleep.

I wasn't around for all that. Didn't want to know how bad things were for him. Worrying about my mother was tough enough. I could identify with her grief, I could blame my brother. An awful situation, but simple too. My role, my responsibilities and loyalties were clear. The *wildness* was to blame, and it was a passing thing, so I just had to help my mother survive the worst of it, then everything would be alright. I'd steel myself for the moments alone with her when she'd tell me the worst. In the kitchen, usually, over a cup of coffee with the radio playing. When my mother was alone in the house on Tokay, either the TV or a radio or both were always on. Atop the kitchen table a small clock radio turned to WAMO, one of Pittsburgh's soul stations, would background with scratchy gospel music whatever we said in the morning in the kitchen. On a morning like that in 1975, while I drank a cup of coffee and part of me, still half-asleep, hidden, swayed to the soft beat of gospel, my mother had explained how upset Robby was over the death of his friend, Garth.

It was a terrible thing. I've known Garth's mother for years. He was a good boy. No saint for sure, but deep down a good boy. Like your brother. Not a mean bone in his body. Out there in the street doing wrong, but that's where most of them are. What else can they do, John? Sometimes I can't blame them. No jobs, no money in their pockets. How they supposed to feel like men? Garth did better than most. Whatever else he was into, he kept that little job over at Westinghouse and helped out his mother. A big, playful kid. Always smiling. I think that's why him and Robby were so tight. Neither one had good sense. Giggled and acted like fools. Garth no wider than my finger. Straight up and down. A stringbean if I ever saw one. When Robby lived here in the house with me, Garth was always around. I know how bad Robby feels. He hasn't said a word but I know. When Robby's quiet, you know something's wrong. Soon as his eyes pop open in the morning he's looking for the party. First thing in the morning he's chipper and chattering. Looking for the party. That's your brother. He had a match in Garth.

Shame the way they did that boy. He'd been down to the clinic two or three times but they sent him home. Said he had an infection and it would take care of itself. Something like that anyway. You know how they are down there. Have to be spitting blood to get attention. Then all they give you is a Band-Aid. He went back two times, but they kept telling him the same dumb thing. Anybody who knew Garth could see something awful was wrong. Circles under his eyes. Sallow look to his skin. Losing weight. And the poor thing didn't have any weight to lose. Last time I saw him I was shocked. Just about shocked out my shoes. Wasn't Garth standing in front of me. Not the boy I knew.

Well, to make a long story short, they finally took him in the hospital but it was too late. They let him walk the streets till he was dead. It was wrong. Worse than wrong how they did him, but that's how those dogs do us every day God sends here. Garth's gone, so nothing nobody can say will do any good. I feel so sorry for his mother. She lived for that boy. I called her and tried to talk but what can you say? I prayed for her and prayed for Garth and prayed for Robby. A thing like that tears people up. It's worse if you keep it inside. And that's your brother's way. He'll let it eat him up and then go out and do something crazy.

Until she told me Garth's story I guess I hadn't realized how much my mother had begun to change. She had always seemed to me to exemplify the tolerance, the patience, the long view epitomized in her father. John French's favorite saying was, Give 'em the benefit of the doubt. She could get as ruffled, as evil as the rest of us, cry and scream or tear around the house fit to be tied. She had her grudges and quarrels. Mom could let it all hang out, yet most of the time she radiated a deep calm. She reacted strongly to things but at the same time held judgment in abeyance. Events, personalities always deserved a second, slower appraisal, an evaluation outside the sphere of everyday hassles and vexations. You gave people the benefit of the doubt. You attempted to remove your ego, acknowledge the limitations of your individual view of things. You consulted as far as you were equipped by temperament and intelligence a broader, more abiding set of relationships and connections.

You tried on the other person's point of view. You sought the other, better person in yourself who might talk you into relinquishing for a moment your selfish interest in whatever was at issue. You stopped and considered the long view, possibilities other than the one that momentarily was leading you by the nose. You gave yourself and other people the benefit of the doubt.

My mother had that capacity. I'd admired, envied, and benefited infinitely from its presence. As she related the story of Garth's death and my brother's anger and remorse, her tone was uncompromisingly bitter. No slack, no margin of doubt was being granted to the forces that destroyed Garth and still pursued her son. She had exhausted her reserves of understanding and compassion. The long view supplied the same ugly picture as the short. She had an enemy now. It was that revealed truth that had given the conversation its edge, its impact. *They* had killed Garth, and his dying had killed part of her son; so the battle lines were drawn. Irreconcilably. Absolutely. The backside of John French's motto had come into play. Giving someone the benefit of the doubt was also giving him enough rope to hang himself. If a person takes advantage of the benefit of the doubt and keeps on taking and taking, one day the rope plays out. The piper must be paid. If you've been the one giving, it becomes incumbent on you to grip your end tight and take away. You turn the other cheek, but slowly, cautiously, and keep your fist balled up at your side. If your antagonist decides to smack rather than kiss you or leave you alone, you make sure you get in the first blow. And make sure it's hard enough to knock him down.

Before she told Garth's story, my mother had already changed, but it took years for me to realize how profoundly she hated what had been done to Garth and then Robby. The gentleness of my grandfather, like his fair skin and good French hair, had been passed down to my mother. Gentleness styled the way she thought, spoke, and moved in the world. Her easy disposition and sociability masked the intensity of her feelings. Her attitude to authority of any kind, doctors, clerks, police, bill collectors, newscasters, whites in general partook of her constitutional gentleness. She wasn't docile or cowed. The power other people possessed or believed they possessed didn't frighten her; she accommodated herself, offered something they could accept as deference but that was in fact the same resigned, alert attention she paid to roaches or weather or poverty, any of the givens outside herself that she couldn't do much about. She never engaged in public tests of will, never pushed herself or her point of view on people she didn't know. Social awkwardness embarrassed her. Like most Americans she didn't like paying taxes, was suspicious of politicians, resented the disparity between big and little people in our society and the double standard that allowed big shots to get away with murder. She paid particular attention to news stories that reinforced her basic political assumption that power corrupts. On the other hand she knew the world was a vale of tears and one's strength, granted by God to deal with life's inevitable calamities, should not be squandered on small stuff.

In spite of all her temperamental and philosophic resistance to extremes, my mother would be radicalized. What the demonstrations, protest marches, and slogans of the sixties had not effected would be accomplished by Garth's death and my brother's troubles. She would become an aggressive, acid critic of the status quo in all its forms: from the President ("If it wasn't for that rat I'd have a storm door to go with the storm windows but he cut the program") on down to bank tellers ("I go there every Friday and I'm one of the few black faces she sees all day and she knows me as well as she knows that wart on her cheek but she'll still make me show my license before she'll cash my check"). A son she loved would be pursued, captured, tried, and imprisoned by the forces of law and order. Throughout the ordeal her love for him wouldn't change, couldn't change. His crime tested her love and also tested the nature, the intent of the forces arrayed against her son. She had to make a choice. On one side were the stark facts of his crime: robbery, murder, flight; her son an outlaw, a fugitive; then a prisoner. On the other side the guardians of society, the laws, courts, police, judges, and keepers who were responsible for punishing her son's transgression.

She didn't invent the two sides and initially didn't believe there couldn't be a middle ground. She extended the benefit of the doubt. Tried to situate herself somewhere in between, acknowledging the evil of her son's crime while simultaneously holding on to the fact that he existed as a human being before, after, and during the crime he'd committed. He'd done wrong but he was still Robby and she'd always be his mother. Strangely, on the dark side, the side of the crime and its terrible consequences, she would find room to exercise her love. As negative as the elements were, a life taken, the grief of the survivors, suffering, waste, guilt, remorse, the scale was human; she could apply her sense of right and wrong. Her life to that point had equipped her with values, with tools for sorting out and coping with disaster. So she would choose to make her fight there, on treacherous yet familiar ground—familiar since her son was there—and she could place herself, a woman, a mother, a grieving, bereaved human being, there beside him.

Nothing like that was possible on the other side. The legitimacy of the other side was grounded not in her experience of life, but in a set of rules seemingly framed to sidestep, ignore, or replace her sense of reality. Accepting the version of reality encoded in *their* rules would be like stepping into a cage and locking herself in. Definitions of her son, herself, of need and frailty and mercy, of blackness and redemption and justice had all been neatly formulated. No need here for her questions, her uncertainty, her fear, her love. Everything was clean and clear. No room for her sense that things like good and evil, right and wrong bleed into each other and create a dreadful margin of ambiguity no one could name but could only enter, enter at the risk of everything because everything is at stake and no one on earth knows what it means to enter or what will happen if and when the testing of the margin is over.

She could love her son, accept his guilt, accept the necessity of punishment, suffer with him, grow with him past the stage of blaming everyone but himself for his troubles, grieve with him when true penitence began to exact its toll. Though she might wish penance and absolution could be achieved in private, without the intervention of a prison sentence, she understood dues must be paid. He was her son but he was also a man who had committed a robbery in the course of which another woman's son had been killed. What would appall her and what finally turned her against the forces of law and order was the incapacity of the legal system to grant her son's humanity. "Fair" was the word she used—a John French word. She expected them to treat Robby fair. Fairness was what made her willing to give him up to punishment even though her love screamed no and her hands clung to his shoulders. Fairness was what she expected from the other side in their dealings with her and her son.

She could see their side, but they steadfastly refused to see hers. And when she realized fairness was not forthcoming, she began to hate. In the lack of reciprocity, in the failure to grant that Robby was first a man, then a man who had done wrong, the institutions and individuals who took over control of his life denied not only his humanity but the very existence of the world that had nurtured him and nurtured her—the world of touching, laughing, suffering black people that established Robby's claim to something more than a number.

Mom expects the worst now. She's peeped their hole card. She understands they have a master plan that leaves little to accident, that most of the ugliest things happening to black people are not accidental but the predictable results of the working of the plan. What she learned about authority, about law and order didn't make sense at first. It went against her instincts, what she wanted to believe, against the generosity she'd observed in her father's interactions with other Homewood people. He was fair. He'd pick up the egg rolls he loved from the back kitchen door of Mr.

Wong's restaurant and not blame Wong, his old talking buddy and card-playing crony, for not serving black people in his restaurant. Wong had a family and depended on white folks to feed them, so Wong didn't have any choice and neither did John French if he wanted those incredible egg rolls. He treated everyone, high and low, the same. He said what he meant and meant what he said. John French expected no more from other people than he expected from himself. And he'd been known to mess up many a time, but that was him, that was John French, no better, no worse than any man who pulls on his britches one leg at a time. He needed a little slack, needed the benefit of that blind eye people who love, or people who want to get along with other people, must learn to cast. John French was grateful for the slack, so was quick to extend it to others. Till they crossed him.

My mother had been raised in Homewood. The old Homewood. Her relations with people in that close-knit, homogeneous community were based on trust, mutual respect, common spiritual and material concerns. Face-to-face contact, shared language and values, a large fund of communal experience rendered individual lives extremely visible in Homewood. Both a person's self-identity ("You know who you are") and accountability ("Other people know who you are") were firmly established.

If one of the Homewood people said, "That's the French girl" or, "There goes John French's daughter," a portrait with subtle shading and complex resonance was painted by the words. If the listener addressed was also a Homewood resident, the speaker's voice located the young woman passing innocently down Tioga Street in a world invisible to outsiders. A French girl was somebody who lived in Cassina Way, somebody you didn't fool with or talk nasty to. Didn't speak to at all except in certain places or on certain occasions. French girls were church girls, Homewood African Methodist Episcopal Zion Sunday-school-picnic and social-event young ladies. You wouldn't find them hanging around anywhere without escorts or chaperones. French girls had that fair, light, bright, almost white redbone complexion and fine blown hair and nice big legs but all that was to be appreciated from a distance because they were nice girls and because they had this crazy daddy who wore a big brown country hat and gambled and drank wine and once ran a man out of town, ran him away without ever laying a hand on him or making a bad-mouthed threat, just cut his eyes a certain way when he said the man's name and the word went out and the man who had cheated a drunk John French with loaded dice was gone. Just like that. And there was the time Elias Brown was cleaning his shotgun in his backyard. Brown had his double-barreled shotgun across his knees and a jug of Dago Red on the ground beside him and it was a Saturday and hot and Brown was sweating through his BVD undershirt and paying more attention to the wine than he was to the gun. Next thing you know,

*Boom!* Off it goes and buckshot sprayed down Cassina Way, and it's Saturday and summer like I said, so chillens playing everywhere but God watches over fools and babies so nobody hit bad. Nobody hit at all except the little French girl, Geraldine, playing out there in the alley and she got nicked in her knee. Barely drew blood. A sliver of that buckshot musta ricocheted off the cobblestones and cut her knee. Thank Jesus she the only one hit and she ain't hit bad. Poor Elias Brown don't quite know what done happened till some the mens run over in his yard and snatch the gun and shake the wine out his head. What you doing, fool? Don't you know no better all those children running round here? Coulda killed one these babies. Elias stone drunk and don't hear nothing, see nothing till one the men say French girl. Nicked the little French girl, Geraldine. Then Elias woke up real quick. His knees, his dusty butt, everything he got starts to trembling and his eyes get big as dinner plates. Then he's gone like a turkey through the corn. Nobody seen Elias for a week. He's in Ohio at his sister's next time anybody hear anything about Elias. He's cross there in Ohio and still shaking till he git word John French ain't after him. It took three men gon over there telling the same story to get Elias back to Homewood. John French ain't mad. He *was* mad but he ain't mad now. Little girl just nicked is all and French ain't studying you, Brown.

You heard things like that in Homewood names. Rules of etiquette, thumbnail character sketches, a history of the community. A dire warning to get back could be coded into the saying of a person's name, and a further inflection of the speaker's voice could tell you to ignore the facts, forget what he's just reminded you to remember and go on. Try your luck.

Because Homewood was self-contained and possessed such a strong personality, because its people depended less on outsiders than they did on each other for so many of their most basic satisfactions, they didn't notice the net settling over their community until it was already firmly in place. Even though the strands of the net—racial discrimination, economic exploitation, white hate and fear—had existed time out of mind, what people didn't notice or chose not to notice was that the net was being drawn tighter, that ruthless people outside the community had the power to choke the life out of Homewood, and as soon as it served their interests would do just that. During the final stages, as the net closed like a fist around Homewood, my mother couldn't pretend it wasn't there. But instead of setting her free, the truth trapped her in a cage as tangible as the iron bars of Robby's cell.

Some signs were subtle, gradual. The A & P started to die. Nobody mopped filth from the floors. Nobody bothered to restock empty shelves. Fewer and fewer white faces among the shoppers. A plate-glass display window gets broken and stays broken. When they finally close the store, they paste the going-out-of-business notice over the jagged, taped crack.

Other signs as blatant, as sudden as fire engines and patrol cars breaking your sleep, screaming through the dark Homewood streets. First Garth's death, then Robby's troubles brought it all home. My mother realized her personal unhappiness and grief were inseparable from what was happening *out there*. Out there had never been further away than the thousand insults and humiliations she had disciplined herself to ignore. What she had deemed petty, not worth bothering about, were strings of the net just as necessary, as effective as the most dramatic intrusions into her life. She decided to stop letting things go by. No more benefit of the doubt. Doubt had been cruelly excised. She decided to train herself to be as wary, as unforgiving as she'd once been ready to live and let live. My mother wouldn't become paranoid, not even overtly prickly or bristling. That would have been too contrary to her style, to what her blood and upbringing had instilled. The change was inside. What she thought of people. How she judged situations. Things she'd say or do startled me, set me back on my heels because I didn't recognize my mother in them. I couldn't account for the stare of pure unadulterated hatred she directed at the prison guard when he turned away from her to answer the phone before handing her the rest-room key she'd requested, the vehemence with which she had cussed Richard Nixon for paying no taxes when she, scraping by on an income of less than four thousand dollars a year, owed the IRS three hundred dollars.

Garth's death and Robby's troubles were at the center of her new vision. Like a prism, they caught the light, transformed it so she could trace the seemingly random inconveniences and impositions coloring her life to their source in a master plan.

I first heard Garth's story in the summer of 1975, the summer my wife carried our daughter Jamila in her belly, the summer before the robbery and killing. The story contained all the clues I'm trying to decipher now. Sitting in the kitchen vaguely distracted by gospel music from the little clock radio atop the table, listening as my mother expressed her sorrow, her indignation at the way Garth was treated, her fears for my brother, I was hearing a new voice. Something about the voice struck me then, but I missed what was novel and crucial. I'd lost my Homewood ear. Missed all the things unsaid that invested her words with special urgency. People in Homewood often ask: You said that to say what? The impacted quality of an utterance either buries a point too obscurely or insists on a point so strongly that the listener wants the meat of the message repeated, wants it restated clearly so it stands alone on its own two feet. If I'd been alert enough to ask that question, to dig down to the root and core of Garth's story after my mother told it, I might have understood sooner how desperate and dangerous Homewood had become. Six years later my brother was in prison, and when he began the story of his troubles with Garth's death, a circle completed itself; Robby was talking to me, but I was still on the outside, looking in.

That day six years later, I talked with Robby three hours, the maximum allotted for weekday visits with a prisoner. It was the first time in life we'd ever talked that long. Probably two and a half hours longer than the longest, unbroken, private conversation we'd ever had. And it had taken guards, locks, and bars to bring us together. The ironies of the situation, the irony of that fact, escaped neither of us.

I listened mostly, interrupting my brother's story a few times to clarify dates or names. Much of what he related was familiar. The people, the places. Even the voice, the words he chose were mine in a way. We're so alike, I kept thinking, anticipating what he would say next, how he would say it, filling in naturally, easily with my words what he left unsaid. Trouble was our minds weren't interchangeable. No more than our bodies. The guards wouldn't have allowed me to stay in my brother's place. He was the criminal. I was the visitor from outside. Different as night and day. As Robby talked I let myself forget that difference. Paid too much attention to myself listening and lost some of what he was saying. What I missed would have helped define the difference. But I missed it. It was easy to half listen. For both of us to pretend to be closer than we were. We needed the closeness. We were brothers. In the prison visiting lounge I acted toward my brother the way I'd been acting toward him all my life, heard what I wanted to hear, rejected the rest.

When Robby talked, the similarity of his Homewood and mine was a trap. I could believe I knew exactly what he was describing. I could relax into his story, walk down Dunfermline or Tioga, see my crippled grandmother sitting on the porch of the house on Finance, all the color her pale face had lost blooming in the rosebush beneath her in the yard, see Robby in the downstairs hall of the house on Marchand, rapping with his girl on the phone, which sat on a three-legged stand just inside the front door. I'd slip unaware out of his story into one of my own. I'd be following him, an obedient shadow, then a cloud would blot the sun and I'd be gone, unchained, a dark form still skulking behind him but no longer in tow.

The hardest habit to break, since it was the habit of a lifetime, would be listening to myself listen to him. That habit would destroy any chance of seeing my brother on his terms; and seeing him in his terms, learning his terms, seemed the whole point of learning his story. However numerous and comforting the similarities, we were different. The world had seized on the difference, allowed me room to thrive, while he'd been forced into a cage. Why did it work out that way? What was the nature of the difference? Why did it haunt me? Temporarily at least, to answer these questions, I had to root my fiction-writing self out of our exchanges. I had to teach myself to listen. Start fresh, clear the pipes, resist too facile an identification, tame the urge to take off with Robby's story and make it my own.

I understood all that, but could I break the habit? And even if I did learn to listen, wouldn't there be a point at which I'd have to take over the telling? Wasn't there something fundamental in my writing, in my capacity to function, that depended on flight, on escape? Wasn't another person's skin a hiding place, a place to work out anxiety, to face threats too intimidating to handle in any other fashion? Wasn't writing about people a way of exploiting them?

A stranger's gait, or eyes, or a piece of clothing can rivet my attention. Then it's like falling down to the center of the earth. Not exactly fear or panic but an uneasy, uncontrollable momentum, a sense of being swallowed, engulfed in blackness that has no dimensions, no fixed points. That boundless, incarcerating black hole is another person. The detail grabbing me functions as a door and it swings open and I'm drawn, sucked, pulled in head over heels till suddenly I'm righted again, on track again and the peculiarity, the ordinariness of the detail that usurped my attention becomes a window, a way of seeing out of another person's eyes, just as for a second it had been my way in. I'm scooting along on short, stubby legs and the legs are not anybody else's and certainly not mine, but I feel for a second what it's like to motor through the world atop these peculiar duck thighs and foreshortened calves and I know how wobbly the earth feels under those run-over-at-the-heel, split-seamed penny loafers. Then just as suddenly I'm back. I'm me again, slightly embarrassed, guilty because I've been trespassing and don't know how long I've been gone or if anybody noticed me violating somebody else's turf.

Do I write to escape, to make a fiction of my life? If I can't be trusted with the story of my own life, how could I ask my brother to trust me with his?

The business of making a book together was new for both of us. Difficult. Awkward. Another book could be constructed about a writer who goes to a prison to interview his brother but comes away with his own story. The conversations with his brother would provide a stage for dramatizing the writer's tortured relationship to other people, himself, his craft. The writer's motives, the issue of exploitation, the inevitable conflict between his role as detached observer and his responsibility as a brother would be at the center of such a book. When I stopped hearing Robby and listened to myself listening, that kind of book shouldered its way into my consciousness. I didn't like the feeling. That book compromised the intimacy I wanted to achieve with my brother. It was as obtrusive as the Wearever pen in my hand, the little yellow sheets of Yard Count paper begged from the pad of the guard in charge of overseeing the visiting lounge. The borrowed pen and paper (I was not permitted into the lounge with my own) were necessary props. I couldn't rely on memory to get my brother's story down and the keepers had refused my request to use a tape recorder, so there I was. Jimmy Olson, cub reporter, poised on the edge of my seat, pen and paper at ready, asking to be treated as a brother.

We were both rookies. Neither of us had learned very much about sharing our feelings with other family members. At home it had been assumed that each family member possessed deep, powerful feelings and that very little or nothing at all needed to be said about these feelings because we all were stuck with them and talk wouldn't change them. Your particular feelings were a private matter and family was a protective fence around everybody's privacy. Inside the perimeter of the fence each family member resided in his or her own quarters. What transpired in each dwelling was mainly the business of its inhabitant as long as nothing generated within an individual unit threatened the peace or safety of the whole. None of us knew how traditional West African families were organized or what values the circular shape of their villages embodied, but the living arrangements we had worked out among ourselves resembled the ancient African patterns. You were granted emotional privacy, independence, and space to commune with your feelings. You were encouraged to deal with as much as you could on your own, yet you never felt alone. The high wall of the family, the collective, communal reality of other souls, other huts like yours eliminated some of the dread, the isolation experienced when you turned inside and tried to make sense out of the chaos of your individual feelings. No matter how grown you thought you were or how far you believed you'd strayed, you knew you could cry *Mama* in the depths of the night and somebody would tend to you. Arms would wrap round you, a soft soothing voice lend its support. If not a flesh-and-blood mother then a mother in the form of song or story or a surrogate, Aunt Geral, Aunt Martha, drawn from the network of family numbers.

Privacy was a bridge between you and the rest of the family. But you had to learn to control the traffic. You had to keep it uncluttered, resist the temptation to cry wolf. Privacy in our family was a birthright, a union card granted with family membership. The card said you're one of us but also certified your separateness, your obligation to keep much of what defined your separateness to yourself.

An almost aesthetic consideration's involved. Okay, let's live together. Let's each build a hut and for security we'll arrange the individual dwellings in a circle and then build an outer ring to enclose the whole village. Now your hut is your own business, but let's in general agree on certain outward forms. Since we all benefit from the larger pattern, let's compromise, conform to some degree on the materials, the shape of each unit.

Because symmetry and harmony please the eye. Let's adopt a style, one that won't crimp anybody's individuality, one that will buttress and enhance each member's image of what a living place should be.

So Robby and I faced each other in the prison visiting lounge as familiar strangers, linked by blood and time. But how do you begin talking about blood, about time? He's been inside his privacy and I've been inside mine, and neither of us in thirty-odd years had felt the need to exchange more than social calls. We shared the common history, values, and style developed within the tall stockade of family, and that was enough to make us care about each other, enough to insure a profound depth of mutual regard, but the feelings were undifferentiated. They'd seldom been tested specifically, concretely. His privacy and mine had been exclusive, sanctioned by family traditions. Don't get too close. Don't ask too many questions or give too many answers. Don't pry. Don't let what's inside slop out on the people around you.

The stories I'd sent to Robby were an attempt to reveal what I thought about certain matters crucial to us both. Our shared roots and destinies. I wanted him to know what I'd been thinking and how that thinking was drawing me closer to him. I was banging on the door of his privacy. I believed I'd shed some of my own.

We were ready to talk. It was easy to begin. Impossible. We were neophytes, rookies. I was a double rookie. A beginner at this kind of intimacy, a beginner at trying to record it. My double awkwardness kept getting in the way. I'd hidden the borrowed pen by dropping my hand below the level of the table where we sat. Now when in hell would be the right moment to raise it? To use it? I had to depend on my brother's instincts, his generosity. I had to listen, listen.

Luckily there was catching up to do. He asked me about my kids, about his son, Omar, about the new nieces and nephews he'd never seen. That helped. Reminded us we were brothers. We got on with it. Conditions in the prisons. Robby's state of mind. The atmosphere behind the prison walls had been particularly tense for over a year. A group of new, younger guards had instituted a get-tough policy. More strip searches, cell shakedowns, strict enforcement of penny-ante rules and regulations. Grown men treated like children by other grown men. Inmates yanked out of line and punished because a button is undone or hair uncombed. What politicians demanded in the free world was being acted out inside the prison. A crusade, a war on crime waged by a gang of gung-ho guards against men who were already certified casualties, prisoners of war. The walking wounded being beaten and shot up again because they're easy targets. Robby's closest friends, including Cecil and Mike, are in the hole. Others who were considered potential troublemakers had been transferred to harsher prisons. Robby was warned by a guard. We ain't caught you in the shit yet, but we will. We know what you're thinking and we'll catch you in it. Or put you in it. Got your buddies and we'll get you.

The previous summer, 1980, a prisoner, Leon Patterson, had been asphyxiated in his cell. He was an asthma sufferer, a convicted murderer who depended on medication to survive the most severe attacks of his illness. On a hot August afternoon when the pollution index had reached its highest count of the summer, Patterson was locked in his cell in a cellblock without windows and little air. At four o'clock, two hours after he'd been confined to the range, he began to call for help. Other prisoners raised the traditional distress signal, rattling tin cups against the bars of their cells. Patterson's cries for help became screams, and his fellow inmates beat on the bars and shouted with him. Over an hour passed before any guards arrived. They carted away Patterson's limp body. He never revived and was pronounced dead at 10:45 that evening. His death epitomized the polarization in the prison. Patterson was seen as one more victim of the guards' inhumanity. A series of incidents followed in the ensuing year, hunger strikes, melees between guards and prisoners, culminating in a near massacre when the dog days of August hung once more over the prison.

One of the favorite tactics of the militant guards was grabbing a man from the line as the prisoners moved single-file through an archway dividing the recreation yard from the main cell blocks. No reason was given or needed. It was a simple show of force, a reminder of the guards' absolute power, their right to treat the inmates any way they chose, and do it with impunity. A sit-down strike in the prison auditorium followed one of the more violent attacks on an inmate. The prisoner who had resisted an arbitrary seizure and strip search was smacked in the face. He punched back and the guards jumped him, knocked him to the ground with their fists and sticks. The incident took place in plain view of over a hundred prisoners and it was the last straw. The victim had been provoked, assaulted, and surely would be punished for attempting to protect himself, for doing what any man would and should do in similar circumstances. The prisoner would suffer again. In addition to the physical beating they'd administered, the guards would attack the man's record. He'd be written up. A kangaroo court would take away his *good time*, thereby lengthening the period he'd have to wait before becoming eligible for probation or parole. Finally, on the basis of the guards' testimony he'd probably get a sixty-day sojourn in the hole. The prisoners realized it was time to take a stand. What had happened to one could happen to any of them. They rushed into the auditorium and locked themselves in. The prisoners held out till armed state troopers and prison guards in riot gear surrounded the building. Given the mood of that past year and the unmistakable threat in the new warden's voice as he repeated through a loudspeaker his refusal to meet with the prisoners and discuss their grievances, everybody inside the building knew that the authorities meant business, that the forces of law and order would love nothing better than an excuse to turn the auditorium into a shooting gallery. The strike was broken. The men filed out. A point was driven home again. Prisoners have no rights the keepers are bound to respect.

That was how the summer had gone. Summer was bad enough in the penitentiary in the best of times. Warm weather stirred the prisoners' blood. The siren call of the streets intensified. Circus time. The street blooming again after the long, cold winter. People outdoors. On their stoops. On the corners. In bright summer clothes or hardly any clothes at all. The free-world sounds and sights more real as the weather heats up. Confinement a torture. Each cell a hotbox. The keepers take advantage of every excuse to keep you out of the yard, to deprive you of the simple pleasure of a breeze, the blue sky. Why? So that the pleasant weather can be used as a tool, a boon to be withheld. So punishment has a sharper edge. By a perverse turn of the screw something good becomes something bad. Summer a bitch at best, but this past summer as the young turks among the guards ran roughshod over the prisoners, the prison had come close to blowing, to exploding like a piece of rotten fruit in the sun. And if the lid blew, my brother knew he'd be one of the first to die. During any large-scale uprising, in the first violent, chaotic seconds no board of inquiry would ever be able to reconstruct, scores would be settled. A bullet in the back of the brain would get rid of troublemakers, remove potential leaders, uncontrollable prisoners the guards hated and feared. You were supremely eligible for a bullet if the guards couldn't press your button. If they hadn't learned how to manipulate you, if you couldn't be bought or sold, if you weren't into drug and sex games, if you weren't cowed or depraved, then you were a threat.

Robby understood that he was sentenced to die. That all sentences were death sentences. If he didn't buckle under, the guards would do everything in their power to kill him. If he succumbed to the pressure to surrender dignity, self-respect, control over his own mind and body, then he'd become a beast, and what was good in him would die. The death sentence was unambiguous. The question for him became: How long could he survive in spite of the death sentence? Nothing he did would guarantee his safety. A disturbance in a cell block halfway across the prison could provide an excuse for shooting him and dumping him with the other victims. Anytime he was ordered to go with guards out of sight of other prisoners, his escorts could claim he attacked them, or attempted to escape. Since the flimsiest pretext would make murdering him acceptable, he had no means of protecting himself. Yet to maintain sanity, to minimize their opportunities to destroy him, he had to be constantly vigilant. He had to discipline himself to avoid confrontations, he had to weigh in terms of life and death every decision he made; he had to listen and obey his keepers' orders, but he also had to determine in certain threatening situations whether it was better to say no and keep himself out of a trap or take his chances that this particular summons was not the one inviting him to his doom. Of course to say no perpetuated his reputation as one who couldn't be controlled, a bad guy, a guy you never turn your back on, one of the prisoners out to get the guards. That rap made you more dangerous in the keepers' eyes and therefore increased the likelihood they'd be frightened into striking first. Saying no put you in no less jeopardy than going along with the program. Because the program was contrived to kill you. Directly or indirectly, you knew where you were headed. What you didn't know was the schedule. Tomorrow. Next week. A month. A minute. When would one of them get itchy, get beyond waiting a second longer? Would there be a plan, a contrived incident, a conspiracy they'd talk about and set up as they drank coffee in the guards' room or would it be the hair-trigger impulse of one of them who held a grudge, harbored an antipathy so elemental, so irrational that it could express itself only in a burst of pure, unrestrained violence?

If you're Robby and have the will to survive, these are the possibilities you must constantly entertain. Vigilance is the price of survival. Beneath the vigilance, however, is a gnawing awareness boiling in the pit of your stomach. You can be as vigilant as you're able, you can keep fighting the good fight to survive, and still your fate is out of your hands. If they decide to come for you in the morning, that's it. Your ass is grass and those minutes, and hours, days and years you painfully stitched together to put off the final reckoning won't matter at all. So the choice, difficult beyond words, to say yes or say no is made in light of the knowledge that in the end neither your yes nor your no matters. Your life is not in your hands.

The events, the atmosphere of the summer had brought home to Robby the futility of resistance. Power was absurdly apportioned all on one side. To pretend you could control your own destiny was a joke. You learned to laugh at your puniness, as you laughed at the stink of your farts lighting up your cell. Like you laughed at the seriousness of the masturbation ritual that romanticized, cloaked in darkness and secrecy, the simple, hungry shaking of your penis in your fist. You had no choice, but you always had to decide to go on or stop. It had been a stuttering, stop, start, maybe, fuck it, bitch of a summer, and now, for better or worse, we were starting up something else. Robby backtracks his story from Garth to another beginning, the house on Copeland Street in Shadyside where we lived when he was born.

I know that had something to do with it. Living in Shadyside with only white people around. You remember how it was. Except for us and them couple other families it was a all-white neighborhood. I got a thing about black. See, black was like the forbidden fruit. Even when we went to Freed's in Homewood, Geraldine and them never let me go no farther than the end of the block. All them times I stayed over there I didn't go past Mr. Conrad's house by the vacant lot or the other corner where Billy Shields and them stayed. Started to wondering what was so different about a black neighborhood. I was just a little kid and I was curious. I really wanted to know why they didn't want me finding out what was over there. Be playing with the kids next door to Freed, you know, Sonny and Gumpy and them, but all the time I'm wondering what's round the corner, what's up the street. Didn't care if it was *bad* or good or dangerous or what, I had to find out. If it's something bad I figured they would have told me, tried to scare me off. But nobody said nothing except, No. Don't you go no farther than the corner. Then back home in Shadyside nothing but white people so I couldn't ask nobody what was special about black. Black was a mystery and in my mind I decided I'd find out what it was all about. Didn't care if it killed me, I was going to find out.

One time, it was later, I was close to starting high school, I overheard Mommy and Geraldine and Sissy talking in Freed's kitchen. They was talking about us moving from Shadyside back to Homewood. The biggest thing they was worried about was me. How would it be for me being in Homewood and going to Westinghouse? I could tell they was scared. Specially Mom. You know how she is. She didn't want to move. Homewood scared her. Not so much the place but how I'd act if I got out there in the middle of it. She already knew I was wild, hard to handle. There'd be too much mess for me to get into in Homewood. She could see trouble coming.

And she was right. Me and trouble hooked up. See, it was a question of being somebody. Being my own person. Like youns had sports and good grades sewed up. Wasn't nothing I could do in school or sports that youns hadn't done already. People said, Here comes another Wideman. He's gon be a good student like his brothers and sister. That's the way it was spozed to be. I was another Wideman, the last one, the baby, and everybody knew how I was spozed to act. But something inside me said no. Didn't want to be like the rest of youns. Me, I had to be a rebel. Had to get out from under youns' good grades and do. Way back then I decided I wanted to be a star. I wanted to make it big. My way. I wanted the glamour. I wanted to sit high up.

Figured out school and sports wasn't the way. I got to thinking my brothers and sister was squares. Loved youall but wasn't no room left for me. Had to figure out a new territory. I had to be a rebel.

Along about junior high I discovered Garfield. I started hanging out up on Garfield Hill. You know, partying and stuff in Garfield cause that's where the niggers was. Garfield was black, and I finally found what I'd been looking for. That place they was trying to hide from me. It was heaven. You know. Hanging out with the fellows. Drinking wine and trying anything else we could get our hands on. And the ladies. Always a party on the weekends. Had me plenty sweet little soft-leg Garfield ladies. Niggers run my butt off that hill more than a couple times behind messing with somebody's piece but I'd be back next weekend. Cause I'd found heaven. Looking back now, wasn't much to Garfield. Just a rinky-dink ghetto up on a hill, but it was the street. I'd found my place.

Having a little bit of a taste behind me I couldn't wait to get to Homewood. In a way I got mad with Mommy and the rest of them. Seemed to me like they was trying to hold me back from a good time. Seemed like they just didn't want me to have no fun. That's when I decided I'd go on about my own business. Do it my way. Cause I wasn't getting no slack at home. They still expected me to be like my sister and brothers. They didn't know I thought youns was squares. Yeah. I knew I was hipper and groovier than youns ever thought of being. Streetwise, into something. Had my own territory and I was bad. I was a rebel. Wasn't following in nobody's footsteps but my own. And I was a hip cookie, you better believe it. Wasn't a hipper thing out there than your brother, Rob. I couldn't wait for them to turn me loose in Homewood.

Me being the youngest and all, the baby in the family, people always said, ain't he cute. That Robby gon be a ladykiller. Been hearing that mess since day one so ain't no surprise I started to believing it. Youns had me pegged as a lady's man so that's what I was. The girls be talking the same trash everybody else did. Ain't he cute. Be petting me and spoiling me like I'm still the baby of the family and I sure ain't gon tell them stop. Thought I was cute as the girls be telling me. Thought sure enough, I'm gon be a star. I loved to get up and show my behind. Must have been good at it too cause the teacher used to call me up in front of the class to perform. The kids'd get real quiet. That's probably why the teacher got me up. Keep the class quiet while she nods off. Cause they'd listen to me. Sure nuff pay attention.

Performing always come natural to me. Wasn't nervous or nothing. Just get up and do my thing. They liked for me to do impressions. I could mimic anybody. You remember how I'd do that silly stuff around the house. Anybody I'd see on TV or hear on a record I could mimic to a T. Bob Hope, Nixon, Smokey Robinson, Ed Sullivan. White or black. I could talk just like them or sing a song just like they did. The class yell out a famous name and I'd do the one they wanted to hear. If things had gone another way I've always believed I could have made it big in show business. If you could keep them little frisky kids in Liberty School quiet you could handle any audience. Always could sing and do impressions. You remember Mom asking me to do them for you when you came home from college.

I still be performing. Read poetry in the hole. The other fellows get real quiet and listen. Sing down in there too. Nothing else to do, so we entertain each other. They always asking me to sing or read. "Hey, Wideman. C'mon man and do something." Then it gets quiet while they waiting for me to start. Quiet and it's already dark. You in your own cell and can't see nobody else. Barely enough light to read by. The other fellows can hear you but it's just you and them walls so it feels like being alone much as it feels like you're singing or reading to somebody else.

Yeah. I read my own poems sometimes. Other times I just start in on whatever book I happen to be reading. One the books you sent me, maybe. Fellows like my poems. They say I write about the things they be thinking. Say it's like listening to their own self thinking. That's cause we all down there together. What else you gonna do but think of the people on the outside. Your woman. Your kids or folks, if you got any. Just the same old sad shit we all be thinking all the time. That's what I write and the fellows like to hear it.

Funny how things go around like that. Go round and round and keep coming back to the same place. Teacher used to get me up to pacify the class and I'm doing the same thing in prison. You said your teachers called on you to tell stories, didn't they? Yeah. It's funny how much we're alike. In spite of everything I always believed that. Inside. The feeling side. I always believed we was the most alike out of all the kids. I see stuff in your books. The kinds of things I be thinking or feeling.

Your teachers got you up, too. To tell stories. That's funny, ain't it.

I listen to my brother Robby. He unravels my voice. I sit with him in the darkness of the Behavioral Adjustment Unit. My imagination creates something like a giant seashell, enfolding, enclosing us. Its inner surface is velvet-soft and black. A curving mirror doubling the darkness. Poems are Jean Toomer's petals of dusk, petals of dawn. I want to stop. Savor the sweet, solitary pleasure, the time stolen from time in the hole. But the image I'm creating is a trick of the glass. The mirror that would swallow Robby and then chime to me: You're the fairest of them all. The voice I hear issues from a crack in the glass. I'm two or three steps ahead of my brother, making fiction out of his words. Somebody needs to snatch me by the neck and say, Stop. Stop and listen, listen to him.

The Behavioral Adjustment Unit is, as one guard put it, "a maximum-security prison within a maximum-security prison." The "Restricted Housing Unit" or "hole" or "Home Block" is a squat, two-story cement building containing thirty-five six-by-eight-foot cells. The governor of Pennsylvania closed the area in 1972 because of "inhumane conditions," but within a year the hole was reopened. For at least twenty-three hours a day the prisoners are confined to their cells. An hour of outdoor exercise is permitted only on days the guards choose to supervise it. Two meals are served three hours apart, then nothing except coffee and bread for the next twenty-one. The regulation that limits the time an inmate can serve in the BAU for a single offense is routinely sidestepped by the keepers. "Administrative custody" is a provision allowing officials to cage men in the BAU indefinitely. Hunger strikes are one means the prisoners have employed to protest the harsh conditions of the penal unit. Hearings prompted by the strikes have produced no major changes in the way the hole operates. Law, due process, the rights of the prisoners are irrelevant to the functioning of this prison within a prison. Robby was sentenced to six months in the BAU because a guard suspected he was involved in an attempted escape. The fact that a hearing, held six months later, established Robby's innocence, was small consolation since he'd already served his time in the hole.

Robby tells me about the other side of being the youngest: Okay, you're everybody's pet and that's boss, but on the other hand you sometimes feel you're the least important. Always last. Always bringing up the rear. You learn to do stuff on your own because the older kids are always busy, off doing their things, and you're too young, left behind because you don't fit, or just because they forget you're back here, at the end, bringing up the rear. But when orders are given out, you sure get your share. "John's coming home this weekend. Clean up your room." Robby remembers being forced to get a haircut on the occasion of one of my visits. Honor thy brother. Get your hair cut, your room rid up, and put on clean clothes. He'll be here with his family and I don't want the house looking like a pigpen.

I have to laugh at the image of myself as somebody to get a haircut for. Robby must have been fit to be tied.

Yeah, I was hot. I mean, you was doing well and all that, but shit, you were my brother. And it was my head. What's my head got to do with you? But you know how Mommy is. Ain't no talking to her when her mind gets set. Anything I tried to say was "talking *back*," so I just went ahead to the man and got my ears lowered.

I was trying to be a rebel but back then the most important thing still was what the grown-ups thought about me. How they felt meant everything. Everything. Me and Tish and Dave were the ones at home then. You was gone and Gene was gone so it was the three of us fighting for attention. And we fought. Every crumb, everytime something got cut up or parceled out or it was Christmas or Easter, we so busy checking out what the other one got wasn't hardly no time to enjoy our own. Like a dogfight or cat fight all the time. And being the youngest I'm steady losing ground most the time. Seemed like to me, Tish and Dave the ones everybody talked about. Seemed like my time would never come. That ain't the way it really was, I know. I had my share cause I was the baby and ain't he cute and lots of times I know I got away with outrageous stuff or got my way cause I could play that baby mess to the hilt. Still it seemed like Dave and Tish was the ones really mattered. Mommy and Daddy and Sis and Geral and Big Otie and Ernie always slipping some change in their pockets or taking them to the store or letting them stay over all night in Homewood. I was a jealous little rascal. Sometimes I thought everybody thought I was just a spoiled brat. I'd say damn all youall. I'd think, Go on and love those square turkeys, but one day I'll be the one coming back with a suitcase full of money and a Cadillac. Go on and love them good grades. Robby gon do it his own way.

See, in my mind I was Superfly. I'd drive up slow to the curb. My hog be half a block long and these fine foxes in the back. Everybody looking when I ease out the door clean and mean. Got a check in my pocket to give to Mom. Buy her a new house with everything in it new. Pay her back for the hard times. I could see that happening as real as I can see your face right now. Wasn't no way it wasn't gon happen. Rob was gon make it big. I'd be at the door, smiling with the check in my hand and Mommy'd be so happy she'd be crying.

Well, it's a different story ain't it. Turned out different from how I used to think it would. The worst thing I did, the thing I feel most guilty behind is stealing Mom's life. It's like I stole her youth. Can't nothing change that. I can't give back what's gone. Robbing white people didn't cause me to lose no sleep back then. Couldn't feel but so bad about that. How you gon feel sorry when society's so corrupt, when everybody got their hand out or got their hand in somebody else's pocket and ain't no rules nobody listens to if they can get away with breaking them? How you gon apply the rules? It was dog eat dog out there, so how was I spozed to feel sorry if I was doing what everybody else doing. I just got caught is all. I'm sorry about that, and damned sorry that guy Stavros got killed, but as far as what I did, as far as robbing white people, ain't no way I was gon torture myself over that one.

I tried to write Mom a letter. Not too long ago. Should say I did write the letter and put it in a envelope and sent it cause that's what I did, but I be crying so much trying to write it I don't know what wound up in that letter. I wanted Mom to know I knew what I'd done. In a way I wanted to say I was sorry for spoiling her life. After all she did for me I turned around and made her life miserable. That's the wrongest thing I've done and I wanted to say I was sorry but I kept seeing her face while I was writing the letter. I 'd see her face and it would get older while I was look- ing. She'd get this old woman's face all lined and wrinkled and tired about the eyes. Wasn't nothing I could do but watch. Cause I'd done it and knew I done it and all the letters in the world ain't gon change her face. I sit and think about stuff like that all the time. It's better now. I think about other things too. You know like trying to figure what's really right and wrong, but there be days the guilt don't never go away.

I'm the one made her tired, John. And that's my greatest sorrow. All the love that's in me she created. Then I went and let her down.

When you in prison you got plenty of time to think, that's for damned sure. Too much time. I've gone over and over my life. Every moment. Every little thing again and again. I lay down on my bed and watch it happening over and over. Like a movie. I get it all broke down in pieces then I break up the pieces then I take the pieces of the pieces and run them through my hands so I remember every word a person said to me or what I said to them and I weigh the words till I think I know what each and every one meant. Then I try to put it back together. Try to understand where I been. Why I did what I did. You got time for that in here. Time's all you got in here.

Going over and over things sometimes you can make sense. You know. Like the chinky-chinky Chinaman sittin' on the fence. You put it together and you think, yes. That's why I did thus and so. Yeah. That's why I lost that job or lost that woman or broke that one's heart. You stop thinking in terms of something being good or being evil, you just try to say this happened because that happened because something else came first. You can spend days trying to figure out just one little thing you did. People out there in the world walk around in a daze cause they ain't got time to think. When I was out there, I wasn't no different. Had this Superfly thing and that was the whole bit. Nobody could tell me nothing.

Seems like I should start the story back in Shadyside. In the house on Copeland Street. Nothing but white kids around. Them little white kids had everything, too. That's what I thought, anyway. Nice houses, nice clothes. They could buy pop and comic books and candy when they wanted to. We wasn't that bad off, but compared to what them little white kids had I always felt like I didn't have nothing. It made me kinda quiet and shy around them. Me knowing all the time I wanted what they had. Wanted it bad. There was them white kids with everything and there was the black world Mommy and them was holding back from me. No place to turn, in a way. I guess you could say I was stuck in the middle. Couldn't have what the white kids in Shadyside had, and I wasn't allowed to look around the corner for something else. So I'd start the story with Shadyside, the house on Copeland.

Another place to start could be December 29, 1950—the date of Robby's birth. For some reason—maybe my mother and father were feuding, maybe we just happened to be visiting my grandmother's house when my mother's time came—the trip to the hospital to have Robby began from

Finance Street, from the house beside the railroad tracks in Homewood. What I remember is the bustle, people rushing around, yelling up and down the stairwell, doors slammed, drawers being opened and shut. A cold winter day so lots of coats and scarves and galoshes. My mother's face was very pale above the dark cloth coat that made her look even bigger than she was, carrying Robby the ninth month. On the way out the front door she stopped and stared back over her shoulder like she'd forgotten something. People just about shoving her out the house. Lots of bustle and noise getting her through the crowded hallway into the vestibule. Somebody opened the front door and December rattled the glass panes. Wind gusting and whistling, everybody calling out last-minute instructions, arrangements, goodbyes, blessings, prayers. My mother's white face calm, hovering a moment above it all as she turned back toward the hall, the stairs where I was planted, halfway to the top. She didn't find me, wasn't looking for me. A thought had crossed her mind and carried her far away. She didn't know why so many hands were rushing her out the door. She didn't hear the swirl of words, the icy blast of wind. Wrapped in a navy-blue coat, either Aunt Aida's or an old one of my grandmother's, which didn't have all its black buttons but stretched double over her big belly, my mother was wondering whether or not she'd turned off the water in the bathroom sink and deciding whether or not she should return up the stairs to check. Something like that crossing her mind, freeing her an instant before she got down to the business of pushing my brother into the world.

Both my grandfathers died on December 28. My grandmother died just after dawn on December 29. My sister lost a baby early in January. The end of the year has become associated with mournings, funerals; New Year's Day arrives burdened by a sense of loss, bereavement. Robby's birthday became tainted. To be born close to Christmas is bad enough in and of itself. Your birthday celebration gets upstaged by the orgy of gift giving on Christmas Day. No matter how many presents you receive on December 29, they seem a trickle after the Christmas flood. Plus there's too much excitement in too brief a period. Parents and relatives are exhausted, broke, still hung over from the Christmas rush, so there just isn't very much left to work with if your birthday comes four short days after Jesus'. Almost like not having a birthday. Or even worse, like sharing it with your brothers and sister instead of having the private oasis of your very own special day. So Robby cried a lot on his birthdays. And it certainly wasn't a happy time for my mother. Her father, John French, died the year after Robby was born, one day before Robby's birthday. Fifteen years and a day later Mom would lose her mother. The death of the baby my sister was carrying was a final, cruel blow, scaring my mother, jinxing the end of the year eternally. She dreaded the holiday season, expected it to bring dire tidings. She had attempted at one point to consecrate the sad days, employ them as a period of reflection, quietly, privately memorialize the passing of the two people who'd loved her most in the world. But the death of my father's father, then the miscarriage within this jinxed span of days burst the fragile truce my mother had effected with the year's end. She withdraws into herself, anticipates the worst as soon as Christmas decorations begin appearing. In 1975, the year of the robbery and murder, Robby was on the run when his birthday fell. My mother was sure he wouldn't survive the deadly close of the year.

Robby's birthday is smack dab in the middle of the hard time. Planted like a flag to let you know the bad time's arrived. His adult life, the manhood of my mother's last child, begins as she is orphaned, as she starts to become nobody's child.

I named Robby. Before the women hustled my mother out the door into a taxi, I jumped down the stairs, tugged on her coattail and reminded her she'd promised it'd be Robby. No doubt in my mind she'd bring me home a baby brother. Don't ask me why I was certain. I just was. I hadn't even considered names for a girl. Robby it would be. Robert Douglas. Where the Douglas came from is another story, but the Robert came from me because I liked the sound. Robert was formal, dignified, important. Robert. And that was nearly as nice as the chance I'd have to call my little brother Rob and Robby.

He weighed seven pounds, fourteen ounces. He was born in Allegheny Hospital at 6:30 in the evening, December 29, 1950. His fingers and toes were intact and quite long. He was a plump baby. My grandfather, high on Dago Red, tramped into the maternity ward just minutes after Robby was delivered. John French was delighted with the new baby. Called him Red. A big fat little red nigger.

December always been a bad month for me. One the worst days of my life was in December. It's still one the worst days in my life even after all this other mess. Jail. Running. The whole bit. Been waiting to tell you this a long time. Ain't no reason to hold it back no longer. We into this telling-the-truth thing so mize well tell it all. I'm still shamed, but here it is. You know that TV of youall's got stolen from Mommy's. Well, I did it. Was me and Henry took youall's TV that time and set the house up to look like a robbery. We did it. Took my own brother's TV. Couldn't hardly look you in the face for a long time after we done it. Was pretty sure youall never knowed it was me, but I felt real bad round youns anyway. No way I was gon confess though. Too shamed. A junkie stealing from his own family. See. Used to bullshit myself. Say I ain't like them other guys. They stone junkies, they hooked. Do anything for a hit. But me, I'm Robby. I'm cool. I be believing that shit, too. Fooling myself. You got to bullshit yourself when you falling. Got to do it to live wit yourself. See but where it's at is you be doing any goddam thing for dope. You hooked and that's all's to it. You a stone junkie just like the rest.

Always wondered if you knew I took it.

Mom was suspicious. She knew more than we did then. About the dope. The seriousness of it. Money disappearing from her purse when nobody in the house but the two of you. Finding a syringe on the third floor. Stuff like that she hadn't talked about to us yet. So your stealing the TV was a possibility that came up. But to me it was just one of many. One of the things that could have happened along with a whole lot of other possibilities we sat around talking about. An unlikely possibility as far as I was concerned. Nobody wanted to believe it was you. Mom tried to tell us how it *could* be but in my mind you weren't the one. Haven't thought about it much since then. Except as one of those things that make me worry about Mom living in the house alone. One of those things making Homewood dangerous, tearing it down.

I'm glad I'm finally getting to tell you. I never could get it out. Didn't want you to think I'd steal from my own brother. Specially since all youall done to help me out. You and Judy and the kids. Stealing youall's TV. Don't make no sense, does it? But if we gon get the story down mize well get it all down.

It was a while ago. Do you remember the year?

Nineteen seventy-one was Greens. When we robbed Greens and got in big trouble so it had to be the year before that, 1970. That's when it had to be. Youns was home for Christmas. Mommy and them was having a big party. A reunion kinda cause all the family was together. Everybody home for the first time in a long time. Tish in from Detroit. David back from Philly. Youns in town. My birthday, too. Party spozed to celebrate my birthday too, since it came right along in there after Christmas. Maybe that's why I was feeling so bad. Knowing I had a birthday coming and knowing at the same time how fucked up I was.

Sat in a chair all day. I was hooked for the first time. Good and hooked. Didn't know how low you could feel till that day. Cold and snowing outside. And I got the stone miseries inside. Couldn't move. Weak and sick. Henry too. He was wit me in the house feeling bad as I was. We was two desperate dudes. Didn't have no money and that Jones down on us.

Mommy kept asking, What's wrong with you two? She was on my case all day. What ails you, Robby? Got to be about three o'clock. She come in the room again: You better get up and get some decent clothes on. We're leaving for Geral's soon. See cause it was the day of the big Christmas party. Geral had baked a cake for me. Everybody was together and they'd be singing Happy Birthday Robby and do. The whole bit and I'm spozed to be guest of honor and can't even move out the chair. Here I go again disappointing everybody. Everybody be at Geral's looking for me and Geral had a cake and everything. Where's Robby? He's home dying cause he can't get no dope.

Feeling real sorry for myself but I'm hating me too. Wrapped up in a blanket like some damned Indin. Shivering and wondering how the hell Ima go out in this cold and hustle up some money. Wind be howling. Snow pitching a bitch. There we is. Stuck in the house. Two pitiful junkies. Scheming how we gon get over. Some sorry-assed dudes. But it's comical in a way too, when you look back. To get well we need to get money. And no way we gon get money less we go outside and get sicker than we already is. Mom peeking in the room, getting on my case. Get up out that chair, boy. What are you waiting for? We're leaving in two minutes.

So I says, Go on. I ain't ready. Youns go on. I'll catch up with youns at Geral's.

Mommy standing in the doorway. She can't say too much, cause youns is home and you ain't hip to what's happening. C'mon now. We can't wait any longer for you. Please get up. Geral baked a cake for you. Everybody's looking forward to seeing you.

Seem like she stands there a hour begging me to come. She ain't mad no more. She's begging. Just about ready to cry. Youall in the other room. You can hear what she's saying but you can't see her eyes and they tearing me up. Her eyes begging me to get out the chair and it's tearing me up to see her hurting so bad, but ain't nothing I can do. Jones sitting on my chest and ain't no getup in me.

Youns go head, Mommy. I'll be over in a little while. Be there to blow them candles out and cut the cake.

She knew better. Knew if I didn't come right then, chances was I wasn't coming at all. She knew but wasn't nothing she could do. Guess I knew I was lying too. Nothing in my mind cept copping that dope. Yeah, Mom. Be there to light them candles. I'm grinning but she ain't smiling back. She knows I'm in trouble, deep trouble. I can see her today standing in the doorway begging me to come with youns.

But it ain't meant to be. Me and Henry thought we come up with a idea. Henry's old man had some pistols. We was gon steal em and hock em. Take the money and score. Then we be better. Wouldn't be no big thing to hustle some money, get the guns outa hock. Sneak the pistols back in Henry's house, everything be alright. Wouldn't even exactly be stealing from his old man. Like we just borrowing the pistols till we score and take care business. Henry's old man wouldn't even know his pistols missing. Slick. Sick as we was, thinking we slick.

A hundred times. Mom musta poked her head in the room a hundred times.

What's wrong with you?

Like a drum beating in my head. What's wrong with you? But the other thing is stronger. The dope talking to me louder. It says get you some. It says you ain't never gon get better less you cop.

We waited long as we could but it didn't turn no better outside. Still snowing. Wind shaking the whole house. How we gon walk to Henry's and steal them pistols? Henry live way up on the hill. All the way up Tokay then you still got a long way to go over into the projects. Can't make it. No way we gon climb Tokay. So then what? Everybody's left for Geral's. Then I remembers the TV youns brought. A little portable Sony black-and-white, right? You and Judy sleeping in Mom's room and she has her TV already in there, so the Sony ain't unpacked. Saw it sitting with youall's suitcases over by the dresser. On top the dresser in a box. Remembered it and soon's I did I knew we had to have it. Sick as I was that TV had to go. Wouldn't really be stealing. Borrow it instead of borrowing the pistols. Pawn it. Get straight. Steal some money and buy it back. Just borrowing youall's TV.

Won't take me and Henry no time to rob something and buy back the TV. We stone thieves. Just had to get well first so we could operate. So we took youns TV and set the house up to look like a robbery.

I'm remembering the day. Wondering why it had slipped completely from my mind. I feel like a stranger. Yet as Robby talks, my memory confirms details of his recollection. I admit, yes. I was there. That's the way it was. But *where* was I? Who was I? How did I miss so much?

His confessions make me uncomfortable. Instead of concentrating on what he's revealing, I'm pushed into considering all the things I could be confessing, should be confessing but haven't and probably won't ever. I feel hypocritical. Why should I allow my brother to repose a confidence in me when it's beyond my power to reciprocate? Shouldn't I confess that first? My embarrassment, my uneasiness, the clinical, analytic coldness settling over me when I catch on to what's about to happen.

I have a lot to hide. Places inside myself where truth hurts, where incriminating secrets are hidden, places I avoid, or deny most of the time. Pulling one piece of that debris to the surface, airing it in the light of day doesn't accomplish much, doesn't clarify the rest of what's buried down there. What I feel when I delve deeply into myself is chaos. Chaos and contradiction. So how up front can I get? I'm moved by Robby's secrets. The heart I have is breaking. But what that heart is and where it is I can't say. I can't depend on it, so he shouldn't. Part of me goes out to him. Heartbreak is the sound of ice cracking. Deep. Layers and layers muffling the sound.

I listen but I can't trust myself. I have no desire to tell everything about myself so I resist his attempt to be up front with me. The chaos at my core must be in his. His confession pushes me to think of all the stuff I should lay on him. And that scares the shit out of me. I don't like to feel dirty, but that's how I feel when people try to come clean with me.

Very complicated and very simple too. The fact is I don't believe in clean. What I know best is myself and, knowing what I know about myself, clean seems impossible. A dream. One of those better selves occasionally in the driver's seat but nothing more. Nothing to be depended upon. A self no more or less in control than the countless other selves who each, for a time, seem to be running things.

Chaos is what he's addressing. What his candor, his frankness, his confession echo against. Chaos and time and circumstance and the old news, the bad news that we still walk in circles, each of us trapped in his own little world. Behind bars. Locked in our cells.

But my heart can break, does break listening to my brother's pain. I just remember differently. Different parts of the incident he's describing come back. Strange thing is my recollections return through the door he opened. My memories needed his. Maybe the fact that we recall different things is crucial. Maybe they are foreground and background, propping each other up. He holds on to this or that scrap of the past and I listen to what he's saved and it's not mine, not what I saw or heard or felt. The pressure's on me then. If his version of the past is real, then what's mine? Where does it fit? As he stitches his memories together they bridge a vast emptiness. The time lost enveloping us all. Everything. And hearing him talk, listening to him try to make something of the nothing, challenges me. My sense of the emptiness playing around his words, any words, is intensified. Words are nothing and everything. If I don't speak I have no past. Except the nothing, the emptiness. My brother's memories are not mine, so I have to break into the silence with my own version of the past. My words. My whistling in the dark. His story freeing me, because it forces me to tell my own.

I'm sorry you took so long to forgive yourself. I forgave you a long time ago, in advance for a sin I didn't even know you'd committed. You lied to me. You stole from me. I'm in prison now listening because we committed those sins against each other countless times. I want your forgiveness. Talking about debts you owe me makes me awkward, uneasy. We remember different things. They set us apart. They bring us together searching for what is lost, for the meaning of difference, of distance.

For instance, the Sony TV. It was a present from Mort, Judy's dad. When we told him about the break-in and robbery at Mom's house, he bought us another Sony. Later we discovered the stolen TV was covered by our homeowner's policy even though we'd lost it in Pittsburgh. A claim was filed and eventually we collected around a hundred bucks. Not enough to buy a new Sony but a good portion of the purchase price. Seemed a lark when the check arrived. Pennies from heaven. One hundred dollars free and clear since we already had the new TV Mort had surprised us with. About a year later one of us, Judy or I, was telling the story of the robbery and how well we came out of it. Not until that very moment when I caught a glimpse of Mort's face out of the corner of my eye did I realize what we'd done. Judy remembers urging me to send Mort that insurance check and she probably did, but I have no recollection of an argument. In my mind there had never been an issue. Why shouldn't we keep the money? But when I saw the look of surprise and hurt flash across Mort's face, I knew the insurance check should have gone directly to him. He's a generous man and probably would have refused to accept it, but we'd taken advantage of his generosity by not offering the check as soon as we received it. Clearly the money belonged to him. Unasked, he'd replaced the lost TV. I had treated him like an institution, one of those faceless corporate entities like the gas company or IRS. By then, by the time I saw the surprise in Mort's face and understood how selfishly, thoughtlessly, even corruptly I'd behaved, it was too late. Offering Mort a hundred dollars at that point would have been insulting. Anything I could think of saying sounded hopelessly lame, inept. I'd fucked up. I'd injured someone who'd been nothing but kind and generous to me. Not intentionally, consciously, but that only made the whole business worse in a way because I'd failed him instinctively. The failure was a measure of who I was. What I'd unthinkingly done revealed something about my relationship to Mort I'm sure he'd rather not have discovered. No way I could take my action back, make it up. It reflected a truth about who I was.

That memory pops right up. Compromising, ugly. Ironically, it's also about stealing from a relative. Not to buy dope, but to feed a habit just as self-destructive. The habit of taking good fortune for granted, the habit of blind self-absorption that allows us to believe the world owes us everything and we are not responsible for giving anything in return. Spoiled children. The good coming our way taken as our due. No strings attached.

Lots of other recollections were triggered as Robby spoke of that winter and the lost TV. The shock of walking into a burgled house. How it makes you feel unclean. How quickly you lose the sense of privacy and security a house, any place you call home, is supposed to provide. It's a form of rape. Forced entry, violation, brutal hands defiling what's personal, and precious. The aftershock of seeing your possessions strewn about, broken. Fear gnawing at you because what you thought was safe isn't safe at all. The worst has happened and can happen again. Your sanctuary has been destroyed. Any time you walk in your door you may be greeted by the same scene. Or worse. You may stumble upon the thieves themselves. The symbolic rape of your dwelling place enacted on your actual body. Real screams. Real blood. A knife at your throat. A stranger's weight bearing down.

Mom put it in different words but she was as shaken as I was when we walked into her house after Geral's party. Given what I know now, she must have been even more profoundly disturbed than I imagined. A double bind. Bad enough to be ripped off by anonymous thieves. How much worse if the thief is your son? For Mom the robbery was proof Robby was gone. Somebody else walking round in his skin. Mom was wounded in ways I hadn't begun to guess at. At the root of her pain were your troubles, the troubles stealing you away from her, from all of us. The troubles thick in the air as that snow you are remembering, the troubles falling on your head and mine, troubles I refused to see . . .

Snowing and the hawk kicking my ass but I got to have it. TV's in a box under my arm and me and Henry walking down Bennett to Homewood Avenue. Need thirty dollars. Thirty dollars buy us two spoons. Looking for One-Arm Ralph, the fence. Looking for him or that big white Cadillac he drives.

Wind blowing snow all up in my face. Thought I's bout to die out there. Nobody on the avenue. Even the junkies and dealers inside today. Wouldn't put no dog out in weather like that. So cold my teeth is chattering, talking to me. No feeling in my hands but I got to hold on to that TV. Henry took it for a little while so's I could put both my hands in my pockets. Henry lookin bad as I'm feeling. Thought I was gon puke. But it's too goddamn cold to puke.

Nobody in sight. Shit and double shit's what I'm thinking. They got to be somewhere. Twenty-four hours a day, seven days a week somebody doing business. Finally we seen One-Arm Ralph come out the Hi Hat.

This TV, man, Lemme hold thirty dollars on it.

Ralph ain't goin for it. Twenty-five the best he say he can do. Twenty-five don't do us no good. It's fifteen each for a spoon. One spoon ain't enough. We begging the dude now. We got to have it, man. Got to get well. We good for the money. Need thirty dollars for two hits. You get your money back.

Too cold to be standing around arguing. The dude go in his pocket and give us the thirty. He been knowing us. He know we good for it. I'm telling him don't sell the TV right away. Hold it till tomorrow we have his money. He say, You don't come back tonight you blow it. Ralph a hard motherfucker and don't want him changing his mind again about the thirty so I say, We'll have the money tonight. Hold the TV till tonight, you get your money.

Now all we got to do is find Goose. Goose always be hanging on the set. Ain't nobody else dealing, Goose be out there for his people. Goose an alright dude, but even Goose ain't out in the street on no day like this.

I know the cat stays over the barbershop on Homewood Avenue. Across from Murphy's five-and-ten. I goes round to the side entrance, the alleyway tween Homewood and Kelly. That's how you get to his place. Goose lets me in and I cop. For some reason I turn up the alley and go toward Kelly instead of back to Homewood the way I came in. Don't know why I did it. Being slick. Being scared. Henry's waiting on the avenue for me so I go round the long way just in case somebody pinned him. I can check out the scene before I come back up the avenue. That's probably what I'm thinking. But soon's I turn the corner of Kelly, Bam. Up pops the devil.

Up against the wall, Squirrel.

It's Simon and Garfunkel, two jive undercover cops. We call them that, you dig. Lemme tell you what kind of undercover cops these niggers was. Both of em wearing Big Apple hats and jackets like people be wearing then but they both got on police shoes. Police brogans you could spot a mile away. But they think they slick. They disguised, see. Apple hats and hippy-dip jackets. Everybody knew them chumps was cops. Ride around in a big Continental. Going for bad. Everybody hated them cause everybody knew they in the dope business. They bust a junkie, take his shit and sell it. One them had a cousin. Biggest dealer on the Hill. You know where he getting half his dope. Be selling again what Simon and Garfunkel stole from junkies. Some rotten dudes. Liked to beat on people too. Wasn't bad enough they robbing people. They whipped heads too.

Soon's I turn the corner they got me. Brams me up against the wall. They so lame they think they got Squirrel. Think I'm Squirrel and they gon make a big bust. We got you, Squirrel. They happy, see, cause Squirrel dealing heavy then. Thought they caught them a whole shopping bag of dope.

Wearing my double-breasted pea coat. Used to be sharp but it's raggedy now. Ain't worth shit in cold weather like that. Pockets got holes and the dope dropped down in the lining so they don't find nothing the first time they search me. Can tell they mad. Thought they into something big and don't find shit. Looking at each other like, What the fuck's going on here? We big-time undercover supercops. This ain't spozed to be happening to us. They roughing me up too. Pulling my clothes off and shit. Hands all down in my pockets again. It's freezing and I'm shivering but these fools don't give a fuck. Rip my goddamn pea coat off me. Shaking it. Tearing it up. Find the two packs of dope inside the lining this time. Ain't what they wanted but they pissed off now. Take what they can get now.

What's this, Squirrel? Got your ass now.

Slinging me down the alley. I'm stone sick now. Begging these cats for mercy. Youall got me. You got your bust. Lemme snort some the dope, man. Little bit out each bag. You still got your bust. I'm dying. Little taste fore you lock me up.

Rotten motherfuckers ain't going for it. They see I'm sick as a dog. They know what's happening. Cold as it is, the sweat pouring out me. It's sweat but it's like ice. Like knives cutting me. They ain't give back my coat. Snowing on me and I'm shaking and sweating and sick. They can see all this. They know what's happening but ain't no mercy in these dudes. Henry's cross the street watching them bust me. Tears in his eyes. Ain't nothing he can do. The street's empty. Henry's bout froze too. Watching them sling my ass in their Continental. Never forget how Henry looked that day. All alone on the avenue. Tears froze in his eyes. Seeing him like that was a sad thing. Last thing I saw was him standing there across Homewood Avenue before they slammed me up in the car. Like I was in two places. That's me standing there in the snow. That's me so sick and cold I'm crying in the empty street and ain't a damn thing I can do about it.

By the time they get me down to the Police Station, down to No. 5 in East Liberty, I ain't no more good, sure nuff. Puking. Begging them punks not to bust me. Just bout out my mind. Must have been a pitiful sight. Then's when Henry went to Geral's house and scratched on the window and called David out on the porch. That's when youall found out I was in trouble and had to come down and get me. Right in the middle of the party and everything. Henry's sick too and he been walking round Homewood in the cold didn't know what to do. But he's my man. He got to Geral's so youall could come down and help me. Shamed to go in so he scratched on the window to get Dave on the porch.

Party's over and youns go to Mommy's and on top everything else find the house broke in and the TV gone. All the stuff's going through my mind. I'm on the bottom now. Low as you can go. Had me in a cell and I was lying cross the cot staring at the ceiling. Bars all round. Up cross the ceiling too. Like in a cage in the zoo. Miserable as I could be. All the shit staring me in the face. You're a dope fiend. You stole your brother's TV. You're hurting Mommy again. Hurting everybody. You're sick. You're nothing. Looking up at the bars on the ceiling and wondering if I could tie my belt there. Stick my neck in it. I wanted to be dead.

Tied my belt to the ceiling. Then this guard checking on me he starts to hollering.

What you doing? Hey, Joe. This guy's trying to commit suicide.

They take my clothes. Leave me nothing but my shorts. I'm lying there shivering in my underwear and that's the end. In a cage naked like some goddamn animal. Shaking like a leaf. Thinking maybe I can beat my head against the bars or maybe jump down off the bed head first on the concrete and bust my brains open. Dead already. Nothing already. Low as I can go.

Must have passed out or gone to sleep or something, cause it gets blurry round in here. Don't remember much but they gave back my clothes and took me Downtown and there was a arraignment next morning.

Mommy told me later, one the cops advised her not to pay my bond.

Said the best thing for him be to stay in jail awhile. Let him see how it is inside. Scare im. But I be steady beggin. Please, please get me out here. Youns got soft-hearted. Got the money together and paid the bond.

What would have happened if you left me to rot in there till my hearing? Damned if I know. I probably woulda went crazy, for one thing. I do know that. Know I was sick and scared and cried like a baby for Mommy and them to get me out. Don't think it really do no good letting them keep me in there. I mean the jail's a terrible place. You can get everything in jail you get in the street. No different. Cept in jail it's more dangerous cause you got a whole bunch of crazies locked up in one little space. Worse than the street. Less you got buddies in there they tear you up. Got to learn to survive quick. Cause jail be the stone jungle. Call prison the House of Knowledge cause you learns how to be a sure nuff criminal. Come in lame you leave knowing all kinds of evil shit. You learn quick or they eats you up. That's where it's at. So you leave a person in there, chances are they gets worse. Or gets wasted.

But Mom has that soft heart anyway and she ain't leaving her baby boy in no miserable jail. Right or wrong, she ain't leaving me in no place like that. Daddy been talking to Simon and Garfunkel. Daddy's hip, see. He been out there in the street all his life and he knows what's to it. Knows those guys and knows how rotten they is. Ain't no big thing they catch one pitiful little junkie holding two spoons. They wants dealers. They wants to look good Downtown. They wants to bust dealers and cop beaucoup dope so's they can steal it and get rich. Daddy makes a deal with them rats. Says if they drop the charges he'll make me set up Goose. Finger Goose and then stay off Homewood Avenue. Daddy says I'll do that so they let me go.

No way Ima squeal on Goose but I said okay, it's a deal. Soon's I was loose I warned Goose. Pretend like I'm trying to set him up so the cops get off my ass but Goose see me coming know the cops is watching. Helped him, really. Like a lookout. Then dumb motherfuckers got tired playing me. Simon got greedy. Somebody set him up. He got busted for drugs. Still see Garfunkel riding round in his Continental but they took him off the avenue. Too dangerous. Everybody hated them guys.

My lowest day. Didn't know till then I was strung out. That's the first time I was hooked. Started shooting up with Squirrel and Bugs Johnson when Squirrel be coming over to Mom's sometimes. Get up in the morning, go up to the third floor, and shoot up. They was like my teachers. Bugs goes way back. He started with Uncle Carl. Been shooting ever since. Dude's old now. Call him King of the Junkies, he been round so long. Bugs seen it all. You know junkies don't hardly be getting old. Have their day then they gone. Don't see em no more. They in jail or dead. Junkie just don't have no long life. Fast life but your average dopehead ain't round long. Bugs different. He was a pal of Uncle Carl's back in the fifties. Shot up together way back then. Now here he is wit Squirrel and me, still doing this thing. Everybody knows Bugs. He the King.

Let me shoot up wit em but they wouldn't let me go out in the street and hustle wit em. Said I was too young. Too green.

Learning from the King, see. That's how I started the heavy stuff. Me and Squirrel and Bugs first thing in the morning when I got out of bed. Mom was gone to work. They getting themselves ready to hit the street. Make that money. Just like a job. Wasn't no time before I was out there, too. On my own learning to get money for dope. Me and my little mob. We was ready. Didn't take us no time fore we was gangsters. Gon be the next Bugs Johnson. Gon make it to the top.

Don't take long. One day you the King. Next day dope got you and it's the King. You ain't nothing. You lying there naked bout to die and it don't take but a minute. You fall and you gone in a minute. That's the life. That's how it is. And I was out there. I know. Now they got me jammed up in the slammer. That's the way it is. But nobody could tell me nothing then. Hard head. You know. Got to find out for myself. Nobody could tell me nothing. Just out of high school and my life's over and I didn't even know it. Too dumb. Too hardheaded. I was gon do it my way. Youns was square. Youns didn't know nothing. Me, I was gon make mine from the curb. Hammer that rock till I was a supergangster. Be the one dealing the shit. Be the one running the junkies. That's all I knew. Street smarts. Stop being a chump. Forget that nickel-dime hoodlum bag. Be a star. Rise to the top.

You know where that got me. You heard that story. Here I sit today behind that story. Nobody to blame but my ownself. I know that now. But things was fucked up in the streets. You could fall in them streets, Brother. Low. Them streets could snatch you bald-headed and turn you around and wring you inside out. Streets was a bitch. Wake up some mornings and you think you in hell. Think you died and went straight to hell. I know cause I been there. Be days I wished I was dead. Be days worser than that.

· · · · · · · · · ·

## QUESTIONS FOR A SECOND READING

1. Wideman frequently interrupts this narrative to talk about the problems he is having as a writer. At one point he says, for example, "The hardest habit to break, since it was the habit of a lifetime, would be listening to myself listen to him. That habit would destroy any chance of seeing my brother

on his terms; and seeing him in his terms, learning his terms, seemed the whole point of learning his story." What might Wideman mean by this—listening to himself listen? As you reread "Our Time," note the sections where Wideman speaks to you directly as a writer. What is he saying? Where and how are you surprised by what he says?

Wideman calls attention to the problems he faces. How does he try to solve them? Are you sympathetic? Do the solutions work, so far as you are concerned?

2. Wideman said that his mother had a remarkable capacity for "trying on the other person's point of view." Wideman tries on another point of view himself, speaking to us in the voice of his brother, Robby. As you reread this selection, note the passages spoken in Robby's voice and try to infer Robby's point of view from them. If you look at the differences between John and Robby as evidenced by the ways they use language to understand and represent the world, what do you notice?

3. Wideman talks about three ways he could start Robby's story: with Garth's death, with the house in Shadyside, and with the day of Robby's birth. What difference would it make in each case if he chose one and not the others? What's the point of presenting all three?

## ASSIGNMENTS FOR WRITING

1. At several points in the essay, Wideman discusses his position as a writer, telling Robby's story, and he describes the problems he faces in writing this piece (or in "reading" the text of his brother's life). You could read this selection, in other words, as an essay about reading and writing.

Why do you think Wideman talks about these problems here?—Why not keep quiet and hope that no one notices? Choose three or four passages where Wideman refers directly or indirectly to his work as a writer, and write an essay defining the problems Wideman faces and explaining why you think he raises them as he does. Finally, what might this have to do with your work as a writer—or as a student in this writing class?

2. Wideman tells Robby's story in this excerpt, but he also tells the story of his neighborhood, Homewood; of his mother; and of his grandfather John French. Write an essay retelling one of these stories and explaining what it might have to do with Robby and John's.

## MAKING CONNECTIONS

1. In his essay, "Entitlement" (p. 94), Robert Coles says, "more than once I have insisted that each individual has his or her own unique way of pulling together the various elements of mental life. I have wanted, however, to suggest a common manner of response toward life among children of a

certain class and background." The tension in Coles's work is between his need to see general processes and his desire to preserve the identity and integrity of the individual. We know little of Robby's early childhood, but the techniques Coles uses to discuss wealthy children can nevertheless be applied to Robby's story. Write an essay in which you examine both Robby's "unique way of pulling together the various elements of mental life" and Robby as an example of a "common manner of response toward life among children of a certain class and background." How does Wideman help you make this distinction between unique and common responses?

2. Both Harriet Jacobs, in "Incidents in the Life of a Slave Girl" (p. 314), and Wideman speak directly to the reader in their excerpts. They seem to feel that there are particular problems of understanding in the stories they have to tell and in their relations to their subjects and their audiences.

Look back over both essays and mark the passages where the authors address you as a reader. Ask yourself why the authors might do this. What are they saying about their work as writers?

After you have completed this preliminary research, write an essay in which you talk about these two acts of writing *as* acts of writing. Both Jacobs and Wideman could be said to be attempting to negotiate the difficult and precarious relationships between a writer and his or her subject matter and a writer and his or her audience. How might you describe the relationships of writer to audience or writer to subject as they are represented in these texts? How might you describe them as evidence of problems of writing? What might you make of the racial differences represented here: both writers are black and yet both write, at least in part, for a white audience?

# VIRGINIA
# WOOLF

*V*IRGINIA WOOLF *is generally considered one of the twentieth century's major British writers. Born in London in 1882, Woolf was the daughter of
prominent figures in London artistic circles, and her parents encouraged the young
girl in her intellectual pursuits. But even as a child Woolf was made aware of the
different expectations her culture held for men and women. For, while the female
children of the household were taught at home by their mother and a series of tutors
and governesses, the boys were sent away to school. Later in her life Woolf expressed
her bitterness over the inequities of this system of education, a system shared by
most Victorian families.*

*Woolf began her literary career studying Greek, reading in her father's library,
and meeting in her parents' home some of the leading figures of British arts and
letters. After her father's death in 1904, Woolf and her sister and two brothers
moved to Bloomsbury, where their home became a center for young writers and
intellectuals trying to shake free from the restrictions of Victorian life and culture.
Woolf began teaching in a working women's college in South London and writing
reviews for the prestigious* Times Literary Supplement.

*Woolf's first review, published in 1904, when she was twenty-two, was the beginning of a distinguished career which ultimately encompassed six volumes of essays and reviews, two biographies, two book-length essays, several volumes of letters and diaries, nine novels, and two collections of short stories. In addition to being one of the cofounders (with her husband, Leonard) of the Hogarth Press, a publishing company which produced editions of the work of the poet T. S. Eliot, short story writer Katherine Mansfield, and English translations of the work of Sigmund Freud, Woolf is considered one of the finest literary critics of her time and arguably one of the most innovative novelists of the twentieth century. Her novels include* Mrs. Dalloway *(1925),* To the Lighthouse *(1927),* Orlando *(1928), and* The Waves *(1931).* Orlando *is the imaginary biography of a character who lives for four hundred years and changes from male to female in the late seventeenth century. It has been called the companion piece to* A Room of One's Own.

*The following selection is the first and last chapter of Woolf's extended essay,* A Room of One's Own, *a revised version of two papers she read at the women's colleges at Oxford, Girton and Newnham. The two chapters here frame Woolf's lecture on the topic "women and fiction." Because the final chapter alludes to what has come before, it is useful to have a brief sketch of the middle chapters.*

*In these chapters Woolf surveys what men have said about women, and she looks over the history of women's writing, from Renaissance England to the early twentieth century. In Chapter 3 she imagines what might have happened if Shakespeare had had a sister. This young woman, Judith, might have been*

> *as adventurous, as imaginative, as agog to see the world as [her brother] was. But she was not sent to school. She had no chance of learning grammar and logic, let alone of reading Horace and Virgil. She picked up a book now and then. . . . But then her parents came in and told her to mend the stockings or mind the stew and not moon about with books and papers. They would have spoken sharply but kindly, for they were substantial people who knew the conditions of life for a woman and loved their daughter—indeed, more likely than not she was the apple of her father's eye.*

*Finally, the young girl is promised in marriage to a man she does not desire, and she runs away to London to try her fortune in the theater.*

> *What is true . . . , so it seemed to me, reviewing the story of Shakespeare's sister as I had made it, is that any woman born with a great gift in the sixteenth century would certainly have gone crazed, shot herself, or ended her days in some lonely cottage outside the village, half witch, half wizard, feared and mocked at. For it needs little skill in psychology to be sure that a highly gifted girl who had tried to use her gift for poetry would have been so thwarted and hindered by other people, so tortured and pulled asunder by her own contrary instincts, that she must have lost her health and sanity to a certainty. No girl could have walked to London and stood at a stage door and*

*forced her way into the presence of actor-managers without doing
herself a violence and suffering an anguish which may have been
irrational—for chastity may be a fetish invented by certain societies
for unknown reasons—but were none the less inevitable. . . . To
have lived a free life in London in the sixteenth century would have
meant for a woman who was poet and playwright a nervous stress
and dilemma which might well have killed her. Had she survived,
whatever she had written would have been twisted and deformed,
issuing from a strained and morbid imagination. And undoubtedly,
I thought, looking at the shelf where there are no plays by women,
her work would have gone unsigned.*

Chapters 1 and 6 establish Woolf's project and her way of addressing her audience. They are marked by a strong and distinctive style. For one thing, Woolf
delivers most of the lecture through the voice of a character ("call me Mary Beton,
Mary Seton, Mary Carmichael or by any name you please—it is not a matter of
any importance"). In a letter to a friend, Dame Ethel Smyth, Woolf once said, "I
didn't write A Room without considerable feeling . . . ; I'm not cool on the subject.
And I forced myself to keep my own figure fictitious, legendary. If I had said, 'Look
here, I am uneducated because my brothers used the family funds'—which is the
fact—'well,' they'd have said, 'she has an axe to grind'; and no one would have
taken me seriously." Although this essay is "signed," Woolf leaves open some questions about the status and the presence of its author. As you read, you will want
to think about the ways this essay might be seen as an example of the problems and
possibilities for a woman's writing.

# A Room of One's Own

## Chapter One

But, you may say, we asked you to speak about women and fiction—
what has that got to do with a room of one's own? I will try to explain.
When you asked me to speak about women and fiction I sat down on the
banks of a river and began to wonder what the words meant. They might
mean simply a few remarks about Fanny Burney; a few more about Jane
Austen; a tribute to the Brontës and a sketch of Haworth Parsonage under
snow; some witticisms if possible about Miss Mitford; a respectful allusion
to George Eliot; a reference to Mrs. Gaskell and one would have done. But
at second sight the words seemed not so simple. The title women and fiction might mean, and you may have meant it to mean, women and what

they are like; or it might mean women and the fiction that they write; or it might mean women and the fiction that is written about them; or it might mean that somehow all three are inextricably mixed together and you want me to consider them in that light. But when I began to consider the subject in this last way, which seemed the most interesting, I soon saw that it had one fatal drawback. I should never be able to come to a conclusion. I should never be able to fulfill what is, I understand, the first duty of a lecturer— to hand you after an hour's discourse a nugget of pure truth to wrap up between the pages of your notebooks and keep on the mantelpiece for ever. All I could do was to offer you an opinion upon one minor point—a woman must have money and a room of her own if she is to write fiction; and that, as you will see, leaves the great problem of the true nature of woman and the true nature of fiction unsolved. I have shirked the duty of coming to a conclusion upon these two questions—women and fiction remain, so far as I am concerned, unsolved problems. But in order to make some amends I am going to do what I can to show you how I arrived at this opinion about the room and the money. I am going to develop in your presence as fully and freely as I can the train of thought which led me to think this. Perhaps if I lay bare the ideas, the prejudices, that lie behind this statement you will find that they have some bearing upon women and some upon fiction. At any rate, when a subject is highly controversial— and any question about sex is that—one cannot hope to tell the truth. One can only show how one came to hold whatever opinion one does hold. One can only give one's audience the chance of drawing their own conclusions as they observe the limitations, the prejudices, the idiosyncrasies of the speaker. Fiction here is likely to contain more truth than fact. Therefore I propose, making use of all the liberties and licenses of a novelist, to tell you the story of the two days that preceded my coming here—how, bowed down by the weight of the subject which you have laid upon my shoulders, I pondered it, and made it work in and out of my daily life. I need not say that what I am about to describe has no existence; Oxbridge is an invention; so is Fernham; "I" is only a convenient term for somebody who has no real being. Lies will flow from my lips, but there may perhaps be some truth mixed up with them; it is for you to seek out this truth and decide whether any part of it is worth keeping. If not, you will of course throw the whole of it into the wastepaper basket and forget all about it.

Here then was I (call me Mary Beton, Mary Seton, Mary Carmichael, or by any name you please—it is not a matter of any importance) sitting on the banks of a river a week or two ago in fine October weather, lost in thought. That collar I have spoken of, women and fiction, the need of coming to some conclusion on a subject that raises all sorts of prejudices and passions, bowed my head to the ground. To the right and left bushes of some sort, golden and crimson, glowed with the color, even it seemed

burnt with the heat, of fire. On the further bank the willows wept in perpetual lamentation, their hair about their shoulders. The river reflected
whatever it chose of sky and bridge and burning tree, and when the undergraduate had oared his boat through the reflections they closed again,
completely, as if he had never been. There one might have sat the clock
round lost in thought. Thought—to call it by a prouder name than it deserved—had let its line down into the stream. It swayed, minute after minute, hither and thither among the reflections and the weeds, letting the
water lift it and sink it, until—you know the little tug—the sudden con-
glomeration of an idea at the end of one's line: and then the cautious haul-
ing of it in, and the careful laying of it out? Alas, laid on the grass how
small, how insignificant this thought of mine looked; the sort of fish that
a good fisherman puts back into the water so that it may grow fatter and
be one day worth cooking and eating. I will not trouble you with that
thought now, though if you look carefully you may find it for yourselves
in the course of what I am going to say.

But however small it was, it had, nevertheless, the mysterious property
of its kind—put back into the mind, it became at once very exciting, and
important; and as if darted and sank, and flashed hither and thither, set
up such a wash and tumult of ideas that it was impossible to sit still. It
was thus that I found myself walking with extreme rapidity across a grass
plot. Instantly a man's figure rose to intercept me. Nor did I at first understand that the gesticulations of a curious-looking object, in a cutaway
coat and evening shirt, were aimed at me. His face expressed horror and
indignation. Instinct rather than reason came to my help; he was a Beadle;
I was a woman. This was the turf; there was the path. Only the Fellows
and Scholars are allowed here; the gravel is the place for me. Such thoughts
were the work of a moment. As I regained the path the arms of the Beadle
sank, his face assumed its usual repose, and though turf is better walking
than gravel, no very great harm was done. The only charge I could bring
against the Fellows and Scholars of whatever the college might happen to
be was that in protection of their turf, which has been rolled for three
hundred years in succession, they had sent my little fish into hiding.

What idea it had been that had sent me so audaciously trespassing I
could not now remember. The spirit of peace descended like a cloud from
heaven, for if the spirit of peace dwells anywhere, it is in the courts and
quadrangles of Oxbridge on a fine October morning. Strolling through
those colleges past those ancient halls the roughness of the present seemed
smoothed away; the body seemed contained in a miraculous glass cabinet
through which no sound could penetrate, and the mind, freed from any
contact with facts (unless one trespassed on the turf again), was at liberty
to settle down upon whatever meditation was in harmony with the moment. As chance would have it, some stray memory of some old essay

about revisiting Oxbridge in the long vacation brought Charles Lamb to mind—Saint Charles, said Thackeray, putting a letter of Lamb's to his forehead. Indeed, among all the dead (I give you my thoughts as they came to me), Lamb is one of the most congenial; one to whom one would have liked to say, Tell me then how you wrote your essays? For his essays are superior even to Max Beerbohm's, I thought, with all their perfection, because of that wild flash of imagination, that lightning crack of genius in the middle of them which leaves them flawed and imperfect, but starred with poetry. Lamb then came to Oxbridge perhaps a hundred years ago. Certainly he wrote an essay—the name escapes me—about the manuscript of one of Milton's poems which he saw here. It was *Lycidas* perhaps, and Lamb wrote how it shocked him to think it possible that any word in *Lycidas* could have been different from what it is. To think of Milton changing the words in that poem seemed to him a sort of sacrilege. This led me to remember what I could of *Lycidas* and to amuse myself with guessing which word it could have been that Milton had altered, and why. It then occurred to me that the very manuscript itself which Lamb had looked at was only a few hundred yards away, so that one could follow Lamb's footsteps across the quadrangle to that famous library where the treasure is kept. Moreover, I recollected, as I put this plan into execution, it is in this famous library that the manuscript of Thackeray's *Esmond* is also preserved. The critics often say that *Esmond* is Thackeray's most perfect novel. But the affectation of the style, with its imitation of the eighteenth century, hampers one, so far as I remember; unless indeed the eighteenth-century style was natural to Thackeray—a fact that one might prove by looking at the manuscript and seeing whether the alterations were for the benefit of the style or of the sense. But then one would have to decide what is style and what is meaning, a question which—but here I was actually at the door which leads into the library itself. I must have opened it, for instantly there issued, like a guardian angel barring the way with a flutter of black gown instead of white wings, a deprecating, silvery, kindly gentleman, who regretted in a low voice as he waved me back that ladies are only admitted to the library if accompanied by a Fellow of the College or furnished with a letter of introduction.

That a famous library has been cursed by a woman is a matter of complete indifference to a famous library. Venerable and calm, with all its treasures safe locked within its breast, it sleeps complacently and will, so far as I am concerned, so sleep forever. Never will I wake those echoes, never will I ask for that hospitality again, I vowed as I descended the steps in anger. Still an hour remained before luncheon, and what was one to do? Stroll on the meadows? sit by the river? Certainly it was a lovely autumn morning; the leaves were fluttering red to the ground; there was no great hardship in doing either. But the sound of music reached my ear. Some service or celebration was going forward. The organ complained magnificently as I passed the chapel door. Even the sorrow of Christianity sounded in that serene air more like the recollection of sorrow than sorrow itself; even the groanings of the ancient organ seemed lapped in peace. I had no wish to enter had I the right, and this time the verger might have stopped me, demanding perhaps my baptismal certificate, or a letter of introduction from the Dean. But the outside of these magnificent buildings is often as beautiful as the inside. Moreover, it was amusing enough to watch the congregation assembling, coming in and going out again, busying themselves at the door of the chapel like bees at the mouth of a hive. Many were in cap and gown; some had tufts of fur on their shoulders; others were wheeled in bath chairs; others, though not past middle age, seemed creased and crushed into shapes so singular that one was reminded of those giant crabs and crayfish who heave with difficulty across the sand of an aquarium. As I leant against the wall the University indeed seemed a sanctuary in which are preserved rare types which would soon be obsolete if left to fight for existence on the pavement of the Strand. Old stories of old deans and old dons came back to mind, but before I had summoned up courage to whistle—it used to be said that at the sound of a whistle old Professor —— instantly broke into a gallop—the venerable congregation had gone inside. The outside of the chapel remained. As you know, its high domes and pinnacles can be seen, like a sailing ship always voyaging never arriving, lit up at night and visible for miles, far away across the hills. Once, presumably, this quadrangle with its smooth lawns, its massive buildings, and the chapel itself was marsh too, where the grasses waved and the swine rootled. Teams of horses and oxen, I thought, must have hauled the stone in wagons from far countries, and then with infinite labor the gray blocks in whose shade I was now standing were poised in order one on top of another, and then the painters brought their glass for the windows, and the masons were busy for centuries up on that roof with putty and cement, spade and trowel. Every Saturday somebody must have poured gold and silver out of a leathern purse into their ancient fists, for they had their beer and skittles presumably of an evening. An unending stream of gold and silver, I thought, must have flowed into this court perpetually to keep the stones coming and the masons working; to level, to ditch, to dig, and to drain. But it was then the age of faith, and money was poured liberally to set these stones on a deep foundation, and when the stones were raised, still more money was poured in from the coffers of kings and queens and great nobles to ensure that hymns should be sung here and scholars taught. Lands were granted; tithes were paid. And when the age of faith was over and the age of reason had come, still the same flow of gold and silver went on; fellowships were founded; lectureships endowed; only the gold and silver flowed now, not from the coffers of the king, but from the chests of merchants and manufacturers, from the purses of men who had made, say, a fortune from industry, and returned, in their wills, a bounteous share of it to endow more chairs, more lectureships, more fellowships in the university where they had learnt their craft. Hence the libraries and laboratories; the observatories; the splendid equipment of costly and delicate instruments which now stands on glass shelves, where centuries ago the grasses waved and the swine rootled. Certainly, as I strolled round the court, the foundation of gold and silver seemed deep enough; the pavement laid solidly over the wild grasses. Men with trays on their heads went busily from staircase to staircase. Gaudy blossoms flowered in window boxes. The strains of the gramophone blared out from the rooms within. It was impossible not to reflect—the reflection whatever it may have been was cut short. The clock struck. It was time to find one's way to luncheon.

It is a curious fact that novelists have a way of making us believe that luncheon parties are invariably memorable for something very witty that was said, or for something very wise that was done. But they seldom spare a word for what was eaten. It is part of the novelist's convention not to mention soup and salmon and ducklings, as if soup and salmon and ducklings were of no importance whatsoever, as if nobody ever smoked a cigar or drank a glass of wine. Here, however, I shall take the liberty to defy that convention and to tell you that the lunch on this occasion began with soles, sunk in a deep dish, over which the college cook had spread a counterpane of the whitest cream, save that it was branded here and there with brown spots like the spots on the flanks of a doe. After that came the partridges, but if this suggests a couple of bald, brown birds on a plate you are mistaken. The partridges, many and various, came with all their retinue of sauces and salads, the sharp and the sweet, each in its order; their potatoes, thin as coins but not so hard; their sprouts, foliated as rosebuds but more succulent. And no sooner had the roast and its retinue been done with than the silent serving man, the Beadle himself perhaps in a milder manifestation, set before us, wreathed in napkins, a confection which rose all sugar from the waves. To call it pudding and so relate it to rice and tapioca would be an insult. Meanwhile the wineglasses had flushed yellow and flushed crimson; had been emptied; had been filled. And thus by degrees was lit, halfway down the spine, which is the seat of the soul, not that hard little electric light which we call brilliance, as it pops in and out upon our lips, but the more profound, subtle, and subterranean glow, which is the rich yellow flame of rational intercourse. No need to hurry. No need to sparkle. No need to be anybody but oneself. We are all going to heaven and Vandyck is of the company—in other words, how good life seemed, how sweet its rewards, how trivial this grudge or that grievance, how admirable friendship and the society of one's kind, as, lighting a good cigarette, one sunk among the cushions in the window seat.

If by good luck there had been an ashtray handy, if one had not knocked the ash out of the window in default, if things had been a little different from what they were, one would not have seen, presumably, a cat without a tail. The sight of that abrupt and truncated animal padding softly across the quadrangle changed by some fluke of the subconscious intelligence the emotional light for me. It was as if some one had let fall a shade. Perhaps the excellent hock was relinquishing its hold. Certainly, as I watched the Manx cat pause in the middle of the lawn as if it too questioned the universe, something seemed lacking, something seemed different. But what was lacking, what was different, I asked myself, listening to the talk. And to answer that question I had to think myself out of the room, back into the past, before the war indeed, and to set before my eyes the model of another luncheon party held in rooms not very far distant from these; but different. Everything was different. Meanwhile the talk went on among the guests, who were many and young, some of this sex, some of that; it went on swimmingly, it went on agreeably, freely, amusingly. And as it went on I set it against the background of that other talk, and as I matched the two together I had no doubt that one was the descendent, the legitimate heir of the other. Nothing was changed; nothing was different save only—here I listened with all my ears not entirely to what was being said, but to the murmur or current behind it. Yes, that was it—the change was there. Before the war at a luncheon party like this people would have said precisely the same things but they would have sounded different, because in those days they were accompanied by a sort of humming noise, not articulate, but musical, exciting, which changed the value of the words themselves. Could one set that humming noise to words? Perhaps with the help of the poets one could. A book lay beside me and, opening it, I turned casually enough to Tennyson. And here I found Tennyson was singing:

> There has fallen a splendid tear
>   From the passion-flower at the gate.
> She is coming, my dove, my dear;
>   She is coming, my life, my fate;
> The red rose cries, "She is near, she is near";
>   And the white rose weeps, "She is late";
> The larkspur listens, "I hear, I hear";
>   And the lily whispers, "I wait."

Was that what men hummed at luncheon parties before the war? And the women?

My heart is like a singing bird
  Whose nest is in a water'd shoot;
My heart is like an apple tree
  Whose boughs are bent with thick-set fruit;
My heart is like a rainbow shell
  That paddles in a halcyon sea;
My heart is gladder than all these
  Because my love is come to me.

Was that what women hummed at luncheon parties before the war?

There was something so ludicrous in thinking of people humming such things even under their breath at luncheon parties before the war that I burst out laughing, and had to explain my laughter by pointing at the Manx cat, who did look a little absurd, poor beast, without a tail, in the middle of the lawn. Was he really born so, or had he lost his tail in an accident? The tailless cat, though some are said to exist in the Isle of Man, is rarer than one thinks. It is a queer animal, quaint rather than beautiful. It is strange what a difference a tail makes—you know the sort of things one says as a lunch party breaks up and people are finding their coats and hats.

This one, thanks to the hospitality of the host, had lasted far into the afternoon. The beautiful October day was fading and the leaves were falling from the trees in the avenue as I walked through it. Gate after gate seemed to close with gentle finality behind me. Innumerable beadles were fitting innumerable keys into well-oiled locks; the treasure house was being made secure for another night. After the avenue one comes out upon a road—I forget its name—which leads you, if you take the right turning, along to Fernham. But there was plenty of time. Dinner was not till half past seven. One could almost do without dinner after such a luncheon. It is strange how a scrap of poetry works in the mind and makes the legs move in time to it along the road. Those words—

There has fallen a splendid tear
  From the passion-flower at the gate.
She is coming, my dove, my dear—

sang in my blood as I stepped quickly along towards Headingley. And then, switching off into the other measure, I sang, where the waters are churned up by the weir:

My heart is like a singing bird
  Whose nest is in a water'd shoot;
My heart is like an apple tree . . .

What poets, I cried aloud, as one does in the dusk, what poets they were!

In a sort of jealousy, I suppose, for our own age, silly and absurd though these comparisons are, I went on to wonder if honestly one could name two living poets now as great as Tennyson and Christina Rossetti were then. Obviously it is impossible, I thought, looking into those foaming waters, to compare them. The very reason why the poetry excites one to such abandonment, such rapture, is that it celebrates some feeling that one used to have (at luncheon parties before the war perhaps), so that one responds easily, familiarly, without troubling to check the feeling, or to compare it with any that one has now. But the living poets express a feeling that is actually being made and torn out of us at the moment. One does not recognize it in the first place; often for some reason one fears it; one watches it with keenness and compares it jealously and suspiciously with the old feeling that one knew. Hence the difficulty of modern poetry; and it is because of this difficulty that one cannot remember more than two consecutive lines of any good modern poet. For this reason—that my memory failed me—the argument flagged for want of material. But why, I continued, moving on towards Headingley, have we stopped humming under our breath at luncheon parties? Why has Alfred ceased to sing

> She is coming, my dove, my dear?

Why has Christina ceased to respond

> My heart is gladder than all these
> Because my love is come to me?

Shall we lay the blame on the war? When the guns fired in August 1914, did the faces of men and women show so plain in each other's eyes that romance was killed? Certainly it was a shock (to women in particular with their illusions about education, and so on) to see the faces of our rulers in the light of the shell fire. So ugly they looked—German, English, French— so stupid. But lay the blame where one will, on whom one will, the illusion which inspired Tennyson and Christina Rossetti to sing so passionately about the coming of their loves is far rarer now than then. One has only to read, to look, to listen, to remember. But why say "blame"? Why, if it was an illusion, not praise the catastrophe, whatever it was, that destroyed illusion and put truth in its place? For truth . . . those dots mark the spot where, in search of truth, I missed the turning up to Fernham. Yes indeed, which was truth about these houses, for example, dim and festive now with their red windows in the dusk, but raw and red and squalid, with their sweets and their bootlaces, at nine o'clock in the morning? And the willows and the river and the gardens that run down to the river, vague now with the mist stealing over them, but gold and red in the sunlight— which was the truth, which was the illusion about them? I spare you the twists and turns of my cogitations, for no conclusion was found on the

649

road to Headingley, and I ask you to suppose that I soon found my mistake about the turning and retraced my steps to Fernham.

As I have said already that it was an October day, I dare not forfeit your respect and imperil the fair name of fiction by changing the season and describing lilacs hanging over garden walls, crocuses, tulips, and other flowers of spring. Fiction must stick to facts, and the truer the facts the better the fiction—so we are told. Therefore it was still autumn and the leaves were still yellow and falling, if anything, a little faster than before, because it was now evening (seven twenty-three to be precise) and a breeze (from the southwest to be exact) had risen. But for all that there was something odd at work:

> My heart is like a singing bird
>    Whose nest is in a water'd shoot;
> My heart is like an apple tree
>    Whose boughs are bent with thick-set fruit—

perhaps the words of Christina Rossetti were partly responsible for the folly of the fancy—it was nothing of course but a fancy—that the lilac was shaking its flowers over the garden walls, and the brimstone butterflies were scudding hither and thither, and the dust of the pollen was in the air. A wind blew, from what quarter I know not, but it lifted the half-grown leaves so that there was a flash of silver gray in the air. It was the time between the lights when colors undergo their intensification and purples and golds burn in windowpanes like the beat of an excitable heart; when for some reason the beauty of the world revealed and yet soon to perish (here I pushed into the garden, for, unwisely, the door was left open and no beadles seemed about), the beauty of the world which is so soon to perish, has two edges, one of laughter, one of anguish, cutting the heart asunder. The gardens of Fernham lay before me in the spring twilight, wild and open, and in the long grass, sprinkled and carelessly flung, were daffodils and bluebells, not orderly perhaps at the best of times, and now windblown and waving as they tugged at their roots. The windows of the building, curved like ships' windows among generous waves of red brick, changed from lemon to silver under the flight of the quick spring clouds. Somebody was in a hammock, somebody, but in this light they were phantoms only, half guessed, half seen, raced across the grass—would no one stop her?—and then on the terrace, as if popping out to breathe the air, to glance at the garden, came a bent figure, formidable yet humble, with her great forehead and her shabby dress—could it be the famous scholar, could it be J—— H—— herself? All was dim, yet intense too, as if the scarf which the dusk had flung over the garden were torn asunder by star or sword— the flash of some terrible reality leaping, as its way is, out of the heart of the spring. For youth——

Here was my soup. Dinner was being served in the great dining hall. Far from being spring it was in fact an evening in October. Everybody was assembled in the big dining room. Dinner was ready. Here was the soup. It was a plain gravy soup. There was nothing to stir the fancy in that. One could have seen through the transparent liquid any pattern that there might have been on the plate itself. But there was no pattern. The plate was plain. Next came beef with its attendant greens and potatoes—a homely trinity, suggesting the rumps of cattle in a muddy market, and sprouts curled and yellowed at the edge, and bargaining and cheapening, and women with string bags on Monday morning. There was no reason to complain of human nature's daily food, seeing that the supply was sufficient and coal miners doubtless were sitting down to less. Prunes and custard followed. And if any one complains that prunes, even when mitigated by custard, are an uncharitable vegetable (fruit they are not), stringy as a miser's heart and exuding a fluid such as might run in miser's veins who have denied themselves wine and warmth for eighty years and yet not given to the poor, he should reflect that there are people whose charity embraces even the prune. Biscuits and cheese came next, and here the water jug was liberally passed round, for it is the nature of biscuits to be dry, and these were biscuits to the core. That was all. The meal was over. Everybody scraped their chairs back; the swing doors swung violently to and fro; soon the hall was emptied of every sign of food and made ready no doubt for breakfast next morning. Down corridors and up staircases the youth of England went banging and singing. And was it for a guest, a stranger (for I had no more right here in Fernham than in Trinity or Somerville or Girton or Newnham or Christchurch), to say, "The dinner was not good," or to say (we were now, Mary Seton and I, in her sitting room), "Could we not have dined up here alone?" for if I had said anything of the kind I should have been prying and searching into the secret economies of a house which to the stranger wears so fine a front of gaiety and courage. No, one could say nothing of the sort. Indeed, conversation for a moment flagged. The human frame being what it is, heart, body, and brain all mixed together, and not contained in separate compartments as they will be no doubt in another million years, a good dinner is of great importance to good talk. One cannot think well, love well, sleep well, if one has not dined well. The lamp in the spine does not light on beef and prunes. We are all *probably* going to heaven, and Vandyck is, we *hope*, to meet us round the next corner—that is the dubious and qualifying state of mind that beef and prunes at the end of the day's work breed between them. Happily my friend, who taught science, had a cupboard where there was a squat bottle and little glasses—(but there should have been sole and partridge to begin with)—so that we were able to draw up to the fire and repair some of the damages of the day's living. In a minute or so we were slipping freely in and out among all those objects of curiosity and interest which form in the mind in the absence of a particular person, and are naturally to be discussed on coming together again—how somebody has married, another has not; one thinks this, another that; one has improved out of all knowledge, the other most amazingly gone to the bad—with all those speculations upon human nature and the character of the amazing world we live in which spring naturally from such beginnings. While these things were being said, however, I became shamefacedly aware of a current setting in of its own accord and carrying everything forward to an end of its own. One might be talking of Spain or Portugal, of book or racehorse, but the real interest of whatever was said was none of those things, but a scene of masons on a high roof some five centuries ago. Kings and nobles brought treasure in huge sacks and poured it under the earth. This scene was forever coming alive in my mind and placing itself by another of lean cows and a muddy market and withered greens and the stringy hearts of old men—these two pictures, disjointed and disconnected and nonsensical as they were, were forever coming together and combating each other and had me entirely at their mercy. The best course, unless the whole talk was to be distorted, was to expose what was in my mind to the air, when with good luck it would fade and crumble like the head of the dead king when they opened the coffin at Windsor. Briefly, then, I told Miss Seton about the masons who had been all those years on the roof of the chapel, and about the kings and queens and nobles bearing sacks of gold and silver on their shoulders, which they shoveled into the earth; and then how the great financial magnates of our own time came and laid checks and bonds, I suppose, where the others had laid ingots and rough lumps of gold. All that lies beneath the colleges down there, I said; but this college, where we are now sitting, what lies beneath its gallant red brick and the wild unkempt grasses of the garden? What force is behind the plain china off which we dined, and (here it popped out of my mouth before I could stop it) the beef, the custard, and the prunes?

Well, said Mary Seton, about the year 1860—Oh, but you know the story, she said, bored, I suppose, by the recital. And she told me—rooms were hired. Committees met. Envelopes were addressed. Circulars were drawn up. Meetings were held; letters were read out; so-and-so has promised so much; on the contrary, Mr. —— won't give a penny. The *Saturday Review* has been very rude. How can we raise a fund to pay for offices? Shall we hold a bazaar? Can't we find a pretty girl to sit in the front row? Let us look up what John Stuart Mill said on the subject. Can anyone persuade the editor of the —— to print a letter? Can we get Lady —— to sign it? Lady —— is out of town. That was the way it was done, presumably, sixty years ago, and it was a prodigious effort, and a great deal of time was spent on it. And it was only after a long struggle and with the utmost difficulty that they got thirty thousand pounds together?[1] So obviously we cannot have wine and partridges and servants carrying tin dishes on their heads, she said. We cannot have sofas and separate rooms. "The amenities," she said, quoting from some book or other, "will have to wait."[2]

As the thought of all those women working year after year and finding it hard to get two thousand pounds together, and as much as they could do to get thirty thousand pounds, we burst out in scorn at the reprehensible poverty of our sex. What had our mothers been doing then that they had no wealth to leave us? Powdering their noses? Looking in at shop windows? Flaunting in the sun at Monte Carlo? There were some photographs on the mantelpiece. Mary's mother—if that was her picture—may have been a wastrel in her spare time (she had thirteen children by a minister of the church), but if so her gay and dissipated life had left too few traces of its pleasures on her face. She was a homely body; an old lady in a plaid shawl which was fastened by a large cameo; and she sat in a basket chair, encouraging a spaniel to look at the camera, with the amused, yet strained expression of one who is sure that the dog will move directly the bulb is pressed. Now if she had gone into business; had become a manufacturer of artificial silk or a magnate on the Stock Exchange; if she had left two or three thousand pounds to Fernham, we could have been sitting at our ease tonight and the subject of our talk might have been archaeology, botany, anthropology, physics, the nature of the atom, mathematics, astronomy, relativity, geography. If only Mrs. Seton and her mother and her mother before her had learnt the great art of making money and had left their money, like their fathers and their grandfathers before them, to found fellowships and lectureships and prizes and scholarships appropriated to the use of their own sex, we might have dined very tolerably up here alone off a bird and a bottle of wine; we might have looked forward without undue confidence to a pleasant and honorable lifetime spent in the shelter of one of the liberally endowed professions. We might have been exploring or writing; mooning about the venerable places of the earth; sitting contemplative on the steps of the Parthenon, or going at ten to an office and coming home comfortably at half past four to write a little poetry. Only, if Mrs. Seton and her like had gone into business at the age of fifteen, there would have been—that was the snag in the argument—no Mary. What, I asked, did Mary think of that? There between the curtains was the October night, calm and lovely, with a star or two caught in the yellowing trees. Was she ready to resign her share of it and her memories (for they had been a happy family, though a large one) of games and quarrels up in Scotland, which she is never tired of praising for the fineness of its air and the quality of its cakes, in order that Fernham might have been endowed with fifty thousand pounds or so by a stroke of the pen? For, to endow a college would necessitate the suppression of families altogether. Making a fortune and bearing thirteen children—no human being could stand it. Consider the facts, we said. First there are nine months before the baby is born. Then the baby is born. Then there are three or four months spent in feeding the baby. After the baby is fed there are certainly five years spent in playing with the baby. You cannot, it seems, let children run about the streets. People who have seen them running wild in Russia say that the sight is not a pleasant one. People say, too, that human nature takes its shape in the years between one and five. If Mrs. Seton, I said, had been making money, what sort of memories would you have had of games and quarrels? What would you have known of Scotland, and its fine air and cakes and all the rest of it? But it is useless to ask these questions, because you would never have come into existence at all. Moreover, it is equally useless to ask what might have happened if Mrs. Seton and her mother and her mother before her had amassed great wealth and laid it under the foundations of college and library, because, in the first place, to earn money was impossible for them, and in the second, had it been possible, the law denied them the right to possess what money they earned. It is only for the last forty-eight years that Mrs. Seton has had a penny of her own. For all the centuries before that it would have been her husband's property—a thought which, perhaps, may have had its share in keeeping Mrs. Seton and her mothers off the Stock Exchange. Every penny I earn, they may have said, will be taken from me and disposed of according to my husband's wisdom—perhaps to found a scholarship or to endow a fellowship in Balliol or Kings, so that to earn money, even if I could earn money, is not a matter that interests me very greatly. I had better leave it to my husband.

At any rate, whether or not the blame rested on the old lady who was looking at the spaniel, there could be no doubt that for some reason or other our mothers had mismanaged their affairs very gravely. Not a penny could be spared for "amenities"; for partridges and wine, beadles and turf, books and cigars, libraries and leisure. To raise bare walls out of the bare earth was the utmost they could do.

So we talked standing at the window and looking, as so many thousands look every night, down on the domes and towers of the famous city beneath us. It was very beautiful, very mysterious in the autumn moonlight. The old stone looked very white and venerable. One thought of all the books that were assembled down there; of the pictures of old prelates and worthies hanging in the paneled rooms; of the painted windows that would be throwing strange globes and crescents on the pavement; of the tablets and memorials and inscriptions; of the fountains and the grass; of the quiet rooms looking across the quiet quadrangles. And (pardon me the thought) I thought, too, of the admirable smoke and drink and the deep armchairs and the pleasant carpets: of the urbanity, the geniality, the dignity which are the offspring of luxury and privacy and space. Certainly our mothers had not provided us with anything comparable to all this—our mothers who found it difficult to scrape together thirty thousand pounds, our mothers who bore thirteen children to ministers of religion at St. Andrews.

So I went back to my inn, and as I walked through the dark streets I pondered this and that, as one does at the end of the day's work. I pondered why it was that Mrs. Seton had no money to leave us; and what effect poverty has on the mind; and what effect wealth has on the mind; and I thought of the queer old gentlemen I had seen that morning with tufts of fur upon their shoulders; and I remembered how if one whistled one of them ran; and I thought of the organ booming in the chapel and of the shut doors of the library; and I thought how unpleasant it is to be locked out; and I thought how it is worse perhaps to be locked in; and, thinking of the safety and prosperity of the one sex and of the poverty and insecurity of the other and of the effect of tradition and of the lack of tradition upon the mind of a writer, I thought at last that it was time to roll up the crumpled skin of the day, with its arguments and its impressions and its anger and its laughter, and cast it into the hedge. A thousand stars were flashing across the blue wastes of the sky. One seemed alone with an inscrutable society. All human beings were laid asleep—prone, horizontal, dumb. Nobody seemed stirring in the streets of Oxbridge. Even the door of the hotel sprang open at the touch of an invisible hand—not a boots was sitting up to light me to bed, it was so late.

## *Chapter Six*

Next day the light of the October morning was falling in dusty shafts through the uncurtained windows, and the hum of traffic rose from the street. London then was winding itself up again; the factory was astir; the machines were beginning. It was tempting, after all this reading, to look out of the window and see what London was doing on the morning of the twenty-sixth of October 1928. And what was London doing? Nobody, it seemed, was reading *Antony and Cleopatra*. London was wholly indifferent, it appeared, to Shakespeare's plays. Nobody cared a straw—and I do not blame them—for the future of fiction, the death of poetry or the development by the average woman of a prose style completely expressive of her mind. If opinions upon any of these matters had been chalked on the pavement, nobody would have stooped to read them. The nonchalance of the hurrying feet would have rubbed them out in half an hour. Here came an errand boy; here a woman with a dog on a lead. The fascination of the London street is that no two people are ever alike; each seems bound on some private affair of his own. There were the businesslike, with their little bags; there were the drifters rattling sticks upon area railings; there were affable characters to whom the streets serve for clubroom, hailing men in carts and giving information without being asked for it. Also there were funerals to which men, thus suddenly reminded of the passing of their own bodies, lifted their hats. And then a very distinguished gentleman came slowly down a doorstep and paused to avoid collision with a bustling lady who had, by some means or other, acquired a splendid fur coat and a bunch of Parma violets. They all seemed separate, self-absorbed, on business of their own.

At this moment, as so often happens in London, there was a complete lull and suspension of traffic. Nothing came down the street; nobody passed. A single leaf detached itself from the plane tree at the end of the street, and in that pause and suspension fell. Somehow it was like a signal falling, a signal pointing to a force in things which one had overlooked. It seemed to point to a river, which flowed past, invisibly, round the corner, down the street, and took people and eddied them along, as the stream at Oxbridge had taken the undergraduate in his boat and the dead leaves. Now it was bringing from one side of the street to the other diagonally a girl in patent leather boots, and then a young man in a maroon overcoat; it was also bringing a taxicab; and it brought all three together at a point directly beneath my window; where the taxi stopped; and the girl and the young man stopped; and they got into the taxi; and then the cab glided off as if it were swept on by the current elsewhere.

The sight was ordinary enough; what was strange was the rhythmical order with which my imagination had invested it; and the fact that the ordinary sight of two people getting into a cab had the power to communicate something of their own seeming satisfaction. The sight of two people coming down the street and meeting at the corner seems to ease the mind of some strain, I thought, watching the taxi turn and make off. Perhaps to think, as I had been thinking these two days, of one sex as distinct from the other is an effort. It interferes with the unity of the mind. Now that effort had ceased and that unity had been restored by seeing two people come together and get into a taxicab. The mind is certainly a very mysterious organ, I reflected, drawing my head in from the window, about which nothing whatever is known, though we depend upon it so completely. Why do I feel that there are severances and oppositions in the mind, as there are strains from obvious causes on the body? What does one mean by "the unity of the mind," I pondered, for clearly the mind has so great a power of concentrating at any point at any moment that it seems to have no single state of being. It can separate itself from the people in the street, for example, and think of itself as apart from them, at an upper window looking down on them. Or it can think with other people spontaneously, as, for instance, in a crowd waiting to hear some piece of news read out. It can think back through its fathers or through its mothers, as I have said that a woman writing thinks back through her mothers. Again if one is a woman one is often surprised by a sudden splitting off of consciousness, say in walking down Whitehall, when from being the natural inheritor of that civilization, she becomes, on the contrary, outside of it, alien and critical. Clearly the mind is always altering its focus, and bringing the world into different perspectives. But some of these states of mind seem, even if adopted spontaneously, to be less comfortable than others. In order to keep oneself continuing in them one is unconsciously holding something back, and gradually the repression becomes an effort. But there may be some state of mind in which one could continue without effort because nothing is required to be held back. And this perhaps, I thought, coming in from the window, is one of them. For certainly when I saw the couple get into the taxicab the mind felt as if, after being divided, it had come together again in a natural fusion. The obvious reason would be that it is natural for the sexes to cooperate. One has a profound, if irrational, instinct in favor of the theory that the union of man and woman makes for the greatest satisfaction, the most complete happiness. But the sight of the two people getting into the taxi and the satisfaction it gave me made me also ask whether there are two sexes in the mind corresponding to the two sexes in the body, and whether they also require to be united in order to get complete satisfaction and happiness. And I went on amateurishly to sketch a plan of the soul so that in each of us two powers preside, one male, one female; and in the man's brain, the man predominates over the woman, and in the woman's brain, the woman predominates over the man. The normal and comfortable state of being is that when the two live in harmony together, spiritually cooperating. If one is a man, still the woman part of the brain must have effect; and a woman also must have intercourse with the man in her. Coleridge perhaps meant this when he said that a great mind is androgynous. It is when this fusion takes place that the mind is fully fertilized and uses all its faculties. Perhaps a mind that is purely masculine cannot create, any more than a mind that is purely feminine, I thought. But it would be well to test what one meant by man-womanly, and conversely by woman-manly, by pausing and looking at a book or two.

Coleridge certainly did not mean, when he said that a great mind is androgynous, that it is a mind that has any special sympathy with women; a mind that takes up their cause or devotes itself to their interpretation. Perhaps the androgynous mind is less apt to make these distinctions than the single-sexed mind. He meant, perhaps, that the androgynous mind is resonant and porous; that it transmits emotion without impediment; that it is naturally creative, incandescent, and undivided. In fact one goes back to Shakespeare's mind as the type of the androgynous, of the man-womanly mind, though it would be impossible to say what Shakespeare thought of women. And if it be true that it is one of the tokens of the fully developed mind that it does not think specially or separately of sex, how much harder it is to attain that condition now than ever before. Here I came to the books by living writers, and there paused and wondered if this fact were not at the root of something that had long puzzled me. No age can ever have been as stridently sex-conscious as our own; those innumerable books by men about women in the British Museum are a proof of it. The Suffrage campaign was no doubt to blame. It must have roused in men an extraordinary desire for self-assertion; it must have made them lay an emphasis upon their own sex and its characteristics which they would not have troubled to think about had they not been challenged. And when one is challenged, even by a few women in black bonnets, one retaliates, if one has never been challenged before, rather excessively. That perhaps accounts for some of the characteristics that I remember to have found here, I thought, taking down a new novel by Mr. A, who is in the prime of life and very well thought of, apparently, by the reviewers. I opened it. Indeed, it was delightful to read a man's writing again. It was so direct, so straightforward after the writing of women. It indicated such freedom of mind, such liberty of person, such a confidence in himself. One had a sense of physical well-being in the presence of this well-nourished, well-educated, free mind, which had never been thwarted, or opposed, but had had full liberty from birth to stretch itself in whatever way it liked. All this was admirable. But after reading a chapter or two a shadow seemed to lie across the page. It was a straight dark bar, a shadow shaped something like the letter "I." One began dodging this way and that to catch a glimpse of the landscape behind it. Whether that was indeed a tree or a woman walking I was not quite sure. Back one was always hailed to the letter "I." One began to be tired of "I." Not but what this "I" was a most respectable "I"; honest and logical; as hard as a nut, and polished for centuries by good teaching and good feeding. I respect and admire that "I" from the bottom of my heart. But— here I turned a page or two, looking for something or other—the worst of it is that in the shadow of the letter "I" all is shapeless as mist. Is that a tree? No, it is a woman. But . . . she has not a bone in her body, I thought, watching Phoebe, for that was her name, coming across the beach. Then Alan got up and the shadow of Alan at once obliterated Phoebe. For Alan had views and Phoebe was quenched in the flood of his views. And then Alan, I thought, has passions; and here I turned page after page very fast, feeling that the crisis was approaching, and so it was. It took place on the beach under the sun. It was done very openly. It was done very vigorously. Nothing could have been more indecent. But . . . I had said "but" too often. One cannot go on saying "but." One must finish the sentence somehow, I rebuked myself. Shall I finish it, "But—I am bored!" But why was I bored? Partly because of the dominance of the letter "I" and the aridity, which, like the giant beech tree, it casts within its shade. Nothing will grow there. And partly for some more obscure reason. There seemed to be some obstacle, some impediment of Mr. A's mind which blocked the fountain of creative energy and shored it within narrow limits. And remembering the lunch party at Oxbridge, and the cigarette ash and the Manx cat and Tennyson and Christina Rossetti all in a bunch, it seemed possible that the impediment lay there. As he no longer hums under his breath, "There has fallen a splendid tear from the passion-flower at the gate," when Phoebe crosses the beach, and she no longer replies, "My heart is like a singing bird whose nest is in a water'd shoot," when Alan approaches what can he do? Being honest as the day and logical as the sun, there is only one thing he can do. And that he does, to do him justice, over and over (I said, turning the pages) and over again. And that, I added, aware of the awful nature of the confession, seems somehow dull. Shakespeare's indecency uproots a thousand other things in one's mind, and is far from being dull. But Shakespeare does it for pleasure; Mr. A, as the nurses say, does it on purpose. He does it in protest. He is protesting against the equality of the other sex by asserting his own superiority. He is therefore impeded and inhibited and self-conscious as Shakespeare might have been if he too had known Miss Clough and Miss Davies. Doubtless Elizabethan literature would have been very different from what it is if the woman's movement had begun in the sixteenth century and not in the nineteenth.

What, then, it amounts to, if this theory of the two sides of the mind holds good, is that virility has now become self-conscious—men, that is to say, are now writing only with the male side of their brains. It is a mistake for a woman to read them, for she will inevitably look for something that she will not find. It is the power of suggestion that one most misses, I thought, taking Mr. B the critic in my hand and reading, very carefully and very dutifully, his remarks upon the art of poetry. Very able they were, acute and full of learning; but the trouble was, that his feelings no longer communicated; his mind seemed separated into different chambers; not a sound carried from one to the other. Thus, when one takes a sentence of Mr. B into the mind it falls plump to the ground—dead; but when one takes a sentence of Coleridge into the mind, it explodes and gives birth to all kinds of other ideas, and that is the only sort of writing of which one can say that it has the secret of perpetual life.

But whatever the reason may be, it is a fact that one must deplore. For it means—here I had come to rows of books by Mr. Galsworthy and Mr. Kipling—that some of the finest works of our greatest living writers fall upon deaf ears. Do what she will a woman cannot find in them that fountain of perpetual life which the critics assure her is there. It is not only that they celebrate male virtues, enforce male values, and describe the world of men; it is that the emotion with which these books are permeated is to a woman incomprehensible. It is coming, it is gathering, it is about to burst on one's head, one begins saying long before the end. That picture will fall on old Jolyon's head; he will die of the shock; the old clerk will speak over him two or three obituary words; and all the swans on the Thames will simultaneously burst out singing. But one will rush away before that happens and hide in the gooseberry bushes, for the emotion which is so deep, so subtle, so symbolical to a man moves a woman to wonder. So with Mr. Kipling's officers who turn their backs; and his Sowers who sow the Seed; and his Men who are alone with their Work; and the Flag—one blushes at all these capital letters as if one had been caught eavesdropping at some purely masculine orgy. The fact is that neither Mr. Galsworthy nor Mr. Kipling has a spark of the woman in him. Thus all their qualities seem to a woman, if one may generalize, crude and immature. They lack suggestive power. And when a book lacks suggestive power, however hard it hits the surface of the mind it cannot penetrate within.

And in that restless mood in which one takes books out and puts them back again without looking at them I began to envisage an age to come of pure, of self-assertive virility, such as the letters of professors (take Sir Walter Raleigh's letters, for instance) seem to forebode, and the rulers of Italy have already brought into being. For one can hardly fail to be impressed in Rome by the sense of unmitigated masculinity; and whatever the value of unmitigated masculinity upon the state, one may question the effect of it upon the art of poetry. At any rate, according to the newspapers, there is a certain anxiety about fiction in Italy. There has been a meeting of academicians whose object it is "to develop the Italian novel." "Men famous by birth, or in finance, industry, or the Fascist corporations" came together the other day and discussed the matter, and a telegram was sent to the Duce expressing the hope "that the Fascist era would soon give birth to a poet worthy of it." We may all join in that pious hope, but it is doubtful whether poetry can come out of an incubator. Poetry ought to have a mother as well as a father. The Fascist poem, one may fear, will be a horrid little abortion such as one sees in a glass jar in the museum of some county town. Such monsters never live long, it is said; one has never seen a prodigy of that sort cropping grass in a field. Two heads on one body do not make for length of life.

However, the blame for all this, if one is anxious to lay blame, rests no more upon one sex than upon the other. All seducers and reformers are responsible, Lady Bessborough when she lied to Lord Granville; Miss Davies when she told the truth to Mr. Greg. All who have brought about a state of sex-consciousness are to blame, and it is they who drive me, when I want to stretch my faculties on a book, to seek it in that happy age, before

Miss Davies and Miss Clough were born, when the writer used both sides of his mind equally. One must turn back to Shakespeare then, for Shakespeare was androgynous; and so was Keats and Sterne and Cowper and Lamb and Coleridge. Shelley perhaps was sexless. Milton and Ben Jonson had a dash too much of the male in them. So had Wordsworth and Tolstoi. In our time Proust was wholly androgynous, if not perhaps a little too much of a woman. But that failing is too rare for one to complain of it, since without some mixture of the kind the intellect seems to predominate and the other faculties of the mind harden and become barren. However, I consoled myself with the reflection that this is perhaps a passing phase; much of what I have said in obedience to my promise to give you the course of my thoughts will seem out of date; much of what flames in my eyes will seem dubious to you who have not yet come of age.

Even so, the very first sentence that I would write here, I said, crossing over to the writing table and taking up the page headed Women and Fiction, is that it is fatal for any one who writes to think of their sex. It is fatal to be a man or woman pure and simple; one must be woman-manly or man-womanly. It is fatal for a woman to lay the least stress on any grievance; to plead even with justice any cause; in any way to speak consciously as a woman. And fatal is no figure of speech; for anything written with that conscious bias is doomed to death. It ceases to be fertilized. Brilliant and effective, powerful and masterly, as it may appear for a day or two, it must wither at nightfall; it cannot grow in the minds of others. Some collaboration has to take place in the mind between the woman and the man before the act of creation can be accomplished. Some marriage of opposites has to be consummated. The whole of the mind must lie wide open if we are to get the sense that the writer is communicating his experience with perfect fullness. There must be freedom and there must be peace. Not a wheel must grate, not a light glimmer. The curtains must be close drawn. The writer, I thought, once his experience is over, must lie back and let his mind celebrate its nuptials in darkness. He must not look or question what is being done. Rather, he must pluck the petals from a rose or watch the swans float calmly down the river. And I saw again the current which took the boat and the undergraduate and the dead leaves; and the taxi took the man and the woman, I thought, seeing them come together across the street, and the current swept them away, I thought, hearing far off the roar of London's traffic, into that tremendous stream.

Here, then, Mary Beton ceases to speak. She has told you how she reached the conclusion—the prosaic conclusion—that it is necessary to have five hundred a year and a room with a lock on the door if you are to write fiction or poetry. She has tried to lay bare the thoughts and impressions that led her to think this. She has asked you to follow her flying into the arms of a Beadle, lunching here, dining there, drawing pictures in the British Museum, taking books from the shelf, looking out of the window. While she has been doing all these things, you no doubt have been observing her failings and foibles and deciding what effect they have had on her opinions. You have been contradicting her and making whatever additions and deductions seem good to you. That is all as it should be, for in a question like this truth is only to be had by laying together many varieties of error. And I will end now in my own person by anticipating two criticisms, so obvious that you can hardly fail to make them.

No opinion has been expressed, you may say, upon the comparative merits of the sexes even as writers. That was done purposely, because, even if the time had come for such a valuation—and it is far more important at the moment to know how much money women had and how many rooms than to theorize about their capacities—even if the time had come I do not believe that gifts, whether of mind or character, can be weighed like sugar and butter, not even in Cambridge, where they are so adept at putting people into classes and fixing caps on their heads and letters after their names. I do not believe that even the Table of Precedency which you will find in Whitaker's *Almanac* represents a final order of values, or that there is any sound reason to suppose that a Commander of the Bath will ultimately walk in to dinner behind a Master in Lunacy. All this pitting of sex against sex, of quality against quality; all this claiming of superiority and imputing of inferiority, belong to the private-school stage of human existence where there are "sides," and it is necessary for one side to beat another side, and of the utmost importance to walk up to a platform and receive from the hands of the Headmaster himself a highly ornamental pot. As people mature they cease to believe in sides or in Headmasters or in highly ornamental pots. At any rate, where books are concerned, it is notoriously difficult to fix labels of merit in such a way that they do not come off. Are not reviews of current literature a perpetual illustration of the difficulty of judgment? "This great book," "this worthless book," the same book is called by both names. Praise and blame alike mean nothing. No, delightful as the pastime of measuring may be, it is the most futile of all occupations, and to submit to the decrees of the measurers the most servile of attitudes. So long as you write what you wish to write, that is all that matters; and whether it matters for ages or only for hours, nobody can say. But to sacrifice a hair of the head of your vision, a shade of its color, in deference to some Headmaster with a silver pot in his hand or to some professor with a measuring rod up his sleeve, is the most abject treachery, and the sacrifice of wealth and chastity which used to be said to be the greatest of human disasters, a mere flea bite in comparison.

Next I think that you may object that in all this I have made too much of the importance of material things. Even allowing a generous margin for symbolism, that five hundred a year stands for the power to contemplate, that a lock on the door means the power to think for oneself, still you may say that the mind should rise above such things; and that great poets have often been poor men. Let me then quote to you the words of your own Professor of Literature, who knows better than I do what goes to the making of a poet. Sir Arthur Quiller-Couch writes: [3]

> What are the great poetical names of the last hundred years or so? Coleridge, Wordsworth, Byron, Shelly, Landor, Keats, Tennyson, Browning, Arnold, Morris, Rossetti, Swinburne— we may stop there. Of these, all but Keats, Browning, Rossetti were University men; and of these three, Keats, who died young, cut off in his prime, was the only one not fairly well to do. It may seem a brutal thing to say, and it is a sad thing to say: but, as a matter of hard fact, the theory that poetical genius bloweth where it listeth, and equally in poor and rich, holds little truth. As a matter of hard fact, nine out of those twelve were University men: which means that somehow or other they procured the means to get the best education England can give. As a matter of hard fact, of the remaining three you know that Browning was well to do, and I challenge you that, if he had not been well to do, he would no more have attained to write *Saul* or *The Ring and the Book* than Ruskin would have attained to writing *Modern Painters* if his father had not dealt prosperously in business. Rossetti had a small private income; and, moreover, he painted. There remains but Keats; whom Atropos slew young, as she slew John Clare in a madhouse, and James Thomson by the laudanum he took to drug disappointment. These are dreadful facts, but let us face them. It is—however dishonoring to us as a nation—certain that, by some fault in our commonwealth, the poor poet had not in these days, nor has had for two hundred years, a dog's chance. Believe me—and I have spent a great part of ten years in watching some three hundred and twenty elementary schools—we may prate of democracy, but actually, a poor child in England has little more hope than had the son of an Athenian slave to be emancipated into that intellectual freedom of which great writings are born.

Nobody could put the point more plainly. "The poor poet has not in these days, nor has had for two hundred years, a dog's chance . . . a poor child in England has little more hope than had the son of an Athenian slave to be emancipated into that intellectual freedom of which great writings are born." That is it. Intellectual freedom depends upon material things. Poetry depends upon intellectual freedom. And women have always been poor, not for two hundred years merely, but from the beginning of time. Women have had less intellectual freedom than the sons of Athenian slaves. Women, then, have not had a dog's chance of writing poetry. That is why I have laid so much stress on money and a room of one's own. However, thanks to the toils of those obscure women in the past, of whom I wish we knew more, thanks, curiously enough, to two wars, the Crimean which let Florence Nightingale out of her drawing room, and the European War which opened the doors to the average woman some sixty years later, these evils are in the way to be bettered. Otherwise you would not be here tonight, and your chance of earning five hundred pounds a year, precarious as I am afraid that it still is, would be minute in the extreme.

Still, you may object, why do you attach so much importance to this writing of books by women when, according to you, it requires so much effort, leads perhaps to the murder of one's aunts, will make one almost certainly late for luncheon, and may bring one into very grave disputes with certain very good fellows? My motives, let me admit, are partly selfish. Like most uneducated Englishwomen, I like reading—I like reading books in the bulk. Lately my diet has become a trifle monotonous; history is too much about wars; biography too much about great men; poetry has shown, I think, a tendency to sterility, and fiction—but I have sufficiently exposed my disabilities as a critic of modern fiction and will say no more about it. Therefore I would ask you to write all kinds of books, hesitating at no subject however trivial or however vast. By hook or by crook, I hope that you will possess yourselves of money enough to travel and to idle, to contemplate the future or the past of the world, to dream over books and loiter at street corners and let the line of thought dip deep into the stream. For I am by no means confining you to fiction. If you would please me— and there are thousands like me—you would write books of travel and adventure, and research and scholarship, and history and biography, and criticism and philosophy and science. By so doing you will certainly profit the art of fiction. For books have a way of influencing each other. Fiction will be much better for standing cheek by jowl with poetry and philosophy. Moreover, if you consider any great figure of the past, like Sappho, like the Lady Murasaki, like Emily Brontë, you will find that she is an inheritor as well as an originator, and has come into existence because women have come to have the habit of writing naturally; so that even as a prelude to poetry such activity on your part would be invaluable.

But when I look back through these notes and criticize my own train of thought as I made them, I find that my motives were not altogether selfish. There runs through these comments and discursions the conviction—or is it the instinct?—that good books are desirable and that good writers, even if they show every variety of human depravity, are still good human beings. Thus when I ask you to write more books I am urging you to do what will be for your good and for the good of the world at large. How to justify this instinct or belief I do not know, for philosophic words, if one has not been educated at a university, are apt to play one false. What is meant by "reality"? It would seem to be something very erratic, very undependable—now to be found in a dusty road, now in a scrap of newspaper in the street, now in a daffodil in the sun. It lights up a group in a room and stamps some casual saying. It overwhelms one walking home beneath the stars and makes the silent world more real than the world of speech—and then there it is again in an omnibus in the uproar of Piccadilly. Sometimes, too, it seems to dwell in shapes too far away for us to discern what their nature is. But whatever it touches, it fixes and makes permanent. That is what remains over when the skin of the day has been cast into the hedge; that is what is left of past time and of our loves and hates. Now the writer, as I think, has the chance to live more than other people in the presence of this reality. It is his business to find it and collect it and communicate it to the rest of us. So at least I infer from reading *Lear* or *Emma* or *La Recherche du Temps Perdu*. For the reading of these books seems to perform a curious couching operation on the senses; one sees more intensely afterwards; the world seems bared of its covering and given an intenser life. Those are the enviable people who live at enmity with unreality; and those are the pitiable who are knocked on the head by the thing done without knowing or caring. So that when I ask you to earn money and have a room of your own, I am asking you to live in the presence of reality, an invigorating life, it would appear, whether one can impart it or not.

Here I would stop, but the pressure of convention decrees that every speech must end with a peroration. And a peroration addressed to women should have something, you will agree, particularly exalting and ennobling about it. I should implore you to remember your responsibilities, to be higher, more spiritual; I should remind you how much depends upon you, and what an influence you can exert upon the future. But those exhortations can safely, I think, be left to the other sex, who will put them, and indeed have put them, with far greater eloquence than I can compass. When I rummage in my own mind I find no noble sentiments about being companions and equals and influencing the world to higher ends. I find myself saying briefly and prosaically that it is much more important to be oneself than anything else. Do not dream of influencing other people, I would say, if I knew how to make it sound exalted. Think of things in themselves.

And again I am reminded by dipping into newspapers and novels and biographies that when a woman speaks to women she should have something very unpleasant up her sleeve. Women are hard on women. Women dislike women. Women—but are you not sick to death of the word? I can assure you that I am. Let us agree, then, that a paper read by a woman to women should end with something particularly disagreeable.

But how does it go? What can I think of? The truth is, I often like women. I like their unconventionality. I like their subtlety. I like their anonymity. I like—but I must not run on in this way. That cupboard there,—you say it holds clean table napkins only; but what if Sir Archibald Bodkin were concealed among them? Let me then adopt a sterner tone. Have I, in the preceding words, conveyed to you sufficiently the warnings and reprobation of mankind? I have told you the very low opinion in which you were held by Mr. Oscar Browning. I have indicated what Napoleon once thought of you and what Mussolini thinks now. Then, in case any of you aspire to fiction, I have copied out for your benefit the advice of the critic about courageously acknowledging the limitations of your sex. I have referred to Professor X and given prominence to his statement that women are intellectually, morally, and physically inferior to men. I have handed on all that has come my way without going in search of it, and here is a final warning—from Mr. John Langdon Davies. [4] Mr. John Langdon Davies warns women "that when children cease to be altogether desirable, women cease to be altogether necessary." I hope you will make a note of it.

How can I further encourage you to go about the business of life? Young women, I would say, and please attend, for the peroration is beginning, you are, in my opinion, disgracefully ignorant. You have never made a discovery of any sort of importance. You have never shaken an empire or led an army into battle. The plays of Shakespeare are not by you, and you have never introduced a barbarous race to the blessings of civilization. What is your excuse? It is all very well for you to say, pointing to the streets and squares and forests of the globe swarming with black and white and coffee-colored inhabitants, all busily engaged in traffic and enterprise and lovemaking, we have had other work on our hands. Without our doing, those seas would be unsailed and those fertile lands a desert. We have borne and bred and washed and taught, perhaps to the age of six or seven years, the one thousand six hundred and twenty-three million human beings who are, according to statistics, at present in existence, and that, allowing that some had help, takes time.

There is truth in what you say—I will not deny it. But at the same time may I remind you that there have been at least two colleges for women in existence in England since the year 1866; that after the year of 1880 a married woman was allowed by law to possess her own property; and that in 1919—which is a whole nine years ago—she was given a vote? May I also remind you that the most of the professions have been open to you for close on ten years now? When you reflect upon these immense privileges and the length of time during which they have been enjoyed, and the fact that there must be at this moment some two thousand women capable of earning over five hundred a year in one way or another, you will agree that the excuse of lack of opportunity, training, encouragement, leisure, and money no longer holds good. Moreover, the economists are telling us that Mrs. Seton has had too many children. You must, of course, go on bearing children, but, so they say, in twos and threes, not in tens and twelves.

Thus, with some time on your hands and with some book learning in your brains—you have had enough of the other kind, and are sent to college partly, I suspect, to be uneducated—surely you should embark upon another stage of your very long, very laborious, and highly obscure career. A thousand pens are ready to suggest what you should do and what effect you will have. My own suggestion is a little fantastic, I admit; I prefer, therefore, to put it in the form of fiction.

I told you in the course of this paper that Shakespeare had a sister; but do not look for her in Sir Sidney Lee's life of the poet. She died young—alas, she never wrote a word. She lies buried where the omnibuses now stop, opposite the Elephant and Castle. Now my belief is that this poet who never wrote a word and was buried at the crossroads still lives. She lives in you and in me, and in many other women who are not here tonight, for they are washing up the dishes and putting the children to bed. But she lives; for great poets do not die; they are continuing presences; they need only the opportunity to walk among us in the flesh. This opportunity, as I think, it is now coming within your power to give her. For my belief is that if we live another century or so—I am talking of the common life which is the real life and not of the little separate lives which we live as individuals—and have five hundred a year each of us and rooms of our own; if we have the habit of freedom and the courage to write exactly what we think; if we escape a little from the common sitting room and see human beings not always in their relation to each other but in relation to reality; and the sky, too, and the trees or whatever it may be in themselves; if we look past Milton's bogey, for no human being should shut out the view; if we face the fact, for it is a fact, that there is no arm to cling to, but that we go alone and that our relation is to the world of reality and not only to the world of men and women, then the opportunity will come and the dead poet who was Shakespeare's sister will put on the body which she has so often laid down. Drawing her life from the lives of the unknown who were her forerunners, as her brother did before her, she will be born. As for her coming without that preparation, without that effort on our part, without that determination that when she is born again she shall find it possible to live and write her poetry, that we cannot expect, for that would be impossible. But I maintain that she would come if we worked for her, and that so to work, even in poverty and obscurity, is worth while.

NOTES

¹ "We are told that we ought to ask for £30,000 at least. . . . It is not a large sum, considering that there is to be but one college of this sort for Great Britain, Ireland, and the Colonies, and considering how easy it is to raise immense sums for boys' schools. But considering how few people really wish women to be educated, it is a good deal." —Lady Stephen, *Life of Miss Emily Davies*.

² Every penny which could be scraped together was set aside for building, and the amenities had to be postponed.—R. Strachey, *The Cause*.

³ *The Art of Writing*, by Sir Arthur Quiller-Couch.

⁴ *A Short History of Women*, by John Langdon Davies.

. . . . . . . . . . .

## QUESTIONS FOR A SECOND READING

1. One of the difficulties in reading "A Room of One's Own" is getting a feel for the tone of voice on the page—or, more properly, the tones of voice. Not only are there different voices speaking to you, but they speak as though they *were* speaking—that is, they rely on inflection and context to give you a sense of how a sentence is to be taken. How, for an example, are you to read a line like this one near the conclusion of the final chapter: "Young women, I would say, and please attend, for the peroration is beginning, you are, in my opinion, disgracefully ignorant?" Who is speaking here? Or in whose voice is the speaker speaking? And to whom? That is, what kind of listener is imagined here? As you reread the essay, think about how its lines might be delivered and pay attention to shifts in tone of voice. You will need to do this to pick up the fine grain of the argument, but also to see the argument about women's writing that is being *enacted* in this prose.

2. There are many unusual gestures and surprises in Woolf's prose. And these could be thought of as part of her argument about women's writing— that is, it is possible to see the writing in the essay as an enactment of her argument about the place of a woman writer in the context of a genre representing the voices and habits of men. The opening word of the book, for example, is "but," itself a bit of a surprise. "But, you may say, we asked you to speak about women and fiction—what has that got to do with a room of one's own?" From the very beginning, the text stands contrary to conventional expectations about style, subject, and presentation.

   As you reread the chapters, mark sections or places that break what you take to be the conventions of the essay, particularly the essay as it could be said to be a masculine genre. And as you mark them, think about what these moments might be said to represent. If they are resisting or revising the genre, why? to what end? with what possible intention?

3. As you read these two chapters you have the sense that you have been taken into someone's thoughts as they are being developed. A sentence is broken, for example, when the speaker misses a turn in the road. Behind this fiction of spontaneous utterance, however, is a writer at work, not walking down the street but sitting somewhere and writing, constructing this moment that you will experience at some other time and place. *This* writer is hard to find, however, behind the "I" of the speaker and the "I" of Mary Seton. At one point, in fact, Woolf says that the "I" in these sentences "is only a convenient term for somebody who has no real being."

As you reread these chapters, mark sections you could use to talk about the strategies of presentation in these pages and how these strategies are consistent (or inconsistent) with the argument the text makes about women's writing.

### ASSIGNMENTS FOR WRITING

1. The title page of the original edition of *A Room of One's Own* said, "This essay is based upon two papers read to the Arts Society at Newnham and the Odtaa at Girton in October 1928. The papers were too long to be read in full, and have since been altered and expanded." As either an essay or the text of a public lecture, *A Room of One's Own* is full of surprises. It doesn't sound like the usual lecture; it doesn't do what essays usually do. At many places and in many ways it takes liberties with the conventions of the genre, with the essay's or the lecture's characteristic ways of addressing the audience, gathering information, and presenting an argument.

As you reread these chapters and prepare to write about them, make note of the ways Woolf (the writer writing the text) constructs a space for speaker and audience, a kind of imaginary place where a woman can do her work, find a way of speaking, think as she might like to think, and prepare others to listen. Look for interesting and potentially significant ways she defies or transforms what you take to be the conventions of the essay. (See the second Question for a Second Reading.) You might especially want to take a look at those places where Woolf seems to be saying, "I know what I should be doing here, but I won't. I'll do this instead."

Choose four such moments and write an essay in which you discuss Woolf's chapters as a performance, a demonstration of a way of writing that pushes against the usual ways of manipulating words. While there is certainly an argument *in* Woolf's essay, your paper will be about the argument represented *by* the essay, an argument enacted in a way of writing. What is Woolf doing? How might you explain what she is doing and why? In what ways might her essay be seen as an example of someone working on the problems of writing? of a woman's writing? And what might this have to do with you, a student in a writing class?

2. In the opening of her essay, Woolf says that the "I" of her text "is only a convenient term for somebody who had no real being." And at the beginning of the last chapter (in reference to a new novel by "Mr. A"), she says,

> But after reading a chapter or two a shadow seemed to lie across the page. It was a straight dark bar, a shadow shaped something like the letter "I." One began dodging this way and that to catch a glimpse of the landscape behind it. Whether that was indeed a tree or a woman walking I was not quite sure. Back one was always hailed to the letter "I." One began to be tired of "I." (p. 658)

It's hard to know what to make of this, as an argument about either the position of women or writing. Read back through Woolf's essay, noting sections you could use to investigate the ways an "I" is or is not present in this text, and to investigate the argument that text makes about a writer's (or speaker's) presence. (See the third Question for a Second Reading.)

Write an essay in which you examine the ways Woolf, a writer, is and is not present in this piece of writing. Where and how does she hide? And why? Whom do you find in her place? How might this difficulty over the presence of the writer be said to be a part of Woolf's argument about women and writing? And what might this have to do with you and the writing you are doing, either in this class or in school generally?

## MAKING CONNECTIONS

1. In a section of the book not included here, Woolf talks about sentences. She says that one of the problems women writers face is that the sentences available to them are men's sentences, unsuitable for a woman's use: "The weight, the pace, the stride of a man's mind are too unlike her own for her to lift anything substantial from him successfully." Moreover, she says, "a book is not made of sentences laid end to end, but of sentences built, if an image helps, into arcades or domes. And this shape too has been made by men out of their own needs for their own uses."

Sentences, and sentences built into shapes—let's take Woolf's line of thought seriously and inquire into the characteristic shapes of some writing that seems "manly" or "womanly." You will need to begin by gathering interesting specimens—sentences, paragraphs, whatever "shapes" seem significant and manageable. Begin with Woolf's essay and turn to two others in this book—one that seems more manly than womanly and one that seems more womanly than manly. You will need to gather sentences, paragraphs, or passages from these essays as well. (Keep in mind that these types of prose are not necessarily determined by the sex of the writer.) Write an essay in which you present and discuss these pieces of writing as representative ways of gathering material, of thinking it through, of presenting oneself and one's thoughts, of imagining a world of speakers and listeners.

2. In "When We Dead Awaken: Writing as Re-Vision" (p. 482), Rich says the following of Woolf's prose:

> In rereading Virginia Woolf's *A Room of One's Own* (1929) for the first time in some years, I was astonished at the sense of effort, of pains taken, of dogged tentativeness, in the tone of that essay. And I recognized that tone. I had heard it often enough, in myself and in other women. It is the tone of a woman almost in touch with her anger, who is determined not to appear angry, who is *willing* herself to be calm, detached, and even charming in a roomful of men where things have been said which are attacks on her very integrity. Virginia Woolf is addressing an audience of women, but she is acutely conscious—as she always is—of being overheard by men: by Morgan and Lytton and Maynard Keynes and for that matter by her father, Leslie Stephen. She drew the language out into an exacerbated thread in her determination to have her own sensibility yet protect it from those masculine presences. Only at rare moments in that essay do you hear the passion in her voice; she was trying to sound as cool as Jane Austen, as Olympian as Shakespeare, because that is the way the men of the culture thought a writer should sound. (p. 485)

Let's assume that this is a way of reading *A Room of One's Own*, but not the last word. It can be seen as opening a space for a response, for a conversation. Write an essay in which you offer a response to Rich, one rooted in your own experience reading (or rereading) these chapters.

Before you begin writing, you should reread the chapters, paying particular attention to tone and voice, looking for passages you can use in forming a response to Rich. You should also reread Rich's essay, not only for what she says about Woolf but for the examples she offers of tone and voice, of a woman writing, conscious, as Rich is too, of the context provided by the men of the culture. You can offer your reading not only of Woolf's prose but of Rich's prose as well.

# Assignment
# Sequences

# WORKING WITH
# ASSIGNMENT
# SEQUENCES

*THE ASSIGNMENT SEQUENCES* that follow are different from the single writing assignments at the end of each essay. The single writing assignments are designed to give you a way back into the works you have read. They define the way you, the reader, can work on an essay by writing about it—testing its assumptions, probing its examples, applying its way of thinking to a new setting or to new material. A single assignment might ask you to read what Paulo Freire has to say about education and then, as a writer, to use Freire's terms and methods to analyze a moment from your own schooling. The single assignments are designed to demonstrate how a student might work on an essay, particularly an essay that is long or complex, and they are designed to show how pieces that might seem daunting are open, manageable, and managed best by writing.

The assignment sequences have a similar function, but with one important difference. Instead of writing one paper, or working on one or two selections from the book, you will be writing several essays and reading several selections. Your work will be sequential as well as cumulative. The work you do on Freire, for example, will give you a way of beginning with Ralph Waldo Emerson, or with Adrienne Rich. It will give you an angle of vision. You won't be a newcomer to such discussions. Your previous reading will make the new essay rich with association. Passages or examples will jump, as if magnetized, and demand your attention. And by reading these essays in context, you will see each writer as a single voice in a larger discussion. Neither Freire, nor Emerson, nor Rich, after all, has had the last word on the subject of education. It is not as though, by working on one of the essays, you have wrapped the subject up, ready to be put on the shelf.

The sequences are designed, then, so that you will be working not only on essays but on a subject, like education (or entitlement, or culture, or the composing process), a subject that can be examined, probed, and understood through the various frames provided by your reading. Each essay becomes a way of seeing a problem or a subject; it becomes a tool for thinking, an example of how a mind might work, a way of using language to make a subject rich and alive. In the assignment sequences, your reading is not random. Each sequence provides a set of readings that can be pulled together into a single project.

The sequences allow you to participate in an extended academic project, one with several texts and several weeks' worth of writing. You are not just adding one essay to another (Freire + Emerson = ?) but trying out an approach to a subject by revising it, looking at new examples, hearing what someone else has to say, and beginning again to take a position of your own. Projects like these take time. It is not at all uncommon for professional writers to devote weeks or even months to a single essay, and the essay they write marks not the end of their thinking on the subject, but only one stage. Similarly, when readers are working on a project, the pieces they read accumulate on their desks and in their minds and become part of an extended conversation with several speakers, each voice offering a point of view on a subject, a new set of examples, or a new way of talking that resonates with echoes from earlier reading.

A student may read many books, take several courses, write many papers; ideally each experience becomes part of something larger, an education. The work of understanding, in other words, requires time and repeated effort. The power that comes from understanding cannot be acquired quickly—by reading one essay or working for a few hours. A student, finally, is a person who choreographs such experiences, not someone who passes one test only to move on to another. And the assignment sequences are designed to reproduce, although in a condensed period of time, the rhythm and texture of academic life. They invite you to try on its characteristic ways of seeing, thinking, and writing. The work you do in one week will not be lost when it has bearing on the work you do in the next. If an essay by Virginia Woolf has value for you, it is not because you proved to a teacher that you read it, but because you have put it to work and made it a part of your vocabulary as a student.

## *Working with a Sequence*

Here is what you can expect as you work with a sequence. You begin by working with a single story or essay. You will need to read each piece twice, the second time with the "Questions for a Second Reading" and the assignment sequence in mind. Before rereading the selection, in other words, you should read through the assignments to get a sense of where you will be headed. And you should read the questions at the end of each selection. (You can use those questions to help frame questions of your own.) The purpose of all these questions, in a sense, is to prepare the text to speak—to prick it to life and insist that it respond to your attention, answer your questions. If you think of the authors as people you can talk to, if you think of their pages as occasions for dialogue (as places where you get to ask questions and insist on responses)—if you prepare your return to those pages in these ways, you are opening up the essays or stories (not closing them down or finishing them off) and creating a scene where you get to step forward as a performer.

While each sequence moves from selection to selection in *Ways of Reading*, the most significant movement in the sequence is defined by the essays you write. Your essays provide the other major text for the course. In fact, when we teach these sequences, we seldom have any discussion of the assigned readings before our students have had a chance to write. When we talk as a group about Rich's "When We Dead Awaken: Writing as Re-Vision," for example, we begin by reproducing one or two student essays, handing them out to the class, and using them as the basis for discussion. We want to start, in other words, by looking at ways of reading Rich's essay—not at her essay alone.

The essays you write for each assignment in a sequence might be thought of as work-in-progress. Your instructor will tell you the degree to which each essay should be finished—that is, the degree to which it should be revised and copy-edited and worked into a finished performance. In our classes, most writing assignments go through at least one revision. After we have had a chance to see a draft (or after a draft has been seen by others in the class), and after we have had some discussion of sample student readings, we ask students to read the assigned essay or story one more time and to rework their essays to bring their work one step further—not necessarily to finish the essays (as though there would be nothing else to say) but to finish up this stage in their work and to feel their achievement in a way a writer simply cannot the first time through. Each assignment, then, really functions as two assignments in the schedule for the course. As a consequence, we don't "cover" as many essays in a semester as students might in another class. But coverage is not our goal. In a sense, we are teaching our students how to read slowly and closely, to return to a text rather than set it aside, to take the time to reread and rewrite and to reflect on what these activities entail.

You will be writing papers that can be thought of as single essays. But you will also be working on a project, something bigger than its individual parts. From the perspective of the project, each piece you write is part of a larger body of work that evolves over the term. You might think of each sequence as a revision exercise, where the revision looks forward to what comes next as well as backward to what you have done. This form of revision asks you to do more than complete a single paper; it invites you to resee a subject or reimagine what you might say about it from a new point of view. You should feel free, then, to draw on your earlier essays when you work on one of the later assignments. There is every reason for you to reuse ideas, phrases, sentences, even paragraphs as your work builds from one week to the next. The advantage of work-in-progress is that you are not starting over completely every time you sit down to write. You've been over this territory before. You've developed some expertise in your subject. There is a body of work behind you.

Most of the sequences bring together several essays from the text and ask you to imagine them as an extended conversation, one with several speakers. The assignments are designed to give you a place in the conversation as well, to allow you to speak in turn and to take your place in the company of other writers. This is the final purpose of the assignment sequence: after several weeks' work on the essays and on the subject that draws them together, you will begin to establish your own point of view. You will develop a position from which you can speak with authority, drawing strength from the work you have done as well as from your familiarity with the people who surround you.

This book brings together some of the most powerful voices of our culture. They speak in a manner that asks for response. The assignments at the end of each chapter and, with a wider range of reference, the assignment sequences here at the end of the book demonstrate that there is no reason for a student, in such company, to remain silent.

# The Aims of Education

Paulo Freire
Adrienne Rich
Ralph Waldo Emerson
Stanley Fish

*YOU HAVE BEEN* in school for several years, long enough for your experiences in the classroom to seem natural, inevitable. The purpose of this sequence is to invite you to step outside a world you may have begun to take for granted, to look at the ways you have been taught and at the unspoken assumptions behind your education. The seven assignments that follow bring together four essays that discuss how people (and particularly students) become trapped inside habits of thought. These habits of thought (they are sometimes referred to as "structures" of thought; Adrienne Rich calls them the "assumptions in which we are drenched") become invisible (or seem natural) because of the ways our schools work or because of the ways we have traditionally learned to use language when we speak, read, or write.

Three of the essays you will read (by Freire, Rich, and Emerson) argue that there are revolutionary ways of using language that can enable a person to break free from limited or limiting ways of thinking. The five assignments that accompany them provide an opportunity for you to test the arguments in individual essays by weighing them against your own experience as a student or to test them by looking at the experience of others. The last two assignments are exercises in revision. The essay by Stanley Fish provides point of view that could be said to oppose those of the other writers in this sequence. You are given a chance to revise one of your earlier essays by bringing in this alternate point of view. The final assignment provides an occasion for you to draw material from all the essays you have written into a final and more comprehensive general statement on the proper uses of reading and writing in a college education.

· · · · · · · · · · ·

A S S I G N M E N T  1

## Applying Freire to Your Own Experience as a Student [Freire]

> The teacher talks about reality as if it were motionless, static, compartmentalized, and predictable. Or else he expounds on a topic completely alien to the existential experience of the students. His task is to "fill" the students with the contents of his narration—contents which are detached from reality, disconnected from the totality that engendered them and could give them significance. Words are emptied of their concreteness and become a hollow, alienated, and alienating verbosity. (pp. 206–07)
>
> — PAULO FREIRE
> *The "Banking" Concept of Education*

Surely all of us, anyone who has made it through twelve years of formal education, can think of a class, or an occasion outside of class, to serve as a quick example of what Freire calls the "banking" concept of education, where students are turned into "containers" to be "filled" by their teachers. If Freire is to be useful to you, however, he must do more than call up quick examples. He should allow you to say more than that a teacher once treated you like a container or that a teacher once gave you your freedom.

Write an essay that focuses on a rich and illustrative incident from your own educational experience and read it (that is, interpret it) as Freire would. You will need to provide careful detail: things that were said and done, perhaps the exact wording of an assignment, a textbook, or a teacher's comments. And you will need to turn to the language of Freire's argument, to take key phrases and passages from his argument and see how they might be used to investigate your case.

To do this you will need to read your account as not simply the story of you and your teacher, since Freire is not writing about individual personalities (an innocent student and a mean teacher, a rude teacher, or a thoughtless teacher) but about the roles we are cast in, whether we choose to be or not, by our culture and its institutions. The key question, then, is not who you were or who your teacher was but what roles you played and how those roles can lead you to better understand the larger narrative or drama of Education (an organized attempt to "regulate the way the world 'enters into' the students").

Freire would not want you to work passively or mechanically, however, as though you were following orders. He would want you to make your own mark on the work he has begun. Use your example, in other words, as a way of testing and examining what Freire says, particularly those passages that you find difficult or obscure.

. . . . . . . . . . . .

A S S I G N M E N T  2

# Studying Rich as a Case in Point
# [Freire, Rich]

The truth is, however, that the oppressed are not "marginals," are not men living "outside" society. They have always been "inside"—inside the structure which made them "beings for others." The solution is not to "integrate" them into the structure of oppression, but to transform that structure so that they can become "beings for themselves." Such transformation, of course, would undermine the oppressors' purposes; . . . (p. 210)

— PAULO FREIRE
*The "Banking" Concept of Education*

For a poem to coalesce, for a character or an action to take shape, there has to be an imaginative transformation of reality which is no way passive. . . . Moreover, if the imagination is to transcend and transform experience it has to question, to challenge, to conceive of alternatives, perhaps to the very life

you are living at that moment. You have to be free to play
around with the notion that day might be night, love might
be hate; nothing can be too sacred for the imagination to turn
into its opposite or to call experimentally by another name.
For writing is renaming. (p. 490)

      — ADRIENNE RICH
*When We Dead Awaken: Writing as Re-Vision*

Both Freire and Rich talk repeatedly about transformations—about
transforming structures, transforming the world, transforming the way language is used, transforming the relations between people. In fact, the
changes in Rich's poetry might be seen as evidence of her transforming the
structures from within which she worked. And, when Freire takes a situation we think of as "natural" (teachers talking and students sitting silent)
and names it "banking education," he makes it possible for students and
their teachers to question, challenge, conceive of alternatives, and transform experience. Each, in other words, can be framed as an example in the
language of the other—Freire in Rich's terms, Rich in Freire's. For both,
this act of transformation is something that takes place within and through
the use of language.

Rich's essay could be read as a statement about the aims of education,
particularly if the changes in her work are taken as evidence of something
the poet learned to do. Rich talks about teachers, about people who helped
her to reimagine her situation as a woman and a poet, and about the work
she had to do on her own.

For this assignment, take three of the poems Rich offers as examples of
change in her writing—"Aunt Jennifer's Tigers," the section from "Snapshots of a Daughter-in-Law," and "Planetarium"—and use them as a way
of talking about revision. What, to your mind, are the key differences between these poems? What might the movement they mark be said to represent? And what do these poems, as examples, have to do with the argument about writing, culture, and gender in the rest of the essay?

As you prepare to write, you might also ask some questions in Freire's
name. For example: What problems did Rich pose for herself? How might
this be taken as an example of a problem-posing education? In what ways
might Rich be said to have been having a "dialogue" with her own work?
Who was the teacher here (or the teachers) and what did the poet learn to
do?

You are not alone as you read these poems, in other words. In fact,
Rich provides her own commentary on the three poems, noting what for
her are key changes and what they represent. You will want to acknowledge what Rich has to say, to be sure, but you should not be bound by it.

You, too, are a person with a point of view on this issue. Rich (with Freire) provides a powerful language for talking about change, but you want to be sure to carve out space where you have the opportunity to speak as well.

• • • • • • • • • • •

ASSIGNMENT 3

## *Tradition and the Writing of the Past* [Rich]

> We need to know the writing of the past, and know it differently than we have ever known it; not to pass on a tradition but to break its hold over us. (p. 484)
> — ADRIENNE RICH
> *When We Dead Awaken: Writing as Re-Vision*

"We need to know the writing of the past," Rich says. The "we" of that sentence can be read as an invitation to you too. Look back over your own writing (perhaps the drafts and revisions you have written for this course), and think back over comments teachers have made, textbooks you have seen; think about what student writers do and what they are told to do, about the secrets students keep and the secrets teachers keep. You can assume, as Rich does, that there are ways of speaking about writing that are part of the culture of schooling and that they are designed to preserve certain ways of writing and thinking and to discourage others. Write an essay in which you reflect on the writing of the past and its presence in your own work as a writer.

One might argue, in other words, that there are ways of writing that are part of schooling. There are traditions here too. As you look at the evidence of the "past" in your own work, what are its significant features: What might you name this tradition (or these traditions)? What are the "official" names? What do these names tell us? What do they hide? What difference might it make to name tradition in terms of gender and call it "patriarchal"?

How would you illustrate the hold this tradition has on your work or the work of students generally? What might you have to do to begin to "know it differently," "to break its hold," or to revise? And, finally, why would someone want (or not want) to make such a break?

. . . . . . . . . . . .

A S S I G N M E N T **4**

# Performing an Emersonian Reading
## of "The American Scholar" [Emerson]

One must be an inventor to read well. As the proverb says, "He that would bring home the wealth of the Indies, must carry out the wealth of the Indies." There is then creative reading, as well as creative writing. When the mind is braced by labor and invention, the page of whatever book we read becomes luminous with manifold allusion. Every sentence is doubly significant, and the sense of our author is as broad as the world. (p. 165)

> — RALPH WALDO EMERSON
> *The American Scholar*

There is no question but that Emerson's text is difficult to read, and the difficulty is not simply a matter of big or unusual words. The text just doesn't do what we expect it to do. Some of its elusiveness can be attributed to the time it was written—expectations were different then—but this should not keep you from making the most of your own responses as a reader. For one thing, it's not completely true; not everyone in the 1830s wrote like Emerson. For another, it assumes that a nonspecialist cannot or should not read works from the past. One way of imagining your connection to the 1830s is to imagine that your encounter with this text is somehow typical—that you, too, are Emerson's contemporary.

Take a section of the essay that you find characteristically difficult. (Section II is an interesting one to work with.) Reread it, paying close attention to the experience of reading. Where are you surprised? Where are you confused? How might this be part of a strategy, part of Emerson's design? What is Emerson doing? What is he asking you to do? This should be an exercise in close reading. You want to pay attention to how paragraph leads to paragraph, sentence leads to sentence; to notice the ways examples or statements are offered and taken away. Emerson's style could be said to call for a different reader and therefore to make an argument about the American scholar. If you want to get beyond a simple statement (that you have to work hard or read creatively to work with Emerson), how might you describe the reader Emerson imagines?

Write an essay in which you describe in close detail what it was like to read this section of "The American Scholar." Tell a story of reading, one where you and Emerson are the main characters—complicated characters, not stick figures (the Innocent Student and the Inscrutable Genius). When you are done, see what connections you can make with Emerson's argument—with what he says about a proper education and the proper relation between readers and writers.

.  .  .  .  .  .  .  .  .  .  .

ASSIGNMENT 5

## *The American Scholar 150 Years Later* [Emerson]

In the three numbered sections of "The American Scholar," Emerson speaks of "the education of the scholar by nature, by books, and by action." Choose the argument he makes that seems to you to be the most powerful or most interesting, and apply it to the curriculum at your own school. If you use your own school as an example, what does the education of an American scholar look like 150 years or so after Emerson's address to students and teachers at Harvard?

You might need to search out your college catalogue or whatever documents your school has prepared to explain its curriculum. As you begin thinking about your essay, you could imagine that you are writing a piece for an alumni magazine, or perhaps a position paper to be presented to a faculty committee charged with reviewing undergraduate education.

.  .  .  .  .  .  .  .  .  .  .

ASSIGNMENT 6

## *Confronting an Alternate Point of View* [Freire, Rich, Emerson, Fish]

The conclusion, therefore, is that all objects are made and not found, and that they are made by the interpretive strategies we set in motion. . . . No one of us wakes up in the morning and (in French fashion) reinvents poetry or thinks up a new educational system or decides to reject seriality in favor of some other, wholly original, form of organization. We do not do these things because we could not do them, because the mental operations we can perform are limited by the institutions in which we are *already* embedded. (p. 186)

— STANLEY FISH
*How to Recognize a Poem When You See One*

Fish seems to be arguing that we cannot make fundamental changes in what we do or what we know "because the mental operations we can perform are limited by the institutions in which we are *already* embedded." This seems to stand in striking opposition to arguments made by Freire, Rich, and Emerson. What can you make of what Fish says in light of the work you have already done in this assignment sequence? Does Fish know something these others don't know? Is he more of a realist? Does he have a better sense of what students can and cannot do? Or could he be said somehow to be wrong? And, if so, how?

Perhaps the best way for you to bring Fish into the work you have done is literally to work him into something that you have already written. For example, you have written in response to Freire, Emerson, and Rich. What would happen to any of those essays if you brought in relevant examples, terms, or arguments from "How to Recognize a Poem When You See One"?

For this assignment, go back to rework one of the essays you have written in this sequence by bringing in Fish. (You might begin by rereading his essay and noting those sections you most want to work with.) You might think of Fish as someone who *also* has something to say about the aims of education, a person who has said something that simply can't be ignored.

You will be revising your earlier essay, but the revision here will require some major changes. Rather than taking what you had written, getting back inside its argument, and making it tighter, you will be bringing in material that has the potential to upset or perhaps transform what you have said. You will have to consider another point of view and establish its position in a discussion you have already begun.

. . . . . . . . . . . .

A S S I G N M E N T   7

# *Putting Things Together*
# [Freire, Rich, Emerson, Fish]

This is the final assignment of this sequence, and it is the occasion for you to step back and take stock of all that you have done. Perhaps the best way for you to do this is by making a statement of your own about the role of reading and writing in an undergraduate education. You might, for example, write a document for students who will be entering your school for the first time, telling them what they should expect or what they should know about reading and writing if they want to make the most of their education. Or, as in assignment 5, this might be an essay written for an alumni magazine or a paper for a faculty committee charged with reviewing undergraduate education.

You should feel free to draw as much as you can from the papers you have already written, making your points through examples you have already examined, perhaps using your own work with these assignments as an example of what students might be expected to do.

S E Q U E N C E   T W O

# Cultural Frames

Jean Franco
Carlos Fuentes
Clifford Geertz

*T*HE THREE ASSIGNMENTS that follow invite you to think about a story
by Carlos Fuentes from two very different perspectives by bringing
forward aspects of it that might be said to represent "cultural interpretations or frames." First, you're asked to read an essay in which Jean Franco
discusses the loss of traditionally sacred territorial spaces in Latin American
culture and to apply her sense of the "Latin American imaginary" to the
Fuentes story. For the second assignment you're asked to read Clifford
Geertz's essay on cockfights and "deep play" so that you can extend his
project and "read" the various moments of play in the Fuentes story as
representative of cultural values and social orders. Finally, you're asked
to reconcile your previous two readings by using them to discuss what
you've learned about the story, about Latin America, about culture and
about reading.

. . . . . . . . . . .

## A S S I G N M E N T 1

# *Applying Franco to Fuentes's Story*
# [Franco, Fuentes]

> Although it is impossible to separate the literary from the so-
> cial, literature is a good place to begin to understand this
> Latin American imaginary with its clearly demarcated spaces.
> In common with Mediterranean countries, public space in
> Latin America was strictly separated from the private space
> of the house (brothel), home, and convent, that is spaces
> which were clearly marked as "feminine." These spaces gave
> women a certain territorial but restricted power base and at
> the same time offered the "felicitous" spaces for the repose
> of the warrior. (pp. 198–99)
>
> — JEAN FRANCO
> *Killing Priests, Nuns, Women, Children*

Franco's essay makes claims about the disappearance of sacred, territorial spaces in Latin American life, and it proceeds through illustrations
and examples drawn from social and literary sources. She uses the phrase
"Latin American imaginary" to identify those acts of imagining protected
and sacred spaces, such as the home or brothel, that "gave women a certain territorial but restricted power base." "In describing these spaces," she
says, "I am not describing categories of women but an imaginary topography in which the 'feminine' was rigidly compartmentalized and assigned
particular territories."

Write an essay in which you extend Franco's project by discussing
Fuentes's story as another possible example of the Latin American imaginary. Take this opportunity either to extend or to comment on or challenge
Franco's conception of the Latin American imaginary and its territorial
spaces. If you see the Fuentes story as an occasion for reproducing and
strengthening Franco's argument, how might you read it to make or extend
her case? If you see the story as an occasion to comment on or challenge
Franco's argument, in what ways does his story present a different scene?
What counter argument does it make? How might you account for these
differences?

One could argue that Franco wouldn't want you to do this as just a
literary exercise or writing assignment without considering the political im-

plications of this process. So as you construct your interpretation, consider how the honoring or violating or "deterritorialization" of protected spaces in the Fuentes story might be said to represent political motives and consequences for readers as well as the inhabitants of Franco's and Fuentes's world.

· · · · · · · · · · · ·

A S S I G N M E N T   2

# Performing a Geertzian Reading of Fuentes's Story
## [Fuentes, Geertz]

> [T]he cockfight renders ordinary, everyday experience comprehensible by presenting it in terms of acts and objects which have had their practical consequences removed and been reduced (or, if you prefer, raised) to the level of sheer appearances, where their meaning can be more powerfully articulated and more exactly perceived. The cockfight is "really real" only to the cocks—it does not kill anyone, castrate anyone, reduce anyone to animal status, alter the hierarchical relations among people, nor refashion the hierarchy; it does not even redistribute income in any significant way. What it does is what, for other peoples with other temperaments and other conventions, *Lear* and *Crime and Punishment* do; it catches up these themes—death, masculinity, rage, pride, loss, beneficence, chance—and, ordering them into an encompassing structure, presents them in such a way as to throw into relief a particular view of their essential nature. (p. 295)
> – CLIFFORD GEERTZ
> *Deep Play: Notes on the Balinese Cockfight*

Geertz talks about "reading" a culture as "an ensemble of texts" while peering over the shoulders of those to whom it belongs. It's possible to say that Franco and Geertz share this sense of interpreting or "reading" culture, but it would be difficult to claim that the events which interest Franco could be called deep play. Yet play in a culture seems to be a telling and important way to understand relationships and values, and although it would also be difficult to claim that Fuentes's short story accurately or completely represents a culture, this assignment asks you to begin with the assumption that it can and does represent at least some aspects of Latin American culture.

Write an essay in which you do a Geertzian reading of the "play"—
those moments when the characters are literally or metaphorically playing—in the Fuentes story. What does their play reveal about the characters'
values and the social order around them? What, for example, might you
say about the three uncles and their shooting games, or their visits to the
factory, or the serious play of the Hawks' training and fighting on the
streets? What values might you see (following in Geertz's footsteps) in the
moments of play here? And how might you read their statements about
the social order of the family, or the barrio, or the city?

· · · · · · · · · · ·

ASSIGNMENT 3

# *Reconciling Readings*
# [Franco, Fuentes, Geertz]

They went to the training camp and El Güero gave Bernabé
a pistol so he could defend himself and told him not to worry,
the Chief was right, there was no way to stop them once they
got rolling, *look at that rock, how it keeps rolling*, shit, said El
Güero with a shrewd and malicious expression Bernabé
hadn't seen before, they could even slip out of the Chief's
hands if they wanted, didn't he know everything there was
to know? how to set things up, how to go to a barrio and
round up the young kids, begin with slingshots if they had
to, then chains, then ice picks like the one you killed the
Burro with, Bernabé. . . . But Bernabé didn't answer, he'd
stopped listening. He was remembering his visit to the cemetery that morning, the Sundays he'd spent making love with
Martincita in the crypt of a wealthy family, remembering a
ragged old man urinating behind a cypress, bald, smiling like
an idiot. . . . Bernabé felt a surge of shame. But don't let it
return. A vague memory, a kind of unknowing would be
enough for this new Bernabé. (p. 267)

> — CARLOS FUENTES
> *The Son of Andrés Aparicio*

This is the final assignment of this sequence, and it is the occasion for
you to reconcile your readings of the Fuentes story. You might see this as
a "putting together" of your two readings, but that would be only partially
right, because the "reconciliation" in this assignment asks that you weave

together both of your readings to comment on this story and the culture it might be said to represent.

You have done two strong readings, both of which could be called anthropological studies, but they focused on quite different things. In reading through Franco's essay, you examined her conception of the Latin American imaginary, and in a sense you tested her ideas with this story. In reading through Geertz's essay, you examined moments of play in the story for what they might be said to say about values in the family or barrio or city.

So you have these two different readings (and more if you're considering others' papers along with yours). Now your job is to write an essay in which you reconcile these readings and bring forward something you've learned or want to comment on or challenge about cultural interpretations—these ways of constructing and changing the world—from working with these essays and the Fuentes story.

# SEQUENCE THREE

# Entitlements

### Robert Coles
### John Edgar Wideman
### Harriet Jacobs

*T*HIS ASSIGNMENT SEQUENCE begins by inviting you to read closely one of the stories that Robert Coles tells in his study of the children of wealthy families and what they feel entitled to because of their positions in society. The second assignment asks you to read an excerpt from John Edgard Wideman's story of his brother Robby and to imagine Robby reading Coles's essay, "Entitlement." How, you are asked, would Robby (or you) revise Coles's work to account for Robby's story and what Robby knows about entitlements that Coles doesn't? For the third assignment, you are asked to read an excerpt from Harriet Jacobs's autobiography, *Incidents in the Life of a Slave Girl,* and to tell her story as a story of entitlements, a narrative that both makes use of and revises Coles's terms and concepts. The final assignment invites you to write an essay that revises Coles's theory based on the three papers you've written and the readings you've done for this sequence.

. . . . . . . . . . . .

# *Awareness of Entitlements* [Coles]

Each child . . . is also influenced by certain social, racial, cultural, or religious traditions, or thoroughly idiosyncratic ones—a given *family's* tastes, sentiments, ideals, say. The issue is "class"; but the issue is not only "class."

I use the word "entitlement" to describe what, perhaps, all quite well-off American families transmit to their children—an important psychological common denominator, I believe: an emotional expression, really, of those familiar, class-bound prerogatives, money and power. The word was given to me, amid much soul-searching, by the rather rich parents of a child I began to talk with almost two decades ago, in 1959. I have watched those parents become grandparents, seen what they described as "the responsibilities of entitlement" get handed down to a new generation. (p. 95)

– ROBERT COLES
*Entitlement*

In his discussion of entitlement, Coles tells a number of stories about families—the lawyer-stockbroker's family, the mine owner's family, the patrician Yankee family from Westchester County, the family from the Garden District of New Orleans, and the powerful Florida grower's family. These families differ in significant ways, even though they share certain traits common to monied, powerful people.

For this assignment, select one of these family stories and write an essay in which you show how an awareness of entitlements is conveyed by the family to its children. Specifically, what are these entitlements? What is their source? How do these entitlements influence the children who receive them? Which of the entitlements are class related and which are "thoroughly idiosyncratic"?

You can imagine that your job here is to perform a close reading, a careful analysis of one family handing down values, traditions, tastes, and sentiments to its children.

. . . . . . . . . . . .

ASSIGNMENT 2

# Reading Coles Through
# Robby Wideman's Eyes [Coles, Wideman]

> I have always burned up in my fervent passions of desire and
> want. My senses at times tingle and itch with my romantic,
> idealistic outlook on life, which has always made me keep my
> distance from reality, reality that was a constant insult to my
> world, to my dream of happiness and peace, to my people-
> for-people kind of world, my easy-cars-for-a-nickel-or-a-dime
> sorta world. And these driving passions, this sensitivity to
> the love and good in people, also turned on me because I
> used it to play on people and their feelings. These aspirations
> of love and desire turned on me when I wasn't able to live
> up to this sweet-self morality, so I began to self-destruct,
> burning up in my sensitivity, losing direction, because no-
> where could I find this world of truth and love and harmony.
> (pp. 596–97)
>
> — JOHN EDGAR WIDEMAN
> *Our Time*

Like the youngsters in Coles's study, Robby Wideman had dreams and
expectations about himself and his future. Like those children, he inherited
values, beliefs, and ideals from his family and from others, but clearly he
is not from a monied, powerful family.

For this assignment, imagine that you have been taken with Coles's
study of entitlements after your initial work with it in the first assignment.
You would like, however, to look beyond his portrait of wealthy families
to examine "entitlements" in the lives of children from different social
strata, different backgrounds. Like Coles, you are interested in the forces
that shape the lives of children, not only the general, large pervasive forces
("social, racial, cultural, or religious traditions") but also the idiosyncratic
ones, like those belonging to a particular family with its "tastes, sentiments, ideals." According to Coles, "The issue is 'class'; but the issue is
not only 'class'."

To begin this project, imagine both John and Robby Wideman reading
Coles and trying to use what Coles says to account for Robby and his experience. How might Robby be seen in Coles's terms? What of Coles's

work would they have to rewrite because something is missing, something particular to Robby or to life in this family or of a black family in the 1960s?

Write an essay in which you tell Robby's story as a story of entitlements, a story that both uses and rewrites Coles's work to give Robby a place in a theory of entitlements. You might imagine doing this as Coles or John Edgar Wideman does by letting Robby speak for himself and then speaking alongside him—commenting, raising questions, pointing out directions and conclusions. Remember that you want to keep the spirit of Coles's work by honoring both Robby's individuality, his unique way of "pulling together various elements of mental life" and his "common manner of response," but you should also imagine that the Widemans know things about entitlements that Coles doesn't, so you'll want to revise (and rename, perhaps) Coles's ideas and terms as they might.

· · · · · · · · · · ·

A S S I G N M E N T  3

## Studying Entitlements Through Jacobs
## [Coles, Wideman, Jacobs]

> He told me I was his property; that I must be subject to his will in all things. My soul revolted against the mean tyranny. But where could I turn for protection? No matter whether the slave girl be as black as ebony or as fair as her mistress. In either case, there is no shadow of law to protect her from insult, from violence, or even from death; all these are inflicted by fiends who bear the shape of men. The mistress, who ought to protect the helpless victim, has no other feelings towards her but those of jealousy and rage. The degradation, the wrongs, the vices, that grow out of slavery, are more than I can describe. They are greater than you would willingly believe. (p. 334)
>
> — HARRIET JACOBS
> *Incidents in the Life of a Slave Girl*

Jacobs, in this excerpt from the opening chapters of her autobiography, *Incidents in the Life of a Slave Girl*, describes how she (under the name of Linda Brent) came to understand her identity as men's property—as a slave and as a woman—and how that identity was determined by her particular situation (her light color, her education, the psychology of her owner, the values of her family) and by the codes governing slavery in the South.

For this assignment, as for the previous one, think of yourself continuing the project that you began when you imagined the Widemans reading Coles. Now you have an excerpt from Harriet Jacobs's autobiography before you and you want to imagine her reading Coles. What would she find useful in Coles's essay to describe her situation as a person with "social, racial, cultural, or religious traditions, or thoroughly idiosyncratic ones"? What might she want to revise and rewrite? What does she know about entitlements, or whatever she might call them, that Coles doesn't?

Write an essay in which you tell Jacobs's story as a story of entitlements, one that both makes use of and revises Coles's terms and ideas. Imagine that her story, like Robby's, will take its place in a project on entitlements that began with Coles's study of wealthy families and has been expanded to include your work in this sequence. And remember, as you did for Robby, that you must keep the careful spirit of Coles's work by honoring Jacobs as both a unique individual and a person with what Coles calls "a common manner of response toward life." But feel free to rename and revise his terms and concepts as you think Jacobs might or as you think they need to be to take into account what Jacobs knows and says.

· · · · · · · · · · ·

A S S I G N M E N T  **4**

## *Putting the Stories Together* [Coles, Wideman, Jacobs]

For this final assignment in the sequence, think of the three stories that you have worked on (the one from Coles, the Wideman's, and Jacobs's) as the material for your final revision of Coles's theory of entitlements. Like his stories of children from wealthy families, your stories will serve as your material for thinking through and presenting your theory. This is a big job, because you have a lot of new material to speak from, but you should allow yourself the freedom to use what you feel is essential from Coles and to revise or reimagine whatever you need to. This has become your theory— you have taken Coles's work beyond its original conception—and although you want to acknowledge him and keep to the spirit of his work, your allegiance now is to a revision of his original theory to include the work you have done in this sequence.

The first question you should ask yourself is how you'll proceed. How will you organize your work? Do you want to examine one story at a time? Or do you want to make comparisons among stories? or look for patterns across stories? Does your work already suggest a way to proceed? How, too, will you refer to Coles's work? What of his theory will you use and what will you revise?

Write an essay that reviews Coles's theory of entitlements, an essay that proceeds from and incorporates the three papers you wrote as you re-imagined his work. Feel free to use whatever you want from Coles (with proper acknowledgments, of course) and from your previous papers, and to revise whatever you want from either Coles's or your own work.

# SEQUENCE FOUR

# Experts and Expertise

John Ruskin
Thomas Kuhn
Adrienne Rich
Clifford Geertz
John Edgar Wideman
Walker Percy

*T*HE FIRST FIVE ASSIGNMENTS in this sequence invite you to look at the world through the eyes of experts: John Ruskin, Thomas Kuhn, Adrienne Rich, Clifford Geertz and John Edgar Wideman. This can be heady and exciting work. You are given the chance to think about familiar settings or experiences through the imaginations of thinkers who have had a profound effect on contemporary culture. In his essay, "The Nature of Gothic," for example, Ruskin looks at the buildings and objects that surround him and thinks about the way they were made and the quality of life of the people who worked to make them. You will be asked to conduct a similar inventory and see what connections you can make between architecture or consumer goods and the values they represent. Kuhn provides a way of charting the "structure" of a discovery. You will be asked to use his terms to chart the "structure of discovery" in your experience reading Ruskin. To gather material for her argument about the relations between an individual and culture, Rich brings poems and personal narrative into her essay. You will be asked to experiment similarly with the conventions of the essay. Geertz, in "Deep Play: Notes on the Balinese

Cockfight," argues that the Balinese cockfight is a story the Balinese tell themselves about themselves. With Geertz as a model, you will be given the opportunity to interpret a characteristic scene from the culture around you. And Wideman, in his attempts to understand and represent his brother's life and thoughts, provides an example of the kind of interpretive expertise that stands outside usual academic conventions for investigation and report.

In each case, you will be given the opportunity to work alongside these thinkers as an apprentice, carrying out work they have begun. The final assignment in the sequence will ask you to look back on what you have done, to take stock, and to draw some conclusions about the potential and consequences of this kind of intellectual apprenticeship.

. . . . . . . . . . . .

A S S I G N M E N T  1

## Going Forth Again to Gaze on a Familiar Setting [Ruskin]

> Go forth again to gaze upon the old cathedral front, where you have smiled so often at the fantastic ignorance of the old sculptors: examine once more those ugly goblins, and formless monsters, and stern statues, anatomiless and rigid; but do not mock at them, for they are signs of the life and liberty of every workman who struck the stone; a freedom of thought, and rank in scale of being, such as no laws, no charters, no charities can secure; but which it must be the first aim of all Europe at this day to regain for her children. (p. 530)
>
> — JOHN RUSKIN
> *The Nature of Gothic*

Ruskin addresses you fairly aggressively as *his* reader: "Go forth and look again at the old cathedral front," he says to you. Or, in another section, "And now, reader, look round this English room of yours."

You are not in an English room. You are not his nineteenth-century contemporary. And you are not, most likely, in a position to have a first-hand look at the front of a Gothic cathedral (although you will find some photographs of a gothic cathedral on pages 537 and 538). Ruskin directs your attention, and he is quite certain about what you will see, about what the "signs" in these landscapes mean. The perfection of the English room, "if read rightly," is a sign of slavery and degradation, while the ugliness and imperfection of the cathedral facade are signs of life and liberty.

For this assignment, see if you can extend Ruskin's challenge to your own immediate surroundings. Look again at something that is part of your local environment—perhaps a building or a room. Look at it for what it says about the life and character of the persons who made it, and for what it says about the culture that values it (or fails to value it). Write an essay in which you explain what you see and how it might be read "rightly." Your job, then, is to extend Ruskin's method of analysis to your world, seen at this point in time.

Note: You should not feel that in carrying on Ruskin's project, you are bound to share Ruskin's politics—to say what he does about industrialization or the working class. There are those who would argue that you cannot adopt a method (a way of seeing) without adopting a political stance. When you have finished your essay, you might ask yourself whether it is possible to imitate Ruskin's way of seeing architectural or domestic detail without coming to similar conclusions about production and consumption.

·   ·   ·   ·   ·   ·   ·   ·   ·   ·   ·

ASSIGNMENT 2

## *A Story of Reading* [Kuhn, Ruskin]

> These features suggest the existence of two normal requisites for the beginning of an episode of discovery. The first, which throughout this paper I have largely taken for granted, is the individual skill, wit, or genius to recognize that something has gone wrong in ways that may prove consequential. (p. 390)
>
> > — THOMAS KUHN
> > *The Historical Structure of Scientific Discovery*

Kuhn says that all three of the discoveries he studied began with an anomaly, with "nature's failure to conform entirely to expectation." Phrases like this are often used to describe the experience of reading, where a reader moves along expecting to hear the sorts of things one usually hears but then is surprised by what a writer does and has to readjust his or her view of what the text is saying. Texts, or sections of texts, that might be called "difficult" or "obscure" or "boring" might also, that is, be called "anomalous," and, as a consequence, the story of reading could be plotted differently.

For this assignment, tell the story of your experience with "The Nature of Gothic." (You may write an essay, but you may find some other form more useful.) You will probably want to reread Ruskin's essay for this assignment, but before you do so you ought to try to reconstruct, at least for your notes, your experience the first few times you sat down with it.

Your primary responsibility in this essay is to be a good historian—to tell a story that is rich in detail and in understanding. This is your story. You are one of the characters, if not the main character. You also want to bring forward the features that make it a story—suspense, action, context, drama. You are writing this history, however, to see the degree to which Kuhn's approach to understanding scientific discovery can be usefully applied to the study of the process of reading. You should use his terms and methods where you can, and where they do not seem appropriate, think about why they don't work and what you need to put in their place.

. . . . . . . . . . . .

A S S I G N M E N T  3

## *Looking Back* [Rich]

Re-vision—the act of looking back, of seeing with fresh eyes, of entering an old text from a new critical direction—is for women more than a chapter in cultural history: it is an act of survival. Until we can understand the assumptions in which we are drenched we cannot know ourselves. (pp. 483–84)

I have hesitated to do what I am going to do now, which is use myself as an illustration. For one thing, it's a lot easier and less dangerous to talk about other[s]. (p. 486)
     – ADRIENNE RICH
     *When We Dead Awaken: Writing as Re-Vision*

In "When We Dead Awaken," Rich is writing not to tell her story but to tell a collective story, the story of women or women writers, a story in which she figures only as a representative example. In fact, the focus on individual experience might be said to run against the argument she has to make about the shaping forces of culture and history, in whose context knowing oneself means knowing the assumptions in which one is "drenched."

Yet Rich tells her story—offering poems, anecdotes, details from her life. Write an essay in which you too (and perhaps with similar hesitation) use your own experience as an illustration, as a way of investigating not just your situation but the situation of people like you. (Think about what materials you might have to offer in place of her poems.) Tell a story of your own and use it to talk about the ways you might be said to have been shaped or named or positioned by an established and powerful culture. You should imagine that this assignment is a way for you to use (and put to the test) some of Rich's key terms, words like "re-vision," "re-naming," "structure," and "patriarchy."

• • • • • • • • • • •

ASSIGNMENT 4

## *Seeing Your World Through Geertz's Eyes* [Geertz]

> The culture of a people is an ensemble of texts, themselves ensembles, which the anthropologist strains to read over the shoulders of those to whom they properly belong. (p. 301)
> – CLIFFORD GEERTZ
> *Deep Play: Notes on the Balinese Cockfight*

Geertz talks about "reading" a culture while peering over the shoulders of those to whom it properly belongs. In "Deep Play," he "reads" the cockfight over the shoulders of the Balinese. But the cockfight is not a single event to be described in isolation. It is itself a "text," one that must be understood in context. Or, as Geertz says, the cockfight is a "Balinese reading of Balinese experience; a story they tell themselves about themselves."

The job of the anthropologist, Geertz says, is "formulating sociological principles, not . . . promoting or appreciating cockfights." And the question for the anthropologist is this: "What does one learn about such principles from examining culture as an assemblage of texts?" Societies, he says, "like lives, contain their own interpretations. One has only to learn how to gain access to them."

Anthropologists are experts at gaining access to cultures and at performing this kind of complex reading. One of the interesting things about being a student is that you get to (or you have to) act like an expert even though, properly speaking, you are not. Write an essay in which you prepare a Geertzian "reading" of some part of our culture you know well (sorority rush, window-shopping in a shopping mall, slam-dancing, studying in the library, decorating a dorm room, tailgate parties at the football game, whatever). Ideally, you should go out and observe the behavior you are studying, looking at the players and taking notes with your project in mind. You should imagine that you are working in Geertz's spirit, imitating his method and style and carrying out work that he has begun.

· · · · · · · · · · ·

A S S I G N M E N T  5

## *Wideman as a Case in Point* [Wideman]

> The hardest habit to break, since it was the habit of a lifetime, would be listening to myself listen to him. That habit would destroy any chance of seeing my brother on his terms; and seeing him in his terms, learning his terms, seemed the whole point of learning his story. However numerous and comforting the similarities, we were different. The world had seized on the difference, allowed me room to thrive, while he'd been forced into a cage. (p. 612)
>
> – JOHN EDGAR WIDEMAN
> *Our Time*

At several points in this selection, Wideman discusses his position as a writer, researching and telling Robby's story, and he describes the problems he faces in writing this piece (and in "reading" the text of his brother's life). You could read this excerpt, in other words, as an essay on reading and writing.

Why do you think Wideman brings himself and these problems into the text? Why not keep quiet and hope no one notices? Choose three or four passages where Wideman refers directly or indirectly to the work he is doing as he writes this piece, and write an essay describing this work and why you think Wideman refers to it as he does. If he confronts problems, what are they and how does he go about solving them? If Wideman is an expert, how might you describe his expertise? And what might his example say to you as you think about your work as a student? as a writer?

. . . . . . . . . . . .

# On Experts and Expertise
## [Ruskin, Kuhn, Rich, Geertz, Wideman, Percy]

The whole horizon of being is staked out by "them," the experts. The highest satisfaction of the sightseer (not merely the tourist but any layman seer of sights) is that his sight should be certified as genuine. The worst of his impoverishment is that there is no sense of impoverishment. (p. 468)

I refer to the general situation in which sovereignty is surrendered to a class of privileged knowers, whether these be theorists or artists. A reader may surrender sovereignty over that which has been written about, just as a consumer may surrender sovereignty over a thing which has been theorized about. The consumer is content to receive an experience just as it has been presented to him by theorists and planners. The reader may also be content to judge life by whether it has or has not been formulated by whose who know and write about life. (p. 469)

– WALKER PERCY
*The Loss of the Creature*

In the last five assignments you were asked to try on other writers' ways of seeing the world. You looked at what you had read or done, and at scenes from your own life, casting your experience in the terms of others.

Percy, in "The Loss of the Creature," offers what might be taken as a critique of such activity. "A reader," he says, "may surrender sovereignty over that which has been written about, just as a consumer may surrender sovereignty over a thing which has been theorized about." Ruskin, Kuhn, Rich, Geertz, and Wideman have all been presented to you as, in a sense, "privileged knowers." You have been asked to model your own work on their examples.

It seems safe to say that, at least so far as Percy is concerned, surrendering sovereignty is not a good thing to do. If Percy were to read over your work in these assignments, how do you think he would describe what you have done? If he were to take your work as an example in his essay, where might he place it? And how would his reading of your work fit with your sense of what you have done? Would Percy's assessment be accurate, or is there something he would be missing, something he would fail to see?

Write an essay in which you describe and comment on your work in this sequence, looking at it both from Percy's point of view and from your own, but viewing that work as an example of an educational practice, a way of reading (and writing) that may or may not have benefits for the reader.

Note: You will need to review carefully those earlier papers and mark sections that you feel might serve as interesting examples in your discussion. You want to base your conclusions on the best evidence you can. When you begin writing, it would be best if you referred to the writer of those earlier papers as a "he" or a "she" who played certain roles and performed his or her work in certain characteristic ways. You can save the first person, the "I," for the person who is writing this assignment and looking back on those texts.

# Gendered Writing

Adrienne Rich
Jean Franco
Harriet Jacobs
Virginia Woolf

*THE ASSIGNMENTS* in this sequence begin with Adrienne Rich's feminist critique of the position of women, and women writers particularly, within a patriarchal culture. The purpose of this sequence is to use gender as a way of talking about differences in the ways people think and speak, read and write. As we use the term "gender," it does not necessarily mean the same thing as "sex." It is possible, in other words, for a woman to write like a man or a man to write like a woman. We can, however, name these differences in terms of gender to refer to ways of thinking and using language, ways of establishing a relationship with a reader or a subject. The assignments in this sequence will ask everyone, men and women alike, to imagine themselves inside and outside gendered ways of thinking and speaking offered as "naturally there" by the culture. If you think, for example, of the disembodied textbook voice of authority (the "When one considers the effects of the Industrial Revolution" voice of a term paper), and if you think of that voice as a version of the voice of a Father, you have a way of thinking about why it is both attractive and unattractive, productive or counterproductive, and you have a way of understanding how to reproduce that voice or resist its reproduction in your own work. This is the kind of interpretation these assignments require.

Rich's essay establishes a powerful way of representing the position of women's writing within the dominant culture. The first two assignments ask you to work closely with her argument and employ it to frame a personal narrative of your own, one that you can use to reflect on your own position within a dominant culture. Jean Franco, who writes about the way public and private space could be said to "belong" differently to men and women in Latin America, demonstrates a way of reading the political or social scene as though it too were a text. Assignment 4 looks at "Incidents in the Life of a Slave Girl," an excerpt from the autobiography of Harriet Jacobs, who spent much of her life as a slave in the Carolinas. The position she occupies as a woman is complicated by her position as a slave, as property in real economic terms. You will be asked to work with Franco's essay, again as a tool for examining your own cultural moment, but also to reflect on the culture of slavery in the Carolinas before the Civil War.

With Virginia Woolf's "A Room of One's Own," the sequence returns to the question of gender and writing. The excerpt in *Ways of Reading* reproduces the opening and closing chapters of Woolf's long essay. In the middle chapters Woolf develops her argument about women and writing. In the chapters included here, however, she enacts an argument about women's writing in the style and method of the essay. You will be asked to work with the essay to see what it says, through its example, about the possibilities of stepping outside a genre historically dominated by men's voices, men's ways of thinking and speaking. And, finally, you will be asked to revise some of your own work, to work against those ways of thinking and writing that reproduce what might be seen to be the habits of male-dominated culture. You will be asked, in other words, to imagine in practice what it would be like to step outside the standard genre. In a final retrospective assignment, you will have a chance to reflect on this experience and how it might bear on your education as a writer.

. . . . . . . . . . . .

ASSIGNMENT 1

## *Writing as Re-Vision* [Rich]

Re-vision—the act of looking back, of seeing with fresh eyes, of entering an old text from a new critical direction—is for women more than a chapter in cultural history: it is an act of survival. Until we can understand the assumptions in which we are drenched we cannot know ourselves. And this drive to self-knowledge, for women, is more than a search for identity: it is part of our refusal of the self-destructiveness of male-dominated society. A radical critique of literature, feminist in its impulse, would take the work first of all as a clue to how we live, how we have been living, how we have been led to imagine ourselves, how our language has trapped as well as liberated us, how the very act of naming has been till now a male prerogative, and how we can begin to see and name— and therefore live—afresh. A change in the concept of sexual identity is essential if we are not going to see the old political order reassert itself in every new revolution. We need to know the writing of the past, and know it differently than we have ever known it; not to pass on a tradition but to break its hold over us. (pp. 483–84)

— ADRIENNE RICH
*When We Dead Awaken: Writing as Re-Vision*

To know the writing of the past and to know it differently; to understand the assumptions in which we are drenched; to take the work as a clue to how we have been living, how we have been led to imagine ourselves, how language has trapped as well as liberated us—Rich's program for political change and political action is rooted in acts of reading and writing, of interpretation and response. Her words put a particular pressure on the work of a writing class. They make it hard to see that work as neutral, as "just" a matter of sentences and paragraphs.

One way to begin thinking about reading and writing as an engagement with history, politics, and culture is to look closely at Rich's example. For this assignment, take three of the poems Rich offers as examples of change in her writing—"Aunt Jennifer's Tigers," the section from "Snapshots of a Daughter-in-Law," and "Planetarium"—and use them as a way of talking about revision, particular revision as "an act of survival." What might this mean? What, to your mind, are the key differences among these poems? What might the development they mark be said to represent? And what do these poems, as examples, have to do with the argument about writing, culture, and gender in the rest of the essay?

You are not alone as you read these poems. Rich provides some commentary of her own, noting changes and commenting on what they represent. You will want to acknowledge what Rich has to say, to be sure, but you should not be bound by it. Does your account agree with hers? What does she fail to say? You will need to make careful and precise use of examples drawn from the poems and from Rich's discussion of those poems. But you should use these as your materials, as starting points in a discussion where there is room for you, too, to speak with authority.

. . . . . . . . . . . .

A S S I G N M E N T  **2**

# *Telling a Story of Your Own* [Rich]

> Re-vision—the act of looking back, of seeing with fresh eyes, of entering an old text from a new critical direction—is for women more than a chapter in cultural history: it is an act of survival. Until we can understand the assumptions in which we are drenched we cannot know ourselves. (pp. 483–84)
>
> I have hesitated to do what I am going to do now, which is to use myself as an illustration. For one thing, it's a lot easier and less dangerous to talk about other[s]. (p. 486)
>
> — ADRIENNE RICH
> *When We Dead Awaken: Writing as Re-Vision*

In "When We Dead Awaken," Rich hesitates to tell her own story, perhaps because she is more interested in a collective story, the story of women or women writers, a story in which she figures only as a representative example. In fact, an exclusive focus on isolated or individual experience runs against the argument she has to make about the shaping forces of culture and history, in whose context knowing oneself means knowing the assumptions in which one is drenched.

Yet Rich tells her story—offering poems, anecdotes, details from her life. Write an essay in which you too (and perhaps with similar hesitation) use your own experience as an illustration, as a way of investigating not just your situation but the situation of people like you. Tell a story of your own and use it to talk about the ways you might be said to have been shaped or named or positioned by an established and powerful culture. You should imagine that this assignment is a way for you to use (and put to the test) some of Rich's key terms, words like "revision," "re-naming," "structure," "culture" and, particularly, "patriarchy."

. . . . . . . . . . .

A S S I G N M E N T **3**

# *Dividing Up the Territory* [Franco]

Bachelard's investigations "seek to determine the human value of the sorts of space that may be grasped, that may be defended against adverse forces, the space we love. For diverse reasons, and with the differences entailed by poetic shadings, this is eulogized space. Attached to its protective value, which can be a positive one, are also imagined values, which soon become dominant." . . . In this essay, I want to give these felicitous spaces a more concrete and historical existence. (p. 198)

– JEAN FRANCO
*Killing Priests, Nuns, Women, Children*

Franco's essay is offered as an attempt to understand a "Latin American imaginary"—that is, a way of thinking and speaking that is rooted in the culture and that could be said to *produce* the world experienced as naturally there: "House, home, and convent are undoubtedly constructions produced by a sex-gender system." There are houses, homes, and convents produced by particular owners and made of brick and mortar, but as terms signifying a particular kind of space properly belonging to men or women, "house," "home," and "convent" are produced by a way of speaking that reproduces a way of thinking about men and women. Franco writes about real examples of an imaginary space, in other words, and about how the "imaginary" is being revised.

Write an essay that explores a contemporary North American "imaginary," a topography or map produced to organize the landscape into clearly demarcated spaces, some belonging to men and some to women. Think of your essay as a response to Franco. You should imagine your essay as an investigation of particular sites or spaces, bringing forward the system or logic that governs the position and significance of these sites in the North American "imaginary." Ideally, you should consider how this system is reproduced, how it might be revised, and what would be lost or gained in its revision.

. . . . . . . . . . .

# ASSIGNMENT 4

## *Mapping the Culture of Slavery* [Franco, Jacobs]

> Reader, I draw no imaginary pictures of southern homes. I am telling you the plain truth. Yet when victims make their escape from this wild beast of Slavery, northerners consent to act the part of bloodhounds, and hunt the poor fugitive back into his den, "full of dead men's bones, and all uncleanness." Nay, more, they are not only willing, but proud, to give their daughters in marriage to slaveholders. The poor girls have romantic notions of a sunny clime, and of the flowering vines that all the year round shade a happy home. To what disappointments are they destined! (p. 340)
>
> — HARRIET JACOBS
> *Incidents in the Life of a Slave Girl*

Franco provides a demonstration of how spaces can be said to be part of a way of thinking and speaking, an imaginary topography. And she demonstrates how these representations of space relate to political struggle, to the borderlines between the personal and the social.

The arrangements of people in "Incidents in the Life of a Slave Girl," are difficult to chart, partly because these arrangements defy easy categorization (that blacks and whites lived separately; that family lines and color lines were distinct markers; that the South was a single, simple place). As you reread this excerpt from Jacobs's autobiography, pay close attention to the ways people are organized by family, love, community, and color. See what you can determine about the codes that govern relations in this representation of slave culture. Ask where and how Jacobs places herself in these networks.

Following Franco's lead, how might you chart and read the distribution of spaces in Jacobs's world, particularly those spaces Jacobs fears and desires, spaces imagined as either safe and free or dangerous and limiting? Write an essay in which you apply this kind of analysis in a close reading of the real and imaginary topography of "Incidents."

. . . . . . . . . . .

A S S I G N M E N T  5

# Man-Womanly/Woman-Manly:
## Gender and Writing [Woolf]

And I went on amateurishly to sketch a plan of the soul so that in each of us two powers preside, one male, one female; and in the man's brain, the man predominates over the woman, and in the woman's brain, the woman predominates over the man. The normal and comfortable state of being is that when the two live in harmony together, spiritually co-operating. If one is a man, still the woman part of the brain must have effect; and a woman also must have intercourse with the man in her. Coleridge perhaps meant this when he said that a great mind is androgynous. It is when this fusion takes place that the mind is fully fertilized and uses all its faculties. Perhaps a mind that is purely masculine cannot create, any more than a mind that is purely feminine, I thought. But it would be well to test what one meant by man-womanly, and conversely by woman-manly, by pausing and looking at a book or two. (p. 657)

— VIRGINIA WOOLF
*A Room of One's Own*

As either an essay or the text of a public lecture, the two chapters from "A Room of One's Own" excerpted in *Ways of Reading* are full of surprises. This lecture doesn't sound like the usual lecture; this essay doesn't do what essays usually do. At many places and in many ways this work revises the conventions of the genre—the essay's or the lecture's characteristic ways of addressing an audience, gathering information, and presenting an argument.

After reading Franco's essay, it seems possible to think of the essay as a space, both a constructed space and a space that constructs. The essay is a space in the culture (in the usual ways of writing essays and giving lectures); it constructs a writer or speaker (teaching him or her how to think and speak and relate to others), but it is also something a writer or speaker constructs (as Woolf could be said to have constructed this text, doing something with the usual ways of writing or speaking).

As you reread these chapters and prepare to write about them, make note of the ways Woolf (the writer writing the text) constructs a space for speaker and audience, a kind of imaginary place where a woman can do her work, find a way of speaking, think as she might like to think, and prepare others to listen. Look for interesting and potentially significant ways she defies or transforms what you take to be the conventions of the essay. You might especially want to look for those places where Woolf seems to be saying, "I know what I should be doing here, but I won't. I'll do this instead."

Choose four of these moments in "A Room of One's Own" and, with them as your material, write an essay in which you discuss Woolf's writing as a performance, an action, a demonstration of a way of writing that pushes against the usual ways of doing things with words. While there is certainly an argument *in* Woolf's essay, your paper will be about the argument represented *by* the essay, an argument enacted in a way of writing. What is Woolf doing? How might you explain what she is doing and why she is doing it? In what ways might her essay be seen as an example of someone working on the problems of writing? of a writer working with a tradition more "manly" than "womanly." And what might all this have to do with you, a student in a writing class?

. . . . . . . . . . .

A S S I G N M E N T  6

# *Writing as Re-Vision*
## [Rich, Woolf]

We need to know the writing of the past, and know it differently than we have ever known it; not to pass on a tradition but to break its hold over us. (p. 484)
— ADRIENNE RICH
*When We Dead Awaken: Writing as Re-Vision*

"We need to know the writing of the past." The "we" of that sentence can be seen as an invitation to you, too. For this assignment, choose one of the papers you have written for this class. As is usually the case with revision, you would do best to choose your favorite paper—the one that you care about most, the one that shows your best work. Read back through it closely, marking the features that seem to reproduce both the best and the worst of what you might call a patriarchal tradition, a writing that seems to come only from a masculine cultural tradition. Remember, you are not looking at what you said but at how you said it. You are looking for ways of writing that could be called more "manly" than "womanly."

After you have completed this exercise, write a major revision of this essay, one that fundamentally changes its mode (or gender) of presentation. Your goal should be to write from what might be called a feminine tradition, even if that means losing the balance between womanly-manly and manly-womanly.

When you have finished, and on a separate page, write a brief commentary on this exercise. What were the most interesting or important changes you made? What was lost and what was gained in your revision? What have you learned from this process that you might carry with you to other assignments or settings?

· · · · · · · · · · ·

A S S I G N M E N T   7

## *Retrospective* [Woolf]

But when I look back through these notes and criticize my own train of thought as I made them, I find that my motives were not altogether selfish. There runs through these comments and discursions the conviction—or is it the instinct?— that good books are desirable and that good writers, even if they show every variety of human depravity, are still good human beings. Thus when I ask you to write more books I am urging you to do what will be for your good and for the good of the world at large. (pp. 664–65)

Here I would stop, but the pressure of convention decrees that every speech must end with a peroration. And a peroration addressed to women should have something, you will agree, particularly exalting and ennobling about it. I should implore you to remember your responsibilities, to be higher, more spiritual; I should remind you how much depends upon you, and what an influence you can exert upon the future. But those exhortations can safely, I think, be left to the other sex, who will put them, and indeed have put them, with far greater eloquence than I can compass. (p. 665)

– VIRGINIA WOOLF
*A Room of One's Own*

Several of the pieces you have read in this sequence are addressed specifically to women. The sequence itself has assumed that men and women can read these pieces with equal interest, success, or difficulty. And it has assumed that they can work to equal ends.

This is the last paper you will write in this sequence, although it is certainly not the last paper you'll write in your career as a student (or, most likely, in your career outside of school).

Write an essay in which you review the work you have done for this sequence. To do this you will need to go back over your essays as though you were preparing to write a research paper. You will need to read carefully, take notes, mark passages, and gather your material. As you review your work, you might look for key moments or points of transition, for things that have changed and things that have remained the same in your reading and writing. You might ask: What sort of reader or writer was I at the beginning? What sort am I now? What is the evidence of my efforts, achievements, and failures? In what ways could I be said to have learned to know and revise "the writing of the past"?

Note: When you begin writing, it would be best if you referred to the writer of those earlier papers as a "he" or a "she" who played certain roles and performed his or her work in certain characteristic ways. You can save the first person, the "I," for the person who is writing this assignment and looking back on those texts.

# SEQUENCE SIX

# Inventing a Methodology

Alice Walker

Gloria Steinem

Julia Kristeva

*T*HE THREE ESSAYS that you are asked to read for this sequence of assignments deal with similar issues from different perspectives—all of them concerning women and motherhood. And although the issues are important and compelling, initially you are asked to give your attention to these writers' methods of working. The first assignment has you examine Alice Walker's methods and comment on how her essay proceeds. The second invites you to compare the methods of Walker and Gloria Steinem, paying particular attention to how those methods might be related to the issues they raise and the conclusions they draw. The third assignment offers you a difficult piece of writing by Julia Kristeva and asks you both to examine her methods and to experiment with your own when discussing hers. The final assignment invites you to enter the conversation framed by these three writers by deliberately experimenting with your own methods of reading and writing.

· · · · · · · · · · ·

A S S I G N M E N T **1**

# *Studying Walker's Methods* [Walker]

> What did it mean for a black woman to be an artist in our
> grandmothers' time? In our great-grandmothers' day? It is a
> question with an answer cruel enough to stop the blood.
> (p. 586)
>
> — ALICE WALKER
> *In Search of Our Mothers' Gardens*

This is the first of a series of assignments that asks you to examine the
methods of three women writing about similar concerns—women and
motherhood. In her essay Walker raises the question of what it meant (and
what it still means) to be a black woman and an artist, and her response
proceeds from examples that take her mother and herself, among others,
into account. As you read her essay, pay particular attention to Walker's
methods of working. How does she build her arguments? Where does her
evidence come from? her authority? To whom is she appealing? What do
her methods allow her to see (and say) and not to see? And, finally, how
might her conclusions be related to her methods?

Write a paper in which you examine Walker's essay in terms of the
methods by which it proceeds. Pay particular attention to the connections
among her arguments, evidence, supposed audience, and conclusions, and
feel free to invent names and descriptions for what you would call her
characteristic ways of working. Remember that your job is to invent a way
of describing how Walker works and how her methods—her ways of gathering materials, of thinking them through, of presenting herself and her
thoughts, of imagining a world of speakers and listeners—might be related
to the issues she raises and the conclusions she draws.

. . . . . . . . . . . .

A S S I G N M E N T  **2**

# *Comparing Steinem's Work with Walker's* [Steinem, Walker]

> The family must have watched this energetic, fun-loving, book-loving woman turn into someone who was afraid to be alone, who could not hang on to reality long enough to hold a job, and who could rarely concentrate enough to read a book.
>
> Yet I don't remember any family speculation about the mystery of my mother's transformation. (pp. 543–44)
> — GLORIA STEINEM
> *Ruth's Song (Because She Could Not Sing It)*

In her essay Steinem is working on a problem similar to the one Walker poses—the treatment of women, in particular of her mother—but Steinem is more concerned with understanding her mother's transformation as a person than with seeing her mother as an artist. As you read Steinem's essay, look closely, as you did in Walker's, at her methods of work. How would you say she proceeds? How might her methods be similar to and different from Walker's? Where does Steinem's authority come from? her arguments? How does she gather materials? think them through? present herself and her thoughts? For whom or to whom do you suppose she's writing? And how might her methods be related to her conclusions? What do they allow her to see (and say) and not to see?

Write an essay in which you compare Steinem's methods of working with Walker's. Pay particular attention to what you find compelling and not compelling about their work (and the reasons you feel the way you do). And be sure to address the questions of where their authority comes from, and how their methods—their ways of gathering materials and thinking them through—might be related to the issues they raise and the conclusions they draw. Again, feel free to invent names and descriptions for the way these writers work and to speculate on reasons for the similarities and differences in their methods.

· · · · · · · · · · ·

## A S S I G N M E N T  3

# *Untangling Kristeva* [Kristeva]

> What is there, in the portrayal of the Maternal in general and particularly in its Christian, virginal, one, that reduces social anguish and gratifies a male being; what is there that also satisfies a woman so that a commonality of the sexes is set up, beyond and in spite of their glaring incompatibility and permanent warfare? (p. 361)
>
> — JULIA KRISTEVA<br>*Stabat Mater*

You are now going to work with a very difficult essay, but one which addresses issues—women and motherhood—similar to those in the Walker and Steinem essays. Kristeva's work is difficult in part because she deals with concepts and cultural forces *as* concepts and forces, rather than as notions drawn from examples of particular people's behavior. But it's also interesting work because of the methods by which it proceeds. Kristeva sets out to work differently. As you read (and reread) her essay, pay particular attention to those methods—her ways of gathering materials, thinking them through, presenting herself and her ideas, imagining a world of speakers and listeners—that make her work different from Walker's and Steinem's.

How would you characterize Kristeva's methods? her authority? her ways of gathering materials and thinking them through? her presentation of herself and her thoughts? Who do you think she imagines as her audience? And what do you find compelling or not compelling about her work? How would you say the issues she raises and the conclusions she draws are related to her methods?

Write an essay in which you examine Kristeva's methods and how those methods might be said to be related to the issues she raises and the conclusions she draws. Feel free to experiment with your own methods (however you might imagine that experimentation), and draw your attention to how Kristeva's work differs from and is similar to that of Walker and Steinem.

. . . . . . . . . . .

A S S I G N M E N T  **4**

# *Experimenting with Your Own Writing*
# [Walker, Steinem, Kristeva]

This final assignment in the sequence is an opportunity for you to enter into this discussion on women and motherhood but within the context of the issues raised by Walker, Steinem, and Kristeva. This is, in other words, a chance for you to speak about what they speak about, to address the issues and concerns and conclusions they do; it is a chance for you to tell some stories of your own, to think about material or sources close to you. And as much as this is an invitation for you to enter into the discussion they frame, it is also an invitation for you to pay attention to your methods, to experiment with the way your essay might proceed.

Write an essay in which you enter into the conversation framed by Walker, Steinem, and Kristeva. This is a conversation in writing, however, and like these other writers you will want to pay particular attention to convention and method. You will want to experiment as they do, in order to do what you can to keep what you want to say from sounding like more of the same old stuff.

# Listening to TV;
# Watching the Radio

Mark Crispin Miller
Simon Frith

*M*ARK CRISPIN MILLER *and* SIMON FRITH are two of the most influential critics of popular culture writing today. While both write for magazines, theirs is not the usual mix of summary and opinion. Their criticism is systematic, disciplined, scholarly, in both cases reflecting the authors' academic training. Their concern is not just to describe a new show or recording but to see it as part of something larger (the culture of TV for Miller, youth culture, for Frith). They try to place individual events against a larger context, where various interested forces in the culture compete and try to preserve and reproduce themselves.

The first two assignments in this sequence ask you to try your hand at the kind of criticism Miller and Frith write. The next two provide a way for you to reflect on what you have done. Assignment 3 asks you to return to the key terms and methods of Miller's and Frith's essays and translate them for an audience new to this kind of criticism. Assignment 4 asks for a personal narrative, in which you see yourself as a character in the story of American TV and rock and roll.

· · · · · · · · · · · ·

A S S I G N M E N T  **1**

# *TV* [Miller]

Miller is an example of a critic who works against the grain of the material he studies (in this case TV) and against the grain of what he assumes to be a common misreading of that material. He reads against the way "The Cosby Show" or the Shield ad want to be read; he writes against what he assumes to be the viewers' blindness to motive and detail.

It seems that this takes considerable effort. Television (and for Miller this is both a culture and an industry) is very sophisticated in diverting our attention. As he said in the essay that introduces *Boxed In*: "Hectic, ironic, and seemingly unintended, the ads do not stand out—and so TV has all but boxed us in. Whereas, out on the walls and billboards, the ads were once overt and recognizable, TV has resubmerged them, by overwhelming the mind that would perceive them, making it only half-aware—as every adman knows: 'People don't watch television like they're taking notes for an exam,' says Lou Centlivre, Executive Creative Director at Foote Cone Belding." And from the very beginning, Miller argues, TV has developed strategies to counter criticism. The most recent is TV's own version of irony—there is no achievement in arguing that a TV show is banal if it never presents itself as serious in the first place. This is how Miller accounts for the impact of figures such as Bruce Willis, David Letterman, or Mariette Hartley. "The generation that once laughed off TV, in short, is trying still to laugh it off while disappearing into it."

Write an essay in which you try your hand at Miller's kind of criticism, developing a close reading of a particular show or ad currently on TV. Like Miller, you will need to present your material carefully and to show how it might be read. The questions you ask should include these: How does it work? What does it assume of its audience? What is its hidden logic? What are its intentions? How and why are these intentions hidden or hard to see? Whose interests might these intentions be said to represent?

Note: This last question is the hardest one. It is possible to talk about the TV ad or show simply as though it were the agent *doing* something (as when Miller says that the Shield ad offers women a fantasy of power and control). But there is, of course, some force behind the ad or the show. You could think about the goals of a particular industry—the soap maker or the TV producer. Miller invites you to think as well about culture (the culture of TV) and history (the history of American TV and American consumerism).

•   •   •   •   •   •   •   •   •   •   •   •

### A S S I G N M E N T  2

## *Rock and Roll* [Frith]

Frith pays attention to the 1950s, 1960s, and 1970s, and he deals most immediately with the English experience of rock and roll. He is trying to "historicize" rock, to argue for its particular character or meaning in a particular culture at a particular point in time. The particulars of his account create a space in which you can offer an account of your own, one that extends his discussion to the 1980s (or the late 1980s) and to the United States (or your particular region of the United States).

Write an essay in which you construct your own account of rock and sexuality. You should begin your work by rereading Frith's essay, and you should pay close attention to the way he accounts for the relationship between culture and individual artists or consumers. He argues against the common notion that music *expresses* feelings or thoughts that are already there. He writes, rather, about the power of rock and roll to shape, construct, or organize experience. As you work back through his essay, mark the terms and phrases that Frith uses to describe the relationships between culture, music, and the individual. These terms and phrases will be useful when you begin writing.

Frith works quickly, painting with broad strokes, moving easily from generalization to generalization, summing up the 1960s in just a few pages, for example. You should work much more slowly in your essay. Before you generalize about rock and roll in the 1980s, turn your attention to more fine-grained detail—the lyrics of two or three songs, a description of an MTV video, a careful representation of a subculture and its music. Work with local material, material you know well and can reproduce in detail.

•   •   •   •   •   •   •   •   •   •   •

### A S S I G N M E N T  3

## *Criticism* [Frith, Miller]

Frith, like Miller, is trying to find a way of talking about how culture "works" in the life of the individual. He is not making a simple argument—

that listening to rock songs makes people do things (be promiscuous or conservative, passive or violent). Yet he wants to argue that culture does something—that it is an agent, a shaping force in our lives, that it is more than an expression of thoughts and feelings, that it does more than articulate, what is already "naturally" there. This is a difficult argument to make for two reasons: it requires a language different from the usual language of cause and effect (in which people are presumed to act by reasoned decision or obvious intent). And it requires that we imagine a shaping force beyond the individual (the force of culture or history, for example). In fact individuals disappear in this account and become "types."

Read back through Miller's and Frith's essays, marking passages you could use to try to define "culture," particularly those passages that describe a particular cultural event or phenomenon: how it works, how it is reproduced or altered, and how its effects can be seen. Choose two or three from each selection and write an essay in which you explain to an audience unfamiliar with Miller, Frith, and their work who these critics are and what they do. You will be writing a kind of beginner's guide to cultural criticism.

•  •  •  •  •  •  •  •  •  •  •  •

A S S I G N M E N T   **4**

# *Culture* [Frith, Miller]

Once you feel you have a way of representing this argument (or these arguments) about culture, write an autobiographical essay telling your story, a story to reflect or illustrate (and then, perhaps, to challenge) the arguments of these critics. Your essay will be, in a sense, a chapter from your autobiography, a chapter on your experience as a participant or consumer in some area of contemporary American culture, perhaps including the ways you might be said to be a product of your culture. This is your chance to represent yourself as a character in the story of American TV and rock and roll. Your story should be rich and detailed—a good story, that is. But a careful reader should also be able to see echoes and allusions to more formal arguments by the critics to whom you are responding.

# The Problems of Difficulty

Ralph Waldo Emerson
Harriet Jacobs
Julia Kristeva
John Ruskin

*THE FOUR ASSIGNMENTS* in this sequence invite you to consider the nature of difficult texts and how the problems they pose might be said to belong simultaneously to language, to readers and to writers. The first assignment asks you to look closely at Ralph Waldo Emerson's "The American Scholar" in order to discuss the position in which he puts you, the reader, as he makes his argument. The second assignment asks you to concentrate on sections of Harriet Jacobs's and Julia Kristeva's essays to chart the sorts of difficulties that each presents and to consider how their writing might be said to be similar and different. The third assignment asks you to turn your attention to John Ruskin's "The Nature of Gothic" so that you might examine the difficulties posed by his terms and the demands he makes on readers. And the last assignment invites you to pull together what you've learned about the nature of difficult texts.

. . . . . . . . . . . .

A S S I G N M E N T  1

# *Turning to Emerson* [Emerson]

There is no question but that Emerson's text is difficult to read, and the difficulty is not simply a matter of big or unusual words. The text just doesn't do what we expect it to do. Some of this elusiveness can be attributed to the time it was written—expectations were different then—but this should not keep you from making the most of your own responses as a reader. For one thing, it's not completely true; not everyone in the 1830s wrote like Emerson. For another, it assumes that a nonspecialist cannot or should not read works from the past. One way of imagining your connection to 1837 is to imagine that your encounter with this text is somehow typical—that you, too, are Emerson's contemporary.

Take a section of the essay that you find characteristically difficult. (Section II is an interesting one to work with.) Reread it, paying close attention to the experience of reading. Where are you surprised? Where are you confused? How might this be part of a strategy, part of Emerson's design? This should be an exercise in close reading. You want to pay attention to how paragraph leads to paragraph, sentence leads to sentence; to notice the ways examples or statements are offered and taken away.

Write an essay in which you describe in close detail what it was like to read this section of "The American Scholar." Tell a story of reading, one in which you and Emerson are the main characters—complicated characters, not stick figures (the Innocent Student and the Inscrutable Genius). When you are done, see what connections you can make with Emerson's argument—with what he says is a proper relation between readers and writers. In what ways might his difficulties and yours be said to be unfortunate? In what ways might they be signs of his attempts to get the language (and a reader) to do what he wants them to do?

• • • • • • • • • • •

A S S I G N M E N T 2

# Continuing the Difficulty
# [Jacobs, Kristeva]

Both Jacobs and Kristeva could be said to have written difficult texts, and in both cases the difficulties could be seen as attempts to thwart or resist conventional desires (the desires of readers; the desires of the culture; the desire at the root of language, which is part of its history, resisting change, insisting on predictability).

For this essay, take a representative section of each selection in order to chart in careful detail the sorts of difficulties each presents—the difficulties that are "in" the text; the difficulties that are "in" the experience of the reader; the difficulties that are "in" the aims and strategies of the writer.

In what ways can Jacobs's and Kristeva's writing be said to be similar? In what ways can they be said to be different? How might you explain the differences? How do you think the authors would like these differences to be explained?

• • • • • • • • • • •

A S S I G N M E N T 3

# Ruskin's Terms [Ruskin]

In "The Nature of Gothic" Ruskin says,

> And it is, perhaps, the principal admirableness of the Gothic schools of architecture, that they thus receive the results of the labor of inferior minds: and out of fragments of imperfection, and betraying that imperfection in every touch, indulgently raise up a stately and unaccusable whole. (p. 528)

> Of human worth none but what is bad can be perfect, in its own bad way. (p. 536)

Inferior, imperfect, betrayal, indulgence: these are strange terms to use to describe what is admirable (or, as Ruskin says, "unaccusable") in a work of art. As you read his chapter, ask yourself what these terms come to represent. Look also at the steps in Ruskin's argument, from the beginning of the essay to the end. This is not the sort of argument that states its point and then quickly gets on with business. Once you've completed your preliminary research, write an essay in which you discuss the difficulties you faced as a reader and what they might or might not have to do with Ruskin and his motives as he presents his argument. What difficulties would you attribute to history—to the historical or cultural distance between you and Ruskin? (Be careful here. And be honest.) What difficulties would you attribute to his "strategy"? What might be said to be failures, more or less, on his part? And, finally, what does a reader have to do to keep up with this writing, to follow, and to make the most of it? What are the rewards?

· · · · · · · · · · · ·

A S S I G N M E N T   4

## Learning from Difficulties
## [Emerson, Jacobs, Kristeva, Ruskin]

Now that you have worked with these four texts, you're in a good position, that of an expert, to sort through them and say something about the difficulties they pose. How would you characterize the various difficulties of these texts? What can you now say about the nature of difficult texts?

Write an essay in which you discuss what you have learned about the nature of difficult texts and how a reader might negotiate the problems they pose. You'll want to work from your previous papers and the specific examples that you chose to study from the four texts, but feel free to extend your discussion beyond these texts to the difficulties of your own work and that of other students.

## S E Q U E N C E   N I N E

# Reading Culture

Roland Barthes

Mark Crispin Miller

John Berger

Simon Frith

Jane Tompkins

*I*N THIS SEQUENCE you will be reading and writing about culture. Not Culture, something you get if you go to the museum or a concert on Sunday, but culture—the images, words, and sounds that pervade our lives and organize and represent our common experience. This sequence invites your reflection on the ways culture "works" in and through the lives of individual consumers. The readings turn to a rich variety of cultural forms—wrestling and striptease, television ads and shows, rock and roll, museum art, academic research.

The difficulty of this sequence lies in the way it asks you to imagine that you are not a sovereign individual, making your own choices and charting the course of your life. This is conceptually difficult, but it can also be distasteful, since we learn at an early age to put great stock in imagining our own freedom. Most of the readings that follow ask you to imagine that you are the product of your culture; that your ideas, feelings, and actions, your ways of thinking and being, are constructed for you by a large, organized, pervasive force (sometimes called history, sometimes called culture, sometimes called ideology). You don't feel this to be the case, but that is part of the power of culture, or so the argument goes. These forces hide themselves. They lead you to believe that their constructions are naturally, inevitably there, that things are the way they are because that is just "the way things are." The assignments in this sequence ask you to read against your common sense. You will be expected to try on the role of the critic—to see how and where it might be useful to recognize complex motives in ordinary expressions.

The authors in this sequence all write as though, through great effort, they could step outside culture to see and criticize its workings. The assignments in this sequence will ask you both to reflect on this type of criticism and to participate in it. Simon Frith, for example, writes about rock and roll and sexuality. He says, "Male sexuality is no more 'naturally' aggressive, assertive, and urgent than female sexuality is 'naturally' passive, meek, and sensitive. But the issue is not the nature of sex but its representations, and they work not by describing feelings but by constructing them." You will be asked to write about representations of sexuality in contemporary rock and roll. This is an extraordinarily varied field—think of the powerful and competing images of women one can see in just thirty minutes' worth of MTV. And you will be asked to consider what it might mean to say that these images "construct" rather than express feelings and beliefs.

. . . . . . . . . . .

## ASSIGNMENT 1

# *Mythologies* [Barthes]

Such a precise finality demands that wrestling should be exactly what the public expects of it. Wrestlers, who are very experienced, know perfectly how to direct the spontaneous episodes of the fight so as to make them conform to the image which the public has of the great legendary themes of its mythology. A wrestler can irritate or disgust, he never disappoints, for he always accomplishes completely, by a progressive solidification of signs, what the public expects of him. In wrestling, nothing exists except in the absolute, there is no symbol, no allusion, everything is presented exhaustively. Leaving nothing in the shade, each action discards all parasitic meanings and ceremonially offers to the public a pure and full signification, rounded like Nature. This grandiloquence is nothing but the popular and age-old image of the perfect intelligibility of reality. What is portrayed by wrestling is therefore an ideal understanding of things; it is the euphoria of men raised for a while above the constitutive ambiguity of everyday situations. (pp. 31–32)

— ROLAND BARTHES
*The World of Wrestling*

The subjects of Barthes's two short essays—wrestling and striptease—could be said to be relatively common. As "spectacles," they seem reasonably self-evident: they are what they are; they don't require elaborate interpretation or commentary. And yet that is what Barthes gives us, elaborate interpretation and commentary. His "mythologies" are at times difficult, obscure, excessive. They are also at times dazzling, witty, and profound.

Who is this "Roland Barthes," and what is he doing? It is important to know what he says about wrestling and striptease, but it is also important to understand his method, how he does what he does when he "reads" these common events and interprets them. Choose one of his excerpts—either "The World of Wrestling" or "Striptease"—reread it, and mark sections that seem to give you insight into Barthes's method, sections where he takes a common feature of wrestling or striptease and finds in it a significance that seems uncommon, surprising.

Once you have located passages to work with, choose two of them and write an essay in which you explain both what Barthes says and how he says what he says. Work closely with the passages you have chosen. You can imagine that you are writing to another student, someone who has read the "mythologies" but who can't quite figure out what Barthes is saying or what this is all about.

. . . . . . . . . . . .

A S S I G N M E N T  2

# *Saying What Needs to Be Said* [Barthes]

The starting point of these reflections was usually a feeling of impatience at the sight of the "naturalness" with which newspapers, art, and common sense constantly dress up a reality which, even though it is the one we live in, is undoubtedly determined by history. . . . I resented seeing Nature and History confused at every turn, and I wanted to track down, in the decorative display of *what-goes-with-*

*out-saying,* the ideological abuse, which, in my view, is hidden there.

– ROLAND BARTHES
*Introduction to* Mythologies

In *Mythologies* Barthes "reads" some characteristic examples of French popular culture. He reads against what he takes to be a common but false understanding (against common sense, what most people think), and he reads in the name of the "public" or the "spectator," whose experience he comes to understand in a way he believes they cannot, because he thinks they fail to pay attention or they take things for granted. He looks for the hidden agenda, the ideology behind objects or events that do not seem to require such attention, that are presented as neutral, value free, naturally and inevitably there, as though their significance to us *"goes-without-saying."*

As a way of testing your sense of Barthes's method, write an essay (or perhaps a series of "mythologies") that provides a similar reading of an example (or related examples) of American culture—MTV, skateboarding, the Superbowl, Pee Wee Herman, and so on. You can imagine that you are either extending and reproducing or commenting on and revising Barthes's project in *Mythologies.* Perhaps you like what he is doing and would like to try your hand at it with some material from your own culture. Or perhaps you think there is something wrong with what he is doing and you'd like to show him a better way. In either case you should make some reference to Barthes and what he would do. What would he notice in your material? What might he say about it?

You should imagine that you are writing to an audience that is as much a part of the culture as you are. You should imagine, that is, that you are talking to people who will be familiar with the example or examples you choose, but whose common-sense understanding you will have to revise or undo.

• • • • • • • • • • •

## ASSIGNMENT 3

# *Watching TV* [Miller]

To read is, in this case, to undo. Such a project, however, demands that we not simply snicker at TV, presuming its stupidity and our own superiority. Rather we need a critical approach that would take TV seriously (without extolling it), a method of deciphering TV's component images, requiring both a meticulous attention to concrete detail, and a sense of TV's historical situation. Genuinely seen through, those details illuminate that larger context, and vice versa, so that the reading of TV contains and necessitates a reading of our own moment and its past.

The essays in this book represent my efforts to set such a critical example.

— MARK CRISPIN MILLER
*Introduction to* Boxed In

You've seen Miller's "reading" of both a Shield ad and "The Cosby Show." Behind both are certain assumptions about how TV works and how viewers typically respond (both consciously and subconsciously). Let's assume (for the sake of this assignment) that Miller has only sort of got it right, that something about the nature of TV (including its "concrete detail," its "historical situation") and something about a viewer's experience of TV is missing or hidden, or displaced or skewed or lost in his reading.

Write an essay in which you respond to Miller, as though you were going to show him where and how his account is wrong or incomplete. As the ground for your response, use a particular ad or show (something similar to Miller's material, something you could put up next to his readings of the Shield ad or "The Cosby Show").

Like Miller, you will need to present your material carefully and to show how it might be read. The questions you ask should include these: How does it work? What does it assume of its audience? What is its hidden logic? What are its intentions? How and why are these hidden or hard to see? Whose interests might these intentions be said to represent?

Note: This last question is the hardest one. It is possible to talk about the TV ad or show simply as though it were the agent *doing* something (as when Miller says that the Shield ad offers women a fantasy of power and control). But there is, of course, some force behind the ad or show. You could think about the goals of a particular industry—the soap maker or the TV producer. Miller invites you to think as well about culture (the culture of TV) and history (the history of American TV and American consumerism).

. . . . . . . . . . . .

A S S I G N M E N T 4

## *Looking at Pictures* [Berger]

> Original paintings are silent and still in a sense that information never is. Even a reproduction hung on a wall is not comparable in this respect for in the original the silence and stillness permeate the actual material, the paint, in which one follows the traces of the painter's immediate gestures. This has the effect of closing the distance in time between the painting of the picture and one's own act of looking at it.
> . . . What we make of that painted moment when it is before our eyes depends upon what we expect of art, and that in turn depends today upon how we have already experienced the meaning of paintings through reproductions. (pp. 86–87)
> — JOHN BERGER
> *Ways of Seeing*

While Berger describes original paintings as silent in this passage, it is clear that these paintings begin to speak if one approaches them properly, if one learns to ask "the right questions of the past." Berger demonstrates one route of approach, for example, in his reading of the Hals paintings, where he asks questions about the people and objects and their relationship to the painter and the viewer. What the paintings might be made to say, however, depends upon the viewer's expectations, his or her sense of the questions that seem appropriate or possible. Berger argues that, because of the way art is currently displayed, discussed, and reproduced, the viewer expects only to be mystified.

For this assignment, imagine that you are working against the silence and mystification Berger describes. Go to a museum—or, if that is not possible, to a large-format book of reproductions in the library (or, if that is not possible, to the reproductions in "Ways of Seeing")—and select a painting that seems silent and still, yet invites conversation. Your job is to figure out what sorts of questions to ask, to interrogate the painting, to get it to speak, to engage with the past in some form of dialogue. Write an essay in which you record this process and what you have learned from it. Somewhere in your essay, perhaps at the end, turn back to Berger's chapter to talk about how this process has or hasn't confirmed what you take to be Berger's expectations.

Note: If possible, include with your essay a reproduction of the painting you select. (Check the postcards at the museum gift shop.) In any event, you want to make sure that you describe the painting in sufficient detail for your readers to follow what you say.

.   .   .   .   .   .   .   .   .   .   .   .

# A S S I G N M E N T   5

## *Listening to Rock and Roll* [Frith]

> Rock is an American music, and much of what I'm going to say will draw on British experience and British examples. I'm not apologetic about this—my rock experience is a British experience, and it is this, ultimately, that I am trying to understand. And there are advantages in my position: rock is both a medium general to capitalist cultures and a specifically American form of music. How American music was generalized, how American sounds—pop and rock—are experienced (and produced) in other cultural contexts are important questions in themselves. The issue here is not just musical meaning, but also the slipperiness, the power, the idea of "America" itself.
>
>             – SIMON FRITH
>             *Introduction to* Sound Effect

Frith pays particular attention to the 1950s, 1960s, and 1970s, and he deals most immediately with the English experience of rock and roll. He is trying to "historicize" rock, to argue for its particular character or meaning in a particular culture at a particular point in time. The range of his account creates a space in which you can offer an account of your own, one that extends his discussion to the 1980s (or the late 1980s) and to the United States (or your particular region of the United States).

Write an essay in which you construct your own account of rock and sexuality. You should begin your work by rereading Frith's essay, and you should pay close attention to the way he accounts for the relationship between culture and individual artists or consumers. He argues against the common notion that music *expresses* feelings or thoughts that are already there. He writes, rather, about the power of rock and roll to shape, construct, or organize experience. As you work back through his essay, mark the terms and phrases that Frith uses to describe the relationships between culture, music, and the individual. These terms and phrases will be useful when you begin writing.

Frith works quickly, painting with broad strokes, moving easily from generalization to generalization, summing up the 1960s in just a few pages, for example. You should work much more slowly in your essay. Before you generalize about rock and roll in the 1980s, turn your attention to more fine-grained detail—the lyrics of two or three songs, a description of an MTV video, a careful representation of a subculture and its music. Work with local material, material you know well and can reproduce in detail.

. . . . . . . . . . .

ASSIGNMENT 6

## *On Schooling* [Tompkins]

> My Indians, like my princesses, were creatures totally of the imagination, and I did not care to have any real exemplars interfering with what I already knew. (p. 561)
>
> Though it is probably true that in certain cases Europeans did consciously tamper with the evidence, in most cases there is no reason to suppose that they did not record faithfully what they saw. And what they saw was not an illusion, was not determined by selfish motives in any narrow sense, but was there by virtue of a *way* of seeing which they could no more consciously manipulate than they could choose not to have been born. (p. 573)
>
> – JANE TOMPKINS
> *"Indians": Textualism, Morality,*
> *and the Problem of History*

You've reached the point in this sequence where it is time to stop and take stock. Tompkins's essay is a fine example of such stocktaking. In it, she tells the story of an academic project, but she also "reads" that story— that is, not only does she describe what she did, or what other people said, but she reflects on what her actions or the work of others might be said to represent. She writes about "point of view" or "frame of reference" and the ways they might be said to determine how people act, what they write, and what they know.

Write an essay that tells a similar story of your own, using Tompkins's essay as a model. Here are two ways you might begin:

1. You could tell the story of a course of study or a research project you prepared for school (perhaps a term paper, perhaps the work you have been doing for this course). You do not have to write a pious or dutiful account. Tompkins, after all, writes against what she takes to be the predictable or expected account of research (the Disinterested Pursuit of Truth). And she writes in a style that is not solemnly academic. Like Tompkins, you can tell what you take to be the untold story of school (your version of going to the library to find Indians); you can reflect on the "problem" of schooling by turning to your own experience.

Your account should begin well before your work "officially" started—that is, you too will want to show the "prehistory" of your project, the possible connections between schoolwork and your life outside school. And you will want to tell the story of your work with other people's writing. The purpose of all this, if you are following Tompkins's lead, is to reflect on how knowledge is constructed and how you, as a student, have participated in that process.

2. You could write an autobiographical essay that is not about school but about your participation generally in the various cultures of contemporary American life. Tompkins's essay begins this way. She tells the story of her childhood and the ways in which images of Indians were far more powerful for her than the real things. She goes on to tell a parallel story of her work as an adult, through which she finds that she is still, in a sense, a product of her culture.

You could tell the story of a moment when you realized the ways you are a product of your culture (or cultures). You could tell the story of a time when "real" exemplars interfered with what you already knew. You could tell the story of a time when something that seemed "natural" suddenly was revealed as a construct, something made and packaged. This is your chance to represent yourself as a character in the story of American culture. Your narrative should be rich and detailed—a good story, that is. But a careful reader should also be able to see in it echoes and allusions to the reading you have done in this sequence.

# Stories and Their Readers

### Saul Bellow
### Joyce Carol Oates
### Carlos Fuentes

*Y*OU HAVE BEEN reading stories for a good part of your life, long enough for you to have a sense of what you like and don't like, and of what works or doesn't work for you as a reader. This sequence of assignments invites you to study three stories and your responses to them as a way of examining the principles and assumptions (as well as the habits and prejudices) that underlie your reading.

The first assignment asks you to discuss whether a story by Saul Bellow "works" for you in terms of what you notice as key moments in the story. The second assignment builds on that task by asking you to compare stories by Carlos Fuentes and Joyce Carol Oates. The final assignment invites you to study your previous papers in this sequence (and those of your classmates) for what you might learn about successful (or unsuccessful) texts.

. . . . . . . . . . . .

A S S I G N M E N T  **1**

## *Noticing Key Moments in a Story* [Bellow]

As you read through "A Silver Dish" for the first time, place check marks (or some other shorthand notation) in the margins next to those moments that you would call key moments in the story, places where you think Bellow is asking for your special attention. And place X's (or some other notation) in the margins next to those places that give you the most pleasure, those that have the most significance for you as a reader.

Once you've made your marginal notations, reread the story again. Then write an essay in which you discuss the differences (or similarities) between the reader Bellow seems to assume and the reader you are. Where does Bellow seem to be working on the reader? And where might the story be said to have worked best for you?

. . . . . . . . . . . .

A S S I G N M E N T  **2**

## *Comparing Two Stories* [Fuentes, Oates]

This assignment builds on the previous one by asking you once again to notice key moments in your readings of "The Son of Andrés Aparicio" by Carlos Fuentes and "Theft" by Joyce Carol Oates. Only this time your job is to compare your responses to these very different stories. Which one worked best for you? Which one gave you the most pleasure? Which one was the most compelling or memorable? Why? To what might you contribute the story's success or failure?

Write a paper, then, in which you explain and compare your responses to the two stories. The point of this exercise is for you to bring forward the assumptions and expectations (as well as the habits and prejudices) that underlie your reading. You need to do more, that is, than state what you liked or didn't like. You need to explore possible reasons for your responses.

. . . . . . . . . . .

ASSIGNMENT 3

# Studying Stories and Yourself as a Reader
## [Bellow, Fuentes, Oates]

You have had a chance to record and discuss your responses to these three stories. With this assignment, you will now have the chance to step outside of your own immediate experience and to think about your relationship to other readers, particularly your colleagues in this class. Gather copies of at least five sets of papers written by other students working on these assignments, study them, looking closely to see the significant moments of similarity and difference among the various readers, both in their responses to the stories and in their accounts of their responses.

Once you have completed this preliminary research, write an essay in which you talk not just about yourself as a reader but about reading in general. What do you see in these papers before you? What have you learned about yourself as a reader? about reading? How might you explain what you see or what you have learned? What relationships are there between what you have learned about reading through this project and the official advice given to readers in school?

# A Way of Composing

Paulo Freire

John Berger

Adrienne Rich

*T*HIS SEQUENCE is designed to offer a lesson in writing. The assignments will stage your work (or the process you will follow in composing a single essay) in a pattern common to most writers: drafting, revising, and editing. You will begin by identifying a topic and writing a first draft; this draft will be revised several times and prepared as final copy.

This is not the usual writing lesson, however, since you will be asked to imagine that your teachers are Paulo Freire, John Berger, and Adrienne Rich and that their essays were addressed immediately to you as a writer, as though these writers were sitting by your desk and commenting on your writing. In place of the conventional vocabulary of the writing class, you will be working from passages drawn from their essays. You may find that the terms these teachers use in a conversation about writing are unusual—they are not what you would find in most composition textbooks, for example—but the language is powerful and surprising. This assignment sequence demonstrates how these writers could be imagined to be talking to you while you are writing, and it argues that you can make use of a theoretical discussion of language—you can do this, that is, if you learn to look through the eyes of a writer eager to understand his or her work.

Your work in these assignments, then, will be framed by the words of Freire, Berger, and Rich. Their essays are not offered as models, however. You will not be asked to write like Freire, Berger, or Rich. Their essays are offered as places where a writer can find a vocabulary to describe the experience of writing. Writers need models, to be sure. And writers need tips or techniques. But above all writers need a way of thinking about writing, a way of reading their own work from a critical perspective, a way of seeing and understanding the problems and potential in the use of written language. The primary goal of this assignment sequence is to show how this is possible.

• • • • • • • • • • •

## ASSIGNMENT 1

# *Posing a Problem for Writing* [Freire]

> Students, as they are increasingly posed with problems relating to themselves in the world and with the world, will feel increasingly challenged and obliged to respond to that challenge. Because they apprehend the challenge as interrelated to other problems within a total context, not as a theoretical question, the resulting comprehension tends to be increasingly critical and thus constantly less alienated. Their response to the challenge evokes new challenges, followed by new understandings; and gradually the students come to regard themselves as committed. (p. 215)
>
> — PAULO FREIRE
> The "Banking" Concept of Education

One of the arguments of Freire's essay, "The 'Banking' Concept of Education," is that students must be given work that they can think of as theirs; they should not be "docile" listeners but "critical co-investigators" of their own situations "in the world and with the world." The work they do must matter, not only because it draws on their experience but also because that work makes it possible for students to better understand (and therefore change) their lives.

This is heady talk, but it has practical implications. The work of a writer, for example, to be real work must begin with real situations that need to be "problematized." "Authentic reflection considers neither abstract man nor the world without men, but men in their relations with the world." The work of a writer, then, begins with stories and anecdotes, with examples drawn from the world you live in or from reading that could somehow be said to be yours. It does not begin with abstractions, with theses to be proven or ideas to be organized on a page. It begins with memories or observations that become, through writing, verbal representations of your situation in the world; and, as a writer, you can return to these representations to study them, to consider them first this way and then that, to see what form of understanding they represent and how that way of seeing things might be transformed. As Freire says, "In problem-posing education, men develop their power to perceive critically *the way they exist* in the world *with which* and *in which* they find themselves; they come to see the world not as a static reality, but as a reality in process, in transformation."

For this assignment, locate a moment from your own recent experience (an event or a chain of events) that seems rich or puzzling, that you feel you do not quite understand but that you would like to understand better (or that you would like to understand differently). Write the first draft of an essay in which you both describe what happened and provide a way of seeing or understanding what happened. You will need to tell a story with much careful detail, since those details will provide the material for you to work on when you begin interpreting or commenting on your story. It is possible to write a paper like this without stopping to think about what you are doing. You could write a routine essay, but that is not the point of this assignment. The purpose of this draft is to pose a problem for yourself, to represent your experience in such a way that there is work for you to do on it as a writer.

You should think of your essay as a preliminary draft, not a finished paper. You will have the opportunity to go back and work on it again later. You don't need to feel that you have to say everything that can be said, nor do you need to feel that you have to prepare a "finished" essay. You need to write a draft that will give you a place to begin.

When you have finished, go back and reread Freire's essay as a piece directed to you as a writer. Mark those sections that seem to offer something for you to act on when you revise your essay.

. . . . . . . . . . .

A S S I G N M E N T **2**

## *Giving Advice to a Fellow Student* [Berger]

Yet when an image is presented as a work of art, the way people look at it is affected by a whole series of learnt assumptions about art. Assumptions concerning:

Beauty
Truth
Genius
Civilization
Form
Status
Taste, etc. (p. 69)

– JOHN BERGER
*Ways of Seeing*

Berger suggests that problems of seeing can also be imagined as problems of writing. He calls this problem "mystification." "Mystification is the process of explaining away what might otherwise be evident." Here is one of his examples of the kind of writing he calls mystification:

Hals's unwavering commitment to his personal vision, which enriches our consciousness of our fellow men and heightens our awe for the ever-increasing power of the mighty impulses that enabled him to give us a close view of life's vital forces.

This way of talking might sound familiar to you. You may hear some of your teachers in it, or echoes of books you have read. Teachers also, however, will hear some of their students in that passage. Listen, for example, to a passage from a student paper:

Walker Percy writes of man's age-old problem. How does one know the truth? How does one find beauty and wisdom combined? Percy's message is simple. We must avoid the distractions of the modern world and learn to see the beauty and wisdom around us. We must turn our eyes again to the glory of the mountains and the wisdom of Shakespeare. It is easy

745

to be satisfied with packaged tours and *Cliff's Notes*. It is more comfortable to take the American Express guided tour than to rent a Land Rover and explore the untrodden trails of the jungle. We have all felt the desire to turn on the TV and watch "Dallas" rather than curl up with a good book. I've done it myself. But to do so is to turn our backs on the infinite richness life has to offer.

What is going on here? What is the problem? What is the problem with the writing—or with the stance or the thinking that is represented by this writing? (The student is writing in response to Walker Percy's essay "The Loss of the Creature," one of the essays in this book. You can understand the passage, and what is going on in the passage, even if you have not read Percy's essay. Similarly, you could understand the passage about Franz Hals without ever having seen the paintings to which it refers. In fact, what it says could probably be applied to any of a hundred paintings in your local museum. Perhaps this is one of the problems with mystification.)

For this assignment, write a letter to the student who wrote that paragraph. You might include a copy of the passage, with your marginal comments, in that letter. The point of your letter is to give advice—to help that student understand what the problem is and to imagine what to do next. You can assume that he or she (you choose whether it is a man or a woman) has read both "The 'Banking' Concept of Education" and "Ways of Seeing." To prepare yourself for this letter, reread "Ways of Seeing" and mark those passages that seem to you to be interesting or relevant in light of whatever problems you see in the passage above.

· · · · · · · · · · · ·

A S S I G N M E N T  **3**

# *Writing a Second Draft* [Freire, Berger]

Problem-posing education, as a humanist and liberating praxis, posits as fundamental that men subjected to domination must fight for their emancipation. To that end, it enables teachers and students to become Subjects of the educational process by overcoming authoritarianism and an alienating intellectualism; it also enables men to overcome their false perception of reality. The world—no longer something to be described with deceptive words—becomes the object of that transforming action by men which results in their humanization. (p. 218)

– PAULO FREIRE
*The "Banking" Concept of Education*

There is a difference between writing and revising, and the difference is more than a difference of time and place. The work is different. In the first case you are working on a subject—finding something to say and getting words down on paper (often finding something to say *by* getting words down on paper). In the second, you are working on a text, on something that has been written, on your subject as it is represented by the words on the page.

Revision allows you the opportunity to work more deliberately than you possibly can when you are struggling to put something on the page for the first time. It gives you the time and the occasion to reflect, question, and reconsider what you have written. The time to do this is not always available when you are caught up in the confusing rush of composing an initial draft. In fact, it is not always appropriate to challenge or question what you write while you are writing, since this can block thoughts that are eager for expression and divert attention from the task at hand.

The job for the writer in revising a paper, then, is to imagine how the text might be altered—and altered, presumably, for the better. This is seldom a simple, routine, or mechanical process. You are not just copying-over-more-neatly or searching for spelling mistakes.

If you take Freire and Berger as guides, revision can be thought of as a struggle against domination. One of the difficulties of writing is that what you want to say is sometimes consumed or displaced by a language that mystifies the subject or alienates the writer. The problem with authoritarianism or alienating intellectualism or deceptive words is that it is not a simple matter to break free from them. It takes work. The ways of speaking and thinking that are immediately available to a writer (what Berger calls "learnt assumptions") can be seen as obstacles as well as aids. If a first draft is driven by habit and assisted by conventional ways of thinking and writing, a second can enable a writer to push against habit and convention.

For this assignment, read back through the draft you wrote for assignment 1, underlining words or phrases that seem to be evidence of the power of language to dominate, mystify, deceive, or alienate. And then, when you are done, prepare a second draft that struggles against such acts, that transforms the first into an essay that honors your subject or that seems more humane in the way it speaks to its readers.

. . . . . . . . . . . .

A S S I G N M E N T  **4**

## *Writing as Re-Vision* [Rich]

> For a poem to coalesce, for a character or an action to take
> shape, there has to be an imaginative transformation of reality
> which is no way passive. And a certain freedom of the mind
> is needed—freedom to press on, to enter the currents of your
> thought like a glider pilot, knowing that your motion can be
> sustained, that the buoyancy of your attention will not be
> suddenly snatched away. Moreover, if the imagination is to
> transcend and transform experience it has to question, to
> challenge, to conceive of alternatives, perhaps to the very life
> you are living at that moment. You have to be free to play
> around with the notion that day might be night, love might
> be hate; nothing can be too sacred for the imagination to turn
> into its opposite or to call experimentally by another name.
> For writing is re-naming. (p. 490)
>    — ADRIENNE RICH
>    *When We Dead Awaken: Writing as Re-Vision*

This is powerful language, and it is interesting to imagine how a writer
might put such terms to work. For this assignment, go back to the draft
you wrote for assignment 3 and look for a section where the writing is
strong and authoritative, where you seemed, as a writer, to be most in
control of what you were doing. If, in that section, you gave shape and
definition (perhaps even a name) to your experience, see what you can do
to "transcend and transform" what you have written. Play around with the
notion that day might be night, love might be hate; nothing should be "too
sacred for your imagination to turn into its opposite or call experimentally
by another name."

Rewrite that section of your essay, but without throwing away or dis-
carding what you had previously written. The section you work on, in
other words, should grow in size as it incorporates this "playful" experimentation with another point of view. Grant yourself the "freedom to press
on," even if the currents of your thought run in alternate directions—or
turn back on themselves.

. . . . . . . . . . .

ASSIGNMENT 5

## *Preparing a Final Draft* [Freire, Berger, Rich]

> Their response to the challenge evokes new challenges, fol-
> lowed by new understandings; and gradually the students
> come to regard themselves as committed. (p. 215)
>                                   — PAULO FREIRE
>                           *The "Banking" Concept of Education*

A piece of writing is never really finished, but there comes a point in time when a writer has to send it to an editor (or give it to a teacher) and turn to work on something else. This is the last opportunity you will have to work on the essay you began in assignment 1. To this point, you have been working under the guidance of expert writers: Freire, Berger, and Rich. For the final revision, you are on your own. You have their advice and (particularly in Rich's case) their example before you. You have your drafts, with the comments you've received from your instructor (or per-haps your colleagues in class). You should complete the work, now, as best you can, honoring your commitment to the project you have begun and following it to the fullest conclusion.

Note: When you have finished working on your essay and you are ready to hand it in, you should set aside time to proofread it. This is the work of correcting mistakes, usually mistakes in spelling, punctuation, or grammar. This is the last thing a writer does, and it is not the same thing as revision. You will need to read through carefully and, while you are reading, make corrections on the manuscript you will turn in.

The hard work is locating the errors, not correcting them. Proofreading requires a slowed-down form of reading, where you pay attention to the marks on the page rather than to the sound of a voice or the train of ideas, and this form of reading is strange and unnatural. Many writers have learned, in fact, to artificially disrupt the normal rhythms of reading by reading their manuscripts backwards, beginning with the last page and moving to the first; by reading with a ruler to block out the following lines; or by making a photocopy, grabbing a friend, and taking turns reading out loud.

# SEQUENCE TWELVE

# Ways of Seeing

## John Berger

*T*HIS SEQUENCE ASKS you to examine claims that John Berger makes about our ways of seeing art. The first assignment invites you to consider what he says about how we look at paintings, pictures, and images, and what all this has to do with "history." The second asks you to write about a painting, giving you an opportunity to demonstrate how the meaning of this piece of art from the past belongs to you. The third assignment then turns you back on your own writing so that you can examine it for the expectations and strategies that came into play when you wrote about the painting you chose. The final assignment invites you to review your first paper in the sequence so that you can enter into the conversation with Berger about what gets in the way when we look at pictures, paintings, and images, and what all this might have to do with "history."

. . . . . . . . . . . . .

## A S S I G N M E N T  **1**

# *Berger's Example of a Way of Seeing*
# [Berger]

We are not saying that there is nothing left to experience before original works of art except a sense of awe because they
have survived. The way original works of art are usually approached—through museum catalogues, guides, hired cassettes, etc.—is not the only way they might be approached.
When the art of the past ceases to be viewed nostalgically,
the works will cease to be holy relics—although they will
never re-become what they were before the age of reproduction. We are not saying original works of art are now useless.
(p. 86)

> – JOHN BERGER
> *Ways of Seeing*

Berger argues that there are problems in the way we see or don't see
the things before us, problems that can be located in and overcome by
strategies or approaches.

For Berger, what we lose if we fail to see properly is history: "If we
'saw' the art of the past, we would situate ourselves in history. When we
are prevented from seeing it, we are being deprived of the history which
belongs to us." It is not hard to figure out who, according to Berger, prevents us from seeing the art of the past. He says it is the ruling class. It *is*
difficult, however, to figure out what he believes gets in our way and what
all this has to do with "history."

For this assignment, write an essay explaining what, as you read Berger,
it is that gets in the way when we look at pictures, paintings, or images,
and what this has to do with history.

. . . . . . . . . . . .

# A S S I G N M E N T 2

## Applying Berger's Methods to a Painting [Berger]

> A people or a class which is cut off from its own past is far less free to choose and to act as a people or class than one that has been able to situate itself in history. This is why— and this is the only reason why—the entire art of the past has now become a political issue. (p. 89)
>
> — JOHN BERGER
> *Ways of Seeing*

Berger says that the real question facing those who care about art is this: "To whom does the meaning of the art of the past properly belong? To those who can apply it to their own lives, or to a cultural hierarchy of relic specialists?" As Berger's reader, you are invited to act as though the meaning of the art of the past belonged to you. Go to a museum or, if that is not possible, to a large-format book of reproductions in the library (and if that is not possible, to the reproduction of Vermeer's *Woman Pouring Milk* that is included in the essay). Select a painting you'd like to write about, one whose "meaning" you think you might like to describe to others. Write an essay that shows others how they might best understand that painting. You should offer this lesson in the spirit of John Berger. That is, how might you demonstrate that the meaning of this piece of art from the past belongs to you or can be applied in some way to your life?

Note: If possible, include with your essay a reproduction of the painting you select. (Check the postcards at the museum gift shop.) In any event, you want to make sure that you describe the painting in sufficient detail for your readers to follow what you say.

. . . . . . . . . . .

A S S I G N M E N T  **3**

# *A Way of Seeing Your Way of Seeing* [Berger]

What we make of that painted moment when it is before our
eyes depends upon what we expect of art, and that in turn
depends today upon how we have already experienced the
meaning of paintings through reproductions. (p. 87)
                                                    — JOHN BERGER
                                                    *Ways of Seeing*

Return to the essay you wrote for assignment 2, and look at it as an
example of a way of seeing, one of several ways a thoughtful person might
approach and talk about that painting. You have not, to be sure, said everything there is to say about the painting. What you wrote should give
you evidence of a person making choices, a person with a point of view,
with expectations and strategies that have been learned through prior
experience.

For this assignment, study what you have written and write an essay
that comments on your previous essay's way of seeing (or "reading") your
painting. Here are some questions that you should address in preparing
your commentary:

1. What expectations about art are represented by the example of the
person you see at work in your essay?

2. What is the most interesting or puzzling or significant thing that
viewer (you) was able to see in this painting? How would you characterize
a viewer who would notice *this* and take it as central to an understanding
of the painting?

3. What do you suppose that viewer must necessarily have missed or
failed to see? What other approaches might have been taken? What are the
disadvantages of the approach you see in the essay?

4. Is there anything you might point to as an example of "mystification"
in that essay? ("Mystification" is the term Berger uses to characterize writing that sounds like this: "Hals's unwavering commitment to his personal
vision, which enriches our consciousness of our fellow men and heightens
our awe for the ever-increasing power of the mighty impulses that enabled

**753**

him to give us a close view of life's vital forces.") Is there anything in your essay you might point to as an example of mystification's opposite?

5. Berger says, "If we 'saw' the art of the past, we would situate ourselves in history." As you look back over your essay, what does any of what you wrote or saw (or failed to write or see) have to do with your position in "history"?

6. Berger says that what you write depends on how you have already experienced the meaning of paintings. What are the characteristic features in the work of a person who has learned from Berger how to "experience the meaning of paintings"? If you were to get more training in this—in the act of looking at paintings and writing about them—what would you hope to learn?

. . . . . . . . . . .

A S S I G N M E N T  **4**

## *Reviewing the Way You See* [Berger]

Now that you have had the opportunity to work with Berger's examples of "seeing" and with your own examination of a painting (and your way of seeing it), this final assignment invites you to return to the first paper you wrote in this sequence, to review it with an eye to revising what you had to say about what gets in the way when we look at pictures, paintings, or images. When you first worked on this assignment, you were untangling Berger's ideas about what gets in the way. This assignment is an occasion for you to speak with him, comment on his ideas, or challenge them. You know more now, after having written about a work of art and then studied that writing for what it could be said to show about your expectations and strategies. You have firsthand experience now with the problem Berger poses, and that experience should inform your review.

Write an essay in which you revise your first essay for this argument. This time you are in a position to add your response. Your revision, in other words, will do more than tighten up or finish that first attempt. The revision is an opportunity for you to come forward as both a speaker and an authority. Berger's text becomes something you can use in an essay of your own. Or, to put it another way, in this draft you are in a position to speak with or from or against Berger. He will not be the only one represented. Your revision should be considerably longer than your first draft and a reader should be able to see (or hear) those sections of the essay which could be said to be yours.

# Whose Text Is It Anyway?

Walker Percy

Richard Rodriguez

Clifford Geertz

*T*HIS SEQUENCE is designed to provide you with a way of reading Walker Percy's essay, "The Loss of the Creature." This is not a simple essay, and it deserves more than a single reading. There are six assignments in this sequence, all of which offer a way of rereading (or revising your reading of) Percy's essay; and, in doing so, they provide one example of what it means to be an expert or a critical reader.

"The Loss of the Creature" argues that people have trouble seeing and understanding the things around them. Percy makes his point by looking at two exemplary groups: students and tourists. The opening three assignments provide a way for you to work on "The Loss of the Creature" as a single essay, as something that stands alone. You will restate its argument, tell a "Percian" story of your own and test the essay's implications. Then Richard Rodriguez and Geertz provide alternate ways of talking about the problems of "seeing." And, in addition, they provide examples you can use to extend Percy's argument further. The last assignment is the occasion for you to step forward as an expert, a person who has something to add to the conversation Percy began and who determines whose text it is that will speak with authority.

. . . . . . . . . . . .

A S S I G N M E N T  1

## Who's Lost What in
## "The Loss of the Creature"? [Percy]

> Our complex friend stands behind the fellow tourists at the Bright Angel Lodge and sees the canyon through them and their predicament, their picture taking and busy disregard. In a sense, he exploits his fellow tourists; he stands on their shoulders to see the canyon.
>
> Such a man is far more advanced in the dialectic than the sightseer who is trying to get off the beaten track—getting up at dawn and approaching the canyon through the mesquite. This stratagem is, in fact, for our complex man the weariest, most beaten track of all. (p. 464)
>
> — WALKER PERCY
> *The Loss of the Creature*

Percy's essay is not difficult to read, and yet there is a way in which it is a difficult essay. He tells several stories—some of them quite good stories—but it is often hard to know just what he is getting at, just what point it is he is trying to make. If he's making an argument, it's not the sort of argument that is easy to summarize. And if the stories (or anecdotes) are meant to serve as examples, they are not the sort of examples that quickly add up to a single, general conclusion or that serve to clarify a point or support an obvious thesis. In fact, at the very moment at which you expect Percy to come forward and talk like an expert (to pull things together, sum things up, or say what he means), he offers yet another story, as though another example, rather than any general statement, would get you closer to what he is saying.

There are, at the same time, terms and phrases to suggest that this is an essay with a point to make. Percy talks, for example, about "the loss of sovereignty," "symbolic packages," "sovereign individuals," "consumers of experience," "a universe disposed by theory," "dialectic," and it seems safe to say that these terms and phrases are meant to name or comment on key scenes, situations, or characters in the examples. You could go to the dictionary to see what these words might mean, but the problem for a reader of this essay is to see what the words might mean for Percy as he is writing the essay, telling those stories, and looking for terms he can use to make the stories say more than what they appear to say (about a trip to the Grand Canyon, or a trip to Mexico, of a Falkland Islander, or a student at Sarah Lawrence College). This is an essay, in other words, that seems to break some of the rules of essay writing and to make unusual (and interesting) demands on a reader. There's more for a reader to do here than follow a discussion from its introduction to its conclusion.

As you begin working on Percy's essay (that is, as you begin rereading), you might begin with the stories. They fall roughly into two groups (stories about students and those about tourists), raising the question of how students and tourists might be said to face similar problems or confront similar situations.

Choose two stories that seem to you to be particularly interesting or puzzling. Go back to the text and review them, looking particularly for the small details that seem to be worth thinking about. (If you work with the section on the tourists at the Grand Canyon, be sure to acknowledge that this section tells the story of several different tourists—not everyone comes on a bus from Terre Haute; not everyone follows the same route.) Then, in an essay, use the stories as examples for your own discussion of Percy's essay and what it might be said to be about.

Note: You should look closely at the differences between the two examples you choose. The differences may be more telling than the similarities. If you look only at the similarities, then you are tacitly assuming that they are both examples of the same thing. If one example would suffice, presumably Percy would have stopped at one. It is useful to assume that he added more examples because one wouldn't do, because he wanted to add another angle of vision, to qualify, refine, extend, or challenge the apparent meaning of the previous examples.

· · · · · · · · · · ·

ASSIGNMENT 2

## *Telling a "Percian" Story of Your Own* [Percy]

The situation of the tourist at the Grand Canyon and the biology student are special cases of a predicament in which everyone finds himself in a modern technical society—a society, that is, in which there is a division between expert and layman, planner and consumer, in which experts and planners take special measures to teach and edify the consumer. (p. 474)

— WALKER PERCY

*The Loss of the Creature*

For this assignment you should tell a story of your own, one that is suggested by the stories Percy tells—perhaps a story about a time you went looking for something or at something, or about a time when you did or did not find a dogfish in your Shakespeare class. You should imagine that you are carrying out a project that Walker Percy has begun, a project that has you looking back at your own experience through the lens of "The Loss of the Creature." You might also experiment with some of his key terms or phrases (like "dialectic" or "consumer of experience," but you should choose the ones that seem the most interesting or puzzling—the ones you would want to work with, that is). These will help to establish a perspective from which you can look at and comment on the story you have to tell.

•  •  •  •  •  •  •  •  •  •  •

A S S I G N M E N T  3

# Complex and Common Readings of *"The Loss of the Creature"* [Percy]

I do not refer only to the special relation of layman to theorist. I refer to the general situation in which sovereignty is surrendered to a class of privileged knowers, whether these be theorists or artists. A reader may surrender sovereignty over that which has been written about, just as a consumer may surrender sovereignty over a thing which has been theorized about. The consumer is content to receive an experience just as it has been presented to him by theorists and planners. The reader may also be content to judge life by whether it has or has not been formulated by those who know and write about life. (p. 469)

> This dialectic of sightseeing cannot be taken into account by
> planners, for the object of the dialectic is nothing other than
> the subversion of the efforts of the planners. (p. 465)
>
> — WALKER PERCY
> *The Loss of the Creature*

Percy charts several routes to the Grand Canyon: you can take the packaged tour, you can get off the beaten track, you can wait for a disaster,
you can follow the "dialectical movement which brings one back to the
beaten track but at a level above it." This last path (or "stratagem"), he
says, is for the complex traveler. "Our complex friend stands behind his
fellow tourists at the Bright Angel Lodge and sees the canyon through
them and their predicament, their picture taking and busy disregard. In a
sense, he exploits his fellow tourists; he stands on their shoulders to see
the canyon."

When Percy talks about students studying Shakespeare or biology, he
says that "there is nothing the educator can do" to provide for the student's
need to recover the specimen from its educational package. "Everything
the educator does only succeeds in becoming, for the student, part of the
educational package."

Percy, in his essay, is working on a problem, a problem that is hard to
name and hard to define, but it is a problem that can be located in the
experience of the student and the experience of the tourist and overcome,
perhaps, only by means of certain strategies. This problem can also be
imagined as a problem facing a reader: "A reader may surrender sovereignty over that which has been written about, just as a consumer may
surrender sovereignty over a thing which has been theorized about."

The complex traveler sees the Grand Canyon through the example of
the common tourists with "their predicament, their picture taking and busy
disregard." He "stands on their shoulders" to see the canyon. What happens if you apply these terms—*complex* and *common*—to reading? What
strategies might a complex reader use to recover his or her sovereignty over
that which has been written (or that which has been written about)?

For this assignment, write an essay that demonstrates a common and
a complex reading of "The Loss of the Creature." Your essay should have
three sections (you could number them, if you choose).

The first two sections should each represent a different way of reading
the essay. One should be an example of the work of a common reader, a
reader who treats the text the way the common tourists treat the Grand
Canyon. The other should be an example of the work of a complex reader,
a reader with a different set of strategies or a reader who has found a different route to the essay. You should feel free to draw on either or both of
your previous essays for this assignment, revising them as you see fit to

make them represent either of these ways of reading. Or, if need be, you may start all over again.

The third section of your paper should look back and comment on the previous two sections. In particular, you might address these questions: What does the complex reader see or do? And why might a person prefer one reading over another? What is to be gained or lost?

• • • • • • • • • • •

## A S S I G N M E N T  4

# Rodriguez as One of Percy's Examples [Percy, Rodriguez]

> Those who would take seriously the boy's success—and his failure—would be forced to realize how great is the change any academic undergoes, how far one must move from one's past. It is easiest to ignore such considerations. So little is said about the scholarship boy in pages and pages of educational literature. Nothing is said of the silence that comes to separate the boy from his parents. Instead, one hears proposals for increasing the self-esteem of students and encouraging early intellectual independence. Paragraphs glitter with a constellation of terms like *creativity* and *originality*. (Ignored altogether is the function of imitation in a student's life.) (p. 516)
>
> — RICHARD RODRIGUEZ
> *The Achievement of Desire*

"The Achievement of Desire" is the second chapter in Rodriguez's autobiography, *Hunger of Memory: The Education of Richard Rodriguez*. The story Rodriguez tells is, in part, a story of loss and separation, of the necessary sacrifices required of all those who take their own education seriously. To use the language of Percy's essay, Rodriguez loses any authentic or sovereign contact he once had with the world around him. He has become a kind of "weary traveler," deprived of the immediate, easy access he once had to his parents, his past, or even his own thoughts and emotions. And whatever he has lost, it can only be regained now—if it can be regained at all—by a complex strategy.

If Percy were to take Rodriguez's story—or a section of it—as an example, where would he place it and what would he have to say about it?

If Percy were to add Rodriguez (perhaps the Rodriguez who read Hoggart's *The Uses of Literacy* or the Rodriguez who read through the list of the "hundred most important books of Western Civilization") to the example of the biology student or the Falkland Islander, where would he put Rodriguez and what would he say to place Rodriguez in the context of his argument?

For this assignment, write two short essays. In the first essay read Rodriguez's story through the frame of Percy's essay. From this point of view, what would Percy notice and what would he say about what he notices?

Rodriguez, however, also has an argument to make about education and loss. For the second essay, consider the following questions: What does Rodriguez offer as the significant moments in his experience? What does he have to say about them? And what might he have to say to Percy? Is Percy one who, in Rodriguez's terms, can take seriously the scholarship boy's success and failure?

Your job, then is to set Percy and Rodriguez against each other, to write about Rodriguez from Percy's point of view, but then in a separate short essay to consider as well what Rodriguez might have to say about Percy's reading of "The Achievement of Desire."

• • • • • • • • • • •

ASSIGNMENT 5

# The Anthropologist as a Person with a Way of Seeing [Geertz]

For the anthropologist whose concern is with formulating sociological principles, not with promoting or appreciating cockfights, the question is, what does one learn about such principles from examining culture as an assemblage of texts? (pp. 298–99)

— CLIFFORD GEERTZ
*Deep Play: Notes on the Balinese Cockfight*

You've gone from tourists to students and now, at the end of this set of readings, you have another travel story before you. This essay, "Deep Play: Notes on the Balinese Cockfight," was written by an anthropologist. Anthropologists, properly speaking, are not really tourists. There is a scholarly purpose to their travel, and, presumably, they have learned or developed the complex strategies necessary to get beyond the preformed "symbolic complex" that would keep them from seeing the place or the people they have traveled to study. They are experts, in other words, not just any "layman seer of sights." One question to ask of "Deep Play" is whether Geertz has solved the problem of seeing that Percy outlines.

Anthropologists are people who observe (or in Geertz's terms "read") the behavior of other people. But their work is governed by methods, by ways of seeing that are complex and sophisticated. They can do something that the ordinary tourist to Bali (or Mexico or the Grand Canyon) cannot. They have different ways of situating themselves as observers, and they have a different way of thinking (or writing) about what they have seen. What is it, then, that anthropologists do, and how do they do what they do?

If this essay were your only evidence, how might you describe the work of an anthropologist? Write an essay in which you look at "Deep Play" section by section, describing on the basis of each what it is that an anthropologist must be able to do. In each case, you have the chance of watch Geertz at work. (Your essay, then, might well have seven sections that correspond to Geertz's.) When you have worked through them all, write a final section that discusses how these various skills or arts fit together to define the expertise of someone like Geertz.

. . . . . . . . . . .

ASSIGNMENT 6

## Taking Your Turn in the Conversation
## [Percy, Rodriguez, Geertz]

I refer to the general situation in which sovereignty is surrendered to a class of privileged knowers, whether these be theorists or artists. A reader may surrender sovereignty over that which has been written about, just as a consumer may surrender sovereignty over a thing which has been theorized about. The consumer is content to receive an experience just as it has been presented to him by theorists and planners. The reader may also be content to judge life by whether it has or has not been formulated by those who know and write about life. (p. 469)

– WALKER PERCY
*The Loss of the Creature*

It could be argued that all of the work you have done in these assignments has been preparing you to test the assumptions of Percy's essay, "The Loss of the Creature." You've read several accounts of the problems facing tourists and students, people who look at and try to understand what is before them. You have observed acts of seeing, reading, and writing that can extend the range of examples provided by Percy. And you have, of course, your own work before you as an example of a student working under the guidance of a variety of experts. You are in a position, in other words, to speak in response to Percy with considerable authority. This last assignment is the occasion for you to do so.

For this assignment, you might imagine that you are writing an article for the journal that first printed "The Loss of the Creature." You can assume, that is, that your readers are expert readers. They have read Percy's essay. They know what the common reading would be and they know that they want something else. This is not an occasion for summary, but for an essay that can enable those readers to take a next step in their thinking. You may challenge Percy's essay, defend and extend what it has to say, or provide an angle you feel others will not have seen. You should feel free to draw as much as you can on the writing you have already done, working sections of those papers into your final essay. Percy has said what he has to say. It is time for you to speak, now, in turn.

SEQUENCE FOURTEEN

# Working Alongside
# an Anthropologist

Clifford Geertz
Saul Bellow

*T*HIS ASSIGNMENT SEQUENCE invites you to participate in the work of an anthropologist by "reading" cultural phenomena, including a short story, "over the shoulders of those to whom they properly belong." The first assignment invites you to do a close reading of Clifford Geertz's study of Balinese cockfights, to reexamine what he thinks cockfights do and do not say about the Balinese. The second assignment asks you to "read" the narrator of Saul Bellow's short story as Geertz might, and the final assignment invites you to use what you have learned to read some part of our culture.

. . . . . . . . . . . .

ASSIGNMENT 1

# *Studying Geertz Studying Cockfights*
## [Geertz]

> What the cockfight says it says in a vocabulary of sentiment—
> the thrill of risk, the despair of loss, the pleasure of triumph.
> Yet what it says is not merely that risk is exciting, loss de-
> pressing, or triumph gratifying, banal tautologies of affect,
> but that it is of these emotions, thus exampled, that society
> is built and individuals put together. (p. 299)
> — CLIFFORD GEERTZ
> *Deep Play: Notes on the Balinese Cockfight*

Geertz says that the cockfight provides a "commentary upon the whole matter of assorting human beings into fixed hierarchical ranks and then organizing the major part of collective existence around that assortment." Cockfights don't reinforce the patterns of Balinese life; they comment on them. Write an essay in which you explain both what the cockfights say (at least according to Geertz) and how Geertz arrives at his conclusion. In a sense you are summarizing Geertz's findings, but you are also explaining how he does the interpretive end of his work. What is the process of interpretation as demonstrated here? What are the steps or stages? (How does he describe what he does? What does he say about the work of other anthropologists, work he feels is limited or reductive?) Once Geertz has gathered his "data," how does he get from notes or observations to meaning?

. . . . . . . . . . .

A S S I G N M E N T  2

# Studying the Narrator of "A Silver Dish"
## [Geertz, Bellow]

As Woody put it, be realistic. Think what times these are. The papers daily give it to you—the Lufthansa pilot in Aden is described by the hostages on his knees, begging the Palestinian terrorists not to execute him, but they shoot him through the head. Later they themselves are killed. And still others shoot others, or shoot themselves. That's what you read in the press, see on the tube, mention at dinner. (p. 39)

> — SAUL BELLOW
> *A Silver Dish*

Geertz, in "Deep Play: Notes on the Balinese Cockfight," approaches cockfights in Bali as a reader might approach a text—he begins by assuming that they "say something of something," that they represent more than just the fact of cockfights. After mapping out his evidence, he concludes that they are dramatizations of status concerns, in other words, that they enact the culture's appointments of power and rank and, as such, that they use emotion for cognitive ends. A cockfight's function, as Geertz says, "is interpretive: it is a Balinese reading of Balinese experience; a story they tell themselves about themselves."

Bellow's narrator in "A Silver Dish" is invisible; we don't see him as a character in the story, but it is his story, and, although he announces that it is the story of a man dealing with his father's death, it could be, if we take a Geertzian perspective, a story about something else as well, a story that says something about the narrator and his culture.

Write an essay in which you take the narrator of this story and make him visible by "reading" him as a cultural artifact, as a particular person telling a particular story that could be said to dramatize or enact something significant about his culture. Like Geertz, you might begin by asking what the narrator offers you for evidence. What, in his terms, is the "central feature" of this way of speaking about a father and about death? What, for example, are his significant metaphors? How do they represent him and the culture he is embedded in? What are the significant events and relationships he offers? How might you read them as "saying something of something"?

. . . . . . . . . . . .

ASSIGNMENT 3

# *Studying Your Culture* [Geertz]

As in more familiar exercises in close reading, one can start anywhere in a culture's repertoire of forms and end up anywhere else. One can stay, as I have here, within a single, more or less bounded form and circle steadily within it. One can move between forms in search of broader unities or informing contrasts. One can even compare forms from different cultures to define their character in reciprocal relief. But whatever the level at which one operates, and however intricately, the guiding principle is the same: societies, like lives, contain their own interpretations. One has only to learn how to gain access to them. (pp. 301–02)

– CLIFFORD GEERTZ
*Deep Play: Notes on the Balinese Cockfight*

Geertz says that "the culture of a people is an ensemble of texts, themselves ensembles, which the anthropologist strains to read over the shoulders of those to whom they properly belong." Anthropologists are expert at "reading" in this way. One of the interesting things about being a student is that you get to (or you have to) act like an expert even though, properly speaking, you are not. Write an essay in which you prepare a Geertzian "reading" of some part of our culture you know well (sorority rush, window-shopping in a shopping mall, studying in the library, decorating a dorm room, whatever). Ideally, you should go out and observe the behavior you are studying, examining it and taking notes with your project in mind. You should imagine that you are working in Geertz's spirit (as you did in the previous assignment with Bellow's story), imitating his method and style and carrying out work that he has begun.

*(continued from page ii)*
in *Human Experience* by Thomas J. Cottle and Stephen L. Klineberg. Copyright © 1974 by The Free Press.

Stanley Fish, "How to Recognize a Poem When You See One." From *Is There a Text in This Class? The Authority of Interpretive Communities* by Stanley Fish, Cambridge, Mass.: Harvard University Press. Copyright © 1980 by the President and Fellows of Harvard College. Reprinted by permission.

Jean Franco, "Killing Priests, Nuns, Women, Children." From *On Signs* edited by Marshall Blonsky (Johns Hopkins University Press, 1985). Reprinted by permission of the author.

Paulo Freire, "The 'Banking' Concept of Education." From Ch. 2 of *Pedagogy of the Oppressed* by Paulo Freire. Copyright © 1970 by the author. Reprinted by permission of the Continuum Publishing Company.

Simon Frith, "Rock and Sexuality." Copyright © 1981 by Simon Frith. Reprinted from *Sound Effects: Youth, Leisure, and the Politics of Rock 'n' Roll* by Simon Frith, by permission of Pantheon Books, a division of Random House, Inc., and Constable Publishers.

Carlos Fuentes, "The Son of Andrés Aparicio." From *Burnt Water* by Carlos Fuentes. Translation copyright © 1969, 1974, 1978, 1979, 1980 by Farrar, Straus and Giroux, Inc. Reprinted by permission of Farrar, Straus and Giroux, Inc.

Clifford Geertz, "Deep Play: Notes on the Balinese Cockfight." Reprinted by permission of *Daedalus*, Journal of the American Academy of Arts and Sciences, Vol. 101, Nos. 1–2 (Winter 1972), Boston, Mass.

Harriet (Brent) Jacobs, "Incidents in the Life of a Slave Girl." From *Incidents in the Life of a Slave Girl* by Harriet (Brent) Jacobs. Reprinted by permission of Mnemosyne Publishing Co.

Julie Kristeva, "Stabat Mater." Copyright © 1988 Columbia University Press. Used by permission.

Thomas S. Kuhn, "The Historical Structure of Scientific Discovery." From *Science*, Vol. 136 (1 June 1962), pp. 760–764. Copyright 1962 by the AAAS.

Mark Crispin Miller, "Getting Dirty." Reprinted by permission of *The New Republic*. "Cosby Knows Best." Excerpt from "Deride and Conquer," by Mark Crispin Miller, as it appeared in *Boxed In: The Culture of TV* by Mark Crispin Miller. Copyright © 1986 by Mark Crispin Miller. Reprinted from *Watching Television*, edited by Todd Gitlin, by permission of Pantheon Books, a division of Random House, Inc. "Getting Dirty" afterword and "Cosby Knows Best" afterword from Mark Crispin Miller in *Boxed In: The Culture of TV* (Evanston, Ill.: Northwestern University Press, 1988), pp. 49–50, 77–78. © 1988 Mark Crispin Miller. Reprinted by permission of Northwestern University Press.

Joyce Carol Oates, "Theft." Copyright © Ontario Review, Inc., 1989. Reprinted by permission of the author.

Walker Percy, "The Loss of the Creature." From *The Message in the Bottle* by Walker Percy. Copyright © 1954, 1956, 1957, 1958, 1959, 1961 1967, 1972, 1975 by Walker Percy. Reprinted by permission of Farrar, Straus and Giroux, Inc.

Adrienne Rich, "When We Dead Awaken: Writing as Re-Vision." Reprinted from *On Lies, Secrets, and Silence, Selected Prose 1966–1978* by Adrienne Rich, by permission of W. W. Norton & Company, Inc. Copyright © 1979 by W. W. Norton & Company, Inc.

Richard Rodriguez, "The Achievement of Desire." From *Hunger of Memory* by Richard Rodriguez. Copyright © 1982 by Richard Rodriguez. Reprinted by permission of David R. Godine, Publisher. Richard Hoggart excerpts appearing in "The Achievement of Desire" by Richard Rodriguez from *The Uses of Literacy* by Richard Hoggart. Copyright 1957. Reprinted by permission of Oxford University Press, the author, and Chatto & Windus.

John Ruskin, "The Nature of Gothic." From *The Stones of Venice* by John Ruskin, Everyman's Library edition. Reprinted by permission of J. M. Dent & Sons. Photos: page 537, The Bettman Archive; page 538, Owen Franken/Stock Boston.

Gloria Steinem, "Ruth's Song (Because She Could Not Sing It)." From *Outrageous Acts and Everyday Rebellions* by Gloria Steinem. Copyright © 1983 by Gloria Steinem. Reprinted by permission of Henry Holt and Company, Inc.

Jane Tompkins, "'Indians': Textualism, Morality, and the Problem of History." From *Critical Inquiry*, Vol. 13, No. 1 (Autumn 1986). Reprinted in Henry Louis Gates, ed., *Race, Writing, and Difference* (1986), pp. 101–119. © 1986 by The University of Chicago. All rights reserved. Reprinted by permission of the publisher.

Alice Walker, "In Search of Our Mothers' Gardens." Copyright © 1974 by Alice Walker, reprinted from her volume *In Search of Our Mothers' Gardens* by permission of Harcourt Brace Jovanovich, Inc. "Women" (internal poem), copyright © 1971 by Alice Walker, reprinted from her volume *Revolutionary Petunias & Other Poems* by permission of Harcourt Brace Jovanovich, Inc.

John Edgar Wideman, "Our Time." From *Brothers and Keepers* by John Edgar Wideman. Copyright © 1984 by John Edgar Wideman. Reprinted by permission of Henry Holt and Company, Inc.

Virginia Woolf, "A Room of One's Own." Chs. 1 and 6 from *A Room of One's Own* by Virginia Woolf, copyright 1929 by Harcourt Brace Jovanovich, Inc., and renewed 1957 by Leonard Woolf, reprinted by permission of the publisher and the Executors of the Virginia Woolf Estate.